HANDBOOK OF ORGANIZATIONAL POLITICS

Handbook of Organizational Politics

Edited by

Eran Vigoda-Gadot

Associate Professor of Organizational Behavior and Public Administration, University of Haifa, Israel

Amos Drory

Professor of Organizational Behavior, School of Management, Ben-Gurion University of the Negev, Israel

Edward Elgar
Cheltenham, UK • Northampton, MA, USA

Published by
Edward Elgar Publishing Limited
Glensanda House
Montpellier Parade
Cheltenham
Glos GL50 1UA
UK

Edward Elgar Publishing, Inc.
136 West Street
Suite 202
Northampton
Massachusetts 01060
USA

A catalogue record for this book
is available from the British Library

Library of Congress Cataloguing in Publication Data

Handbook of organizational politics/edited by Eran Vigoda-Gadot, Amos Drory.
    p. cm.
   Includes bibliographical references and index.
   1. Office politics—Handbooks, manuals, etc. 2. Organizational behavior—
Political aspects—Handbooks, manuals, etc. 3. Business and politics—
Handbooks, manuals, etc. I. Title: Organizational politics. II. Vigoda-Gadot,
Eran, 1966– . III. Drory, Amos.
  HF5386.5.H36   2006
  302.3'5—dc22   2005052090

ISBN-13: 978 1 84376 995 8 (cased)
ISBN-10: 1 84376 995 6 (cased)

Printed and bound in Great Britain by MPG Books Ltd, Bodmin, Cornwall

Contents

Contributors

Simon Albrecht, Department of Psychology, Monash University, Australia

Constant D. Beugré, School of Management, Delaware State University, USA

Astrid I. Boogers-van Griethuijsen, Faculty of Management and Organization, University of Groningen, The Netherlands

Robyn L. Brouer, Department of Management, Florida State University, USA

David Butcher, Cranfield School of Management, UK

Chu-Hsiang Chang, Department of Psychology, Buchtel College of Arts and Sciences, University of Akron, USA

Stephen Chen, National Graduate School of Management, Australian National University, Australia

Martin Clarke, Cranfield School of Management, UK

Russell Cropanzano, Department of Psychology, Colorado State University, USA

Mary Dana Laird, Department of Management, Florida State University, USA

Amos Drory, School of Management, Ben-Gurion University of the Negev, Israel

Yinnon Dryzin-Amit, Division of Public Administration and Policy, University of Haifa, Israel

Ben J.M. Emans, Faculty of Management and Organization, University of Groningen, The Netherlands

Gerald R. Ferris, Department of Management, Florida State University, USA

David C. Gilmore, Department of Psychology, University of North Carolina at Charlotte, USA

Robert T. Golembiewski, School of Public and International Affairs, Department of Public Administration and Policy, University of Georgia, USA

Jane Gunn, Australian National University, National Graduate School of Management, Australia

Jonathon R.B. Halbesleben, College of Business, California State University, USA

Angela T. Hall, Department of Management, Florida State University, USA

Wayne A. Hochwarter, Department of Management, Florida State University, USA

Keith James, Department of Psychology, Colorado State University, USA

Michele K. Kacmar, Department of Management and Marketing, University of Alabama, USA

Robert W. Kolodinsky, Department of Management, James Madison University, USA

Ronnie Kurchner-Hawkins, President, Kurchner-Hawkins Associates, Philadelphia, USA

Paul E. Levy, Department of Psychology, Buchtel College of Arts and Sciences, University of Akron, USA

Andrew Li, Department of Psychology, Colorado State University, USA

Yongmei Liu, Department of Management, Florida State University, USA

Patrick R. Liverpool, School of Business and Industry, Florida A&M University, USA

John P. Meriac, University of Tennessee, Appalachian State University, USA

Rima Miller, Vice-President, Performa Global Ltd, Bangkok, Thailand

Pamela L. Perrewé, Department of Management, Florida State University, USA

Melita L. Prati, Department of Management, East Carolina University, USA

Chris Provis, School of International Business, University of South Australia, Australia

Christopher C. Rosen, Department of Psychology, Buchtel College of Arts and Sciences, University of Akron, USA

Arndt M. Sorge, Faculty of Management and Organization, University of Groningen, The Netherlands

Janka I. Stoker, Faculty of Management and Organization, University of Groningen, The Netherlands

Darren C. Treadway, School of Business Administration, University of Mississippi, USA

Eran Vigoda-Gadot, Division of Public Administration and Policy and the Center for Public Management and Policy, University of Haifa, Israel

Peter D. Villanova, University of Tennessee, Appalachian State University, USA

Anthony R. Wheeler, Foster College of Business Administration, Bradley University, USA

Lawrence A. Witt, Department of Management, University of New Orleans, USA

Nurit Zaidman, School of Management, Ben-Gurion University of the Negev, Israel

Preface: Challenges and new frontiers for organizational politics in modern worksites

Eran Vigoda-Gadot and Amos Drory

Studies in organizational politics: past, present and future

Organizational politics has been a fruitful field of academic writing and research for more than three decades. Dozens of papers, book chapters, and other publications as well as numerous conference presentations and symposia have been devoted to what was once considered the hidden dynamics of power and influence in organizations, those that create the politicized worksite. In the past decade, the flow of studies has intensified, reflecting the growing interest in this arena. More than 150 studies have been published in professional academic journals that have explored the meaning of this phenomenon, its antecedents, implications, and significance for managers and employees in various fields and sectors and across cultures.

This book is an attempt to provide a comprehensive understanding of a field that for many years seemed interesting, but almost impossible to study empirically. As with other handbooks, we seek to paint the broad picture. Therefore, we have approached most of the scholars who have written about this phenomenon in recent decades and offered them the opportunity to contribute their unique perspectives. Many have agreed to join our journey and have contributed original papers, pre-published works, or updated versions of previously published papers. In sum, approximately thirty chapters were considered for possible inclusion in this volume, of which 19 were finally selected. These articles were carefully chosen for their quality, their clarity and their ability to provide the reader with an integrative look at workplace politics from various perspectives. The result is 19 chapters of what we see as a thoughtful and lucid analysis written by the leading researchers in the field.

The *Handbook of Organizational Politics* is therefore designed to offer a broad perspective on the fascinating phenomenon of power, influence and politics in modern worksites. This phenomenon has proven meaningful for individuals, groups and other organizational stakeholders, as it is related to various aspects of organizational outcomes and performances. However, politics in organizations is difficult to study because employees, middle managers and corporate leaders are not eager to reveal the political secrets and dynamics that help them get ahead in the workplace and advance their personal agendas. Organizational politics has many definitions, but all of them relate to the use of personal or aggregate power to influence others and achieve one's goals in the workplace. Throughout the years, scholars have studied not only the positive and negative aspects of politics and its internal structure, but also its antecedents and potential outcomes. The book discusses most, if not all, of these themes, as detailed in the partial list below. The book is intended as a comprehensive collection of original or re-worked studies that together comprise a current picture of our knowledge about this area. This portrait is based on both theoretical ideas and empirical findings from around the globe.

The art of workplace politics

Organizational politics has been studied empirically for more than two decades, but its theoretical foundations can be traced back as far as half a century ago. In a previous book (Vigoda, 2003), we stated that organizational politics represents a unique domain of inter-personal relations in the workplace. Its main characteristic is the readiness of people to use power in their efforts to influence others and secure personal or collective interests or, alternatively, avoid negative outcomes within the organization (Bozeman et al., 1996).

In recent decades, organizational politics has become a topic of prime importance in management literature. In the late 1950s, Lasswell claimed that politics is important because it represents the secret of 'who gets what, when, and how' in a social system (Lasswell, 1958). However, until the 1970s, politics in organizations received little or no attention. Only with the recognition that, as in the national arena, organizations also have to deal with conflicts, resource-sharing processes, and power struggles among their members and units has organizational politics begun to attract growing attention. In the late 1970s and early 1980s, some studies established a theoretical framework for the inquiry into the role of politics in the workplace (Bacharach and Lawler, 1980; Mayes and Allen, 1977; Mintzberg, 1983; Pfeffer, 1981).

In the early 1990s, Pfeffer (1992, p. 8) argued that organizations, particularly large ones, are like governments in that they are fundamentally political entities. To understand them one needs to understand organizational politics, just as to understand governments one needs to understand governmental politics. As interest in organizational politics grew, so did the variety of approaches to its study (Vigoda, 2003). For example, some studies have tried to typologize the various influence tactics found in the workplace (for example, Kipnis et al., 1980), while others have used a theory of organizational conflict to explain power struggles and influence tactics (for example, Putnam, 1995). Most of these studies have focused on the nature and expressions of organizational politics and have done so using a negative perspective that equates organizational politics with the dark side of human behavior, such as manipulation, coercive influence, or other subversive and semi-legal actions (for example, Ferris and King, 1991; Mintzberg, 1983, 1989). Few have used a balanced approach to determine the effects of organizational politics on employees' atti-tudes, behavior and performance in the workplace. The relationship between organiza-tional politics and organizational outcomes is important because every member of an organization has power and exercises it in a unique way to benefit himself/herself in his/her work environment. Power, influence and politics have at least some effect on every member of an organization and thus on the entire organizational unit. Therefore, many scholars have argued that the relationship between organizational politics and organiza-tional outcomes is an important one that deserves further inquiry (Bozeman et al., 1996; Ferris and Kacmar, 1992; Kacmar and Carlson, 1994). During the 1990s and on into the twenty-first century, the interest in organizational politics began to focus on people's per-ceptions about the political maneuvers in their workplaces. This shift in focus was based on the assumption that the reality of politics is best understood through the perceptions of individuals.

Indeed, most of the relatively few studies on organizational politics have concentrated on employees' perceptions of politics (Vigoda, 2003, pp. 7–8). To date, two approaches to organizational politics have dominated the literature. The first focuses on employees' influence tactics at work as the best expression of political behavior. This line of research proposes a variety of typologies for influence tactics as well as possible antecedents and consequences of various influence tactics (i.e. Allen et al., 1979; Brass, 1984; Burns, 1961; Cheng, 1983; Erez and Rim, 1982; Izraeli, 1975; Kipnis et al., 1980). The second approach is more recent and focuses on employees' subjective *perceptions* of organizational politics rather than on political behavior or influence tactics (i.e. Ferris et al., 1994, 1996, 1998; Kacmar and Ferris, 1991; Vigoda, 2000, 2001, 2002; Vigoda-Gadot and Kapun, 2005). As was suggested by Kacmar and Ferris (1991, pp. 193–4) and Kacmar and Carlson (1994, p. 3), perceptions of organizational politics represent the degree to which respondents view their work environment as political in nature, promoting the self-interests of others, and therefore unjust and unfair from the individual's point of view. These studies proposed a scale for the measurement of political perceptions called the 'Perceptions of Organizational Politics Scale' (POPS). Many of the chapters included in this volume have used this scale in their research, making their studies quite comparable with one another. Notwithstanding, one should clearly distinguish between *actual* political behavior in the workplace and the *perceptions* of this behavior. Actual political behavior differs conceptually from perceptions of politics. It is, however, related to perceptions, and the nature of both phenomena is posited and tested in this volume, along with some relationships between them.

In an earlier work we indicated that organizational politics is a controversial concept (Vigoda, 2003). While there is no doubt that internal politics is a common phenomenon in every organization, too little is known about the exact nature and boundaries of such machinations even today (Cropanzano et al., 1997; Kipnis et al., 1980; Mayes and Allen, 1977). Clearly, there is a growing need to fill in the missing pieces of this puzzle. This volume is intended as a major step in that direction.

The framework of the book
The book is presented in five sections that embody the core areas of research in modern studies of organizational politics. These five sections focus on the individual's viewpoint: values issues including ethics, justice and trust; emotions and stress; systems and performance analysis; and professional perspectives on organizational politics. We believe these areas to be representative of many research approaches in this field. In recent years, we have seen a veritable explosion of studies that have introduced a broad range of perspectives, methods and research tools to the study of organizational politics. All of them have contributed to advancing our knowledge in this area. This book, two years in the making, tries to do justice to the wide variety of approaches to the study of organizational politics by selecting representative material created by an influential list of contributors.

Part I: The individual's perspective
The first part of this volume deals with the micro level and sub-topics of organizational politics that, by nature, relate to individuals and their role in the workplace. It consists of five chapters. The first, by Eran Vigoda-Gadot and Yinnon Dryzin-Amit, deals with the significance of organizational politics for managers in their role as leaders. The authors argue that for many years studies have dealt with the relationship between leadership and organizational performance, but have paid little attention to workplace politics as a mediating factor. This chapter proposes that perceptions of politics among public sector employees are a possible mediator between the supervisor's leadership style and formal and

informal aspects (organizational citizenship behavior – OCB) of the employees' performance. The chapter develops a theoretical framework that should be tested empirically in
future studies. Its main contribution is in taking the theory of organizational politics into
different realms and exploring its usefulness beyond what is already known in the literature.

    The second chapter, by John P. Meriac and Peter D. Villanova, is intended to study agree-
ableness and extraversion as moderators of the political influence compatibility–work outcomes relationship. The objectives of this study were threefold: to provide additional
support for the notion that political tactics relate differently to work outcomes, to test
whether political influence compatibility (PIC) explains incremental variance in the same
work outcomes better than perceived political climate, and to explore whether agreeableness or extraversion moderated the PIC–outcomes relationship. Mariac and Villanova
used an impressive sample of 479 employees of a large southeastern US merchandising
company who completed questionnaires designed to measure their political influence
climate perceptions, orientation toward influence tactics and work attitudes. The interesting results indicated that political tactics were related to work outcomes in a variety of
ways. Furthermore, while PIC explained incremental variances in work outcomes over and
above those explained by political climate, extraversion moderated this relationship only
partially. This chapter is unique in using the concept of Person Organization Fit (POF) in
relation to organizational politics. Its use raises the issue of people's political fit with the
organization and the impact that fit has on their work performance.

    The third chapter, by Christopher C. Rosen, Chu-Hsiang Chang and Paul E. Levy,
deals with organizational politics and personality. The purpose of this insightful chapter
is threefold. First, the authors present a review of the literature that relates personality to
perceptions of organizational politics. This review discusses personality as an antecedent
to perceptions of politics, as well as the role of personality variables in moderating the
relationships between politics and outcomes. Second, they use the perspective of an individual to discuss the multiplicity of effects that personality variables have on the relationship between politics and outcomes. Finally, the authors present an empirical study
to illustrate this approach, focusing on the interactive effects of perceptions of politics,
self-monitoring and agreeableness. Results supported the proposed three-way interaction
and suggested that perceptions of politics have positive effects on organizational citizenship behaviors for employees who report having higher levels of self-monitoring and
agreeableness. Finally, the authors speculate on the implications of these findings and
discuss them within the context of a process-oriented framework that is used to link
organizational politics to work-related attitudes and behaviors.

    The fourth chapter in this part, written by Keith James, offers a different look at the
individual's perception of politics. Through his middle-level research on the behavior of
individuals as part of larger bodies such as work groups, James suggests that fully understanding and managing organizational politics requires considering group-level (collective) politics as well as politics at the individual level. He argues that while most studies of
organizational politics consider only the perspective of the individual, the causes, mechanisms and results of collective politics in the workplace are key issues that must be
considered as well. James defines politics as the use of means other than formal organizational systems, policies, or procedures to try to control resources, people, or decisions.
This definition is rather unusual, but it paves the way for the argument that collective politics can yield both positive outcomes (e.g. flexibility, broad representation) and negative

ones (e.g. inequitable distributions, polarization of factions). The chapter successfully integrates intergroup and intragroup political processes. Its examination of context influences on the tone and direction of politics in the workplace helps explicate the circumstances that lead to positive rather than negative collective organizational political outcomes. James reviews the limited literature focusing directly on collective organizational politics. He highlights a number of relevant ideas and findings from studies that have examined organizational politics from the point of view of the individual. In addition, he extrapolates some works on collective politics in non-organizational (e.g. national) settings to collective politics in organizations. Finally, James suggests a new, integrative model with which to study the causes, moderators and process of collective politics in organizations.

The final chapter in this part, by Amos Drory and Nurit Zaidman, highlights the concept of impression management in organizations as a political behavior. It suggests that impression management in organizations has been widely recognized among researchers and organizational behavior scholars as behavior performed by the individual attempting to control or manipulates others' attributions and impressions of him or her. In the organizational context impression management is therefore considered a subset of political tactics focusing on influencing others in order to serve the needs of the individual. The chapter by Drory and Zaidman discusses the ways in which individuals use impression management at work to serve their own interests and the factors which determine the choice of impression management tactics. The main thrust of this chapter is to discuss the role of contextual factors in determining how self-impression is manipulated in organizations. The chapter presents both qualitative and quantitative findings to demonstrate the relationship between contextual variables such as organizational norms culture, and sociocultural characteristics and impression management tactics.

Part II: Ethics and fairness
The second part of the volume looks at values and moral considerations in organizational politics. Three chapters are included in this part. The first chapter, by Chris Provis, offers a fresh definition of organizational politics from a philosophical viewpoint, with an eye to a direct discussion about ethical considerations. Provis proposes addressing some of the normative and ethical issues in organizational politics in the same sorts of ways that political theory has addressed issues that arise in the politics of nation-states. To do so, he suggests that we must eschew definitions of organizational politics that incorporate common negative assumptions. Those assumptions hinder us from a full theoretical understanding of organizational politics, in particular from seeing similarities between organizational politics and other varieties of politics. They also obscure a number of genuine ethical dilemmas and problems. Hence, Provis suggests that we should not evaluate tactics by how well they conform to organizational demands or promote organizational objectives. One may take issue with a definition because the definition itself may play a part in political processes. However, any definition should leave open the possibility of viewing organizational politics as an important activity that is subject to ethical analysis, but can still be important and even praiseworthy. Evaluation of specific cases will often be hindered by the fact that it is hard to discern people's real motives and intentions, but that does not mean that evaluation is impossible or that we should abandon efforts to work out principles that underlie sound ethical evaluations.

From the vantage point of the philosopher, we advance to that of the psychologist who, in the second chapter, is looking at organizational justice as a mediator between organizational politics, organizational support and organizational commitment. The study by Simon Albrecht extends the research on the relationship between organizational politics, organizational support, organizational trust and organizational commitment. Moreover, the study tests whether or not organizational trust mediates the influence of organizational politics and organizational support on organizational commitment. The sample on which the conclusions are based consisted of 306 full-time employees occupying a diverse number of roles within a large medical facility. Confirmatory factor analysis showed that employees could clearly discriminate between organizational politics, organizational support, organizational trust and organizational commitment. Structural equations modeling showed that, as predicted, organizational politics was inversely related to organizational support and organizational trust. Organizational trust strongly influenced organizational commitment. Contrary to expectations and previous research findings, organizational support did not mediate the relationship between organizational politics and organizational commitment and did not directly influence organizational commitment. Rather, the results showed that organizational trust fully mediated the relationship between organizational support and organizational commitment. However, organizational trust did not mediate the relationship between organizational politics and organizational commitment. Albrecht discusses the results in terms of the important role that politics plays in shaping trust and support, and the important role that organizational trust plays in shaping organizational commitment.

Finally, Constant D. Beugré and Patrick R. Liverpool deal with organizational politics as a determinant of perceptions of fairness in organizations. In this chapter, the authors focus on the possibility that politics and trust are separate phenomena and question the extent to which perceptions of politics influence perceptions of fairness, equity and justice in organizations. While this is an unusual approach to organizational behavior theory, the authors argue that understanding the impact of politics on justice is important. Just as politics is ubiquitous in organizational life, they claim, so are issues of fairness and unfairness. Beugré and Liverpool maintain that the literature of both organizational politics and organizational justice may enrich each other because the two concepts tend to have similar antecedents and produce similar consequences. Moreover, organizational politics and organizational justice are both perceptual phenomena. Given that people are more likely to act based on their *perception* of reality rather than on reality itself (Lewin, 1936), it is important to understand how perceptions of politics influence notions of fairness. The chapter is divided into four sections. In the first, the authors define the concepts of politics and justice. This is followed by an explanation of the relationship between perceptions of politics and perceptions of justice. In the third, they develop and explain a theoretical model of the relationship between the two concepts. The fundamental premise of this model is that perceptions of organizational politics negatively affect perceptions of justice. Finally, the authors discuss the model's implications for practice and research.

Part III: Emotions and stress
The third part moves beyond the individual and ethical levels to explore the mental and physical consequences of highly politicized modern worksites. It concentrates on the emotions and stress that are involved in the political process in organizations. The three

chapters included in this part provide cutting-edge theories and empirical findings about the covert aspects of power and politics and their consequences for the mental health of the individual and his/her surroundings. The first chapter, by Russell Cropanzano and Andrew Li, elaborates on the meaning and implications of the relationship between organizational politics and stress. In this chapter, the authors systematically and thoroughly review the research literature relating organizational politics to workplace stress. They open the discussion by considering three different definitions of stress. First, stress is depicted as an environmental event that may engender negative reactions from employees. Second, stress is defined as a cognitive appraisal that one's resources are overwhelmed by environmental demands. Third, stress is considered as a response to adverse working conditions. A review of each of these definitions provides insights into the dynamics of organizational politics, but each one also raises unanswered questions. After considering stress, Cropanzano and Li turn their attention to organizational politics. They begin by discussing the treatment of politics as a neutral event, rather than as a negative occurrence. They then turn their attention to the distinction between actual political behavior and perceived organizational politics. As they demonstrate, each of these conceptualizations of organizational politics has different implications for the etiology of stress. The chapter concludes with a thought-provoking, integrative model that underscores conceptual needs and acts as an impetus for future research.

The second chapter, by Yongmei Liu, Gerald R. Ferris, Darren C. Treadway, Melita L. Prati, Pamela L. Perrewé and Wayne A. Hochwarter, explores affective and cognitive reactions to politics as a stressor and proposes a discussion of the 'emotion of politics and the politics of emotions'. The authors suggest that despite the increased interest in organizational politics in recent years, only minimal research has examined the role of emotion in organizational politics processes. In this chapter, the authors propose a conceptualized linking of perceptions of organizational politics with emotion, which is focused at both the individual and dyadic levels of analysis. They argue that emotion and emotional behaviors serve as intermediate linkages in the relationships between perceptions of organizational politics and both attitudinal and behavioral outcomes. Specifically, the chapter draws from research on organizational politics, affective events theory, and social-psychological studies of emotion in an effort to advance an emotions-based approach to organizational politics. The authors convincingly demonstrate that there is emotion in organizational politics and organizational politics in emotion, and that the intersection of the two has to be recognized in order to obtain a more complete understanding of both.

The third chapter, by Robyn L. Brouer, Gerald R. Ferris, Wayne A. Hochwarter, Mary Dana Laird and David C. Gilmore, expands the study of stress-related reactions to perceptions of organizational politics. Following Vigoda (2002), this chapter argues that perceptions of politics play the role of a workplace stressor, which produces associated reactions. In keeping with earlier studies, the authors suggest that this relationship holds only for those individuals who have weak political skills. For those with stronger political skills, perceptions of politics should be associated with less negative attitudes and reactions. The chapter is the outcome of a three-tiered investigation into political skill as a moderator of the relationship between perceptions of politics and strain, where strain was defined as symptoms of depression in employees. The convergence of results across the three studies demonstrated that, for those with strong political skills, increases in perceptions of politics were associated with decreases in symptoms of depression. The opposite was true for those who were politically less savvy. The authors discuss these results clearly and suggest their thoughts on the implications of the study as well as directions for future research in this area.

Part IV: Systems and performance

The fourth part of the book is devoted to a macro view of organizational politics and deals with system and performance analysis using issues such as strategy, change and decision making. Five chapters are included in this part, the first of which is an intriguing chapter by Jane Gunn and Stephen Chen devoted to the question of how organizational politics influences strategic decision making. This chapter highlights strategic management from a political perspective. The authors suggest that early strategic management literature assumed strategy making as a rational, logical process. However, they continue, the impact of organizational politics on strategy processes has received little attention. Although many of the rational assumptions have been challenged in academic literature, they continue to influence practice, and research linking strategic management and organizational politics remains limited. Focusing on organizational politics at the micro or intra-organizational level, this chapter critically reviews the literature on strategic management and organizational politics in order to investigate strategic management as a political activity. Gunn and Chen provide a micro-political perspective on strategic management and identify areas for future research. Their unconventional explorations of and explanations for politics at the strategic system level of analysis lay the groundwork for continued studies in this field.

The following chapter, by Simon Albrecht, discusses affective reactions to organizational politics, cognitive assessments and their influence on organizational commitment, and cynical attitudes toward change. This chapter is in keeping with the previous chapter in this part, as it deals with attitudes towards systematic change and performance in organizations. Albrecht begins by suggesting that although there is substantial empirical evidence supporting the important role that politics plays in organizational contexts, there is limited empirical evidence that focuses on the distinction between how employees *feel* about organizational politics and what they *think* about organizational politics. Exploratory and confirmatory factor analysis of survey data ($N = 365$) collected from full-time workers employed in a broad range of organizations showed that respondents could reliably discriminate between what they think about organizational politics (as measured by POPS), and how they feel about organizational politics. Newly developed measures of affective reactions to organizational politics identified two distinct dimensions – one positive and one negative. Regression analyses showed that the affective dimensions of organizational politics predicted variance in affective commitment and attitudes to change beyond that accounted for by what employees think about politics (as measured by the POPS) and by how they perceive organizational support (as measured by the Survey of Perceived Organizational Support – SPOS). More specifically, positive feelings about organizational politics explained variance in organizational commitment beyond that explained by perceptions of organizational politics and organizational support. Negative feelings about organizational politics explained variance in cynicism toward change beyond that explained by perceptions of organizational politics and organizational support. Supplementary analysis showed that negative affective reactions to politics partially mediated the relationship between cognitive perceptions of politics

(POPS) and cynicism toward change. Finally, Albrecht provides implications for further research on organizational politics.

The third chapter, by Jonathon R.B. Halbesleben and Anthony R. Wheeler, explores the relationship between perceptions of politics, social support, withdrawal and perform-ance at the organizational level. In this chapter, the authors view withdrawal and perfor-mance as significant factors with considerable effects on system-level outcomes. They hypothesize that social support moderates the relationship between perceptions of polit-ics (POP) and employee withdrawal behaviors (the depersonalization component of burnout), which in turn mediates the relationship between POP and employee perform-ance. Study 1 was based on a sample of 83 firefighters and found support for the hypothe-sized relationship between the variables. Study 2 was more ambitious and sampled 521 full-time employees from two geographic regions in the USA. It in essence replicated the findings of Study 1. Both studies supported the proposed model, indicating a process underlying the relationship between POP and performance that is linked to the conserva-tion of resources. Helbesleben and Wheeler conclude that the inclusion of social support and withdrawal behaviors in the POP–performance relationship extends the literature on politics. They also offer practical recommendations to assist human resource managers in handling the system consequences of politics in organizations.

The fourth chapter, by Wayne A. Hochwarter, Robert W. Kolodinsky, Lawrence A. Witt, Angela T. Hall, Gerald R. Ferris and Michele K. Kacmar, offers competing views about the role that understanding plays in the relationship between perceptions of pol-itics and job performance. The authors argue that to date, research examining the role of understanding as a moderator of the relationship between organizational politics perceptions and work outcomes has paid disproportionate attention to attitudinal or affective worker reactions, largely ignoring behavioral outcomes, such as job performance. To fill this void, the authors tested two competing hypotheses. The first posited that better understanding serves as an *antidote* and reduces the negative effects of politics on job per-formance. The second took a different tack, arguing that better understanding *distracts* employees from their work and hinders their performance. Hierarchical, moderated, mul-tiple regression analyses results from three studies convincingly support the 'distraction' hypothesis. The chapter concludes with a discussion about the contributions of these results, the study's strengths and limitations, practical implications and directions for future research, all of which underscore the potential that testing moderators hold for the study of organizational politics.

The final chapter in this part, by David Butcher and Martin Clarke, elaborates on the relationship between organizational politics and organizational democracy and ques-tions whether the two can exist symbiotically or are by nature at war with one another. In the last 20 years, substantial changes in the structure of the economy have forced busi-nesses to rethink the way they approach the distribution of organizational influence. However, despite these developments there is still increasing evidence that employees do not always see themselves as beneficiaries of such change. Surveys and reports regularly highlight unacceptable levels of employee cynicism, disillusionment and alienation. Attempts to install democratic principles in organizations do not always work. Much has changed, but much has also remained the same. Some piece of the jigsaw puzzle is missing. It is a piece that has long been viewed as integral to governmental democracy, but strangely enough, has been seen as illegitimate in organizational democracy – it is politics. The chapter explores this increasing tension between democratized organization forms and the realities of bureaucracies. In this context Clark and Butcher argue that organizational politics is not only an important and necessary managerial discipline, but that models of political behavior are also central to the development of real organizational democracy. The inherent compatibility of organizational politics and democracy is considered. The authors draw on recent research to delineate how the adoption of constructive political behavior derived from a political institutional leadership setting offers a robust model for those the leadership of more democratic organizational forms. They also offer advice on how to work with a constructive political 'mindset' and consider how the progress toward redistributing organizational influence may be accelerated through individual action.

Part V: The professional's perspective
In the final part of the book we decided to take a more practical look at organizational politics and consider issues related to human resource management and counseling that frequently arise when power and influence are involved in the daily life of managers and employees. We found four articles that addressed these topics very effectively. First, a stimulating chapter by one of the major contributors to organizational development theory and practice, Robert T. Golembiewski, focuses on consulting. He notes that the literature on consulting for and reporting to hierarchical superiors does not address power phenomena, even though there is strong evidence that one ignores such issues at his/her own peril. Golembiewski finds no adequate explanation for the failure to deal with this issue. He suggests that the emphasis on legitimacy may be to blame, especially because this view is so attractive to formal elites in all collective systems. He further suggests that perhaps 'power' or 'politics' in organizations is considered unworthy of attention, with connotations of being 'dirty' or underhand. Golembiewski characterizes power as a necessity of collective life, whose manifestations may be good, bad, or somewhere in between. His chapter goes a long way to remedying this tendency to define power topics as off limits in most organizational theory and practice, as well as in consulting. The chapter also sketches two related practical methods of ameliorating the traditional neglect of this topic. It asks whether 'power' is viewed as derived from legitimate or formal authority or from skills, personality, or other bases. The primary focus of the chapter is on public organizations, but it has general applicability to public sector and NGO contexts as well.

In keeping with Golembiewski's arguments, the chapter by Astrid I. Boogers-van Griethuijsen, Ben J.M. Emans, Janka I. Stoker and Arndt M. Sorge deals with sources of consultants' personal power. Twelve foundations for the power position of consultants are suggested and are based on the assumption that a management consultant is often hired in order to promote organizational change. Therefore, the consultant should possess the qualities deemed necessary to that end. One of those qualities is power *vis-à-vis* involved organizational members. In this study, the authors contribute to the knowledge of organizational politics by developing a model that explains the sources of power of management consultants. Based on interviews with management consultants, they enumerate expert power, personal power, reputation of the consultancy firm, professional status symbols, indirect formal power, network power, means of exchange, reward power, coercive power, power based on persuasive skills, power based on communicative skills, and power based on analytic skills as relevant power bases for consultants.

Finally, Ronnie Kurchner-Hawkins and Rima Miller present their experience-based view about the need to build positive strategies of organizational politics in turbulent times. They start with the well-accepted assertion that politics is an organizational reality and develop a chapter that explores how individuals can construct positive strategies for managing organizational politics. The authors view organizational politics neutrally as the exercise of power and influence that primarily occurs outside of formal organizational processes and procedures. A mindset shift continuum is presented describing the attitude and behavior changes that support positive political action. The authors' model of organizational politics provides a context for understanding and constructing positive political strategies. The model identifies eight factors that impact organizational politics. Four behavioral factors – influence, communication/information, relationships/alliances, and networks – serve as 'levers' that can be activated when constructing political strategies. Four additional mediating factors – history, culture, 'past plays' and ethics – provide a context for determining political action. The chapter concludes with a discussion of the implications of implementing positive political strategies for individuals and organizations and emphasizes a practical approach for the management of politics in modern worksites.

Target readers
This book is intended as a collection of up-to-date, original studies on organizational politics conducted around the world at various levels of analysis and from manifold disciplinary perspectives. It encompasses theoretical, empirical and practical approaches contributed by the leading scholars in the field. Hence it offers serious, analytical material for scholars, students and practitioners alike. Such a collection should be of greatest interest to scholars in various fields of the behavioral and social sciences such as organizational behavior, management and business, occupational psychology, sociology and political science. The book's focus on the internal politics of organizations makes it a useful tool for academics and managers from the public and private sectors looking for better explanations of internal processes in businesses, as well as in large federal or state organizations. However, the mid-level and macro-level analysis of some of the chapters can be used for policy studies and strategic management as well.

While most of the book's readers will probably be academics, the chapters included provide a wealth of information that may prove useful for other audiences. For example, the second section may be of interest to scholars in the humanistic disciplines, and the fifth part of the book is oriented towards practitioners. Many of the empirical data provided throughout the other chapters should help scholars and graduate students in the social sciences seeking a better understanding of intra-organizational dynamics, the development of conflicts in organizations, and the nature of power influence and authority in various worksites. Finally, the book, with its strong academic and empirical orientation, delineates some important current developments in an area that is both covert and hard to study, but which holds great potential and promise for the future understanding of human political behavior in modern worksites and its implications for personal, group and system-level performance.

References

Allen, R.W., Medison, D.L., Porter, L.W., Renwick, P.A. and Mayes, B.T. (1979). Organizational politics: Tactics and characteristics of political actors. *California Management Review*, **22**, 77–83.

Bacharach, S.B. and Lawler, E.J. (1980). *Power and politics in organizations*. San Francisco: Jossey-Bass.

Bozeman, D.P., Perrewe, P.L., Kacmar, K.M., Hochwarter, W.A. and Brymer, R.A. (1996). An examination of reactions to perceptions of organizational politics. Paper presented at the Southern Management Association Meeting, New Orleans, LA.

Brass, D.J. (1984). Being in the right place: A structural analysis of individual influence in an organization. *Administrative Science Quarterly*, **29**, 518–39.

Burns, T. (1961). Micropolitics: Mechanisms of institutional change. *Administrative Science Quarterly*, **6**, 257–81.

Cheng, J.L. (1983). Organizational context and upward influence: An experimental study of the use of power tactics. *Group and Organizational Studies*, **8**, 337–55.

Cropanzano, R., Howes, J.C., Grandey, A.A. and Toth, P. (1997). The relationship of organizational politics and support to work behaviors, attitudes, and stress. *Journal of Organizational Behavior*, **18**, 159–80.

Erez, M. and Rim, Y. (1982). The relationship between goals, influence tactics and personal and organizational variables. *Human Relations*, **35**, 877–8.

Ferris, G.R. and Kacmar, K.M. (1992). Perceptions of organizational politics. *Journal of Management*, **18**, 93–116.

Ferris, G.R. and King, T.R. (1991). Politics in human resources decisions: A walk on the dark side. *Organizational Dynamics*, **20**, 59–71.

Ferris, G.R., Fedor, D.B. and King, T.R. (1994). A political conceptualization of managerial behavior. *Human Resource Management Review*, **4**, 1–34.

Ferris, G.R., Frink, D.D., Bhawuk, D.P.S. and Zhou, J. (1996). Reactions of diverse groups to politics in the workplace. *Journal of Management*, **22**, 23–44.

Ferris, G.R., Harrell-Cook, G. and Dulebohn, J.H. (1998). Organizational Politics: The nature of the relationship between politics perceptions and political behavior. In S.B. Bacharach and E.J. Lawler (eds), *Research in the sociology of organizations*, Greenwich, CT: JAI Press.

Izraeli, D.N. (1975). The middle manager and the tactics of power expansion: A case study. *Sloan Management Review*, **16**, 57–70.

Kacmar, K.M. and Carlson, D.S. (1994). Further validation of the Perceptions of Politics Scale (POPS): A multiple sample investigation. Paper presented at Academy of Management Meeting, Dallas, Texas.

Kacmar, K.M. and Ferris, G.R. (1991). Perceptions of Organizational Politics Scale (POPS): Development and construct validation. *Educational and Psychological Measurement*, **51**, 193–205.

Kipnis, D., Schmidt, S.M. and Wilkinson, I. (1980). Intraorganizational influence tactics: exploration in getting one's way. *Journal of Applied Psychology*, **65**, 440–52.

Lasswell, H.D. (1958). *Politics: who gets what, when, how*. Cleveland, OH: World Publishing.

Lewin, K. (1936). *Principles of topological psychology*. New York: McGraw-Hill.

Mayes, B.T. and Allen, R.W. (1977). Toward a definition of organizational politics. *Academy of Management Review*, **2**, 672–8.

Mintzberg, H. (1983). *Power in and around organizations*. Englewood Cliffs, NJ: Prentice-Hall.

Mintzberg, H. (1989). *Mintzberg on management*. New York: Free Press.

Pfeffer, J. (1981). *Power in organizations*. Marshfield, MA: Pitman Publishing.

Pfeffer, J. (1992). *Management with power*. Boston: Harvard Business School Press.

Putnam, L.L. (1995). Formal negotiations: The productive side of organizational conflict. In A.M. Nicotera (ed.), *Conflict and organizations* (pp. 183–200). New York: State University of New York.

Vigoda, E. (2000). The relationship between organizational politics, job attitudes, and work outcomes: Exploration and implications for the public sector. *Journal of Vocational Behavior*, **57**, 326–47.

Vigoda, E. (2001). Reactions to organizational politics: A cross-cultural examination in Israel and Britain. *Human Relations*, **54**, 1483–518.

Vigoda, E. (2002). Stress-related aftermaths to workplace politics: An empirical assessment of the relationship among organizational politics, job stress, burnout, and aggressive behavior. *Journal of Organizational Behavior*, **23**, 571–91.

Vigoda, E. (2003). *Developments in organizational politics: How political dynamics affect employee performance in modern work sites*. Cheltenham, UK and Northampton, MA: Edward Elgar.

Vigoda-Gadot, E. and Kapoon, D. (2005). Perceptions of politics and performance in public and private organizations: A test of one model across two sectors. *Policy and Politics*, **33** (2), 251–76.

PART I

THE INDIVIDUAL'S PERSPECTIVE: POLITICS, PERSONALITY AND LEADERSHIP

1 Organizational politics, leadership and performance in modern public worksites: A theoretical framework*
Eran Vigoda-Gadot and Yinnon Dryzin-Amit

Introduction
In the last few decades much attention has been given to theories of leadership in organizations. Leadership is considered to have a major influence on the performance of organizations, managers and employees. Early theories tried to define effective leadership styles (democratic or autocratic, socially oriented or target oriented etc.). More recently, researchers have focused mainly on the subordinates' perspective. This perspective was suggested by Burns (1978) and Bass (1985) and was called the transformational leadership theory. The theory claims that transformational leadership has a positive effect on employees' attitudes towards their job and their job environment, and ultimately affects their work performance.

Consequently studies have also pointed to organizational politics as an important antecedent of employees' performance. Organizational politics relates to feelings of fairness and justice in the workplace. Other studies describe organizational politics as a power game and influence tactics designed to achieve the best outcomes for the user (Pfeffer, 1992). This phenomenon occurs frequently in business corporations, factories, hospitals, military organizations, governmental ministries and many other organizations (Vigoda, 2000) and different studies emphasize its importance for understanding the performance of both the individual and the organization.

This chapter develops a theory about the relationship between leadership and employees' performance and argues that organizational politics mediates in this relationship. The chapter focuses on two fundamental aspects of performance: formal and informal. Formal performance refers to those aspects of an employee's job that are defined as compulsory by the organization. Informal performance refers to the acts that an employee performs above and beyond the contractual requirements of his/her position. Smith et al. (1983) established the concept of organizational citizenship behavior as a unique phenomenon that describes informal performance in the organization. This phenomenon was defined as an individual behavior that is not included in the job's formal definition, a behavior for which the employee is not compensated and the absence of which would incur no sanctions (Organ, 1988). Nevertheless, the employee chooses to perform it and by so doing contributes to the organization's effectiveness. Our study tries to relate aspects of leadership to aspects of performance by examining organizational politics as a mediating factor.

* An empirical examination of the theoretical framework presented in this chapter is forthcoming in *Personnel Review*; Emerald Publishers.

Leadership in organizations

An investigation of the scientific knowledge about leadership shows that throughout the years, reference has been made to two leading factors: (1) the leader's characteristics and behavior, and (2) the circumstances necessitating the demonstration of leadership. The Scottish historian Thomas Carlyle (1907) relates the leadership phenomenon to the leader only. He claims that history is an expression of combinations of many biographies about different leaders. Carlyle highlights the leader's role. He claims that the leader is first and foremost a spiritual leader whose purity of vision elevates him above society in general. The leader is brave and original, and can discern the truth.

This romantic attitude was the basis for the characteristic and charismatic approach. According to this, the leader is born with characteristics that mark him as a leader. A meta-analysis by Stogdill (1984) revealed no common or consistent set of characteristics for all leaders. Stogdill concluded that different situations require different kinds of leadership, thereby paving the way for the behavioral and situational approaches that were developed later.

Karl Marx approached leadership from a situational rather than a characteristic viewpoint. According to this approach, social and financial situations have a deterministic constancy. Circumstances and not characteristics define who will become a leader. Just as a baby's body develops and grows with time, so does the shared awareness of the masses, developing to the point where a new reality is created. According to the situational approach, leaders do not dictate circumstances, but are led by them. Many researchers, disappointed with the characteristic approach, adopted this methodology, only to find it equally unsatisfying. While it explained the results of lab studies, it was not adequate to describe the leadership phenomenon in a more general way (Heifetz, 1994).

A new focus has emerged in studies that have centered on different leadership styles. According to this research theory, the leader's effectiveness is dependent on his behavioral style, which can be learned and made part of his psyche (Lewin et al., 1939; Blake and Mouton, 1964). The main contribution of this theory was to conceptualize different leadership styles, for example, the missionary style (including both the social missionary and the autocratic missionary), the democratic style, and the *laissez-faire* style. These categories remain in effect even today. Since the 1960s, studies on leadership have focused on the interaction between the leader's style and the situations he/she encounters that require the exercise of leadership. Gradually, the question of the leader's effectiveness has become a main focus in organizational research. There were attempts to characterize the most effective leadership styles, but these studies reached the same dead end as the characteristic approach. The attempt to identify a more or less effective leadership style did not take into account the fact that the leader has to cope with different situations that have a major influence on his effectiveness.

To rectify this problem, the contingency theory of leadership was devised, which contended that leadership derives from the interaction of the leader's characteristics with environmental and circumstantial factors. These studies have tried to conceptualize the situational circumstances in which each type of leadership style will be most effective. Using this approach, three central models were identified: (1) Reddin's (1967) three-dimensional theory, which claims that the leader is a person who analyzes the situation and adjusts himself accordingly; (2) Hersey and Blanchard's (1972) life-cycle model, which suggests the group's maturity level as a variable that mediates between the style of leadership and its effectiveness; and (3) Fiedler's (1978) dependent model.

Today, the starting point of most studies is the notion that organizational leadership is first and foremost an influence on people's motivation to perform missions throughout time while utilizing motivation methods and little use of force (Yammarino and Dubinsky, 1994; Kotter, 1996). This definition emphasizes the subordinate's choice to perform a task of his own free will and rejects the use of force. Such a definition makes a clear distinction between leadership and rule. In addition, it connects leadership with the processes of influence, strength, power and authority, which comprise the political environment in organizations. When people act out of obedience to authority, it is difficult to decide whether they are acting of their own free will or out of fear of punishment.

The current chapter adopts this leadership definition and focuses on two of its main aspects: transformational leadership and transactional leadership. These aspects were first developed by Burns (1978) and were improved by Bass and Avolio to become the 'full range model of leadership' (Bass, 1985; Avolio and Bass, 1991; Bass and Avolio, 1993). According to this theory, there are two basic levels of influence evident in the interaction between the leader and the led. One influence comes from the understanding that the leader creates a cost–benefit concept in his constituency. Burns (1978) called this influence transactional leadership, meaning that the employees will function in accordance with the leader's wishes because they believe they will benefit by such actions. The second influence of the leader is the 'sensation awakening,' which Burns called transformational or charismatic leadership. This style is based on a relationship between the leader and his employees that is inspirational and breaks the cycle of subordinates' basic expectations. This leadership style can captivate employees and urge them on to new and challenging objectives. Transformational leadership raises the employees' awareness of their need to grow, validates their self-expression, and motivates them to perform at new and higher levels. A transformational leader influences the expectations of his subordinates, changes their beliefs and values, and raises them in the hierarchy of needs. According to Burns (1978), the hierarchy of needs is the foundation of the transformational process. He suggests that the outcome of transformational leadership is a relationship of mutual stimulus that transforms the led into leaders and the leaders into 'moral agents.' Transformational leadership is a result of the leader's character, the strength of his belief and his ability to express a compelling vision.

Bass (1985) used the behavioral descriptions derived from Burns's theory to build a research tool, called the MLQ – The Multifactor Leadership Questionnaire. In studies that used this tool, a high correlation was found between the leader's transformational style and the organizational performance level. This correlation was consistently higher than the positive correlation between the leader's transactional style and the organizational performance. In these studies, a negative correlation was usually found between the absent and passive style and organizational performance (Gaspar, 1992; Lowe et al., 1996; Geyer and Steyrer, 1998; MacKenzie et al., 2001; Parry, 2003).

Avolio and Bass (1991) expanded the leadership model to include eight styles of leadership behavior, the most differentiated model ever devised. The model is based on the outcome of their research with 78 managers who were asked in an open-ended questionnaire to describe the most remarkable characteristics of leaders who had influenced them personally. After analyzing the results, Avolio and Bass expanded Bass's original model to what they called the 'Full Range of Leadership Model.' This model includes (1) a leadership style of *'laissez-faire'* or no leadership, (2) transactional leadership which is based on passive and active aspects, and (3) transformational leadership which is based on personal relationships, intellectual challenge, inspirational motivation and behavioral charisma. These three categories create a hierarchical sequence of leadership styles according to the extent of activity that the leader expresses in his action and according to the extent of effectiveness. In this model, transformational leadership ranks as the most effective style, followed by transactional leadership and then the *laissez-faire* style. The basic assumption of the Full Range of Leadership model claims that in every leader all styles can be found. Den Hertog et al. (1997) tested this approach in a study of Dutch managers where only three factors were found (transformational leadership, transactional leadership and no leadership) out of the eight measurements that were described in the Full Range of Leadership model.

Leadership and performance in the public sector

The relationship between leadership and performance has received considerable scholarly attention, but its study in the public sector is still quite limited. Parry (2003) claims that a structural paradox exists between the demand that a manager as leader conduct himself with innovation and flexibility and also provide a wide range of quality services to the public. Parry examines the leadership style that copes best with the complexity that characterizes public management. His review reveals that most studies emphasize the supervision method, that is, the method by which the leader inspects his subordinates' work and gives them feedback about it. These studies suggest that the key to influencing performance in public organizations is the leader's (the manager's) ability to use positive reinforcements (gratitude and recognition) and negative reinforcements (reproaches and punishments). Over time, the leader's ability to respond consistently and coherently to behaviors of the subordinates creates an involuntary connection that guides the subordinates in their performance. These interactions between the leaders and the led are based on 'give and take' and imply the ability of the leader to have an impact on his subordinates.

Most studies on transactional leadership's ability to influence organizational performance have yielded disappointing findings (Gaspar, 1992; Lowe et al., 1996; Geyer and Steyrer, 1998; MacKenzie et al., 2001; Parry, 2003). These studies found that the leadership behaviors that were examined explained a relatively low percentage of the variance of the performance criteria that were studied. This led to leadership theories putting more emphasis on the leader's charismatic/transformational ability to influence (Bass, 1985). Employees choose to perform the tasks out of identification with the leader or with the organization. This relationship results in the employees' basic agreement with the norms to which they are required to perform. Bass claims that transformational leadership can create identification with and internalization of desirable values, as opposed to the limited goal of transactional leadership to create a compliant workforce. Parry (2003) suggests that in public sector organizations there is an inherent tension between the demands to change the managerial strategy for improving the organization's ability to cope with the changing reality and the demand to establish fair, national standards for providing service to all citizens. He examined the influence of the transformational leadership style on the innovation and effectiveness of public organizations and found that the leadership style had a positive influence on their performance. In addition, Theobald (1997) emphasizes the managerial paradox that characterizes public administration organizations. He argues that a comparison between private and public organizations cannot be made because there are significant differences in production processes, marketing and service between them. He further suggests that the transactional leadership style may actually be more beneficial for a public organization because it offers elements that compensate for the lack of more sophisticated rewards systems such as those that exist in the private sector.

Leadership and organizational politics
The importance of organizational politics lies in its potential for helping us understand informal processes of conflict and cooperation in the organization, the relationship between them, and their impact on performance. Kurt Lewin et al. (1939) suggested that people respond to reality as it is perceived by them, not to the reality itself. One can make a similar claim about organizational politics. In other words, the concept of organizational politics is an important stage in the employee's reality perspective. It is customary to define organizational politics as influence tactics used by organization members to improve personal or organizational interests (Vigoda, 2003). Thus the perception of organizational politics reflects feelings of fairness and justice in resource distribution. The stronger the perception of organizational politics, the more the organization is acting in accordance with the interests of its influence holders rather than advancing the organization's goals (Ferris et al., 1989; Ferris and Kacmar, 1992; Vigoda, 2003).

Ferris et al. (1989) suggested the Perceptions of Organizational Politics Scale (POPS) that became very popular and has been used in many studies. A large number of these studies point to the negative influences of the political phenomenon on employees' performance. Studies that used POPS found that strong levels of organizational politics were linked with negative perceptions about the organization's procedural justice, distributional justice, fairness and decency toward employees. In recent studies, relationships were found between organizational politics perspectives and the inefficiency of divisions in the organization (Kacmar and Ferris, 1991; Folger et al., 1992; Ferris and Kacmar, 1992; Ferris et al., 1996). Ferris et al. (1989) pointed to a number of expected outcomes from organizational politics. Such outcomes include: psychological outcomes (employee stress and exhaustion), a negative change in employees' attitudes (trust, dissatisfaction, organizational commitment, etc.), and, finally, an impact on actual behaviors (tardiness, absenteeism, neglecting work, job turnover).

Luthans et al. (1985) have observed successful managers in different organizations. Their findings show that a significant relationship exists between successful managers and the frequency of the use of political behaviors by these managers. This study supported Mintzberg's (1973) findings that managers dedicate most of their time to activities that entail social interactions and power broking rather than classic managerial activities such as decision-making, negotiation and representation. Kumar and Ghadially (1989) also claimed that organizational politics has positive and negative influences. On the positive side, researchers list results such as performance improvement, goals fulfillment, recognition, position improvement, authority enlargement and promotion. On the negative side, researchers list results such as the waste of organizational resources, the damage to reliability, the increase in negative attitudes of others, the development of guilt feelings, and overall damage to the organization's performance.

Today, most researchers agree with the assumption that members of organizations do make use of political behavior at work in order to promote their long- or short-term interests. These interests can, on one hand, advance the organization's goals and benefit its members. For example, Randolph (1985) claimed that organizational politics is not necessarily bad. It is another tool that employees and managers have for promoting goals that cannot be achieved in other ways.

Organizational politics and performance

Performance in organizations comprises different variables that include not only direct, measurable tasks but also attitudinal variables, behavioral tendencies, behaviors and motivation. Motowidlo et al. (1986) also distinguished between task components and background variables that affect the performance of individuals, groups, or the organization. These studies defined the task components as in-role performance or core task and attitudes, including behavioral and motivational variables such as contextual performance. In addition, they pointed to another group of behaviors called extra-role performance, which included behaviors that support the social fabric of the organization. These behaviors are not unique to a specific role, but their frequency significantly affects the organization's outputs.

O'Connor and Morrison (2001) found that the organizational climate has an effect on organizational politics perceptions and on the organization's performance. Witt et al. (2002) suggest that perceptions of the organization's politics are a subjective scale that is dependent on the employees' interpretation of the organizational climate. This scale is supposed to influence employees' behavior and performance. Researchers suggest that employees who believe that their workplace is rife with politics tend to interpret every behavior in the organization in light of that perception. For example, junior employees will avoid transmitting information that is opposed to senior management's decisions, assuming that it could damage their promotion. In these cases, the negative outcomes for the organization's performance could be highly significant and could damage the organizational goals. New employees tend to learn quickly by observing and mimicking the customary behaviors and know when to withhold comment or ignore situations so that they will not have to defy their superior's decisions or deviate from the acceptable political standards.

In fact, high levels of organizational politics may damage the organization's performance in a number of ways. First, employees may interpret the presence of organizational politics as an indicator of a problem with the leadership or management of the organization itself. As a result, employees tend to feel that a certain violation of the 'psychological contract' between themselves and the leaders/managers has occurred. This 'psychological contract' is composed of a social–economic interaction and is influenced by organizational politics perceptions. Therefore, when some employees are rewarded or promoted as a result of what is perceived as a successful political maneuver, the other employees may see the decision as unfair. The result will be an increased distrust towards the 'political player' and the supervisor. Second, political behaviors tend to damage the social relations between the members of the organization. In a political working environment, employees may withhold voluntary behaviors such as offering help to others for fear that their efforts will be perceived by others as political capital (Organ, 1990). Third, employees who perceive their working environment as political in a negative sense may act in different ways to avoid taking part in the 'political game.' Bartunk (1994) claims that employees who recoil at the behaviors of organizational politics tend to focus on just doing their jobs and keep their social interaction or professional collaboration with other members of the organization to a minimum. Finally, a political climate in an organization may lead to hiring unqualified people, just because they possess political power in the organization. The implications of inappropriate hiring on the organization's performance are clear. It seems that in a working environment that is perceived as political, a relationship of distrust is created between the employees and the management. Social connections in the organization are unstable. Communication channels are blocked and the tendency to act above and beyond the minimum requirements of the job definition is squelched. As a result, organizational performance may be seriously damaged.

The relationship between organizational politics, leadership and performance: a theoretical model

The research model depicted in Figure 1.1 suggests a relationship between leadership, organizational politics and employees' performance. The model argues that perceptions of organizational politics mediate the relationship between leadership and performance.

Pillai et al. (1999) examined the relationship between transformational and transactional leadership, procedural justice and distributive justice, and trust to organizational obligation, OCB, and satisfaction from work. He found that an indirect relationship exists between transformational leadership and OCB. The studies of MacKenzie et al. (2001) examined the effect of transformational and transactional leadership on marketing personnel's performance at an insurance company. Findings showed that transformational leadership has more influence on performance than transactional leadership. This finding supports assumptions that the transformational leadership style has a stronger relationship with in-role performance and with OCB compared with transactional leadership.

Most studies on the relationship between leadership and performance show a stronger relationship between transformational leadership and performance than between transactional leadership and performances. Transactional leadership explains a relatively low percentage of the researched performance criterion's variance. On the other hand, the

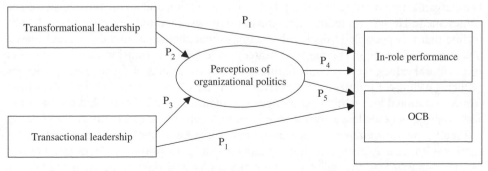

Figure 1.1   The research model

relationship between transformational leadership and the measurement of performance is positive and quite strong (Gaspar, 1992; Lowe et al., 1996; Geyer and Steyrer, 1998; Pillai et al., 1999; MacKenzie et al., 2001; Parry, 2003). It seems that in many organizations, especially public ones, transformational leadership is more effective than transactional leadership. Skilled transformational managers have the ability to support and educate employees, while challenging them to stretch themselves in order to do their jobs. By their own behavior, such transformational managers offer an imitation model and help encourage the employees in their efforts to promote aims and goals. Transformational leadership pushes employees to contribute to the organization beyond the basic requirements of their job description out of personal motivation, out of a challenge, or out of their desire to resemble the leader and be regarded as one of his successful protégés. Nonetheless, it seems that transactional leadership has the ability to strengthen the effectiveness of performance, especially formal performance, which can be quantitatively measured and accurately rewarded. Some studies have found that there is a significant relationship between the conditional gratitude measure (one of the transactional leadership components) and in-role performance (for example, MacKenzie et al., 2001). Therefore, the first proposition suggests that:

P_1 There is a positive relationship between leadership, both transformational and transactional, and in-role performance and OCB. Transformational leadership will have a stronger relationship with and more influence on formal performance and OCB than transactional leadership.

The literature identifies a number of factors that are related to perceptions of organizational politics among employees. Women, junior employees, middle managers and people with a lower level of education tend to perceive their working environment as more political. Similar to them are employees who have a low level of organizational obligation and satisfaction, as well as those who feel less involved in the decision-making process (Vigoda, 2003). In addition, other variables such as position definition, task characteristics, organizational climate, leadership style and supervision are all related to perceptions of organizational politics (Ferris et al., 1989; Witt et al., 2002). Given that leadership in an organization is strongly related to most of the variables presented here, we suggest that a possible relationship between patterns of leadership and organizational politics may exist.

First, a transformational managerial leader may reduce the perceptions of politics in an organization because he/she offers a vision, a mission and an operative plan for goal achievement. He/she can reduce ambiguity and professional uncertainty and validate the feeling that it is possible to deal with organizational challenges in a decent and reasonable way. In addition, the managerial strategy underlying the transformational style reinforces moral values, thereby contributing positively to feelings of fairness and justice and reducing feelings of inferiority that derive from a lack of recourse to political alternatives. Transformational leadership creates a positive organizational climate that supports professionalism and excellence, resulting in a reduced perception of organizational politics.

Finally, the transparency in decision-making processes that characterizes the transformational leader may also contribute to reducing the perceptions of organizational politics by strengthening the belief that both the leader and the organization are fair and trustworthy (Ferris et al., 1989; Kacmar and Ferris, 1991; Ferris and Kacmar, 1992; Folger et al., 1992; Ferris et al., 1996; Pillai et al., 1999, Vigoda, 1999; Witt et al., 2002; Parry, 2003). In sum, transformational leadership has characteristics that can reduce perceptions of organizational politics among employees. Therefore, it is expected that a transformational leader will create a better understanding among employees as to what is expected from them in the framework of their job. In addition, they should have a more positive outlook on their workplace and be willing to invest effort in work, even beyond that which is required by their job definition.

On the other hand, it seems that transactional leadership contributes to strengthening perceptions of organizational politics. This leadership style is characterized by negotiation skills that are suitable for a political environment, by the ability to build systems from various types of components, and by the management of a reward system that will increase employees' motivation. Therefore, we suggest that the transactional leadership style creates negotiation about interests and puts a price tag on everyone and everything. In this environment, the interest struggle is clear, and employees will tend to promote their interests more aggressively. An organizational environment that is in the middle of a dynamic struggle over limited resources and competing interests tends to be more 'political' than other organizations experiencing lower levels of negotiation and struggle. Findings from Pillai et al.'s (1999) research show that there is a positive relationship between aspects of transactional and transformational leadership on the one hand and expressions of fairness and justice on the other. These findings strengthen the idea that there is a relationship between leadership and organizational politics. Nonetheless, and in contrast to Pillai et al.'s (1999) research, we claim that the nature of the relationship changes and will be positive for transactional leadership and negative for transformational leadership. Based on the above, we formulated the following propositions:

P_2 There is a negative relationship between transformational leadership and perceptions of organizational politics.

P_3 There is a positive relationship between transactional leadership and perceptions of organizational politics.

Studies show that there is an established relationship between organizational politics and a long series of organizational performance measurement scales. High perceptions of organizational politics may damage the organization's performance in a number of ways. First, they are related to negative attitudes towards the organization (such as lower levels of trust, satisfaction, or commitment, etc.). Second, relationships were found between perceptions of organizational politics and various negative employee behaviors such as the withholding of information, neglect of one's work, tardiness, absenteeism, turnover, etc. (Vigoda, 2003). Finally, high perceptions of organizational politics may damage the organization's social fabric by reducing social cohesion and enhancing the tendency to act in one's personal interests, even if they are at odds with those of the organization (Ferris et al., 1989; Kacmar and Ferris, 1991; Ferris and Kacmar, 1992; Folger et al., 1992; Ferris et al., 1996; Pillai et al., 1999, Vigoda, 1999; MacKenzie et al., 2001; O'Connor and Morrison, 2001; Witt et al., 2002; Parry, 2003; Poon, 2003). It seems that in an organization where employees interpret reality as politically charged, the relationship created between employees and management encourages attitudes and behaviors that damage the organization's performance. Therefore, employees are expected to reduce their participation in activities that are important to the organization's development, such as spontaneous behavior and OCB (Vigoda, 2003). Accordingly, we suggest that:

P₄ There is negative relationship between the perception of organizational politics and employee's in-role performance.

P₅ There is a negative relationship between the perception of organizational politics and OCB.

Various studies have further examined the effect of mediating variables on the relationship between leadership and performance. Pillai et al. (1999) found that trust, procedural justice and distributive justice are mediating factors between leadership, OCB and satisfaction. MacKenzie et al. (2001) found that trust and job ambiguity are mediator variables between leadership, in-role performance and OCB. Parry (2003) showed that organizational climate is a mediating factor between leadership and performance in a public organization. These findings are significant because they improve our understanding of the complex relations between transactional and transformational leadership and in-role or extra-role performance in the organization.

In addition, the direct relationship between leadership and organizational politics has not been explored sufficiently. The most significant contribution of the proposed model in this research is its examination of the influence of transactional and transformational leadership on employees' perceptions of organizational politics. According to studies in leadership theory (Avolio and Bass, 1991), it seems that transformational leadership should reduce the perception of politics because the transformational leader is by definition an exemplar and a role model. In addition, a transformational leader tends to educate, guide and treat every employee to personal attention in his effort to motivate them to perform above and beyond what is required of them. In contrast, a transactional leadership style should strengthen perceptions of organizational politics among employees because it does not emphasize these values. The transactional leader is characterized by his ability to create a system of rewards and punishments that are necessary for economic and social interactions within the organization. The interactions are influence bases for the transactional leader and for the political phenomenon itself. Therefore, even when a transactional leader seems to be promoting his/her subordinate's interests, the subordinate may be tempted to interpret this support as strategic in nature. Such an interpretation may affect the employee's performance. This theoretical rationale is in line with Ehrhart's (2004) research, which found that a climate of organizational justice mediates in the relationship between leadership and OCB. Accordingly, we suggest a final proposition:

P₆ Perceptions of organizational politics mediate the relationship between transactional and transformational leadership, on one hand, and in-role performance and OCB on the other.

Summary and discussion

This chapter proposes a theoretical framework for the study of relationship between organizational politics, leadership and performance in the workplace. Although this framework is not yet put to empirical test it draws substance from similar studies that have found relationships between leadership and performance (Gaspar, 1992; Lowe et al., 1996; Geyer and Steyrer, 1998; Pillai et al., 1999; MacKenzie et al., 2001; Parry, 2003) and between perceptions of organizational politics and performance (Ferris et al., 1989; Kacmar and Ferris, 1991; Ferris and Kacmar, 1992; Folger et al., 1992; Ferris et al., 1996; Vigoda, 1999; O'Connor and Morrison, 2001; Witt et al., 2002; Poon, 2003). In light of these studies, we suggest that the relationship between leadership and performance may be not only direct but also indirect. Organizational politics is suggested as a mediating factor between leadership and formal and informal performance.

This chapter follows the ideas developed by Pillai et al. (1999), MacKenzie et al. (2001), and Parry (2003), who showed that there are different situational variables that mediate in the relationship between leadership and performance in the organization. Building on this approach, we suggested that employees' perception of organizational politics is a significant perceptual variable that may impact the quality of the relationship between leadership and performance. The chapter offers a rationality to support the idea that such a mediation relationship exists, but it also suggests that a direct relationship exists between leadership and performance.

Our chapter and theoretical framework also support Organ's (1988) claim that as long as the employee believes that the organization is managed fairly, he/she will be willing to improve OCB and formal performance. In contrast, high levels of internal politics yield a low level of trust and negatively affect the level of performance. We believe that this situation is possible mainly because of the transactional leadership pattern. In this situation, the employee may change his/her performances according to the direct rewards received. When the reward system is not balanced, it will be translated into a reduction in performance level. Our chapter follows Pillai et al.'s (1999) findings that perceptions of trust and procedural and distributive justice are mediators in the relationship between leadership (transactional and transformational) and OCB. Similarly, perceptions of trust and justice, particularly procedural and distributive justice, indicate the level of organizational politics (Ferris et al., 1989). Also, our arguments are in line with prior studies on the relationship between leadership and performance (Podsakoff, 2000; MacKenzie et al., 2001; Parry, 2003). It seems that the use of the organizational politics for explaining the mediating process between leadership and performance in organizations contributes significantly to the understanding of all three phenomena altogether: leadership, politics and performance in the organization.

Finally, the theoretical framework as suggested here follows ideas previously suggested by Burns (1978), who identified two basic factors in the interaction between leadership and employees. One factor stems from the leader's ability to deliver rewards and punishments (transactional leadership). The second factor is the leader's ability to rally his staff and urge them to cooperate in achieving the organization's goals (transformational leadership). The current chapter suggested a relationship between leadership and performance in the light of the knowledge accumulated in recent years regarding organizational politics. Future studies are encouraged to test this model empirically. Proving the model by which organizational politics mediates between leadership and performance beyond the direct relationship between leadership and performance may be a significant contribution by itself. A support to this idea may suggest that organizational politics serves as a persistent background variable. It may show that constant tension is created between the individual's aspiration to develop and promote himself and his tendency to fulfill the organization's goals out of loyalty and commitment. According to the ideas proposed in this chapter, it seems that transformational leadership may influence employees, change their positions, create feelings of trust in the leader and in the organization's goals, and promote a perception that the organization operates in a moral way. In this environment, where the managerial policy is consistent with the principles of transformational leadership, employees assimilate the understanding that the road to personal development and progress passes through the fulfillment of the organization's goals, without the need for power relationships, power plays, or internal politics.

References

Avolio, B.J. and Bass, B.M. (1991). *The full-range of leadership development*. Binghamton, NY: Center for Leadership Studies.

Bartunk, J.M. (1994). Changing the interpretive schemes and organizational restructuring: The example of a religious order. *Journal of Administrative Science Quarterly*, **29**, 355–72.

Bass, B.M. (1985). *Leadership and performance beyond expectations*. New York: Free Press.

Bass, B.M. and Avolio, B.J. (1993). Transformational leadership theory: A response to critiques, in M.M Chemmers and R. Ammons (eds), *Leadership & research: Perspectives and direction*, 49–80, California Academic Press.

Blake, J.J. and Mouton, J.S. (1964). *The managerial grid*. Houston, TX: Gulf Publications.

Burns, J.M. (1978). *Leadership*. New York: Harper and Row.

Carlyle, T. (1907). *On heroes, hero worship & the heroic history*. Boston: Houghton Mifflin.

Den Hertog, D.N., Van Muijen, J.J. and Koopman, P.L. (1997). Transactional versus transformational leadership: An analysis of the MLQ. *Journal of Occupational and Organizational Psychology*, **70**, 19–34.

Ehrhart, M.G. (2004). Leadership and procedural justice climate as antecedents of unit-level organizational citizenship behavior. *Personnel Psychology*, **57**, 61–94.

Ferris, G.R. and Kacmar, K.M. (1992). Perceptions of organizational politics. *Journal of Management*, **18** (1), 93–116.

Ferris, G.R, Russ, G.S. and Fandt, P.M. (1989). Politics in organizations, in R.A. Giacalone and P. Rosenfeld (eds), *Impression management in the organization*, 143–170, Hillsdale, NJ: Lawrence Erlbaum.

Ferris, G.R., Frink, D.D., Bhawuk, D.P.S. and Zhou, J. (1996). Reactions of diverse groups to politics in the workplace. *Journal of Management*, **22**, 23–44.

Fiedler, F.E. (1978). The contingency model and the dynamics of the leadership process, in L. Berkowitz (ed.), *Advances in experimental social psychology*, 60–112, Vol. 11, New York: Academic Press.

Folger, R., Konovsky, M.A. and Cropanzano, R. (1992). A due process metaphor for performance appraisal, in L. Cummings and B. Staw (eds), *Research in organizational behavior*, 129–77, Vol. 14, Greenwich, CT: JAI Press.

Gaspar, S. (1992). *Transformational leadership: An integrative review of the literature*, Ph.D., Western Michigan University.

Geyer, A.L. and Steyrer, J.M. (1998). Transformational leadership and objective performance in banks. *Journal of Applied Psychology*, **47**, 397–420.

Heifetz, R.A. (1994). *Leadership without easy answers*. Cambridge, MA: Harvard University Press.

Hersey, P. and Blanchard, K.H. (1972). *Management of organizational behavior: Utilizing human resources*. Englewood Cliffs, NJ: Prentice Hill.

Kacmar, K.M. and Ferris, G.R. (1991). Perceptions of organizational politics scale (POPS): Development and construct validation. *Educational and Psychological Measurement*, **51**, 193–205.

Kotter, J.P. (1996). *Leading change*. Cambridge, MA: Harvard Business School Press.

Kumar, P. and Ghadially, R. (1989). Organizational politics and its effects on members of organizations. *Journal of Human Relations*, **42**, 305–14.

Lewin, K., Lippit, R. and White R.K. (1939). Patterns of aggressive behavior in experimentally created social cultures. *Journal of Social Psychology*, **10**, 271–99.

Lowe, K.B., Kroeck, K.G. and Sivasubramaniam, N. (1996). Effectiveness correlates of transformational and transactional leadership: A meta- analytic review of MLQ literature. *Leadership Quarterly*, **7**, 385–425.

Luthans, F., Rosenkrantz, S.A. and Harry, W.H. (1985). What do successful managers really do? An observation study of managerial activities. *The Journal of Applied Behavioral Science*, **2**, 255–70.

MacKenzie, S.B., Podssakoff, P.M. and Rich, G.A. (2001). Transformational and transactional leadership and salesperson performance. *Journal of Academy of Marketing Science*, **2**, 115–34.

Mintzberg, H. (1973). *The nature of managerial work*. New York: Harper and Row.

Motowidlo, S.J., Packard, J.S. and Manning, M.A. (1986). Occupational stress, its causes and consequences for job performance. *Journal of Applied Psychology*, **71**, 618–29.

O'Connor, W.E. and Morrison T.G. (2001). A comparison of situational and dispositional predictors of perceptions of organizational politics. *The Journal of Psychology*, **135**, 301–12.

Organ, D.W. (1988). *Organizational citizenship behavior: The good soldier syndrome*. Lexington, MA: Lexington Books.

Organ, D.W. (1990). The subtle significance of job satisfaction. *Clinical Laboratory Management Review*, **4**, 94–8.

Parry, K.W. (2003). Leadership, culture and performance: The case of the New Zealand public sector. *Journal of Change Management*, **4**, 376–99.

Pfeffer, J. (1992). *Management with power*. Boston: Harvard Business School Press.

Pillai, R., Schriesheim, C.A. and Williams, E.S. (1999). Fairness perceptions and trust as mediators for transformational and transactional leadership: A two-sample study. *Journal of Management*, **25**, 897–933.

Podsakoff, P.M. (2000). Organizational citizenship behaviors: A critical review of the theoretical and empirical literature and suggestions for future research. *Journal of Management*, **58**, 423–65.

Poon, J.M.L. (2003). Situational antecedents and outcomes of organizational politics perceptions. *Journal of Managerial Psychology*, **18**, 138–55.

Randolph, W.A. (1985). *Understanding and managing organizational behavior*. Homewood, IL: Richard D. Irwin.

Reddin, W.J. (1967). The 3-D management style theory. *Training and Development Journal*, **4**, 8–17.

Smith, C.A., Organ, D.W. and Near, J.P. (1983). Organizational citizenship behavior: Its nature and antecedents. *Journal of Applied Psychology*, **68**, 656–63.

Stogdill, R.M. (1984). Personal factors associated with leadership: A survey of literature. *Journal of Psychology*, **25**, 35–71.

Theobald, R. (1997). Enhancing public service ethics: More culture, less bureaucracy? *Administration and Society*, **29**, 490–504.

Vigoda, E. (1999). Organizational politics, job attitudes and work outcomes: exploration and implications for the public sector. *Journal of Vocational Behavior*, **57**, 326–47.

Vigoda, E. (2000). Internal politics in public administration systems: An empirical examination of its relationship with job congruence, organizational citizenship behavior and in-role performance. *Public Personnel Management*, **29**, 185–201.

Vigoda, E. (2003). *Developments in Organizational Politics*. Cheltenham, UK and Northampton, MA, USA: Edward Elgar Publishing.

Witt, L.A., Kacmar K.M., Carlson, D.S. and Zivnuska, S. (2002). Interactive effect of personality and organizational politics on contextual performance. *Journal of Organizational Behavior*, **23**, 911–26.

Yammarino, F.J. and Dubinsky, A.J. (1994). Transformational leadership theory: Using levels of analysis to determine boundary condition. *Personnel Psychology*, **47**, 787–811.

2 Agreeableness and extraversion as moderators of the political influence compatibility–work outcomes relationship

John P. Meriac and Peter D. Villanova

Introduction

Social influence is a common phenomenon in virtually any organizational setting (Jones, 1995). However, social influence that is not authorized by the formal hierarchy of an organization is often viewed as unnecessary and counterproductive by management. Behavior with the aim of influencing the perceptions or future actions of others that lie beyond the formal power system and are often self-serving in nature can be defined as political behavior (Yoffie and Bergenstein, 1985).

Management often takes a negative view of such occurrences and attempts to minimize their presence. Mintzberg's (1983) extensive review of political behavior in organizations facilitated an era of interest in the empirical study of this phenomenon. Despite 20 years of attention, however, much of the published literature is very limited in scope (Jex, 2002). Only recently have theories of political behavior begun to resemble the complexity of better-understood work behavior concepts (Christiansen et al., 1997) or approximate the empirical rigor of more mainstream topics in organizational behavior.

In the current study, political behavior is operationalized through informal social influence tactics. More specifically, these tactics are: reason, friendliness, bargaining, assertiveness, appeals to higher authority and coalition formation (Kipnis and Schmidt, 1982). Reason is the practice of using facts and data to influence a target person's behavior, by trying to rationalize a particular decision. Friendliness, also known as ingratiation, is a strategy characterized by attempting to change the impression a target has of the influencer so the target may be more inclined to give the influencer what he or she wants. Bargaining is a political influence tactic which is characterized by an exchange of favors; an example of this may be an offer for the influencer to support the target in a future instance if they show support for the influencer at the present moment. Assertiveness is a tactic which is used when influencing others in a forceful manner, so as to show that the influencer is 'in charge.' Appealing to higher authority is an influence tactic where the influencer relies on the chain of command, and uses the power of individuals with more legitimate authority above that of the target to change the target individual's behavior. Finally, coalition formation is a tactic which involves forming an alliance of individuals to confront another individual in an attempt to get them to change their behavior.

Implications of political climate

The organizational environment surrounding political behavior can be referred to as its political climate (Ferris et al., 1994). Studies in the domain of political behavior have largely concluded that more politicized environments produce more unfavorable work environments (Cropanzano et al., 1997; Kumar and Ghadially, 1989; Witt, 1998). Furthermore, published studies have focused more on general perceptions of politics rather than observable political behaviors. A better understanding of the nature of organizational politics and how different individuals behave within political climates may provide insight into how to assess and manage its outcomes more effectively to facilitate positive organizational functioning (Christiansen et al., 1997).

While two climates may be described as political, it does not necessarily follow that the same forms of influence behaviors predominate in both settings. For example, the political climate of one organization may be characterized by an institutionalized practice of bargaining and exchange as the basis of political behavior whereas the influence behaviors in another equally politicized climate may reflect greater reliance on assertiveness. Because political behavior is a multidimensional construct characterized by several forms of social influence tactics (Schriesheim and Hinkin, 1990) and these tactics have been shown to be related differently to work outcomes (Christiansen et al., 1997), it is necessary to understand what tactics predominate in an organization described as politicized.

Interpretation of what makes a situation or climate 'political' in nature depends on contextual factors such as the situation itself and the actor, individual characteristics of the observer, and, most importantly, the evaluations of the observer (Ferris et al., 1994; Lewin, 1935). To one observer the simple promise of exchange of favors may not only be perceived as political but also suggest some insidious unethical relationship that may imperil organizational success. To another observer, such an interaction could be considered quite mundane and be attributed to 'greasing the wheels' of efficient operation. Surely, some individuals must benefit from the presence of a political climate; otherwise there would be no motive for engaging in any type of political behavior.

Who then may benefit from different tactics that prevail in a political environment? Might there be tactics that better suit the predilections of some organizational members that are not equally acceptable or beneficial as influence practices to other members? Just as no two people have identical personality profiles, we maintain that individuals exhibit some degree of variance in their preferences for aspects of the political climate. Answering such a question requires information about both the relative frequency of political tactics that dominate attempts at social influence and information about member preferences for the different political tactics. Valle (1997) proposed that individuals maintain personal orientations toward political behavior, and such orientations impact both behavioral and affective reactions to the perceived presence of political behavior. With this orientation in mind, congruence with the environment is one approach toward gaining a better understanding of how individuals function in the presence of political behavior.

Congruence or 'fit' models are suited to providing answers to such questions with some degree of accuracy because they take into account both personal and situational characteristics (Nadler and Tushman, 1997). The basic premise of fit approaches is that individuals who maintain preferences or attributes that are more highly correspondent with situational characteristics tend to experience more beneficial outcomes than those whose personal features on key attributes are at odds with the situation (Chatman, 1989; Christiansen et al., 1997; O'Reilly et al., 1991). An approach that considers individual preferences for particular organizational climates may provide a deeper understanding of how political climates and individuals affect each other than traditional approaches that simply characterize organizational climates as more or less political.

Person–climate/organization fit

A harmonious fit between employee preferences and elements of the work environment such as climate can create highly effective relationships with positive implications for various types of desirable work outcomes (Chatman, 1989). In this context, fit can be defined as the congruence between the norms and values of organizations (situational characteristics) and the values or expectancies of persons (individual characteristics) (Kristof, 1996).

Fit models emphasize the importance of the congruence between individual preferences and the various parts of the organization rather than simply the presence or absence of factors that impact an employee's attitudes or behaviors. A good fit with the climate of the organization is positively related to job satisfaction, organizational commitment and lower turnover rates (O'Reilly et al., 1991). A poor fit between the employee and organization is associated with unfavorable work outcomes such as poor work performance, various types of dissatisfaction and intention to turnover (Cable and Parsons, 2001; Villanova et al., 1994).

Political influence compatibility

The consideration of a fit model in political climate research could be a meaningful alternative to popular main effect perspectives that have largely been used in the study of organizational politics. Christiansen et al. (1997) investigated the viability of a person-political climate fit model, dubbed 'political influence compatibility (PIC).' PIC is the congruence between a person's orientation toward influence tactics and the political climate of an organization. PIC maintains that workers will not merely view organizational politics negatively, but rather exhibit responses to the work environment correspondent to their fit with the political climate of the organization. This supports the notion that a

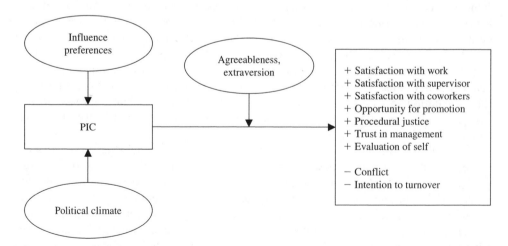

Figure 2.1   Model of personality moderators of the PIC–work outcomes relationship

political climate in an organization will not influence all workers in an identical manner, but instead individuals will be affected in different ways. Christiansen et al. (1997) found that PIC explained incremental validity above that of political climate alone, and was predictive of several employee attitudes, such as satisfaction with work, procedural fairness, conflict and trust in management.

As in Christiansen et al. (1997), the current study investigates the concept that the relationship an individual has with the political climate of an organization is most rationally examined by taking a fit approach. Furthermore, other factors besides orientation toward the political climate of the organization may also play a role in determining differences in work outcomes. In the relevant literature, assertions have been made that dispositional factors such as an individual's personality may also influence the climate of an organization (Schneider, 1987). The current study therefore also investigates how an individual's personality may influence the relationship between PIC and work outcomes.

Personality assessment
Today, personality testing is a component of the selection process in approximately 40 percent of Fortune 500 companies (Bates, 2002). Internationally, personality assessment is also becoming a more integral component of the selection process (Yoon, 2002). With over 2500 tests available and currently in use, personality assessment has become a widespread phenomenon in the workplace and is utilized globally. One of the widely applied measures of personality assessment in the workplace is the five-factor model or 'Big Five' (Smith et al., 2001). The most popular titles used for these factors are: neuroticism, extraversion, openness to experience, agreeableness and conscientiousness (Goodstein and Lanyon, 1999). The current study focuses on two of these variables: agreeableness and extraversion.

Agreeableness is generally associated with altruism and sympathy towards others. Highly agreeable individuals are best characterized as people who act as team players, supporting the goals of a group over their own. Reviews on the predictive validity of personality have shown that of the Big Five, agreeableness is one of the strongest predictors of job performance (Goodstein and Lanyon, 1999). Furthermore, Caldwell and Burger (1997) found agreeableness to be negatively correlated with assertiveness and exchange.

Extraverted individuals prefer to be in settings comprising large groups and are characterized as talkative, outgoing and assertive (Costa and McCrae, 1991). Extraversion predicts job success where interaction with others is a determinant of performance (Barrick and Mount, 1991). In studies of organizational influence, extraversion was positively correlated with involvement and self-reported use of rational persuasion (Caldwell and Burger, 1997).

Another way in which personality may influence the relationship between two variables is as a moderator (Baron and Kenny, 1986), where the direction or magnitude of the relationship between two variables can be influenced by a third 'moderating' variable. Research has demonstrated the capacity of personality variables to moderate relationships between variables in organizational settings (Skarlicki et al., 1999; Tepper et al., 2001). Hochwarter et al. (2000) found that 'perceptions of organizational politics' moderated the relationship between conscientiousness and job performance, signifying that moderating relationships may exist. However, other personality factors may also explain variance in work outcomes, and alternative models may demonstrate that these variables function in different ways. Literature reviews have postulated that individual dispositions may moderate the relationship between person–organization fit and work outcomes (Kristof, 1996); however, this has not yet been empirically tested. The current study aims to explore the extent to which personality dispositions moderate the relationship between PIC and work outcomes.

Hypotheses

Christiansen et al. (1997) demonstrated that congruence with social influence tactics is significantly related to work outcomes exhibited by individuals. To determine the extent to which personality variables moderate the relationship between PIC and work outcomes, it is first necessary to demonstrate that a relationship exists between PIC and work outcomes.

> **Hypothesis 1**   The pattern of relationships among political tactics and outcome variables will largely replicate the findings of Christiansen et al. (1997), who found that reason and ingratiation tended to positively correlate with favorable outcomes and negatively with unfavorable work outcomes, whereas assertiveness, upward appeals and coalition formation tended to correlate positively with unfavorable outcomes and negatively with favorable outcomes.

Therefore, it is proposed that political influence tactics will not relate in an identical manner to work outcomes.

> **Hypothesis 2**   Political influence compatibility will correlate positively with satisfaction with work, coworkers, supervisor and opportunity for promotion, trust in management and evaluation of self and negatively with unfavorable work attitudes such as intention to turnover and conflict. PIC will explain significant incremental variance in work outcomes above political climate perceptions and influence orientation.

Once the PIC–work outcomes relationship is established, it is possible to examine the extent to which moderator variables influence the relationship between PIC and work outcomes (see Figure 2.1). In particular, agreeableness and extraversion, the two key domains of the Big Five that relate to interpersonal tendencies, will be investigated in their capacity to moderate the relationship between PIC and work outcomes.

> **Hypothesis 3**   Agreeableness will moderate the PIC–work outcomes relationship in that this relationship will be stronger for individuals higher in agreeableness.

When a poor fit exists between influence orientation and the political climate, high agreeableness individuals may have even more negative views of work. In contrast, when individuals who are high in agreeableness have a good match with the political climate of the organization, they may report more positive work outcomes due to a good match between their drive for affiliation and a climate that is consistent with their views on political behavior. Thus individuals who score higher in agreeableness should report more extreme scores in relation to PIC.

Hypothesis 4   Extraversion will moderate the PIC–work outcomes relationship in that this relationship will be stronger for individuals higher in extraversion.

Individuals who are high in extraversion may more openly exhibit unfavorable work outcomes when there is a poor fit between their orientation and the climate, and more openly exhibit favorable work outcomes and when a good fit exists. Individuals who are low in extraversion may be less likely to exhibit their favor or disfavor with the environment. Thus individuals who are more extraverted should report more extreme scores as a function of PIC.

Method

Participants
Participants were employees of a large southeastern merchandising company. The sample comprised 52 percent male employees ranging from 16 to 71 years of age. Also, participants spanned a broad range of both managerial and non-managerial job categories. Approximately 625 questionnaires were distributed, and 530 were returned. Of those returned, 33 questionnaires were not sufficiently completed to include in the analyses, resulting in a sample size of $N = 497$.

Measures

Political climate   Political climate scales retained a format utilized by Christiansen et al. (1997), which were adaptations of the Schriesheim and Hinkin (1990) 18-item measure. Scores indicated the extent to which individuals perceived that others used the following political influence tactics: coalition formation, upward appeals, assertiveness, ingratiation, exchange and reason. Each item was rated on a five-point summated frequency scale, indicating frequency of occurrence, ranging from 'never' to 'very often.' Means were computed for the three items that corresponded to each subscale, and a composite score was computed by averaging all political climate items to determine a global rating of the political climate of the organization. Internal consistency estimates of each subscale ranged from $\alpha = 0.66$ to 0.76.

Personal orientation towards influence   An adaptation of the Kipnis and Schmidt (1982) Profiles of Organizational Influence Strategies (POIS) subscales by Christiansen et al. (1997) was used to determine participants' orientation towards influence processes exhibited. This measure had 36 items with six subscales, rated on a five-point summated frequency scale ranging from 'unfavorably' to 'favorably.' Each subscale measured individuals' orientation toward one of six types of social influence processes: reason, friendliness, bargaining, assertiveness, appeals to higher authority and coalition formation. For each individual, a composite score was calculated for the general orientation towards political influence. POIS dimensions corresponded to climate dimensions and were compared so that they can be used to compute the PIC index. Internal consistency estimates of the subscales were found to be quite high, ranging from $\alpha = 0.89$ to 0.94.

Political influence compatibility index   An index was constructed utilizing the climate scores and orientation scores as in Christiansen et al. (1997). To compute the index, the climate and orientation items for each participant were given rank-order scores, which corresponded to the relative frequency which these influence tactics were perceived to be used in the organization and the orientation that individuals had towards the usage and effectiveness of the influence strategies. Spearman's rho correlation was used to compute the index scores (Howell, 2001), and scores ranged from -1.0 to $+1.0$. Upon construction of the PIC index, the usable sample size was further reduced to $N = 461$, since the PIC index could not be computed for some individuals due to the mathematical properties of Spearman's rho. PIC scores were standardized using Fisher's Z transformation before conducting the analyses (Howell, 2001).

Work outcomes   The dependent variables in the study consisted of several organizational/work attitudes, measured across 30 items via a five-point summated frequency scale in which participants either agreed or disagreed with statements, or rated each item's frequency of occurrence. The work outcome variables selected were suggested by the majority of the literature to be related to political behaviors (Christiansen et al., 1997). Variables included: conflict, trust in management, evaluation of self, intention to turnover, and job satisfaction dimensions (Cammann et al., 1983). Job satisfaction items were variations of 15 items of the Job Descriptive Index (JDI) (Smith et al., 1969), which measured the employee's satisfaction with work itself, supervision, salary, coworkers, and opportunity for promotion. Internal consistency estimates are presented in Table 2.1.

Personality assessment   Personality variables were assessed using the Big Five Inventory (BFI) (Benet-Martinez and John, 1998), a 44-item measure. The BFI is a five-factor inventory which assesses the following personality dimensions: neuroticism, extraversion, openness to experience, agreeableness and conscientiousness. Internal consistency estimates of this scale ranged from $\alpha = 0.75$ to 0.78.

Demographic information   Demographic information was obtained through a 9-item measure investigating the gender of the participant, education level, occupational category, salary, tenure within the company, tenure within the current department, level of supervisory responsibility and the size of department. Demographic information was obtained for the purpose of ensuring that the sample was representative of the population and industry. As the respective demographic variables were each entered into the regression equations in the analyses, no incremental variance was explained in the work outcomes with the exception of age; however, this did not impact the direction of the relationships among the independent and dependent variables; subsequently the overall results were unaffected.

Procedure
Paper-based questionnaires with cover letters were distributed to employees at the place of employment. Sealable return envelopes absent of any identifying information were provided with questionnaires to maintain confidentiality. Employees were asked to read the cover letter, complete the questionnaire, and return them via inter-office mail where they would be collected at the company's headquarters. The cover letter asked respondents to complete the questionnaire and disclosed the purpose of the study, its importance, confidentiality, and that participation was voluntary.

Table 2.1 Means, standard deviations, reliabilities and correlations among influence, work outcomes and personality variables

	M	S.D.	1	2	3	4	5	6	7	8	9	10	11	12	13	14	15
1. PIC	0.50	0.61	—														
2. Climate	2.61	0.67	-0.10	—													
3. Orientation toward influence	2.87	0.62	-0.05	0.52	—												
4. Evaluation of self	4.19	0.69	0.04	-0.02	0.10	(0.75)											
5. Conflict	2.48	1.17	-0.15	0.24	0.08	-0.37	(0.87)										
6. Trust in management	3.44	1.21	0.10	-0.19	-0.06	0.36	-0.61	(0.67)									
7. Intention to turnover	1.85	0.99	-0.08	0.18	0.12	-0.27	0.37	-0.31	(0.83)								
8. Satisfaction with work	4.03	0.90	0.14	-0.18	-0.15	0.37	-0.42	0.36	-0.59	(0.74)							
9. Satisfaction with coworkers	4.18	0.83	0.11	-0.18	-0.04	0.35	-0.49	0.36	-0.43	0.50	(0.65)						
10. Satisfaction with supervisor	3.90	0.93	0.11	-0.16	-0.04	0.48	-0.49	0.50	-0.48	0.55	0.58	(0.79)					
11. Satisfaction with pay	3.05	1.02	0.08	-0.04	0.01	0.20	-0.17	0.18	-0.26	0.38	0.21	0.24	(0.65)				
12. Opportunity for promotion	3.54	1.13	0.07	-0.08	0.01	0.39	-0.33	0.37	-0.49	0.54	0.41	0.53	0.30	(0.80)			
13. Procedural justice	3.65	0.93	0.10	-0.11	-0.04	0.44	-0.41	0.40	-0.41	0.45	0.38	0.55	0.25	0.42	(0.74)		
14. Agreeableness	4.29	0.53	0.03	-0.15	-0.06	0.29	-0.25	0.23	-0.30	0.40	0.37	0.38	0.14	0.21	0.28	(0.76)	
15. Extraversion	3.67	0.68	-0.03	-0.02	-0.04	0.32	-0.16	0.14	-0.15	0.21	0.24	0.23	0.09	0.15	0.14	0.32	(0.78)

Note: $N = 461$, internal consistency estimates shown in parentheses, $|r| > 0.09$ are statistically significant at $p < 0.05$ or less.

Table 2.2   Correlations among frequency of use of political tactics and work outcomes

Work attitudes	Political behavior dimensions					
	Assertiveness	Ingratiation	Reason	Exchange	Upward appeals	Coalition formation
Coworker satisfaction	−0.35*	−0.02	0.01	−0.17*	−0.19*	−0.14*
Supervisor satisfaction	−0.34*	0.05	0.02	−0.12*	−0.20*	−0.16*
Work satisfaction	−0.29*	0.00	0.02	−0.20*	−0.19*	−0.14*
Pay satisfaction	−0.08	0.04	0.00	−0.04	−0.08	0.01
Opportunity for promotion	−0.21*	0.03	0.02	−0.09	−0.08	−0.04
Evaluation of self	−0.19*	0.09	0.08	−0.07	−0.02	−0.01
Procedural justice	−0.25*	0.03	0.04	−0.06	−0.16*	−0.13*
Trust in management	−0.28*	−0.07	0.00	−0.17*	−0.19*	−0.18*
Conflict	0.43*	0.04	0.01	0.19*	0.22*	0.22*
Intention to turnover	0.27*	0.06	−0.01	0.19*	0.16*	0.16*

Note: $N = 461$, * $p < 0.05$ or less.

Data analysis
To investigate the differential relationships that might exist between dimensions of
the political climate and work outcomes, Pearson product–moment correlations were
computed; these were also computed to evaluate the overall main effects between political climate, PIC, work outcomes and personality variables. Moderated multiple regression was used to analyze the effects of PIC and personality variables on the relationship
between political climate and work outcomes (Cohen et al., 2003).

Results
Table 2.1 provides means, standard deviations and correlations for scores of political
climate perceptions, influence orientation, PIC, work outcomes, agreeableness and extraversion. The relationships among overall political climate and the work outcomes were
consistent with the majority of the literature in that political behavior overall was positively correlated with more unfavorable work outcomes and negatively correlated with
positive work outcomes.

Differential relationship of political tactics with work outcomes
An examination of the relationships among dimensions of political behavior and work
outcomes revealed that political influence tactics were not related to work outcomes in an
identical manner, but varied in their relationships with work outcomes. Table 2.2 reports
the correlations among the perceived frequency of use of each of the six political tactics
and the work outcomes. Hypothesis 1 was generally supported in that upward appeals,
coalition formation and assertiveness were negatively correlated with favorable work outcomes and were positively correlated with unfavorable work outcomes. However, reason
and ingratiation did not significantly correlate with outcomes as expected. In addition,
exchange correlated significantly with several of the work outcomes, although this was
not hypothesized.

Table 2.3   Hierarchical regression output for Hypothesis 2

	Step 1			Step 2	
	Climate β	Orientation β	R^2	PIC β	ΔR^2
Satisfaction with work	−0.15*	0.07	0.04*	0.19*	0.01*
Satisfaction with coworkers	−0.23	0.08	0.04*	0.09*	0.01*
Satisfaction with supervisor	−0.19	0.06	0.03*	0.10*	0.01*
Opportunity for promotion	−0.12*	0.07	0.01	0.06	0.01
Satisfaction with pay	−0.06	0.04	0.00	0.08	0.00
Procedural justice	−0.13*	0.03	0.01*	0.09*	0.01*
Conflict	0.27*	−0.06	0.06*	−0.13*	0.02*
Trust in management	−0.22*	0.05	0.04*	0.08	0.01
Evaluation of self	−0.10	0.15*	0.01*	0.04	0.00
Intention to turnover	0.16	0.04	0.03*	−0.06	0.00

Note: $N = 461$, * $p < 0.05$ or less.

Variance in work outcomes explained by PIC
PIC explained a significant ΔR^2 at $p < 0.05$ for each respective work outcome, supporting Hypothesis 2 (see Table 2.3). More specifically, PIC explained significant incremental variance above perceived climate and influence orientation in satisfaction with work, coworkers and supervisor, and with procedural justice and conflict. Also, PIC did not explain incremental variance in satisfaction with pay as expected. The incremental variance PIC explained in opportunity for promotion and trust in management did not reach statistical significance, but was only marginally non-significant. The overall pattern of results supported the hypothesis.

Moderating effect of agreeableness on the PIC–work outcomes relationship
In the regression analyses conducted for each work outcome variable, the PIC × agreeableness interaction did not significantly explain incremental variance above PIC, extraversion and agreeableness. Thus Hypothesis 3 was not supported, as agreeableness did not significantly moderate the relationships among PIC and any of the work outcome variables.

Moderating effect of extraversion on the PIC–work outcomes relationship
The analyses provided only partial support for Hypothesis 4, where extraversion significantly moderated the relationship between PIC and trust in management scores ($\Delta R^2 = 0.01$, $F(4, 461) = 3.97$, $p < 0.05$). None of the other predicted relationships between PIC and work outcomes was moderated by extraversion.

Discussion
PIC explained more variance in work outcomes than did political climate and orientation, thus supporting the notion that main effect relationships are one explanation of the relationship between political behavior and work outcomes. Although the results supported the PIC model, the analyses revealed that neither agreeableness nor extraversion moderated the relationships between PIC and work outcomes as expected. Extraversion was found to significantly moderate only one relationship, between PIC and trust in management.

An interesting finding of the study was that Hypothesis 1 was only partially supported in its extension of Christiansen et al. (1997). However, even though different relationships exist among the presence of influence tactics and work outcomes, PIC still explained incremental variance in the work outcomes as expected. Thus the current study provides support for the explanatory power of PIC over the presence of a political climate alone.

While Hypothesis 2 was generally supported, the resulting effect sizes were somewhat smaller than those reported in the Christiansen et al. (1997) study. This may be a result of volunteer bias, which is impacted by responses of individuals that have more extreme views on an issue, potentially magnifying the effect sizes of relationships by failing to capture the responses of more 'moderate' respondents (Rosenthal and Rosnow, 1975). In the Christiansen et al. (1997) study, questionnaires were mailed to employees of a university and returned through campus mail. The current study also collected data using voluntary self-report questionnaires, but instead of randomly mailing them to individuals, supervisors distributed them to participants, and they were then returned via an intra-organization mail system. A comparison of the response rates reveals that the current study maintained an 82 percent response rate versus the 35 percent response rate of Christiansen et al. (1997). The results of the current study may have provided a more realistic analysis of the dynamics of a political climate by obtaining a more representative sample.

Although the data failed to support the inquiry into personality moderators of the PIC–outcome relationship as hypothesized, the first two hypotheses were supported, providing an extension of Christiansen et al. (1997) into a broader domain. The previous study utilized non-student employees of a midwestern university with a sample size of 138, whereas the current study's participants consisted of 461 employees of a privately owned southern company. This confirmatory evidence in support of Christiansen et al.'s (1997) hypotheses may help researchers better understand the complexity of organizational politics research and that behavior is not sufficiently explained by main effects between perceptions of the presence of a political climate and its correlates. Even partial support for a hypothesis may at least allow researchers to build upon the theory by investigating the effects of other variables. Furthermore, this confirmatory evidence supports the premise that it is the correspondence between individual orientation toward influence tactics and the prevailing political climate that is most powerful in explaining differences in work outcomes, not simply the perceived presence of a political climate.

Implications for future research
Future research on PIC should investigate the relationship between an individual's fit and objective criteria, such as work performance and actual turnover rates. In addition, contextual performance should be explored as a work outcome, as it has already been demonstrated as a function of a political climate in previous research (Witt et al., 2002). Other factors such as implicit motives and self-determination may be related to the use of social influence tactics (Deci and Ryan, 2000; Kehr, 2004). Although the Big Five are generally regarded as the most popular measures of personality, other personality dispositions exist and may provide meaningful insight into how individuals function in political environments. The consideration of implicit motives as dispositional factors may further

enhance our understanding of how individuals will interact with the social influence climate of an organization.

In addition to the inclusion of different variables, the location of the interaction may occur at other positions in the model. For example, Vigoda (2003) found that person–organization fit effectively mediated the relationship between influence tactics and perceptions of organizational politics, which subsequently influenced work outcomes. Witt et al. (2002) found that personality variables and perceptions of politics interact to influence contextual performance. With the presence of different models, including an interaction, in the literature, a comprehensive analysis of these various models is needed to clarify which is most appropriate.

Overall, the current study advances our understanding of political behavior in organizations, and provides support for a previously proposed model. However, this study by no means fully explains how individuals function in political climates. More research investigating the individual differences of employees is needed to better conceptualize the organizational behavior of employees in political climates, specifically focusing on individual differences and interactions between individual differences and the prevailing climate.

References

Baron, R. and Kenny, D. (1986). The moderator–mediator variable distinction in social psychological research: Conceptual, strategic, and statistical considerations. *Journal of Personality and Social Psychology*, **51**, 1173–82.

Barrick, M.R. and Mount, M.K. (1991). The big five personality and job performance: a meta-analysis. *Personnel Psychology*, **44**, 1–27.

Bates, S. (2002). Personality counts. *HR Magazine*, **47**, 28–34.

Benet-Martinez, V. and John, O.P. (1998). Los cinco grandes across cultures and ethnic groups: Multitrait multimethod analyses of the big five in Spanish and English. *Journal of Personality and Social Psychology*, **75**, 729–50.

Cable, D.M. and Parsons, C.K. (2001). Socialization tactics and person–organization fit. *Personnel Psychology*, **54**, 1–23.

Caldwell, D.F. and Burger, J.M. (1997). Personality and social influence strategies in the workplace. *Personality and Social Psychology Bulletin*, **23**, 1003–12.

Cammann, C., Fichman, M., Jenkins, G.D. and Klesh, J.R. (1983). Assessing the attitudes and perceptions of organizational members. In S.E. Seashore, E.E. Lawler, P. Mervis and C. Cammann (eds), *Assessing Organizational Change*, New York: Wiley.

Chatman, J.A. (1989). Improving interactional organizational research: a model of person–organization fit. *Academy of Management Review*, **14**, 333–49.

Christiansen, N., Villanova, P. and Mikulay, S. (1997). Political influence compatibility: fitting the person to the climate. *Journal of Organizational Behavior*, **18**, 709–73.

Cohen, J., Cohen, P., West, S.G. and Aiken, L.S. (2003). *Applied Multiple Regression/Correlation Analysis for the Behavioral Sciences*. Mahwah, NJ: Lawrence Erlbaum.

Costa, P.T. and McCrae, R.R. (1991). *NEO PI-R Professional Manual*. Odessa, FL: Psychological Assessment Resources.

Cropanzano, R., Howes, J., Grandey, A. and Toth, P. (1997). The relationship of organizational politics and support to work behaviors, attitudes, and stress. *Journal of Organizational Behavior*, **18**, 159–80.

Deci, E.L. and Ryan, R.M. (2000). The 'what' and 'why' of goal pursuits: human needs and the self-determination of behavior. *Psychological Inquiry*, **11**, 227–68.

Ferris, G.R., Fedor, D.B. and King, T.R. (1994). A political conceptualization of managerial behavior. *Human Resource Management Review*, **4**, 1–34.

Goodstein, L.D. and Lanyon, R.I. (1999). Applications of personality assessment to the workplace: a review. *Journal of Business and Psychology*, **13**, 291–322.

Hochwarter, W.A., Witt, L.A. and Kacmar, M.K. (2000). Perceptions of organizational politics as a moderator of the relationship between conscientiousness and job performance. *Journal of Applied Psychology*, **85**, 472–8.

Howell, D. (2001). *Statistical Methods for Psychology*. Pacific Grove, CA: Wadsworth.

Jex, S. (2002). *Organizational Psychology: A scientist–practitioner approach*. New York: John Wiley & Sons.

Jones, G. (1995). *Organizational Theory: Texts and cases*. Reading, MA: Addison-Wesley.

Kehr, H. (2004). Implicit/explicit motive discrepancies and volitional depletion among managers. *Journal of Personality and Social Psychology*, **30**, 315–27.

Kipnis, D. and Schmidt, S. (1982). *Profiles of Organizational Influence Strategies*. San Diego, CA: University Associates.

Kristof, A. (1996). Person–organization fit: an integrative review of its conceptualizations, measurement, and implications. *Personnel Psychology*, **49**, 1–49.

Kumar, P. and Ghadially, R. (1989). Organizational politics and its effects on members of organizations. *Human Relations*, **42**, 305–14.

Lewin, K. (1935). *A Dynamic Theory of Personality: Selected papers* (D.K. Adams and K.E. Zener, trans.). New York: McGraw-Hill.

Mintzberg, H. (1983). *Power in and Around Organizations*. Englewood Cliffs, NJ: Prentice-Hall.

Nadler, D.A. and Tushman, M.L. (1997). *Competing by Design*. New York: Oxford University Press.

O'Reilly, C.A., Chatman, J. and Caldwell, D.F. (1991). People and organizational culture: A profile comparison approach to assessing person–organization fit. *Academy of Management Journal*, **34**, 487–516.

Schneider, B. (1987). The people make the place. *Personnel Psychology*, **40**, 437–53.

Schriesheim, C. and Hinkin, T. (1990). Influence tactics used by subordinates: A theoretical and empirical analysis and refinement of the Kipnis, Schmidt, and Wilkerson subscales. *Journal of Applied Psychology*, **75**, 246–57.

Skarlicki, D., Folger, R. and Tesluk, P. (1999). Personality as a moderator in the relationship between fairness and retaliation. *Academy of Management Journal*, **42**, 100–108.

Smith, B.S., Hanges, P.J. and Dickson, M.W. (2001). Personnel selection and the five-factor model: Reexamining the effects of applicant's frame of reference. *Journal of Applied Psychology*, **86**, 304–15.

Smith, P., Kendall, L. and Hulin, C. (1969). *The Measurement of Satisfaction of Work and Retirement*. Chicago, IL: Rand McNally.

Tepper, B., Duffy, M. and Shaw, J. (2001). Personality moderators of the relationship between abusive supervision and subordinates' resistance. *Journal of Applied Psychology*, **86**, 974–83.

Valle, M. (1997). The effects of political orientation on attributions of co-worker success/failure. *Social Behavior and Personality*, **25**, 211–22.

Vigoda, E. (2003). *Developments in Organizational Politics*. Cheltenham, UK and Northampton, MA, USA: Edward Elgar.

Villanova, P., Bernardin, H.J., Johnson, D.L. and Dahmus, S.A. (1994). The validity of a measure of job compatibility in the prediction of job performance and turnover of motion picture theater personnel. *Personnel Psychology*, **47**, 73–90.

Witt, L.A. (1998). Enhancing organizational goal congruence: a solution to organizational politics. *Journal of Applied Psychology*, **83**, 666–74.

Witt, L., Kacmar, M., Carlson, D. and Zivnuska, S. (2002). Interactive effects of personality and organizational politics on contextual performance. *Journal of Organizational Behavior*, **23**, 911–26.

Yoffie, D. and Bergenstein, S. (1985). Creating political advantage: The rise of corporate entrepreneurs, *California Management Review*, 124–39.

Yoon, S. (2002). Will your personality win over employers? Retrieved 3 April 2002 from the World Wide Web: http://www.careerjournal.com/jobhunting/workabroad/20010322-yoon.html.

3 Personality and politics perceptions: A new conceptualization and illustration using OCBs

Christopher C. Rosen, Chu-Hsiang Chang and Paul E. Levy

Introduction

Organizational politics are generally defined as activities that are self-serving, not officially sanctioned by the organization, and that often have detrimental effects (Ferris et al., 2002; Ferris and Kacmar, 1992; Randall et al., 1999). Since the publication of Ferris et al.'s (1989) now classic model of perceptions of organizational politics and Kacmar and Ferris's (1991) development of the Perceptions of Organizational Politics Scale (POPS), research in the area of organizational politics perceptions has flourished. Another topic in the organizational sciences that has seen a recent increase in attention is personality research. Researchers have begun to examine personality in relation to a variety of organizational phenomena, including perceptions of organizational politics. Ferris et al. (1989) suggested that personality serves as an antecedent to perceptions of politics and, until recently, most of the studies relating these two constructs have been limited to this conceptualization (Kacmar and Baron, 1999). In the present chapter, we present a review of the literature in which personality traits are examined as an antecedent to politics perceptions. Following this review, we discuss recent studies that have viewed personality characteristics as moderators of the politics–outcomes relationship. Finally, we present a recent study to illustrate the new directions in which this research should be extended. In particular, we believe that the study of personality in relation to politics has been limited by its focus on personality as an antecedent to politics perceptions. Furthermore, viewing single personality characteristics as moderating the relationship between politics and outcomes may be overly simplistic. Therefore, we suggest that researchers should begin to examine how various aspects of personality interact with each other to moderate the relationship between politics and work outcomes.

Personality as an antecedent to politics perceptions

Ferris et al.'s (1989) model is often cited as the catalyst for contemporary research in the area of perceptions of organizational politics (Ferris et al., 2002). In fact, this model has been so influential that Kacmar et al. (1999) suggested that the literature has been limited to examining only relationships that were specified by Ferris et al. (1989). For example, Ferris et al. (1989) suggested that personality (e.g. Machiavellianism and self-monitoring) serves as an antecedent to POPS and, for nearly a decade, few researchers have considered personality in any other way. In the following section, we review the literature that has examined personality as an antecedent to politics perceptions (see Figure 3.1). Some of these early studies served as influences on Ferris et al. (1989), whereas others were published following the development of the POPS (Kacmar and Ferris, 1991), which allowed researchers to examine many of the relationships specified by Ferris et al. (1989).

In terms of organization, this section of the chapter discusses: (1) adjective checklists in relation to organizational politics research, (2) Vredenburgh and Maurer's (1984) suggestion that personality characteristics serve as antecedents to political sensitivity, and (3) personality research in the context of the Ferris et al. (1989) model.

Adjective lists
Over two decades ago, Mayes and Allen (1977) first suggested that researchers identify the personality characteristics of political actors and examine the interaction between personality and situational factors to determine how political processes affect employees. Consequently, early studies examining the relationship between personality and organizational politics involved the development of adjective lists used to describe effective organizational politicians (Allen et al., 1979; Vredenburgh and Maurer, 1984). For example, Allen et al. (1979) developed a list of 13 personal characteristics associated with effective political actors from employees' responses to a survey. Empirical studies directly assessing the relationship between these personality adjectives and organizational politics are lacking. However, some recent studies have utilized contemporary conceptualizations of personality characteristics and organizational politics (e.g. Big Five measures; the POPS) to examine these relationships. Personality characteristics included in these adjective lists are discussed in relation to politics perceptions in a later section that reviews contemporary conceptualizations of personality in relation to organizational politics perceptions.

Personality and political sensitivity
Vredenburgh and Maurer (1984) were among the first to suggest that individual differences serve as antecedents to perceptions of organizational politics. In particular, they identified several individual needs (e.g. needs for power and autonomy) and personality characteristics (e.g. expedient–conscientious, locus of control) that might serve as antecedents to political sensitivity. Of the personality characteristics that Vredenburgh and Maurer (1984) identified as antecedents to political sensitivity, only need for power and locus of control have received attention from the empirical literature (Kacmar and Baron, 1999). Therefore, we now discuss the empirical research relating locus of control and need for power to organizational politics.

Locus of control   Moberg (1978) was among the first to mention locus of control within the context of organizational politics. According to the framework used in his study, people having an external locus of control are more likely to attribute outcomes to environmental forces, resulting in an increased tendency to attribute work outcomes to organizational politics. Supporting this idea, Moberg's results indicated that people having an external locus of control reported heightened perceptions of politics. Recently, the empirical literature has returned to the ideas of Moberg (1978) and started to re-examine the relationship between locus of control and perceptions of organizational politics. Researchers (O'Connor and Morrison, 2001) have suggested that external locus of control is positively related to perceptions of politics because externals view themselves as unable to manipulate the work environment, which results in heightened perceptions of vulnerability to the politicking of their coworkers. Additionally, O'Connor and Morrison (2001) reiterated the suggestions of Moberg (1978) by stating that external locus of control is positively related to perceptions of organizational politics because employees who believe that they have less control over organizational events are more likely to make attributions that the organizational environments in which they work are politically controlled.

Supporting Moberg's (1978) ideas, several empirical studies (Andrews and Kacmar, 2001; O'Connor and Morrison, 2001; Valle and Perrewé, 2000) have indicated that external locus of control is positively related to perceptions of organizational politics. In Valle and Perrewé's (2000) study, there was support for a positive relationship between both internal and external locus of control and perceptions of politics. However, multiple regression results indicated that only external locus of control accounted for a significant portion of variance beyond other personal influences in perceptions of politics. O'Connor and Morrison (2001) found that external work locus of control was positively related to perceptions of organizational politics. In addition, the structural equation models presented by Andrews and Kacmar (2001) provided further evidence that external locus of control serves as an antecedent to perceptions of politics. In sum, studies working within Moberg's (1978) framework have consistently provided evidence that external locus of control is positively related to perceptions of organizational politics. Therefore, external locus of control should continue to be further integrated into future models (Valle and Perrewé, 2000).

Need for power   Vredenburgh and Maurer (1984) discussed need for power as being 'germane' to political actors (p. 55) and positively related to political sensitivity. Expanding this idea, Kirchmeyer (1990) suggested that managers with high power needs are motivated to engage in political activities and to enter into political arenas in order to accumulate power. Empirical studies have provided some support for a relationship between need for power and individuals' political activities (Kirchmeyer, 1990). However, studies examining the relationship between need for power and politics perceptions have failed to provide conclusive evidence that need for power is an antecedent to perceptions of politics (Valle and Perrewé, 2000). Nonetheless, there is evidence that alternative forms of perceptions of politics (e.g. Tziner et al.'s 1996 measure of perceptions of politics in performance appraisal) may be related to need for power.

Personality and the classic model of organizational politics perceptions
A review of prior research led Ferris et al. (1989) to develop a theoretical model which emphasized the role of employee *perceptions* of politics in organizational life. Because the focus of this model is employee perceptions, the network of variables expected to be associated with politics typically includes individual level beliefs, attitudes and behaviors. Ferris et al.'s (1989) model detailed the antecedents and consequences of such employee perceptions. This model described organizational (e.g. centralization, formalization), environmental (e.g. feedback, interactions with others) and personal influences (e.g. Machiavellianism, locus of control) on perceptions of organizational politics. In the present discussion, we focus on personality as it was included in Ferris et al.'s (1989) antecedent category of personal influences.

Following Vredenburgh and Maurer's (1984) ideas that personality characteristics serve as predispositions to political sensitivity, Ferris et al. (1989) suggested that Machiavellianism and self-monitoring are personal influences that are antecedents to politics perceptions. They theorized that people high in Machiavellianism would be more inclined to interpret actions and events in political terms because 'manipulation and opportunism are such personally salient issues' for people who are high in Machiavellianism (p. 161). Additionally, Ferris et al. (1989) proposed that high self-monitors should be better able to detect political nuances of the behaviors of those around them since they have heightened environmental scanning skills. Shortly after the publication of the politics perceptions model, Kacmar and Ferris (1991) developed and validated a measure of perceptions of organizational politics which made it possible for researchers to examine Ferris et al.'s (1989) idea that certain personality characteristics (e.g. Machiavellianism and self-monitoring) serve as antecedents to perceptions of politics. In the following sections, we review empirical studies that have related Machiavellianism and self-monitoring to organizational politics.

Machiavellianism   The construct of Machiavellianism was derived from the belief that people differ in their willingness and ability to gain and maintain interpersonal power (McHoskey et al., 1998). Individuals who are high in Machiavellianism are best described as more rational than sensitive, willing to lie to achieve personal goals, placing little value on friendship at work, and finding enjoyment in the manipulation of others (Moorhead and Griffin, 1995). Therefore, it is not surprising that the empirical literature has provided consistent support for a relationship between Machiavellianism and politics. In fact, in their review of the work of Ferris et al. (1989, 2002), Dipboye and Foster (2002) claim that 'The only personal influence variable that appears to have been shown to have a consistent relation to perceived politics is Machiavellianism' (pp. 257–8).

Early research (Biberman, 1985) on this relationship indicated that individuals scoring high on a scale measuring Machiavellianism also had high scores on the office politics questionnaire (DuBrin, 1978; OPQ). In fact, the authors mention that the strength of this relationship is such that the OPQ may serve as 'a surrogate to the Mach scale' (Biberman, 1985; p. 1309). Additionally, recent studies (Valle and Perrewé, 2000; O'Connor and Morrison, 2001) that have used variations of the POPS to examine the relationship between Machiavellianism and politics perceptions have also provided support for this linkage. For example, in their replication and extension of the Ferris et al. (1989) model, Valle and Perrewé (2000) found that Machiavellianism was an antecedent that was positively related to perceptions of politics. Tziner et al. (1996) also demonstrated that Machiavellianism is positively related to politics perceptions in the performance appraisal process.

Self-monitoring   As previously mentioned, Mayes and Allen (1977) and Allen et al. (1979) suggested that characteristics such as social adeptness and sensitivity should be related to organizational politics. These characteristics are subsumed by the construct of self-monitoring, which is generally defined as the extent to which individuals monitor and control the images that they present to better fit with the social climate around them (Day et al., 2002). Ferris et al. (1989) suggested that self-monitoring is an antecedent to perceptions of organizational politics because high self-monitors possess a heightened environmental scanning ability. Valle and Perrewé (2000) further speculated that there is a heightened sense of self associated with self-monitoring and this 'would lead to increased perceptions of behaviors that could be perceived as political' (Valle and Perrewé, 2000, p. 367). However, the two published empirical studies (Ferris and Kacmar, 1992, Study 2;

Valle and Perrewé, 2000) that have examined self-monitoring as an antecedent to perceptions of organizational politics have failed to support such a relationship.

Nonetheless, studies have demonstrated that self-monitoring is related to alternative measures of organizational politics. For example, Kirchmeyer (1990) found that
self monitoring was related to self reports of political activity for men ($r = 0.31$), but a
weaker relationship for women ($r = 0.22$). More recently, Ferris et al. (2005) suggested that
the emerging construct of political skill should overlap with self-monitoring because they
both reflect measures of social effectiveness. Ferris et al.'s (2005) results supported this
idea. Based on these findings, we recommend that researchers do not prematurely dis-
continue research on self-monitoring in relation to organizational politics. Rather, we
suggest that future studies consider how self-monitoring moderates the relationships
between perceptions of organizational politics and individual-level outcomes. This point
is illustrated in the study that we present in a later section.

The Zeitgeist: personality as a moderator of the politics–outcome relationship
Thus far, we have discussed how several personality characteristics (e.g. locus of control,
need for power, Machiavellianism and self-monitoring) have been construed as antecedents to perceptions of organizational politics (see Figure 3.1). However, there is a bur-
geoning stream of research that has begun to examine how perceptions of organizational
politics interact with personality characteristics to predict work outcomes. In particular,
the inconsistent results of empirical studies (Ferris et al., 1996; Kacmar et al., 1999; Poon,
2003; Randall et al., 1999) linking politics perceptions to aspects of performance have led
contemporary researchers (Valle et al., 2002; Witt et al., 2002) to suggest that it is likely
that individual differences predispose people to respond in different ways to their perceptions of organizational politics (see Figure 3.2). Therefore, it is necessary that researchers
move away from emphasizing a focus on personality as an antecedent to perceptions of
politics and begin to examine the role of personality characteristics in moderating the
relationship between perceptions of organizational politics and work-related outcomes.

In this section, a review of the few studies that have examined personality characteristics (e.g. Big Five Personality Traits and Affect) as moderators of the politics–outcome
relationship is provided. Following this review, we discuss a recent study in which
Hochwarter et al. (2003) suggest that the relationship between politics and work outcomes
will be best explained by research that examines how interactions among multiple variables moderate this relationship. We then present a study as an exemplar for future
research relating personality and politics. Specifically, we propose that interactions among
multiple personality characteristics (e.g. self-monitoring and agreeableness) moderate the

Figure 3.1   Personality as an antecedent to politics perceptions

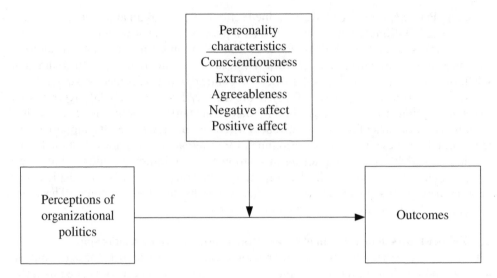

Figure 3.2   Personality as a moderator of the politics–outcomes relationship

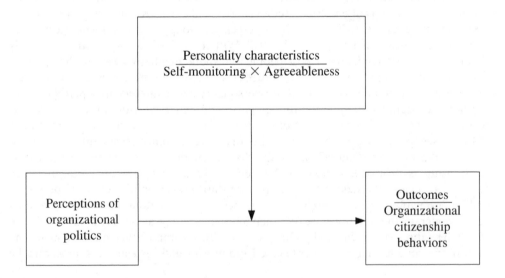

Figure 3.3   The interaction between self-monitoring and agreeableness moderates the relationship between politics perceptions and OCBs

relationship between POPS and outcomes (see Figure 3.3). By focusing on understanding how interactions that occur among combinations of personality variables moderate the relationship between perceived politics and work outcomes, researchers can more accurately capture the dynamic relationship between perceptions of politics and work outcomes.

Big Five traits
Contemporary researchers have speculated that Big Five personality traits interact with organizational politics to predict work attitudes and outcomes. For example, Witt et al. (2002) predicted that the relationship between perceptions of organizational politics and facets of contextual performance would be moderated by conscientiousness, extraversion and agreeableness. They hypothesized that the negative effects of perceptions of organizational politics on supervisor ratings of contextual performance would be stronger among individuals low in conscientiousness, introverts, and people low in agreeableness. However, results of this study indicated that only the interaction between politics and agreeableness explained a significant amount of incremental variance in contextual performance (Witt et al., 2002). As such, these results provided partial support to the prediction that personality traits moderate the relationship between perceptions of politics and contextual performance.

Coming from a slightly different perspective, Hochwarter et al. (2000) examined the interaction between conscientiousness and perceptions of organizational politics in predicting in-role performance. They took an interactionist approach and identified organizational politics as a situational factor that moderates the relationship between the Big Five trait conscientiousness and performance. In particular, they speculated that individuals who are high in conscientiousness are more likely to overcome barriers to their performance and find ways to complete their work tasks. The results of this study indicated that perceptions of politics moderate the relationship between conscientiousness and job performance such that conscientiousness was related to job performance among workers perceiving high levels of organizational politics but unrelated to performance for workers perceiving low levels of politics.

These two studies (Witt et al., 2002; Hochwarter et al., 2000) provide evidence that conscientiousness and agreeableness moderate the relationship between politics and performance. However, more research is necessary to determine the precise nature of the relationship between politics and all of the Big Five personality traits. In addition, future researchers should explore the role of personality profiles, represented by constellations of personality traits, in moderating the relationship between politics perceptions and work-related outcomes.

Affect   Recently, Hochwarter and colleagues have advanced a stream of research examining the relationship between perceptions of organizational politics and affective dispositions. In this literature, affect has been construed as an antecedent to perceptions of politics (Valle et al., 2002), and more recently as a moderator of the relationship between perceptions of politics and job attitudes (Hochwarter, 2003; Hochwarter and Treadway, 2003; Hochwarter et al., 2003). In the following section, we discuss the empirical literature that has examined affect as a moderator of the relationship between politics and work-related outcomes.

Based on the theory that levels of negative affect (NA) and positive affect (PA) determine the extent to which organizational politics is viewed as a threat or opportunity by the individual, it has been suggested (Hochwarter and Treadway, 2003; Valle et al., 2002) that affective dispositions moderate the relationship between perceptions of politics and work-related attitudes. Valle et al. (2002) described politics as more threatening and associated with negative outcomes and attitudes for people high in NA and more associated with positive outcomes and attitudes for people high in PA. They further suggested that dispositional characteristics of high NA individuals predispose them to perceive the ambiguity surrounding political environments as more threatening. In the only empirical study examining the moderating role of NA in the perceptions of politics–job satisfaction relationship, Hochwarter and Treadway (2003) hypothesized that high NAs would be more sensitive to the adverse effects of politics, causing high NAs to perceive political environments as more threatening. Results provided support for the moderating role of NA such that the negative relationship between politics and job satisfaction was strongest for people high in NA (Study 1: Hochwarter and Treadway, 2003).

However, the literature is not as clear when it comes to describing the moderating role of PA in the relationship between perceptions of politics and work attitudes. Some researchers have suggested that PA reduces the magnitude of the negative relationship between POPS and work attitudes (e.g. Hochwarter et al., 2003), whereas others have suggested that PA serves to increase the magnitude of this relationship (Hochwarter and Treadway, 2003). Valle et al. (2002) mentioned that people high in PA may have more 'social power,' and political environments represent opportunities for people high in PA to achieve positive outcomes by engaging in social activities. Hochwarter et al. (2003) also suggested that the positive emotions associated with PA should buffer the stress associated with perceptions of politics. However, other researchers (Hochwarter and Treadway, 2003) have suggested that reduced reward expectancies, associated with ambiguity in political environments, are related to lower levels of satisfaction for employees high in PA because people high in PA are more sensitive to reward signals (Shaw et al., 1999).

Empirical studies (Hochwarter and Treadway, 2003; Hochwarter et al., 2003) generally support the proposition that PA moderates the relationship between perceptions of politics and job attitudes such that high PA is related to a stronger magnitude inverse relationship between perceived politics and job satisfaction. For example, Hochwarter and Treadway (2003) performed two studies in which they examined affect as a moderator in the relationship between organizational politics and job satisfaction. They hypothesized that the adverse effects of politics on job satisfaction would be strongest for participants high in PA. Results of these two studies indicated that perceptions of politics were more strongly related to low job satisfaction scores for people reporting high PA. As such, the literature supports the idea that people higher in PA are more affected by the decrease in reward expectancies that are associated with heightened politics perceptions.

Interactions among moderators of the politics–outcomes relationship
In a recent study, Hochwarter et al. (2003) attempted to identify factors that buffer the harmful effects of organizational politics on employees and suggested that 'employing only one moderating variable may fail to fully capture the dynamics of organizational life' (Hochwarter et al., 2003, p. 1010). They further suggested that researchers look at the multiplicative effects of numerous moderators in the relationship between POPs and work outcomes. Therefore, Hochwarter et al. (2003) examined how personality variables (e.g., positive affect; PA) and characteristics of the situation (e.g., perceived collective efficacy; PCE) interact with politics to predict job satisfaction. They predicted that the negative relationship between politics perceptions and job satisfaction would be strongest for employees low in PCE and that this relationship would be weakest for employees high

in PA and high in PCE. The results of this study indicated the presence of a significant three-way interaction. However, this interaction contradicted the authors' hypotheses because it indicated that people high in PA and high in PCE reported a stronger inverse relationship between POPS and job satisfaction than people low in PA and low in PCE. These findings were, however, consistent with the suggestions of Hochwarter and Treadway (2003) that the inverse relationship between politics and job satisfaction would be stronger for people high in PA due to the relationship of PA to heightened sensitivity to reward expectancies.

Politics, the multiplicative effects of personality, and OCBs: An illustrative example

Vigoda (2003) suggested that our understanding of organizational politics may be enhanced by examining political activities and citizenship behaviors within the context of general political behavior. From a political theory perspective, it has been suggested that there is a relationship between an individual's participation in national and governmental political activities (e.g. political participation and community involvement) and certain aspects of citizenship behavior within organizations (Brady et al., 1995; Cohen and Vigoda, 1998, 1999, 2000; Peterson, 1990; Vigoda, 2003). This perspective is based on the ideas of political scientists and sociologists who have suggested that experiences in one domain can be transferred into other similar, or congruent, domains (Brady et al., 1995; Cohen and Vigoda, 2000; Sobel, 1993). Based on the arguments put forth by Almond and Verba (1963), theorists (Cohen and Vigoda, 2000; Sobel, 1993) have suggested that the spheres in which politics and work activities occur are congruent and both domains have 'analogous formal authority patterns' (Cohen and Vigoda, 2000, p. 600) which enhance transference of behaviors across domains. As such, there is reason to believe that general political activity will spill over into work activities, which take the form of specific organizational citizenship behaviors (Cohen and Vigoda, 2000, 1998). Thus an innate desire for political participation, associated with general citizenship activities, may directly spill over into voluntary work behaviors (Graham, 1991; Sobel, 1993). Supporting this perspective, research has provided evidence that there is a complex relationship between levels of general political activity and certain citizenship behaviors within the organization (Cohen and Vigoda, 1998, 2000). Thus, based on the political science literature, there is reason to believe that political participation in one domain will transfer to the other (Cohen and Vigoda, 2000; Peterson, 1990; Sobel, 1993) and, relevant to the present study, that individuals probably have predispositions that are related to how they experience and engage in political activities outside of and within the organization.

In the present study, ideas relating predispositions (see Sobel, 1993; Verba and Nie, 1972) to general political activities are extended to the domain of perceptions of organizational politics. Despite the array of research relating general political behavior to organizational citizenship behaviors, researchers have had difficulty providing consistent results supporting a relationship between perceptions of organizational politics and OCBs. In the present study, we integrate the idea that individuals may have certain predispositions that make them more sensitive and responsive to political environments with Hochwarter et al.'s (2003) suggestion that researchers employ an interactionist perspective to enhance our understanding of the relationship between politics and work-related outcomes. Specifically, we recommend that researchers extend the personality and politics perceptions literature by examining how interactions among sets of personality traits moderate the relationship between politics perceptions and outcomes. This recommendation is based on a person approach to understanding individual differences, an interactionist perspective of personality, and the idea that examining single moderators is not sufficient for understanding the complexity of work relationships (Hochwarter et al., 2003).

Magnusson (1995) proposed that researchers utilize a person approach to understand individual differences. According to this perspective, individual functioning is best understood in terms of patterns of personality variables which are relevant for the problem under consideration. The person approach was developed in response to the notion that current approaches are too simplistic to accurately explain differences in how individuals function in their environments. Supporting the use of the person approach, constellations of personality traits have been used to make predictions across a range of domains, including leadership (Smith and Foti, 1998) and performance appraisal (Bernardin et al., 2000). In addition, personality researchers have advocated an interactionist perspective which emphasizes the relationship between aspects of the situation and personality traits in determining work-related behaviors such as performance (Tett and Burnett, 2003). This technique has become especially popular since Chatman (1989) presented the interactionist perspective within the context of person–organization fit. Another influence on the present study was Hochwarter et al.'s (2003) recent suggestion that a more complete understanding of complex work relationships requires that investigations go beyond the use of only one moderator variable. Therefore, we suggest that a person approach, which utilizes an interactionist perspective, should be applied to understanding the role of multiple personality variables (e.g. self-monitoring and Big Five traits) in moderating the relationship between perceived politics and citizenship behaviors. Taking such an approach will allow us to better understand the dynamic relationship between politics, personality and aspects of work performance.

As an example of this approach, we present a study in which we extended the ideas of Hochwarter et al. (2003) by examining how the joint relationship between personality characteristics (e.g. agreeableness and self-monitoring) moderates the relationship between politics and organizational citizenship behaviors (OCBs). This study extends the literature in three ways. First, we specified that self-monitoring and agreeableness serve as moderators in the relationship between perceptions of politics and work-related outcomes, which is in contrast to the majority of studies that have specified that personality characteristics are an antecedent to perceptions of organizational politics. Second, the few studies that have examined the moderating role of personality in the politics–outcomes relationship have generally focused only on how personality moderates the relationship between politics and work attitudes (e.g. job satisfaction). However, we examined how the multiplicative effects of these personality characteristics moderate the relationship between perceptions of politics and employees' demonstration of citizenship behaviors, as rated by supervisors. Another contribution of this study is that it aims to rectify a number of inconsistencies in the literature. In particular, previous studies (e.g. Cropanzano et al., 1997) failed to support a relationship between perceptions of politics and OCBs, and the literature has not provided empirical support for a relationship between self-monitoring and organizational politics (Ferris and Kacmar, 1992; Valle and Perrewé, 2000). If the results support the relationships proposed in this study, then they will indicate that the relationship between politics and work outcomes is more complex than previous models have specified (e.g. Ferris et al., 1989; Valle and Perrewé, 2000). Furthermore, these results would support further examination of the multiplicative effects of personality character-istics in the politics–outcomes relationship.

The perceptions of organizational politics–OCB relationship

Cropanzano and colleagues (Cropanzano et al., 1997; Randall et al., 1999) suggested that organizations are a social marketplace and that organizational politics are likely related to citizenship behaviors through their influence on exchange relationships that exist between employers and employees. Cropanzano et al. (1997) suggested that the quality of this exchange relationship manifests itself through employees' demonstration of OCBs, which are a response to employees' perceptions that the organization will meet their needs. In particular, employees view highly political organizations as risky invest-ments and respond to these perceptions by reducing the OCBs that they perform. Similarly, Vigoda (2000) suggested that decreases in OCBs that are related to perceptions of politics are the result of employees' beliefs that highly political systems are innately unfair and employees' decreases in performance and OCBs are a reaction to perceived unfairness in the work environment. However, only a few empirical studies have explored the linkages between organizational politics and OCBs as evaluated by a supervisor, and these studies have produced inconsistent results (Cropanzano et al., 1997; Randall et al., 1999; Vigoda, 2000, Witt et al., 2002). For example, Cropanzano et al. (1997) found no relationship between politics and supervisor ratings of OCBs, whereas studies by Randall et al. (1999) and Vigoda (2000) both provided evidence that OCBs were inversely related to perceptions of politics. These inconsistent findings suggest the presence of moderators (Ferris et al., 2002).

Recently, Witt et al. (2002) suggested that in politically charged environments, employ-ees who demonstrate fewer OCBs are likely not sufficiently skilled self-managers to have learned effective political skills. This lack of self-management skills makes it more difficult for these employees to adjust their behavior to fit their environments (Witt et al., 2002). As such, these employees do not know how to interact with others in political situations and will likely perceive organizational politics as more threatening because they are less capable of achieving success in political environments. On the other hand, it has been sug-gested that some employees are likely predisposed to respond in a positive way to politics due to dispositional factors (Ferris et al., 2005). In the following section, we explore these ideas in more detail and consider specific dispositions that moderate the POPS–OCB relationship.

Personality, politics and OCBs

Researchers have suggested that personality can be used to predict OCBs (Podsakoff, et al., 2000). Furthermore, politics researchers (Fedor et al., 1998; Witt et al., 2002) have suggested that interpersonal factors color how individuals interpret and respond to their work environments. Based on previous research in the area of organizational politics, and a theoretically derived rationale, we performed a study intended to examine the role of agreeableness and self-monitoring in moderating the relationship between perceived politics and supervisor ratings of OCBs.

Although self-monitoring was originally specified as an antecedent to politics percep-tions (Ferris et al., 1989), empirical studies (Valle and Perrewé, 2000; Ferris and Kacmar,

1992) have failed to provide support for this relationship. However, recent work by Ferris and colleagues (Ferris et al., 2002, 2005) has shown that self-monitoring is related to political skill, which is likely related to performance in political environments because it is an indicator of social effectiveness (Ferris et al., 2005). As such, high self-monitors are likely to interpret their perceptions of politics as less threatening. Therefore, we suggest that self-monitoring serves as a moderator, rather than an antecedent, in the relationship between POPs and outcomes. Furthermore, this prediction is based on the idea that high self-monitors are adept at recognizing what behaviors are required and adapting them to fit the situation (Day et al., 2002). Day et al. (2002) further suggested that the higher performance ratings of self-monitors may be due to impression management. Therefore, the positive correlation between self-monitoring and measures of work performance should be higher when performance is measured subjectively. Previous studies (Allen and Rush, 1998; Johnson, 2001) have indicated that higher levels of OCBs are related to higher performance ratings although OCB-related behaviors have not traditionally shown up on actual performance evaluations. As such, employees possessing higher levels of self-monitoring likely engage in OCBs to increase performance ratings in political environments.

However, just because an employee can identify what behaviors are necessary to achieve success does not mean that he or she can effectively or efficiently engage in those behaviors. We suggest that there are probably predispositions that make it easier for certain employees to achieve success in political environments. In the present study, we focused on agreeableness, which is composed of traits indicating that the individual is courteous, trusting, good-natured, cooperative, tolerant, altruistic and modest (Barrick and Mount, 1991). As such, agreeableness predisposes people to develop certain orientations with other people via their expressed behaviors. In support of this idea, Witt et al. (2002) suggested that individuals who are high in agreeableness are acting in ways that are congruent with their personalities when they engage in OCBs. Therefore, it is easier for individuals high in agreeableness to demonstrate these behaviors and they can do so more efficiently (e.g. with less conscious effort) than employees who are low in agreeableness. In support of these ideas, Witt et al. (2002) found an interaction between politics and agreeableness such that the negative effect of organizational politics on supervisor ratings of interpersonal facilitation was stronger for individuals who were low in agreeableness.

As an extension of Witt et al.'s (2002) findings regarding agreeableness and Ferris et al.'s (2002) suggestions that self-monitoring is an indicator of social effectiveness, we propose that a three-way interaction between perceptions of politics, self-monitoring and agreeableness explains significant incremental variance in supervisor ratings of OCBs (see Figure 3.3). Highly political environments are described as having ambiguous and subjective measures of performance (Graddick and Lane, 1998). Furthermore, individuals who are high in the agreeableness personality trait will be acting in a way that is more congruent with their personalities when they engage in OCBs (Witt et al., 2002). Therefore, employees who are high in self-monitoring will be able to recognize the need to change their behavior to fit the political environment (Day et al., 2002). Additionally, employees who are more agreeable will be more capable of engaging in OCBs because those types of behaviors are more inherent to their personalities than to those of individuals who are low in agreeableness. Therefore, we predict that the interaction between self-monitoring and perceptions of politics will be moderated by agreeableness such that the positive relationship between politics perceptions and organizational citizenship behaviors will be strongest for those who are high in both self-monitoring and agreeableness.

Method

Participants
One hundred and eighty-three undergraduate students at a large, midwestern university who worked at least part-time and full-time participated in the study for class credit. Participants approached their direct supervisors and asked them to fill out a different questionnaire. One hundred and three supervisors returned the survey, yielding a response rate of 53 percent and a total of 103 usable matched supervisor–subordinate pairs.

The average age of participants was 24.4 years. Women made up 72.8 percent of the sample. Approximately 74.8 percent of the sample identified themselves as Caucasian, 14.6 percent identified themselves as African American, and 10.6 percent identified themselves as Asian, Hispanic, Native American or Other. Their average tenure at the present job was 33.1 months, and they estimated that they worked an average of 30 hours per week.

The average age of supervisors was 39.3 years. About 55 percent of the supervisors were female and 78.8 percent were Caucasian, 12.1 percent were African American, and 9.1 percent indicated that they belonged to Asian, Hispanic, Native American or Other racial groups. The average time they spent supervising the participant was 31.5 months, while the average time spent at their current managerial position was about 6.5 years.

Measures

Perceptions of organizational politics We used Kacmar and Carlson's (1997) revised Perceptions of Organizational Politics Scale to measure the extent to which employees view their work environment as political. Following Witt et al.'s (2002) rationale, we used only the 'going along to get ahead' subscale in our data analysis. A sample item from this scale is 'Agreeing with powerful others is the best alternative in this organization.' The subscale has seven items, and participants responded on a seven-point Likert scale (1 = strongly disagree, 7 = strongly agree). Participants' responses were averaged across the items to calculate their perceptions of organizational politics. The reliability (α) coefficient of this subscale was 0.77.

Personality Agreeableness was measured by Goldberg's unipolar trait marker (Saucier, 1994). Eight trait markers tap into agreeableness. Participants indicated how well each trait marker describes themselves on a nine-point Likert scale (1 = extremely inaccurate, 9 = extremely accurate). Example trait markers include 'cooperative,' 'kind' and 'sympathetic.' An average was calculated to represent each participant's level of agreeableness. The agreeableness scale yielded a reliability (α) coefficient of 0.78.

Self-monitoring The subscale of 'ability to modify self-representation' from the revised self-monitoring scale (Lennox and Wolfe, 1984) was used in the study to measure participants' ability to modify self-presentation when situations require such change. An example item is 'In social situations, I have the ability to alter my behavior if I feel that something else is called for.' The reliability coefficient of the seven-item subscale was 0.81.

Organizational citizenship behavior   Supervisors were asked to complete the OCB scale developed by Williams and Anderson (1991). This scale has been validated for use by supervisors in rating the two dimensions of OCBs: OCBI and OCBO. OCBIs were measured using seven items (e.g. 'Helps others who have been absent') intended to measure those OCBs that benefit specific individuals in the organization. OCBOs, OCBs that benefit the organization as a whole, were measured using six items (e.g. 'Adheres to informal rules devised to maintain order'). The reliabilities of the OCBI ($\alpha = 0.92$) and OCBO ($\alpha = 0.85$) scales were both acceptable.

Procedure
Participants who were currently employed volunteered to complete the survey in exchange for class credit. They completed measures assessing their perceptions of organizational politics, personality, self-monitoring and demographics. After finishing the survey, participants filled out a consent form allowing their supervisors to be contacted regarding their work performance. Participants were then instructed to bring a survey to their direct supervisor. The supervisor survey assessed supervisors' demographic information, and their ratings of participants' organizational citizenship behaviors. Supervisors then mailed the completed surveys directly to the researchers.

Results
Table 3.1 presents the means, standard deviations and correlations between the variables. OCBI and OCBO were not related to participants' demographic information. Participants' perceptions of organizational politics did not have significant direct relationships with supervisor-rated OCBI or OCBO. This was similar to what past research has found (Rosen et al., in press). It also indicated that the relationship between perceptions of politics and OCBI or OCBO was potentially much more complicated than a direct relationship. Participants' agreeableness had a positive significant relationship with participants' OCBI ($r = 0.31$, $p < 0.001$). However, its relationship with OCBO

Table 3.1   Means, standard deviations and correlation coefficients between variables

Variables	M	S.D.	1	2	3	4	5	6	7	8
1. Age (year)	24.33	8.21	–							
2. Tenure (month)	33.09	50.41	0.66***	–						
3. Working hour	29.56	12.23	0.44***	0.41***	–					
4. Politics	3.60	1.10	−0.09	0.11	0.02	0.77				
5. Agreeableness	7.57	0.97	0.03	−0.07	−0.07	−0.18	0.78			
6. Self-monitoring	5.16	0.91	0.17	−0.04	−0.11	0.02	0.25**	0.81		
7. OCBI	5.68	1.05	0.06	0.11	0.10	−0.12	0.31***	−0.02	0.92	
8. OCBO	5.90	1.02	−0.03	0.04	−0.09	−0.06	0.05	−0.15	0.60***	0.85

Note: $N = 102-3$; ** $p < 0.01$; *** $p < 0.001$; numbers on the diagonal represent the reliability coefficients.

was not significant ($r = 0.05$, $p > 0.05$). As such, the results provided partial support for a relationship between agreeableness and OCBs. Employees' self-monitoring ability did not have a significant relationship with their supervisor-rated OCBI or OCBO.

Moderated multiple regression analyses were used to assess the hypothesized moderated relationships. Since all the predictor variables were continuous, we followed the recommendations of Aiken and West (1991) to first center the variables to reduce the effects of multicollinearity, then calculate the interaction terms between predictors. The results are shown in Table 3.2. Two separate regression analyses were run to examine the interaction effects of predictors on supervisor-rated OCBI and OCBO. For OCBI, participants' age, tenure and working hours were entered at the first model as control variables. These control variables explained a total of 2 percent of the variance in OCBI ($R^2 = 0.02$, $p > 0.05$). Participants' perceptions of politics, agreeableness and self-monitoring were included in the second model. This second model accounted for an additional 12 percent of explained variance. ($\Delta R^2 = 0.14$, $p < 0.05$). Specifically, participants' agreeableness level appeared to be a strong predictor ($\beta = 0.33$, $p < 0.001$), suggesting that the more agreeable participants were, the more likely they were to engage in OCBI. The two-way interaction terms between the three predictors were entered in step three. Only the two-way interaction between politics and agreeableness was statistically significant, and these interaction terms did not explain a significant amount of additional variance ($\Delta R^2 = 0.05$, $p > 0.05$). Finally, the three-way interaction term between perceptions of politics, agreeableness and self-monitoring was included in the last model. This final model explained significant incremental variance ($\Delta R^2 = 0.06$, $p < 0.01$) in OCBI, suggesting the three-way interaction between perceptions of politics, agreeableness and self-monitoring was a significant predictor of OCBs directed towards coworkers.

Figures 3.4a and 3.4b illustrate the three-way interaction between politics, self-monitoring, agreeableness and OCBIs. Overall, results indicated that there was a strong positive relationship between politics and OCBI only for participants who were both high in self-monitoring and agreeableness (Figure 3.4a). When self-monitoring and agreeableness were not both high, the relationship between politics and OCBIs was negative. These results support our prediction that an interaction between self-monitoring and agreeableness would moderate the relationship between politics and OCBI.

For predicting OCBO, participants' age, tenure and working hours were entered at the first model as control variables. Similar to OCBI, these control variables did not explain the significant amount of variance in OCBO ($R^2 = 0.02$, $p > 0.05$). Neither the second model, which included participants' centered perceptions of organizational politics, agreeableness and self-monitoring, nor the third model, which included two-way interaction terms between the three predictors, predicted OCBO significantly (model 2: $R^2 = 0.06$, $p > 0.05$; model 3: $R^2 = 0.10$, $p > 0.05$). The final model, which included the three-way interaction, explained a significant amount of incremental variance in OCBO ($\Delta R^2 = 0.05$, $p < 0.05$), suggesting that the three-way interaction between perceptions of politics, agreeableness and self-monitoring was a significant predictor.

Figures 3.5a and 3.5b illustrate the three-way interaction between politics, self-monitoring, agreeableness and OCBOs. Similar to the results found for the relationship between politics and OCBI, there was a strong positive relationship between politics and OCBO only for participants who were high in both self-monitoring and agreeableness (Figure 3.5a). When self-monitoring and agreeableness were not both high, the

Table 3.2   Multiple regression predicting OCBI and OCBO with perceptions of organizational politics, agreeableness and self-monitoring

Predictors	OCBI				OCBO			
	Model 1	Model 2	Model 3	Model 4	Model 1	Model 2	Model 3	Model 4
Age	−0.04	−0.09	−0.11	−0.08	−0.06	−0.02	−0.02	0.01
Tenure	0.11	0.17	0.16	0.18	0.13	0.12	0.13	0.14
Working hour	0.07	0.09	0.10	0.09	−0.13	−0.16	−0.16	−0.16
R^2	0.02				0.02			
Politics		−0.09	−0.05	−0.09		−0.06	−0.05	−0.09
Agreeableness		0.33***	0.34***	0.35***		0.08	0.10	0.12
Self-monitoring		−0.07	−0.12	−0.07		−0.19	−0.22*	−0.17
R^2		0.14*				0.06		
ΔR^2		0.12**				0.04		
Politics × agreeableness			0.21*	0.21*			0.19a	0.19a
Agreeableness × self-monitoring			0.06	0.00			0.13	0.08
Politics × self-monitoring			−0.12	−0.03			−0.05	0.04
R^2			0.18*				0.10	
ΔR^2			0.05				0.04	
Politics × agreeableness × self-monitoring				0.28**				0.27*
R^2				0.24**				0.15a
ΔR^2				0.06**				0.05*

Note: $N = 102$–3; * $p < 0.05$; ** $p < 0.01$; *** $p < 0.001$; a = $p < 0.10$.

(a) Higher self-monitoring

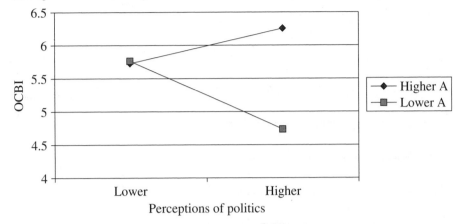

(b) Lower self-monitoring

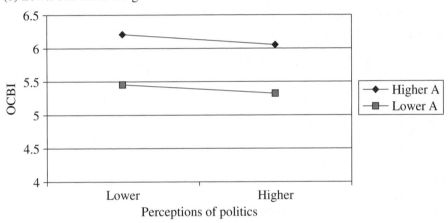

*Figure 3.4   Three-way interaction between perceptions of organizational politics,
agreeableness and self-monitoring on OCBI*

relationship between politics and OCBOs was negative. Overall, these results support our prediction that an interaction between self-monitoring and agreeableness would moderate the relationship between politics and OCBO.

Discussion
The results of this study supported our predictions that in political environments, high self-monitors are likely more adept at identifying when behaviors need to be changed to fit the environment and agreeable individuals are more capable of changing their behaviors when the situation calls for increased OCBs. In particular, a positive relationship between perceptions of politics and engagement of OCBs was found only in employees who were higher in both self-monitoring and agreeableness. These results bolster the

(a) Higher self-monitoring

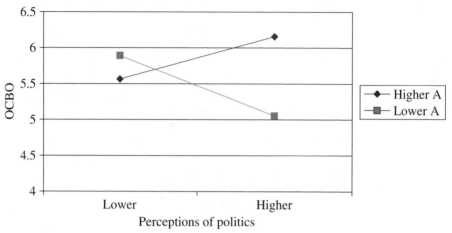

(a) Lower self-monitoring

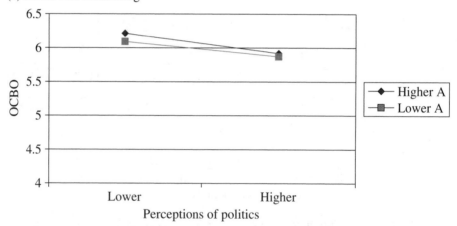

Figure 3.5   *Three-way interaction between perceptions of organizational politics,*
agreeableness and self-monitoring on OCBO

findings of Witt et al. (2002) and extend the literature by identifying another important
individual difference – self-monitoring – that serves as a moderator in the politics–OCB
relationship. Furthermore, our results support the notion that there may be aspects of
personality which predispose individuals to experience and respond to politics in certain
ways (Verba and Nye, 1972; Sobel, 1993). When integrated with the work of political theorists (Cohen and Vigoda, 1998, 2000; Peterson, 1990; Sobel, 1993; Verba and Nye, 1972),
our results provide support for the notion that some people may be more politically oriented than others and thus more active in different aspects of politics inside and outside
of organizational life.

The whole is greater than the sum of its parts
The empirical study presented in this chapter indicated that the multiplicative effects of personality characteristics moderate the relationship between politics and certain aspects of performance. Therefore, we provided an example of how a person-based, interactionist approach can be applied to understanding the role of personality traits in moderating the relationship between politics and work-related outcomes. This approach provides a framework that helps to clarify the politics–work outcomes relationship by demonstrating that organizational politics do not always lead to negative outcomes. Rather, due to personality differences, some people respond in more positive ways to perceptions of politics than do others. Furthermore, our results support the notion that previous models identifying self-monitoring as an antecedent to politics perceptions may have been misspecified. As such, previous studies may have failed to find a relationship between personality, politics and OCBs.

More importantly, the current study applies a person-based approach (Magnusson, 1995) to the investigation of how personality characteristics moderate the effects of perceptions of politics on employee behaviors. Previous studies have generally examined only how single personality characteristics (e.g. Witt et al., 2002: agreeableness) moderate the effects of perceived politics. While this line of research has helped organizational scientists identify potential personality variables as moderators, it may be too narrow a focus. Each employee should be considered as possessing a collection of multiple traits (Magnusson, 1995). Thus, examining the interaction effect of multiple dispositional variables at the same time may not only advance theoretical model building, but also better represent the real-life situation and carry practical implications.

Theoretical model building
While the current study asserted the importance of considering the individual as a whole when examining employee responses to perceptions of organizational politics, it does not clarify the underlying mechanisms relating politics to employee outcomes. However, there are other studies (e.g. Rosen et al., in press; Rosen et al., 2005) that have focused on the processes by which perceptions of organizational politics influence employee attitudes and behaviors. It is possible to combine these two lines of research to construct a more complete theoretical model that will provide a framework to guide future research.

As previously mentioned, one possible explanation for self-monitoring acting as a moderator of the effects of perceived politics on OCBs is through impression management (Day et al., 2001). Specifically, individuals with high levels of self-monitoring may see the political environment as an opportunity to enhance their images in front of their supervisors. As a result, they take advantage of this chance and engage in OCBs to create a more positive impression. However, those with low levels of self-monitoring may be unable to seize this opportunity to bolster their images by engaging in OCBs, and thus may perceive organizational politics as a more threatening aspect of their work environments. As such, employees' interpretations of their perceptions of organizational politics are likely related to how they respond to politics, which is congruent with the ideas presented by Ferris et al. (1989) regarding politics perceptions as a source of environmental stress.

In contrast, Rosen and his colleagues (Rosen et al., in press; Rosen et al., 2005) have focused on employees' more negative construal of organizational politics as a threatening aspect of the organizational environment. They argued that perceptions of organizational politics violate the balance of exchange relationships between the organization and employees and thus reduce the instrumentality of employees' performance. As a result, employees likely interpret organizational politics as a threat to achieving expected and desired rewards and may lead to the development of negative attitudes and decreased performance.

When the ideas presented in the current chapter are integrated with the suggestions of Rosen et al. (in press, 2005), it appears that individuals' interpretations of perceptions of organizational politics may explain how employees respond to politics perceptions and that there may be individual differences that moderate both the link between perceived politics and interpretation, and the link between interpretation and attitudinal and behavioral outcomes. Such a process-oriented model is presented in Figure 3.6. For example, from the current study it can be argued that while self-monitoring interacts with perceptions of organizational politics to shape employees' interpretation of organizational politics as an opportunity, agreeableness may also interact with this interpretation to increase employees' tendency to engage in OCBs. Arguably, this interpretation process occurs *within* each individual and the interactive effect of multiple traits observed in the current study represents only an indirect way to capture this process.

This model also helps integrate previous research on the moderating effects of various aspects of personality on the relationship between perceived politics and employee attitudes and behaviors. For example, positive and negative affect have been found to moderate the relationship between perceptions of politics and outcomes (e.g. Hochwarter and Treadway, 2003; Valle et al., 2002). Based on the assertion that affective dispositions influence how individuals perceive and process information (e.g. Bies et al., 1997; Zautra and Reich, 1983), positive and negative affectivity can be seen as important moderators of the relationship between perceived organizational politics and the construal of such perceptions. While those with high PA may interpret perceived politics as opportunities to advance their personal gains, those with high NA may consider perceived politics as more threatening to their success in organizations.

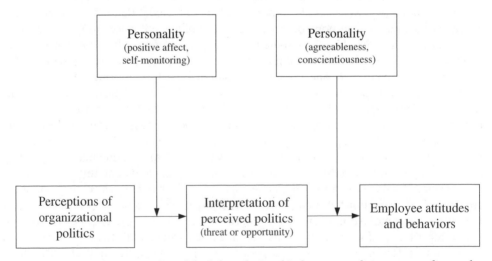

Figure 3.6   Process-oriented model of the relationship between politics, personality and employee outcomes

This model also helps explain the moderating effect of conscientiousness and agreeableness found in previous studies (e.g. Hochwarter et al., 2000; Witt et al., 2002). It can be argued that these effects observed in previous studies are better considered as the interaction between personality traits and the *interpretation* of perceived politics, rather than the interaction between personality and perceived politics directly. In other words, the buffer effect of higher levels of conscientious or agreeableness can be seen as enhancing the interpretation of politics as an opportunity or as alleviating the interpretation of perceived organizational politics as a threat. Thus we believe that this model combines a process-oriented perspective to specify the mechanism linking perceived organizational politics with outcomes *and* a person-based approach to understanding how a constellation of personality traits moderates the effect of such perceptions on work-related attitudes and behaviors.

Practical implications
An important practical implication of the present chapter is that from an individual perspective, personality traits may have diagnostic value in terms of helping organizations identify the type of employees that may be most effective in politically charged environments. Particularly, it appears that those with higher self-monitoring may interpret their perceptions of politics more positively and thus respond with more positive attitudes and behaviors, especially when they are predisposed to do so (i.e. higher agreeableness and conscientiousness). On the other hand, those with lower levels of self-monitoring may construe the perceived politics more negatively, and have a particularly hard time coping with such a negative interpretation when they possess a different set of personality characteristics (e.g. lower agreeableness and conscientiousness). Thus the pattern of personality traits may help set apart those who are likely to function more effectively in political environments.

Limitations
A limit of the present study was the relatively small sample size (although it was adequate for the statistical tests used in the study). The reliance on a younger sample of subordinates, of modest job tenure, may also place some boundary conditions on the generalizability of the study. Replication using a more varied sample of subordinates would further extend our knowledge of personality as a moderator of the relationship between politics and work outcomes. However, the collection of data from subordinates from different organizations does work to increase the generalizability of the findings. A second limitation is that we have captured a cross-sectional snapshot of the relationships among these variables. Although the results are quite strong and consistent, there are certainly other variables beyond the politics perceptions which may have an as large or potentially larger effect on organizational citizenship behaviors.

Conclusion
In the present chapter, we reviewed the existing literature that discusses personality in relation to organizational politics perceptions. Our review indicated that the vast majority of early research focused on identifying personality variables that serve as antecedents to organizational politics (e.g. behaviors and perceptions). However, researchers have recently started to examine how personality traits may serve to moderate the relationship

between organizational politics and work attitudes and behaviors. We suggest that this literature should be extended to focus on an examination of the multiplicative effects among variables moderating the politics perceptions–OCB relationship. We presented a recent study as an example of our recommendation that future researchers explore how interactions among personality characteristics moderate employees' reactions to perceptions of organizational politics. Results of this study supported our predictions and demonstrated the importance of examining alternative ways in which personality is related to politics perceptions.

In addition, we also proposed a process-oriented theoretical model that takes a person-based approach to link perceptions of organizational politics and outcomes. We argue that by using this model as a framework for future research, organizational scientists will acquire a clearer understanding of why employees react in different ways to political environments and will be able to further clarify relationships between politics and important work outcomes. This area of research is quite promising and future researchers should continue to test and refine the models presented in this study. In accord with the suggestions of Kacmar et al. (1999), pursuit of this line of research will expand our knowledge of politics perceptions beyond the relationships specified by Ferris et al. (1989) and will provide a more complete picture of how different individuals are affected by organizational politics.

References

Aiken, L.S. and West, S.G. (1991). *Multiple regression: Testing and interpreting interactions*. London: Sage.

Allen, R.W., Madison, D.L., Porter, L.W., Renwick, P.A. and Mayes, B.T. (1979). Organizational politics: Tactics and characteristics of its actors. *California Management Review*, **22**, 77–83.

Allen, T.D. and Rush, M.C. (1998). The effects of organizational citizenship behavior on performance judgments: A field study and a laboratory experiment. *Journal of Applied Psychology*, **83**, 247–60.

Almond G. and Verba, S. (1963). *The Civic Culture: Democracy in Five Nations*, Princeton, NJ: Princeton University Press.

Andrews, M.C. and Kacmar, K.M. (2001). Discriminating among organizational politics, justice, and support. *Journal of Organizational Behavior*, **22**, 347–66.

Barrick, M.R. and Mount, M.K. (1991). The big five personality dimensions and job performance: A meta-analysis. *Personnel Psychology*, **44**, 1–26.

Bernardin, H.J., Cooke, D.K. and Villanova, P. (2000). Conscientiousness and agreeableness as predictors of rating leniency. *Journal of Applied Psychology*, **85**, 232–6.

Biberman, G. (1985). Personality and characteristic work attitudes of persons with high, moderate, and low political tendencies. *Psychological Reports*, **57**, 1303–10.

Bies, R.J., Tripp, T.M. and Kramer, R.M. (1997). At the breaking points: Cognitive and social dynamics of revenge in organizations. In R.A. Giacalone and J. Greenberg (eds), *Anti-social behavior in organizations* (pp. 18–36). Thousand Oaks, CA: Sage.

Brady, H.E., Verba, S. and Schlozman, K.L. (1995). Beyond SES: A resource model of political participation. *American Political Science Review*, **89**, 271–94.

Chatman, J.A. (1989). Improving interactional organizational research: A model of person–organization fit. *Academy of Management Review*, **14**, 333–49.

Cohen, A. and Vigoda, E. (1998). An empirical assessment of the relationship between general citizenship and work outcomes. *Public Administration Quarterly*, **4**, 401–31.

Cohen, A. and Vigoda, E. (1999). Politics and the workplace: An empirical examination of the relationship between political behavior and work outcomes. *Public Productivity and Management Review*, **22**, 389-406.

Cohen, A. and Vigoda, E. (2000). Do good citizens make good organizational citizens? An empirical examination of the relationship between general citizenship and organizational citizenship behavior in Israel. *Administration and Society*, **32**, 596–624.

Cropanzano, R., Howes, J.C., Grandey, A.A. and Toth, P. (1997). The relationship of organizational politics and support to work behaviors, attitudes, and stress. *Journal of Organizational Behavior*, **18**, 159–80.

Day, D.V., Shleicher, D.J., Unckless, A.L. and Hiller, N.J. (2002). Self-monitoring personality at work: A meta-analytic investigation of construct validity. *Journal of Applied Psychology*, **87**, 390–401.

Dipboye, R.L. and Foster, J.B. (2002). Multi-level theorizing about perceptions of organizational politics. In F.J. Yammarino and Dansereau, F. (eds), *The many faces of multi-level issues* (pp. 255–70). Amsterdam, Netherlands: JAI Press.

Dubrin, A.J. (1978). *Winning at office politics*. New York: Van Nostrand Reinhold Company.

Fedor, D.B., Ferris, G.R., Harrell-Cook, G. and Russ, G.S. (1998). The dimensions of politics perceptions and their organizational and individual predictors. *Journal of Applied Social Psychology*, **28**, 1760–97.

Ferris, G.R. and Kacmar, K.M. (1992). Perceptions of organizational politics. *Journal of Management*, **18**, 93–116.

Ferris, G.R., Russ, G.S. and Fandt, P.M. (1989). Politics in organizations. In R.A. Giacalone and P. Rosenfeld (eds), *Impression management in the organization* (pp. 143–70). Hillsdale, NJ: Lawrence Erlbaum.

Ferris, G.R., Frink, D.D., Galang, M.C., Zhou, J., Kacmar, K.M. and Howard, J.L. (1996). Perceptions of organizational politics: Prediction, stress-related implications, and outcomes. *Human Relations* **49**, 233–66.

Ferris, G.R., Adams, G., Kolodinsky, R.W., Hochwarter, W.A. and Ammeter, A.P. (2002). Perceptions of organizational politics: Theory and research directions. In F. Dansereau and F.J. Yammarino (eds), *Research in multi-level issues*. Oxford, UK: Elsevier Science/JAI Press.

Ferris, G.R., Treadway, D.C., Kolodinsky, R.W., Hochwarter, W.A., Kacmar, C.J., Douglas, C. and Frink, D.D. (2005) Development and validation of the political skill inventory. *Journal of Management*, **31**, 126–53.

Graddick, M.M. and Lane, P. (1998). Evaluating executive performance. In J.W. Smither (ed.), *Performance appraisal: State of the art in practice* (pp. 370–403). San Francisco, CA: Jossey-Bass.

Graham, J.W. (1991). An essay on organizational citizenship behavior. *Employee Responsibilities and Rights Journal*, **4**, 249–70.

Hochwarter, W.A. (2003). The interactive effects of pro-political behavior and politics perceptions on job satisfaction and affective commitment. *Journal of Applied Social Psychology*, **33**, 1360–78.

Hochwarter, W.A. and Treadway, D.C. (2003). The interactive effects of negative and positive affect on the politics perceptions–job satisfaction relationship. *Journal of Management*, **29**, 551–67.

Hochwarter, W.A., Witt, L.A. and Kacmar, K.M. (2000). Perceptions of organizational politics as a moderator of the relationship between conscientiousness and job performance. *Journal of Applied Psychology*, **85**, 472–8.

Hochwarter, W.A., Kiewitz, C., Castro, S.L., Perrewé, P.L. and Ferris, G.R. (2003). Positive affectivity and collective efficacy as moderators of the relationship between perceived politics and job satisfaction. *Journal of Applied Social Psychology*, **33**, 1009–35.

Johnson, J.W. (2001). The relative importance of task and contextual performance dimensions to supervisor judgments of overall performance. *Journal of Applied Psychology*, **86**, 984–96.

Kacmar, K.M. and Baron, R.A. (1999). Organizational politics: The state of the field, links to related processes, and an agenda for future research. In K.M. Rowland and G.R. Ferris (eds), *Research in personnel and human resources management* (Vol. 17, pp. 1–39). Greenwich, CT: JAI Press.

Kacmar, K.M. and Carlson, D.S. (1997). Further validation of the Perceptions of Politics Scale (POPS): A multiple sample investigation. *Journal of Management*, **23**, 627–58.

Kacmar, K.M. and Ferris, G.R. (1991). Perceptions of organizational politics scales (POPS): Development and construct validation. *Educational and Psychological Measurement*, **51**, 193–205.

Kacmar, K.M., Bozeman, D.P., Carlson, D.S. and Anthony, W.P. (1999). An examination of the perceptions of organizational politics model: Replication and extension. *Human Relations*, **52**, 383–416.

Kirchmeyer, C. (1990). A profile of managers active in office politics. *Basic and Applied Social Psychology*, **11**, 339–56.

Lennox, R.D. and Wolfe, R.N. (1984). Revision of the self-monitoring scale. *Journal of Personality and Social Psychology*, **46**, 1349–64.

Magnusson, D. (1995). Individual development: A holistic, integrated model. In P. Moen, G.L. Elder, Jr and K. Luscher (eds), *Examining lives in context* (pp. 19–60). Washington, DC: American Psychological Association.

Mayes, B.T. and Allen, R.W. (1977). Toward a definition of organizational politics. *Academy of Management Review*, **2**, 672–8.

McHoskey, J.W., Worzel, W. and Szyarto, C. (1998). Machiavellianism and psychopathy. *Journal of Personality and Social Psychology*, **74**, 192–210.

Moberg, D.J. (1978). Factors which determine the perception and use of organizational politics. Paper presented at the National Meeting of the Academy of Management, San Francisco, CA.

Moorhead, G. and Griffin, R.W. (1995). *Organizational behavior managing people and organizations*. Boston, MA: Houghton Mifflin.

O'Connor, W.E. and Morrison, T.G. (2001). A comparison of situational and dispositional predictors of perceptions of organizational politics. *Journal of Psychology*, **135**, 301–12.

Peterson, S.A. (1990). *Political behavior*. Beverly Hills, CA: Sage.

Podsakoff, P.M., MacKenzie, S.B., Paine, J.B. and Bacharach, D.G. (2000). Organizational citizenship behaviors: A critical review of the theoretical and empirical literature and suggestions for future research. *Journal of Management*, **26**, 516–63.

Poon, J.M.L. (2003). Situational antecedents and outcomes of organizational politics perceptions. *Journal of Managerial Psychology*, **18**, 138–55.

Randall, M.L., Cropanzano, R., Bormann, C.A. and Birjulin, A. (1999). Organizational politics and organizational support as predictors of work attitudes, job performance, and organizational citizenship behavior. *Journal of Organizational Behavior*, **20**, 159–74.

Rosen, C.C., Chang, C., Johnson, R.E. and Levy, P.E. (2005). Psychological contract as a mediator of the relationships between politics, justice, and work attitudes. In P. Ohlott (Chair) Symposium, *Re-Visioning Organizational Politics* as part of the annual Academy of Management Meeting, Honolulu, Hawaii.

Rosen, C.C., Levy, P.E. and Hall, R.J. (in press). Placing perceptions of politics in the context of the feedback environment, employee attitudes, and performance. *Journal of Applied Psychology*.

Saucier, G. (1994). Mini-markers: A brief version of Goldberg's unipolar Big-Five markers. *Journal of Personality Assessment*, **63**, 506–16.

Shaw, J.D., Duffy, M.K., Jenkins, G.D. and Gupta, N. (1999). Positive and negative affect, signal sensitivity, and pay satisfaction. *Journal of Management*, **25**, 189–205.

Smith, J.A. and Foti, R.J. (1998). A pattern approach to the study of leader emergence. *Leadership Quarterly*, 147–60.

Sobel, R. (1993). From occupational involvement to political participation: An exploratory analysis. *Political Behavior*, **15**, 339–53.

Tett, R.P. and Burnett, D.D. (2003). A personality trait-based interactionist model of job performance. *Journal of Applied Psychology*, **88**, 500–517.

Tziner, A., Latham, G.P., Price, B.S. and Haccoun, R. (1996). Development and validation of a questionnaire for measuring perceived political considerations in performance appraisal. *Journal of Organizational Behavior*, **17**, 179–90.

Valle, M. and Perrewé, P.L. (2000). Do politics perceptions relate to political behaviors? Tests of an implicit assumption and expanded model. *Human Relations*, **53**, 359–86.

Valle, M., Witt, L.A. and Hochwater, W.A. (2002). Dispositions and organizational politics perceptions: The influence of positive and negative affectivity. *Journal of Management Research*, **2**, 121–8.

Verba, S. and Nye, N. (1972). *Participation in America.* New York: Harper & Row.

Vigoda, E. (2000). Internal politics in public administration systems: An empirical examination of its relationship with job congruence, organizational citizenship behavior, and in-role performance. *Public Personnel Management*, **29**, 185–210.

Vigoda, E. (2003). *Developments in organizational politics: How political dynamics affect employee performance in modern work sites*. Chetenham, UK and Northampton, MA, USA: Edward Elgar.

Vredenburgh, D.J. and Maurer, J.G. (1984). A process framework of organizational politics. *Human Relations*, **37**, 47–66.

Williams, L.J. and Anderson, S. (1991). Job satisfaction and organizational commitment as predictors of organizational citizenship and in-role behaviors. *Journal of Management*, **17**, 601–17.

Witt, L.A., Kacmar, M., Carlson, D.S. and Zivnuska, S. (2002). Interactive effects of personality and organizational politics on contextual performance. *Journal of Organizational Behavior*, **23**, 911–26.

Zautra, A.J. and Reich, J.W. (1983). Life events and perceptions of life quality: Developments in a two-factor approach. *Journal of Community Psychology*, **11**, 121–32.

4 Antecedents, processes and outcomes of collective (group-level) politics in organizations
Keith James

Introduction
Psychological and organizational behavior theory and research on workplace politics have generally focused on the individual and interpersonal levels of political action and poltical outcomes (for reviews, see Ferris et al., 2002; and Kacmar and Baron, 1999). Recently, however, there have been arguments for the importance, for full understanding and effective practice, of integrating group- and organizational-level phenomena with micro-level organizational politics theories and research (e.g. Darr and Johns, 2004; Dipboye and Foster, 2002; Walsh, 2004; Witt et al., 2002). In keeping with those arguments, the current chapter focuses on group-level organizational political behavior. By group-level, I mean largely *collective* political perceptions and actions in organizations – what Gummer (1987) labeled 'Social (group) agency' politics. Politics *within* (intra-) organizational groups (see e.g. Maslyn and Fedor, 1998) will be considered here only to the extent that it may cast light on politics that an organizational group engages in relative to another group, to the organization as a whole, or to extra-organizational entities.

Organizational politics is accordingly defined here as those relatively informal tactics and approaches that groups within organizations use to try to influence other groups; or to influence organizational goals, decisions, resource allocations, policies and practices; or to influence individuals or groups outside of the organization. By 'informal,' I mean that political behaviors by and large either occur outside of the 'official' governance apparatus and procedures of an organization, or are aimed at gaining power over that official apparatus. Informal is not meant to imply, however, that organizational politics need be unsystemic; politics can, in fact, involve complex strategies and tactics that play out over an extended period of time.

In the academic literature on workplace politics, one sometimes finds the suggestion that organizational politics is inherently harmful (e.g. Cropanzano et al., 1993; Drory and Romm, 1988). Some common definitions of organizational politics describe it as involving undermining of official policies and procedures, and devious manipulation toward selfish resource and power accumulations (Cropanzano et al., 1993; Drory and Romm, 1990). Others, however (e.g. Provis, 2004; Vigoda, 2003), argue that politics can serve either positive or negative goals, and can support either ethical or unethical individual, group and organizational action.

Collective politics can help insure, for example, that the views of various groups and individuals are represented when important decisions are being made (Butcher and Clarke, 2002). It is widely agreed that disputations centered on ideas or possible courses of action can help to promote good decisions, organizational effectiveness and ethical organizational action (Provis, 2004; Rahim, 2001; Whyte, 1998). Organizational politics is often the means through which such disputations occur (Butcher and Clarke, 2002; Provis, 2004).

Politics is also adaptive in the sense that formal systems and structures cannot be designed with all possible contingencies in mind. When organizations are faced with new and unanticipated circumstances, the informal decision and action mechanisms of politics can be critical to successful adaptation. Similarly, organizational change is often forced by turbulence in the organizations' environment but successful change requires internal political coalition building to garner the support and insure the resources needed to put into effect changes needed for survival or success (Frost and Egri, 1992).

Politics can also, however, be the means through which individuals or groups seek to control resources, decision making, policies, or collective action toward goals that do not serve the best interests of the organization or of society (Ashforth and Anand, 2003; Cropanzano et al., 1997). In this chapter, a generally neutral view of politics will be taken. The focal question here is under what circumstances group-level organizational politics will tend to produce, on the one hand, generally beneficial outcomes, and, on the other, negative results.

Groups and organizational politics

Why group-level politics?
Individuals and groups engage in political behavior in organizations because they need sense-making guidance, social support, resources and power. Organizational politics is a major mechanism through which those things can be obtained (Ferris and Judge, 1991; Darr and Johns, 2004; Walsh, 2004). For instance, Bamberger et al. (1999) developed a theory of organizational subgroup (specifically, union) loyalty that indicates that it and its outcomes, including collective politics, are substantially shaped by two factors: perceived group instrumentality (i.e. utility for aiding attainment of valued outcomes such as resource, power and social support); and socialization (i.e. information-processing and meaning-provision effects). A meta-analysis conducted by Bamberger et al. (1999) supported that theory (see also Tan and Aryee, 2002).

Organizational subgroup memberships and subgroup processes influence who will receive positive treatment in the form of encouragement, non-verbal and verbal support, information, and resource and opportunity access (James, 2004). Those who are perceived as belonging to the same group as oneself are more likely to be liked, listened to, empathized with, and supported with social and material resources (Ferris and Judge, 1991; James, 1993, 2004). Subordinates, for instance, who have effective political relationships with superiors tend to, relative to apolitical or ineffectively political subordinates, receive higher performance evaluations, better social support and greater rewards (Zivnuska et al., 2004). They also tend be more satisfied with their organizations and less likely to leave them (Ferris and Judge, 1991; Gerstner and Day, 1997; Poon, 2003).

Figure 4.1 depicts the precursors, mechanisms and moderators that seem to shape the levels and direction (i.e. positive outcomes versus negative) of group-level organizational politics. The elements of the figure are discussed in the remaining sections of this chapter, beginning with the antecedents of collective politics shown in the box at the left of the figure.

Antecedents of group politics
Various organizational context factors that help shape the level, as well the direction (positive versus negative), of collective political efforts in organizations have been identified

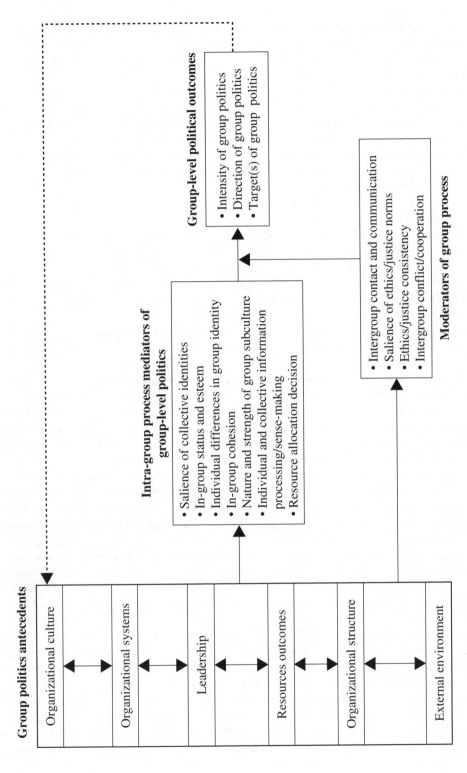

Figure 4.1   *Precursors, mechanisms and outcomes of group-level politics*

in the literature. Those factors include: (1) organizational culture; (2) internal organizational structures, systems and leadership; (3) an organization's external environment; (4) the combination of a highly valued in-group identity and a highly valued outcome that seems group-related (Walker and Pettigrew, 1984); (5) a strong within-group ideology that promotes collective action (Guimond and Dube-Simard, 1983; Taylor and McKirnan, 1984); (6) lack of perceived individual options for meeting needs or achieving goals (Martin, 1981, 1986); (7) intergroup conflicts and competition (Deutsch, 1985; James, 1993); and (8) attention-grabbing procedural and distributive injustices based on group memberships (James, 1993; Taylor et al., 1986). Environmental and organizational determinants of the levels, the nature and the targets of intergroup politics in organizations are the subject of the next subsections.

Organizational cultures and systems
Organizations' cultural norms can include guides on the general acceptability of politics in each (Ashforth and Anand, 2003; Tilly, 2003). When an organization is generally highly politicized or is perceived as such, any given potential collective political action should be made more likely. At the individual level, perceptions that an organization's existing culture is highly politicized seem to make it more likely that members will engage in political behavior (Ferris and Judge, 1991; Ferris et al., 2002).

   Cultural forces also seem to help generally to determine whether organizational subgroups will tend to develop and be powerful, or whether common organizational identities and processes will tend to outweigh subgroup effects (Hogg and Terry, 2000; Martin and Siehl, 1983; Walsh, 2004). For instance, cultures can make potent or deemphasize intergroup boundaries, status differences and norms of differential subgroup treatment. Cultures can also promote high-level valuing of, and conformity to, work-unit or ethnic subgroups. Organizational cultures can also influence which types of groups are most likely to be the focus of collective politics when they do occur (Allen et al., 1983; James, 1993; Tilly, 2003; Triandis, 1988). Similarly, cultures differ in the extent to which they normatively encourage positive versus negative emotions. Those two major categories of emotion should help determine whether partisan politics, when they do occur, will involve intergroup hostilities and negative intergroup actions, or positive intergroup relations and positive intergroup outcomes. Organizational cultures also influence the levels of shared stress experienced by organizational groups (Lansisalmi et al., 2000). Higher stress levels can make negative political actions more likely, while relatively low levels of collective stress may predispose groups toward more positive versions of collective politics (James et al., 1999). Thus organizational cultural values can promote or diminish the overall likelihood of group politics and, also, shape the direction that collective politics will take.

Structural influences on group politics
A model from A.F.C. Wallace (1971) provides a good framework for discussing the impact of organizational structures on group-politics levels and direction. Based on examination of a number of different societies, Wallace identified five basic approaches to producing positive relationships among the subgroups of a larger entity. Wallace's first approach is what he calls the zero principle. This states that entities can attempt to deal with internal differences by reducing them, with reduction being more effective the closer it gets to yielding zero difference. Systems that minimize intergroup boundaries, status differences

and intergroup competition would move an organization toward a zero-principle approach to partisan politics. For instance, detailed and uniform policies and procedures that are consistently applied and any other factors that promote consistent treatment of organization members are zero-principle structural elements. Minimizing power hierarchies across categories such as work units or professions also helps prevent them from becoming more closely linked to identities and outcomes than are shared goals.

The second approach Wallace identified as *ad hoc* (i.e. casual; unstructured) communications to cement relations. Although this type of communication cannot, by definition, be mandated or systematized, it can be facilitated or inhibited by organizational and professional cultures, structures, procedures, and leader and organizational actions. For instance, eliminating physical divisions among groups helps promote social interaction. Walsh (2004) examined identity and political dynamics in several community groups and found that those groups whose internal operations took place in settings where out-group members tended to be present (even if not interacting or spatially distant) had more inclusionary identities and politics. Following the same logic, one organization that the current author worked with eliminated separate cafeterias for workers and for managers in order to promote informal interactions and, they hoped, positive politics across the organization's hierarchy-based groups.

Another of Wallace's unifying structural approaches – what he calls the 'administrative approach' – also ties in with promoting intergroup connections and communications. In this, some individual or set of individuals is given the role of facilitating and coordinating intergroup relations. High-level leaders often have this as part of their responsibilities. Organizations can also, though, specifically assign non-leadership individuals or committees the duties of planning and coordinating intergroup ferment and synthesis. Research results indicate that effective group boundary spanners facilitate communication of important information across groups, and help to cement intergroup ties. Allocating some control over important resources (decision-making power, information, materials and money) to boundary spanners can facilitate their acceptance by others and their influence over them (James, 2004). In fact, administrative systems that reward non-political or positive political behavior and punish negative political behavior should generally be useful for increasing the former and reducing the latter (Vigoda, 2003).

Wallace's fourth approach is inclusion. Broad inclusion in decision making, goal setting and power structures are among the major reasons that individuals and groups accept and identify with formal organizational systems (Farrell, 1983). Inclusionary institutional structures and systems, and over-arching identities, provide mechanisms for both wide input and for acceptable resolutions of differing perspectives and desires. Acceptable resolutions are those that are thought to have been arrived at through honest, carefully considered means derived from organizational missions and goals. We can add that transparency about resource allocations and other decisions and the processes that produced them helps to reduce negative partisan politics (Vigoda, 2003). Behind-the-scenes decision making and hidden allocations will promote them.

Wallace's final approach he calls end-linkage, which is similar to vision and mission. End-linkage involves creating connections among the activities, goals, ideals and identities of the subgroups within a organization. It is the equivalent of invoking a higher-level identity that helps subsume and integrate multiple lower-level identities (Turner, 1985; Fry, in press).

Resources/power and collective politics

Power and status differentials are associated with multiple forms of institutionalized social discrimination and other types of organizational corruption (Pratto et al., 2000). Currently held resources/power are generally most concrete and salient. They are integral to how a group that holds them functions and to its assumptions about how to succeed. Growing out of the latter (and other influences on in-group processes, identity and identification), current resources become symbolic of individuals' and groups' self-images, cultures and values. Threats to current resources are, therefore, especially likely to trigger strong emotional and cognitive forces that can easily lead to the types of aggressive, devious, or unethical actions that take organizational political behavior into the realms of divisiveness and destructiveness (James, 2004; James et al., 1999; Tilly, 2003).

It may sometimes be relatively high-status and high-power groups that are most likely to exhibit out-group negative politicized behavior (Greenberg et al., 1986; Kipnis, 1989; Tajfel and Turner, 1979; Sachdev and Bourhis, 1991). Members of such groups are most able to derive esteem (status) from the group and all that it stands for and controls. High-status groups are frequently, therefore, most likely to exhibit negative attitudes and actions toward out-groups that threaten either in-group power or the symbolic value of the in-group (Greenberg et al., 1986; Tajfel and Turner, 1979; Tilly, 2003).

High-status, high-power groups in organizations are, of course, also most able to translate their beliefs, expectations and fears into direct negative political action (Er, 1989; Kipnis, 1976, 1989; Tajfel and Turner, 1979). Thus Kipnis (1976, 1989; Kipnis et al., 1980; Wilkinson and Kipnis, 1978) reports that high-power, high-status individuals and groups are most likely to use threats and sanctions to get their way.

At the extreme, perceived high power and status can lead to negative organizational politics such as efforts to exclude lower-status out-groups from involvement in decisions important to them (Kanter, 1977; Fernandez, 1981; James, 2004). Efforts by advantaged groups to preserve status and resource differences also tend to lead to efforts to institutionalize them into organizational norms, values, policies and rules regardless of their relevance to organizational mission or professed ethics (Ashforth and Anand, 2003; Kanter, 1977; Feagin and Feagin, 1986; Tilly, 2003). Low-power, low-status individuals and groups, on the other hand, seem more likely to use less harmful/more positive political techniques such as ingratiation, upward appeals (to, i.e. inclusive identities or values) and positive reinforcement (Kipnis, 1976, 1989). Thus, power/status levels (or perceptions) of groups may partly determine the likelihood of use of negative (greater with relatively high power/status) versus positive (greater with relatively low power/status) political tactics.

In truth, though, both high- and low-power groups seem likely to engage in collective politics that will sometimes be negative; they simply tend toward different types of political strategies. For instance, James et al. (1999) discuss how hidden and indirect political attacks are more likely where direct and open conflict is unfeasible. Thus relatively low-power groups should be, given circumstances such as intergroup resource conflict, more likely to engage in *covert* negative collective political activity (e.g. dirty tricks such as indirect slurs or sabotage), while high-power groups should be more likely to engage in *overt* negative political action.

Finally, some authors (Tajfel and Turner, 1979; Taylor et al., 1986; Walker and Pettigrew, 1984) have argued that low perceived power *differentials* between two contending groups or a relatively unstable system of social status will, when combined with high salience of group categories, yield a very high likelihood of collective political action. Those authors do not contend, though, that such action will always be negative. Other context factors seem to combine with low intergroup power differentials to shape the levels and directions of collective organizational politics. Leadership is one of those other context factors.

Leadership and group politics
A leader is 'one who guides or directs' (Webster's *New World Dictionary*, p. 343). Leaders must largely act through organizational subgroups and individuals' social identities to influence subordinates' performance (Lord and Brown, 2003; Luthans and Avolio, 2003). Thus organizational groups and group identities become implicated in political behavior by leaders.

Power corrupts (Kipnis, 1989), but so can lack of power. Often lacking power to make changes or influence individuals', groups' or organizations' outcomes using official procedures and policies, supervisors and administrators can easily be tempted to exert influence through under-the-table means, trading of favors, coercion and bribery (Ashforth and Anand, 2003). They may also try to polarize subgroups as a means of exercising and obtaining power through collective politics (James, 2004; Tilly, 2003).

Leader–member exchange theory and collective politics Leader–member exchange (LMX) theory supports the relation of leadership and subordinate subgroups to politics. In LMX, the quality of leader–subordinate exchange relationships is posited to determine the nature of many outcomes for the organization and subordinates (see Graen and Uhl-Bien, 1995). As Ferris and Judge (1991) make clear, much of such an exchange process is political in nature. More directly relevant to the group-level focus of the current chapter, LMX theory also indicates that there tend to be in-groups and out-groups of subordinates, depending on whether their relationship with their supervisor/leader is generally positive (in-group) or neutral-to-negative (out-group). In-group members identify with their leader, and their leader identifies with them. Out-group members are alienated from their leader, who also distances her- or himself from them.

It is easy to conceive that the quality of exchange relationships can just as easily devolve from in-group/out-group perceptions and relations as from in-group/out-group patterns developing from the nature of interpersonal exchanges. That is, LMX groups seem likely to initially develop in part based on social-categorization and social-identity processes. Perceptions of shared group membership by subsets of organization members (including subordinates and superiors) promote liking, support and positive political coalitions. Those processes and effects can promote within-group solidarity and support. For instance, concern over equitable allocations of organizational resources extends to those with whom one identifies, not just to oneself (Tyler and Lind, 1990; Folger, 1987). Those same in-group and leader–member exchange processes and effects also, though, provide the foundation on which political 'parties' form in organizations (Provis, 2004).

It seems likely that LMX-oriented leaders will generally engage in and provoke collective political activity in their organizations. One might expect, for instance, that out-groups would be on the losing end of political allocations and decisions by LMX-oriented leaders and organizations, and would perceive the organizations' culture to be more political than would LMX in-group members. However, Andrews and Kacmar (2001) found exactly the opposite – LMX *in*-group members reported higher levels of organizational politics than did LMX *out*-group members. Andrews and Kacmar speculated that in-group members may simply be more privy to political war stories from leaders/supervisors and that the political nature of their organization might be more salient to them than to LMX out-group members. Differences in political perceptions of LMX in-group and LMX out-group members should be further investigated, along with the processes that may produce differences in their political perceptions, actions and outcomes.

More generally, the possibility that LMX-oriented leaders may promote general polit-icization of organizations' cultures and systems warrants research attention, as does the possibility that politicized organizational cultures and processes may make LMX-based leadership more likely than leadership of other sorts. Leader (and follower) characteris-tics other than an LMX orientation may also influence both political perceptions and political behaviors in organizations. For instance, O'Connor and Morrison (2001) report that higher levels of Machiavellianism are associated with both perceptions of overall levels of politics in organizations and with self-reported personal political behavior. Machiavellian leaders may be particularly inclined to engage in political behavior, to manipulate subordinates toward political ends, and to activate collective politics among organizational groups. Narcissistic leaders have also been reported to use manipulative politics to a greater extent than leaders with personalities of other sorts (Kipnis, 1976; Stone and Schaffner, 1988). The relation of these and other leader characteristics to levels and types of collective politics in organizations is an area ripe for future investigation.

The converse of leader actions promoting collective politics is that the leader who func-tions as an honest broker of group politics will reduce the likelihood of negative politics and increase the probability of integrative solutions (Poon, 2003). Such a leader would need to be widely accepted, based on communicated ethics and demonstrated action, as just, neutral relative to partisan groups, and focused on organizational mission and/or unifying human values (Fry, in press). This brings us to transformational leadership and related concepts.

Transformational leadership and collective politics   Transformational leaders inspire fol-lowers through charisma and vision to adhere to leader or collective goals and exert rela-tively high effort toward achieving them (Bass, 1996; Conger and Kanungo, 1998; Shamir et al., 1993). Transformational leaders may be capable of triggering either high levels of positive intergroup politics, or high levels of negative partisan politics in organizations.

'Authentic' (Bass and Steidlmeier, 1999; Luthans and Avolio, 2003) transformational leaders are those who invoke goals that have broad positive implications while 'pseudo-transformational' (Bass, 1996) leaders are those who invoke goals that benefit a few at the expense of others. Pseudo-transformational leaders promote activation of narrower iden-tities and divisive intergroup processes in (or between) organizations. Authentic transfor-mational leaders promote activation of inclusive identities and integrative intergroup processes. Through modeling, self-sacrifice, vision articulation and vision implementation behaviors, the genuine transformational leader brings the needs and values that define the self into alignment with the leader's goals and the organization's mission (Sarros et al., 2002; Shamir et al., 2000).

Authentic transformational leaders, according to Bass and Steidlmeier (1999) and Luthans and Avolio (2003), form their vision and engage in charismatic behaviors out of morally based principles and values. Authentic leaders tend to bring organizational sub-groups together under a common vision and through win–win goals. Because their thoughts and behaviors are guided by moral principles and values, they promote fair systems and allocations, collaborative decision making and status equalization.

Follower attributions of charisma to a transformational leader can promote identi-fication with that individual; identification triggers an inclination to accept her/his vision and goals. Charismatic leaders are viewed by followers as trusted, respected role models, and followers identify with and seek to emulate such leaders (House and Shamir, 1993). The inspiration from vision is theorized to derive from leaders' articulation of an 'ideo-logical goal' that followers can feel morally satisfied in pursuing (House and Shamir, 1993). Subordinate selves focused around ideological values activate strong emotional attach-ment to a leader and a collective, and strong motivation to perform on tasks and goals valued by that leader and group.

Authentic transformational leaders will tend to create and activate a common organ-izational identity as a chronic 'working self' that will help guide goal setting, information processing and behavior. By doing so, they will reduce the overall volume of partisan pol-itics in their organizations, and push such partisan politics as do occur toward promoting win–win solutions and generally positive organizational outcomes.

Effective leaders often, in fact, go beyond single ideological goals to full ideologies – cultural narratives and scripts that help followers find links between what they have experienced in the past, current circumstances and their hopes for the future (Safford, 1988; Schein, 1985; Tilly, 2003). A positive or broadly inclusive ideology from an effective leader will push politics in positive directions; negative and parochial ideology from the same type of leader will tend to evoke negative collective political actions.

Those whom Bass (1996) refers to as 'pseudo-transformational leaders,' however, use charisma or ideology to achieve self- or group-serving ends that are not widely beneficial (Crane, 2000). Many such individuals, such as Adolf Hitler or Usama bin Laden, use out-group hostility to strengthen the conformity of followers to the leaders' vision and goals. Others invoke values or symbolic causes for cynical reasons of attaining compliance, resources, or power (Crane, 2000).

Tilly (2003) presented the related construct of 'political entrepreneurs'. These are indi-viduals who engage in political manipulation of conditions, cultures, individuals and groups in order to advance themselves and their own power. Divide-and-conquer tactics and cronyism are two classic strategies of political entrepreneurs that help to trigger destructive collective politics.

Kark et al. (2003) similarly proposed that identification with a transformational leader may yield either dependency or empowerment. Transformational leaders who acti-vate 'empowering' identities in subordinates promote striving for positive ideals and ethics. 'Pseudo-transformational' (Bass, 1996) leaders, on the other hand, promote/activate 'dependent' identities in subordinates that make them more inclined to selfish or partisan politics. Both types of subordinate identification may yield short-term high moti-vation for performance of leader/organization-specified goals and tasks. 'Empowering' identification will, however, facilitate better intergroup relationships and greater focus on the overall, long-term organizational mission rather than the immediate goals of sub-groups.

External environments and internal politics
Because resource patterns influence the general likelihood and direction of partisan politics, the overall availability of resources to an organization will influence the levels and direction of collective politics occurring within it. The greater the total amount of resources an organization has access to, the more easily the needs and desires of all of the groups in it can be at least partially satisfied. Competition and conflict over resources should tend to be lower, and political polarizations along group lines should be substantially less likely, when resources are plentiful.

One implication of this is that the *external* competitive pressures that large numbers of organizations now experience because of globalized economies and technological changes may be helping to increase *internal* organizational politics. With pressure to enhance efficiency and reduce costs should come, all other things being equal, greater internal resource competition from which greater group-level political factionation is likely to result. This is, however, an empirical question that does not seem to have been subjected to empirical tests as yet. It should be. A slightly different but related effect of external competitive pressures is that they often push organizations to change patterns of internal resource use. The more that environmental threats begin to put groups' currently held resources at risk, the greater the odds should be that group-level political activity will increase (Frost and Egri, 1992).

Another impact of the environmental munificence that substantially determines organizations' internal resource levels is that it influences leaders' and dominant groups' abilities to consolidate power and control (Tilly, 2003). Tilly (2003) analyzed intergroup political conflicts within nations and found that extreme and overt negative politics (including, in the cases Tilly examined, intergroup violence) were most likely in relatively low-resource countries. His analysis led him to conclude that this is partly the case because leaders and dominant organizational groups with access to relatively high levels of resources are able to use more resources on effective control mechanisms. Overall, the odds of negative politics may generally be lower in relatively high-resource organizations both because there is less need for conflict over resources, and because dominant organizational groups are better able to institutionalize their control and co-opt non-dominant groups.

In addition, salient external ethics and regulations can help prevent some negative internal collective political actions around resources. For example, lax oversight by the board of directors, auditors and government regulators of the publicly traded (US) Adelphi Corporation allowed the Rigas family that ran Adelphi to direct company assets toward supporting their lavish personal lifestyles. Publicity about that case and a series of other corporate scandals has, however, led to both changes in regulatory approaches and market and investor pressures on boards of directors and auditors to increase their oversight. Both effects should make it less likely that a public company in the USA can have substantial amounts of its resources diverted toward a family's (or any other subgroup's) personal use. So, variations in external ethical and regulatory oversight and constraints can influence the likelihood of some types of collective political machinations within organizations.

In-group and collective identity process mediators of group-level politics
The center box in Figure 4.1 shows those within-group and individual-identity processes that seem to largely mediate the effects of the organizational and environmental factors

that were reviewed above on group-level organizational politics. Those mediating processes are the focus of the next few sections.

The nature of organizational social identities

Identity, as the term is used here, refers to a complex, non-linear, adaptive cognitive schema for defining the self. Identification with groups, the internalization of schemas for group identities, and group-process influences are the means by which organizational sub-groups affect individuals' political thoughts and behaviors in ways that shape the enactment of collective politics in an organization.

Social identities in organizations tend to be defined on the basis of shared, socially recognized, category memberships (Tsui and O'Reilly, 1989); on values and attitudes (e.g. Kramer, 1991); on shared genetic heritage (Rushton, 1989); or on interaction patterns determined by such things as proximity or cohort entry into the organization (Williams and O'Reilly, 1998). In fact, those four tend to co-vary to some extent and make for particularly strong effects to the extent that more than one of them helps to define a social identity (James, 2004). Social identities largely operate at unconscious and emotional levels, making it difficult to fully comprehend or manage them.

Social identity, organizational subcultures and collective politics

According to Rokeach (1970), values serve as terminal standards or end-states. As such, they seem to form the core around which a sub-self (i.e. a distinct identity) is organized (for a partly divergent view, see Koestner and Losier, 2002). Values and social categories often go together. For example, the value of achievement may be at the core of a 'leader' identity and its associated cognitive sub-self. The value basis of identities provides individuals with meaning-based guides to thinking and behavior. Conversely, sub-groups within organizations tend to begin to develop subcultures that can contain either destructive or constructive value and norm sets (Martin and Siehl, 1983; Schein, 1985). Strong subcultures associated with powerful organizational subgroups will tend to promote political behavior. In organizations as in society, subgroup identities, sub-cultures, and social-group-based values and norms can end up trumping formal institutional ideals, goals, policies and rules and, to the extent that that occurs, the organizational system will become politicized. Organizational subcultures tend to create, in short, informal organizational systems that operate in parallel to, and either in harmony or dissonance with, formal systems. Therefore, the more and the stronger the subcultures in an organization, the greater should be the likelihood of collective political activity.

In addition to promoting higher volumes of political behavior by promoting informal systems that compete with formal ones, the link of values, norms and subcultures to group and individual identities can also push politics in either positive or negative directions. For instance, cultures are often characterized by a distinctive emotional tone (Babad and Wallbott, 1986). Subcultures that promote intergroup stereotyping, hostility and competition, or that undermine individual ethical and moral standards will promote negative forms of collective political behavior (Ashforth and Anand, 2003; James, 1993, 2004); subcultures that promote intergroup solidarity and harmony will promote positive forms of collective political behavior (Tilly, 2003; Walsh, 2004).

Information-processing effects of social identities and organizational subcultures   Collective social identities serve cognitive- and behavioral-regulation functions. Individuals use social categorizations as fundamental mechanisms for organizing their understanding of the world and of the workplace (Turner, 1985; Van Dick, 2004). Identities seem to provide an organizational framework on which all aspects of perception (self-perceptions included), cognition, belief, motivation and complex behavior are built. As Walsh (2004, p. 31) says, 'Identities function as links between one's social location and one's view of the world.'

Us–them, or in-group/out-group distinctions seem to have particular cognitive power and are, therefore, likely to be used to structure attitudes, judgments and behaviors (Tajfel and Turner, 1979; Walsh, 2004). Perceived identity similarities and differences are fundamental to our understanding of who we are, who we are not, where we fit in social systems (with all of the preceding constituting our sense of identity), and how the world operates. Political decisions and actions in organizations are, therefore, likely to be linked to sub-organizationial social identities partly for purely cognitive reasons.

Wegner (1982) proposed that certain situational conditions make it likely that one's organization will be viewed through the 'lens' of group norms, values, goals and outcomes. According to Wegner (1982), that is likely to occur when one's group is seen as a unitary entity because of factors such as member proximity, similarity or attraction; when there is a perception of a common agency or common fate for the group; and when there are strong 'figure/ground' effects due to situational variations in in-group and out-group proportions, group competition, or other cues for group salience.

Social categorization exerts several effects on individual and collective information processing that can influence political behaviors. For instance, groups who share a common identity are more likely to try to restrict certain types of information and decisions to their members. Important information is one source of power, and the tendency to share it with in-group members and to prevent outsiders from accessing it increases as subgroup social identities and intergroup politics become more important in an organization (James, 2004). If information is withheld from individuals who have a right to it according to organizational policies and systems or a need for it to advance organizational goals, then the information-processing effects of social categorization become a major corrupting force of formal organizational systems (Ashforth and Anand, 2003; Williams and O'Reilly, 1998).

Another possible information-processing effect of group identities and group politics in organizations is that evaluations of the costs and benefits of actions and policies may be positively influenced more by benefits accruing to the in-group. Similarly, costs borne by organizational out-groups are likely to have less negative influence on judgments than similar costs for in-groups (Dooley, 1984; James, 1993; Schein, 1985). The possibility that group-identity-related cost–benefit evaluations may help shape political thought and action does not, however, seem to have been subjected to direct quantitative examination. It should be.

Strong in-group identification, promoted and enhanced by out-group conflict or denigration, can also promote faulty *within*-group problem solving by restricting problem analysis and generation of possible alternatives. This can take the form of active intentional or quasi-intentional efforts to restrict within-group consideration of some information or principles, as well as the form of active generation of rationalizations that support biased, out-group harmful, decisions (Ashforth and Anand, 2003; Kipnis, 1976).

Or it can be more of a passive, unintentional outcome of within-group social processes. That is, in cohesive groups, members of a group tend to assume agreement among themselves and to conform to any consensus that appears to be developing. They are likely, therefore, quickly and strongly to adopt a collective opinion or action plan. Those effects on within-group problem solving and decision making are commonly referred to as groupthink (Janis, 1982; Whyte, 1998; see, however, Aldag and Fuller, 1993; and Wekselberg, 1996, for critiques and reformulations of the groupthink construct). Groupthink supposedly involves development of relatively strong group norms and expectations that limit members' information processing, members' openness to new ideas, as well as the quality and depth of a group's discussion and deliberation of options. Contradictory information is suppressed within the group but also, and especially, rejected when it comes from those considered outsiders.

Groupthink has been invoked as an explanation for a variety of historical organizational and political disasters. Perhaps the most famous recent case it has been applied to is as an explanation of the lack of information sharing among, and poor decision making by, US intelligence groups in the lead-up to the 11 September 2001 terrorist attacks (The 9/11 Commission, 2004). In that case, politics within (e.g. regional FBI bureaus not sharing threat data with each other) and between (e.g. the CIA not informing the FBI that a particular terror suspect had entered the USA) intelligence agencies contributed to failure to detect and prevent the 11 September attacks.

Paradoxically, party politics in organizations should also be able to help reduce groupthink. When subgroups in organizations engage in political disputations with each other, they can potentially be forced to justify the logic of their positions and the thoroughness of their analysis. When such justifications are demanded or even merely anticipated, information should be gathered, shared and analyzed more carefully within the group. Similarly, more decision alternatives are likely to be generated and they are more likely to be carefully evaluated when decisions are seen as subject to political challenges focused on logical and factual support for each group's position.

Clearly, though, the potential positive effect of partisan politics in organizations on groupthink just outlined is only likely to occur if (1) the system(s) of the organization or (2) some key leader or (3) a compelling cultural narrative focuses attention on, justifies and promotes the valuing of shared organizational goals and missions. Organizational subgroups must also believe (trust) that either organizational policies and procedures or some leader can and will serve as an honest broker such that the final resolution of collective differences will, indeed, be based on organizational mission and goals rather than simply on the political positions of, and political benefits to, the most powerful organizational entities.

Salience of ethic/justice norms   Organizational justice and organizational politics seem to be two somewhat distinct; but mutually influential, constructs (e.g. Aryee et al., 2004; Andrews and Kacmar, 2001). One important impact of in-group cohesiveness (especially when mixed with intergroup competition) on information processing can be inconsistent application of justice rules or organizational policies and procedures (Deutsch, 1985; James, 1993, 2004; Kramer, 1991). One common manifestation of this is the development and use of two sets of rules for allocations or procedures – one for 'them' and one for 'us.' Group-related dual standards of that sort mean that the organization's systems of allocations or decision-making have become politicized and corrupted by the effects of political partisanship.

These differences in justice applications with in-group and out-group members involve what Deutsch (1985) and Opotow (1995), among others, refer to as inclusionary and exclusionary justice. To the extent that individuals apply justice principles only to members of the in-group, justice becomes exclusionary. To the extent that justice principles and procedures are seen as universally applicable, they are inclusionary. At extremes of exclusion, the rules of justice are seen as not applying at all to some out-group. In such cases, members of the in-group are treated according to the moral code/values the individual has internalized, while out-groups are used and abused as circumstances allow.

Zero-principle organizational structures and systems should help to promote broad application of inclusionary justice and, by doing so, reduce some types of negative collective political thinking and behavior. Strong zero-principle organizations should also reduce the likelihood of subcultures developing, weaken those that do occur, and help to reduce collective politics by way of impacts on organizational subcultures. End-linkage organizational structures, on the other hand, should be unrelated to the number or strength of subcultures but should make for more positive (integrative) relations among those organizational subcultures that do occur. End-linkage, therefore, should more moderate the direction (positive versus negative) of politics than affect the overall level of politics.

(Authentic) transformational leaders should affect subculture development by presenting a compelling organization-wide vision that carries with it an organizational-level identity, but should also promote integration across subcultures to the extent that the latter occur. Through those effects on organizational subcultures, transformational leadership should help to reduce subgroup formation and within-group groupthink and, through both means, the overall level of collective politics in an organization. Transformational leadership should also reduce intergroup conflict and, by doing so, help to direct whatever collective politics does occur in positive directions.

Individual differences in social identities   Multiple identities (and associated subcultural guides to thinking and behavior) are likely for any given person (for further discussion of this point, see Allen et al., 1983; Hogg and Terry, 2000; and Turner, 1985). Many of those identities are based on group memberships. Some one identity (called the 'working self' by Markus and Wurf, 1987), however, will tend to be more active than the rest at any particular time and, therefore, to exert the greatest influence on thinking and behavior at that point (for further discussion of this point, see Cropanzano et al., 1993; Hogg and Terry, 2000; Hong et al., 2000). Individuals differ in the nature and number of identities because of innate, cultural and personal-history factors (Martindale, 1980; Triandis, 1989). They also differ in which identities are chronically more accessible (Markus, 1977; Markus and Wurf, 1987; Martindale, 1980). Strong identities are more chronically accessible and more likely to influence thinking and behavior than are weak ones (James and Cropanzano, 1994; Martindale, 1980; Triandis, 1995).

Individual differences in which organizational identities tend to be chronically active may impact on political perceptions and actions. For instance, Witt et al. (2002) found that the organizational commitment levels of those individuals who tended to identify with professional groups were less influenced by perceived organizational politics than were the organizational commitment levels of individuals who identified with their work units. Little research exists on the effects of different chronic collective identities in organizations on political perceptions and political behaviors and the outcomes of collective politics (see, however, the discussion of high- versus low-power/status identities and politics earlier in this chapter). More such research should be done.

Context and salience of social identities　Along with relatively stable individual differences in workplace identities, they are also partially situationally specific based on activation by environmental factors. Relatively enduring circumstances within a particular organization can make certain identities generally relatively active and influential. For instance, in an organization in which sex ratios are highly skewed, sex categories will tend to become more salient unless some acute event or chronic feature of the organization makes another type of social identity strong enough to override it (Kanter, 1977). Walsh (2004), though, reports that sex groups may be less likely than some other social categories to serve as the basis of intense collective politics because most women and men have close personal relationships with some members of the opposite sex, even if not in the workplace. That argument by Walsh is similar to Wallace's principle of promoting *ad hoc* communications to undermine and, to some extent, constrain the likelihood that collective politics might tend to become organized around certain salient social categories.

On the other hand, even chronically weak identities can temporarily substantially influence behavior and thinking when the proper circumstances cause them to become relatively strongly active and accessible (Hogg and Terry, 2000; James and Cropanzano, 1994; Lord et al., 1999; Triandis, 1989). For example, strong situational competition between an in-group and an out-group will make those groups more powerful influences on members' behavior (see, e.g. James and Cropanzano, 1994).

Identity theorists such as Tajfel and Turner (1979) and Allport (1954) have long acknowledged that the dynamics of in-groups are inextricably linked to relations with out-groups, and vice versa. Strong in-group identifications are promoted by out-group threat. Individuals and groups who present a different identity (be it based on demographic, professional or unit subcultural group membership) threaten all of the functions an identity serves for individuals (Greenberg et al., 1986). Such threat promotes both greater adherence to in-group identity and values, along with increased tendency to denigrate and aggress toward out-groups. Perceived differences are exacerbated and negative feelings about and behaviors toward out-groups become likely. At the same time, the tendency to conform to in-group thinking, emotional states and behavioral norms is also enhanced.

One determinant of the degree and direction of collective organization politics should be whether organizational subgroup identities are relatively prominent and embedded in a context of intergroup conflict (over, i.e., resources), or relatively weak and embedded in a context of cooperation. Oakes (1987) argues and reviews evidence indicating that intergroup effects are determined by a combination of cognitive accessibility of social categories and the fit of such categories to situational conditions. Thus, identity accessibility plus situations that promote intergroup competition may make it particularly likely that group-based politics will occur. When subgroups are both prominent (salient) and exist in a context of conflict, they should tend to promote higher levels of negative politics. When subgroups are both prominent (salient) and exist in a context of cooperation, they should tend to produce positive collective politics. When they are low in salience, only low levels of collective politics are likely to exist.

Intergroup processes, intergroup politics and situational/organizational context actually feed off each other, however, so group salience and intergroup competition/cooperation are neither entirely independent of each other nor independent in their effects on politics. The dashed line in Figure 4.1 represents the feedback cycle between collective politics and organizational/environmental conditions and system.

Organizational social identities and organizational resources   Social identity groups often converge with concrete resource and power interests to encourage the members to engage in collective political behavior. Identities centered around functional categories (e.g. professional group membership), for instance, will largely co-vary with shared goals, tasks, power levels and resource needs (Kipnis, 1989). Frost and Egri (1992), for example, discuss how management in a part of the General Electric Corporation resisted the introduction of a technology that would have reduced the need for administrative control of production despite demonstrated productive benefits of that technology. The threat to managers' power was compounded by an ongoing general dispute between management and the workers' unions, as well as by class and value differences between the managerial and worker groups. Thus, in that case, multiple levels of social identity differences converged and overlapped with power issues to produce political conflict over technological innovation.

Even social–biological categories such as sex or race or religion are often linked to organizational resources, positions and power (e.g. the heavy sex polarization of nurse and doctor professions in US medicine; the concentration of Muslim workers in certain lower-level job types in some European organizations). Thus even identity groups that originate in settings other than work are relevant to the work factors (e.g. influence; power; resources) that organizational politics target.

Resource (including power as a resource) needs and desires across organizational entities can be: (1) common (shared); (2) convergent (different but linked); (3) compatible; (4) non-contingent (neither consistently related nor consistently unrelated); or (5) competitive/conflictual. Organizational political activity is often driven by the co-occurrence of an *intragroup* resource pattern of type numbers 1–3, above, with an *intergroup* pattern of type number 5. For instance, individuals with common interests (1) will lobby and pool power in an effort to secure resources when the organization contains a second group with interests common among themselves but conflictual (5) with those of the first group. Similarly, individuals whose interests diverge but do not clash (2 or 3) also sometimes form political coalitions around agreements to support each other on the resources that matter most to each against out-groups with whom they share competition (5). The current author directly observed an example of the last-mentioned possibility recently. The members of four units of an organization that had either convergent or non-contingent resource allocation interests among themselves voted as a bloc (based on an informally negotiated agreement) to take the some of the resources they desired away from a fifth organizational unit with which they were all in some respect in competition.

The linkage of within-group, between-group and organizational dynamics creates the possibility of a downward spiral into intense and negative partisan politics. When social group membership or friendships are major determinants of fair treatment or good resource access, and the members of powerful organizational subgroups help each other cover up unethical practices, the result is 'cronyism'. Cronyism is the result of a group of people working together to develop and maintain a corrupt informal system that benefits them by circumventing or supplanting formal rules and procedures, and so is a major subtype of negative collective politics.

At the extreme, negative collective politics can produce a completely corrupted organizational system. When collective politics is continuously used to exclude individuals or groups, to create unproductive or unfair allocations of organizational resources, or to harm out-groups (be they within or outside of the organization), then a general culture and system of corrupt organizational politics will exist. Isabella (1986), for instance, describes several cases in which groups within organizations or whole organizations developed cultural systems that justified cheating or injuring members of the public. Similarly, Ashforth and Anand (2003) analyze the organizational subgroup cultural processes and rationalizations that helped encourage ethical and legal violations in the Enron Corporation and other famous millennial business fiascoes. Negative politics and cronyism feed off of each other: cronyism corrupts institutional systems, and corrupt systems support cronyism and negative political behaviors (Ashforth and Anand, 2003; Sims, 1979).

Where cronyistic politics becomes common, power tends to be used to set up selection, socialization, reward and other systems that validate and reinforce cronyism. For example, in crony systems, individuals are vetted during the hiring process for in-group membership and likely fit with a politicized culture and, if they are hired, they are socialized toward accepting that ethical violations are a normal, required part of successful business (Ashforth and Anand, 2003). Such systematization forms a major component of organizational culture, what Safford (1988) called 'artifactual penetration.' Where there is substantial artifactual penetration of supports for group-based partisan political activity in the systems and structure of an organization, the organization will have a culture characterized by high levels of cronyism.

Conclusions

The nature, mechanisms and results of group-level politics in organizations are issues that have not yet received the theoretical or research attention they seem to deserve. Studies of politics within and between nations, as well as anecdotal and indirect evidence from organizations, seem to indicate that politics at the collective level is both relatively common, and can potentially yield important results for individuals, groups, organizations and societies. Yet not much conceptual or empirical work has directly considered collective politics in organizations.

In an effort to help rectify the relative neglect of collective politics in organizational science, in the current chapter a preliminary conceptual review and analysis was presented of influences on the likelihood and direction (positive or negative) of collective (group) political perceptions and actions in organizations. Some intra-organizational and external-environment influences on the processes and outcomes of partisan politics were described, followed by a description of intragroup and individual-level mechanisms that seem to mediate organizational and environmental influences on collective politics. Influences on both the extent (degree) of collective politics that occurs in organizations and on the direction (positive versus negative) of political actions were reviewed.

Within the organizational politics literature, the distinction between those two components of politics has often been ignored. It is hoped that the analysis presented here makes it clear that considering those two components of politics is important for theories of politics, for designing organizational politics research and for application. More studies are needed, for example, that examine how any given influence on politics affects both its level and potential positive and negative outcomes. The model shown in Figure 4.1 and the various sections of this chapter provide guidance for studies of that sort. An added subtlety discussed here (especially in the section on resources, power and collective politics) is the idea that politics can be either overt or covert. It was suggested, for instance, that low-power groups may, when circumstances provoke them toward negative political action, mainly take such action in covert ways. Additional theoretical and empirical work is needed on how individual and group characteristics and circumstances come together to influence the likelihood of overt versus covert political action in organizations, as well as to influence selection of particular types of overt or covert action by collectives.

Most of the organizational and environmental factors described here as likely to influence collective politics have, in fact, been subjected to very few direct research tests. Many were extrapolated either from work on individual-level political perceptions and behaviors, or from literatures on topics such as organizational justice and conflict that seem relatively closely related to politics. The same is generally true of the potential intragroup and individual-level mediators of collective politics that were outlined. Clearly, however, research that directly examines their impact on collective-level political thought and behavior is required to determine the utility of the theoretical ideas about them that were presented in this chapter. Several explicit and specific suggestions were offered for future research on the antecedents, dynamics and outcomes of collective politics.

Finally, Figure 4.1 shows collective politics feeding back to influence organizational and environmental factors. Various specific examples of where and how that occurs (for instance, from collective politics to organizational culture) were offered. Studies that examine those feedback processes and their outcomes would be of interest and value.

A complex pattern of influences on and outcomes of collective politics in organizations was outlined here. Many of the ideas presented no doubt require further refinement and elaboration, and some may be challenging to research rigorously. It is hoped that they will be, though, of heuristic value in stimulating future research and conceptual development on the dynamics of collective politics in the workplace.

References

Aldag, R.J. and Fuller, S.R. (1993). Beyond fiasco: a reappraisal of the groupthink phenomenon and a new model of group decision processes. *Psychological Bulletin*, **113**, 533–52.

Allen, V.L., Wilder, D.A. and Atkinson, M.L. (1983). Multiple group membership and social identity. In T.R. Sarbin and K.E. Scheibe (eds), *Studies in social identity* (pp. 83–110). New York: Praeger.

Allport, G.W. (1954). *The nature of prejudice*. Oxford: Addison-Wesley.

Andrews, M.C. and Kacmar, K.M. (2001). Discriminating among organizational politics, justice, and support. *Journal of Organizational Behavior*, **22**, 347–66.

Aryee, S., Chen, Z.X. and Budhwar, P.S. (2004). Exchange fairness and employee performance: An examination of the relationship between organizational politics and procedural justice. *Organizational Behavior and Human Decision Processes*, **94**, 1–14.

Ashforth, B.E. and Anand, V. (2003). The normalization of corruption in organizations. In B.M. Staw and L.L. Cummings (eds), *Research in Organizational Behavior* (Vol. 25, pp. 1–52). Amsterdam: Elsevier.

Babad, E.Y. and Wallbott, H.G. (1986). The effects of social factors on emotional reactions. In K.S. Scherer, H.G. Wallbott and A.B. Summerfield (eds), *Experiencing emotion: A cross-cultural study* (pp. 154–72). Cambridge, UK: Cambridge University Press.

Bamberger, P.A., Kluger, A.N. and Suchard, R. (1999). The antecedents and consequences of union commitment: A meta-analysis. *Academy of Management Journal*, **42**, 304–18.

Bass, B.M. (1996). *A new paradigm for leadership: An inquiry into transformational leadership*. Alexandria, VA: US Army Research Institute for the Behavioral and Social Sciences.

Bass, B.M. and Steidlmeier, P. (1999). Ethics, character, and authentic transformational leadership behavior. *Leadership Quarterly*, **10**, 181–217.

Butcher, D. and Clarke, M. (2002). Organizational politics: The cornerstone for organizational democracy. *Organizational Dynamics*, **31**, 35–46.

Conger, J.A. and Kanungo, R.N. (1998). *Charismatic leadership in organizations*. Thousand Oaks, CA: Sage Publications.

Crane, A. (2000). Corporate greening as amoralization. *Organization Studies*, **21**, 673–96.

Cropanzano, R., Howes, J.C., Grandey, A.A. and Toth, P. (1997). The relationship of organizational politics and support to work behaviors, attitudes, and stress. *Journal of Organizational Behavior*, **18**, 159–80.

Cropanzano, R., James, K. and Citera, M. (1993). A goal-hierarchy model of personality, motivation, and leadership. In L.L. Cummings and B.M. Staw (eds), *Research in organizational behavior* (Vol. 15, pp. 267–322). Greenwich, CT: JAI Press.

Darr, W. and Johns, G. (2004). Political decision-making climates: Theoretical processes and multi-level antecedents. *Human Relations*, **57**, 169–200.

Deutsch, M. (1985). *Distributive justice: A social psychological perspective*. New Haven, CT: Yale University Press.

Dipboye, R.L. and Foster, J.B. (2002). Multi-level theorizing about perceptions of organizational politics. In F.J. Yammarino and F. Dansereau (eds). *The many faces of multi-level issues. Research in multi-level issues* (Vol. 1, pp. 255–70). Greenwich, CT: Elsevier Science/JAI Press.

Dooley, D. (1984). Program evaluation. In D. Dooley, *Social research methods* (pp. 302–26). Hillsdale, NJ: Prentice-Hall.

Drory, A. and Romm, T. (1988). Politics in organization and its perception within the organization. *Organization Studies*, **9**, 165–79.

Drory, A. and Romm, T. (1990). The definition of organizational politics: A review. *Human Relations*, **43**, 1133–52.

Er, M.C. (1989). Assertive behavior and stress. *Advanced Management Journal*, **54**, 4–8.

Farrell, D. (1983). Exit, voice, loyalty, and neglect as responses to job dissatisfaction: A multidimensional scaling study. *Academy of Management Journal*, **26**, 596–607.

Feagin, J.R. and Feagin, C.B. (1986). *Discrimination American style: Institutional racism and sexism*. Malabar, FL: R.E. Krieger.

Fernandez, J.P. (1981). *Racism and sexism in corporate life*. Lexington, MA: Lexington Books.

Ferris, G.R. and Judge, T.A. (1991). Personnel/human resources management: A political influence perspective. *Journal of Management*, **17**, 447–88.

Ferris, G.R., Adams, G., Kolodinsky, R.W., Hochwarter, W.A. and Ammeter, A.P. (2002). Perceptions of organizational politics: Theory and research directions. In F.J. Yammarino and F. Dansereau (eds), *Research in multi-level issues, volume 1: The many faces of multi-level issues* (pp. 287–97). New York: Elsevier Science.

Folger, R. (1987). Reformulating the preconditions of resentment: The referent cognitions model. In J.C. Masters and W.P. Smith (eds), *Social comparison, justice, and relative deprivation: Theoretical, empirical, and policy perspectives* (pp. 183–215). Hillsdale, NJ: Erlbaum.

Frost, P.J. and Egri, C.P. (1992). The political nature of innovation. In P.J. Frost, V. Mitchell and W. Nord (eds), *Organizational reality: Reports from the firing line* (pp. 449–60). New York: HarperCollins.

Fry, L.W. (in press). Toward a theory of ethical and spiritual well-being, and corporate social responsibility through spiritual leadership. In R.A. Giacalone and C.L. Jurkiewicz (eds), *Positive psychology in business ethics and corporate responsibility*. Greenwich, CT: Information Age Publishing.

Gerstner, C.R. and Day, D.V. (1997). Meta-analytic review of leader-member exchange theory: Correlates and construct issues. *Journal of Applied Psychology*, **82**, 827–44.

Graen, G.B. and Uhl-Bien, M. (1995). Relationship-based approach to leadership: Development of leader–member exchange (LMX) theory of leadership over 25 years: Applying a multi-level multi-domain perspective. *Leadership Quarterly*, **6**, 219–47.

Greenberg, J., Pyszcynski, T. and Solomon, S. (1986). The causes and consequences of need for self-esteem: A terror management theory. In R.F. Baumeister (ed.), *Public self and private self* (pp. 189–212). New York: Springer-Verlag.

Guimond, S. and Dube-Simard, L. (1983). Relative deprivation theory and the Quebec nationalist movement: The cognitive–emotion distinction and personal–group deprivation issue. *Journal of Personality and Social Psychology*, **44**, 526–35.

Gummer, B. (1987). Groups as substance and symbol: Group processes and organizational politics. *Social Work with Groups*, **10**, 25–39.

Hogg, M.A. and Terry, D.J. (2000). Social identity and self-categorization processes in organizational contexts. *Academy of Management Review*, **25**, 121–40.

Hong, Y.Y., Morris, M.W., Chiu, C.Y. and Benet-Martinez, V. (2000). Multicultural minds: A dynamic constructivist approach to culture and cognition. *American Psychologist*, **55**, 709–20.

House, R.J. and Shamir, B. (1993). Toward an integration of charismatic, transformational, and visionary theories. In M.M. Chemers and R. Ayman (eds), *Leadership theory and research: Perspectives and directions* (pp. 81–107). Orlando, FL: Academic Press.

Isabella, L.A. (1986). Culture, key events, and corporate social responsibility. In J.E. Post and L.E. Preston (eds), *Research in corporate social performance and policy* (Vol. 8, pp. 175–92). Greenwich, CT: JAI Press.

James, K. (1993). The social context of organizational justice: Cultural, inter-group and structural effects on justice behaviors and perceptions. In R. Cropanzano (ed.), *Justice in the workplace: Approaching fairness in human resource management* (pp. 21–50). Hillsdale, NJ: Lawrence Erlbaum.

James, K. (2004). Corruption in academe: The organizational psychology of Native experiences in higher education. In D. Mishesuah and A.C. Wilson (eds), *Indigenizing the academy* (pp. 48–68). Lincoln, NE: University of Nebraska Press.

James, K. and Cropanzano, R. (1994). Dispositional group loyalty and individual action for the benefit of an ingroup: Experimental and correlational evidence. *Organizational Behavior and Human Decision Processes*, **60**, 179–205.

James, K., Clark, K. and Cropanzano, R. (1999). Positive and negative creativity in groups, institutions, and organizations: A model and theoretical extension. *Creativity Research Journal*, **12**, 211–27.

Janis, I.L. (1982). *Groupthink: Psychological studies of policy decisions and fiascoes* (2nd edn). Boston, MA: Houghton-Mifflin.

Kacmar, K.M. and Baron, R.A. (1999). Organizational politics: The state of the field, links to related processes, and an agenda for future research. In G.R. Ferris (ed.), *Research in human resources management* (Vol. 17, pp. 1–39). Greenwich, CT: Elsevier Science/JAI Press.

Kanter, R.M. (1977). *Men and women of the corporation*. New York: Basic Books.

Kark, R., Shamir, B. and Chen, G. (2003). The two faces of transformational leadership: Empowerment and dependency. *Journal of Applied Psychology*, **88**, 246–55.

Kipnis, D. (1976). *The powerholders*. Chicago, IL: University of Chicago Press.

Kipnis, D. (1989). *Technology and power*. New York: Springer.

Kipnis, D., Schmidt, S.M. and Wilkinson, I. (1980). Intraorganizational influence tactics: Explorations in getting one's way. *Journal of Applied Psychology*, **65**, 440–52.

Koestner, R. and Losier, G.F. (2002). Distinguishing three ways of being highly motivated: A closer look at introjection, identification, and intrinsic motivation. In E.L. Deci and R.M. Ryan (eds), *Handbook of self-determination research* (pp. 101–21). Rochester, NY: University of Rochester Press.

Kramer, R.M. (1991). Intergroup relations and organizational dilemmas: The role of categorization processes. In L.L. Cummings and B.M. Staw (eds), *Research in organizational behavior* (Vol. 13, pp. 191–228). Greenwich, CT: JAI Press.

Lansisalmi, H., Peiró, J.M. and Kivimäki, M. (2000). Collective stress and coping in the context of organizational culture. *European Journal of Work and Organizational Psychology*, **9**, 527–59.

Lord, R.G and Brown, D.J. (2003). *Leadership processes and follower self-identity*. Mahwah, NJ: Lawrence Erlbaum.

Lord, R.G, Brown, D.J and Freiberg, S.J. (1999). Understanding the dynamics of leadership: The role of follower self-concepts in the leader/follower relationship. *Organizational Behavior and Human Decision Processes*, **78**, 167–203.

Luthans, F. and Avolio, B. (2003). Authentic leadership development. In K.S. Cameron, J.E. Dutton and R.E. Quinn (eds), *Positive organizational scholarship* (pp. 241–62) San Francisco, CA: Berrett-Koehler.

Markus, H. (1977). Self-schemata and processing information about the self. *Journal of Personality and Social Psychology*, **35**, 63–78.

Markus, H. and Wurf, E. (1987). The dynamic self-concept: A social psychological perspective. In M.A. Rosenzweig and L.W. Porter (eds), *Annual Review of Psychology* (Vol. 38, pp. 299–337). Palo Alto, CA: Annual Reviews, Inc.

Martin, J. (1981). Relative deprivation: A theory of distributive injustice in an era of shrinking resources. In L.L. Cummings and B.M. Staw (eds), *Research in Organizational Behavior* (Vol. 3, pp. 53–107). Greenwich, CT: JAI Press.

Martin, J. (1986). When expectations and justice do not collide: Blue-collar visions of a just world. In H.W. Bierhoff, R.L. Cohen and J. Greenberg (eds), *Justice in social relations* (pp. 317–35). New York: Plenum.

Martin, J. and Siehl, C. (1983). Organizational culture and counter culture: An uneasy symbiosis. *Organizational Dynamics*, **12**, 52–64.

Martindale, C.C. (1980). Subselves: The internal representation of situational and personal dispositions. In L. Wheeler (ed.), *Review of Personality and Social Pychology* (Vol. 1, pp. 193–218). Beverley Hills, CA: Sage.

Maslyn, J.M. and Fedor, D.B. (1998). Perceptions of politics: Does measuring different foci matter? *Journal of Applied Psychology*, **83**, 645–53.

Oakes, P. (1987). The salience of social categories. In J.C. Turner and Associates, *Rediscovering the social group: A self-categorization theory* (pp. 117–41). Oxford, UK: Basil Blackwell.

O'Connor, W.E. and Morrison, T.G. (2001). A comparison of situational and dispositional predictors of perceptions of organizational politics. *Journal of Psychology: Interdisciplinary and Applied*, **135**, 301–12.

Opotow, S. (1995). Drawing the line: Social categorization, moral exclusion, and the scope of justice. In B. Bunker and J.Z. Rubin (eds), *Conflict, cooperation, and justice: Essays inspired by the work of Morton Deutsch* (pp. 347–69). San Francisco, CA: Jossey-Bass.

Poon, J.M.L. (2003). Situational antecedents and outcomes of organizational politics perceptions. *Journal of Managerial Psychology*, **18**, 138–55.

Pratto, F., Liu, J.H., Levin, S., Sidanius, J., Shih, M., Bachrach, H. and Hegarty, P. (2000). Social dominance orientation and the legitimization of inequality across cultures. *Journal of Cross-Cultural Psychology*, **31**, 369–409.

Provis, C. (2004) *Ethics and organisational politics*. Cheltenham, UK and Northampton, MA, USA: Edward Elgar.

Rahim, M.A. (2001). Managing organizational conflict: Challenges for organization development and change. In R.T. Golembiewski (ed.), *Handbook of organizational behavior* (2nd edn, pp. 365–87). New York: Marcel Dekker.

Rokeach, M. (1970). *The nature of human values*. New York: Free Press.

Rushton, J.P. (1989). Genetic similarity, human altruism, and group selection. *Behavioral and Brain Sciences*, **12**, 503–59.

Sachdev, I. and Bourhis, R.Y. (1991). Power and status differentials in minority and majority group relations. *European Journal of Social Psychology*, **21**, 1–24.

Safford, G.S. (1988). Culture traits, strength, and organizational performance: Moving beyond 'strong' culture. *Academy of Management Review*, **13**, 546–58.

Sarros, J.C., Tanewski, G.A., Winter, R.P., Santora, J.C and Densten, I.L. (2002). Work alienation and organizational leadership. *British Journal of Management*, **13**, 285–304.

Schein, E. (1985). *Organizational culture and leadership*. San Francisco, CA: Jossey-Bass.

Shamir, B., House, R.J. and Arthur, M. (1993). The motivational effects of charismatic leadership: A self-concept based theory. *Organization Science*, **4**, 577–94.

Shamir, B., Zakay, E., Brainin, E. and Popper, M. (2000). Leadership and social identification in military units: Direct and indirect relationships. *Journal of Applied Social Psychology*, **30**, 612–40.

Sims, H.P. (1979). Organizational philosophy, policies, and objectives related to unethical decision behavior: A laboratory experiment. *Journal of Applied Psychology*, **64**, 331–8.

Stone, W.F. and Schaffner, P.E. (1988). *The psychology of politics* (2nd edn). New York: Springer-Verlag.

Tajfel, H. and Turner, J.C. (1979). An integrative theory of intergroup conflict. In W.G. Austin and S. Worchel (eds), *The social psychology of intergroup relations* (pp. 33–47). Monterey, CA: Brooks/Cole.

Tan, H.H. and Aryee, S. (2002). Antecedents and outcomes of union loyalty: A constructive replication and an extension. *Journal of Applied Psychology*, **87**, 715–22.

Taylor, D.M. and McKirnan, D.J. (1984). A five-stage model of intergroup relations. *British Journal of Social Psychology*, **23**, 291–300.

Taylor, D.M., Moghaddam, F.M., Gamble, I. and Zellerer, E. (1986). Disadvantaged group responses to perceived inequality: From passive acceptance to collective action. *Journal of Social Psychology*, **127**, 259–72.

The 9/11 Commission (2004). *The 9/11 Commission Final Report: Final Report of the Commission on Terrorist Attacks upon the United States*. Washington, DC: US Government Printing Office. (Also available at: http://a257.g.akamaitech.net/7/257/2422/05aug 20041050/www.gpoaccess.gov/911/pdf/fullreport.pdf)

Tilly, C. (2003). *The politics of collective violence*. Cambridge, UK: Cambridge University Press.

Triandis, H.C. (1988). Collectivism v. individualism: A reconceptualisation of a basic concept in cross-cultural social psychology. In G.K. Verma and C. Bagley (eds), *Cross-cultural studies of personality, attitudes and cognition* (pp. 60–95). New York: St. Martin's Press.

Triandis, H.C. (1989). The self and social behavior in differing cultural contexts. *Psychological Review*, **96**, 506–20.

Triandis, H.C. (1995). *Culture and social behavior*. New York: McGraw-Hill.

Tsui, A.S. and O'Reilly, C.A. (1989). Beyond simple demographic effects: The importance of relational demography in superior/subordinate dyads. *Academy of Management Journal*, **32**, 402–23.

Turner, J.C. (1985). Social categorization and the self-concept: A social cognitive theory of group behavior. In E.J. Lawler (ed.), *Advances in group processes: Theory and research* (Vol. 2, pp. 77–122). Greenwich, CT: JAI Press.

Tyler, T.R. and Lind, E.A. (1990). Intrinsic versus community-based justice models: When does group membership matter? *Journal of Social Issues*, **46**, 83–94.

Van Dick, R. (2004). My job is my castle: Identification in organizational contexts. *International Review of Industrial and Organizational Psychology*, **19**, 171–203.

Vigoda, E. (2003). *Developments in organizational politics: How political dynamics affect employee performance in modern work sites*. Cheltenham, UK: Edward Elgar.

Walker, I. and Pettigrew, T.F. (1984). Relative deprivation theory: An overview and conceptual critique. *British Journal of Social Psychology*, **23**, 301–10.

Wallace, A.F.C. (1971). *Culture and personality* (2nd edn). New York: Random House.

Walsh, K.C. (2004). *Talking about politics: Informal groups and social identity in American life*. Chicago, IL: University of Chicago Press.

Wegner, D.M. (1982). Justice and the awareness of social entities. In J. Greenberg and R. Cohen (eds), *Equity and justice in social behavior* (pp. 77–117). New York: Academic Press.

Wekselberg, V. (1996). Groupthink: A triple fiasco in social psychology. In C.W. Tolman, F. Cherry, R. Van Hezewijk and I. Lubek (eds), *Problems of theoretical psychology* (pp. 217–27). North York, ON, Canada: Captus Press.

Whyte, G. (1998). Recasting Janis's groupthink model: The key role of collective efficacy in decision fiascoes. *Organizational Behavior and Human Decision Processes*, **73**, 185–209.

Wilkinson, I. and Kipnis, D. (1978). Interfirm uses of power. *Journal of Applied Psychology*, **63**, 315–20.

Williams, K.Y. and O'Reilly, C.A. (1998). Demography and diversity in organizations: A review of 40 years of research. *Research in Organizational Behavior* (Vol. 20, pp. 77–140). Greenwich, CT: JAI Press.

Witt, L.A., Patti, A.L. and Farmer, W.L. (2002). Organizational politics and work identity as predictors of organizational commitment. *Journal of Applied Social Psychology*, **32**, 486–99.

Zivnuska, S., Kacmar, K.M., Witt, L.A., Carlson, D.S and Bratton, V.K. (2004). Interactive effects of impression management and organizational politics on job performance. *Journal of Organizational Behavior*, **25**, 627–40.

5 The politics of impression management in organizations: Contextual effects
Amos Drory and Nurit Zaidman

Introduction

The behavioral expression of organizational politics consists of deliberate influence attempts applied by individual actors for purposes of attaining personally desirable goals. The nature of political tactics has been studied extensively (Kipnis et al., 1980; Rao et al., 1995). Impression management has been identified as a specific form of social influence behavior applied by individuals in various contexts (Tadeschi and Melburg, 1984; Jones and Pittman, 1982; Rosenfeld et al., 2002; Wayne and Ferris, 1990).

It is widely accepted that the power of the individual in the organization stems not only from his formal position and actual control of resources, but also from the image that person has in the eyes of other members in the organization. One's ability to influence others and affect decision-making processes in the organization therefore depends greatly on the extent to which others believe in this image. Creating it is the practice of impression management.

Impression management occurs within specific contexts. The purpose of this chapter is to discuss the impact of national culture, organizational characteristics and personal and group circumstances on impression management behavior. The chapter opens with a survey of the research about the role of contextual determinants of this behavior. The second section includes qualitative and quantitative findings demonstrating the relevance of contextual variables to the understanding of impression management behavior in work organizations.

Impression management has attracted the attention of behavioral scientists and organizational researchers in a variety of contexts. The concept refers to the process by which people attempt to influence the image others have of them. Rosenfeld et al. (2002) define impression management as 'any behavior by the individual attempting to control or manipulate others' attributions and impressions of him.' Impression management occurs when a person wishes to create and maintain a specific identity. This goal is achieved by intentionally exhibiting certain behaviors, both verbal and nonverbal, that will lead others to view the actor as desired.

Many researchers (Tadeschi and Melburg, 1984; Jones and Pittman, 1982; Rosenfeld et al., 2002; Wayne and Ferris, 1990) have identified various strategies of impression management. Assertive strategies, for example, are designed to establish a given desirable identity. Among such strategies, ingratiation has received the most empirical research attention (Ralston, 1985; Wayne and Kacmar, 1991). Defensive or protective strategies, on the other hand, consist of the use of excuses and justifications to repair spoiled identities (Rosenfeld et al., 2002).

Jones and Pittman (1982) identified five categories of impression management behavior: (1) ingratiation – the attempt to appear likable; (2) exemplification – the attempt to appear dedicated; (3) intimidation – the attempt to appear threatening; (4) self-promotion – the attempt to appear competent; and (5) supplication – the attempt to appear in need of assistance.

Naturally, the work organization is one of the major arenas in which impression management is exercised. The use of impression management in the work organization has been well documented (Bozeman and Kacmar, 1997; Gardner, 1992; Giacalone and Rosenfeld, 1991; Rosenfeld et al., 2002). Perhaps the most common organizational relationship in which impression management occurs is that of superior and subordinate. The structural dependence of the subordinate in this relationship leads to a natural desire among subordinates to create a positive impression on their superior. Some of the specific organizational practices where impression management was found relevant are interviewing (Stevens and Kristof, 1995), performance appraisal (Wayne and Ferris, 1990) and feedback (Ashford and Northcraft, 1992).

Career advancement is also an area where impression management is a relevant explanatory variable. Feldman and Klich (1991) suggest that career orientation commonly includes the beliefs that merit alone is not enough for advancement in organizations and that much work cannot be directly observed and accurately assessed. Social relations thus are perceived as a critical factor in facilitating career advancement. They conclude that such beliefs may serve to justify the use of impression management.

Other researchers also agree that impression management could have a considerable effect on individual success and promotion opportunities at work (Kacmar et al., 1992; Gilmore et al., 1999). Specific findings show that impression management may indeed effectively help career advancement. Gould and Penley (1984), for example, found that impression management strategies were positively associated with salary progression. Judge and Bretz (1994) found similar relationships between impression management and career development.

Contextual causes of impression management

Beyond the attempts to define, describe and measure impression management in organizations as a subset of the political arena, research has naturally focused on the causes and determinants of this behavior. Many researchers agree that contextual variables play an important role in determining the way in which an organization's members attempt to impress others in their surroundings. Yet relatively little empirical research has been devoted to this topic. In this chapter we attempt to highlight the potential role of contextual variables in determining the actual choices made by individuals in organizations in regard to their impression management behavior. There are three levels of context that are worth noting:

- Organizational characteristics: structure, norms and rules, organizational culture.
- Personal and group circumstances: socioeconomic conditions, demographic characteristics.
- National culture: norms and values.

Contextual variables can enhance our understanding of impression management behavior with respect to three general issues or research questions. The first issue focuses on motivation. What motivates individuals to engage in impression management attempts?

What factors affect the intensity and frequency of these attempts? The second issue pertains to the nature of the image the individual seeks to create. The third deals with the process by which individuals attempt to create the desirable impression. This question involves the specific strategies chosen to impress other individuals (Leary and Kowalski, 1990).

In what follows, we first briefly demonstrate how contextual variables are related to the three issues described above. We then present some of our own findings in this regard.

Contextual effects and the motivation to engage in impression management behavior
People construct a favorable image of themselves because they wish to maximize their rewards (Schlenker, 1980), maintain their self-esteem (Schneider, 1969) or create a desired identity (Swann, 1987). Several contextual variables have an impact on the motivation to engage in impression management behavior.

Power relations in the organization   When an individual's dependence on others for valued outcomes is greater, the individual will be more motivated to engage in impression management (Leary and Kowalski, 1990; Schlenker, 1980). People are thus more likely to ingratiate their bosses and teachers than their friends (Bohra and Pandey, 1984; Hendricks and Brikman, 1974; Schlenker, 1980). In addition, people are more likely to ingratiate these authorities when the authorities have greater power to dispense valued outcomes (Jones et al., 1965; Stires and Jones, 1969) or when desired resources are scarce (Beck, 1983; Pandey and Rastagi, 1979).

Limited economic and political opportunities (of subgroups)   Pandey (1986) suggests that impression management may be more common in societies with limited economic and political opportunities. This argument is empirically supported by studies that find that Hispanics and blacks in the USA may be more likely than whites to engage in impression management by making socially desirable responses on surveys and questionnaires (Ross and Mirowsky, 1984; Adams and Krasnoff, 1989; Bachman and O'Malley, 1984). This behavior has to do with their relative lack of social power in American society. It may therefore be suggested that minorities in organizations will more frequently engage in impression management because they are relatively less powerful (Zaidman and Drory, 2001). In addition, minorities in organizations may be more uncertain about the range of acceptable behaviors. This uncertainty may increase their impression management behavior (Gardner and Martinko, 1988).

Culture-specific cultural codes   Rosenfeld et al. (1994) suggest that impression management among Hispanics may be due to a culture-specific Hispanic script known as *simpatia* (i.e. the need for behaviors that promote smooth and pleasant interpersonal relations). Other cultural groups may have other scripts that enhance the legitimacy of impression management (Zaidman and Drory, 2001).

Power distance   Power distance characterizes the extent to which less powerful members of organizations accept unequal distribution of power (Hofstede, 1980). Individuals in societies with great power distance will attribute greater legitimacy to impressing their superiors than individuals in societies with a small power distance (Bond, 1991).

Contextual effects and the desired impression

Organizational roles   Role constraints influence the public image of individuals. Most roles are associated with particular personal characteristics (Leary and Kowalski, 1990; Sarbin and Allen, 1968). Impression management in role-governed situations is often based on a prototype-matching process: people try to make their social images conform as closely as possible to prototypic characteristics of the role they are playing (Leary and Kowalski, 1990).

Occupational status   Individuals who hold low-status jobs are more likely to use impression management toward their superiors in order to improve their conditions. Foley (2005) suggests that because midwifery in the USA is an occupation at the margins of medicine, midwives must frequently negotiate competing identity claims, so they use impression management to establish their desired public identity.

National culture   Individualistic societies are characterized by an emphasis on individual identity, individual goals and individual welfare. On the other hand, collectivist societies stress membership within groups or communities, emphasize communal goals, and consider group welfare more important than an individual's welfare (Hofstede, 1980; Riordan and Vandenberg, 1994). According to Triandis (1989), in individualistic cultures it is assumed that the generalized other will value autonomy, independence and self-reliance. By contrast, in collectivists cultures, conformity to the other in public settings is valued. One can therefore argue that the desired impression in individualistic cultures will be that of an independent and self-reliant individual, and in collectivist cultures it will be that of a person who displays politeness and harmony (Zaidman and Drory, 2001).

Contextual effects on the choice of impression management strategies
Although several researchers have discussed the potential influence of contextual variables on the choice of impression management strategies, little rigorous attention has been given to this link.

Organizational characteristics   Rosenfeld et al. (2002) suggest that organizational behavior is highly responsive to the interpersonal cues and social aspects of the situation. They argue that greater emphasis should be placed on issues of organizational characteristics and culture. They claim that so far we know little about which strategies predominate in particular organizational settings. Gardner and Martinko (1988) suggest that organizational strategies, policies and symbols serve to support the behavior and attitudes considered appropriate, thus placing constraints on the range of impression management behaviors available. Other related factors that may influence the choice of impression management strategies are the existence of formal rules and procedures, task and role ambiguity, and the scope for novelty in the organization (Gardner and Martinko, 1988; Ralston, 1985).

   Rao et al. (1995) compare managers in private sector organizations and municipal government and educational organizations. They hypothesize that the differences in formalization and routinization between the two types of organizations would affect the types of influence strategies used by subordinates, but their empirical results do not support this hypothesis.

Limited economic and political opportunities   Pandey (1986) argues that manipulative behavior such as ingratiation becomes more common in circumstances of inequality, deprivation, limited resources and sociopolitical uncertainty.

Culture   Pandey (1986) suggests that specific cultural traits influence the choice of impression management strategies. His findings in India show four different ingratiating tactics that had not been identified in studies that took place in the West: self-degradation, instrumental dependence, name dropping, and changing with the situation.

Asian-American managers report using significantly lower levels of self-disclosure and self- and supervisor-focused impression management tactics but more job-focused impression management tactics than European-American managers do (Xin, 2004).

Examples
During the past few years we have accumulated some empirical data based on both qualitative and quantitative methods in relation to some of the issues described above. In the following sections we provide evidence to demonstrate the impact of contextual variables on impression management behavior.

Our research focused on two levels of variables. In the first study we compared Russian immigrants to Israel with Israeli-born employees. The comparison between these two groups highlighted the effects of both national culture and socioeconomic differences between the two groups. In the second study we examined the differences in impression management behavior in two organizational cultures.

The impact of job security and limited economic resources on impression management behavior
We asked 20 immigrants from the former USSR to describe the difference between their impression management behavior toward their superiors in their previous job, in the former USSR, and their current job in Israel. Participants had immigrated to Israel between 1992 and 1997. The majority were people over the age of 38, who had worked in the USSR and had limited or no exposure to the Israeli education system. The interviewees had a variety of occupations, including doctors, engineers, secretaries, cooks and laborers.

Half of the participants said that their impression management behavior had not changed since their immigration. For example, a doctor said: 'Basically I try to make the same impression, although my relationships with my Israeli superiors are more friendly, and there is less distance between me and them. But the behavior that is required from medical doctors is the same.' In this example, in spite of differences in power distance, the employee's status as a physician seems to be more important and to cross cultural boundaries. Another person, who works in construction, said: 'I am the same. This is who I am. It has nothing to do with being in Israel or in the former USSR, it has to do with who I am.'

Yet the other participants said that they put more effort in impression management in Israel than they did before, generally to increase their job security. The following are a few examples: 'In the former USSR, I put less effort into impression management because

I was also a university lecturer, and there was no risk that they would fire me. Here the situation is different. I am a simple physician, and I am dependent on my superiors.' Another person said: 'In the former USSR, there was no need to convey an impression. There, if a person had been accepted for a job, there is a very small chance that his superiors would kick him out. Here, everyone is afraid to lose their jobs.'

Thus the qualitative data show that job security has an impact on the motivation to create a positive impression. Future research should focus on quantitative analysis with larger samples.

The impact of national culture on the legitimacy of impression management
We conducted a focus group and 24 interviews with Israeli employees. The average age of the participants was 43. The major occupational categories ranged from highly professional jobs, such as doctor and engineer, through technical jobs, including technician, to such positions as production worker and cashier. The results show that Israelis perceived impression management as immoral and deceptive. Participants drew a distinction between honest behavior, which is good and legitimate, and impression management behavior, which is dishonest and illegitimate. Participants referred negatively to employees who tried to impress superiors. An example is the following: 'People often say that making a good impression is flattery. I know that it is so. Flattery is temporary. After some time, the real person surfaces. For me, a good impression is hard work; it means trying harder.'

Often the responses to the question, 'What is the impression that you would like to convey to your superiors?' were 'I do not want to make any impression,' or 'I do not work to make impressions but to get results.'

Yet, at the same time, a secondary viewpoint surfaced that acknowledged the importance of upward impression management. The following statement demonstrates how participants reject, and at the same time acknowledge, the positive aspects of impression management behavior: 'Often when an employee is ingratiating it only makes a bad impression because it is clear that there is nothing beyond his or her words. In my experience at work, only those who had nothing to contribute behaved in such a shallow way. Perhaps the boss liked it. But I wanted to get away from it, to do exactly the opposite.'

Thus, although the dominant argument among the participants was that impression management is shallow and deceptive, they nevertheless acknowledged that it could yield benefits, at least in the short term.

Two major cultural characteristics explain this position. First, informality and low level of power distance characterize Israeli society. As a group with a small power distance (Hofstede, 1980), Israelis reject the possibility that relationships between superior and subordinate can be based on impression management behavior. The natural, real and desirable relationship between an employee and a superior, from their point of view, should be based on equality, formality and closeness. Impression management behavior cannot be effective in the long run in such a climate.

The Dugri code, which influences social relationships toward simple behavior and equality, is another factor explaining the illegitimacy of impression management behavior. Two major components of this code are directness and simplicity in communication and in relationships. It is expressed in impatience with verbal polish or circumlocution and with the complexities and frivolities of a cultured life (Katriel, 1986, p. 29). Dugri talk is characterized by a rejection of pathos, cliché, and long and sophisticated words. Manners are perceived as an expression of hypocrisy (Almog, 1997).

The impact of organizational culture on the choice of impression management strategies
Our second study focused on the impact of organizational characteristics on impression management by comparing two distinct organizational systems, namely, the organic and the mechanistic systems described by Burns and Stalker (1961).

The mechanistic system is typically highly centralized. It is supported by a strong hierarchical structure with a high level of formalization. The system is designed to strengthen the formal power of management in terms of information, control and decision making. Subordinates' dependence on their superiors is naturally high. Jobs in the mechanistic system are rigid, well structured and routine. Loyalty to the organization and obedience to superiors are considered prerequisites to organizational membership. Innovation is not encouraged.

Organic organizations emphasize lateral responsibilities rather than rigid job definitions and the exchange of information rather than the giving of directions (Burns and Stalker, 1961). The organization of workflows in organic firms requires frequent contact across vertical levels (Burns and Stalker, 1961; Hage, 1988). Frequent interaction, in and of itself, generates closer social bonds (Homans, 1950; Newcomb, 1961). Thus vertical relations in organic organizations tend to be characterized by a close social distance and a small power distance (Morand, 1996). Here, status distinctions are not considered reflective of underlying differences in terms of superiority or inferiority. Rather, the hierarchy simply reflects an 'inequality of roles, established for convenience' (Hofstede, 1980, p. 75).

In our study, the mechanistic system is represented by a sample taken from the military. Altman and Baruch (1998) suggest that the main thread of any armed force is an emphasis on structure, hierarchy and discipline. They further suggest that one characteristic of an armed forces organization is its rigidity, that is, the extent to which behavior is constrained by a normative role differentiation. The organic system is represented by a sample of employees from research and development units in several technology businesses. Such units typically deal with a high level of uncertainty and are characterized by a flexible structure, teamwork and a low level of formal control. It seems likely that the differences between the two organizational systems will lead to substantial differences in the patterns of impression management behavior.

We conducted in-depth, half-structured interviews with 11 employees in R&D organizations (seven men and four women) and 12 employees of the armed forces (seven men and five women). We selected participants who had been working in their organization for at least one year. The participants came from different levels within their organization. Their ages ranged between 24 and 50.

We asked the subjects from the military to describe the unique characteristics of impression management in their organization. The majority of the respondents emphasized the constraints imposed by military policies and symbols on their ability to manage impressions: 'In the army you work according to instructions and cannot change them. For example, in non-military organizations you can work more hours if you want to create a good impression, but in the army you cannot do that.' Another person said: 'In the army there are predetermined work procedures, and there is no room for interpretation, while in non-military organizations one can be more flexible in using them to impress others.'

Other participants discussed the specific symbols that are used in the army and how they affect impression management: 'One has to wear a uniform in the army. The possibility to create an impression through the way you dress does not exist.' Moreover, according to another participant, 'The ranks are very important in the army. People use their officer rank as a very strong tool to make an impression.'

The responses of employees from organic organizations to the same open question were different. Participants said that professionalism and performing tasks are properties that characterize their organization in terms of impression management behavior. Thus, while the responses of participants from mechanistic organizations reflect the centrality of the constraints of the military policies and symbols, the responses of employees in organic organizations reflect low levels of formal control.

We hypothesized that members of mechanistic organizations will be significantly less likely to engage in impression management toward their peers than toward their superiors; we expected no such difference for employees of organic systems. This hypothesis was based on the assumption that the hierarchical and autocratic management style in a mechanistic organization will lead to a high dependence on one's superior and therefore to greater attempts to try to make a good impression on that person. In the organic system, on the other hand, the emphasis is on team work and collaboration rather than on obedience to superior ranks. In this climate it should be more natural for the employee to assign the same importance to peers and superiors alike. Both interview data and a questionnaire survey lent support to this hypothesis.

We asked employees from both organic and mechanistic organizations an open question regarding normative and non-normative impression management behavior in their organizations. The question was framed in the following way: 'What are the common ways to manage impressions in your organization? What ways are not considered acceptable? Please give examples and explain your response.'

Six of 11 interviewees from organic systems gave examples that showed the importance attributed to peers in these organizations. Two people said that ingratiating behavior toward superiors is not accepted. The other four expressed a complementary view that one should not hurt a colleague in an attempt to impress a superior (or that one should be a part of the team). The following are a few examples:

'It is not acceptable to step over dead bodies on the way up.'

'It is not acceptable to tell about the failures of others on the same project on which you have been successful.'

'It is not acceptable to be unsocial, or to be alien to the people around you. It does not impress the superiors. It is acceptable to be socially active, to be part of a group with your colleagues.'

No clear trends emerged from the responses of employees in mechanistic systems regarding normative and non-normative behavior. One person indicated that it is not acceptable to ignore others in order to make a good impression on superiors. Another said that ingratiating behavior is acceptable, as is telling negative things about peers. Others mentioned various acceptable ways to create a good impression in the organization: gaining professional knowledge, ingratiation, and using networks with superiors to create good impression on others. There were only a few remarks about non-normative behavior and impression management.

In order to further examine our hypothesis, we administered an 18-item scale measuring the use of impression management tactics to a sample of 107 technology employees from 20 different organizations and 101 army officers from non-combat administrative units.

The authors developed this scale on the basis of a large sample of statements from employees in various organizations describing impression management tactics. Factor analysis revealed three factors comparable to those suggested by Jones and Pittman (1982) and described earlier in this chapter. The three factors were *exemplification* (alpha = 81), *ingratiation* (alpha = 0.83), and *self-promotion* (alpha = 0.78). The response to each statement was given on a five-point scale ranging from 'almost never' to 'very often.' We compared the extent to which the respondents reported directing impression management attempts at their superiors and at their peers.

The results suggested that, in the mechanistic sample, there was a significantly higher number of impression management attempts directed at superiors than at peers with respect to all three factors: exemplification: $F = 113.9$, $df = 1206$, $p < 0.00$; ingratiation: $F = 164.56$, $df = 1206$, $p < 0.00$; self-promotion: $F = 89.78$, $df = 1206$, $p < 0.00$. We found no significant differences in impression management toward superiors and toward peers for the employees of the organic systems: exemplification: $F = 0.39$, $df = 1206$; ingratiation: $F = 0.157$, $df = 1206$; self-promotion: $F = 0.42$, $df = 1206$.

Conclusions

In this chapter we have suggested a two-dimensional framework for the study of the contextual aspects of impression management behavior (see Figure 5.1).

Existing research has considered several of these topics but there is little or no work yet on others. Yet contextual variables play an important role in shaping impression

Levels of context

		Personal and group circumstances	Organizational characteristics	National culture
Impression management characteristics	Motivation and intensity			
	The desirable image			
	Choice of strategies			

Figure 5.1   Framework for study of impression management behavior

management in organizations, and their study can contribute greatly to our understanding of the dynamics of such behavior. We therefore recommend that future research specifically focus on this area, for both practical and theoretical reasons.

Practically, decisions about benefits, promotions, placement and assignments clearly are affected by the impression a person manages to establish on superiors, peers and even subordinates. In addition, personal power may be at stake. By creating a desirable impression, an individual can obtain a better opportunity to influence decisions. A person who manages to impress others that his/her virtues are relevant to a given decision-making process could have a greater impact on those decisions.

From the organizational viewpoint the impact of impression management may be undesirable and even detrimental, particularly when the impression created is misleading or false. It is therefore important to develop a more comprehensive understanding of the dynamics of this behavior and to increase the awareness of managers and organizational leaders regarding the dynamics of impression management, what motivates it, and how it is achieved.

References

Adams, C.J. and Krasnoff, A.G. (1989). Social desirability effects in male prisoners. *Journal of Research in Personality*, **23**, 421–34.

Almog, A. (1997). *The Zabbar*. Tel Aviv, Israel: Am Oved.

Altman, Y. and Baruch, Y. (1998). Cultural theory and organizations: Analytical method and cases. *Organization Studies*, **19**, 769–85.

Ashford, S.J. and Northcraft, G.B. (1992). Conveying more (or less) than we realize: The role of impression management in feedback seeking. *Organizational Behavior and Human Decision Processes*, **53**, 310–34.

Bachman, J.G. and O'Malley, P.M. (1984). Yea-saying, nay-saying and going to extremes: Black–White differences in response style. *Public Opinion Quarterly*, **48**, 491–509.

Beck, R.C. (1983). *Motivation: Theory and principles* (2nd edn). Englewood Cliffs, NJ: Prentice-Hall.

Bohra, K.A. and Pandey, J. (1984). Ingratiation toward strangers, friends, and bosses. *Journal of Social Psychology*, **122**, 217–22.

Bond, M.H. (1991). Cultural influences on modes of impression management, implication for the culturally diverse organization. In R.A. Giacalone and P. Rosenfeld (eds), *Applied impression management: How image making affects managerial decisions* (pp. 195–215). Newbury Park, CA: Sage Publications.

Bozeman, D.P. and Kacmar, K.M. (1997). A cybernetic model of impression management processes in organizations. *Organizational Behavior and Human Decision Processes*, **69** (1), 9–30.

Burns, T. and Stalker, G.M. (1961). *The management of innovation*. London: Tavistock.

Feldman, D.C. and Klich, N. (1991). Impression management and career strategies. In R.A. Giacalone and P. Rosenfeld (eds), *Applied impression management: How image-making affects managerial decisions* (pp. 67–80). Newbury Park, CA: Sage Publications.

Foley, L. (2005). Midwives, marginality, and public identity work. *Symbolic Interaction*, **28**, 183.

Gardner, W.L. (1992). Lessons in organizational dramaturgy: The art of impression management. *Organizational Dynamics*, **21** (1), 33–46.

Gardner, W.L. and Martinko, M.J. (1988). Impression management in organizations. *Journal of Management*, **14** (2), 321–38.

Giacalone, R.A. and Rosenfeld, P. (eds) (1991). *Applied impression management: How image making affects managerial decisions*. Newbury Park, CA: Sage Publications.

Gilmore, D.C., Stevens, C.K., Harrell-Cook, G. and Ferris, G.R. (1999). Impression management tactics. In R.W. Eder and M.M. Harris (eds), *The employment interview handbook*. Newbury Park, CA: Sage Publications.

Gould, S. and Penley, L.E. (1984). Career strategies and salary progression: A study of their relationship in a municipal bureaucracy. *Organizational Behavior and Human Performance*, **34**, 244–65.

Hage, J. (1988). The pathways of evolution in organizations. In J. Hage (ed.), *Futures of organizations* (pp. 44–65). Lexington, MA: Lexington Books.

Hendricks, M. and Brikman, P. (1974). Effects of status and knowledge ability of audience on self-presentation. *Sociometry*, **37**, 440–9.

Hofstede, G. (1980). *Culture's consequences: International differences in work-related values*. Beverly Hills, CA: Sage.

Homans, G.C. (1950). *The human group*. New York: Harcourt, Brace and World.

Jones, E.E. and Pittman, T.S. (1982). Toward a general theory of strategic self-presentation. In *Psychological Perspectives of the self* (pp. 231–62). Hillsdale, NJ: Erlbaum.

Jones, E.E., Gargen, K.J., Gumbert, P. and Thibaut, J.W. (1965). Some conditions affecting the use of integration to influence performance evaluation. *Journal of Personality and Social Psychology*, **1**, 613–25.

Judge, T.A. and Bretz, R.D. (1994). Political influence behavior and career success. *Journal of Management*, **20**, 43–65.

Kacmar, K.M., Delery J.E. and Ferris, G.R. (1992). Differential effectiveness of applicant impression management tactics on employment interview decisions. *Journal of Applied Social Psychology*, **22**, 1250–72.

Katriel, T. (1986). *Talking straight, Dugri speech in Israeli Sabra culture*. Cambridge: Cambridge University Press.

Kipnis, D., Schmidt, S. and Wilkinson, I. (1980). Intraorganizational influence tactics: Explorations in getting one's way. *Journal of Applied Psychology*, **65**, 444–52.

Leary, M.R. and Kowalski, R.M. (1990). Impression management: A literature review and two-component model. *Psychological Bulletin*, **107**, 34–47.

Morand, D.A. (1996). What's in a name? An exploration of the social dynamics of forms of address in organizations. *Management Communication Quarterly*, **9**, 422–49.

Newcomb, T. (1961). *The acquaintance process*. New York: Holt, Rinehart & Winston.

Pandey, J. (1986). Sociological perspectives on ingratiation. *Progress in Experimental Personality Research*, **14**, 205–29.

Pandey, J. and Rastagi, R. (1979). Machiavellianism and ingratiation. *The Journal of Social Psychology*, **108**, 221–5.

Ralston, D.A. (1985). Employee ingratiation: the role of management. *Academy of Management Review*, **10**, 477–87.

Rao, A., Schmidt, S.M. and Murray, L.H. (1995). Upward impression management: Goals, influence strategies and consequences. *Human Relations*, **48** (2), 147–67.

Riordan, C.M. and Vandenberg, R.J. (1994). A central question in cross-cultural research: Do employees of different cultures interpret work-related measures in an equivalent manner? *Journal of Management*, **20**, 643–71.

Rosenfeld, P., Booth-Kewley, S., Edwards, J.E. and Alderton, D.L. (1994). Linking diversity and impression management. *American Behavioral Scientist*, **37**, 672–81.

Rosenfeld, P., Giacalone, R.A. and Riordan, C.A. (2002). *Impression management: Building and enhancing reputations at work*. London: Thomson Learning.

Ross, C.E. and Mirowsky, J. (1984). Social-desirable response and acquiescence in a cross-cultural survey of mental health. *Journal of Health and Social Behavior*, **25**, 189–97.

Sarbin, T.R. and Allen, V.L. (1968). Role theory. In G. Lindzey and E. Aronson (eds), *The handbook of social psychology* (3rd edn, vol. 1, pp. 488–567). Reading, MA: Addison-Wesley.

Schlenker, B.R. (1980). *Impression management*. Monterey, CA: Brooks/Cole.

Schneider, D.J. (1969). Tactical self-presentation after success and failure. *Journal of Personality and Social Psychology*, **13**, 262–8.

Stevens, C.K. and Kristof, A.L. (1995). Making the right impression: A field study of applicant impression management during job interviews. *Journal of Applied Psychology*, **80**, 587–606.

Stires, L.D. and Jones, E.E. (1969). Modesty vs. self-enhancement as alternative forms of ingratiation. *Journal of Experimental Social Psychology*, **5**, 172–88.

Swann Jr, W.B. (1987). Identity negotiation: Where two roads meet. *Journal of Personality and Social Psychology*, **53**, 1038–51.

Tadeschi J.T. and Melburg, V. (1984). Impression management and influence in organizations. In S.B. Bacharach and E.J. Lawler (eds), *Research in the sociology of organizations* (pp. 31–58). Greenwich, CT: JAI Press.

Triandis, H.C. (1989). The self and social behavior in differing cultural contexts. *Psychological Review*, **96**, 506–20.

Wayne, S.J. and Ferris, G.R. (1990). Influence tactics, effect and exchange quality in supervisor–subordinate interactions: A laboratory experiment and field study. *Journal of Applied Psychology*, **75**, 487–99.

Wayne, S.J. and Kacmar, K.M. (1991). The effects of impression management on the performance appraisal process. *Organizational behavior and human decision processes*, **48**, 70–88.

Xin, K.R. (2004). Asian American Managers: An impression gap?: An investigation of impression management and supervisor–subordinate relationships. *The Journal of Applied Behavioral Science*, **40**, 160–82.

Zaidman, N. and Drory, A. (2001). Upward Impression Management in the Work Place – Cross Cultural Analysis. *International Journal of Intercultural Relations*, **25**, 671–90.

PART II

ETHICS AND JUSTICE: VALUES, FAIRNESS AND THE POSSIBILITIES FOR TRUST IN WORKPLACE POLITICS

6 Organizational politics, definitions and ethics
Chris Provis

Introduction
The theme of this chapter is that there are substantial ethical issues about organizational politics that need careful examination. However, only toward the end of the chapter do I touch on the ways that we might try to answer the sorts of questions that such examination may disclose. Most of my discussion argues that such issues are complex, difficult and important, despite the fact that they often are ignored or that some answers that actually are problematic are taken for granted.

I shall suggest to begin with that it may be helpful to consider analogies with the politics of nation-states. For thousands of years, consideration has been given to ethical issues regarding the politics of nation-states, and I shall contend that there is room for a similar approach to the politics of organizations. On this view, organizational politics can be an important and constructive part of organizational life, just as the politics of a nation-state can be an important aspect of citizenship and involvement in community life.

This approach is contrary to a widespread approach which I then go on to discuss: the sort of approach that sees organizational politics as inherently unethical, perhaps even unethical by definition. I argue that such an approach tends to obscure both some dynamics of organizational politics and some genuine ethical issues. The analogy with the politics of nation-states discloses some such issues, like the question when it is legitimate to dissent from official authority and the question to what extent political necessity may free us from usual moral constraints.

The idea that organizational politics is inherently unethical may have some roots in unitarist positions about organizations, and so the discussion will then consider some unitarist views, both in comparison with pluralist views about organizations and in comparison with analogous approaches to the politics of nation-states.

That discussion draws our attention to the complexity for ethical analysis that definition and interpretation are often tactics of organizational politics, which simultaneously bear on ethical appraisal. What constitutes 'politics' itself may be contested, and so may be the definition of specific actions like 'backstabbing' and 'nepotism'. When we start to look at some examples of specific tactics, we can see that both definition and ethical appraisal may require us to pay close attention to the detailed circumstances, including the motives and perceptions of individuals involved. Perceptions are an important part of organizational politics, even though we sacrifice possibilities of ethical appraisal if we focus only on people's perceptions.

That sort of complexity makes ethical appraisal very difficult in organizational politics, and I conclude with a suggested way forward. It is tempting to utilize some general ethical theory like utilitarianism, but such general theories tend themselves to be contentious at critical points. It is desirable to find a systematic approach, but we may achieve that best by identifying some ethical principles that apply to various sorts of cases, without trying to base appraisal on a single over-arching ethical theory. Ultimately, I suggest, what is important is for us each to accept our individual responsibility for judgment and action in the complex and difficult situations in which we find ourselves.

Varieties of politics

For several hundred years the central preoccupation of political theorists has been the politics of nation-states. There has been a special preoccupation with the rights and obligations of citizens and the state, whether the state has been conceived as the person of the monarch or an abstract constitutional authority. Hobbes, Locke, Rousseau and others grappled with issues about the source and extent of political authority within the nation-state. These are problems of ethics, in so far as they concern the question of what moral obligations we have to comply with that authority (cf. Benn and Peters 1959: 318). Perhaps the explanation for the emphasis on nation-states has been the assumption that they alone may use physical coercion to enforce their authority, but, whatever the explanation, the emphasis has been clear.

It is true that other political environments have been examined in academic study. Anthropologists have studied power arrangements in small communities (e.g. Gluckman 1965), sociologists and psychologists have studied power dynamics within families (e.g. Laing 1971) and other social groupings, and management theorists have considered power within work organizations (e.g. French and Raven 1960; Bacharach and Lawler 1980; Pfeffer 1981, 1992). But by and large these studies have been descriptive rather than normative. That is, they have focused on the causal dynamics, the factors that have explained how things have happened one way rather than another, and not on what ought to happen, on how individuals ought to cope with the dilemmas and ethical difficulties that arise for them. It is also true that in the 1960s and 1970s, some writers addressed such issues, but recently their work seems to have been put aside (for some references to that work, see Velasquez 2002: chap. 8; Velasquez is one author who has drawn a comparison between organizational politics and the politics of nation-states, as I advocate in what follows).

In some ways, this emphasis on the empirical reminds us of Machiavelli's work. In the Italian city-states, modern empirical study of politics began when Machiavelli wrote *The Prince* by way of advice to political actors about the best ways for them to conduct themselves. For Machiavelli, empirical descriptive study was crucial, and normative conclusions followed straightforwardly. He was impatient with ethical qualms that might detract from effectiveness, and explicitly argued that the political leader could not afford traditional virtues (Hampshire 1989: 162–7). In this, he was aided by a limited conception of what is good for people: 'glorious worldly achievements which will be recognized in history' (ibid.: 165). It was only later that political theorists were bemused by such questions as the extent to which ends can justify means, or whether individuals have rights that may not be infringed for the good of the state.

The present situation in the study of organizational politics is rather similar to the study of the politics of nation-states in Machiavelli's time. Antony Jay wrote a book titled *Management and Machiavelli*, in which he noted that 'Machiavelli . . . is in fact bursting with urgent advice and acute observations for top management of the great private and public corporations all over the world' (Jay 1967: chap. 1), and approaches today do not seem so very different from when Jay wrote. Machiavelli's great achievement was to articulate some of the causal relationships that are important in political life, and Jay has pointed out how some of them are as significant for modern corporate political life as they were for the politics of Italian city-states. For us, however, it may be a concern that normative inferences that have been drawn by theorists about organizational politics have often been as straightforward and uninhibited as Machiavelli's.[1] Much less attention has been given to normative issues in organizational politics than to normative issues in the politics of the nation-state since Machiavelli's time. Medieval Christian theorists had tried to articulate principles of political actions and political arrangements that were systematic and consistent with their theology, but in doing so they neglected empirical detail. Machiavelli focused on the empirical detail but pushed aside ethical reservations or dilemmas. Subsequent theorists restored some balance in studying the politics of nation-states, but theorists have only recently started to consider ethical dilemmas in the politics of organizations.

On the surface, there seems to be no reason why we should not approach ethical issues about organizational politics along similar lines to ethical issues in the politics of nation-states. One requirement of a good theory is that it will help us to see similarities and relationships between processes that may on the surface seem different, or at least will not mask such similarities and relationships. A satisfactory approach to organizational politics would leave it open to us to see similarities and relationships with other political processes, and in particular, for our purposes, any ethical similarities or differences.

There is plenty of scope to consider similarities and differences of organizational politics and other politics. Jay's book is a quite explicit effort to show the similarities between the politics of corporate organizations and the politics of nation-states. Political anthropologists have examined the political processes in tribes, villages and other small communities, which show similarities in their political processes both to modern western organizations and to traditional monarchies or feudal empires. Gluckman says of such communities that 'the unifying force of ritual symbols is most important' (1965: xxii), just as other writers have emphasized the importance of such things in modern organizations (e.g. Deal and Kennedy 1988). Gluckman notes the interaction between politics and means of production, the way in which organizational structures can be in conflict with a principle of government, and how 'palace intrigues become more isolated from the main mass of people' (1965: xxii). Any of these might equally well be a possibility worth considering in corporate politics or the politics of nation-states. The sorts of factors that may figure in causal explanations may be similar in the different cases, and if they are, then that casts light on them all.

This is not to suggest that there are no differences amongst political processes in different contexts. For example, background culture and belief can play an important part in people's behaviour, and in their political activities. Gluckman notes that in the communities of which he is writing,

> Not all disturbances of social relations arise from open breaches of rules of right conduct. A marked characteristic of tribal society is that 'natural' misfortunes are ascribed to the evil wishes of witches or sorcerers, to the anger of spirits affronted by neglect of themselves or of the sufferer's obligations towards kin, to breaches of taboo and omission of ritual, and to rightful curses by appropriate persons. (1965: xxiii)

While 'rightful curses by appropriate persons' may often play a part in modern western organizational politics, probably there is less belief in witches, sorcerers or spirits. (Perhaps it has been replaced by belief in the gurus and wizards of information technology and their associated hardware or software gremlins.)

There may be these and other differences amongst political processes in different contexts, but the key point is that we are ill advised to adopt any approach to organizational politics that would hinder us from observing similarities or differences relative to other forms of politics. It is potentially useful to accept with Miller that 'There is politics in the board room, in the inter-departmental conference, in the school staff meeting, and in the annual conference of the dog-lovers' association' (Miller 1962: 15). If we do, we are better placed to develop our theoretical understanding of such processes. We can hope to see just how far background beliefs and culture affect such processes, and how much they are affected by the type of community or association in which they occur. So far as ethical issues are concerned, we may consider how far the approaches we take to such issues in other politics may be appropriate also in organizational politics.

Definition and ethics
It would be implausible to suggest that the politics of nation-states is inherently unethical. It would be widely accepted that such politics contains scope for good action as well as bad, and biographies of political leaders often show them to embody virtues as well as faults, including virtues that they can be seen to have exercised in politics (see e.g. examples cited in Provis 2004: 65, 217). On the other hand, a good deal of literature still contains the suggestion that organizational politics is inherently unethical. This provides one of the biggest obstacles to constructive discussion of ethical issues in organizational politics. Drory and Romm (1990) found definitions that refer to outcomes that are 'self-serving' and 'against the organization', and which had a variety of other adverse connotations. Cropanzano et al. say that we use the term 'organizational politics' to refer to attempts to gain influence that are 'covert, crafty, and behind the scenes' (1995: 17). Their statement is prompted by definitions of organizational politics found in various authors, where 'the idea that these behaviors are designed to promote or protect one's own self-interests is continually noted' (p. 7).

This conception of organizational politics has some clear shortcomings. It can lead to circularity, for example. When Kacmar and Baron say by way of definition that 'organizational politics involves actions by individuals which are directed toward the goal of furthering their own self-interests without regard for the well-being of others or their organization' (1999: 4), then it is hardly surprising that later they find that 'politics appears to be a negative force in organizations. That is, many of the consequences of organizational politics are negative for the individual and the organization' (p. 21). The approach also seems unduly restrictive. If we build into our definition of organizational politics that it is 'covert and crafty', then consider the situation where a boss says quite openly, 'Do this, or I'll fire you!' The definition excludes it from being considered 'organizational politics'.

More generally, such approaches to definition have two defects. One is that they are problematic as a basis for analysing the dynamics of organizational politics. If organizational politics must by definition be self-interested, then we are impeded from seeing similarities and differences amongst pieces of behaviour that embody varying degrees of self-interest. For a manager to require his own signature on all outgoing correspondence may be a self-interested effort at maintaining his own position, or it may be an attempt to counteract the unprincipled behaviour of an underling. In either case, it is a way of managing power, and its dynamics may be similar. Certainly, there may also be differences. His intentions and motives will affect our explanations and predictions, and to the extent that they are accurately discerned by others around him they may respond differently and the whole course of events may be different. But there will be a whole series of possibilities, affected in part by the whole range of motives and intentions he may have. If we wish to understand the dynamics of such processes, we are not assisted by an attempt to quarantine just a few of them as 'organizational politics'. The same problem occurs if we include a requirement like 'covert and crafty' in a definition: there is a wide range of possibilities about how covert or open, how crafty or straightforward, actions are, and to draw an arbitrary line does us no good as students or theorists of organizational processes.

The second general defect of such definitions is that they obscure genuine ethical dilemmas and problems. Labels such as 'self-interested' or 'covert and crafty' suggest that it is straightforward to discern what is ethical. Those phrases have clear negative overtones, and suggest that it is unproblematic what ethical stance to adopt toward episodes of organizational politics. In fact, though, there are many cases where things are not so simple.

One sort of example that has become well known is where an individual in an organization sees a technical or moral problem about a decision or line of conduct that has become part of official organizational policy. In his extended study of several US corporations, Robert Jackall recounts a number of cases of political conflict within organizations. One is that of 'Joe Wilson', an engineer who was eventually fired after his increasingly forceful opposition to the ways his organization was going about clean-up after the 1979 Three Mile Island nuclear accident (Jackall 1988: 112–19). Wilson's dilemma was at least partly how to act in a way that he could accept as ethical where there were conflicts between organizational decisions and what he took to be wider values, as well as conflicts between obligations he had to his own staff and obligations to other managers in the organization. Other managers in the organization felt that Wilson's perceptions and priorities were awry. One of the points of conflict with other managers was their view that

> Authority has the prerogative to resolve technical disputes. Whether Wilson liked it or not, Bechtel had won the power struggle and they had the right, that is the power, to call the shots on the cleanup. (Jackall 1988: 118)

In other words, the issue was the scope of legitimate authority, and an individual's right to dissent. It is an ethical issue in organizational politics that has close analogies in the politics of nation-states. Such matters have preoccupied political theorists in other contexts from the Lutheran Reformation, through the English Civil War and the American War of Independence to the Campaign for Nuclear Disarmament and the Vietnam Moratorium Campaign.

Here we see an example of a moral issue that may often be important in discussions of organizational politics (and one which often comes to prominence in cases of whistleblowing, for example), but one which can be ruled out of court by some definitions of organizational politics. Just as some definitions may build in ideas of self-interest, or of covert, crafty behaviour, a related approach is to build into the definition the idea that organizational politics is illegitimate. Mintzberg says that politics refers to individual or group behavior that is informal, ostensibly parochial, typically divisive, and above all, in the technical sense, illegitimate – sanctioned neither by formal authority, accepted ideology, nor certified expertise. (1983: 172)

Mintzberg's position has been questioned elsewhere (see e.g. Vigoda 2003: 23–5). However, Vigoda notes that such an approach 'characterizes most researchers' attitudes' (ibid.: 19). It is worth special attention because of what it implies as an attitude to the ethics of organizational politics. If organizational politics is by definition illegitimate, then by definition there is no scope in discussions of organizational politics for considering ethical questions about when dissent from formal authority may be morally right and proper. Referring to 'accepted' ideology begs the question: accepted by whom? It is circular to say: 'by legitimate authorities'. Similarly for 'certified' expertise: certified by whom? These are exactly the sorts of questions that theorists of state authority have grappled with for many years.

Like some of the other definitions, the idea that politics in an organization is necessarily illegitimate is conceptually a very difficult one to sustain. What about lobbying before a meeting? It may not be until a decision is taken at the meeting that there is any policy or behaviour that is 'sanctioned' on a particular matter. Another problem with such a restriction occurs when people in an organization take opposed courses; we would sometimes have to say that one side was but the other was not engaged in organizational politics. In Wilson's case, he and his opponents in the organization took different points of view and pursued opposed courses of action. It is hard to see how we could say that his opponents' actions were organizational politics while his own were not, or vice versa: they were interacting with one another in the same environment, actions on each side responding to the others.

Legitimacy is one example where an issue about the politics of nation-states carries over to the politics of organizations. Another example is the problem that has recently concerned theorists of politics and the ethics of politics under the title of the 'dirty hands' problem: the idea that 'the vocation of politics somehow rightly requires its practitioners to violate important moral standards which prevail outside politics' (Coady 1991: 373). That idea is clearly reminiscent of Machiavelli, and we have already noted that Machiavelli's idea of what is good for people is echoed by some modern management writers. The idea that the vocation of politics requires practitioners to get their hands dirty is echoed by the idea that the vocation of management does so also, when managers have to engage in organizational politics.[2] Jackall notes the view of Joe Wilson's ex-colleagues that 'Sunday school ethics – the public espousal of lofty principles – do not help managers cut the sometimes unpleasant deals necessary to make the world work' (1988: 118). The suggestion has been made more formally that 'managers, consultants, and organizational interventionists may have to adopt behaviours towards others which initially could be distasteful to them, but may in the long term prove to be an effective approach to achieving their goals' (Kakabadse and Parker 1984: 101; attributing the suggestion to Pettigrew 1975 and Schein 1977). Like the issue of legitimacy, questions about whether otherwise culpable actions can be acceptable because of the political context in which they occur are questions that may be salient in organizational as in other politics. There can be differences that affect the answers, but the questions are discernibly similar.

Unitarism, pluralism and definition

Overall, we should not at the outset assume too much about the problems, but we should avoid any definitions that tend to foreclose options about the sorts of issues that we may wish to address. Thus, we do not want to assume that all of the activities to be considered are self-interested, or covert and crafty, or illegitimate, because including those ideas in definitions may obscure things that are important. For example, it may obscure the fact that actions may figure in precisely similar ways in the political dynamics of organizations, but some of them be ethically questionable because of the motives with which they are performed, while the others are ethically quite proper.

We also want to avoid any assumption that the problems are primarily issues about efficiency or organizational effectiveness. There is a tendency by at least some theorists to make that assumption, rather like Machiavelli's assumption that worldly success is the criterion of value. Kacmar and Baron introduce their survey of literature about organizational politics with the comment that 'Virtually all human resources decisions (e.g., promotions, hiring) have the potential to be impacted by political actions and agendas. . . . When this occurs, the best decisions are not always made' (1999: 1). Here is at least some orientation toward a 'unitary' conception of organizations: the idea that in general an organization can be conceived of as a harmonious environment, with members united by common goals and values.[3] In such an environment, political activity can well seem aberrant and dysfunctional.

Such a unitary view of organizations has been common, often reflected in approaches to organizations that treat them as machines that ought to be made to function smoothly and effectively to produce good-quality outputs at low cost and with little stress for the individuals who comprise them. The organizational machine will not function well if there are worn components, grit in the bearings, or parts out of alignment. Thus Frederick Taylor's idea of 'scientific management' (Taylor 1911) is sometimes taken as a good approach to organizations, to ensure that their machinery is as well designed as possible to process raw materials and turn them into goods and services.

Some academic writers seem to have accepted that ostensible organizational aims are a criterion of what should be accepted, even where behaviour seems ethically questionable: Schein suggested that in cases of information distortion and other covert means of influence, 'what needs to be investigated is whether the powerholder's intent is in line with organizational concerns' (1977: 67).[4] To many of us, it may seem problematic to make organizational concerns such a predominant criterion for ethical assessment. In a market economy, it may be common to accept that organizations can determine what their own concerns are, and that forces of competition will then rule out any that are problematic. However, in most countries there is a wide variety of organizational aims that are ruled out not by market forces but by law, aims that range from terrorism to paedophilia, and it seems reasonable to suggest that organizational aims or concerns must remain ethically contestable, even if we can expect immediate consensus that many are good and proper.

If so, we cannot rely on consistency with organizational aims to provide any straightforward or simple touchstone for whether actions of organizational politics are ethical or unethical. In many areas, we would often accept that the ends of action are relevant to ethical appraisal, and they may be so in organizational politics as much as elsewhere, but consistency with organizational aims cannot determine whether actions are ethical. The aims themselves may be ethically questionable, and even where they are unproblematic, unethical means might be used to achieve them, just as unethical actions may be used to achieve the proper aims of nation-states.

It is widely accepted that there is scope for ethical appraisal of aims of nation-states, and of the means they use to achieve them: editorial writers and media commentators invite their audiences to conduct such appraisal on a regular basis. Why would academic writers suggest that the aims of organizations or organizational power holders are a criterion by which to determine whether actions are ethical? Perhaps they might be influenced by the popularity of the unitary view of organizations with managers who seek compliance and consensus among their subordinates. The popularity of that approach with managers may remind us of similar attitudes that have been shown by some national leaders: for example, it has been written of one leader that 'the questioning of his assumptions or of his facts rattled him and threw him out of his stride . . . The introduction of intellectual processes of criticism and analysis marked the intrusion of hostile elements which disturbed the exercise of this power' (Bullock 1962: 372–3). There may be few organizational leaders who would go so far as Hitler in their suppression of dissent, but the unitary view of organizations can still be favoured because it functions to bolster the authority of incumbent leaders, and it is then associated with the idea that political activity within an organization is necessarily dysfunctional, since it is inherently at odds with harmony and consensus. The fact that such ideas are common in practice emerges in the comment made by Glazer and Glazer that

> Several people in our study regretfully learned that their professional assessment sometimes had to be tempered or even submerged because opposition was not welcome in organizations largely characterized by hierarchy and the absence of a democratic culture. Their superiors had a tendency to define dissent as insubordination and disobedience as rebellion. (1989: 71)

In the analogous politics of nation-states, such a position would be tantamount to totalitarianism.[5] Most of us would question such intolerance of dissent in civil society, and so the question inevitably arises why it is not to be questioned also in organizations.

The 'unitary' conception of organizations has been given other names, such as the 'rationalist' perspective. Bradshaw-Camball and Murray say that this 'simplifies and deemphasizes the structural dimension of politics by assuming that top management holds power based primarily on its legitimate and formal organizational authority and also, to some extent, on its expertise' (1991: 381). Like Alan Fox, they contrast this with other perspectives such as the 'pluralist' perspective, which acknowledges interest group conflict as inevitable and acceptable within organizations (Bradshaw-Camball and Murray 1991: 381; Fox 1974: 255–70; see also Provis 1996: 480–83; and Buchanan and Badham 1999: 46, 167–70).

The pluralist view that organizations are always a venue for interest group conflict is itself an echo of the approach to political theory that sees wider society as an arena for contestation among interest groups. In the wider context, that view underpins the constitutional structures and political arrangements of many modern liberal democracies. In recent times, the general political theory of liberal pluralism has been questioned from a variety of directions, but generally in ways that continue to accept the necessity and importance of diverse opinions being respected in the community (see e.g. Offe 1985; Phillips 1993). If we agree that both societies and organizations ought to accept diversity of opinion, it is difficult to see how we can avoid accepting also that political activity is to be accepted and respected. Bernard Crick makes the point in his book *In Defence of Politics* that it has been in systems of tyranny and oppression that the term 'political activity' has most often been used pejoratively (e.g. Crick 1964: 19; see also Crick 1967). Tyranny and oppression can have difficulty with diversity of opinions and views because respecting people's opinions seems to involve not only allowing them to hold those opinions, but also the political activity of putting the opinions to others and seeking agreement, contrary to the dominant regime.

Perhaps putting one's opinions to others and seeking agreement does not sound like the type of thing often connoted by 'politics', certainly not by 'organizational politics'. Here, again, however, we come to issues about satisfactory definition. The connotations of terms often have to be ignored in order to give useful definitions of them. 'Flower' connotes something colourful and attractive, but plants may have flowers that are drab and ugly. 'Dinosaur' has the connotation of something large and unwieldy, but some dinosaurs were small and agile. And so on. Connotations of terms are associated with common perceptions and preconceptions, which may be incomplete or influenced by stereotypes. Various studies have examined perceptions and attitudes about organizational politics (e.g. Kacmar and Ferris 1991; Ralston et al. 1994), but care needs to be taken in assessing their implications. Learning about people's perceptions and attitudes towards flowers may be useful and informative for some purposes, but it may be possible to learn more about flowers by studying them directly.[6]

The case of organizational politics is different from that of flowers or dinosaurs to the extent that a human social activity like organizational politics will be affected by the perceptions and expectations of the people who participate in it. What people believe is normal and acceptable has a major influence on what they do and what they accept from others as 'legitimate' behaviour.[7] But this is not to go so far as the suggestion that 'organizational politics is a subjective perception, not necessarily an objective reality' (Ferris et al. 1993: 86). If we accept that there is such a thing as political behaviour in general, we can expect it to occur in organizations. It is likely to be more open in pluralist organizations than in unitarist ones. In pluralist organizations, it may then be easier to scrutinize and easier to evaluate different political tactics as ethical or unethical. In unitarist organizations, it may be forced underground, harder to scrutinize, and more likely to be 'covert, crafty and behind the scenes'.

Because in unitarist organizations political activity is likely to be condemned as illegitimate, it follows that identifying some behaviour there as a piece of organizational politics is likely to delegitimize it, weakening support for those who do it and even rendering them liable to official sanction. It further follows, then, that in such a context to identify something as a piece of organizational politics can itself be a political tactic.[8] Because the distinction between unitarist and pluralist organizations is not a perfectly clear and precise one, but in some respects a matter of degree, it will also be a matter of degree to what extent politics is openly accepted. This can result in complexity of political processes themselves, as actors assess what is and is not acceptable, and how it may be labelled. Buchanan and Badham devote a chapter to 'the terminology game' (1999: chap. 2). They note a variety of ways in which the terms used to describe organizational politics or to recommend approaches to it may serve political purposes or embody covert ethical judgments, and suggest that 'the essence of political behaviour thus lies . . . in the ways in which it is represented by the players in the game' (p. 70).

Definition and contestation

The different attitudes pluralists and unitarists have towards organizational politics may reflect the fact that 'organizational politics', like 'politics' in general, is an 'essentially contested concept' (see Connolly 1993: chap. 1). The implication may be that we cannot hope to give a precise definition that will gain universal acceptance. All we can do is try to make reasonably clear the general area of discussion. Above, it has been implied that organizational politics is a variety of politics more generally understood, albeit perhaps a variety that involves more personal relationships than the phenomena that have been the focus of political theorists since Machiavelli. It has been suggested further that putting one's views to others to elicit agreement is one example, and some other examples have been mentioned. Then it may suffice to conceive of organizational politics as political activity within organizations, so that the issue of definition is at least pushed back to the wider one of how to define politics in general.

We can assume that political activity typically involves attempts to influence others, as recognized by many definitions of organizational politics (Vigoda 2003: 31), that it has to do with power relationships (which is to some extent a corollary of the fact that it involves attempts to influence others), also recognized by a number of definitions of organizational politics, and that often it has to do with the distribution of resources. To assume these characteristics would achieve wide although not universal consensus. They are also consistent with the idea Aristotle had of politics when at the outset of the *Nicomachean Ethics* he characterizes it as the 'master-craft' (1934: 5, Book I, chap. ii). This is a more exalted view of politics than the idea that it is necessarily 'covert, crafty, and behind the scenes', or that it necessarily aims to further people's self-interest regardless of others. It accepts that it can be 'an acceptable, common and socially functional phenomenon' (Vigoda 2003: 10).

Nevertheless, some problems still remain as the result of the contestability of specific terms and concepts in political processes. Even if we have some broad agreement on the overall scope of discussion, similar problems come up as we move to more detail. In broad terms, we may agree with Robert Solomon that 'the ideal is thus not to eliminate politics but to democratize and civilize our power relationships, to avoid jungle and battlefield metaphors and promote a culture in which politics is mutually supportive instead of antagonistic and destructively competitive' (Solomon 1992: 131). We know there are difficulties of implementation in doing that: even when we know what to do, problems can arise in doing it, individual problems like weakness of will or communal problems like mistrust and suspicion. But there are also difficulties in becoming clear about what to do, before we even start implementation. What, in practice, is it for politics to be mutually supportive? What, in concrete organizational terms, are democratic and civilized power relationships? Even here there are difficulties with terms and definitions. Cavanagh et al. noted the need to distinguish between forms of organizational politics that are ethically acceptable and others that are not, and suggested that the latter may include 'such Machiavellian techniques as "situational manipulation," "dirty tricks," and "backstabbing."' (1981: 364). Well, fine, but what tricks are dirty? What is the difference between 'situational manipulation' and 'organizing'? If I report your adverse comments to the boss, is that backstabbing? What if I report threats you have made, threats perhaps against me, as well as others? We may sometimes have clear intuitions when we are confronted with these in practice, but if we are trying to clarify underlying principles about ethics and organizational politics then it can hinder us if we build ethical presuppositions into the terms we use to refer to tactics and strategies.

Thus we can expect that the sorts of examples of organizational politics that may be useful at this point will be ones that do not seem in their very description to carry over-tones of moral condemnation or approbation. In their survey, Kacmar and Baron report a number of examples other authors have identified that seem to satisfy that requirement. Thus, for instance, Allen and colleagues found that those most often mentioned by their respondents were: 'attacking or blaming others', 'selective use of information', 'impres-sion management or image building', 'generating support for ideas', 'praising others and ingratiating', 'building powerful coalitions and strong allies', 'associating with influential others' and 'creating obligations and using reciprocity' (Kacmar and Baron 1999: 8). By and large, these do not seem to have strong in-built presuppositions of ethical praise or blame. 'Attacking or blaming others' might seem to be something we generally ought to avoid, but it would be hard to suggest that blaming others is necessarily wrong: it seems as though that may depend on how, when and for what purpose it is done. 'Selective use of information' is hardly a description of something that is unethical in itself: selecting the information that is relevant and appropriate for a particular purpose is often a key part of work, including managerial work. Again, the issue is how and for what purpose. It seems clear that impression management is at least not straightforwardly unethical (see Moberg 1989; Provis 2004: chaps 8–10). If it may seem that impression management has some connotation of unethical deceit or manipulation, 'generating support for ideas', on the other hand, appears to have a quite positive air: it is, after all, what academics and authors often make their primary task.

Overall, the sorts of tactics and strategies in the list are enough to show that there is room for serious discussion about what is ethical and what is not. Some of the difficulties we need to overcome emerge clearly in regard to the strategy of 'creating obligations and using reciprocity'. This builds on strategies of influence that have become well known in social psychology:

> A few years ago, a university professor tried a little experiment. He sent Christmas cards to a sample of perfect strangers. Although he expected some reaction, the response he received was amazing – holiday cards addressed to him came pouring back from people who had never met nor heard of him. The great majority of those who returned cards never inquired into the iden-tity of the unknown professor. They received his holiday greeting card, *click*, and *whirr*, they automatically sent cards in return . . .
>
> While small in scope, this study shows the action of one of the most potent of the weapons of influence around us – the rule of reciprocation. The rule says that we should try to repay, in kind, what another person has provided for us . . . By virtue of the reciprocity rule, then, we are *oblig-ated* to the future repayment of favors, gifts, invitations, and the like. (Cialdini 1993: 19–20; citing Kunz and Woolcott 1976, italics in original)[9]

It is important that, at least on some occasions, reciprocity grounds genuine obligations, and is not just a mechanism of influence. On the other hand, it has limitations in that respect. Cialdini notes that sometimes people who want to influence others can trade on the mechanism of reciprocity (for instance, by the use of 'free samples'). In practice, what we want to say about the ethics of influencing people through reciprocity may again depend on the circumstances and manner in which the mechanism is used, but our atti-tude towards it can be embodied in terms we use. In one case, we may commend someone for accepting some ties of reciprocal obligation by referring to the person's 'loyalty' to another. In another case we may condemn it, by referring to 'nepotism' when someone's appointment to a position is fulfilling an obligation or trying to create one.

Essentially the same reciprocity mechanism has been referred to as one person 'squaring' another. Miller quotes F.M. Cornford's amusing account of this process, where among other things 'we shall emphasize the fact that there is *no connexion* whatever between my supporting your Job and your supporting mine. This absence of connexion is the essential feature of Squaring' (Miller 1962: 120, quoting F.M. Cornford's *Microcosmographia Academica*). The 'absence' is of course an ostensible but not a genuine absence. Here, as in much other organizational politics, some arrangements are made by 'a nod and a wink', using tacit understandings, paralanguage such as tone of voice or timing of utterance, and other mechanisms that leave no clear, reportable trace. Such concealment of the relationship between one action and another may boost organizational politics' reputation for being 'covert' or 'crafty'.

At the same time, that example also brings us to a complexity in the discussion of organizational politics which reflects similar complexity in politics generally (see Connolly 1993). It is sometimes very hard to discern people's real intentions and motives, and hard to determine whether actions are motivated by considerations like reciprocation of favours or authentic concern for common goals. An action by one manager that benefits another might be reciprocation of a favour, but it might also be justified by organizational purposes. If a manager appoints a protégé to a position, that might show favouritism, or it might show accurate perception of merit. That sort of ambiguity is common. It allows room for political tactics that consist of depicting actions in one way rather than another, and makes ethical appraisal of particular actions especially difficult.

Interpretation and ethical assessment
As with so many other issues, in organizational politics and elsewhere, the fact that there are vague or ambiguous cases does not imply that there are no clear or well-defined cases. Nevertheless, even though in many cases there is some well-defined reality behind possible interpretations of people's motives and intentions, the frequent difficulty of identifying it has wide ramifications. As we have seen, just as it is difficult to give an uncontentious definition of organizational politics, so it may be difficult to give a comprehensive list of tactics or strategies of organizational politics, because whether or not something is a political tactic may be inherently contestable, and the contestation of the issue may itself be part of the political process. Such contestation and contestability can pose great problems for ethical analysis and appraisal in organizational politics.

It is not only with such *prima facie* questionable tactics like 'attacking or blaming others', 'selective use of information' and the like, that this point arises. Fairholm takes 'developing others' and 'training and orienting others' both to be strategies of organizational politics (1993: chap. 8). He says that they 'are the most effective tactics used with subordinates to get them to behave in desired ways' (p. 102). Clearly, though, they are often necessary and important activities that would be commended, and not categorized as organizational politics at all. They *may* be so categorized because they affect the distribution of power within the organization. A manager who trains and develops others increases their skill and experience, but also enables them to increase their power. The manager's own power may be enhanced if they subsequently display loyalty in exchange for the training and development they have received. Others might accuse the manager of 'empire-building' (Mintzberg 1983: 188). And so it might be. But it might also be aimed at the good of the organization, or aimed at the good of the subordinates. It might even be all three.[10]

In a similar way, almost any activity within an organization might be a tactic of organizational politics, given certain circumstances and participants' motives. Increasing the pay of an individual or group, purchasing new technology, allocating an order to one supplier rather than another; the list is endless. In this context just as elsewhere there will be a spectrum for the interpretation of events that ranges from cynicism at one end through realism to naïveté at the other. As elsewhere, one's own interpretation of some particular set of events will be affected both by one's current personal situation relative to the events, and by one's generally charitable or suspicious inclinations. Once more, however, that does not entail that all interpretations are equally well grounded. That things' appearance is affected by the colour of one's spectacles does not entail that there are no optimal viewing conditions or that one can see things however one wishes.

However, we have also noted that people's perceptions of the facts may be a causally important part of the facts. What is politically possible or necessary will often be determined by people's perceptions or expectations, but that does not mean that it is not really possible or necessary. The fact that people would perceive an appointment to be an act of nepotism might mean that it would be received with so much resentment that it is never made. It is not whether it is an act of nepotism that stops it being made, but the fact that it would be perceived so. But assuming that the resentment would be so great, it really is impossible, even though its impossibility is the result of people's perceptions.

This is not unique to organizational politics. It is a characteristic of politics in general. A political leader may appoint a member of a rival faction to a position in order to be seen by the faction as ready to compromise on other matters, or may refrain from doing so for fear of anger from members of the leader's own faction. Support for a particular bill, approval of some measure, alliance with some group – all might be effected or avoided in part because of the way the action would be perceived and the motives that would be seen to lie behind it, regardless of the action's inherent merits. Those perceptions could make passage of the bill inevitable or impossible, the measure necessary or impracticable, the alliance unavoidable or unworkable, depending on the circumstances. That is sometimes the very thrust of the phrase 'politically impossible'. We have already noted cases where effects on people's perceptions can be important for political strategies and tactics. Unitarists may contend that what they are doing is not 'political', because it is just part of their organizational role (as though prime ministers might say that what they do is not 'politics', but 'prime ministering'). Not only in unitarist organizations, but in very many contexts, political action will only be effective if it is not noticed as such. No analysis of such situations is straightforward or easy, and that goes for ethical analysis, in organizational politics and other politics. At worst, for example, it can be hypocrisy or cowardice to accept something as necessary or impossible just because of people's widespread perceptions: sometimes, the ethical thing to do may be to embark on the impossible, for the sake of the future or one's own integrity.

How do we decide what is the ethical thing to do, in these complex and contestable situations?

We might turn to widely accepted approaches to ethics like utilitarian theory, theories based on human rights, or theories of justice like the one put forward so persuasively by John Rawls in *A Theory of Justice* (1972). Unfortunately, though, such theories are at odds with one another at significant points. We cannot simply accept any one of them as a full account that will deal satisfactorily with all the instances that confront us.

On the other hand, it can also be problematic to provide an account of the ethics of organizational politics that does not have a systematic underlying basis. A number of authors give accounts that provide plausible comments and worthwhile insights into such processes, but often those comments rest on direct and unconnected moral intuition, or resort to pointing out the imprudence or ineffectiveness of some arguably unethical behaviour. The absence of a systematic account of why the behaviour is unethical once again leaves the way open for disagreement, this time not so much because claims rest on some general theory as because they can seem like mere opinion.

We might try to proceed by a method of 'reflective equilibrium' (Rawls 1972: 20–21), an iterative comparison of our ethical theory and our considered ethical judgments, aspiring to reconcile the two by gradual adjustments. Or we might fall back on the fact that agents in organizational politics characteristically share commitments at least to some norms and values.[11] Williams shows how these approaches might be combined, by considering the reflective equilibrium that may be reached by individuals who 'are irreversibly committed to living closely together in one society' (1985: 99).

Nevertheless, that leaves open the question of how to proceed in concrete terms, and all that can be done here is to suggest a way that may be fruitful. It may be possible to identify some cases where it seems as though there may be difficulty in making an ethical choice, and considering what principles may be relevant. It is possible that various considerations may come into play in different circumstances. For example, it is likely that in some situations the good or harm that may accrue from an action will be very salient. In other circumstances, different considerations may be salient, such as the extent to which some proposal would be fair to all parties, the extent to which others have consented to some course of action, or the extent to which some behaviour is inconsistent with expectations we have induced in them.[12]

If we proceed in this way, then we need to avoid some of the traps we have noted already. We may identify some situation in concrete terms as ethically culpable, on any terms. For example, deliberately to spread false rumours about someone is unethical, and we can probably identify several reasons why. But what of something like 'backstabbing'? The problem with this is that the very term is unclear: it is more a term of rhetoric than a useful term to identify a piece of behaviour. We might identify quite different sorts of things as 'backstabbing': on the one hand, perhaps, acting contrary to expectations we have induced in someone; on the other hand, going to a third party to complain about someone, whatever their expectations may be. In our ethical analysis we need to be alert for the ambiguity or vagueness of many terms, which leaves the way open for contrary interpretations and conflicting ethical appraisals.

We can also see some of the sorts of cases that need to be considered, which are analogous to cases that arise in the politics of nation-states. One example is the issue of legitimacy: to what extent do requirements of the state or the organization have legitimate moral force? Another is the problem of dirty hands: to what extent can the requirements of political life in the organization or the state demand that we sacrifice principles of morality?

It may be possible to give analyses of these cases in terms of some wider, more general principles, such as an ethical requirement to let others make responsible decisions, to avoid bad consequences, to be fair, and so on. If this approach is correct, there are a few such principles that do not constitute a general ethical theory, but which do provide a more systematic account of what is ethical than relying on separate, relatively disconnected judgments in different cases. However, the extent to which such an approach may be successful can only be seen by trying to implement it in detail (Provis 2004 makes some efforts in that direction).

Of course, there are some other sorts of ethical issues, such as the important question of how to support and encourage ethical behaviour. If a manager threatens subordinates with dismissal unless they support some personal aim of the manager's, that may be unjust, infringe their rights, and be against the long-term interests of the organization and its stakeholders. That sort of case may be a hard one to deal with in practice if the manager has sufficient power, but it is not hard to deal with in terms of ethical appraisal: it is straightforwardly wrong, and that is all there is to it. The practical problem of how to deal with that and other unethical behaviour in organizations is a significant one, and one to which we ought to devote both intellectual and other resources (two books that attempt to deal with some such issues are Treviño and Nelson 1995 and Nielsen 1996). However, it is not the only sort of question that is important. There are at least some cases where there are significant questions about what actually is ethical. It is that sort of question that I have primarily been referring to, and which I believe is worth substantial attention, both for practical and for theoretical reasons. The central theme of this chapter is that the ethical issues of organizational politics are complex and often do not have simple answers, but are important enough to merit careful attention, both for theorists and participants.

Conclusion
Martin Buber begins *I and Thou* by saying:

> Man's world is manifold, and his attitudes are manifold. What is manifold is often frightening because it is not neat and simple. Men prefer to forget how many possibilities are open to them. They like to be told that there are two worlds and two ways. This is comforting because it is so tidy. Almost always one way turns out to be common and the other one is celebrated as superior. (1970: 9)

He might have been referring specifically to organizational politics. Sometimes the temptation to look for just two worlds and just two ways is overwhelming. But if we do so, then we may fall into error: we think that all cases are the same, and we don't bother to look at the detail; or we decide that ethics is too hard, and not to be bothered with, and we hand responsibility to superior authority; but ultimately, then, we abandon our status as moral subjects in a moral community.

'Man's world is manifold', and nowhere more so than in organizational politics. We have there to come to conclusions and make decisions in an environment that is fluid or ambiguous; we are subject to conflicting demands which all seem to have some legitimate call on us; we have to persuade others without misleading them; we have to convey information in ways that are honest but which guard us against chicanery and exploitation; we have to deal with expectations others have of us that we do not regard as reasonable. These and a variety of other problems are endemic to organizations and may give pause to anyone who wishes to act in an ethical way. They are political problems to the extent that they arise especially in situations where organization members compete for power and resources. None of the problems is confined to life in organizations, but there they may come to special prominence.

Then there is an all-too-understandable temptation to over-simplify, to look for simple rules or standard processes or definitions that remove the problems. But there is an increasing acceptance that in management generally there are shortcomings to rule-based approaches (see e.g. Petersen 2002), and that the challenges confronting us there often require 'moral imagination' (see e.g. Werhane 1999). Nowhere is this more so than in organizational politics. We can benefit from seeing similarities among situations, so long as we do not ignore the differences. We can benefit from seeing the sorts of principles that may help us identify morally relevant differences among situations. We can approach organizations as moral communities and not just as machines for production. But ultimately we shall have to accept responsibility for judgment and action in the situations that confront us, in all their manifold complexity. We ought not try to put that responsibility aside by over-simplification or by definition or by reliance on the organization as a source of moral authority.[13]

Notes

1. See, for example, Pfeffer (1992, pp. 7–8), where he emphasizes the importance of individuals understanding and using power if they are to gain success for themselves and their organizations.
2. The point is reflected in the title of McCalman's article (2001).
3. Alan Fox most clearly identified this 'unitary' conception of organizations and contrasted it with alternatives: in particular see Fox (1974, pp. 249–50).
4. Cf. Drory and Romm (1990, p. 1133), who draw attention to how much 'the goal orientation of the firm' has tended to predominate over other considerations in much theorizing. This idea emerges in a number of ways, including even the idea that effects on 'employee performance' are the primary reason for study of organizational politics.
5. 'A form of government that permits no rival loyalties or parties': *Concise Oxford Dictionary*, 6th edn.
6. Cf. Vigoda (2003), who comments in his Preface that all of his studies reported in that volume 'are predicated on the belief that actual organizational politics substantially differ from perceived organizational politics' (p. xi).
7. As can perhaps be seen most vividly in Milgram's well-known studies: see Milgram (1974); on the general point see also Provis (2004, pp. 43–7), and references given there.
8. Cf. Buchanan and Badham (1999, p. 102): 'Every change process requires the "management of meaning", and the delegitimation of opponents and opposing arrangements.'
9. The extent to which reciprocity produces genuine obligations is discussed in Barry (1980). See also Aristotle (1934, Book V, chap. iv, p. 279).
10. It is not uncommon for actions to have more than one aim. Sometimes, then, there are difficulties in ethical evaluation: see, for example, Davis (1984).
11. Bailey says of political competition that 'the restraint upon manoeuvre which distinguishes a competition from a fight entails that the contestants have some values in common' (1969, p. 21).
12. An approach somewhat like this is suggested by Velasquez et al. (1983), but theirs differs from the suggestion made here in giving greater prominence to considerations that are salient in different ethical theories, rather than focusing on what considerations may be relevant in problematic cases, regardless of whether such considerations are highlighted in established ethical theories.
13. This chapter is based on Chapter 1 of Provis (2004). For assistance in revising it to be included in the present volume I thank Kate Leeson, Michael Pembroke, Eran Vigoda and Amos Drory.

References

Aristotle (1934). *Nicomachean ethics*. Translated by H. Rackham. Cambridge, MA: Harvard University Press.
Bacharach, S.B. and E.J. Lawler (1980). *Power and politics in organisations*. San Francisco, CA: Jossey-Bass.

Bailey, F.G. (1969). *Stratagems and spoils*. Oxford: Basil Blackwell.

Barry, B. (1980). Justice as reciprocity. In E. Kamenka and A.E.-S. Tay (eds), *Justice* (pp. 50–78). New York: St Martin's Press.

Benn, S.I. and R.S. Peters (1959). *Social principles and the democratic state*. London: George Allen & Unwin.

Bradshaw-Camball, P. and V.V. Murray (1991). Illusions and other games: A trifocal view of organizational politics. *Organization Science*, **2** (4), 379–97.

Buber, M. (1970). *I and thou*. Translated by W. Kaufmann. New York: Charles Scribner's Sons. First published in German in 1923.

Buchanan, D. and R. Badham (1999). *Power, politics, and organizational change*. London: Sage.

Bullock, A. (1962). *Hitler: A study in tyranny*. 2nd edn. Harmondsworth: Penguin.

Cavanagh, G.F., D.J. Moberg and M. Velasquez (1981). The ethics of organizational Politics. *Academy of Management Review*, **6** (3), 363–74.

Cialdini, R.B. (1993). *Influence: science and practice*. 3rd edn. New York: HarperCollins.

Coady, C.A.J. (1991). Politics and the problem of dirty hands. In P. Singer (ed.), *A companion to ethics* (pp. 373–83). Oxford: Blackwell.

Connolly, W.E. (1993). *The terms of political discourse*. 3rd edn. Oxford: Blackwell.

Crick, B. (1964). *In defence of politics*. rev. edn. Harmondsworth: Penguin. Originally published 1962.

Crick, B. (1967). Freedom as politics. In P. Laslett and W.G. Runciman (eds), *Philosophy, politics and society: Third series* (pp. 194–214). Oxford: Basil Blackwell.

Cropanzano, R.S., K.M. Kacmar and D.P. Bozeman (1995). The social setting of work organizations: Politics, justice and support. In R.S. Cropanzano and K.M. Kacmar (eds), *Organizational politics, justice, and support* (pp. 1–18). Westport, CT: Quorum Books.

Davis, N. (1984). The doctrine of double effect: Problems of interpretation. *Pacific Philosophical Quarterly*, **65** (2), 107–23.

Deal, T.E. and A.A. Kennedy (1988). *Corporate cultures: The rites and rituals of corporate life*. Harmondsworth: Penguin.

Drory, A. and T. Romm (1990). The definition of organizational politics: A review. *Human Relations*, **43** (11), 1133–54.

Fairholm, G.W. (1993). *Organizational power politics*. Westport, CT: Praeger.

Ferris, G.R., J.F. Brand, S. Brand, K.M. Rowland, D.C. Gilmore, T.R. King, K.M. Kacmar and C.A. Burton (1993). Politics and control in organizations. In *Advances in group processes* (Vol. 10, pp. 83–111). Greenwich, CT: JAI Press.

Fox, A. (1974). *Beyond contract: Work, power and trust relations*. London: Faber and Faber.

French, J.R.P. and B. Raven (1960). The bases of social power. In D. Cartwright and A. Zander (eds), *Group dynamics* (2nd edn, pp. 607–23). London: Tavistock Publications. Reprinted from D. Cartwright (ed.), *Studies in social power*, 1959.

Glazer, M.P. and P.M. Glazer (1989). *The whistleblowers*. New York: Basic Books.

Gluckman, M. (1965). *Politics, law and ritual in tribal society*. Oxford: Basil Blackwell.

Hampshire, S. (1989). *Innocence and experience*. London: Penguin.

Jackall, R. (1988). *Moral mazes*. New York: Oxford University Press.

Jay, A. (1967). *Management and Machiavelli*. London: Hodder & Stoughton.

Kacmar, K.M. and R.A. Baron (1999). Organizational politics: The state of the field, links to related processes, and an agenda for future research. In G.R. Ferris (ed.), *Research in personnel and human resources management* (Vol. 17, pp. 1–39). Stamford, CT: JAI Press.

Kacmar, K.M. and G.R. Ferris (1991). Perceptions of organizational politics scale (POPS): Development and construct validation. *Educational and Psychological Measurement*, **51**, 193–205.

Kakabadse, A. and C. Parker (1984). Towards a theory of political behaviour in organizations. In A. Kakabadse and C. Parker (eds), *Power, politics, and organisations: A behavioural science view* (pp. 87–108). Chichester: John Wiley & Sons Ltd.

Kunz, P.R. and M. Woolcott (1976). Season's greetings: From my status to yours. *Social Science Research*, **5**, 269–78.

Laing, R.D. (1971). *The politics of the family and other essays*. London: Tavistock.

McCalman, J. (2001). But I did it for the company! The ethics of organisational politics. *Reason in Practice: The Journal of Philosophy of Management*, **1** (3), 57–66.

Milgram, S. (1974). *Obedience to authority*. New York: Harper & Row.

Miller, J.D.B. (1962). *The nature of politics*. Harmondsworth: Penguin.

Mintzberg, H. (1983). *Power in and around organisations*. Englewood Cliffs, NJ: Prentice-Hall.

Moberg, D.J. (1989). The ethics of impression management. In R.A. Giacalone and P. Rosenfeld (eds), *Impression management in the organization* (pp. 171–87). Hillsdale, NJ: Lawrence Erlbaum.

Nielsen, R.P. (1996). *The politics of ethics*. New York: Oxford University Press.

Offe, C. (1985). *Disorganised capitalism*. Cambridge: Polity Press.

Petersen, V.C. (2002). *Beyond rules in society and business*. Cheltenham, UK and Northampton, MA: Edward Elgar.

Pettigrew, A.M. (1975). Towards a political theory of organisational intervention. *Human Relations*, **28** (3), 191–208.

Pfeffer, J. (1981). *Power in organizations* Boston, MA: Pitman.

Pfeffer, J. (1992). *Managing with power*. Boston, MA: Harvard Business School Press.

Phillips, A. (1993). *Democracy and difference*. Cambridge, UK: Polity Press.

Provis, C. (1996). Unitarism, pluralism, interests and values. *British Journal of Industrial Relations*, **34** (4), 473–95.

Provis, C. (2004). *Ethics and organisational politics*. Cheltenham, UK and Northampton, MA: Edward Elgar.

Ralston, D.A., R.A. Giacalone and R.H. Terpstra (1994). Ethical perceptions of organizational politics: A comparative evaluation of American and Hong Kong managers. *Journal of Business Ethics*, **13**, 989–99.

Rawls, J. (1972). *A theory of justice*. Oxford: Clarendon Press.

Schein, V.E. (1977). Individual power and political behaviour in organizations: An inadequately explored reality. *Academy of Management Review*, **2**, 64–72.

Solomon, R.C. (1992). *Ethics and excellence*. New York: Oxford University Press.

Taylor, F.W. (1911). *Scientific management*. New York: Harper.

Treviño, L.K. and K.A. Nelson (1995). *Managing business ethics: Straight talk about how to do it right*. New York: John Wiley & Sons.

Velasquez, M.G. (2002). *Business ethics: Concepts and cases*. 5th edn. Upper Saddle River, NJ: Prentice-Hall.

Velasquez, M.G., D.J. Moberg and G.F. Cavanagh (1983). Organizational statesmanship and dirty politics: Ethical guidelines for the organizational politician. *Organizational Dynamics*, **12** (2), 65–80.

Vigoda, E. (2003). *Developments in organizational politics*. Cheltenham, UK and Northampton, MA: Edward Elgar.

Werhane, P.H. (1999). *Moral imagination and management decision-making*. New York: Oxford University Press.

Williams, B.A.O. (1985). *Ethics and the limits of philosophy*. London: Fontana Press.

7 The direct and indirect influence of organizational politics on organizational support, trust and commitment
Simon Albrecht

Introduction

Organizational politics is being increasingly recognized as an important dimension of organizational experience (Hochwarter et al., 2003; Vigoda, 2000). Over time progress has been made in developing a nomological net defining the antecedents, correlates, moderators, mediators and consequences of organizational politics. Andrews and Kacmar (2001) for example identified leader–member exchange, centralization of decision making, formalization of rules, policies and procures and co-worker cooperation as predictors of organizational politics. In terms of consequences, and consistent with its negatively laden connotation (Kacmar and Carlson, 1997), organizational politics has been shown to have an adverse impact on attitudinal outcomes such as job stress (Cropanzano et al., 1997), job satisfaction (Witt et al., 2000) and organizational commitment (Cropanzano et al., 1997; Drory, 1993; Randall et al., 1999). Organizational politics has also been shown to have an adverse, albeit modest, impact on behavioural outcomes such as negligent behaviour and performance (Vigoda, 2000). Despite clear advances in establishing the nomological net surrounding the construct of organizational politics, more research needs to be conducted to help clarify the pattern of influence among variables associated with organizational politics.

Organizational commitment is probably one of the most frequently researched outcomes associated with organizational politics. Along with organizational politics, organizational support and organizational trust have each been shown, either directly or indirectly, to influence commitment (Cropanzano et al., 1997; Vigoda, 2000; Eisenberger et al., 1990; Dirks and Ferrin, 2001). Organizational commitment is an important outcome variable because it has consistently been shown to be negatively associated with absenteeism and labour turnover (Mathieu and Zajac, 1990; Meyer et al., 2002; Rhoades et al., 2001) and shown to be positively associated with increased extra role performance, dedication, loyalty and supervisor-rated job performance (Meyer and Allen, 1988; Meyer et al., 2002; Rhoades et al., 2001). While researchers have looked at the individual or paired effects of organizational politics, organizational support and organizational trust on commitment, no published studies have assessed the pattern of influence among all three constructs nor mapped their direct or indirect associations with commitment. Furthermore, apart from some notable exceptions (Chen et al., 2005; Eisenberger et al., 2001; Hochwarter et al., 2003), very little published research has looked to identify the factors which mediate the influence of politics and support on organizational commitment. This chapter sets out to extend the nomological net pertaining to organizational politics by examining the mediating role of organizational trust in the relationships between organizational politics, organizational support and organizational commitment.

Organizational support and affective organizational commitment
Organizational commitment refers to the extent to which an employee feels involved in, emotionally attached to, and a sense of belonging to, their organization (Allen and Meyer, 1990). Organizational commitment manifests itself as a willingness to work towards and accept organizational goals and values (Mowday et al., 1979).

Meyer et al.'s (2002) meta-analysis, combining the results of more than 18 studies and 7128 participants, identified organizational support as a particularly salient predictor of affective organizational commitment ($\rho = 0.63$). Conversely, Rhoades and Eisenberger's (2002) meta-analysis, combining the results of more than 42 studies and 11 706 participants, identified affective commitment as the most salient outcome ($r = 0.73$) of perceived organizational support (POS). Overall, the accumulated research clearly shows a strong and direct relationship between organizational support and affective organizational commitment.

Social exchange theory (Blau, 1964) provides a theoretical explanation for the association between organizational support and organizational commitment. Social exchange theory predicts that an employee's commitment to their organization arises out of generalized beliefs that their organization appreciates their contributions and is concerned about their well-being (Armeli et al., 1998; Eisenberger et al., 1986, 2002; Hutchison and Garstka, 1996; Settoon et al., 1996). In effect, employees develop a 'felt obligation' (Eisenberger et al., 2001) to 'reciprocate' (Gouldner, 1960) the organization's demonstration of good will and support with prosocial attitudes and positive behaviour. Felt obligation and prosocial attitudes often find expression in the form of organizational commitment.

Organizational politics, organizational support and commitment
Organizational politics has been shown to directly or indirectly influence organizational commitment. Ferris et al. (1989), Vigoda (2000) and Randall et al. (1999) found strong negative associations between organizational politics and affective commitment. Other researchers, however, have found that when the influences of organizational support and organizational politics on affective commitment are jointly considered, more often than not, the influence of one of the variables is cancelled out (Cropanzano et al., 1997; Randall et al., 1999). By way of resolving these findings, Hochwarter et al. (2003) showed that organizational support fully mediates the relationship between organizational politics and affective commitment. Explaining their results in terms of social exchange theory, Hochwarter et al. concluded that any negative outcomes which accrue from organizational politics do so because politics erodes employees' confidence that their organization values their contribution and is concerned about their well-being.

Organizational trust and commitment
Mayer et al. (1995) defined trust as 'a willingness of a party to be vulnerable to the actions of another party based on the expectation that the other will perform a particular action important to the trustor, irrespective of the ability to monitor or control that party' (p. 712). Albrecht and Travaglione (2003) defined employee trust in terms of their willingness to act on the basis of the words, actions and decisions of organizational decision makers under conditions of uncertainty or risk. Common to both these definitions is the notion that organizational trust is predicated on feelings of vulnerability, uncertainty and risk.

Dirks and Ferrin (2002), in their meta-analysis of the antecedents, correlates and con-sequences of trust identified organizational commitment as a key outcome of trust in organizational leadership. They reported, on the basis of results aggregated from over 18 studies and 5592 participants, a mean corrected correlation of 0.57 between the two con-structs.

Organizational trust has also elsewhere been shown to directly influence organizational commitment. Cook and Wall (1980), for example, reported a sizeable correlation ($r = 0.61$) between trust in management and organizational commitment. Similarly, Konovsky and Cropanzano (1991), Tan and Tan (2000), Armstrong-Stassen (2002) and Whitener (2001) all reported sizeable correlations between trust in management and organizational commitment. Overall, on the basis of these and other studies, there is clear evidence of a strong association between organizational trust, or trust in management, and affective organizational commitment.

Organizational trust as a mediator
Hochwarter et al. acknowledged the research of Parker et al. (1995) and argued that trust is often damaged in a politically charged organizational environment. More explicitly, Witt et al. (2002) suggested that it is the uncertainty and risk resulting from increasingly politicized organizational environments that provides the mediating psychological mech-anisms through which negative outcomes may accrue. As already noted, uncertainty and risk are central to the definition of trust. As employees feel increasingly uncertain about whether or not they can trust individuals and processes within their organization, they are more likely to contribute less, engage in some form of withdrawal behaviour, and reduce their commitment. It is therefore here proposed that organizational trust will fully mediate the relationship between organizational politics and organizational commitment.

A case can also be made that trust will also mediate the relationship between organ-izational support and affective commitment. Eisenberger et al. (1990) argued that orga-nizational trust provides the mechanism through which outcomes associated with organizational support can be explained. Again drawing from social exchange theory (Blau, 1964), Eisenberger et al. argued that 'perceived support would create trust that the organization will fulfil its exchange obligations of noticing and rewarding employee efforts made on its behalf' (p. 57). Aryee et al. (2003) noted that Blau himself argued for the centrality of trust in any conceptualization of social exchange and noted a paucity of research on trust in organizational social exchange processes. Given that Hochwarter et al. (2003) also noted that trust is 'an essential element of the exchange relationship asso-ciated with POS' (p. 440), it is here contended that trust will either partially or fully mediate the relationship between organizational support and affective organizational commitment.

Research model
The research model, as shown in Figure 7.1, derived from the foregoing review of the lit-erature, shows organizational trust fully mediating the relationship between organiza-tional politics and organizational commitment, and partially mediating the relationship between organizational support and organizational affective commitment.

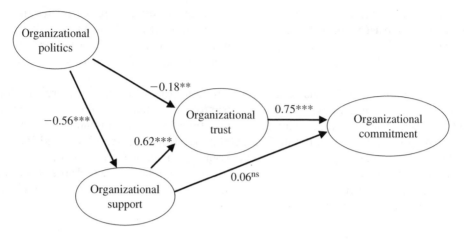

Note: ** $p < 0.01$; *** $p < 0.001$; ns = not significant.

Figure 7.1   Proposed model

Method

Samples

Survey data were collected from a large Australian public sector metropolitan medical facility. Of the 3115 surveys distributed to all full-time, part-time, casual, contract and sessional employees, 915 (29 per cent) were returned. Four hundred and twenty-three of these responses came from full-time employees who had been employed by the organization for a year or longer. These respondents would probably have a more clearly defined sense of organizational politics, organizational trust and organizational support. The final subsample consisted of the 306 full-time employees who had been with the organization for a year or more and who completed all items on the questionnaire relevant to the present study. Two hundred and twenty-nine (75 per cent) of these respondents were female and 71 (23 per cent) were male. Six respondents (2 per cent) did not record their gender. Eighty-eight per cent of respondents were aged between 25 and 54 years and had an average organizational tenure of 9.1 years (SD = 6.7). The majority of respondents identified themselves as salaried officers (53 per cent) and nursing and midwifery staff (35 per cent). The remaining respondents identified themselves as support workers (6 per cent), medical staff (4 per cent) and trades staff (1 per cent). Independent assessment of HR data showed that the sample was generally representative of the organization's overall demographic in terms of age and gender.

Procedure

Data were collected through an employee opinion survey. Hard copy questionnaires were attached to employees' pay slips and accompanied by a cover letter, a participant information sheet and a reply-paid envelope. Employees were also provided with the option of posting their completed responses in designated sealed collection boxes. The participant information sheet assured participants that the researcher would retain all data and would provide no information to the host organizations that could identify any individual employee.

Measures

Organizational politics was measured using the five highest-loading items of a prelimi-nary exploratory factor analysis of Kacmar and Ferris's (1991) 31-item Perceptions of Organizational Politics Scale (POPS). Cropanzano et al. (1997) reported an alpha of 0.79 and Nye and Witt (1993) reported an alpha of 0.93 using similar adaptations of the POPS. Example items included: 'Favoritism rather than merit determines who gets ahead around here', 'There has always been an influential group in this department that no one ever crosses' and 'People here usually don't speak up for fear of retaliation by others'. Response alternatives ranged from 'strongly disagree' (1) to 'strongly agree' (7).

Organizational support was measured using the six highest-loading positively worded items of Kottke and Sharafinski's (1988) adaptation of Eisenberger et al.'s (1986) Survey of Perceived Organizational Support (SPOS). Rhoades and Eisenberger (2002) noted that it is generally accepted practice for researchers to select a subset of high-loading items from within the full-scale SPOS. Example items included: 'The organization really cares for my well-being', 'Help is available from the organization when I have a problem' and 'The organization values my contribution to its well-being'. Response alternatives ranged from 'strongly disagree' (1) to 'strongly agree' (7).

Organizational trust was measured using the four highest-loading items of a prelimi-nary exploratory factor analysis of Tan and Tan's (2000) adaptation of a scale developed by Gabarro and Athos (1976). Robinson and Rousseau (1994) and Tan and Tan reported alpha reliability coefficients greater than 0.80 for the full seven-item scale. Example items included: 'I believe my organization has high integrity', 'In general, I believe my organ-ization's motives and intentions are good' and 'I can expect my organization to treat me in a consistent and predictable fashion'. Response alternatives ranged from 'strongly dis-agree' (1) to 'strongly agree' (7).

Organizational commitment was measured using the five highest-loading items of a preliminary exploratory factor analysis of Bishop and Scott's (2000) adaptation of Mowday et al.'s (1979) Organizational Commitment Questionnaire. Bishop and Scott showed that their nine-item scale had an acceptable alpha reliability coefficient ($\alpha = 0.90$). Consistent with arguments proposed by Magazine et al. (1996), all items used in the present research were positively phrased. Example items included: 'I really care about this organization', 'I am proud to tell others that I am part of this organization' and 'For me, this is the best of all possible organizations for which to work'. Response alternatives ranged from 'strongly disagree' (1) to 'strongly agree' (7).

Results

Before testing structural relations between constructs, it is important to verify the psy-chometrics of the measures used to capture the constructs of interest (Anderson and Gerbing, 1988). Confirmatory factor analysis (CFA) was used to assess the overall fit of alternative measurement models, the convergent validity of items on their proposed con-structs, and the discriminant validity between the various constructs. CFA, using AMOS (5) (Arbuckle, 2003) and the raw data as the input, was applied to the data.

Table 7.1 shows how competing measurement models compared against a number of recommended 'fit indices' (Marsh et al., 1996): the comparative fit index (CFI), the normed fit index (NFI), the goodness-of-fit index (GFI) and the root-mean-square error of approximation (RMSEA). NFI and GFI values greater than 0.90, CFI values of 0.95

and above, and RMSEA values less than 0.08 indicate relatively good fit between a hypothesized model and observed data (Browne and Cudeck, 1993).

Table 7.1 shows that the proposed four-factor model, which had four items loading on commitment, four items loading on organizational trust, six items loading on organizational support and five items loading on organizational politics, provided an acceptable fit to the data. Neither the null model, nor the one-factor model, where all 19 items loaded on a single factor, provided an acceptable fit to the data.

The convergent validity of the items in the proposed four-factor model was assessed by examining the factor loadings of the items on their specified dimensions. The standardized parameter estimates ranged from 0.54 to 0.89 and were all statistically significant. Given that standardized values greater than 0.50 demonstrate reasonably high factor loadings (Kline, 1998), the results suggest convergent validity within the proposed measurement model.

Descriptive statistics, reliabilities and correlations
The means, standard deviations, and Cronbach's alpha for all four measures are shown in Table 7.2. The mean scores for organizational commitment, organizational politics and organizational trust corresponded to ratings between 'not sure' and 'agree just a little'. The mean score for organizational support corresponded to a rating between 'disagree just a little' and 'not sure'. Alpha reliability coefficients for all four scales clearly exceeded Nunnally's (1978) criterion of $\alpha = 0.70$.

Table 7.1   Fit indices of the four-factor measurement model (n = 306)

Model	χ^2	DF	NFI	GFI	CFI	RMSEA	RMSEA (90% CI)
Null model	3987.88	190					
1 factor	1441.80	170	0.64	0.60	0.66	0.157	(0.149–0.164)
4 Factor	352.119	164	0.91	0.90	0.95	0.061	(0.053–0.070)

Note: NFI = Normed fit index, GFI = Goodness-of-fit index, CFI = Comparative fit index, RMSEA = Root-mean-square error of approximation, 90% CI = RMSEA 90% confidence interval.

Table 7.2   Descriptives, alpha and inter-correlations between organizational commitment, organizational support, organizational politics and organizational trust (n = 306)

	Mean	S.D.	Possible range	Alpha	1	2	3	4
1. Organizational commitment	4.40	1.43	1–7	0.89	–			
2. Organizational politics	4.78	1.44	1–7	0.87	−0.38	–		
3. Organizational support	3.67	1.43	1–7	0.92	0.60	−0.56	–	
4. Organizational trust	4.36	1.26	1–7	0.79	0.80	−0.60	0.77	–

Note: *** $p < 0.001$ (two-tailed).

Given the relatively high correlations between some of the study variables (see Table 7.2), the independence of the constructs was assessed by conducting tests of discriminant validity. The discriminant validity between each pair of constructs was assessed by comparing chi-square values when the covariance between two constructs was fixed at one to when the covariance between the two constructs was freely estimated (Anderson and Gerbing, 1988). A significant difference in chi-square (with 1 degree of freedom) assures discriminant validity (Bagozzi and Phillips, 1982). Table 7.3 shows that the six tests yielded statistically significant differences in chi-square (ranging from 4.08 to 229.34), and thus provided additional evidence in support of the proposed four-factor measurement model.

Having established a theoretically viable measurement model with CFA, the next step in the analysis was to examine the proposed structural relations between the constructs. The fit statistics (see Table 7.4) for the proposed structural suggested a good fitting model: χ^2 (165, $n = 306$) = 313.139, CFI = 0.96, NFI = 0.92, GFI = 0.90, RMSEA = 0.054 (0.045, 0.063). The path estimates, representing the strength and direction of influence between the constructs, and their significance values are shown in Figure 7.2. Kline (1998) noted that standardized path coefficients less than 0.10 indicate a 'small' effect; coefficients around 0.30 indicate a 'medium' effect; and coefficients of 0.50 or more indicate a 'large' effect.

Table 7.3 Discriminant validity among pairs of constructs (n = 306)

	χ^2 covariance set free	df	χ^2 covariance fixed at 1	df	χ^2 difference per 1 df
Organizational politics with:					
Organizational support	117.760	43	330.987	44	213.287***
Organizational trust	90.563	26	319.901	27	229.338***
Organizational commitment	76.285	34	218.137	35	211.852***
Organizational support with:					
Organizational trust	124.278	34	135.036	35	10.756**
Organizational commitment	114.868	43	118.841	44	4.083*
Organizational trust with:					
Organizational commitment	87.945	26	94.982	27	7.037**

Note: * $p < 0.05$; ** $p < 0.01$; *** $p < 0.001$.

Table 7.4 Fit indices of alternative structural models (n = 306)

Model	χ^2	DF	NFI	GFI	CFI	RMSEA	RMSEA (90% CI)
Proposed model	313.139	165	0.921	0.903	0.961	0.054	(0.045–0.063)
Model B	352.127	165	0.912	0.895	0.951	0.061	(0.052–0.070)
Model C	394.518	166	0.900	0.885	0.939	0.067	(0.059–0.076)
Model D	313.651	166	0.921	0.903	0.961	0.054	(0.045–0.063)

Note: NFI = Normed fit index, GFI = Goodness-of-fit index, CFI = Comparative fit index, RMSEA = Root-mean-square error of approximation, 90% CI = RMSEA 90% confidence interval.

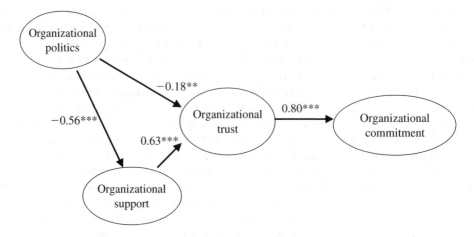

Note: * $p<0.05$; ** $p<0.01$; *** $p<0.001$; ns = not significant.

Figure 7.2   Respecified model (Model D)

Consistent with the proposed model, all but one of the paths were statistically significant (see Figure 7.1). The strongest paths, with values of 0.50 or more, were from organizational politics to organizational support, organizational trust to organizational commitment, and organizational support to organizational trust. The path from organizational support to organizational commitment was not significant.

Consistent with recommended structural modelling practice (Kline, 1988), theoretically viable alternative structural models were evaluated against the proposed model. First, Model B, including a path connecting organizational politics to organizational commitment, was estimated (see Table 7.4). The chi-square for Model B was significantly different to that of the proposed model and the fit indices suggested a less acceptable fit. The paths connecting organizational politics to organizational commitment and organizational support to organizational commitment were not significant.

A third alternative model was tested in order to evaluate the mediating effects of trust on the relationship between organizational support and organizational commitment. In Model C, the path connecting organizational support to organizational trust was fixed to zero. By fixing this path to zero, the direct effect of organizational support on commitment, independent of the mediating influence of trust, could be assessed. As shown in Table 7.4, Model C provided a significantly worse fit to the data than the proposed model. It is noteworthy, however, that the path connecting organizational support and organizational commitment was here significant (standardized coefficient of 0.207, significant at $p<0.001$). Given that in the estimation of the proposed model this path was not significant, this result suggests that organizational trust may fully mediate the influence of organizational support on organizational commitment (Baron and Kenny, 1986).

Finally, given that in the proposed model the path from organizational support to organizational commitment was non-significant, a respecified model (Model D), with the path from organizational support to organizational commitment fixed to zero, was estimated. Table 7.4 shows that, given a difference of one degree of freedom, the chi-square for Model D was not significantly different from the proposed model and yielded virtually identical fit indices. Overall, Model D, in providing an acceptable and more parsimonious fit to the data, becomes the preferred model. The parameter estimates for the respecified model are shown in Figure 7.2.

In order to test the mediating effect of organizational trust on the relationship between organizational politics and organizational commitment in the respecified model, Model D was re-estimated after adding a path linking organizational politics and organizational commitment and fixing at zero the mediating path leading from organizational politics to organizational trust. The model estimation yielded acceptable fit: χ^2 (166, $n = 306) = 321.479$, CFI $= 0.96$, NFI $= 0.92$, GFI $= 0.90$, RMSEA $= 0.055$ (0.064, 0.159). However, the path directly connecting organizational politics and organizational commitment was non-significant (standardized coefficient of -0.03). This result suggests that organizational politics has no influence, either directly or indirectly, on organizational commitment.

In order to test the mediating effect of organizational trust on the relationship between organizational support and organizational commitment in the respecified model, Model D was re-estimated after adding a path linking organizational support and organizational commitment and fixing at zero the mediating path leading from organizational trust to organizational commitment. The model estimation yielded acceptable fit: χ^2 (166, $n = 306) = 393.267$, CFI $= 0.94$, NFI $= 0.90$, GFI $= 0.89$, RMSEA $= 0.067$ (0.058, 0.076). The path directly connecting organizational support and organizational commitment was significant (standardized coefficient of 0.63, $p < 0.001$). This result, in combination with previously reported results, clearly suggests that organizational support indirectly influences organizational commitment through organizational trust.

Discussion

The results showed that, although the relationship between politics and trust was not as strong as the relationship between politics and support, organizational politics directly influenced organizational support and organizational trust. These results clearly suggest that the more that employees perceive that diligence and hard work will not be enough to get them ahead, the more that 'cliques' or 'in-groups' are perceived to have influence, and the more that favouritism rather than merit determines who gets ahead, the more likely it will be that employees feel vulnerable, at risk and unsupported.

The results also showed that organizational politics, beyond having a direct effect on trust and support, also indirectly influenced trust through its influence on perceived organizational support. Organizational support provides an additional indirect link through which organizational politics can influence organizational trust. This suggests that organizations are able to exacerbate or ameliorate the negative effects that perceived political activity might have on organizational trust by managing organizational support. The extent, for instance, to which an organization is perceived to care about employee satisfaction and well-being, the extent to which it demonstrates a willingness to listen to employee opinions, and the extent to which it is seen to value employee contributions, will probably ameliorate the negative impact that politics may have on organizational trust.

The results also extend the literature describing the influence of organizational support on organizational commitment. Although Eisenberger et al. (2001) demonstrated that felt obligation and positive mood mediate the relationship between POS and organizational commitment, researchers have only very recently addressed the potential mediating influence of trust with respect to this relationship (Chen et al., 2005). Contrary to most previous research findings, no direct relationship between organizational support and organizational commitment was evidenced. Rather, it appears that organizational trust fully mediates the influence of organizational support on organizational commitment such that the experience of organizational support leads to organizational trust which in turn leads to employee commitment. In effect, and extrapolating from Hochwarter et al.'s conclusions, organizational trust acts as an explanatory factor or conduit through which organizational support influences organizational commitment. Consequently organizations need to ensure that provision of organizational support is associated with trust. Provision of organizational support that is perceived to be in any sense tokenistic, inconsistent or inauthentic will not result in organizational commitment.

Hochwarter et al. reported that the influence of organizational politics on organizational commitment was fully mediated by organizational support. The present results contradict this finding. As previously noted, in the presence of organizational trust, organizational support had no direct effect on organizational commitment. In the absence of a direct effect from organizational support to organizational commitment, politics cannot influence commitment through support. Further research is needed to assess the cross-validity of this finding.

The proposed research model showed organizational trust having a direct influence on organizational commitment. Results of structural equations modelling showed that organizational trust indeed exerted a strong and direct influence on organizational commitment. The strength of this association suggests that trust is a key determinant of commitment and that without the development and maintenance of organizational trust it is unlikely that employees will feel emotionally connected to, be positive about, or proactive within their particular organizational setting. It is noteworthy that this relationship has not been widely acknowledged. Meyer et al. (2002), for example, did not include organizational trust in their widely cited meta-analysis of the antecedents, correlates and consequences of organizational commitment. The present results suggest that further cross-validation research needs to be conducted to verify the key role that trust plays in the development and maintenance of organizational commitment.

In sum, the results provide new insights into the psychological mechanisms through which organizational politics influences organizational trust and organisational support influences organizational commitment. While organizational support, in the context of social exchange theory, has been widely cited as accounting for the development of employee commitment (Eisenberger et al., 1986, 2002; Hutchison and Garstka, 1996; Lynch et al., 1999), the claim that trust is 'an essential element of the exchange relationship associated with POS' (Hochwarter et al., 2003, p. 440) has gone largely untested. As such the present research goes some way toward addressing the paucity of research involving trust in organizational social exchange processes and goes some way toward establishing the centrality of trust in any conceptualization of social exchange. The research also extends current understanding of the mediating roles of organizational trust and organizational support within a social exchange framework.

Beyond extending the nomological net of the variables associated with organizational politics by contributing a new model defining the relationships between organizational politics, organizational support, organizational trust and organizational commitment, the present research also makes a contribution to the literature with respect to the measurement of these social-exchange-related constructs. Consistent with Warr's (1990) call for short and generally applicable measures of organizational constructs, confirmatory factor analyses demonstrated the psychometric adequacy of all four measures. Respondents were clearly able to distinguish between the constructs and alpha reliabilities for each of the measures met criterion levels. Such measures can therefore be used with confidence in related research endeavours.

At a practical level, the monitoring and managing of organizational politics, organizational support, organizational trust and organizational commitment can be achieved through a range of organizational development initiatives. For example, all four measures could routinely be included in climate surveys to diagnose and monitor employee perceptions of the social exchange relationship. Survey feedback processes (Golombiewski and Hilles, 1979) could then be used to involve employees in developing strategies aimed at fostering and maintaining a positive social exchange climate. At the same time, an inclusive review of the effectiveness of human resource practices and processes could be conducted. Selection, promotion and performance management systems need to reflect an organizational climate where negative politics is absent and where a climate of support is present. Again, climate surveys would provide a broad-level indicator that such systems are in place (Kraut, 1996). Furthermore, at an individual level, individual performance management and development processes need to have politics, support, trust relations and commitment as key performance criteria. Communication audits (Goldhaber, 1993) and multi-rater feedback processes (Cacioppe and Albrecht, 2000) could be used to routinely assess or monitor the extent to which individuals are leading and managing in a way consistent with a high commitment culture.

While the present research has provided new insights into the relationships between organizational politics, organizational support, organizational trust and organizational commitment, some limitations need to be acknowledged. Cross-sectional, as opposed to longitudinal, analyses were conducted for this study. Although rigorous confirmatory and structural modelling technologies were used, cross-sectional data do not enable the determination of causal relations. Longitudinal analyses, preferably drawn over three time periods (Willet, 1989), enable much stronger claims to be made about causality and potential reciprocality of influence among the variables.

Another potential limitation centres on the method of data collection. Given that all of the data were collected through self-report procedures, 'common method variance' may have inflated correlations between the variables (Spector, 1987). However, given that the measurement model demonstrated acceptable fit to the data, given that the correlations between the different measured constructs varied quite considerably, and given that the discriminant validity between each pair of measured constructs was established, the issue of common method variance appears not to be problematic.

Overall, given the increasing status of social exchange as a paradigm for understanding the motivational underpinnings of employee work attitudes and behaviours (Aryee et al., 2003), additional research on a more fully elaborated social exchange model is indicated. Additional antecedent variables focused on the psychological contract (Robinson and Morrison, 1995; Rousseau, 1990), distributive justice (McFarlin and Sweeney, 1992) and procedural justice (Cropanzano and Greenberg, 1997; Folger and Konovsky, 1989; Moorman, 1991; Collquitt, 2001) could be included in the model. The influence of personality variables such as extraversion, openness to experience and altruism (Judge and Bono, 2000; Judge et al., 1999) on the social exchange dynamic could also be modelled. Similarly, additional mediating variables such as felt obligation, positive mood and leader–member exchange could be included in the model. In general, researchers should also look to link social-exchange-related constructs with important organizational outcomes such as organizational citizenship behaviour (Robinson and Morrison, 1995), turnover intention (Wayne et al., 1997) and attitudes toward change (Rousseau and Tijoriwala, 1999) and with more objectively defined criteria. Structural equations modelling within longitudinal designs would provide the most appropriate means of testing these potential relationships within alternative and expanded models.

In conclusion, the present findings reinforce the important part that trust plays in the way that employees evaluate organizational experience. As argued by Aryee et al. (2003), trust can be regarded as the central axis on which social-exchange-based employment relationships revolve. Trust appears to be a critical determinant of employee commitment and is an essential medium by which demonstrations of organizational support and organizational politics translate into commitment and commitment concomitant outcomes. Organizations clearly need to learn how to effectively manage trust. The present results suggest that beyond building trust through individual demonstrations of integrity, competence, consistency, benevolence and openness (Albrecht and Travaglione, 2003; Mayer and Davis, 1999; Mishra, 1996; Shaw, 1997), trust can be enhanced by managing the negative consequences of organizational politics and by building organizational supports.

References

Albrecht S.L. and Travaglione, T. (2003). Trust in public sector senior management. *International Journal of Human Resource Management*, **14** (2), 1–17.
Allen, N.J. and Meyer, J.P. (1990). The measurement and antecedents of affective, continuance and normative commitment. *Journal of Occupational Psychology*, **63**, 1–18.
Anderson, J.C. and Gerbing, D.W. (1988). Structural equation modeling in practice: A review and recommended two-step approach. *Psychological Bulletin*, **49**, 411–23.
Andrews, M.C. and Kacmar, K.M. (2001). Discriminating among organizational politics, justice, and support. *Journal of Organizational Behavior*, **22**, 347–66.
Arbuckle, J.L. (2003). *Amos 5.0: Update to the Amos User's Guide*. Chicago, IL: Smallwaters.
Armeli, S., Eisenberger, R., Fasolo, P. and Lynch, P. (1998). Perceived organizational support and police performance: The moderating influence of socioemotional needs. *Journal of Applied Psychology*, **83** (2), 288–97.
Armstrong-Stassen, M. (2002). Designated redundant but escaping a lay-off: A special group of lay-off survivors. *Journal of Occupational and Organizational Psychology*, (75), 1–13.
Aryee, S., Budhwar, P.S. and Chen, Z.X. (2003). Trust as a mediator of the relationship between organizational justice and work outcomes: Test of a social exchange model. *Journal of Organizational Behavior*, **23** (3), 267–85.
Bagozzi, R.P. and Phillips, L.W. (1982). Representing and testing organizational theories: A holistic construal. *Administrative Science Quarterly*, **27**, 459–89.
Baron, R.M. and Kenny, D.A. (1986). The moderator–mediator variable distinction in social psychological research: Conceptual, strategic, and statistical considerations. *Journal of Personality and Social Psychology*, **51**, 1173–82.
Bishop, J.W. and Scott, K.D. (2000). An examination of organizational and team commitment in a self-directed team environment. *Journal of Applied Psychology*, **85** (3), 439–50.
Blau, P.M. (1964). *Exchange and power in social life*. New York: John Wiley.
Browne, M.W. and Cudeck, R. (1993). Alternative ways of assessing model fit. In K.A. Bollen and J.S. Long (eds), *Testing structural equation models* (pp. 136–62). Newbury Park, CA: Sage.

Cacioppe, R.L. and Albrecht, S.L. (2000). Using 360° feedback and the integral model to develop leadership and management skills. *The Leadership and Organizational Development Journal*, **21**, 390–404.

Chen, Z.X., Aryee, S. and Lee, C. (2005). Test of a mediation model of perceived organizational support. *Journal of Vocational Behavior*, **66**, 457–70.

Collquitt, J.A. (2001). On the dimensionality of organizational justice: A construct validation of a measure. *Journal of Applied Psychology*, **86** (3), 386–400.

Cook, J. and Wall, T. (1980). New work attitude measures of trust, organisational commitment and personal need non-fulfilment. *Journal of Occupational Psychology*, **53**, 39–52.

Cropanzano, R. and Greenberg, J. (1997). Progress in organizational justice: Tunnelling through the maze. *International Review of Industrial and Organizational Psychology*, **12**, 317–72.

Cropanzano, R., Howes, J.C., Grandey, A.A. and Toth, P. (1997). The relationship of organizational politics and support to work behaviors, attitudes, and stress. *Journal of Organizational Behavior*, **18**, 159–80.

Dirks, K.T. and Ferrin, D.L. (2001). The role of trust in organizational settings. *Organization Science*, **12** (4), 450–67.

Drory, A. (1993). Perceived political climate and job attitudes. *Organization Studies*, **14**, 59–71.

Eisenberger, R., Huntington, R., Hutchison, S. and Sowa, D. (1986). Perceived organizational support. *Journal of Applied Psychology*, **71**, 500–507.

Eisenberger, R., Fasolo, P. and Davis-LaMastro, D. (1990). Perceived organizational support and employee diligence, commitment, and innovation. *Journal of Applied Psychology*, **75** (1), 51–9.

Eisenberger, R., Armeli, S., Rexwinkel, B., Lynch, P.D. and Rhoades, L. (2001). Reciprocation of perceived organizational support. *Journal of Applied Psychology*, **86** (1), 42–51.

Eisenberger, R., Stinglhamber, F., Vandenberghe, C., Sucharski, I. and Rhoades, L. (2002). Perceived supervisor support: Contributions to perceived organizational support and employee retention. *Journal of Applied Psychology*, **87** (3), 565–73.

Ferris, G.R. and Kacmar, K.M. (1992). Perceptions of organizational politics. *Journal of Management*, **18** (1), 93–116.

Ferris, G.R., Russ, G.S. and Fandt, P.M. (1989). Politics in organizations. In R.A. Giacalone and P. Rosenfeld (eds), *Impression management in organizations*. Newbury Park, CA: Sage, pp. 143–70.

Folger, R. and Konovsky, M. (1989). Effects of procedural and distributive justice on reactions to pay raise decisions. *Academy of Management Journal*, **32**, 115–30.

Gabarro, J. and Athos, J. (1976). *Interpersonal relations and communications*. Englewood Cliffs, NJ: Prentice-Hall.

Goldhaber, G.M. (1993). *Organizational Communication*. New York: McGraw-Hill.

Golembiewski, R.T. and Hilles, R.J. (1979). *Toward the responsive organization: The theory and practice of survey feedback*. Salt Lake City, UT: Brighton.

Gouldner, A. (1960). The norm of reciprocity: A preliminary statement. *American Sociological Review*, **25**, 161–78.

Hochwarter, W.A., Kacmar, C., Perrewé, P.L. and Johnson, D. (2003). Perceived organizational support as a mediator of the relationship between politics and work outcomes. *Journal of Vocational Behavior*, **63**, 438–56.

Hutchison, S. and Garstka, M.L. (1996). Sources of perceived organizational support: Goal setting and feedback. *Journal of Applied Social Psychology*, **26** (15), 1351–66.

Judge, T.A. and Bono, J.E. (2000). Five-factor model of personality and transformational leadership. *Journal of Applied Psychology*, **84** (5), 751–65.

Judge, T.A., Thoresen, C.J., Pucik, V. and Welbourne, W. (1999). Managerial coping with organizational change: A dispositional perspective. *Journal of Applied Psychology*, **84**, 107–22.

Kacmar, K.M. and Carlson, D.S. (1997). Further validation of the perceptions of organizational politics scale (POPS): A multiple sample investigation. *Journal of Management*, **23**, 627–58.

Kacmar, K.M. and Ferris, G.R. (1991). Perceptions of organizational politics scale (POPS): Development and construct validity. *Educational and Psychological Measurement*, **51**, 193–205.

Kline, R.B. (1998). *Principles and practice of structural equation modeling*. New York: The Guilford Press.

Konovsky, M.A. and Cropanzano, R. (1991). Perceived fairness of employee drug testing as a predictor of employee attitudes and job performance. *Journal of Applied Psychology*, **76**, 698–707.

Kottke, J.L. and Sharafinski, C.E. (1988). Measuring perceived supervisory and organizational support. *Educational and Psychological Measurement*, **48**, 1075–9.

Kraut, A.I. (ed.) (1996). *Organizational surveys: Tools for assessment and change*. San Francisco, CA: Jossey-Bass.

Lynch, P., Eisenberger, R. and Armeli, R. (1999). Perceived organizational support: Inferior versus superior performance by wary employees. *Journal of Applied Psychology*, **84**, 467–83.

Magazine, S.L., Williams, L.J. and Williams, M.L. (1996). A confirmatory factor analysis of reverse coding effects in Meyer and Allen's affective and continuance commitment scales. *Educational and Psychological Measurement*, **56**, 241–50.

Marsh, H.W., Balla, J.R. and Hau, K.-T. (1996). An evaluation of incremental fit indices: A clarification of mathematical and empirical properties. In G.A. Marcoulides and R.E. Schumacker (eds), *Advanced structural equation modeling* (pp. 315–52). Mahwah, NJ: Lawrence Erlbaum.

Mathieu, J.E. and Zajac, D.M. (1990). A review and meta-analysis of the antecedents, correlates, and consequences of organizational commitment. *Psychological Bulletin*, **108**, 171–94.

Mayer, R.C. and Davis, J.H. (1999). The effect of the performance appraisal system on trust for management: A field quasi-experiment. *Journal of Applied Psychology*, **84**, 123–36.

Mayer, R.C., Davis, J.H. and Schoorman, F.D. (1995). An integrative model of organizational trust. *Academy of Management Review*, **20**, 709–34.

McFarlin, D.B. and Sweeney, P.D. (1992). Distributive and procedural justice as predictors of satisfaction with personal and organizational outcomes. *Academy of Managemant Journal*, **35**, 626–37.

Meyer, J.P. and Allen, N.J. (1988). Links between work experiences and organizational commitment during the first year of employment: A longitudinal analysis. *Journal of Occupational Psychology*, **61**, 195–209.

Meyer, J.P., Stanley, D.J., Herscovitch, L. and Topolnytsky, L. (2002). Affective, continuance, and normative commitment to the organization: A meta-analysis of antecedents, correlates and consequences. *Journal of Vocational Behavior*, **61** (1), 20–52.

Mishra, A. (1996). Organizational responses to crisis. In R.M. Kramer and T.R. Tyler (eds), *Trust in organizations: Frontiers of theory and research* (pp. 261–87). Thousand Oaks, CA: Sage Publications.

Moorman, R.H. (1991). Relationship between organizational justice and organizational citizenship behavior: Do fairness perceptions influence employee citizenship? *Journal of Applied Psychology*, **76** (6), 845–55.

Mowday, R.T., Steers, R.M. and Porter, L.W. (1979). The measurement of organizational commitment. *Journal of Vocational Behavior*, **14**, 224–47.

Nunnally, J. (1978). *Psychometric theory*. New York: McGraw-Hill.

Nye, L.G. and Witt, L.A. (1993). Dimensionality and construct validity of the Perceptions of Politics Scale (POPS). *Educational and Psychological Measurement*, **53**, 821–9.

Parker, C.P., Dipboye, R.L. and Jackson, S.L. (1995). Perceptions of organizational politics: An investigation of antecedents and consequences. *Journal of Management*, **21**, 891–912.

Parker, C.P., Baltes, B.B., Young, S.A., Huff, J.W., Altmann, R.A., Lacost, H.A. and Roberts, J.E. (2003). Relationship between psychological climate perceptions and work outcomes: A meta-analytic review. *Journal of Organizational Behavior*, **24**, 389–416.

Randall, M.L, Cropanzano, R., Bormann, C.A. and Birjulin, A. (1999). Organizational politics and organizational support as predictors of work attitudes, job performance, and organizational citizenship behavior *Journal of Organizational Behavior*, **20**, 159–74.

Rhoades, L. and Eisenberger, R. (2002). Perceived organizational support: A review of the literature. *Journal of Applied Psychology*, **87** (4), 698–714.

Rhoades, L., Eisenberger, R. and Armeli, S. (2001). Affective commitment to the organization: The contribution of perceived organizational support. *Journal of Applied Psychology*, **86** (5), 825–36.

Robinson, S.L. and Morrison, E.W. (1995). Psychological contracts and OCB: The effect of unfulfilled obligations on civic virtue behaviour. *Journal of Organizational Behavior*, **16**, 289–98.

Robinson, S.L. and Rousseau, D.M. (1994). Violating the psychological contract: Not the exception but the norm. *Journal of Organizational Behavior*, **15**, 245–59.

Rousseau, D.M. (1990). Assessing organizational culture: The case for multiple methods. In B. Schneider (ed.), *Organizational climate and culture* (pp. 153–94). San Francisco, CA: Jossey-Bass.

Rousseau, D.M. and Tijoriwala, S.A. (1999). What's a good reason to change? Motivated reasoning and social accounts in promoting organizational change. *Journal of Applied Psychology*, **84**, 514–28.

Settoon, R.P., Bennett, N. and Liden, R.C. (1996). Social exchange in organizations: Perceived organizational support, leader–member exchange and employee reciprocity. *Journal of Applied Psychology*, **81**, 219–27.

Shaw, R.B. (1997). *Trust in the balance: Building successful organizations on results, integrity and concern*. San Francisco, CA: Jossey-Bass.

Spector, P.E. (1987). Method variance as an artifact in self-reported affect and perceptions at work: Myth or significant problem. *Journal of Applied Psychology*, **72**, 438–43.

Tan, H.H. and Tan, C.S.F. (2000). Toward the differentiation of trust in supervisor and trust in organization. *Genetic, Social, and General Psychology Monographs*, **126** (2), 241–60.

Vigoda, E. (2000). Organization politics, job attitudes, and work outcomes: Exploration and implications for the Public Sector. *Journal of Vocational Behavior*, **57**, 326–47.

Warr, P. (1990). The measurement of well-being and other aspects of mental health. *Journal of Occupational Psychology*, **63**, 193–210.

Wayne, S.J., Shore, L.M. and Liden, R.C. (1997). Perceived organizational support and leader–member exchange: A social exchange perspective. *Academy of Management Journal*, **40**, 82–111.

Whitener, E.M. (2001). Do high commitment human resource practices affect employee commitment? A cross-level analysis using hierarchical linear modelling. *Journal of Management*, **27** (5), 515–35.

Willett, J.B. (1989). Some results on the reliability for the longitudinal measurement of change: Implications for the design of individual growth. *Educational and Psychological Measurement*, **49**, 587–602.

Witt, L.A., Andrews, M.C. and Kacmar, K.M. (2000). The role of participation in decision-making in the organizational politics–job satisfaction relationship, *Human Relations*, **53** (3), 341–58.

Witt, L.A., Kacmar, K.M., Carlson, D.S. and Zivnuska, S. (2002). Interactive effects of personality and organizational politics on contextual performance. *Journal of Organizational Behavior*, **23**, 911–26.

8 Politics as determinant of fairness perceptions in organizations

Constant D. Beugré and Patrick R. Liverpool

Introduction

A workplace can be conceptualized as a social marketplace in which multiple individuals engage in several transactions each seeking to obtain a favorable return on their investment (Cropanzano et al., 1997; Randall et al., 1999). In pursuit of this favorable return on investment, organizational members may engage in self-serving behaviors without regard for the welfare of other organizational members or the organization itself. One such self-serving behavior is organizational politics – a self-serving interpersonal influence behavior, not formally sanctioned by the organization and designed to maximize self-interest at the expense of others (Mintzberg, 1985). The importance of organizational politics lies in its potential consequences and effect on work outcomes (Vigoda, 2003). Indeed, the perceptions individuals hold about the political nature of their work environment influence the way they do their jobs (Kacmar and Carlson, 1997). Thus, both the occurrence of political behavior and individuals' perceptions of politics are important to our understanding of organizations (Parker et al., 1995).

Several authors have underscored the ubiquitous nature of organizational politics (e.g. Gandz and Murray, 1980; Ferris et al., 1989; Ferris and Kacmar, 1992; Kacmar and Baron, 1999; Vigoda, 2003). Talk about politics is common in the workplace (Gandz and Murray, 1980). Politics in organizations is simply a fact of life (Ferris and Kacmar, 1992) and the use of political tactics in organizations is widespread (Kacmar and Carlson, 1997). Organizational politics scholars have assessed the impact of political behavior on employee attitudes and behaviors. Specifically, they have shown a direct link between perceptions of politics and attitudinal and behavioral outcomes, such as job satisfaction, commitment and stress (Maslyn and Fedor, 1998; Ferris et al., 1996; Kacmar et al., 1999; Zhou and Ferris, 1995; Cropanzano et al., 1997; Vigoda, 2002). The common thread of this stream of research is that organizational politics is dysfunctional because it reduces employee commitment (Maslyn and Fedor, 1998), job satisfaction (Ferris et al., 1996; Kacmar et al., 1999; Zhou and Ferris, 1995), and increases stress (Cropanzano et al., 1997; Vigoda, 2002).

However, most research in organizational politics has neglected to assess its potential impact on employee perceptions of justice (or fairness – in this chapter we use the terms interchangeably). This is astonishing in view of the conceptual closeness between organizational politics and organizational justice. For instance, perceptions of organizational politics and organizational justice are two constructs germane to the allocation process (Aryee et al., 2004). Although there are recent attempts to explore the link between organizational politics and justice (Aryee et al., 2004), these efforts are inadequate compared to the vast body of conceptual and empirical research on the consequences of organizational politics.

Our objective in writing this chapter is to analyze the extent to which perceptions of organizational politics influence perceptions of fairness in organizations. Three reasons at least motivate our work. First, the extant literature on the consequences of organizational politics tends to overlook its effects on employee perceptions of fairness. Understanding such linkage is important because as politics is ubiquitous to organizational life, so are issues of fairness and unfairness. The main thesis in this chapter is that perceptions of organizational politics influence perceptions of justice. Second, we strongly believe that both the organizational politics literature and the organizational justice literature may enrich each other because the two concepts tend to have similar antecedents and produce similar consequences. It is also possible to envision a strong correlation between the two concepts. For instance, perceptions of organizational politics may strongly influence perceptions of justice. Employees who perceive their organization as highly political may tend to report situations of unfairness. Likewise, employees who feel unfairly treated may consider their organization as more political than those who feel fairly treated.

Third, organizational politics and organizational justice are both perceptual phenomena. Since people act more based on their perception of reality than on reality itself (Lewin, 1936), it is important to understand how perceptions of politics influence fairness. As justice lies in the eye of the beholder, so does organizational politics. As Andrews and Kacmar (2001, p. 350) put it, 'Organizational politics is often in the eye of the beholder. An action viewed by one individual as political may be viewed as completely fair by another.' Such understanding may have both theoretical and practical implications. From a theoretical standpoint, such an understanding may advance our knowledge of the fields of organizational politics and organizational justice. In discussing the link between politics and fairness, we add another outcome variable to Ferris et al.'s (1989) model of the antecedents and consequences of organizational politics. From a practical perspective, managers may enhance employee perceptions of fairness by reducing perceived political activities. Likewise, managers may reduce perceptions of political activity by creating fair working environments.

The present chapter is divided into four sections. In the first section, we define the concept of organizational politics. We also explore the various means through which political behavior takes place in organizations. In the second section, we analyze the relationship between organizational politics and justice. In the third section, we present and discuss a model of the relationship between politics perceptions and justice. Finally, in the fourth section we discuss the model's implications for management practice and research.

Understanding organizational politics

Defining organizational politics

Although organizational politics is ubiquitous, there is no single definition of political behavior in organizations. Organizational politics is generally conceived as an intentional social influence process in which behavior is strategically designed to maximize short-term or long-term self-interest (Ferris et al., 1989). Political activities are a means of exercising social influence and promoting and protecting one's self-interests (Kacmar and Carlson, 1997). For Kacmar and Baron (1999, p. 4), organizational politics involves actions by individuals, which are directed toward the goal of furthering their own self-interest without regard for the well-being of others or their organization. The common thread of these definitions is that they all imply that organizational politics is a self-serving behavior and as such is antisocial. When people engage in political behavior, they do so for their own self-interest without regard for the interest of others or the organization. Thus organizational politics is a self-serving behavior.

Organizational politics takes several forms. Examples include bypassing the chain of command to gain approval, going through improper channels to obtain special equipment, and lobbying high-level managers just prior to promotion decisions (Andrews and Kacmar, 2001). Other forms of organizational politics include attacking and blaming others, using information as a political tool, creating and maintaining a favorable image (impression management), developing a base of support, ingratiating and praising others, developing power coalitions, associating with influential persons, and creating obligations and reciprocity (Kipnis et al., 1980). One must, however, differentiate organizational politics from perceptions of organizational politics. Indeed, some organizational politics scholars differentiate political behavior in organizations from perceptions of organizational politics.

Perceptions of politics
Actual political behavior differs conceptually from perceptions of politics (Ferris and Kacmar, 1992; Kacmar and Baron, 1999; Vigoda and Cohen, 2001; Vigoda, 2003). The former refers to the objective political behavior engaged in by organizational members, whereas the latter deals with the feelings and/or subjective evaluation of political activities. When members of the organization define their work environment as political in nature, they are expressing a feeling that some people, owing to their power resources and influence skills, receive preferential treatment over others who actually deserve the same benefits as everyone else, but lack similar political assets (Vigoda-Gadot et al., 2003, p. 769). Although political behaviors may be objective and observable, perceptions of those behaviors vary substantially across individuals, situations and time (Ferris and Kacmar, 1992). Similarly, behaviors that may be judged as political in some situations may be seen as effective leadership in others (Davis and Gardner, 2004).

Perceptions of politics usually reflect employees' views about the level of power and influence used by other organizational members to gain advantages and secure their interests in conflicting situations (Vigoda-Gadot et al., 2003). Ferris et al. (2000) defined perceptions of politics as an individual's subjective evaluation about the extent to which the work environment is characterized by co-workers and supervisors who demonstrate self-serving behaviors. The definition of organizational politics we adopt in this chapter is restricted to the action of individuals alone. Political perceptions are formed in reference to one's co-workers and superiors; they are about other individuals (Randall et al., 1999). Moreover, organizational politics continues to be conceptualized as an individual-level construct (Darr and Johns, 2004).

For Gandz and Murray (1980), organizational politics is a subjective state in which organizational members perceive themselves or others as intentionally seeking selfish ends in an organizational context when such ends are opposed to those of others. This definition construes organizational politics as a subjectively experienced phenomenon. Although we are cognizant of the fact that organizational groups may collectively behave in a political manner based on some mutual consensus (Drory and Romm, 1990), we limit our analysis to the actions of individuals to better capture the impact of political behavior on perceptions of fairness. We also focus on perceptions of politics because it is the cognitive evaluation of perceptions of events that determines people's responses and the outcomes of those responses (Ferris et al., 1995).

Operationalizing perceptions of politics

Kacmar and Ferris (1991) developed the Perceptions of Organizational Politics Scale (POPS) to measure employee perceptions of political activities in organizations. This instrument includes three dimensions, 'General political behavior,' 'Going along to get ahead' and 'Pay and promotion.' The first dimension, 'General political behavior,' includes actions such as policy changes that help only a few, the existence of groups that always get their way, and building oneself by tearing others down. The second dimension, 'Going along to get ahead,' is considered as a career-planning political behavior (Witt et al., 2002). In situations where employees perceive the organizational reality as politicized, they may behave accordingly, deliberately withholding important information from executives when that information is thought to be contrary to the executive agenda. 'By remaining silent or even misleading executives by telling them what they want to hear, employees are attempting to be seen as "team players" who do not "rock the boat." In essence, they are "going along to get ahead" to the detriment of business operations and employee morale' (Witt et al., 2002, p. 913). The dimension 'Pay and promotion' deals with the extent to which policies related to those outcomes are arbitrary and inconsistent.

Organizational politics can be functional or dysfunctional. A fundamental issue in work on organizational politics concerns its largely negative interpretation (Ferris and Kacmar, 1992). Indeed, most studies view organizational politics as negative – being construed as a negative force contributing to negative affective and behavioral outcomes (Cropanzano et al., 1997; Parker et al., 1995). However, under some circumstances, organizational politics may have positive effects. Politics is essential to the effective functioning of organizations (Pfeffer, 1981). Wayne and Ferris (1990) contend that individuals who are effective in playing politics can advance their careers. Similarly, Ferris and Kacmar (1992) note that perceptions of organizational politics increase job involvement. It is, therefore, important to adopt a neutral perspective on organizational politics (Ferris and Kacmar, 1992). Kacmar and Ferris (1993) recognize that in some circumstances, political behaviors enacted by an individual can align with departmental and organizational goals as well as with the individual's. For example, if managers who are responsible for negotiating a contract with a vendor can withhold certain information during the negotiation process that allows them to win a better price, the managers, departments and organization will all benefit (Kacmar and Ferris, 1993, p. 70). It is important to recognize that organizational politics need not be bad, though in general usage the term has a pejorative connotation. Political skills such as coalition building, compromise trade-offs and negotiation may be desirable in an organization (Kacmar et al., 1999). Before presenting the conceptual model of the perceptions of politics and justice link, we explain the differences between the two concepts. Specifically, we argue that perceptions of organizational politics and perceptions of justice are conceptually different.

Organizational politics and organizational justice

Although organizational politics may be closely related to fairness, the two concepts are different (Aryee et al., 2004). Organizational politics refers to self-serving behavior to the detriment of other organizational members or the organization itself. The purpose of political behavior is to obtain some advantage, such as promotion, power, or better performance evaluation. Justice (or fairness), however, refers to organizational members' perceptions of fair treatment (Greenberg, 1987). These perceptions may be related to the fairness of outcome distribution (Adams, 1965), the fairness of formal procedures (Lind and Tyler, 1988), or the fairness of interpersonal treatment (Bies and Moag, 1986). Justice is mostly a judgment related to the fairness of the outcomes one receives, the fairness of formal procedures underlying outcome distribution, or the extent to which one is treated with respect and dignity by others within the organization, especially those in positions of power.

The similarity between the two concepts lies in the fact that they are both perceptual phenomena. Organizational politics and organizational justice have both objective and subjective components. Organizational justice may well exist in an organization. However, employees' perceptions give meaning to the sense of justice or injustice. As Vigoda and Cohen (2001) put it, 'Politics in organizations should be understood in terms of what people think the politics is than what it actually is' (p. 312). Organizational politics and organizational justice are also multifaceted phenomena. Perceptions of organizational politics include three forms: 'General political behavior,' 'Going along to get ahead' and 'Pay and promotion' (Kacmar and Ferris, 1991). Similarly, organizational justice includes three components: distributive justice, procedural justice and interactional justice. In the following paragraphs, we briefly discuss the key assumptions of each of the three dimensions of organizational justice. (For more detail on these constructs, see Thibaut and Walker, 1975; Lind and Tyler, 1988; Bies and Moag, 1986; and Cropanzano and Greenberg, 1997.)

Distributive justice
Distributive justice refers to perceptions of outcome fairness (Adams, 1965). When an individual compares his or her input/output ratio to that of a comparison other (Adams, 1965), he or she experiences equity when the two ratios are equal and inequity when they are unequal. Individuals may restore equity by lowering their inputs, enhancing their outputs (in case of over-reward inequity), changing the comparison other or leaving the exchange relationship (Adams, 1965). Distributive injustice occurs when a person does not get the amount of reward he or she expects in comparison with the reward some other gets (Deutsch, 1985). People are concerned about the fairness of the outcomes they receive as well as the fairness of the process leading to these outcomes – thus introducing the construct of procedural justice.

Procedural justice
Procedural justice focuses on the fairness of decisions underlying the outcome distribution (Leventhal, 1976; Thibaut and Walker, 1975). Leventhal (1976) and Leventhal et al. (1980) identified six procedural justice rules: consistency (procedures must be consistent to ensure fairness), bias suppression (procedures must be developed and implemented without considering the self-interests of those who elaborated them), rule of accuracy (procedures must be based on accurate information), rule of correctability (procedures must allow room for correction), rule of representativeness (procedures must integrate the interests of all parties), and rule of ethicality (procedures must follow moral and ethical standards). Organizational rules and procedures that are biased and

inconsistent may create feelings of procedural injustice. Procedural justice theories include the self-interest model (Thibaut and Walker, 1975) and relational model (Lind and Tyler, 1988; Tyler and Lind, 1992). The self-interest model contends that people value justice because it helps them control decision outcomes (Thibaut and Walker, 1975). The relational model, however, argues that people value justice because fair treatment provides a standing and status within groups (Lind and Tyler, 1988). It expands the definition of procedural justice beyond the fairness of formal procedures and includes a social component. This relational component of procedural justice is referred to as interactional justice.

Interactional justice
Interactional justice refers to the quality of interpersonal treatment people receive during the enactment of organizational procedures (Bies and Moag, 1986). Interactional justice also includes providing adequate information regarding decision making (Bies, 1987). Interactional justice acknowledges that people prefer to be treated with respect and dignity (Cropanzano and Greenberg, 1997). These three components of distributive, procedural and interactional justice may be influenced by perceptions of politics. To account for the relationship between the constructs of perceptions of politics and organizational justice, we developed a conceptual model, which is discussed next.

Politics perceptions and justice: A conceptual model
The fundamental premise of the model (see Figure 8.1) is that perceptions of organizational politics negatively affect perceptions of justice. In making such a prediction, the model essentially construes organizational politics as dysfunctional. The model includes the three forms of perceptions of politics identified by Kacmar and Ferris (1991), 'General political behavior,' 'Going along to get ahead' and 'Pay and promotion.' Each of these three dimensions is likely to negatively affect perceptions of distributive, procedural

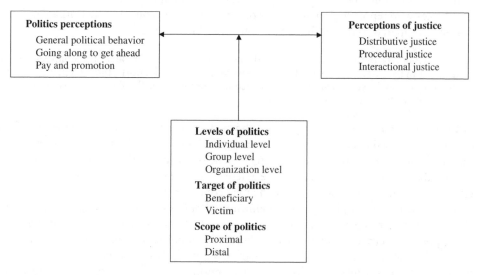

Figure 8.1   A model of the relationship between politics perceptions and justice

and interactional justice. In anticipating a direct relationship between the two constructs, we reassert the view that there are conceptually different. Perceptions of politics refer to some employees' perceptions that others within the organization are using unauthorized (often illegitimate) means for personal gains, whereas perceptions of fairness refer to the fairness of outcomes distribution, formal procedures, and treatment with respect and dignity. Although politics may entail perceptions of unfairness, lack of justice does not always mean that politics is present (Ferris et al., 1995).

In addition to these direct effects, the model postulates moderating effects. Indeed, the model also contends that three variables, targets of organizational politics, levels of organizational politics and scope of organizational politics, may moderate the perceptions of the politics–fairness relationship. The first moderator, level of politics, includes three dimensions: individual level, group level and organizational level. The extent to which politics occurs at each level may moderate the perceptions of the politics–fairness relationship. The same holds true for the second moderator, target of politics. An individual may be a beneficiary or a victim of political behavior. A beneficiary of political behavior is someone who gets some types of advantages from political actions. A victim of political behavior is one who does not get any advantage from the political behavior. The extent to which a person is a beneficiary or a victim of organizational politics may also moderate the perceptions of the politics–fairness relationship. Finally, the third moderator, scope of politics, includes proximal and distal politics. Politics is proximal when it occurs in one's work unit and distal when it occurs somewhere else. It may also moderate the perceptions of the politics–fairness relationship.

The two-way arrow between perceptions of politics and justice in Figure 8.1 indicates that the relationship between the two variables may be circular – implying that they may mutually influence each other. For instance, perceptions of politics may influence perceptions of justice. Similarly, employees who feel unfairly treated may consider that their work unit or organization is more political than those who feel fairly treated. As perceptions of politics influence perceptions of fairness, so might the latter influence the former. Employees who report high perceptions of unfairness may consider their organization as political compared to those who report low levels of unfairness.

> Politics might be perceived or be enhanced when one feels unfairly treated. If employees feel that decision-makers are not appreciating and rewarding their work efforts, they might work behind the scenes to make sure their efforts are called into attention, or the shortcomings of others are highlighted. (Ferris et al., 2002, p. 223)

Take the example of an employee who expected a promotion. Suppose that this employee is passed over for the promotion (loss of outcomes). If the employee perceives this situation as unfair (distributive injustice), he or she may question the fairness of the process that led to that outcome. To the extent that the employee considers the process as unfair (procedural unfairness), he or she may conclude that the process was arbitrary or based on favoritism, implying that organizational politics has contaminated this process. The distribution of resources is closely tied to conflict and as such is likely to bring about more political activity than most other organizational situations (Drory and Romm, 1990). Since we have hypothesized a direct relationship between the two constructs, we discuss in the following paragraphs how perceptions of politics might affect perceptions of fairness.

Perceptions of politics and justice

The three dimensions of politics perceptions illustrated by the three components of the Perceptions of Politics Scale, 'General politics behavior,' 'Going along to get ahead' and 'Pay and promotion' (Kacmar and Ferris, 1991), may affect differently the three dimensions of organizational justice. For instance, most of the items comprising the dimension 'General political behavior' pertain to issues of process and interactions between individuals. Examples of such items include 'people in this organization attempt to build themselves up by tearing others down' and 'there has always been an influential group in this department that no one ever crosses.' Not only do people adopting such behaviors fail to treat others with respect and dignity, but they also attempt to circumvent formal procedures. This may happen when organizations lack formal procedures and policies. In the absence of specific rules and policies for guidance, individuals have few clues as to acceptable behavior, and therefore develop their own – often self-serving (Kacmar and Carlson, 1997). Thus one may posit that when political behavior occurs at this level, it may undermine feelings of procedural and interactional justice. For instance, Andrews and Kacmar (2001) found negative correlations between perceptions of politics and procedural justice ($r = -0.48$) and distributive justice ($r = -0.43$). They conclude that perceptions of politics undermine fairness in the organization because not everyone engages in politicking to meet their own objectives. Those who do not engage in such political behavior would experience resentment and feelings of procedural and interactional injustice.

The subscale 'Going along to get ahead' includes items such as 'employees are encouraged to speak out frankly even when they are critical of well-established ideas,' 'agreeing with powerful others is the best alternative in this organization' and 'telling others what they want to hear is sometimes better than telling the truth,' to name just a few. These items indicate a lack of formal procedures. Thus people engage in behaviors that are self-serving. Those behaviors violate two justice principles, the procedural principle and the distributive principle. They violate the procedural principle in that they do not observe any formal procedures. They also violate the distributive principle because their purpose is to secure a personal outcome.

Finally, the subscale 'Pay and promotion' deals directly with rewards and outcomes. Thus, when political behavior infiltrates the compensation and promotion process, it may negatively affect perceptions of distributive justice. Pay and promotion may raise issues of distributive and procedural justice (e.g. Witt and Nye, 1992; Saal and Moore, 1992; Kaplan and Ferris, 2001; Lemons and Jones, 2001) because they represent outcomes valued by most employees. For instance, in a merit-pay system, the likelihood of political behavior on the part of a few or many is great, and problems of perceived fairness are not uncommon (Ferris et al., 1995). Ferris et al. (1995) also note that the mobility or promotion channels are more likely related to procedural justice than distributive justice because they specify elements of the process regarding how promotions are awarded rather than who receives them. When an employee does not get an expected pay raise, he/she may experience feelings of inequity (Adams, 1965). Similarly, an employee who is passed over for a promotion he/she thinks is deserved may experience feelings of inequity. In both cases, the disgruntled employee may start questioning the process underlying the pay or promotion decision (issues of procedural fairness). Thus, we formulated the following proposition.

Proposition 1   Perceptions of 'General political behavior' and 'Going along to get ahead' would negatively affect perceptions of procedural and interactional justice, whereas perceptions of politics for 'Pay and promotion' would negatively affect perceptions of distributive justice.

Organizational politics may influence perceptions of fairness for at least two reasons. First, for a sense of justice or injustice to occur, one should hold another responsible for the action. Fairness theory (Folger and Cropanzano, 1998, 2001) may explain this phenomenon. According to fairness theory, the central topic of social justice is the assignment of blame (Folger and Cropanzano, 1998, 2001). 'When people identify an instance of unfair treatment, they are holding someone accountable for an action (or inaction) that threatens another person's material or psychological well-being. If no one is to blame, there is no social injustice. For this reason, the process of accountability, or how another social entity comes to be considered blameworthy, is fundamental to justice. When people ascertain the fairness of someone's actions, they are trying to decide whether to hold that person accountable for those actions' (Folger and Cropanzano, 2001, p. 1). If a person cannot attribute blame, no injustice has occurred. Perceptions of organizational politics may lead to perceptions of injustice in so far as the person 'playing politics' can be identified and blamed for the action.

Second, in an exchange relationship, members tend to maximize their personal return on investment. In doing so, they may engage in behaviors that are perceived as self serving – leading to feelings of exploitation. Since political behaviors have the capacity to alter both process and outcome fairness, we would expect that perceptions of politics would have a strong, inverse relationship with justice (Ferris et al., 2002). Fairness heuristics theory (Lind, 2001) helps explain the extent to which politics may affect employee perceptions of fairness in organizations. The basis of fairness heuristic theory is the recognition that virtually all social relationships, including most relationships in organizations, involve repeated encounters with a very basic dilemma – 'the fundamental social dilemma' (Lind, 2001). People routinely resolve the fundamental social dilemma by using impressions of fair treatment as a heuristic device (Lind, 2001).

> If people believe they have been treated fairly by others in a given social context, then this prompts a 'short-cut' decision to subordinate personal desires to the needs of the group, team, or organization . . . Fair treatment leads people to respond cooperatively to the demands and requests of others and the group as a whole. On the other hand, if they believe that they have been treated unfairly, this cooperative orientation is rejected in favor of a self-interested orientation that decides every request on the basis of its implications for short-term self-interest. (Lind, 2001, p. 65)

Thus perceptions of politics may create the impression that one is manipulated and his or her interests are ignored, sparking a self-serving behavior.

In addition to this direct effect, we anticipated that three types of variables, the targets of political behavior, the level of political activity, and the scope of political activity, may mitigate the negative impact of perceptions of politics on fairness. We discuss the moderating role of these variables next.

The role of moderators

Although organizational politics is generally conceived as a negative phenomenon (Aryee et al., 2004), the personal consequences of political activities for an employee may affect his or her reactions to it. Employees who are 'victims' of organizational politics may view it in a negative manner, whereas those who benefit from it may view it as a normal part of organizational life. Thus, perceptions of fairness based on perceptions of politics may be shaped by the extent to which an employee is a beneficiary or a victim of organizational politics. This corresponds to the egocentric bias in fairness decisions. Indeed, people tend to view their own actions as fair compared to the actions of others. The egocentric fairness bias contends that people tend to remember their own fair behaviors and others' unfair behaviors and attribute more fair behaviors to themselves than to others (Tanaka, 1999). An egocentric fairness judgment represents an example of self-serving behavior (Paese and Yonker, 2001). In expanding this construct, we consider that an egocentric politics bias may influence individuals' perceptions of politics. People may be more likely to view their own actions as less political than the actions of others.

Organizational politics occurs at three levels: individual, group and organizational (Ferris et al., 1989). We anticipated that the occurrence of politics at each of these three levels might moderate the relationship between perceptions of politics and fairness. For instance, perceptions of politics at the individual level may affect perceptions of interactional justice, whereas perceptions of politics at the group and organizational levels may affect perceptions of distributive and procedural justice. Indeed, procedures are often enacted by entities, such as groups or organizations, not single individuals (although managers are often perceived as agents of groups or organizations).

Finally we anticipated that the scope of politics might also moderate the relationship between perceptions of politics and fairness. We used two constructs, proximal organizational politics and distal organizational politics, to explain the extent to which employees are close to or removed from political activities in their organizations. The former refers to perceptions of organizational politics occurring in one's unit, whereas the latter refers to perceptions of organizational politics occurring in a different organizational unit. For example, employees who view their own work unit as more political than other work units would report high levels of perceptions of unfairness. However, when they view other work units as more political than their own work unit, they may be less likely to report high levels of unfairness. Ambrose and Harland (1995), Dulebohn (1997) and Aryee et al. (2004) found that organizational politics reduced procedural justice. The extent to which an employee is close to or removed from the occurrence of political behavior may affect his or her perceptions of organizational politics. Maslyn and Fedor (1998) argue that one should distinguish the political behavior that occurs within one's own work group from what occurs in the larger organization. Even in a highly political organization, one can be partially insulated within the work group setting. In contrast, the larger organization can be nonpolitical while one experiences high levels of politics in his or her immediate work group (Maslyn and Fedor, 1998, p. 645).

In discussing the scope of justice, we suggest that the extent to which some employees view their unit as political may moderate the relationship between perceptions of politics and perceptions of fairness. People would experience a strong sense of unfairness when their own work units are seen as more political than when other work units are described as political. The occurrence of both proximal and distal politics may moderate the relationship between perceptions of politics and fairness. Thus, we formulated the following proposition:

Proposition 2   The three moderating variables, levels of politics, target of politics and scope of politics, would moderate the relationships between perceptions of organizational politics and perceptions of fairness.

Implications for research and practice
The fundamental assumption in this chapter is that perceptions of organizational politics affect perceptions of justice (or fairness). Both organizational politics and organizational justice are multifaceted concepts. Perceptions of organizational politics include the three dimensions outlined by the Perceptions of Politics Scale (Ferris and Kacmar, 1991). Organizational justice includes distributive justice, procedural justice and interactional justice. The model we developed presents several implications for research and practice.

Implications for research
In assessing the link between perceptions of organizational politics and perceptions of fairness, we made two research propositions that warrant empirical inquiry. First, we suggested a direct relationship between perceptions of organizational politics and justice. Empirical research may assess the extent to which perceptions of politics affect particular dimensions of justice. Research using Kacmar and Ferris's (1991) version of the Perceptions of Organizational Politics Scale may assess what particular subscale is related to specific justice dimensions. Moreover, researchers may also investigate the justice dimension which is most affected by employee perceptions of politics. Do perceptions of politics affect more the fairness of outcomes, procedures, or treatment with respect and dignity? The answer to this question remains an empirical one.

Second, we suggested that the relationship between perceptions of politics and justice might be moderated by three variables: level of politics, scope of politics and targets of politics. Future research might assess the moderating role of these variables. Although our model did not include it, future research should also explore another approach to organizational politics – a cross-cultural perspective. Very few studies have analyzed the cultural impact of organizational politics perceptions. Yet one may speculate that fairness reactions to politics may be influenced by cultural norms. In a comparative study of British and Israeli public sector employees, Vigoda (2001) found that Israeli employees were more tolerant of political behaviors than British employees, viewing them as a natural means by which an employee can gain advantages and achieve personal interests in the workplace. Based on these findings, one may speculate that British employees may have perceived politics as less fair than their Israeli counterparts. Empirical cross-cultural studies are needed in attempting to understand the relationship between perceptions of politics and justice. In conducting such studies, researchers may look at both differences and similarities across cultures. For instance, a recent study conducted on a sample of 208 Malaysian employees found that employees who perceived a high level of politics in their workplace reported higher levels of stress, lower levels of job satisfaction, and higher levels of intention to quit than did employees who perceived a low level of politics

(Poon, 2002). These findings are consistent with those of research conducted in North American organizational settings.

It is also possible that the widespread use of e-mail and other information technologies may facilitate the occurrence of political behavior in organizations. E-mail is an enabler of political behavior (Kuzmits et al., 2002). The authors used the construct of e-politics to refer to political activities based on the use of electronic means, such as e-mail. By facilitating the occurrence of political behavior in the workplace, e-politics may indirectly affect the relationship between perceptions of politics and justice.

Implications for practice
Our discussion of the relationship between perceptions of politics and organizational justice has implications for management practice. We consider that since politics is ubiquitous to organizational life, managers may reduce its detrimental effects by understanding its impact on another ubiquitous perceptual phenomenon – organizational justice. Since 'political' organizations do little to satisfy employees equally and create fair compensation systems (Vigoda-Gadot et al., 2003), managers may reduce perceptions of unfairness by reducing not only perceptions of politics in organizations but also actual political behavior. If organizational politics influences perceptions of fairness and leads particularly to perceptions of unfairness, then one may reduce unfairness by reducing employee perceptions of politics. When political behavior is rewarded in organizations, not only do beneficiaries tend to repeat it but others may get involved in it as well (Kacmar and Carlson, 1997).

Organizations may teach managers and employees alike how to recognize political behavior. Specifically, organizations may teach managers to recognize the realities of perceptions of politics. Since people with more power are in a better position to satisfy their interests and needs at the expense of others who have fewer political resources and influence (Vigoda-Gadot et al., 2003, p. 766), they may be less likely to perceive politics in their organizations. Compared to employees, managers may be less likely to recognize the existence of political activity in their organizations. Thus, they would be less likely to take actions required to curtail such activities. To the extent that they recognize the existence of political behavior, they may be likely to take corrective actions.

Organizations may also reduce perceptions of political behavior by creating fair working environments. To the extent that employees feel fairly treated, they would be less likely to incriminate political activities. Cropanzano et al. (1995) suggest that organizational justice may be an effective way to manage organizational politics. By introducing distributive, procedural and interactional fairness, managers may curtail perceptions of organizational politics. For instance, what fair procedures do best is help maintain a social system such as a business firm, even in the face of the inevitable bruised feelings and ill outcomes (Cropanzano et al., 1995).

Despite our model's implications for research and practice, we recognize some of its limitations. It is after all a conceptual model and its assumptions can only be speculative. We strongly hope that the issues raised in this chapter will spark future empirical studies and conceptual developments on the link between politics perceptions and organizational justice. This is particularly important since perceptions of organizational politics represent a growing area of scientific inquiry and an area of 'real-world' relevance as well (Ferris et al., 2002). We hope that this chapter is an important step in that direction.

References

Adams, S.J. (1965). Inequity in social exchange. In L. Berkowitz (ed.), *Advances in social experimental psychology* (Vol. 2, pp. 267–99). New York: Academic Press.

Ambrose, M.L. and Harland, L.K. (1995). Procedural justice and influence tactics: Fairness, frequency, and effectiveness. In R.S. Cropanzano and K.M. Kacmar (eds), *Organizational politics, justice, and support: Managing the social climate of the workplace* (pp. 97–130). Westport, CT: Quorum Books.

Andrews, M.C. and Kacmar, K.M. (2001). Discriminating among organizational politics, justice, and support. *Journal of Organizational Behavior*, **22**, 347–66.

Aryee, S., Chen, Z.X. and Budhwar, P. (2004). Exchange fairness and employee performance: An examination of the relationship between organizational politics and procedural justice. *Organizational Behavior and Human Decision Processes*, **94**, 1–15.

Bies, R.J. (1987). The predicament of injustice: The management of moral outrage. In L.L. Cummings and B.M. Staw (eds), *Research in organizational behavior* (pp. 289–319). Greenwich, CT: JAI Press.

Bies, R.J. and Moag, J.S. (1986). Interactional justice: Communication criteria of fairness. In R.J. Lewicki, B.H. Sheppard and M.H. Bazerman (eds), *Research on negotiation in organizations* (Vol. 1, pp. 43–55). Greenwich, CT: JAI Press.

Cropanzano, R. and Greenberg, J. (1997). Progress in organizational justice: Tunneling through the maze. In C.L. Cooper and I.T. Robertson (eds), *International review of industrial and organizational psychology* (pp. 317–72). New York: John Wiley & Sons.

Cropanzano, R., Kacmar, K.M. and Bozeman, D.P. (1995). The social setting of work organizations: Politics, justice, and support. In R.S. Cropanzano and K.M. Kacmar (eds), *Organizational politics, justice, and support: Managing the social climate of the workplace* (pp. 1–18). Westport, CT: Quorum Books.

Cropanzano, R., Howes, J.C., Grandey, A.A. and Toth, H.P. (1997). The relationship of organizational politics and support to work behaviors, attitudes, and stress. *Journal of Organizational Behavior*, **18**, 159–80.

Darr, W. and Johns, G. (2004). Political decision-making climates: Theoretical processes and multi-level antecedents. *Human Relations*, **57**, 169–200.

Davis, W.D. and Gardner, W.L. (2004). Perceptions of politics and organizational cynicism: An attributional and leader–member exchange perspective. *Leadership Quarterly*, **15**, 439–65.

Deutsch, M. (1985). *Distributive justice: A social-psychological perspective*. New Haven, CT: Yale University Press.

Drory, A. and Romm, T. (1990). The definition of organizational politics: A review. *Human Relations*, **43**, 1133–54.

Dulebohn, J.H. (1997). Social influence in justice evaluations of human resources systems. In G.R. Ferris (ed.), *Research in personnel and human resources management* (Vol. 15, pp. 241–91). Greenwich, CT: JAI Press.

Ferris, G.R. and Kacmar, K.M. (1992). Perceptions of organizational politics. *Journal of Management*, **18**, 93–116.

Ferris, G.R., Russ, G.S. and Fandt, P.M. (1989). Politics in organizations. In R.A. Giacalone and R. Rosenfeld (eds), *Impression management in the organization* (pp. 143–70). Hillsdale, NJ: Erlbaum.

Ferris, G.R., Frink, D.D., Beehr, T.A. and Gilmore, D.C. (1995). Political fairness and fair politics: The conceptual integration of divergent constructs. In R.S. Cropanzano and K.M. Kacmar (eds), *Organizational politics, justice, and support: Managing the social climate of the workplace* (pp. 21–36). Westport, CT: Quorum Books.

Ferris, G.R., Frink, D.D., Bhawuk, D., Zhou, J. and Gilmore, D.C. (1996). Reactions of diverse groups to politics in the workplace. *Journal of Management*, **22**, 23–44.

Ferris, G.R., Harrell-Cook, G. and Dulebohn, J.H. (2000). Organizational politics: The nature of the relationship between politics and political behavior. In S.B. Bacharach and E.J. Lawler (eds), *Research in the sociology of organizations* (Vol. 17, pp. 89–130). Stamford, CT: JAI Press.

Ferris, G.R., Adams, G., Kolodinsky, R.W., Hochwarter, W.A. and Ammeter, A.P. (2002). Perceptions of organizational politics: Theory and research directions. In F.J. Yammarino and F. Dansereau (eds), *The many faces of multi-level issues* (pp. 179–254). New York: JAI Elsevier Science.

Folger, R. and Cropanzano, R. (1998). *Organizational justice and human resource management*. Beverly Hills, CA: Sage.

Folger, R. and Cropanzano, R. (2001). Fairness theory: Justice as accountability. In J. Greenberg and R. Cropanzano (eds), *Advances in organizational justice* (pp. 1–55). Stanford, CA: Stanford University Press.

Gandz, J. and Murray, V.V. (1980). The experience of workplace politics. *Academy of Management Review*, **23**, 237–51.

Greenberg, J. (1987). A taxonomy of organizational justice theories. *Academy of Management Review*, **12**, 9–22.

Kacmar, K.M. and Baron, R.A. (1999). Organizational politics: The state of the field, links to related research, and an agenda for future research. In G. Ferris (ed.), *Research in personnel and human resources management* (Vol. 17, pp. 1–39). Greenwich, CT: JAI Press.

Kacmar, K.M. and Carlson, D.S. (1997). Further validation of the perceptions of politics scale (POPS): A multiple sample investigation. *Journal of Management*, **23**, 627–58.

Kacmar, K.M. and Ferris, G.R. (1991). Perceptions of organizational politics scale (POPS): Development and construct validation. *Educational and Psychological Measurement*, **51**, 193–205.

Kacmar, K.M. and Ferris, G.R. (1993). Politics at work: Sharpening the focus of political behavior in organizations. *Business Horizons* (July–August), 70–74.

Kacmar, K.M., Bozeman, D.P., Carlon, D.S. and Anthony, W.P. (1999). An examination of perceptions of organizational politics model: Replication and extension. *Human Relations*, **52**, 383–416.

Kaplan, D.M. and Ferris, G.R. (2001). Fairness perceptions of employee promotion systems: A two-study investigation of antecedents and mediators. *Journal of Applied Social Psychology*, **31**, 1204–22.

Kipnis, D., Schmidt, S.M. and Wilkinson, I. (1980). Intraorganizational influence tactics: Explorations in getting one's way. *Journal of Applied Psychology*, **65**, 440–52.

Kuzmits, F., Sussman, L., Adams, A. and Raho, L. (2002). Using information and e-mail for political gain. *The Information Management Journal* (September–October), 76–80.

Lemons, M.A. and Jones, C.A. (2001). Procedural justice in promotion decisions: Using perceptions of fairness to build employee commitment. *Journal of Managerial Psychology*, **16**, 268–80.

Leventhal, G.S. (1976). The distinction of rewards and resources in groups and organizations. In L. Berkowitz and E. Walster (eds), *Advances in experimental social psychology* (Vol. 9, pp. 91–131). New York: Academic Press.

Leventhal, G.S., Karuza, J. and Fry, W.R. (1980). Beyond fairness: A theory of allocation preferences. In G. Mikula (ed.), *Justice and social interaction* (pp. 167–218). New York: Springer-Verlag.

Lewin, K. (1936). *Principles of topological psychology*. New York: McGraw-Hill.

Lind, E.A. (2001). Fairness heuristic theory: Justice judgments as pivotal cognitions in organizational relations. In J. Greenberg and R. Cropanzano (eds), *Advances in organizational justice* (pp. 56–88). Stanford, CA: Stanford University Press.

Lind, E.A. and Tyler, T.R. (1988). *The social psychology of procedural justice*. New York: Plenum Press.

Maslyn, J.M. and Fedor, D.B. (1998). Perceptions of politics: Does measuring different foci matter? *Journal of Applied Psychology*, **84**, 645–53.

Mintzberg, H. (1985). The organization as political arena. *Journal of Management Studies*, **22**, 133–54.

Paese, P.W. and Yonker, R.D. (2001). Toward a better understanding of egocentric fairness judgments in negotiation. *The International Journal of Conflict Management*, **12**, 114–31.

Parker, C.P., Dipboye, R.L. and Jackson, S.L. (1995). Perceptions of organizational politics: An investigation of antecedents and consequences. *Journal of Management*, **21**, 891–912.

Pfeffer, J. (1981). *Power in organizations*. Boston, MA: Pitman.

Poon, J.M.L. (2002). Situational antecedents and outcomes of organizational politics perceptions. *Journal of Managerial Psychology*, **18**, 138–55.

Randall, M.L., Cropanzano, R., Bormann, C.C. and Birjulin, A. (1999). Organizational politics and organizational support as predictors of work attitudes, job performance, and organizational citizenship behavior. *Journal of Organizational Behavior*, **20**, 159–74.

Saal, F.E. and Moore, S.C. (1992). Perceptions of promotion fairness and promotion candidates' qualifications. *Journal of Applied Psychology*, **78**, 105–12.

Tanaka, K.I. (1999). Judgments of fairness by just world believers. *The Journal of Social Psychology*, **139** (5), 631–8.

Thibaut, J.W. and Walker, L. (1975). *Procedural Justice: A psychological analysis*. Hillsdale, NJ: Lawrence Erlbaum.

Tyler, T.R. and Lind, E.A. (1992). A relational model of authority in groups. In M.P. Zanna (ed.), *Advances in experimental social psychology* (Vol. 25, pp. 115–91). San Diego, CA: Academic Press.

Vigoda, E. (2001). Reactions to organizational politics: A cross-cultural examination in Israel and Britain. *Human Relations*, **54**, 1482–518.

Vigoda, E. (2002). Stress-related aftermaths to workplace politics: The relationship among politics, job distress, and aggressive behavior in organizations. *Journal of Organizational Behavior*, **23**, 571–91.

Vigoda, E. (2003). *Developments in organizational politics*. Cheltenham, UK and Northampton, MA, USA: Edward Elgar.

Vigoda, E. and Cohen, A. (2001). Influence tactics and perceptions of organizational politics: A longitudinal study. *Journal of Business Research*, **55**, 311–24.

Vigoda-Gadot, E., Vinarski-Peretz, H. and Ben-Zion, E. (2003). Politics and image in the organizational landscape: An empirical examination among public sector employees. *Journal of Managerial Psychology*, **18** (8), 764–87.

Wayne, S.J. and Ferris, G.R. (1990). Influence tactics, affect, and exchange quality in supervisor–subordinate interactions. *Journal of Applied Psychology*, **75**, 487–99.

Witt, L.A. and Nye, L.G. (1992). Gender and the relationship between perceived fairness of pay or promotion and job satisfaction. *Journal of Applied Psychology*, **77**, 910–17.

Witt, L.A., Kacmar, K.M., Carlson, D.S. and Zivnuska, S. (2002). Integrative effects of personality and organizational politics on contextual performance. *Journal of Organizational Behavior*, **23**, 911–26.

Zhou, J. and Ferris, G.R. (1995). The dimensions and consequences of organizational politics perceptions: A confirmatory analysis. *Journal of Applied Social Psychology*, **25**, 1747–64.

PART III

EMOTIONS AND STRESS: ORGANIZATIONAL POLITICS AND EMPLOYEES' WELL-BEING

9 Organizational politics and workplace stress
Russell Cropanzano and Andrew Li

Introduction

Sitting at the computer to begin a chapter on politics and stress, one is immediately confronted by a sense of daunting. The sensation surprises, for one can be sure that politics and stress *should* be related. Ferris, Frink, Galang et al. (1996), Ferris et al. (1994), Harris and Kacmar (2005) and Vigoda (2003) list good reasons why. For one thing, 'politics' and 'stress' are both phenomenological concepts. That is, each is a sort of subjective appraisal of one's work environment or perhaps of one's response to one's work environment. A thing is 'stressful' or 'political' when someone decides that it is. Second, stress and politics are both suffused with ambiguity and unpredictability. Both involve a certain perplexity as to *what* is going on and *when* it will occur. Politics creates ambiguity in various ways. For example, it undermines (or runs parallel to) formal decision structures and tends not to be transparent to all. Such uncertainty can be unsettling, engendering a sense of ill-ease. Third, both concepts involve weighing the opportunity for gains against the potential for losses, and the tipping of that scale is at least partially dependent on the employee's response. In sum, politics and stress involve how people subjectively construe uncertain situations where an appropriate action is necessary to avoid a harm or to realize a gain. With so much in common, why is there such an off-putting feeling?

The reason has to do with one other attribute shared by 'politics' and 'stress' – both concepts lend themselves to multiple definitions. Since each term can have multiple meanings, then what we can learn from these constructs depends on the denotation intended by the speaker. This creates conceptual confusion and makes it difficult to integrate findings and build theory. With these thoughts in mind, our present chapter will discuss the sundry definitions – those for stress and those for politics. In the course of this, we pledge to review relevant empirical evidence, but do so through the lens of each definition. The empirical evidence, therefore, should be more informative once these different perspectives are made salient.

The definition of 'stress'

Keil (2004) tells us that our modern term 'stress' traces back to the Latin *stringere*, meaning 'to draw tight.' Keil further observes that by the 1300s, Old English included the word *destresse* (in Middle English the term was *stresse, American Heritage Dictionary*, 1981), which conveyed a sense of psychological hardship. By the 1800s, however, the word 'stress' was used within the physical sciences to convey the process by which a physical object is distorted by the application of a force (Kahn and Byosiere, 1992). As Kahn and Byosiere (p. 573) put it, 'Stress referred to the internal resisting force . . . Strain or distortion was the resulting change in the object.' The word 'stress' and its progenitors have long vacillated between connotations of the physical (*stringere*, the nineteenth-century usage of 'stress') and the psychological (*destresse, stresse*). Even today a good dictionary will include both of these meanings (and a few others).

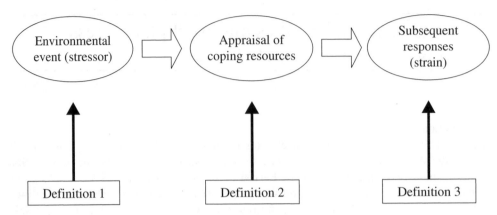

Figure 9.1   Heuristic model of workplace stress, showing possible definitions

The common theme in this definitional history is that some external force presses against an object, thereby altering its shape. Depending on the connotations, that 'object' might be a physical structure, a human body, or a condition of one's psychology. The key ideas of (1) external stimulus, (2) applying pressure, and (3) changing of form were captured in the early usages of 'stress' by medical researchers (Osler, 1910; Cannon, 1935; Selye, 1936). What then is the core of 'stress'? As we shall see, our chronicle has given us three plausible candidates, and these are illustrated in Figure 9.1. Each of these has been defined as 'stress' by some researchers but not by others (for reviews see Jex and Beehr, 1991; Kahn and Byosiere, 1992).

Stress definition 1: Stress as environmental events

Overview   One possibility listed by Kahn and Byosiere (1992) is to define stress in terms of events that provoke responses. In this lexicon, a 'stressful' event might be something that causes anxiety, dissatisfaction, or poor health. For example, Kahn et al. (1964) term role ambiguity and role conflict 'stresses,' even though these constructs are presumed to cause other reactions (for similar usage, see Fisher and Gitelson, 1983; Peterson et al., 1995). Within the literature on organizational politics, Dipboye and Foster (2002, p. 261) suggest that some individuals might conceptualize 'politics as stress.' This way of approaching politics would treat politics/stress as a source of potentially harmful individual responses.

Unanswered questions   The problem with this definition is that this use of the word 'stress' as a cause (i.e. our stress definition 1) proceeds in lockstep with the use of the word 'stress' as a response (i.e. our stress definition 3 – see below). This problem has been recognized for some time. For example, we just saw how some scholars referred to role conflict and role ambiguity as role 'stress.' However, when Rizzo et al. (1970) developed scales to measure role conflict and role ambiguity, the authors referred to role ambiguity as one of the '*sources* of stress' (p. 151, italics added).[1] Notice that no one disagrees as to the causal status of these two variables. They are presumed to engender negative responses, such as tension (e.g. Netemeyer et al., 1990). The question is whether role ambiguity and role conflict *cause* stress or *are* stresses.

In reviewing his own work, Selye (1976, p. 50) mentioned a *British Medical Journal* article which maintains that 'according to Selye, "stress is its own cause." ' Selye seems to have acknowledged the criticism by fixing the conceptual problem. Specifically, he says (p. 51) that he 'was forced to create a neologism and introduce the word *stressor*, for the causative agent, into the English language, retaining *stress* for the resulting condition.' In other words, Selye solved the problem by abandoning the first definition.

For politics researchers, Selye's (1976) insight is critical. Researchers tend not to see politics as stress *per se*. Instead, politics is treated as a stressor, or the cause, of some individual reaction (e.g. anxiety, burnout, etc.). However, we should understand that Selye's solution is incomplete. The reason is that there are two possible 'resulting conditions' to which one might reasonably apply the term 'stress.' One is the immediate cognitive appraisals made by the individual. The other is the longer-term responses engendered by those appraisals. We will examine this issue when we discuss our second and third definitions of stress.

Advantages of using this definition   The key advantage of this first definition is that it focuses our attention on the nature of the stressor. In other words, it urges us to examine why politics is or should be related to workplace stress. In this regard, our theoretical models to date remain incomplete and further conceptual development is of vital importance. Different scholars have proposed different models and these frameworks, while not fundamentally in contradiction, have yet to be fully integrated.

One perspective focuses on individuals' abilities to control valuable outcomes and prevent harm. For example, according to Witt et al. (2000; see also Cropanzano et al., 1997; Witt, 1998), political environments run the risk of violating the social contract between an individual and an employing organization. The politicized setting can become chaotic and uncertain. This disordered and uncertain situation produces stress. Other authors have made similar observations (e.g. Ferris and Judge, 1991; Ferris et al., 1989; Randall et al., 1999; Vigoda, 2003). Stated somewhat loosely, politics (the stressor) produces negative reactions (e.g. tension, burnout) by jeopardizing benefits and threatening individuals with harm. This lack of predictability and control as to the outcomes subsequently produces adverse psychological states. These sorts of reactions should be familiar to students of workplace stress. To take but two examples, this analysis is generally consistent with the already-reviewed research on role ambiguity and role conflict (Jackson and Schuler, 1985) and learned helplessness (Seligman, 1992).

While this analysis is important, it only tells us part of the story. Political environments may have other effects which are equally destructive. Various authors have argued that workplace politics might engender a sense of injustice (e.g. Ferris et al., 2002; Ferris and Kacmar, 1992; Kacmar and Ferris, 1991). In this regard, evidence exists suggesting that injustice harms a worker's sense of well-being (Cropanzano et al., 2005). With these considerations in mind, Vigoda (2002, pp. 575–6) has suggested that injustice might provide an additional mechanism by which politics creates stress. Notice that Vigoda's model suggests a mediator that is different from (perhaps 'in addition to' would be a better way to put this) the one proposed earlier. According to Vigoda, the sense of unfairness or inequity might be important for understanding how politics produces stress. We shall return to this possibility in more detail when we discuss the definition of politics and again when we build our integrative model.

Stress definition 2: Stress as an assessment of coping resources

Overview   A second definition of stress concerns the subjective judgment of one's resources relative to the demands one has to meet (Hobfoll, 1989, 1993). When demands exceed resources, one is likely to experience work tension, anxiety, and so on. Most notable here is the idea that stress is a mediating variable that carries the influence of the stressor on to some response (cf. Edwards, 1992; Folkman and Lazarus, 1991). From this perspective, the response is generally termed 'strain' (Kahn and Byosiere, 1992). Indices of strain can include such things as physical symptoms, health symptoms, negative affect and so forth.

Within the literature on organizational politics, Ferris, Frink, Galang et al. (1996) come close to this definition when they refer to politics as a source of stress (p. 242, that is, not *as* stress) and strain as a possible *outcome* of stress (p. 243). Likewise, Ferris et al. (1994, pp. 1206–7) emphasize that stress involves 'uncertainty' and is 'an individually-experienced phenomenon.' Moreover, definition 2 was explicitly used by Cropanzano et al. (1997) and reviewed (though not employed) by Vigoda (2002).

Unanswered questions   The key problem with this definition is that it has not been used unambiguously. To understand why, consider how one would measure stress if it were understood to be a mediating variable that caused strain. Stress in this sense would involve some appraisal of coping capacity and/or an assessment of perceived environmental demands. However, this was not the operational definition that was utilized by Cropanzano et al. (1997). These authors (see especially pp. 171–2) measured 'stress' as tension, fatigue and uneasiness. These are emotional and physical symptoms that should *result* from stress – were stress taken to be the aforementioned mediator. In other words, Cropanzano et al. defined stress in accordance with definition 2 but operationalized it with an emphasis on definition 3. This is similar to the mix-up we observed when we discussed the work of Rizzo et al. (1970) – two definitions are simultaneously in play.

This muddle is unfortunate because it implies that scholars have not measured an essential mediator. One might or might not reasonably choose to define stress as the perception that demands exceeded capacity. However, as shown in Figure 9.1, most would agree that such a mediator is worthy of consideration. Therefore, by not directly assessing these appraisals, we are left with an unoperationalized variable in our causal model.

Advantages of this definition   We are in a quandary! The key strength of this second definition is that it draws our attention to the role of cognitive appraisals as mediators of the strain (Edwards, 1992). However, since to our knowledge no one has directly assessed this intervening variable, this strength would seem to be undermined. Despite this, our conceptual dilemma is not insoluble. There is literature available that allows us to approach the matter from a different perspective. If, as we have argued here, employees' perceptions of resources relative to demands intervene between the stressors and strain, then there should be particular variables that moderate this effect. Politics may be a threat, but it can also be an opportunity for those with the *savoir-faire* to manage potentially contentious environments. For these individuals, politics could provide a prospect for success (Drory, 1993; Ferris et al., 1995). In this regard, Ferris and his colleagues are quite explicit: politics sometimes engenders anxiety, but this is by no means always true.

In a survey of 310 workers from four organizations, Ferris et al. (1993, Study 1) provided an initial test of these ideas. Politics was assessed using a shortened version of the Perceptions of Organizational Politics Scale (POPS) validated by Ferris and Kacmar (1992, Study 2), Kacmar and Ferris (1991), and Nye and Witt (1993). While politics tended to predict job anxiety, this relationship was qualified by an interaction with perceived control over the work environment. In particular, politics was more strongly related to job anxiety for those with less perceived control, and less strongly related to job anxiety for those with more perceived control. In a later study, Ferris et al. (1994) evaluated the role of understanding one's workplace environment in moderating the relationship between perceived politics at work and stress. Using a sample of 310 employees from four organizations, Ferris and colleagues (Ferris et al., 1994) predicted and found that understanding, operationalized as organizational tenure, moderated the relationship between perceived politics and anxiety.

Ferris, Frink, Galang et al. (1996) also examined the politics/anxiety relationship. These authors found that when predicting job anxiety, politics exhibited two two-way interactions – one with perceived control over the work environment and the other with understanding of organizational politics. For the politics by control interaction, politics was strongly and positively related to job anxiety for those who perceived that they had little control over their work environment. However, the smallest association between politics and anxiety was when perceived control was high. The interaction between politics and understanding exhibited a similar pattern.

In another field study, Ferris et al. (1996) replicated the moderating effects of understanding, but did so in a way that extended previous research. Ferris and his colleagues maintained that white males are more likely to have the status of workplace 'insiders.' As a consequence of this advantageous position, they are more likely to learn critical skills necessary for survival in a politically charged environment. Individuals from other ethnic backgrounds, and to a lesser but still appreciable extent white women, are more likely to occupy the status of 'outsiders,' and have fewer opportunities to learn these political skills than do their white male coworkers.

Given these considerations, Ferris et al. (1996) argued that an understanding of workplace events would ameliorate the impact of politics on anxiety, but only for white males. For other groups the moderating effect of understanding would be weaker. These predictions were supported among a large sample of nonacademic employees at a large university. In other words, for groups other than white males, politics was positively related to job anxiety, regardless of understanding. For white males, on the other hand, understanding events in organizations weakened the relationship between politics and anxiety.

Nevertheless, we should be mindful that the evidence, while generally strong, is not fully consistent. The moderating effects of understanding on the relationship between workplace politics and anxiety were not replicated in another study by Kacmar et al. (1999). Kacmar and her colleagues found that although anxiety was positively correlated with politics perceptions, this relationship was not moderated by employees' understanding of their work environment.

Hochwarter et al. (1999) approached the issue of organizational politics and job tension from a different perspective. Unlike previous research that focused on situational factors that moderate the consequences of politics, Hochwarter and his colleagues argued that dispositional factors may also play a critical role. One such dispositional factor suggested by Hochwarter et al. is individuals' commitment to their organizations. The authors predicted that the relationship between tension and organizational politics is strong for low-commitment employees but weak for those who have high commitment. Hochwarter and his colleagues tested this hypothesis in a sample of 141 middle- and upper-level managers in the hotel industry. Consistent with their hypothesis, low-commitment employees reported a higher level of tension as they perceived more politics at work. The moderating effect was so robust that it was replicated in their second study with 418 employees in a large university.

The work of Ferris and his colleagues, which has demonstrated these important moderation effects, suggests that there is some utility in considering the second definition. That is, the effects of politics become pernicious when individuals feel they lack understanding or cannot control the situation. Treating stress as a mediator calls scholars' attention to an important intervening variable. Researchers should attend to this variable, even if they elect to define stress in some other way.

Stress definition 3: Stress as an individual's response

Overview   A third definition that has gained currency among politics researchers is what Vigoda (2002, p. 574) terms the 'response definition.' Stress is 'an individual's response to work-related environmental stressors, one of which would be politics' (ibid.). Vigoda's response definition is shown in Figure 9.1 of our model. In accordance with this definition, stress is the outcome of environmental pressure, though these effects may be mediated through a subjective appraisal of resources relative to work demands. Notice that this third definition of stress roughly corresponds to what some scholars have termed 'strain' (see Jex et al., 1992, as well as our discussion above). As before, either nomenclature is reasonable, so long as we are clear about our definitions. Nevertheless, among scholars of politics it is probably most common to define stress as a response. For example, Anderson (1994) also treats stress as a response.

An especially interesting example is provided by Ferris et al. (1993). These authors (p. 83) refer to stress as an outcome, thereby implying the response definition. However, as we have already seen, Ferris et al. (1993) presented evidence that perceived control moderated the ill-effects of organizational politics. In other words, these authors used the third (or response) definition, but presented evidence generally consistent with the second (or mediated) approach. Once again this shows the general difficulty the field has in agreeing upon a definition of stress. Politics researchers are forced to pick and choose among a set and, as such, are sometimes inconsistent in their usage.

Nevertheless, in the case of Ferris et al. (1993) this should not trouble us. The key point, as discussed earlier, is that virtually all models of stress recognize (at least) the three stages presented in Figure 9.1 – an event, an appraisal, and a response. Which of these stages is termed 'stress' is less important than the realization that all stages (by whatever name) are useful explanatory variables. Seen from this perspective, it is perfectly reasonable to define 'stress' as a response and then examine potential moderators. The important thing is for scholars to recognize the entire framework. In this regard, a variety of nomenclatures is acceptable, so long as we clearly define our terms and so long as the names we choose do not lead us astray.

Unanswered questions The use of the third definition raises an important theoretical question. Heretofore, our comments (as well as our Figure 9.1) have presupposed that some cognitive appraisal lies between an initial event and a response (or between the strain and stressor, if one prefers the second definition). Many scholars elect not to call this variable 'stress,' preferring some other appellation. This is probably a reasonable representation of the literature, as theories of organizational stress also tend to include cognitive appraisals as mediators (for a review, see Kahn and Byosiere, 1992, especially pp. 580–93). However, we should mind the hazards of overstatement. The intervening variable might not exist at all, or at least it might be less important than one might infer from Figure 9.1.

Technically, if one defined stress as a response to environmental stressors (cf. Vigoda, 2002), then it would not be conceptually necessary to include cognitive appraisals as a mediator. This would change the theory from what we have presented in Figure 9.1. Absent such a mediator, one would be arguing that reactions are caused by the *objective* effects of politics rather than by one's *subjective* evaluation of these effects. In other words, it is theoretically possible to re-draw Figure 9.1, erasing the intermediate Step 2. It strikes us as plausible that the cognitive appraisal of coping capacity is only a partial mediator. That is, politics may have some direct effects on responses, as well as some mediated ones.

Advantages of this definition The key advantage of the response definition is that it calls our attention to what workers feel and do as a result of experiencing politics in the workplace. As such, researchers working from this definition have sometimes provided the most important and straightforward evidence relating politics to workplace stress. The reader should notice, of course, that the studies reviewed here are in no way inconsistent with the tests of moderation reviewed above. The difference is that this current set of papers is for the most part less concerned with what lies between politics and responses, leaving that as an issue for other research.

One example of this research is provided by Anderson (1994). In the course of developing his measure of Dysfunctional Office and Organizational Politics (DOOP), Anderson validated these new measures by correlating the long and short form of the DOOP with a measure of job stress. These were correlated at $r = 0.25$ and $r = 0.27$, respectively. Another study worth considering is that of Cropanzano et al. (1997, Study 2). As we saw earlier, this study *defined* stress as an intervening variable, but *measured* stress as a response. Hence, from a methodological (though not a definitional) point of view, it is best considered here. Cropanzano and his colleagues surveyed 185 working students. All were part-time employees, working for less than 40 hours per week. These respondents were administered two stress measures. The first was Pines and Aronson's (1988) 21-item Burnout Index (BI, for a review of validation evidence, see Shirom, 1989). The second was a 17-item measure of work stress constructed and validated by House and Rizzo (1972). The House and Rizzo instrument contains three scales: (a) job tension, (b) somatic tension, and (c) general fatigue and uneasiness. Cropanzano and his colleagues found that perceptions of politics were significantly correlated with all four of these stress variables (*r*s ranged from 0.29 to 0.37). Moreover, these relationships remained significant even beyond the effect of organizational support.

The goal of these earlier studies was to establish straightforward main effect relationships. While no one would gainsay the importance of this goal, especially in the initial stages of research on politics and stress, recent work has gone further, looking at the relationship among different responses.

In this regard, one interesting study was conducted by Valle and Perrewé (2000). Valle and Perrewé surveyed 260 individuals working at six different organizations. The authors found that perceptions of organizational politics predicted job stress (operationalized as job anxiety; see p. 372). Additionally, as Valle and Perrewé predicted, the ill-effects of politics were stronger for employees who responded with reactive political behaviors. As Valle and Perrewé used the term, reactive political behaviors are those that include 'avoiding action,' 'avoiding blame' and 'avoiding change.'

Another informative study was conducted by Vigoda (2002). Vigoda examined three samples of employees. Across all of these samples perceptions of politics were related to job distress. (The specific distress measure did vary across samples, see p. 581. However, the basic relationships were consistent with one another and with Vigoda's predictions.) In his third sample, Vigoda also included a measure of workplace aggression. Vigoda found that politics predicted aggression and that this relationship was partially mediated by job distress. Vigoda's model is intriguing, for it suggests that politics increases job distress and this distress, in turn, results in aggressive behaviors. In other words, a behavioral response to politics (aggression) is caused by an affective one (distress).

There is another interesting implication of Vigoda's (2002) findings. Since one's coworkers no doubt dislike being victims of aggression, the perpetrator is, in effect, spreading his or her stress around the office. This study simply added one step to Vigoda's causal model. Politics creates distress, distress creates aggression, and aggression likely creates more distress in one's fellow employees. The implication, of course, is that a political climate can have negative ramifications even for those who are not directly touched by the original events.

A criterion-oriented caveat before we move on   While some progress has been made on the criterion side, we should not leave this section without observing that more work needs to be done. Vigoda (2002) lamented that only a limited set of stress-related outcomes, such as anxiety, job satisfaction and organizational commitment, have been examined in the current literature, while little attention has been given to other consequences such as burnout or somatic tension. We concur with Vigoda's conclusions, though for convenience here we emphasize affective and health-related consequences, leaving work attitudes and behaviors to other chapters in this book.

The narrow range of criterion variables is unfortunate because empirical research has documented a wide range of consequences associated with stress. Indeed, Kahn and Byosiere (1992) suggested that stress may generate three categories of responses, including physiological, psychological and behavioral responses. Physiological responses to stress include, but are not limited to, such outcomes as high blood pressure, high heart rates and high cholesterol level (Fried et al., 1984). Psychological responses are related to such outcomes as anxiety, burnout, confusion, depression, job dissatisfaction, health problems and fatigue (Beehr et al., 1976; Cooper and Roden, 1985; Davidson and

Cooper, 1986; Fisher, 1985; Kobasa, 1982). Finally, behavioral responses to stress entail a wide variety of outcomes, such as absence at work, counterproductive behavior, job performance, turnover and drug use on the job (Blau, 1981; Mangione and Quinn, 1975).

Apparently most of the literature investigating stress-related outcomes caused by workplace politics concentrated on the psychological responses and to a lesser extent behavioral responses. Studies that investigate physiological responses to stress are largely absent in the workplace politics literature, and when such data are collected they are usually via self-report (e.g. Cropanzano et al., 1997).

The limited range of stress-related outcomes reported in the politics literature warrants concern for two reasons. First, given that most of the physiological and behavioral responses to stress are largely unexplored, it is possible that the consequences may extend well beyond what is delineated in the existing literature. In other words, stress-related consequences may be understated due to the restricted focus in the current literature. Second, as most of the studies employed self-report questionnaire methods, common method variance may inflate the underlying correlation between politics-induced stress and the psychological responses (Crampton and Wagner, 1994; Podsakoff et al., 2003; Podsakoff and Organ, 1986). The inclusion of nonself-report consequences to stress such as physiological symptoms or performance rated by supervisors may help ascertain the extent of method variance. This would place scholars on a stronger empirical footing regarding conclusions about politics and worker stress.

Some closing thoughts

We have completed our sojourn through the stress literature, from the perspective of three definitions. From our point of view, any of these designations is reasonable; we would simply caution scholars to define their terms as carefully as possible. Given this, the easiest convention is to settle on the definition that is most widely used in the literature. From our reading that would seem to be the response definition. Hence we would encourage scholars to employ that approach and to do so explicitly. In that spirit, we will adopt the response definition for the remainder of this chapter. We emphasize that this is not intended as a critique of other approaches, nor does it gainsay the importance of findings generated by scholars using alternative perspectives. We encourage researchers to learn from each other.

Each definition contains a point of view or an area of emphasis. The first definition encourages us to attend carefully to the theoretical mechanism by which politics creates stress. The second calls our attention to the cognitive appraisal of coping capacity as a mediating variable. The third leads us to delineate and measure the particular responses that are produced by politics. For practical purposes it is confusing to call them all 'stress,' but by whatever name they are all worthy of our consideration.

The definition of 'politics'

The term 'organizational politics' has received many definitions over the years (Drory and Romm, 1990; Kacmar and Baron, 1999; Mayes and Allen, 1977). There are two definitional issues that are especially important. First, we examine what precisely is meant by the term 'politics,' at least in the context of stress research. Second, we need to examine the implications of defining politics as a subjective perception. Afterwards, we will attempt to solve some conceptual problems by considering these two issues together.

The meaning of 'politics': neutral vs bad

Overview   As discussed elsewhere (e.g. Fedor and Maslyn, 2002; Ferris et al., 2000; Kacmar and Baron, 1999), operational definitions of politics can fall into at least two families. The first family treats politics quite generally, viewing it as a manifestation of social influence processes within organizations (e.g. Mintzberg, 1985; Pfeffer, 1981). In this tradition one influential definition was offered by Pfeffer (1981), who defined politics as 'power in action' (p. 7). Scholars in this tradition would agree that politics is not necessarily a bad thing, and could even have a positive impact on organizational functioning. Fedor and Maslyn (p. 272) refer to such benefits as 'positive politics.'

Politics has also been defined more narrowly. Rather than viewing all influence attempts as political, the term 'politics' has been sometimes limited to those attempts to influence that are unsanctioned and serve individual (as opposed to organizational) goals (e.g. Ferris and Judge, 1991; Gandz and Murray, 1980). Witt et al. (2000, p. 343) summarize this idea nicely when they 'view politics in a pejorative sense.' Another good statement of this position is nicely summarized by Kacmar and Baron (1999): '*Organizational politics involves actions by individuals which are directed toward the goal of furthering their own self-interests without regard for the well-being of others or their organization*' (p. 4, italics in original). Harris and Kacmar (2005, p. 253) explicitly employ this definition in their thorough review of the politics and stress literature. Likewise, Anderson (1994, p. 159) refers to these sorts of behaviors as 'dysfunctional office and organizational politics.'

Theoretical implications of the first definition   Once more, we can see that we have multiple definitions, each of which is reasonable but takes us in a different theoretical direction. If politics is seen as essentially neutral (Pfeffer, 1981), then the primary challenge for the employee is likely to be one of understanding and control. Consequently, workers who have grasped the situation and know how to manage it are likely to experience less stress and greater job satisfaction. As we have seen, evidence supports this contention (Ferris et al., 1993; Ferris, Frink, Bhawuk et al., 1996; Ferris, Frink, Galang et al., 1996).

It is intriguing to consider this matter in light of the definitions of stress we reviewed earlier. Essentially, politics behaves like any other stressor, in the sense that it carries the potential to make demands that exceed the employee's ability to cope. To present the matter more precisely, this approach suggests that the mechanism by which politics creates stress is by causing one or more other stressors to appear. In other words, the demands it induces are things that are well known to stress researchers, such as uncertainty and conflict. As we turn our attention to the second definition, the reader should attend to how the causal mechanism linking politics to stress begins to change.

Theoretical implications of the second definition   The second definition has some interesting properties of its own. Notice that the behaviors designated by the second definition are a subset of those designated by the first. Specifically, Kacmar and Baron's (1999) and Harris and Kacmar's (2005) approach explicitly notes that the 'well-being of others' is not a consideration, thereby overtly excluding actions that *are* undertaken for the benefit of others. For this reason, it should not surprise us that employees who work in political

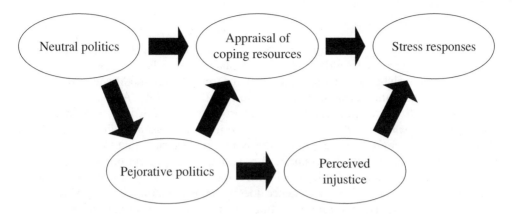

Figure 9.2   The relationship of organizational politics to perceived injustice

climates often have their own needs trampled. Indeed, a certain trampling over the needs of coworkers is implied in the definition.

This suggests an intriguing possibility. It is illustrated in the bottom half of Figure 9.2. As Vigoda (2002) observes, the actions implied by the second definition are apt to be viewed as unfair by those pitiable victims caught in the political cross-fire. Evidentially, the pejorative view of politics raises a second possibility of an additional mediator. As we alluded to earlier, Vigoda (p. 575) has argued that politics engenders a feeling of inequity. Vigoda further observes that unfairness is associated with stress. Given all these, it could be that politics might adversely impact well-being by creating a sense of injustice. Furthermore, *neutral* politics exerts its effects (in part) by increasing the level of *pejorative* politics.

Notice that Figure 9.2 treats perceptions of politics as only a partial mediator. This follows from the 'part/whole' relationship between the two views of politics. Since pejorative politics is only a part of neutral politics, the latter might well persist in having independent effects beyond the former. Of course, this is an empirical question.

Vigoda's (2002) model strikes us as promising, though it is not shared by all researchers. For example, in their Revised Model of Organizational Politics Perceptions, Ferris and his colleagues (2002, p. 235) treat both 'job anxiety/tension' (what have been called stress or stress responses) and 'justice reactions' as consequences of politics perceptions. However, these authors show no causal arrow between them. This is an important idea and could benefit from primary research. Vigoda, on the other hand, sees injustice as a potential cause of stress responses.

Unfortunately, to date there is little empirical evidence providing a direct test. Andrews and Kacmar (2001) presented evidence suggesting that politics and justice, though correlated, are distinct constructs. Likewise, in three studies Aryee et al. (2004) demonstrated that procedural justice and organizational politics have somewhat different nomological networks. None of this, however, provides a direct test of mediation. Clearly, this should be a priority for future research. For our part, we will return to this issue after we consider another definitional issue.

Reality vs perception

Overview   Throughout this chapter we have been emphasizing the subjective or phenomenological approach to understanding workplace politics. This is reasonable enough, as such an approach has dominated research on the topic (Fedor and Maslyn, 2002; Ferris et al., 2002; Harris and Kacmar, 2005; Kacmar and Baron, 1999). Available work tends to measure politics through perceptual/self-report instruments. Strictly speaking, we are not correlating *politics* to stress; we are correlating *perceptions of politics* to stress. As Dipboye and Foster (2002, p. 259) put it, this is akin to declaring 'that the crucial mediator and the most immediate determinant of outcomes is the perceptions, not the reality.' In other words, the event is not harmful until it has been recognized and interpreted as political. As we have already seen, evidence does not contradict this view (e.g. Ferris et al., 2002): we have reviewed literature indicating that perceptions of organizational politics predict stress responses (Harris and Kacmar, 2005; Kacmar and Baron, 1999).

There is also encouraging evidence suggesting that workers' perceptions of politics are at least partially based on some political behaviors. In effect, we are assuming that measures of political perceptions have nontrivial construct validity. While questions have been raised regarding the measurement of politics (e.g. by Dipboye and Foster, 2002), there is enough validation evidence to give us sufficient comfort to proceed (e.g. Fedor and Maslyn, 2002, especially pp. 275–6; Ferris et al., 2000; Witt, 1995).

Given this, it would seem that the bulk of our problem is solved since political behaviors predict perceptions of politics as well as stress. But there is a matter left that concerns us. What is the proper interpretation of the relationship between political behavior and political perceptions? While one might imagine an open frontier of conceptual possibilities, in practice two seem especially likely. In the first case, we could say that our self-report surveys are valid, though admittedly imperfect, measures of actual political behavior. If one adopts this perspective, then perceptual politics is related to actual politics as a scale is related to one's weight. Hence it would seem likely that political behavior is more important than perceived politics in our understanding of the stress response. But there is another possibility. It might be that actual political behavior *causes* perceptions of politics. If one adopts this perspective, then perceptual politics and political behavior are related to one another as effect is related to cause. From this vantage point, perceptions of politics would be no less important than political behaviors for understanding the stress response. Let us consider the implication of these two interpretations. We shall see again the recurring problem we have identified in this chapter – our causal theories change with the definitions we employ.

The first interpretation: Reality matters

The basic model   One possibility would be to treat political perceptions as a 'summary variable' that estimates what actually goes on in the workplace. This hypothetical model appears in Figure 9.3. Notice that political behavior, as imperfectly indexed by perceptual measures, is the conceptual driver of the stress response. The crude self-report measure is a substitute for a more essential reality. There is no fundamental reason to include perceptual politics in our causal model; it is simply one way to gauge how much actual political behavior is occurring in the workplace. There are no doubt other estimates, such as

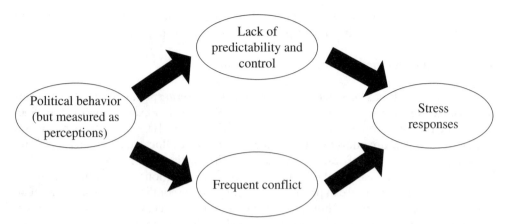

Figure 9.3   A strong realist model of politics and stress

behavioral observation or experimental manipulation, though they have not been widely used in this research area.

Inspired by this realist interpretation, one might begin identifying mediators that lie between actual political behavior and stress. Let us consider a simple illustration. In view of the research reviewed earlier, it seems reasonable to suppose that actual political behavior (even if not so identified by a respondent) creates an environment with at least two negative attributes: (a) lack of predictability and control, and (c) more frequent conflict with others. These environmental attributes, in turn, create stressful working conditions. The reader should not become too enamored of the particulars of this hypothetical model. Though the mediators were adapted from previous theorizing (e.g. Cropanzano et al., 1997; Ferris, Frink, Bhawuk et al., 1996), Figure 9.3 is almost certainly not comprehensive and is only presented as an example of how this realist interpretation might impel a scholar to proceed. We will begin raising questions shortly.

The critical point is what is *not* to be found in this causal flow. Notice that, as presented in Figure 9.3, perceived organizational politics has no separate functional status apart from actual political behavior. Perceptions are important because they can provide important insights into actual political behavior, but they are not causes of stress in their own right. By extension, one who took this realist view could even go so far as to maintain that politics is about equally painful, regardless of whether it is correctly labeled by its victims.

Unanswered questions   The realist model provides a simple interpretation of the relationship between political behavior and perceived politics. Nevertheless, it does not seem to have been widely adopted by scholars who study politics and stress. There is a good reason for this. While political perceptions seem to be influenced by political behaviors (Ferris et al., 2000), there are myriad other causes of these perceptions (Ferris et al., 2002). Ferris et al. (1989) divide these influences into three families: organizational influences (e.g. centralization, formalization), job/work environment influences (e.g. interactions with others), and personal influences (e.g. age, gender). Scholars would probably agree that political behaviors are one source of their perceptual counterparts (e.g. Fedor and Maslyn, 2002), but they would probably not maintain that there is a clean one-to-one mapping of behavior to perception. Given these considerations, our causal models need to distinguish between political perceptions and political behaviors.

The second interpretation: Perceptions as a mediator

The basic model   It has been common for scholars to *describe* politics (partially) in terms of objective events, but *measure* it in terms of perceptions. For example, in the introduction to their study, Cropanzano and his colleagues (1997, p. 160) justify their prediction by describing environmental conditions where 'rewards are allocated based on power' and marked by the existence of 'cabals.' Similarly, in the Ferris, Frink, Bhawuk et al. (1996, p. 26) paper reviewed earlier, the authors discuss 'Organizations as "Political Arenas"' and refer to 'behavior [that] can prove divisive and produce conflict.' Likewise, Ferris et al. (1995, pp. 28–33) provide a thorough review of political behaviors in various human resource systems, and refer specifically to 'Individuals Engaging in Political Activity' (see their Figure 2.1, p. 33). These discussions describe political behaviors in the real world, rather like the realist view discussed above. However, both Cropanzano et al. (1997) and Ferris, Frink, Bhawuk et al. (1996) measured only political perceptions. Such an approach is common. While not gainsaying the value of studying actual behaviors, researchers have also tended to emphasize the importance (not just the necessity) of measuring perceptions when studying stress politics (e.g. Dipboye and Foster, 2002; Ferris et al., 2002; Harris and Kacmar, 2005; Kacmar and Baron, 1999).

This might initially seem confusing, but it makes sense when one recognizes that researchers are actually proposing a sort of mediated model. Political behavior (and other causes) impacts political perceptions; political perceptions, in turn, impact workplace stress. For instance, in their influential 1989 chapter, Ferris et al. (pp. 157–63) pose a framework that places political perceptions in this sort of intervening role. Ferris et al. recognize the importance of interpersonal interactions, but in their model interpersonal interactions affect stress (these authors use the term 'job anxiety') only by way of perceived politics. In a more recent paper, Ferris and his colleagues (2002) revise and expand their earlier model, but the mediated path (or more properly, paths) remains. The model proposed by Ferris and his colleagues (2002) has an important strength. It recognizes that the behavior of others can be one cause of political perceptions, but it also acknowledges other important causes. Hence this model does not assume that perceptions always match reality, but instead treats the matter as an empirical question. This mediated approach has at least one other advantage – scholars have amassed a good deal of evidence attesting to the relationship between perceived politics and stress (for reviews see Ferris et al., 2002; Harris and Kacmar, 2005; Kacmar and Baron, 1999). This suggests that a model relating workplace stress to politics must take into account employees' political perceptions.

In terms of understanding workplace stress, the mediated model carries some fascinating theoretical implications. As illustrated in Figure 9.4, if actual political behavior causes perceived politics, and perceived politics predicts stress, then perceived politics conveys the impact of the work environment on stress.[2] Consequently, it seems that the social environment begins to exert at least some of its effects on an employee *after* that individual has labeled it political. This is shown in Figure 9.4. This approach has been widely employed in the study of politics and worker stress.

Figure 9.4   *Perceived organizational politics mediating the relationship between actual political behavior and stress*

This framework emphasizes how events are interpreted and, by extension, suggests that the stress-provoking effects of actual political behavior can be allayed by managing one's interpretations of the situation. This is because an individual's stress is not directly compelled by environmental events. Rather, it is how those events are interpreted and understood that creates potential problems. The same objective environment may not have the same effects on different persons (Dipboye and Foster, 2002).

Adopting the mediated model presented in Figure 9.4, rather than the realist model presented in Figure 9.3, obliges us to make changes in our thinking. Each model suggests a somewhat different research program as well as distinct (though overlapping) interventions. As a practical matter, to understand the etiology of stress in Figure 9.4 requires theories that explain the causes of political perceptions alongside our theories that explain the causes of actual political behavior. Likewise, to reduce the impact of stress we would need interventions that teach employees to manage their perceptions, as well as interventions that improve their work environment.

In the mediated model, one would explicitly accept that political behavior causes stress. However, it does so by way of our perceptions. As we have already seen, the actual event would then be more likely to produce stress after it has been interpreted as political. By extension, the same event would be less stressful before it is interpreted as political. These conclusions seem generally consistent with the work of others (cf. Ferris et al., 1989, 2000).

Understanding the relationship between perceptions and reality   By making explicit the link between political behavior and perceived politics, we can make sense of the earlier research which described politics as a behavior but measured it as a perception. However, we are now stymied by the available research evidence. The model we are discussing proposes that perceived politics mediates actual political behavior and stress. However, this mediational path is in need of substantially more research attention. It requires some indicators of actual political events (perhaps obtained through observation or laboratory manipulation), some indicators of perceptions, and a stress-relevant criterion variable. The relationship between actual political behavior and stress should be tested with and without the proposed mediator. As Baron and Kenny (1986) and Holmbeck (2002) remind us, the relationship between actual political behavior and stress responses should be larger when perceived politics is not used as a predictor. The relationship of actual political behavior with stress should be smaller, or perhaps nonsignificant, when perceived politics is also used as a predictor.

There is more to the matter than this. Let us suppose that political behaviors are one cause of stress, as was implied by Cropanzano et al. (1997) and Ferris, Frink,

Bhawuk et al. (1996), as well as by the mediated models presented by Ferris et al. (1989, 2002) and discussed above. We also have reasons to suppose that political behavior impacts perceptions of politics (Ferris et al., 2000; Witt, 1995). If these conditions are met, then when predicting stress from political perceptions, political behavior is associated with both the predictor (perceptions) and the criteria (stress responses).

In other words, political behaviors might well be a relevant cause of stress (for details, see James et al., 1982, especially chap. 1). If political behavior is a relevant cause, then excluding it from prediction equations will cause one to misestimate the size of the relationship between perceptions and stress. In essence, political behaviors will function as an unmeasured third variable. Consequently, measuring actual behavior could lead us to learn more about perceived politics. The seriousness of this matter can only be determined by research, for there are circumstances in which these conditions can be met while not biasing the estimated relationship between political perceptions and stress.

Most obviously, there might be a zero correlation between actual political behavior and perceived politics. This would, of course, fly in the face of most theoretical speculation (e.g. Ferris et al., 1989, 2002; Kacmar and Baron, 1999; Vigoda, 2003), as well as empirical evidence (Ferris et al., 2000). Given these considerations it seems likely that the association between political behavior and perceptions is at least nontrivial.

There is another scenario in which actual political behavior could predict political perceptions and stress, while not biasing estimates of the perception/stress association. If the relationship of political behavior and stress is fully mediated by political perceptions, then the behavior is no longer a relevant cause, since its impact is fully determined by the other predictor (James et al., 1982). To state the matter in path-analytic terms, full mediation would imply that there is no direct path from political behavior to stress, only an indirect route through perceptions. Partial mediation would imply a direct path that remains significant alongside the indirect route. Consequently, partial mediation, with its direct path from behavior to stress, could threaten our estimates of the association between political perceptions and stress.

For this reason it is important that scholars explore the possibility of a direct path between political behavior and stress. While the evidence does not allow us to say for certain whether such a route exists, it does not strike us as unlikely that political behavior may have an effect on stress that is unmediated by perceptions. Keep in mind that the informal social influence attempts that characterize political behavior may affect financial well-being, promotion opportunities and work loads regardless of whether we take the trouble to define them as political. It would seem that working in an environment where one could be hurt would be stressful even if the harm were not attributed to politics. Notice that these observations do not deny that perceived politics produces stress, but they suggest a place for actual political behavior as well.

Remaining questions

We are aware that we have yet to provide the reader with a model relating organizational politics to workplace stress. More needs to be said about the missing (direct) path from actual political behavior to stress. The available evidence is not conclusive, but we think that a direct path from actual political behavior might complement the indirect path observed by previous scholars (such as Ferris et al., 1989, 2002). Fortunately, our prior analysis can inform this discussion. Let us begin by considering two points of simplification in our earlier discussion. We will here qualify some things that were stated earlier.

A harder look at Figure 9.3
Figure 9.3 presented a hypothetical model displaying a strong realist position. Actual social influence processes cause unpredictability and conflict, and unpredictability and conflict, in turn, cause stress. Other than the obvious underspecification, this framework may have another problem. It does not seem entirely consistent with previous work. Most notably, Ferris and his colleagues (1989, 2002) have convincingly argued that *perceived* politics produces stress. Such constructs as ambiguity and conflict, therefore, should mediate the relationship between perceived politics and stress, not the relationship between actual political behavior and stress.

Imagine finding out that you were working in a politically charged environment. (In our present language, that actual political behavior is high.) Even if nothing negative had happened, the future might be suspect. You could risk losing desirable benefits, would have to learn more about the social network, may not know the 'real' reward criteria, and are at risk for additional conflict. In each of these examples, *perceived* politics raises the level of uncertainty and conflict (to say nothing of adding additional work demands!), and these states could subsequently engender stress.

But can we go further? It is easy to see why perceiving these events as political would make them worse. For example, as Vigoda (2002) observes, politics can also imply injustice. A random event, or one for which you blamed yourself, might be unfortunate but probably not unfair. Nonetheless, it also seems that unpredictability and conflict would create at least some stress even when they are attributed to some other source. Put into the stress terms we were employing earlier, unpredictability and conflict should be able to overwhelm an individual's resources even if they are not political.

Perceived/pejorative politics
As we show in Figure 9.4, and based on the theoretical models presented by Ferris and his colleagues (1989, 2000), actual political behavior is one cause of perceived politics. Perceived politics, in turn, may overwhelm coping resources. However, a close reading of previous research (e.g. Vigoda, 2002, 2003) raises an additional conceptual question. Perceived politics is most likely to increase stress when it is seen as pejorative for the individual in question.

Consider the nature of perceived politics. The same political machinations may be positive for one person and negative for another. For example, beneficiaries are less apt to cry foul than are those who are harmed (cf. Fedor and Maslyn, 2002). This suggests that politics can be perceived as either positive or negative. However, it seems to be the negative effects of politics that increase the level of stress (Vigoda, 2002, 2003). As an example, consider the aforementioned work of Ferris and his colleagues. These authors show that politics is less harmful when individuals are in a position to cope with it (e.g. Ferris et al., 1994; Ferris, Frink, Bhawuk et al., 1996; Ferris, Frink, Galang et al., 1996).

Armed with these observations, we are prepared to return to Figure 9.4. In that figure, and in the accompanying discussion, we have maintained that actual political behavior is one cause of perceived politics. Political behavior occurs in the real world, and it may or may not overwhelm one's coping resources. In addition, the presence of actual political behavior raises the likelihood that someone will perceive that politics exists. If this behavior is viewed as political and pejorative, then it is likely to increase one's level of stress. This would seem to be what Witt and his colleagues (2000) have in mind when they refer to 'politics in a pejorative sense' (p. 343) and measure it as a set of perceptions. This is also consistent with the work of Cropanzano et al. (1997) and Randall et al. (1999), who define and measure politics in a similar fashion.

An integrative model of politics and workplace stress
Based on our analysis so far, we should be able to assemble the pieces of a model relating politics to stress. This framework is not intended to be a comprehensive listing of every variable that might cause politics perceptions, nor of the moderators among them. This is an important topic, but beyond the scope of the present chapter. Instead, we would refer the reader to the thorough reviews by Ferris and his colleagues (2002), Harris and Kacmar (2005) and Kacmar and Baron (1999). Our goal here is only to identify those constructs that link environmental events to stress responses, as well as to specify the relationships among these variables. Let us present our model by summarizing what we have found in the stress and politics literatures.

What we learned from the stress literature
Figure 9.1 suggests that stress models have three core features. Starting first with the consequence, there must obviously be a response or else there is nothing of interest to predict. Moving our attention to the left side of the figure, the model should specify the event or events that cause the response. If we are concerned with politics and stress, then this cause must be some type of politics. Below we will examine when it is best to think of this political cause as actual or perceived. For now, it should suffice to note that the stress literature specifies that we need some mechanism to carry the influence of politics on to individual responses.

An intermediate cognitive appraisal lies between the precipitating event (in this case, politics) and the resulting consequences (in this case, the stress response). Specially, it is an appraisal that one's coping ability is exceeded by the demands of one's environment (Edwards, 1992; Folkman and Lazarus, 1991; Hobfoll, 1989, 1993). There is evidence that such a judgment intervenes between politics and stress. Notably, we reviewed considerable research suggesting that when individuals feel they understand or can manage politics (in our stress jargon, when their coping resources are not overwhelmed) politics has less pernicious effects. When they cannot understand and manage politics, the effects are worse (Drory, 1993; Ferris et al., 1993; Ferris, Frink, Bhawuk et al., 1996; Ferris, Frink, Galang et al., 1996). This supports the idea of a critical cognitive appraisal linking politics to stress.

If one accepts our argument, then this allows us to make an implicit distinction explicit. The cognitive appraisal that lies between stressor and stress is a subjective judgment. However, the content of this judgment is distinct from perception of politics. In the latter, the individual decides whether or not politics exists. In the former, the individual decides whether or not he or she can cope with the politics. These ideas are presented in our Figure 9.5, which is closely modeled on Figure 9.2.

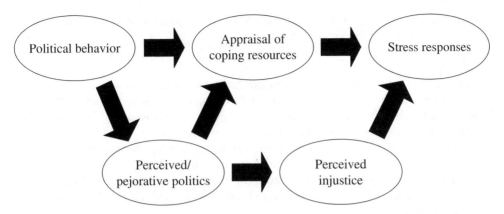

Figure 9.5   Our integrative model of organizational politics and workplace stress

What we learned from the politics literature

Actual behavior and perceived politics   Earlier in this chapter we had much to say about actual and subjective politics. Clearly, perceived politics is important and it is reasonable to assign it a central place in our conceptual thinking. However, we would add that actual political behavior needs to be considered as well, Figure 9.5 includes all of these paths. There are two reasons for this.

The first reason concerns the causal impact of political behavior. The direct effects of a political work environment are well known to stress researchers. They include such things as ambiguity, conflict and so on (Ferris et al., 2002; Kacmar and Baron, 1999). However, work settings characterized by these attributes may well be stressful even if there is no attribution of politics. In other words, political events may create stress even if one does not know they are political. If this is so, then our current models, which tend to emphasize political perceptions, are underspecified. As we already discussed, since political behavior may be correlated with both perceptions of politics and stress, the inclusion of political behaviors in our causal models might impact the association observed between perceptions and stress (James et al., 1982).

The second reason concerns the causal impact of perceived/pejorative politics. Vigoda (2002) has emphasized that politics can produce injustice perceptions. However, for a political act to be seen as unfair, it must first be perceived. That is, if one does not know that politics exists, then one cannot know whether or not it is just. Consequently, Vigoda's work strongly implies an important place for perceived politics. As shown in Figure 9.5, we would expect injustice perceptions to mediate the impact of perceived politics but not the impact of political behavior.

The role of injustice   We have added two other paths to our model. These trace a route from perceived/pejorative politics to perceived injustice, and then proceeds from perceived injustice to stress. These paths were added based on the work of scholars who have observed that perceptions of politics can predict justice (e.g. Ferris et al., 2002; Ferris and Kacmar, 1992; Kacmar and Ferris, 1991). We are positing that injustice will partially mediate the relationship between perceived/pejorative politics and stress. This is, of course, what was found by Vigoda (2002).

Conclusions

In our effort to understand the relationship between politics and stress, we began by disassembling existing conceptual models, and looking closely at the nature of the parts. This led us to identify various points of conceptual confusion and needs for further development. After working through these issues we were able to reassemble the pieces into a new model. We hope that our integrative framework will provide a clearer and more exact understanding of both organizational politics and workplace stress. But we recognize that this chapter is only one small stopping point in a longer journey. There is much more that we need to learn. We hope our chapter has contributed to this exciting and important topic.

Notes

1. To further complicate matters, Rizzo and his colleagues (1970, pp. 154–5) suggest that 'role conflict and role ambiguity are important intervening variables that mediate the effects of various organizational practices on individual and organizational outcomes.' This is quite close to the second possible definition of 'stress.'
2. Of course, it is not absolutely necessary to adopt something like Figure 9.4 as one's theoretical posture. Most notably, it could plausibly be argued that actual political behavior causes both stress and political perceptions. As such, the observed association between perceived politics and stress responses may be due to an unmeasured variable problem. By this reckoning, perceptions of politics do not cause stress. Rather, perceptions and stress are related to each other only by virtue of the fact that both are caused by the objective environment. This possibility is logically consistent with the considerations reviewed thus far in the chapter. However, it does not take us much further than we have already gone. Treating actual political behavior as a third variable assumes that the objective political environment is a more important cause, while perceived politics is demoted in status to an incidental variable. In terms of predicting workplace stress, it brings us back to a model that for most practical purposes looks much like Figure 9.3.

References

Anderson, T.P. (1994). Creating measures of dysfunctional office and organizational politics. *Psychology*, **18**, 159–80.

Andrews, M.C. and Kacmar, K.M. (2001). Discriminating among organizational politics, justice and support. *Journal of Organizational Behavior*, **22**, 347–66.

Aryee, S., Chen, Z.X. and Budhwar, P.S. (2004). Exchange fairness and employee performance: An examination of the relationship between organizational politics and procedural justice. *Organizational Behavior and Human Decision Processes*, **94**, 1–14.

Baron, R.M. and Kenny, D.A. (1986). The moderator–mediator variable distinction in social psychological research: Conceptual, strategic, and statistical considerations. *Journal of Personality and Social Psychology*, **51**, 1173–82.

Beehr, T.A., Walsh, J.T. and Taber, T.D. (1976). Relationships of stress to individually and organizationally valued states: Higher order needs as a moderator. *Journal of Applied Psychology*, **61**, 41–7.

Blau, G. (1981). Organizational investigation of job stress, social support, service length, and job strain. *Organizational Behavior and Human Performance*, **27**, 279–302.

Cannon, W.B. (1935). Stress and strains of homeostasis. *American Journal of Medical Science*, **189**, 1.

Cooper, C.L. and Roden, J. (1985). Mental health and satisfaction among tax officers. *Social Science & Medicine*, **21**, 747–51.

Crampton, S.M. and Wagner, J.A. (1994). Percept–percept inflation in microorganizational research: An investigation of prevalence and effect. *Journal of Applied Psychology*, **79**, 67–76.

Cropanzano, R., Howes, J.C., Grandey, A.A. and Toth, P. (1997). The relationship of organizational politics and support to work behaviors, attitudes, and stress. *Journal of Organizational Behavior*, **18**, 159–80.

Cropanzano, R., Goldman, B. and Benson, L., III (2005). Organizational justice. In J. Barling, K. Kelloway and M. Frone (eds), *Handbook of work stress* (pp. 63–87). Beverly Hills, CA: Sage.

Davidson, M.J. and Cooper, C.L. (1986). Executive women under pressure. Occupational and life stress and the family (special issue). *International Review of Applied Psychology*, **35**, 301–26.

Dipboye, R.L. and Foster, J.B. (2002). Multi-level theorizing about perceptions of organizational politics. In F.J. Yammarino and F. Dansereau (eds), *The many faces of multi-level issues* (pp. 255–70). Amsterdam: JAI Press.

Drory, A. (1993). Perceived political climate and job attitudes. *Organization Studies*, **14**, 59–71.

Drory, A. and Romm, T. (1990). The definition of organizational politics: A review. *Human Relations*, **43**, 1133–54.

Edwards, J.R. (1992). A cybernetic theory of stress, coping, and well-being. *Academy of Management Review*, **17**, 238–74.

Fedor, D.B. and Maslyn, J.M. (2002). Politics and political behavior: Where else do we go from here? In F.J. Yammarino and F. Dansereau (eds), *The many faces of multi-level issues* (pp. 271–85). Amsterdam: JAI Press.

Ferris, G.R. and Judge, T.A. (1991). Personnel/human resources management: A political influence perspective. *Journal of Management*, **17**, 447–88.

Ferris, G.R. and Kacmar, K.M. (1992). Perceptions of organizational politics. *Journal of Management*, **18**, 93–116.

Ferris, G.R., Russ, G.W. and Fandt, P.M. (1989). Politics in organizations. In R.A. Giacalone and P. Rosenfield (eds), *Impression management in organizations* (pp. 143–70). Hillsdale, NJ: Lawrence Erlbaum.

Ferris, G.R., Brand, J.F., Brand, S., Rowland, K.M., Gilmore, D.C., King, T.R., Kacmar, K.M. and Burton, C.A. (1993). Politics and control in organizations. In E.J. Lawler, B. Markovsky, J. O'Brien and K. Heime (eds), *Advances in group processes* (Vol. 10, pp. 83–111). Greenwich, CT: JAI Press.

Ferris, G.R., Frink, D.D., Gilmore, D.C. and Kacmar, K.M. (1994). Understanding as an antidote for the dysfunctional consequences of organizational politics as a stressor. *Journal of Applied Social Psychology*, **24**, 1204–20.

Ferris, G.R., Frink, D.D., Beehr, T.A. and Gilmore, D.C. (1995). Political fairness and fair politics: The conceptual integration of divergent constructs. In R. Cropanzano and M.K. Kacmar (eds), *Organizational politics, justice, and support: Managing the social climate of work organizations* (pp. 21–36). Westport, CT: Quorum.

Ferris, G.R., Frink, D.D., Bhawuk, D.P.S., Zhou, J. and Gilmore, D.C. (1996). Reactions of diverse groups to politics in the workplace. *Journal of Management*, **22**, 23–44.

Ferris, G.R., Frink, D.D., Galang, M.C., Zhou, J., Kacmar, K.M. and Howard, J.L. (1996). Perceptions of organizational politics: Prediction, stress-related implications, and outcomes. *Human Relations*, **49**, 233–66.

Ferris, G.R., Harrell-Cook, G. and Dulebohn, J.H. (2000). Organizational politics: The nature of the relationship between politics perceptions and political behavior. In S.B. Bacharach and E.J. Lawler (eds), *Research in the sociology of organizations*, Vol. 17 (pp. 89–130). Stamford, CT: JAI Press.

Ferris, G.R., Adams, G., Kolodinsky, R.W., Hochwarter, W.A. and Ammeter, A.P. (2002). Perceptions of organizational politics: Theory and research directions. In F.J. Yammarino and F. Dansereau (eds), *The many faces of multi-level issues* (pp. 179–254). Amsterdam: JAI Press.

Fisher, C.D. (1985). Social support and adjustment to work: A longitudinal study. *Journal of Management*, **11**, 39–53.

Fisher, C.D. and Gitelson, R. (1983). A meta-analysis of the correlates of role conflict and ambiguity. *Journal of Applied Psychology*, **68**, 320–33.

Folkman, S. and Lazarus, R.S. (1991). Coping and emotion. In A. Monat and R.S. Lazarus (eds), *Stress and coping: An anthology* (pp. 207–27). New York: Columbia University Press.

Fried, Y., Rowland, K.M. and Ferris, G.R. (1984). The physiological measurement of work stress: A critique. *Personnel Psychology*, **37**, 583–615.

Gandz, J. and Murray, V.V. (1980). The experience of workplace politics. *Academy of Management Journal*, **23**, 237–51.

Harris, K. and Kacmar, M.K. (2005). Organizational politics. In J. Barling, E.K. Kelloway and M.R. Frone (eds), *Handbook of work stress* (pp. 353–74). Thousand Oaks, CA: Sage.

Hobfoll, S.E. (1989). Conservation of resources: A new attempt at conceptualizing stress. *American Psychologist*, **44**, 513–24.

Hobfoll, S.E. (1993). Conservation of resources: A general stress theory applied to burnout. In W.B. Schaufeli, C. Maslach and T. Marek (eds), *Professional burnout: Recent developments in theory and research* (pp. 115–29). New York: Taylor and Francis.

Hochwarter, W.A., Perrewé, P.L., Ferris, G.R. and Guercio, R. (1999). Commitment as an antidote to the tension and turnover consequences of organizational politics. *Journal of Vocational Behavior*, **55**, 277–97.

Holmbeck, G.N. (2002). Post-hoc probing of significant moderational and mediational effects in studies of pediatric populations. *Journal of Pediatric Psychology*, **27**, 87–96.

House, R.J. and Rizzo, J.R. (1972). Role conflict and ambiguity as critical variables in a model of organizational behavior. *Organizational Behavior and Human Performance*, **7**, 467–505.

Jackson, S.E. and Schuler, R.S. (1985). A meta-analysis and conceptual critique of research on role ambiguity and role conflict in work settings. *Organizational Behavior and Human Decision Processes*, **36**, 16–78.

James, L.R., Mulaik, S.A. and Brett, J.M. (1982). *Causal analysis: Assumptions, models, and data*. Beverly Hills, CA: Sage.

Jex, S.M. and Beehr, T.A. (1991). Emerging theoretical and methodological issues in the study of work-related stress. In G.R. Ferris and K.M. Rowland (eds), *Research in organizational behavior* (Vol. 2, pp. 81–127). Greenwich, CT: JAI Press.

Jex, S.M., Beehr, T.A. and Roberts, C.K. (1992). The meaning of occupational stress items to survey respondents. *Journal of Applied Psychology*, **77**, 623–8.

Kacmar, K.M. and Baron, R.A. (1999). Organizational politics: The state of the field, links to related processes, and an agenda for future research. In J. Ferris (ed.), *Research in personnel and human resources management* (Vol. 17, pp. 1–39). Greenwich, CT: JAI Press.

Kacmar, K.M. and Ferris, G.R. (1991). Perceptions of organizational politics scale (POPS): Development and construct validation. *Educational and Psychological Measurement*, **51**, 193–205.

Kacmar, K.M., Bozeman, D.P., Carlson, D.S. and Anthony, W.P. (1999). An examination of the perceptions of organizational politics model: Replication and extension. *Human Relations*, **52**, 383–416.

Kahn, R.L. and Byosiere, P. (1992). Stress in organizations. In M.D. Dunnette and L. M. Hough (eds), *Handbook of industrial and organizational psychology* (2nd edn, Vol. 2, pp. 571–650). Palo Alto, CA: Consulting Psychologists Press.

Kahn, R.L., Wolfe, D.M., Quinn, R.P., Snoek, J.D. and Rothenthal, R.A. (1964). *Organizational stress: Studies in role conflict and ambiguity*. Oxford, UK: John Wiley.

Keil, R.M.K. (2004). Coping and stress: A conceptual analysis. *Journal of Advanced Nursing*, **45**, 659–65.

Kobasa, S. (1982). Commitment and coping in stress among lawyers. *Journal of Personality and Social Psychology*, **42**, 707–17.

Mangione, B.L. and Quinn, R.P. (1975). Job satisfaction, counterproductive behavior, and drug use at work. *Journal of Applied Psychology*, **63**, 114–16.

Mayes, B.T. and Allen, R.W. (1977). Toward a definition of organizational politics. *Academy of Management Review*, **2**, 672–8.

Mintzberg, H. (1985). The organization as a political arena. *Journal of Management Studies*, **22**, 133–54.

Netemeyer, R.G., Johnston, M.W. and Burton, S. (1990). Analysis of role conflict and role ambiguity in a structural equations framework. *Journal of Applied Psychology*, **75**, 148–57.

Nye, L.G. and Witt, L.A. (1993). Dimensionality and construct validity of the perceptions of organizational politics scale (POPS). *Educational and Psychological Measurement*, **53**, 821–9.

Osler, W. (1910). The Lumleian lectures on angina pectoris. *Lancet*, **1**, 696–700, 839–44, 974–7.

Peterson, M.F., Smith, P.B., Akande, A., Ayestaran, S., Bochner, S., Callan, V. et al. (1995). Role conflict, ambiguity, and overload: A 21-nation study. *Academy of Management Journal*, **38**, 429–52.

Pfeffer, J. (1981). *Power in organizations*. Cambridge, MA: Ballinger.

Pines, A. and Aronson, E. (1988). *Career burnout*. New York: The Free Press.

Podsakoff, P.M., MacKenzie, S.B., Lee, J.-Y. and Podsakoff, N.P. (2003). Common method bias in behavioural research: A critical review of the literature and recommended remedies. *Journal of Applied Psychology*, **88**, 879–903.

Podsakoff, P.M. and Organ, D.W. (1986). Self-reports in organizational research: Problems and prospects. *Journal of Management*, **12**, 69–82.

Randall, M.L., Cropanzano, R., Bormann, C.A. and Birjulin, A. (1999). Organizational politics and organizational support as predictors of work attitudes, job performance, and organizational citizenship behaviors. *Journal of Organizational Behavior*, **20**, 159–74.

Rizzo, J.R., House, R.J. and Lirtzman, S.I. (1970), Role conflict and ambiguity in complex organizations. *Administrative Science Quarterly*, **15**, 150–63.

Seligman, M.E.P. (1992). *Helplessness: On development, depression and death*. New York: W.H. Freeman.

Selye, H. (1936). A syndrome produced by diverse noxious agents. *Nature*, **138**, 32.

Selye, H. (1976). *The stress of life* (rev. edn). New York: McGraw-Hill.

Shirom, A. (1989). Burnout in work organizations. In C.L. Cooper and I.T. Robertson (eds), *International review of industrial and organizational psychology* (Vol. 4, pp. 26–48). New York: John Wiley and Sons.

Valle, M. and Perrewé, P.L. (2000). Do politics perceptions relate to political behaviors? Test of an implicit assumption and an expanded model. *Human Relations*, **53**, 359–86.

Vigoda, E. (2002). Stress-related aftermaths of workplace politics: The relationships among politics, job distress, and aggressive behavior in organizations. *Journal of Organizational Behavior*, **23**, 571–91.

Vigoda, E. (2003). *Developments in organizational politics: How political dynamics affect employee performance in modern worksites*. Cheltenham, UK and Northampton, MA, USA: Edward Elgar.

Witt, L.A. (1995). Influences of supervisor behaviors on the levels and effects of workplace politics. In R.S. Cropanzano and K.M. Kacmar (eds), *Organizational politics, justice, and support: Managing the social climate of work organizations* (pp. 37–53). Westport, CT: Quorum Books.

Witt, L.A. (1998). Enhancing organizational goal congruence: A solution to organizational politics. *Journal of Applied Psychology*, **83**, 666–74.

Witt, L.A., Andrews, M.C. and Kacmar, K.M. (2000). The role of participation in decision-making in the organizational politics–job satisfaction relationship. *Human Relations*, **53**, 341–58.

10 The emotion of politics and the politics of emotions: Affective and cognitive reactions to politics as a stressor

Yongmei Liu, Gerald R. Ferris, Darren C. Treadway, Melita L. Prati, Pamela L. Perrewé and Wayne A. Hochwarter

Introduction

> The importance of emotions both for the individual and for the society can scarcely be over-estimated. For the individual, emotions are both ends in themselves and means for the attainment of other ends. For society, emotions are involved critically in social control, role performance, and interpersonal interaction. (Rosenberg, 1990, p. 4)

Emotions are most frequently discussed as an intrapersonal phenomenon. However, human emotions are indeed social in nature (Parkinson, 1996). Emotions serve critical social functions across the individual, interpersonal, group and cultural level (Keltner and Haidt, 1999). At the individual level, emotions are often reactions to *social* events; by experiencing emotions arising from such social events, individuals become mentally, psychologically and physically prepared to respond to opportunities or threats in their social environment (Clore, 1994; Frijda, 1986; Schwarz, 1990). At the dyadic or interpersonal level, emotions help communicate the intentions, needs and thoughts of the individuals involved (Andersen and Guerrero, 1998; Jones and Rittman, 2002), and therefore coordinate social interactions (Keltner and Haidt, 1999). At the group level, collective emotions help define group identity and strengthen between-group boundaries (Heise and O'Brien, 1993; Frijda and Mesquita, 1994). And at the culture level, emotions both structure and are structured by cultural practices and norms (Markus and Kitayama, 1994; Lutz, 1988).

Just as in other social contexts, emotions play important roles in the context of organizational politics. At the individual level, people experience a variety of emotions at work (e.g. anger, embarrassment, envy and joy), frequently a result of the political behaviors by others or themselves. At the dyadic level, people use their emotions strategically as mechanisms of interpersonal influence (e.g. to induce good mood in others, or to put others in an embarrassing situation). Indeed, in many situations, the success of certain influence tactics depends on the ability of an actor to influence others' emotions. At the group level, coalitions or other collective political activities may be accomplished through facilitating collective emotions of anger or excitement. At the cultural level, the legitimacy or appropriateness of certain political behaviors may be sanctioned or denied by the implicit emotional norms of the organizations in question. It is the purpose of this chapter to explore these social roles of emotions in the organizational politics process. We focus on the individual and dyadic levels of analysis.

To date, only minimal research has examined the role emotion plays in organizational politics. Past research in the area has mainly focused on attempts to influence targets' attitudes and behaviors, leaving emotion, at best, an implied element in the process (Drory and Romm, 1990; Ferris, Hochwarter et al., 2002). In the workplace, the focus is primarily on individuals' efforts to manage their own emotions in adherence to organizationally prescribed norms (i.e. display rules – Ekman, 1973; see also, Hochschild, 1983) rather than the proactive behaviors as influence attempts in interpersonal encounters.

In this chapter, we propose a conceptualization linking perceptions of organizational politics with emotion. We argue that emotion and emotional behaviors serve as intermediate linkages in the relationships between organizational politics perceptions and both attitudinal and behavioral outcomes. Specifically, we draw from research on organizational politics (e.g. Drory and Romm, 1990; Ferris et al., 1989; Ferris, Hochwarter et al., 2002; Vigoda, 2000), affective events theory (Weiss and Cropanzano, 1996), and previous social psychology research on emotion (e.g. Clark, 1990; Rosenberg, 1990) to advance an emotion perspective of organizational politics. The main contention is that there is emotion in organizational politics, and that there is organizational politics in emotion, and that the intersection of the two has to be recognized in order to obtain a more complete understanding of both.

Before presenting the model, we begin with a brief overview of organizational politics research. We then briefly discuss previous emotion research conducted in organizations. Next, we develop our integrative conceptualization of politics and emotion. Finally, we discuss the implications of the model and issues raised for future research. Throughout this chapter, following the tradition of the influence literature, we refer the person who initiates the influence attempt as the 'actor,' and the recipient of influence as the 'target.'

Organizational politics
In recent decades, the political perspective of organizations has become prominent in the organizational sciences. In contrast to the rational model view of organizations, the political perspective maintains that organizations, by nature, are political arenas (Ferris et al., 1989; Mintzberg, 1985), and people behave in ways that cannot be explained by rational prescriptions. One of the main messages conveyed by the political perspective is that there is a social influence process in organizations in which individuals exercise tactical and strategic influences to promote self-interest (Ferris et al., 1989; Valle and Perrewé, 2000; Vigoda and Cohen, 2002).

Organizational political behavior promotes an individual's self-interests, with or without regard for the promotion of the objectives or concerns of co-workers or organizations (Mintzberg, 1983; Kacmar and Carlson, 1997). The understanding of political activity has developed along two, relatively independent, streams of research. The first is predicated on the belief that organizational participants act on their perceptions of political activity, not necessarily on actual political activity (Vigoda, 2000). The second addresses the nature of politicking in the workplace and has been investigated within the realms of influence tactics, impression management, social influence and political behavior. Recently, scholars have initiated a third stream of research investigating the interpersonal characteristic of political skill that may prove to affect both the interpretation and enactment of political behaviors in organizations (e.g. Drory, 1993; Ferris, Perrewé et al., 2000).

Political behavior
Whereas one could trace the study of political activity in organizations to the work of Machiavelli (Grams and Rogers, 1990), modern organizational scholars are indebted to

French and Raven's (1959) early notions of political behavior in organizations. These scholars identified five bases of power from which an organizational actor may operate: referent power, expert power, legitimate power, reward power and coercive power. Subsequent work has attempted to distinguish among classes of political activity. For example, Kipnis et al. (1980) defined eight dimensions of personal influence that were unique in their characteristics, specifically, assertiveness, ingratiation, rationality, sanctions, upward appeals, exchange of benefits, blocking and coalition building.

Some authors have argued that influence strategies are not isolated events and, in fact, organizational participants engage in strategic patterns of influence behavior (Perreault and Miles, 1978; Farmer et al., 1997). These strategies have been defined by the types of behavior used, the frequency of the behavior, and toward whom the behavior is directed. For example, Kipnis and colleagues (1980) found that whereas assertiveness, ingratiation, rationality and sanctions are directed toward targets at all levels, upward appeals, blocking and exchange of benefits are directed at superiors, whereas coalition building is directed at subordinates.

Moreover, Kipnis and Schmidt (1983) discussed downward influence styles as being defined by the frequency of tactic usage. Their work suggested that the styles of downward influence could be classified into three distinct groupings: shotgun, tactician and bystander. Shotgun managers use a greater degree of influence behavior with their subordinates, and primarily focus their tactics on assertiveness and bargaining. Tactician managers influence their subordinates through influence behaviors that emphasize reasoning. Bystander managers use little, if any, influence behavior with their subordinates. Subsequent research (Kipnis and Schmidt, 1988) evaluated the use of influence behavior directed toward supervisors and identified a fourth influence style, the ingratiator. This influence style is distinguished by the use of 'friendly' or 'soft' influence tactics such as ingratiation or praise.

Despite a relative abundance of research devoted to identifying the situational and individual antecedents of influence tactical choice (e.g. Dillard and Burgoon, 1985; O'Hair and Cody, 1987), and the consequences of using particular tactics (e.g. Yukl and Tracey, 1992), only a few studies have explicitly discussed the role emotion plays in the organizational politics process. For example, Liden and Mitchell (1988) suggested that target-oriented ingratiation tactics are sometimes used to make the target feel good so that a favorable impression of the ingratiator is made. Kipnis (1984) and Kipnis and Schmidt (1983) also noted that people might use expressions of hostility and irritation as one of the strong influence tactics. Wayne and Liden's (1995) study on leader–member exchange found that subordinates' impression management behavior influenced performance ratings through their supervisor's positive affect (i.e. liking). However, to date, emotion remains a relatively uninvestigated source of influence that could emerge in political contexts, although the role of emotion in the interpersonal influence process has long been both implicitly and explicitly discussed.

Perceptions of politics
Another independent research stream has taken a decidedly different view of political activity in organizations. In agreement with the belief that individuals act on their perceptions of reality rather than 'actual' reality *per se* (Lewin, 1936), Gandz and Murray (1980) suggested that political activity in organizations is best viewed as the perceived

politicization of organizational policies. Thus perception of organizational politics 'involves an individual's attribution to behaviors of self-serving intent, and is defined as an individual's subjective evaluation about the extent to which the work environment is characterized by co-workers and supervisors who demonstrate such self-serving behavior' (Ferris, Harrell-Cook and Dulebohn, 2000, p. 90).

Ferris et al. (1989) developed the first integrative model of perceived organizational politics. This model positioned perceived politics as the product of organizational, job and individual forces. Furthermore, it was argued that elevated levels of politics would lead to a host of negative outcomes. Subsequent research empirically corroborated several linkages in the model. For example, centralization has consistently demonstrated a positive relationship with perceptions of organizational politics (Fedor et al., 1998; Ferris et al., 1996; Kacmar et al., 1999), whereas opportunity for promotion (Ferris and Kacmar, 1992; Valle and Perrewé, 2000; Ferris et al., 1996) has displayed an inverse relationship with perceived politics. Furthermore, research indicates a significant inverse relationship between politics perceptions and job satisfaction (Cohen and Vigoda, 1999; Harrell-Cook et al., 1999; Nye and Witt, 1993; Ferris and Kacmar, 1992; Vigoda-Gadot et al., 2003), and a direct relationship with tension and aggressive behavior (Vigoda, 2002).

Despite its conceptual merit, not all linkages in the perceived politics model (Ferris et al., 1989) have been unequivocally supported by empirical research. Indeed, central aspects of the model (i.e. hierarchical level, autonomy, age and gender) have produced inconsistent results. Recently, Ferris and his colleagues (Ferris, Adams et al., 2002) attempted to reconcile these findings by developing a model of politics perceptions that revised and updated the original Ferris et al. (1989) model, and better integrated the multilevel and interactive nature of the phenomenon. Unique to this model was the introduction of political skill as an important interpersonal quality that affects individual reactions to perceived politics.

Political skill

It was not until very recently that researchers started systematically to investigate the role of interpersonal acuity in the politics process. Ferris and colleagues (Ferris, Anthony et al., 2002; Ferris et al., 1999; Ferris, Perrewé et al., 2000; Perrewé et al., 2000; Perrewé et al., 2004) identified political skill as an important individual difference variable that influences how individuals exert their influence attempts in interpersonal interactions. Political skill refers to 'the ability to effectively understand others at work, and to use such knowledge to influence others to act in ways that enhance one's personal and/or organizational objectives' (Perrewé et al., 2004, p. 142).

Rigorous empirical testing validated the existence of four underlying dimensions of political skill (Ferris et al., 2005). These four dimensions are labeled social astuteness, interpersonal influence, network building/social capital and genuineness (Ferris, Hochwarter et al., 2002). Social astuteness is the ability of the individual to comprehend social cues and accurately attribute the behavioral intentions of others. Interpersonal influence relates to the ability of the actor to control individuals and situations with only moderate levels of effort. The ability to build networks and social capital, the third element of political skill, comes easily to politically skilled individuals. Finally, politically skilled individuals are able to act in a manner that disguises their true intentions and casts their actions as genuine. Due to their ability to exercise situationally appropriate influence tactics in a manner that facilitates positive interpersonal relationships (Ferris, Hochwarter et al., 2002; Ferris, Anthony et al., 2002), highly politically skilled individuals should be at an advantage in trying to use emotions to influence others. In this chapter, we examine how political skill influences emotional reactions to perceived politics in the workplace.

Emotion in organizations

Although emotion has been an implicit theme in organizational research since the early 1930s (e.g. Hearsey, 1932; Rothlisberger and Dickson, 1949), its influence has been largely ignored by organizational scholars until very recently (Ashforth and Humphrey, 1995). Emotion has been rediscovered as a major influence on individuals' attitudes and behaviors at work (Ashforth and Humphrey, 1995; Fisher and Ashkanasy, 2000). The notion that organizational behaviors cannot be completely understood by rational explanations alone has been widely recognized among researchers (Weiss and Cropanzano, 1996). In support, emotions have been identified as an underlying mechanism that may help explain the variance in a wide range of organizational outcomes including performance, leadership, and group and organizational change processes (e.g. Arvey et al., 1998; Ashforth and Humphrey, 1995; Barsade and Gibson, 1998; Huy, 2002; Weiss and Cropanzano, 1996).

Two related, but distinct, streams of research have emerged in the literature: one is primarily concerned with the emotional experience (also commonly referred as emotion, or felt emotion), and the other is the emotional expression (also commonly referred as emotional display) (Fisher and Ashkanasy, 2000). The former focuses on individuals' inner emotional states, and their antecedents and consequences. The latter focuses on the communications function in social interactions.

Emotional experience

Research that focuses on emotional experiences has examined how emotion influences individuals' attitudes and behavior, as well as the relationship with cognition. This stream of research either examines various discrete emotions (e.g. happiness, anger, sadness, etc., Fitness, 2000; Tiedens, 2001), or takes a structural approach and examines emotion in terms of its hedonic tone (i.e. positive versus negative emotion) and level of arousal (cf. Diener, 1999). In this tradition, research has examined the differential influences of positive versus negative emotions on individuals with regard to decision making, creativity and helping behaviors (e.g. George and Zhou, 2002; Isen, 1987; Isen and Means, 1983).

Research has examined the role of emotion as a key variable in explaining organizational phenomena in addition to, or in place of, rationality. In this stream of research, affective events theory proposed by Weiss and Cropanzano (1996) has served as the most influential theoretical framework, due to its conceptual power and consistent empirical support (Ashkanasy et al., 2002). According to this theory, people experience a variety of emotions at work in response to the daily hassles and uplifts they encounter (i.e. affective events). Such emotional experiences significantly influence both short-term and long-term attitudinal and behavioral outcomes. The main point of the theory is that emotion mediates the affective events–outcomes relationships.

A moderate amount of empirical research has been devoted to exploring this mediating role of emotional experiences. For example, it has been found that emotional experiences partly explained organizational or individual factors' influence on job satisfaction (Fisher, 1998, 2000), organizational citizenship behavior (Spector and Fox, 2002), counterproductive work behavior (Fox et al., 2001; Spector and Fox, 2002), helping behavior (Fisher, 2002), organizational commitment and intention to quit (Fisher, 1998, 2002), as well as evaluation of leadership effectiveness (Lewis, 2000).

Emotional expression
Although, typically, emotional expressions serve as genuine demonstrations of one's inner emotional state, there are circumstances when this is not the case. The fact that people can manipulate their facial expressions and other emotional behaviors makes it possible that individuals' emotional expressions can deviate from their real inner feelings (Buller and Burgoon, 1998; Staw et al., 1994). For example, a subordinate who is angry with his or her boss may choose not to suppress the anger, or even express appreciation and warmth to the boss in order to avoid subsequent revenge or establish positive impressions. Here, the subordinate consciously exerts emotional self-control, and the individual strategically uses emotional expression to maintain and develop interpersonal relationships at work. In such situations, emotional expressions become 'a purposive human activity' that represents an interpersonal process, rather than intrapersonal feelings (Rosenberg, 1990).

The examination of emotion from this perspective most frequently appears in the emotional labor literature. Emotional labor refers to individuals' presenting certain emotional expressions in compliance with organizations' requirements, namely, display rules (Hochschild, 1983). Frequently, organizations require or expect employees to display pleasant emotions to customers to generate favorable reactions (e.g. Hochschild, 1983; Van Maanen and Kunda, 1989). Due to the effort to adhere to organizationally prescribed norms, employees' emotional expressions often become inconsistent with their real feelings, causing a disconnect between their public and real selves when performing emotional labor.

The main stream of emotional labor research has focused on this intrapersonal process, that is, how the separation between one's real self and displayed self influences physical and psychological well-being (e.g. Hochschild, 1983; Morris and Feldman, 1996; Schaubroeck and Jones, 2000). This has left the social consequences of emotional labor less well investigated (Thoits, 1996). However, emotional labor is an interpersonal influence process in which the actor tries to use emotional expressions to induce the target to respond favorably (Pugh, 2001). Due to such interpersonal effects of emotional labor, employees' positive emotional expressions have frequently been associated with positive reactions from customers such as bigger tips and higher perceptions of service quality (e.g. Parkinson, 1991; Pugh, 2001).

In fact, as is discussed later in more detail, emotion as a mechanism for social influence is not a new concept. Individuals will self-regulate their emotions from moment to moment for a variety of reasons and purposes (Rosenberg, 1990; Gibson and Schroeder, 2002). Thus we draw attention to this feature by arguing that emotion can be used as a type of influence tactic in the organizational politics process.

Integration of politics and emotion
In light of the foregoing review and discussion, we propose an integrative conceptualization of politics and emotion. In doing so, we demonstrate how previously unexamined emotional reactions to politics perceptions mediate the relationships between politics perceptions and the affective and attitudinal consequences. Furthermore, we discuss how

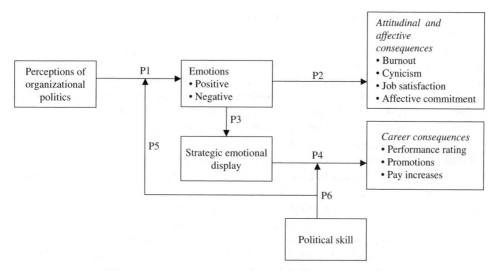

*Figure 10.1   The role of emotion and emotional behaviors in the POP–outcome
relationship*

emotional display, as a strategic influence tactic linked to emotional reactions, can alter
career-related outcomes. Finally, we examine the role of political skill as an influential
variable in our emotions and politics model (see Figure 10.1).

Emotional reactions in the politics process
Ferris et al. (1989) suggested that a politically charged work environment might induce
three potential reactions among employees: they may withdraw from the organization;
they may remain a member of the organization and immerse themselves in work; or they
may stay with the organization and become engaged in the political activities. Regardless
of the chosen reaction, it was argued that, in general, employees who perceive the organization as political tend to view their work environment as stressful, ambiguous and frus-
trating (Ferris et al., 1989; Harrell-Cook et al., 1999; Vigoda, 2002).

Consistent with this view, a variety of outcomes has been found to be associated with
perceptions of organizational politics, such as higher job anxiety, lowered job satisfaction
and more withdrawal behaviors (see Ferris, Adams et al., 2002 for a detailed review;
Vigoda, 2001). The theoretical explanations for such relationships have been provided
from the rational and behavioral perspective (Ferris et al., 1989). However, the role of emotional reactions to perceptions of organizational politics has not yet been examined. We
argue that organizational politics leads to emotional reactions and these emotional reactions affect individual outcomes as well as strategic behaviors aimed at displaying emotion.

Drawing on affective events theory (Weiss and Cropanzano, 1996), it could be argued
that political acts by oneself (i.e. political behavior) or others (i.e. politics perceptions) serve as work events in the forms of daily hassles and uplifts. For example, individuals perceive that political activities occurring in their organization have immediate
relevance to their self-interest, and that such events will trigger a host of emotional
reactions. Consequently, emotional experiences may serve as one of the core mechanisms

through which perceptions of organizational politics influence consequent attitudes and behaviors.

For example, the relationship between perceptions of organizational politics and withdrawal behavior could be explained by arguing that anger leads one to withdraw from the organization. As indirect support for this argument, work events that reflect organizational injustice, often closely related to political behaviors and/or organizational politics perceptions (Fedor and Maslyn, 2002), have been argued to cause feelings of anger, sadness, guilt, or pride, depending on whether the procedure and outcome are favorable to the actor (Cropanzano et al., 2000).

Emotional experiences caused by politics perceptions differ by the amount of relevance others' self-serving behaviors have on strain (cf. Lazarus, 1991). For example, when political acts are perceived as distal to one's self-interests, the emotions induced may be of low intensity. Conversely, when the political acts are perceived to have the potential either to harm or benefit one's self-interest, high-intensity emotions may result. Due to the functional role of emotion, different emotional experiences in reaction to politics perceptions will foster distinct attitudinal and behavioral reactions (Frijda, 1986; Scherer, 1984). Thus emotions are important mediators in the organizational politics process.

We acknowledge that there are situations where perceptions of organizational politics may have no emotional significance for individuals, for example, when the political acts associated with such perceptions are physically or psychologically remote. However, people react emotionally to person–environment encounters in which they have a personal stake (Lazarus, 1991). Political acts of self or others, with few exceptions, imply gain or loss of desired outcomes. Thus, in this chapter, we focus on perceptions of organizational politics that initiate significant emotional responses.

Although individuals tend to view organizational politics negatively, it is noteworthy that reactions may not always be negative (Fedor and Maslyn, 2002; Vredenburgh and Maurer, 1984). For example, some individuals may genuinely enjoy the political game (Ferris et al., 1989). Moreover, organizational politics may represent an opportunity, rather than a constraint, for many individuals. Shuler (1980) suggested that opportunity stressors induce fewer negative and more positive responses from individuals. In these situations, individuals see organizational politics as opportunities rather than threats. Accordingly, Ferris et al. (1989) argued that when employees feel that they understand the 'political game' and perceive a high level of control in the process, they may perceive organizational politics as an opportunity, which gives rise to fewer negative reactions.

Based on prior research findings, Fedor and Maslyn (2002) suggested that organizational politics is less problematic if one's immediate situation remains positive or unaffected (i.e. individuals view themselves as 'players' in the 'political game'). They further argued that the 'distance' of the political behavior from the individual has an inverse relationship with perceptions of organizational politics and its negativity.

In fact, actors who benefit from political behavior in organizations may well experience feelings of joy and excitement in this process. For example, there are situations in organizations where favorable results can be secured only through the use of unsanctioned tactics. In such situations, perceptions of politics may send cues to individuals signaling that there are unique behaviors, although not sanctioned by organizational rules, that can be undertaken to secure desired effects (Fedor and Maslyn, 2002; Ferris et al., 1989). Such possibilities may bring people hope and positive expectations. Consistently, political activities have been found to be necessary and, sometimes, effective acts in organizational change processes (Buchanan and Badham, 1999). Thus, we propose the following:

Proposition 1 Perceptions of organizational politics induces both positive and negative emotional reactions.

Emotions have been closely linked with behaviors (Frijda, 1986; Lazarus, 1991; Plutchik, 1980). Consistently, affective events theory (Weiss and Cropanzano, 1996) argued that the repetitive emotional experiences in reaction to work events influence one's work attitudes over time. Researchers have warned of deleterious outcomes resulting from negative emotions (Elliott et al., 1996; Frost, 2004; Lewis, 2000; Thoresen et al., 2003). Others have touted the benefits of positive emotions for organizational members and the organization as a whole (Elliott et al., 1996; Fisher, 2002; Fredrickson, 1998; Staw and Barsade, 1993; Staw et al., 1994; Thoresen et al., 2003). We argue that the positive or negative emotional reactions to organizational politics result in a number of affective and attitudinal consequences for individuals, including burnout, cynicism, job satisfaction and affective commitment to the organization.

Burnout   Thoresen and colleagues (2003) considered the emotional exhaustion dimension of burnout as a stress reaction associated with negative emotions, such as frustration and irritability. Elliott and colleagues (1996) posited that a negative orientation, including consistently negative emotional states, may cause individuals to be more susceptible to burnout. However, a positive orientation, including positive emotional states, may cause individuals to be less vulnerable to burnout. Based on the limited information available regarding burnout and emotional states, we may assume that negative emotions have a positive association with burnout, and positive emotions have a negative association with burnout.

Cynicism   Cynicism is an attitude composed of beliefs, affect and behavioral tendencies toward a target (Davis and Gardner, 2004). It involves a general mistrust regarding the motivations and honesty of a particular entity of focus. In the literature, negative emotions are consistently linked with the cynicism concept. Andersson and Bateman (1997) stated that a cynical attitude is composed of 'an affective component (negative feelings and disillusionment) as well as a belief (distrust)' (p. 451). Davis and Gardner (2004) stated that cynicism is accompanied by negative feelings, such as anger and contempt. Dean et al. (1998) noted that cynics possess negative feelings, such as contempt, frustration and hopelessness. From this information, it is reasonable to conclude that negative emotions are positively related to cynicism and positive emotions are negatively related to cynicism.

Job satisfaction   Job satisfaction has been strongly linked with emotions. In fact, job satisfaction has been defined as 'a pleasurable or positive emotional state resulting from the appraisal of one's job or job experiences' (Locke, 1976, p. 1300). Negative emotions have been associated with job dissatisfaction (Fisher, 2000) and it is evident that emotions and job satisfaction are inextricably linked (Weiss, 2002; Weiss and Cropanzano, 1996). Furthermore, Thoresen et al. (2003) found state and trait positive affect (negative affect) to have a positive (inverse) correlation with job satisfaction.

Affective commitment   People are successful in negotiating their own places relative to their interactional partners to the extent that they successfully induce desired emotions. Fisher (2002) argued that positive affective events contribute to the development of affective commitment. Thoresen et al. (2003) found state and trait positive affect to have a positive correlation with commitment and a negative correlation between state and trait negative affect and commitment. This evidence leads to the assumption that positive emotions are directly related to commitment, and negative emotions are inversely related to commitment.

We propose that emotions mediate the relationship between perceptions of organizational politics and attitudinal and affective consequences. Specifically, when individuals experience positive emotions due to perceived organizational politics, negative consequences are less likely to occur. Indeed, if individuals perceive organizational politics to be an opportunity and they experience positive emotions, positive consequences such as job satisfaction are more likely to occur. However, when individuals experience negative emotions due to be perceived organizational politics, negative consequences such as cynicism and burnout are more likely to occur.

> **Proposition 2**   Emotional reactions to perceptions of organizational politics influence work-related affective and attitudinal outcomes including burnout, job satisfaction, cynicism and affective commitment.

Emotion as an influence mechanism
Research from a variety of disciplines maintains that people express emotions for purposes other than responding to their inner feelings. Goffman (1959) argued that emotional expressions are guided by conscious self-presentation strategies that convey certain impressions to others. Bowlby (1979) suggested that individuals express emotions that are not felt in order to establish, maintain, or terminate interpersonal relationships. Rosenberg (1990) explicitly distinguished between emotional expression and emotional display. He argued that emotional display 'involves the self-regulation of emotional exhibition for the purpose of producing intended effects on others' minds' (p. 4). He further indicated that individuals use emotional display either to persuade others that they are moral actors who conform to the societal norms, or to influence others and attain their ends. Collectively, this suggests that emotions can serve as mechanisms of influence.

Empirically, the emotional labor literature demonstrated (albeit, indirectly) that emotions could be used to influence the feelings of others. In this tradition, the most appealing case was made by Hochschild (1983), who studied flight attendants and found that they, by the requirement of their occupation and the organizational norms and rules, frequently have to express feelings that are not actually felt in order to put customers in positive emotional states. Hochschild (1983) coined the term 'emotional dissonance' to describe the psychological experiences of individuals resulting from displaying emotions that are not inherently felt. Although her main focus was on the influences of norms and exertion of self-regulation, the concept of emotional labor itself indicates that emotions play a role in interpersonal influence (cf. Thoits, 1996).

Individuals' proactive practices of such influence attempts have been directly examined by a small number of researchers. For example, Rafaeli and Sutton's (1991) research on the use of emotional contrast strategies demonstrated that emotional displays could be used as social influence attempts. They found that criminal interrogators and bill collectors routinely used emotions as a way to induce compliance from suspects and debtors. Specifically, the purposeful expressions of positive emotions and negative emotions in sequence (e.g. the 'good cop, bad cop' strategy) makes the person who expresses positive emotions more likeable and trustworthy, and the person who expresses negative emotions more fear-inducing, both of which help trigger targets' compliance. Similarly, Thoits (1996) also observed that healing groups used a variety of techniques to induce emotions as an attempt to help the target person to regain emotional balance and a sense of emotional well-being.

The conceptual work of other behavioral scientists is more directly indicative of the significance of emotion in organizational politics (Clark, 1990; Collins, 1981, 1990; Gordon, 1990; Kemper, 1984, 1990). Collectively, these scholars argued that emotions represent power and status. For example, it has been proposed that the experience of positive emotions is associated with an increase in one's power and/or status, and the experience of negative emotions is associated with a decrease in one's power and/or status (Kemper, 1984).

Building on the notion of emotion as a reflection of one's power and status, Clark (1990) examined the role of emotions in the micro-politics process. He discussed emotion in terms of its relationship with one's social 'place' (i.e. one's power and status). He argued that self-target emotions (e.g. shame, pride) are associated with people's sense of identity and value. Such emotions 'mark' people's place in interpersonal encounters; that is, they indicate one's relative standing to the interactional partner. Besides the 'place-marker' function of emotion, individuals also 'claim' their place in interpersonal interactions by expressing other-target emotions (e.g. anger, love, or sympathy) and eliciting corresponding emotions in others.

Because emotions both mark and claim places, people are successful in negotiating their own place relative to the interactional partner to the extent that they successfully induce desired emotions in others. For example, consider the first example given at the beginning of the chapter. The boss was successful at negotiating a superior place relative to the subordinate because of the ability to induce feelings of embarrassment. Clark's (1990) work, together with that of others (e.g. Collins, 1990; Gordon, 1990; Kemper, 1990), indicates that emotions can be used as a conscious and strategic mechanism of influence. We refer to this as 'strategic emotional display.'

Following Rosenberg (1990), we define strategic emotional display as an individual's intentional expression of emotion with the purpose of interpersonal influence. By doing so, we are able to conceptualize strategic emotional display as a type of emotion-focused political behavior. It is noteworthy that our concept of strategic emotional display is conceptually different from emotional labor. Whereas emotional labor concerns primarily individuals' adherence to display norms in the service context, strategic emotional display is a type of influence attempt initiated by individuals that may be applied to any interpersonal settings (cf. Buller and Burgoon, 1998). Furthermore, whereas the tactic used by emotional labor is usually limited to the expression of pleasant emotions, individuals attempting to influence others via these means have a wider range of tactics at their disposal, including the expression of negative emotions.

Emotional reaction – strategic emotional display linkage
Frequently, organizations establish display norms that encourage positive emotions and suppress negative ones (Hochschild, 1983; Van Maanen and Kunda, 1989). Thus, when individuals feel fewer positive emotions, they are more likely to use strategic emotional display to disguise their real feelings and to maintain an image that is desirable to the organization. Moreover, social groups, in general, often exert strong norms in terms of emotional display (Andersen and Guerrero, 1998; Thoits, 1996). When their emotional state is not deemed socially appropriate, individuals are likely to hide their real emotions and choose to display strategic emotions in order to be accepted by their immediate social groups. For example, a recipient of a high pay raise may find it useful to express a sense of guilt to others in order to keep being liked and accepted. Alternatively, people may hide their irritation in order not to negatively influence the relationship with another individual who is annoying.

Thus the 'social inappropriateness' of certain emotions sometimes serves as the very reason why people strategically display emotions. When emotional reactions are not in tune with the overall display rules in the organization or the immediate social group, individuals are not likely to act emotionally. We argue that when positive emotions give rise to strategic emotional display, the purpose is primarily to gain an expected advantage. Conversely, when the emotional reactions are negative, the purpose is primarily to cope with situational demands. Thus,

> **Proposition 3**   Emotional reactions induce individuals' strategic emotional displays as either ways of coping (for negative emotions) or gaining expected advantage (for positive emotions).

Strategic emotional display
Strategies of emotional display can be classified in terms of the emotions that are expressed by the focal individual. Although there are different conceptions as to how many strategies people use, three categories have received an adequate level of consensus. These are: positive emotional expression, negative emotional expression and masking emotions (Clark, 1990; Gibson and Schroeder, 2002; Kemper, 1984; Rafaeli and Sutton, 1991; Wharton and Erickson, 1993). Below we discuss each of these three strategies.

Positive emotional expression   Expressing positive emotions is by far the most frequently used emotional strategy for interpersonal influence. This research suggests that organizations impose display rules on employees by requiring them to express positive emotions to customers in order to promote positive organizational image and customer satisfaction and loyalty (e.g. Gatta, 2002; Hochschild, 1983; Van Maanen and Kunda, 1989). Research also has examined the individual and organizational consequences of such efforts (e.g. Grandey, 2003; Pugh, 2001; Shuler and Sypher, 2000; Tsai, 2001). Accumulative research evidence suggests that expressing positive emotions to others leads to positive interpersonal outcomes, such as liking, good will and social support (e.g. Fredrickson, 1998; George and Brief, 1992; Gross, 2002; Gross and John, 2003; Staw et al., 1994).

Rafaeli and Sutton (1991) argued that expressing positive emotions is a tool of social influence because encounters with friendly people are positively reinforcing. That is, individuals prefer to be around others who make them feel good, and will take steps, such as complying with their wishes or requests, to prolong interactions. Clark (1990) suggested that actors who express positive emotions tend to gain the target's acceptance. Furthermore, Wharton and Erickson (1993) suggested that positive emotions bind individuals together by helping establish positive interpersonal relationships. In this sense, expressing positive emotions may enhance one's social standing, which in turn may influence one's career positively.

As empirical support, Staw and Barsade (1993) found that individuals displaying positive emotions were rated as being more effective at managerial decision making than those with negative emotions. Staw et al. (1994) ascertained that positive emotions are associated with favorable supervisor evaluations and higher pay. We expect that individuals displaying positive emotions would be better able to positively affect the mediating processes of liking and perceived similarity in dyadic exchange relationships (Wayne et al., 1997). In support, the use of emotionally friendly tactics such as ingratiation (Strutton and Pelton, 1998) and inspirational appeals (Yukl and Tracey, 1992) has been found to have a positive impact on career-related outcomes. As such, it seems that the use of positive emotional influence strategies may positively influence performance ratings, pay increases and promotions.

However, it should be noted that inappropriate expressions of positive emotions may jeopardize one's career. The choice of influence tactic is partly a function of the characteristics of the target (Kipnis et al., 1980) and setting. For example, individuals who are cynical or suspicious may tend to question the intention and sincerity of others' positive emotional expressions. Therefore expressing positive emotions to these persons may not achieve the same effects as it would for others. In addition, the target may perceive expressing positive emotions as inappropriate, or even offensive in some situations. For example, one's expression of hope and enthusiasm for a project may lead to a supervisor's disliking if the supervisor already has lost interest in the project, or if it is believed that the project cannot be successful. To react with a smiling face to an angry person also may be interpreted as being resentful or scornful. In these instances, one's emotional behavior will influence others' perceptions as to his or her competence, potential and likeability, which may influence subsequent career outcomes. Thus we argue that the strategic display of positive emotions influences one's career. However, the effectiveness of these attempts may vary across different situations.

Negative emotional expression   Research examining the expression of negative emotions is modest relative to that investigating positive ones. However, in daily organizational life, negative emotions often are used to claim or protect one's social place. For example, anger warns others that they are acting inappropriately (Lazarus, 1991). Expressions of guilt relate to the meaning of one's 'having transgressed a moral imperative against another' (Lazarus, 1991), and indicate that one is willing to make amends. When used appropriately, expressions of guilt can cue the target that the actor is of a high moral standard.

In service encounters, individuals' emotional display is more or less prescribed by the organization. However, in daily interpersonal interactions among employees, individuals usually have more discretion as to what emotions to express. In such circumstances, expressing negative emotions as an influence strategy is less inappropriate in terms of display norms. Rather, they may induce positive outcomes for individuals. For example, expressions of anger are associated with others' perceptions of the actor being strong, powerful and competent (Tiedens, 2001; Tiedens et al., 2000).

Prior research suggests both positive and negative effects of expressing negative emotions as influence attempts. On the positive side, early work on tax collectors and criminal interrogators indicated that, for certain occupations, expressing negative emotions help to achieve desired effects on targets (Hochschild, 1983; Rafaeli and Sutton, 1991; Sutton, 1991). For example, Adolf Hitler was well known for his routine expressions of negative emotions, which provides support for the argument that expressions of negative emotion can be an effective way to influence followers. Moreover, negative emotional expressions have also been linked with lower subordinate assessment of a leader's effectiveness (Lewis, 2000).

Rafaeli and Sutton (1991) suggested that the reason why negative emotions influence targets is that negative emotions are repelling to them; therefore targets tend to comply with the actors' requests so that they can escape from the taxing interpersonal encounters. Consistently, Coyne (1976) found that men who talked with a depressed woman on the phone quickly became depressed themselves and refused to talk with her again. Putting this into the organizational context, although expressing negative emotions may help one to achieve the goal of influence at one occasion, it may have a long-term detrimental effect on interpersonal relationships (Tiedens, 2001).

In addition, different negative emotions also have different effects in interpersonal encounters given the variability in their underlying message. For example, expressions of anger and sadness have differential effects on targets, although they both belong to the negative category. Whereas targets tend to perceive actors who express anger as dominant, strong and competent, they tend to perceive actors who express sadness as weak, submissive and incompetent (Tiedens, 2001).

Based on the above discussion, we argue that strategic displays of negative emotions influence one's career, and the effects may vary from positive to negative, depending on the situations and individuals involved, as well as the specific emotions displayed.

Masking emotions   Wharton and Erickson (1993) suggested that the masking of emotions is another strategy that people use to influence. This is comparable to what Clark (1990) called controlling the balance of emotional energy, which refers to one's effort to evoke the target's emotions while regulating one's own. Emotional display may disclose information that the actor may not be willing to share with others, or information that others will use to counter influence attempts. In such situations, it is in the actor's best interest to appear to be emotionally neutral. For example, doing so may help a leader to maintain control over crisis situations. In the work environment, one's emotional expressions may send cues to others as to one's standing with certain issues, which often is not desirable given the political risk. In such situations, masking emotions appears to be a useful strategy to achieve or maintain one's power and status, which in turn leads to a better opportunity to receive a positive performance rating, pay increase and/or promotion.

However, there is also a negative side of emotional masking. Emotional expressions convey important information based on which others infer one's characteristics, beliefs and thoughts (Tiedens, 2001). Being less emotionally expressive, individuals who suppress and mask their emotions lower their own chances of being better understood and appreciated by others, which in turn may lead to performance ratings, pay increase and promotion decisions not reflecting their real skills and competence. Thus,

Proposition 4   Strategically expressing or masking emotions will influence career consequences such as performance ratings, pay increases and promotions.

Combination of multiple strategies   It is worth noting that individuals may use a combination of strategies to influence others. For example, when an actor perceives that one emotional display strategy (e.g. expressing positive emotions) did not achieve the desired effects, he or she may switch to using another strategy (e.g. expressing negative emotions). In fact, using multiple strategies may at times be very effective in inducing desired effects. As noted, Rafaeli and Sutton (1991) found criminal interrogators and tax collectors who used emotional contrasting strategy achieved better results in terms of inducing compliance, as compared to when only one type of emotion was strategically used. Thus it is reasonable to expect that a political actor's use of multiple emotional display strategies also will be effective in many situations.

Political skill

We argue that political skill is influential to the politics process in two ways. First, politically skilled individuals react less negatively (and even positively) to perceptions of organizational politics than others (Perrewé et al., 2004). Second, they are more likely to demonstrate strategic emotional displays effectively. We discuss each in detail below.

Political skill and emotional reactions to perceptions of organizational politics   Ferris, Perrewé and colleagues (2000) suggested that politically skilled people have a strong and convincing personal style that exerts a powerful influence on others. Perhaps because of the ability to influence, politically skilled individuals enjoy a sense of personal security and self-confidence derived from prior successful experiences in interacting with others in their work environments (Ferris et al., 1999). This success reinforces their ability to cope with difficult situations and exert their influence over issues in the intended direction (Greenberger and Strasser, 1986), and achieve desired results (Perrewé et al., 2004). Such personal security and self-confidence also leads politically skilled individuals to experience less stress and strain at work by making their work environment more predicable and controllable (Ferris et al., 1999; Perrewé et al., 2000).

In fact, individuals who are politically skilled not only experience organizational politics perceptions less negatively than others; they may even find politicking rather satisfying. To these individuals, organizational politics may be something that brings fun and a sense of competence and accomplishment to the job. As evidence, Perrewé et al. (2004, p. 149) concluded, 'Perhaps individuals with high political skill require a certain amount of stimuli or activation in their environment to feel comfortable. Stimuli that are stressful for some may be perceived as welcome challenges for individuals with high political skill.'

According to motivation theory, positive emotions are associated with forward progression toward objectives, and negative emotions are associated with failure to progress towards the objectives (Jones and Rittman, 2002; Seo et al., 2004). Because organizational politics often is disruptive to the formal organizational rules and practices, individuals may perceive organizational politics as something that prevents them from achieving their goals. These individuals are likely to experience negative emotions, such as anger, sadness and anxiety, in reaction to organizational politics perceptions. However, because politically skilled individuals tend to take advantages of organizational politics, they are more likely to expect that they will able to realize their desired objectives in this setting.

Proposition 5   Political skill moderates the perception of organizational politics–emotional reactions relationships, such that people who are politically skilled will experience emotions that are less negative (or even ones that are positive) in reaction to organizational politics perceptions, as compared to individuals who are low on political skill.

Political skill and effectiveness of strategic emotional display   We define the effectiveness of strategic emotional display as the degree to which such emotional display is perceived as situationally appropriate and achieves the desired effects on others. People choose specific influence tactics as a result of several factors, such as the different kind of relationships with others, for different purposes, and when in different situations (Kipnis et al., 1980). Individuals need to be skillful and flexible in their political acts, because a certain influence tactic may be effective in one situation but not another. For example, Yukl and Tracey (1992) found that ingratiation and exchange were effective for influencing subordinates and peers, but were not effective for influencing superiors. We expect the same to be true in terms of the strategic use of emotional display. Emotional norms differ across settings, and each situation calls for unique emotional behaviors. Thus the appropriateness of emotional expressions is situationally based. One has to read and comprehend the situation in order to convey one's emotions appropriately. It is likely that politically skilled individuals are better able to display situationally appropriate emotions.

With an ability to perceive others and the situation accurately, politically skilled individuals possess an intuitive savvy and understanding of people and events in organizations (Ahearn et al., 2004). Ferris and colleagues (Ferris, Anthony et al., 2002; Ferris et al., 2005) proposed that individuals possessing political skill are keenly attuned to diverse social situations and have the ability to adapt their behaviors as a function of changing situational demands. Further, they are adept at recognizing and using the appropriate influence tactics for a given situation to achieve their goals. These may contribute to their ability to better determine the appropriate emotions to display in a given situation. For example, in trying to persuade someone, one may try to induce either positive emotions (e.g. liking) or negative emotions (e.g. fear) in the target person. However, in one situation, politically skilled individuals may choose to induce liking rather than fear because they wish to maintain positive interactions in the future. In another situation, they may choose to induce fear rather than liking if they need to 'mark' a higher place (e.g. a young new boss). In addition, they may also use emotional contrasting strategy or simply try different strategies because they can read what is, or is not, working.

Thus, depending on their intentions, politically skilled individuals have the ability to flexibly choose situationally appropriate emotional behaviors. Due to their perceptiveness in immediate interactive situations, politically skilled individuals are presumably able to discern other people's emotional states, and adjust their ways of influencing accordingly.

In sum, politically skilled individuals have the ability to adjust their emotional displays based on their motives, the characteristics of the target of influence (e.g. relative status, emotional state) and the immediate social setting.

Besides demonstrating situationally appropriate emotions, actors also have to 'reach' the target emotionally in order to achieve the desired effects. Influence attempts may fail because people become suspicious about individuals' intentions. Jones (1990) noted that influence attempts will be successful only when actors are perceived as possessing no ulterior motives. Consistently, Liden and Mitchell (1988) argued that in order for ingratiation attempts to be successful, the target has to perceive the actors as being sincere. The same is true for strategic emotional display. In order for the strategic emotional display to be effective, an actor has to ensure perceived authenticity of their intentional displays of emotions in the eyes of the target. We argue that politically skilled individuals know exactly how to reach this goal.

It has been argued that politically skilled individuals know how to exert interpersonal influences in a sincere manner that disguises any ulterior motives and inspires believability, trust and confidence, and renders the influence attempt successful (Ferris, Anthony, et al., 2002; Ferris, Hochwarter et al., 2002). They appear to others as congruent, sincere and genuine (or, honest, open and forthright) (Ferris, Hochwarter et al., 2002). Because their actions are not interpreted as manipulative or coercive, individuals high in apparent sincerity inspire trust and confidence in and from those around them (Ferris, Hochwarter et al., 2002; Ferris et al., 2005). Thus it is reasonable to expect that emotional expressions will be perceived as reflecting real feelings. In addition, due to their ability to accurately read interpersonal cues from others, politically skilled individuals also are likely to alter their influence strategies depending on how well one strategy is working, that is, to use multiple emotional strategies in one influence attempt to make it more effective. Thus,

Proposition 6   Political skill moderates the relationship between strategic emotional display and career consequences, such that people who engage in strategic emotional displays and who are politically skilled are more likely than others to obtain favorable career outcomes.

Discussion and conclusion
In this chapter, we argued that emotion mediates the perceptions of organizational politics–work outcome relationships, and that emotions can be used strategically for political purposes. This chapter represents one of the first discussions linking organizational politics with workplace emotions. By arguing that emotions and politics are intertwined and have to be examined in each other's domain, we intend to encourage scholarly interest in both research fields.

Limitations of the model
There are a number of model limitations that warrant mention. First, for the reason of parsimony, we have chosen to focus on perceptions of organizational politics that have emotional significance for individuals. However, there might be situations where such perceptions lead directly to emotional strategic display, in which cases individuals make the conscious choice to become involved in the political milieu. In addition, there are other variables that may be influential for the proposed links. For example, one's affective

reactions, besides influencing the affective and attitudinal consequences discussed in the model, also may influence career consequences.

It has been found that individuals who feel good also tend to do well at work (e.g. George and Brief, 1992; Staw et al., 1994). Therefore, individuals who enjoy positive affective and attitudinal outcomes at work also should have an advantage in gaining favorable career outcomes. Furthermore, depending on how willingly one tends to become involved in political activities, one's strategic emotional display may also have an influence on affective consequences. In the spirit of parsimony, and to better focus on the intertwining features of politics and emotion, however, we chose to forgo these links.

Finally, to keep the scope of the model manageable, we have omitted the construct of emotional intelligence. However, given the significant influences of emotional intelligence on the way individuals handle emotionally charged situations, it is obvious that emotional intelligence may play an important role in the proposed relationships in the model. For example, an emotionally intelligent individual is likely to make accurate attributions to ambiguous situations (Jordan et al., 2002), such as those in which politics are involved and, therefore, react with more functional emotional responses. Further, it is also likely that emotionally intelligent individuals will react to the same political situation differently from those who are politically skilled. Thus, future research may consider the differential roles of political skill and emotional intelligence in the model. It is important to note that political skill and emotional intelligence are two distinct constructs, although they are also closely related to each other (Ferris et al., 2005). Whereas emotional intelligence concerns one's emotional competency, and therefore the way one deals with one's own and others' emotions, political skill is associated with a wider range of skills and capabilities an individual has in handling his or her social surroundings, such as networking, and influence tactics other than emotion-focused ones. Practically, it is likely that an individual is emotionally intelligent but not politically skilled, or vice versa. For example, whereas they can cast a sincere and trustworthy image in public, politically skilled individuals can nonetheless suffer from a sense of inauthenticity in private, if they are not emotionally intelligent. Given these subtle differences between the two constructs, the roles of the two may at times be different, or overlap. And it is an interesting empirical question to answer as to in what situations they will predict the same or different behaviors and social outcomes for individuals in political situations. For example, it is likely that in situations with implications for self-interest, political skill may predict self-centered considerations and behaviors, whereas emotional intelligence may predict more altruistic behaviors. In all, it represents a fruitful area for future research to consider the role emotional intelligence plays in emotion–politics relationships.

Implications of the model

Implications for organizational politics   Recently, scholars have argued that much can be gained from integrating the emotional and political perspectives of organizational action (Ferris, Hochwarter et al., 2002). The current conceptualization extends one of the suggestions put forth by these authors, that there is a strategic component to emotional display. There appear to be two implications of this model for the future of organizational politics research. Specifically, this model provides the first integrative explanation of the link between perceived politics and political behavior. Although regarded as largely parallel and independent streams of work, there has been an implicit assumption that politics perceptions and political behavior are related (Ferris, Adams et al., 2002; Ferris et al., 1989; Ferris and Kacmar, 1992).

Consistently, a number of studies reported a significant relationship between the two constructs (e.g. Cheng, 1983; Ferris, Harrell-Cook et al., 2000; Harrell-Cook et al., 1999; Valle and Perrewé, 2000; Liu et al., in press). In support of these empirical results, we have argued that the emotional reactions evoked by the perceived existence of political activity energize emotion-focused political behavior as a reaction to the opportunity or threat presented by the environment. By positing emotional reactions as a mediating factor between perceptions of organizational politics and organizational behaviors, it seems reasonable to suggest that, other things being equal, perceptions of politics should encourage more political behaviors.

This model also has implications for the measurement of political activity in organizations. We suggested that people use emotion-focused influence tactics. As such, some work needs to be conducted that distinguishes these tactics from the traditional influence tactics of Kipnis and colleagues (1980). It may be that these emotion-focused influence tactics represent an empirically distinct dimension of interpersonal influence. Or it may be equally plausible that the structure of influence tactics is hierarchically ordered to represent emotional components as higher-order factors of interpersonal influence. Evident in these options is the need to empirically develop the content and structure of emotional influence strategies. Without the development of sound measures of emotion-focused influence tactics, researchers will be unable to assess the impact of emotion in the influence process.

Implications for workplace emotions　The model also has important implications for the literature on emotion in organizations. Thoits (1996) argued that Hochschild (1983) focused only on part of emotional labor, the exertion of emotion self-control. Thoits (1996) called for more research attention to other components, including the influence of others' emotions. However, to date, not much progress has been made in this direction. To understand the role of emotions in organizational life, researchers should begin putting more effort into examining the social function of emotion. Specifically, it may be useful to assess how individuals proactively seek advantage by strategically expressing emotions in their daily interactions with others. In fact, because emotions are usually seen as spontaneous and natural rather than as strategic and manipulative, targets are less likely to question the intentionality or sincerity of emotion-focused influence attempts as compared to other forms of interpersonal influence (Hochschild, 1983; Tiedens, 2001). As such, strategic emotional display could be more effective than other forms of influence tactics examined previously.

In addition, Ferris, Hochwarter and colleagues (2002) noted that the emotions literature has been concerned more with individuals' psychological well-being (e.g. stress-related outcomes, job satisfaction, or burnout), as compared to individuals' performance scores or promotability. Recently, more research has been emerging that focuses on emotion's influence on individual and collective performance (e.g. Gross and John, 2003; Huy, 2002; Reus and Liu, in press). Along with this new outlook of emotion, we argued in this chapter that one way that emotion may influence career success is when people strategically use it to influence their interpersonal standings.

Directions for future research

There are a number of issues that need further research attention. First of all, the model proposed in the chapter needs to be empirically tested. One of the challenges is the operationalization of strategic emotional display. This is problematic because individuals strategically using emotional expressions may not be doing so consciously (Buller and Burgoon, 1998). Instead, they may have developed the skills required for strategic emotional display through earlier socialization or through genetics. As such, it has become habitual, such that when asked in surveys to recall the experiences, they do not recognize them.

To use peer report measures is also problematic in that emotional display has to be intentionally used in order for it to be 'strategic.' Nevertheless, it is difficult for an observer to determine whether one's emotional expressions are intentional or natural. To make matters worse, an actor's emotional display, as observed by others, not only includes the strategic elements that the actor wants others to perceive, but also some non-strategic emotional information that the actor leaks in the communication process (cf. Ekman and Friesen, 1969).

One possible approach to avoid these problems is to start with experimental designs. For example, researchers might use film clips in which the actor practices common-sense types of effective emotional display strategies, and the target's reactions, either positive or negative, are recorded at the same time. The clip can then be shown to the audience, who rate their perceptions of the actor. Successful strategic emotional displays should be those in which: (1) the actor is perceived to have used an appropriate emotional display strategy, and (2) the target's reaction is in the desired direction of the actor, indicating the success of the influence attempt.

Second, the identification of factors that predict the type(s) of strategic emotional display actors tend to use represents another useful direction for future research. The selection of specific emotional display strategies may be influenced by many factors, which include gender and the relative status of the actor as compared to the target. Emotions are gendered (Shields, 2002); that is, different gender roles are associated with different emotional norms. Frequently, societies expect women to be more emotionally sensitive, and express 'soft' emotions such as love, liking, empathy and warmth; and men to be less emotionally sensitive, and express 'strong' emotions such as anger (Hochschild, 1983; Shields, 2002).

In a study of leadership, Lewis (2000) found that male leaders received lower effectiveness ratings when expressing sadness compared to neutrality, while female leaders received lower ratings when expressing either sadness or anger. Thus it is reasonable to expect that effective male actors will use expressions of negative emotions or emotion masking more frequently, and effective female actors will use expressions of positive emotions more frequently, as compared to their female and male counterparts, respectively.

The relative status of the actor as compared to the target is another influential factor that may affect the choice of emotional influence strategies. The influence literature has consistently identified the status of the target as an influential factor on an actor's choices of influence tactics (Kipnis et al., 1980; Kipnis and Schmidt, 1983). Rafaeli and Sutton (1991) suggested that, when using emotion-contrast strategies, actors who have higher status than the targets (e.g. criminal interrogators) are likely to start with expressing negative emotions, whereas actors who have more or less equal status with the targets (e.g. tax collectors) are likely to start with expressing positive emotions. Gibson and Schroeder (2002) also suggested that those with higher position power are more likely to express their authentic feelings than are their lower power counterparts.

Third, influence is an interpersonal process. Therefore it is critical to examine how the target's emotional and behavioral reactions may affect the actor in the process of influence. Fourth, the identification of second-level outcome variables, such as one's power and status, also merits further scholarly attention. Fifth, in terms of strategic emotional display, we have focused on how individuals can work on the hedonic tones of emotions expressed. However, individuals can also influence others by manipulating the intensity of the emotions they express (Andersen and Guerrero, 1998). Thus the exaggeration and minimization of expressed emotional arousal also should be examined in future research.

Fourth, emotions are associated with different meanings in different cultures. For example, although in the American culture fear is associated with a lower social status and indicates weakness, the Ifaluk view people who are fearful as being harmless, and therefore as deserving respect (Lutz, 1988). Individuals' emotional expressions also are under strong influences of culture-specific emotional norms (Ekman, 1972; Matsumoto et al., 1998). For example, it has been found that Japanese men are more likely to cover up their negative emotions with smiles than are American men (Ekman, 1972), probably due to the emphasis on harmony in interpersonal relationships in collectivist cultures. People not only experience and express what they believe to be appropriate emotions; they also expect others to behave according to similar rules (Averill, 1980). Thus individuals who understand and adhere to the cultural emotional norms are more likely to be effective in their influence attempts in a cross-cultural context. As such, culture not only influences how one's emotional expressions will be understood, but also defines its appropriateness, which further determines the effectiveness of certain strategic emotional displays. For example, it is likely that in cultures high on masculinity, expressing negative emotions such as anger is an effective way to generate respect from others, whereas in more feminine cultures expressing positive emotions such as passion and love are more effective ways to gain higher status in groups. In sum, the influences of culture, on emotion make it a more complex task for one to exert influence attempts successfully in a cross-cultural context. Thus another interesting future research question is how culture may influence the interpretations and reactions to one's emotion-focused influence attempts in cross-cultural organizations.

Finally, the notion of positive politics (Fedor and Maslyn, 2002) is most relevant when examined from an emotional perspective. For example, it would be interesting to investigate how strategic emotional display may play a role in making politics more positive in terms of its influence on intrapersonal and interpersonal outcomes. In sum, the examination of the emotion of politics and the politics of emotion will contribute to a more informed understanding of both phenomena.

References

Ahearn, K.K., Ferris, G.R., Hochwarter, W.A., Douglas, D. and Ammeter, A.P. (2004). Leader political skill and team performance. *Journal of Management*, **30**, 309–27.

Andersson, L.M. and Bateman, T.S. (1997). Cynicism in the workplace: Some causes and effects. *Journal of Organizational Behavior*, **18**, 449–69.

Andersen, P.A. and Guerrero, L.K. (1998). Principles of communication and emotion in social interaction. In P.A. Andersen and L.K. Guerrero (eds), *Handbook of communication and emotion: Research, theory, applications, and contexts* (pp. 49–96). San Diego, CA: Academic Press.

Arvey, R.D., Renz, G.L. and Watson, T.W. (1998). Emotionality and job performance: Implications for personnel selection. In G.R. Ferris (ed.), *Research in personnel and human resources management* (Vol. 16, pp. 103–47). Greenwich, CT: JAI Press.

Ashforth, B.E. and Humphrey, R.H. (1995). Emotion in the work place: A reappraisal. *Human Relations*, **48**, 97–125.

Ashkanasy, N.M., Zerbe, W.J. and Hartel, C.E.J. (2002). Managing emotions in a changing workplace. In N.M. Ashkanasy, C.E.J. Hartel and W.J. Zerbe (eds), *Managing emotions in the workplace* (pp. 3–22). New York: M.E. Sharpe.

Averill, J.R. (1980). A construct view of emotion. In R. Plutchik and H. Kellerman (eds), *Emotion: Theory, research, and experience* (Vol. 1, pp. 305–39). New York: Academic Press.

Barsade, S.G. and Gibson, D.E. (1998). Group emotion: A review from top and bottom. In M.A. Neale and E.A. Mannix (eds), *Research on managing groups and teams* (Vol. 1, pp. 81–102). Stamford, CT: JAI Press.

Bowlby, J. (1979). *The making and breaking of affectional bonds*. London: Tavistock Publications.

Buchanan, D. and Badham, R. (1999). Politics and organizational change: The lived experience. *Human Relations*, **52**, 609–29.

Buller, D.B. and Burgoon, J.K. (1998). Emotional expression in the deception process. In P.A. Andersen and L.K. Guerrero (eds), *Handbook of communication and emotion: Research, theory, applications, and contexts* (pp. 381–401). San Diego, CA: Academic Press.

Cheng, J.L. (1983). Organizational context and upward influence: An experimental study of the use of power tactics. *Group and Organization Studies*, **8**, 337–55.

Clark, C. (1990). Emotions and micropolitics in everyday life: Some patterns and paradoxes of 'place'. In T.D. Kemper (ed.), *Research agendas in the sociology of emotions* (pp. 305–33). Albany, NY: State University of New York Press.

Clore, G. (1994). Why emotions are felt. In P. Ekman and R.J. Davidson (eds), *The nature of emotions* (pp. 103–11). New York: Cambridge University Press.

Cohen, A. and Vigoda, E. (1999). Politics and the workplace. *Public Productivity and Management Review*, **22**, 389–407.

Collins, R. (1981). On the microfoundations of macrosociology. *American Journal of Sociology*, **86**, 984–1014.

Collins, R. (1990). Stratification, emotional energy, and the transient emotions. In T.D. Kemper (ed.), *Research agendas in the sociology of emotions* (pp. 27–57). Albany, NY: State University of New York Press.

Coyne, J.C. (1976). Depression and the response of others. *Journal of Abnormal Psychology*, **85**, 186–93.

Cropanzano, R., Weiss, H.M., Suckow, K.J. and Grandey, A. (2000). Doing justice to workplace emotion. In N.M. Ashkanasy, C.E.J. Hartel and W.J. Zerbe (eds), *Emotions in the workplace* (pp. 49–62). Westport, CT: Quorum Books.

Davis, W.D. and Gardner, W.L. (2004). Perceptions of politics and organizational cynicism: An attributional and leader–member exchange perspective. *Leadership Quarterly*, **15**, 439–65.

Dean, J.W., Brandes, P. and Dharwadkar, R. (1998). Organizational cynicism. *Academy of Management Review*, **23**, 341–53.

Diener, E. (1999). Introduction to the special section on the structure of emotion. *Journal of Personality and Social Psychology*, **76**, 803–4.

Dillard, J.P. and Burgoon, M. (1985). Situational influences on the selection of compliance-gaining messages: Two tests of the predictive utility of the Cody–McLaughlin typology. *Communication Monographs*, **52**, 289–304.

Drory, A. (1993). Perceived political climate and job attitudes. *Organization Studies*, **14**, 59–71.

Drory, A. and Romm, R. (1990). The definition of organizational politics: A review. *Human Relations*, **43**, 1133–54.

Ekman, P. (1972). Universals and cultural differences in facial expression of emotion. In J.R. Cole (ed.), *Nebraska symposium on motivation* (pp. 207–83). Lincoln, NE: University of Nebraska Press.

Ekman, P. (1973). Cross culture studies of facial expression. In P. Ekman (ed.), *Darwin and facial expression: A century of research in review* (pp. 169–72). New York: Academic Press.

Ekman, P. and Friesen, W.V. (1969). Nonverbal leakage and clues to deception. *Psychiatry*, **32**, 88–106.

Elliot, T.R., Shewchuk, R., Hagglund, K., Rybarczyk, B. and Harkins, S. (1996). Occupational burnout, tolerance for stress, and coping among nurses in rehabilitation units. *Rehabilitation Psychology*, **41**, 267–84.

Farmer, S.M., Maslyn, J.M., Fedor, D.B. and Goodman, J.S. (1997). Putting upward influence strategies in context. *Journal of Organizational Behavior*, **18**, 17–42.

Fedor, D.B. and Maslyn, J.M. (2002). Politics and political behavior: Where else do we go from here? In F. Dansereau and F.J. Yammarino (eds), *Research in multi-level issues* (Vol. 1, pp. 271–85). Oxford, UK: JAI Press/Elsevier Science.

Fedor, D.B., Ferris, G.R., Harrell-Cook, G. and Russ, G.S. (1998). The dimensions of politics perceptions and their organizational and individual predictors. *Journal of Applied Social Psychology*, **28**, 1760–97.

Ferris, G.R. and Kacmar, K.M. (1992). Perceptions of organizational politics. *Journal of Management*, **18**, 93–116.

Ferris, G.R., Russ, G.S. and Fandt, P.M. (1989). Politics in organizations. In R.A. Giacalone and P. Rosenfeld (eds), *Impression management in the organization* (pp. 143–70). Hillsdale, NJ: Lawrence Erlbaum.

Ferris, G.R., Frink, D.D., Galang, M.C., Zhou, J., Kacmar, M.K. and Howard, J.L. (1996). Perceptions of organizational politics: Prediction, stress-related implications and outcomes. *Human Relations*, **49**, 233–66.

Ferris, G.R., Berkson, H.M., Kaplan, D.M., Gilmore, D.C., Buckley, M.R., Hochwarter, W.A. and Witt, L.A. (1999). Development and initial validation of the political skill inventory. Paper presented at the 59th Academy of Management Meetings, Chicago, IL.

Ferris, G.R., Harrell-Cook, G. and Dulebohn, J.H. (2000). Organizational politics: The nature of the relationship between politics perceptions and political behavior. In S.B. Bacharach and E.J. Lawler (eds), *Research in the sociology of organizations* (Vol. 17, pp. 89–130). Stamford, CT: JAI Press.

Ferris, G.R., Perrewé, P.L., Anthony, W.P. and Gilmore, D.C. (2000). Political skill at work. *Organization Dynamics*, **28**, 25–37.

Ferris, G.R., Adams, G., Kolodinsky, R.W., Hochwarter, W.A. and Ammeter, A.P. (2002). Perceptions of organizational politics: Theory and research directions. In F. Dansereau and F.J. Yammarino (eds), *Research in multi-level issues* (Vol. 1, pp. 179–254). Oxford, UK: JAI Press/Elsevier Science.

Ferris, G.R., Anthony, W.P., Kolodinsky, R.W., Gilmore, D.C. and Harvey, M.G. (2002). Development of political skill. In C. Wankel and R. DeFillippi (eds), *Research in management education and development* (Vol. 1, pp. 3–25). Greenwich, CT: Information Age Publishing.

Ferris, G.R., Hochwarter, W.A., Douglas, C., Blass, R., Kolodinsky, R.W. and Treadway, D.C. (2002). Social influence processes in organizations and human resources systems. In G.R. Ferris and J.J. Martocchio (eds), *Research in personnel and human resources management* (Vol. 21, pp. 65–127). Oxford, UK: JAI Press/Elsevier Science.

Ferris, G.R., Treadway, D.C., Kolodinsky, R.W., Hochwarter, W.A., Kacmar, C.J., Douglas, C. and Frink, D.D. (2005). Development and validation of the political skill inventory. *Journal of Management*, **31**, 126–53.

Fisher, C.D. (1998). A preliminary test of affective events theory. Paper presented at the First Conference on Emotions and Organizational Life, San Diego, CA.

Fisher, C.D. (2000). Mood and emotions while working: Missing pieces of job satisfaction? *Journal of Organizational Behavior*, **21**, 185–202.

Fisher, C.D. (2002). Antecedents and consequences of real-time affective reactions at work. *Motivation and Emotion*, **26**, 3–30.

Fisher, C.D. and Ashkanasy, N.M. (2000). The emerging role of emotions in work life: an introduction. *Journal of Organizational Behavior*, **21**, 123–9.

Fitness, J. (2000). Anger in the workplace: An emotion script approach to anger episodes between workers and their superiors, co-workers and subordinates. *Journal of Organizational Behavior*, **21**, 147–62.

Fox, S., Spector, P.E. and Miles, D. (2001). Counterproductive work behavior (CWB) in response to job stressors and organizational justice: Some mediator and moderator tests for autonomy and emotions. *Journal of Vocational Behavior*, **59**, 291–309.

Fredrickson, B.L. (1998). What good are positive emotions? *Review of General Psychology*, **2**, 300–319.

French, J.R.P. and Raven, B.H. (1959). The bases of social power. In D. Cartwright (ed.), *Studies in social power*. Ann Arbor, MI: University of Michigan Press.

Frijda, N.H. (1986). *The emotions*. Cambridge, UK: Cambridge University Press.

Frijda, N.H. and Mesquita, B. (1994). The social roles and functions of emotions. In S. Kitayama and H.R. Markus (eds), *Emotion and Culture: Empirical studies of mutual influence*. Washington, DC: American Psychological Association.

Frost, P.J. (2004). Handling toxic emotions: New challenges for leaders and their organization. *Organizational Dynamics*, **33**, 111–27.

Gandz, J. and Murray, V. (1980). The experience of workplace politics. *Academy of Management Journal*, **23**, 237–51.

Gatta, M.L. (2002). *Juggling food and feelings: Emotional balance in the workplace*. Lanham, MD: Lexington Books.

George, J. and Brief, A.P. (1992). Feeling good–doing good: A conceptual analysis of the mood at work–organizational spontaneity relationship. *Psychological Bulletin*, **112**, 310–29.

George, J.M. and Zhou, J. (2002). Understanding when bad moods foster creativity and good ones don't: The role of context and clarity of feelings. *Journal of Applied Psychology*, **87**, 687–97.

Gibson, D.E. and Schroeder, S.J. (2002). Grinning, frowning, and emotionless: Agent perceptions of power and their effect on felt and displayed emotions in influence attempts. In N.M. Ashkanasy, W.J. Zerbe and C.E.J. Hartel (eds), *Managing emotions in the workplace* (pp. 184–211). New York: M.E. Sharpe.

Goffman, E. (1959). *The presentation of self in everyday life*. Garden City, NY: Doubleday Anchor.

Gordon, S.L. (1990). Social structural effects on emotions. In T.D. Kemper (ed.), *Research agendas in the sociology of emotions* (pp. 145–79). Albany, NY: State University of New York Press.

Grams, W. and Rogers, R. (1990). Power and personality: Effects of Machiavellianism, need for approval, and motivation on the use of influence tactics. *Journal of General Psychology*, **117**, 71–82.

Grandey, A. (2003). When 'the show must go on': Surface acting and deep acting as determinants of emotional exhaustion and peer-rated service delivery. *Academy of Management Journal*, **46**, 86–96.

Greenberger, D.B. and Strassser, S. (1986). Development and application of a model of personal control in organizations. *Academy of Management Review*, **11**, 164–77.

Gross, J.J. (2002). Emotion regulation: Affective, cognitive, and social consequences. *Psychophysiology*, **39**, 281–91.

Gross, J.J. and John, O.P. (2003). Individual differences in two emotion regulation processes: Implications for affect, relationships and well-being. *Journal of Personality and Social Psychology*, **85**, 348–62.

Harrell-Cook, G., Ferris, G.R. and Dulebohn, J.H. (1999). Political behaviors as moderators of the perceptions of organizational politics–work outcomes relationships. *Journal of Organizational Behavior*, **20**, 1093–105.

Hearsey, R.B. (1932). *Worker's emotions in shop and home: A study of individual workers from the psychological and physiological standpoint*. Philadelphia, PA: University of Pennsylvania Press.

Heise, D.R. and O'Brien, J. (1993). Emotion expression in groups. In M. Lewis and J.M. Haviland (eds), *Handbook of emotions* (pp. 489–98). New York: Guilford Press.

Hochschild, A.R. (1983). *The managed heart: Commercialization of human feeling*. Berkeley, CA: University of California Press.

Huy, Q.N. (2002). Emotional balancing of organizational continuity and radical change: The contribution of middle managers. *Administrative Science Quarterly*, **47**, 31–69.

Isen, A.M. (1987). Positive affect, cognitive processes, and social behavior. *Advances in experimental social psychology*, **20**, 203–53.

Isen, A.M. and Means, B. (1983). The influence of positive affect on decision-making strategy. *Social Cognition*, **2**, 18–31.

Jones, E.E. (1990). *Interpersonal perception*. New York: W.H. Freeman.

Jones, G.R. and Rittman, A.L. (2002). A model of emotional and motivational components of interpersonal interactions in organizations. In N.M. Ashkanasy, W.J. Zerbe and C.E.J. Hartel (eds), *Managing emotions in the workplace* (pp. 98–110). New York: M.E. Sharpe.

Jordan, P.J., Ashkanasy, N.M. and Hartel, C.E.J. (2002). Emotional intelligence as a moderator of emotional and behavioral reactions to job insecurity. *Academy of Management Review*, **27**, 361–72.

Kacmar, K.M. and Carlson, D.S. (1997). The dysfunctional aspect of political behavior in organizations. In R.W. Griffin, A.M. O'Leary-Kelly and J. Collins (eds), *Dysfunctional behavior in organizations* (Vol. 23(b), pp. 195–218). Greenwich, CT: JAI Press.

Kacmar, K.M., Bozeman, P., Carlson, D.S. and Anthony, W.P. (1999). A partial test of the perceptions of organizational politics model. *Human Relations*, **52**, 383–416.

Keltner, D. and Haidt, J. (1999). Social functions of emotions at four levels of analysis, *Cognition and Emotion*, **13**, 505–21.

Kemper, T.D. (1984). Power, status, and emotions: A sociological contribution to a psychophysiological domain. In K. Scherer and P. Ekman (eds), *Approaches to emotion* (pp. 369–84). Hillsdale, NJ: Lawrence Erlbaum.

Kemper, T.D. (1990). Social relations and emotions: A structural approach. In T.D. Kemper (ed.), *Research agendas in the sociology of emotions* (pp. 207–37). Albany, NY: State University of New York Press.

Kipnis, D. (1984). The use of power in organizations and in interpersonal settings. In S. Oskamp (ed.), *Applied social psychology annual* (Vol. 5, pp. 179–210). Beverly Hills, CA: Sage.

Kipnis, D. and Schmidt, S.M. (1983). An influence perspective on bargaining. In M. Bazerman and R. Lewicki (eds), *Negotiating in organizations* (pp. 303–19). Beverly Hills, CA: Sage.

Kipnis, D. and Schmidt, S.M. (1988). Upward influence styles: Relationship with performance evaluations, salary, and stress. *Administrative Science Quarterly*, **33**, 528–42.

Kipnis, D., Schmidt, S.M. and Wilkinson, I. (1980). Intraorganizational influence tactics: Explorations in getting one's way. *Journal of Applied Psychology*, **65**, 440–52.

Lazarus, R.S. (1991). *Emotion and adaptation*. New York: Oxford University Press.

Lewin, K. (1936). *Principles of topological psychology*. New York: McGraw-Hill.

Lewis, K.M. (2000). When leaders display emotion: How followers respond to negative emotional expression of male and female leaders. *Journal of Organizational Behavior*, **21**, 221–34.

Liden, R.C. and Mitchell, T.R. (1988). Ingratiatory behaviors in organizational settings. *Academy of Management Review*, **13**, 572–87.

Liu, Y., Perrewé, P.L., Hochwarter, W.A. and Kacmar, C.J. (in press). Dispositional antecedents and consequences of emotional labor at work. *Journal of Leadership and Organizational Studies*.

Locke, E.A. (1976). The nature and causes of job satisfaction. In M.D. Dunnette (ed.), *Handbook of industrial and organizational psychology* (pp. 1297–349). Chicago, IL: Rand McNally.

Lutz, C.A. (1988). *Unnatural emotions*. Chicago, IL: University of Chicago Press.

Markus, H.R. and Kitayama, S. (1994). The cultural construction of self and emotion: Implications for social behavior. In S. Kitayama and H.R. Markus (eds), *Emotion and culture: Empirical studies of mutual influence* (pp. 89–130). Washington, DC: American Psychological Association.

Matsumoto, D., Takeuchi, S., Andayani, S., Kouznetsova, N. and Krupp, D. (1998). The contribution of individualism–collectivism to cross-national differences in display rules. *Asian Journal of Social Psychology*, 1, 147–65.

Mintzberg, H. (1983). *Power in and around organizations*. Englewood Cliffs, NJ: Prentice-Hall.

Mintzberg, H. (1985). The organization as political arena. *Journal of Management Studies*, 22, 133–54.

Morris, J.A. and Feldman, D.C. (1996). The dimensions, antecedents and consequences of emotional labor. *Academy of Management Review*, 9, 257–74.

Nye, L.G. and Witt, L.A. (1993). Dimensionality and construct validity of the perceptions of organizational politics scale (POPS). *Educational and psychological measurement*, 53, 821–9.

O'Hair, D. and Cody, M.J. (1987). Machiavellian beliefs and social influence. *Western Journal of Speech Communication*, 51, 279–303.

Parkinson, B. (1991). Emotional stylists: Strategies of expressive management among trainee hairdressers. *Cognition and Emotion*, 5, 419–34.

Parkinson, B. (1996). Emotions are social. *British Journal of Psychology*, 87, 663–83.

Perreault, W.D. and Miles, R.H. (1978). Influence strategy mixes in complex organizations. *Behavioral Science*, 23, 86–98.

Perrewé, P.L., Ferris, G.R., Frink, D.D. and Anthony, W.P. (2000). Political skill: An antidote for workplace stressors. *Academy of Management Executive*, 14, 115–23.

Perrewé, P.L., Zellars, K.L., Ferris, G.R., Rossi, A.M., Kacmar, C.J. and Ralston, D.A. (2004). Neutralizing job stressors: Political skill as an antidote to the dysfunctional consequences of role conflict stressors. *Academy of Management Journal*, 47, 141–52.

Plutchik, R. (1980). A general psychoevolutionary theory of emotion. In R. Plutchik and H. Kellerman (eds), *Emotion: Theory, research and experience* (Vol. 1, pp. 3–33). San Diego: CA: Academic Press.

Pugh, D. (2001). Service with a smile: Emotional contagion in service encounters. *Academy of Management Journal*, 44, 1018–27.

Rafaeli, A. and Sutton, R.I. (1991). Emotional contrast strategies as means of social influence. *Academy of Management Journal*, 34, 749–75.

Reus, T.H. and Liu, Y. (in press). Rhyme or reason: The role of emotion in the performance of knowledge-intensive work groups. *Human Performance*, 17, 245–66.

Rosenberg, M. (1990). Reflexivity and emotions. *Social Psychology Quarterly*, 53, 3–12.

Rothlisberger, F. and Dickson, W. (1949). *Management and the worker*. Cambridge, MA: Harvard University Press.

Scherer, K. (1984). On the nature and function of emotion: A component process approach. In K. Scherer and P. Ekman (eds), *Approaches to emotion* (pp. 293–318). Hillsdale, NJ: Lawrence Erlbaum.

Schaubroeck, J. and Jones, J.R. (2000). Antecedents of workplace emotional labor dimensions and moderators of their effects on physical symptoms. *Journal of Organizational Behavior*, 21, 163–83.

Schwarz, N. (1990). Feelings as information: Informational and motivational functions of affective states. In E.T. Higgins and R.M. Sorrentino (eds), *Handbook of motivation and cognition: Foundations of social behavior* (Vol. 2, pp. 527–61). New York: Guilford Press.

Seo, M., Feldman Barrett, L. and Bartunek, J.M. (2004). The role of affective experience in work motivation. *Academy of Management Review*, 29, 423–39.

Shields, S.A. (2002). *Speaking from the heart: Gender and the social meaning of emotion*. New York: Cambridge University Press.

Shuler, R.S. (1980). Definition and conceptualization of stress in organizations. *Organizational Behavior and Human Decision Process*, 25, 184–215.

Shuler, S. and Sypher, B.D. (2000). Seeking emotional labor: When managing the heart enhances the work experience. *Management Communication Quarterly*, 14, 50–89.

Spector, P.E. and Fox, S. (2002). An emotion-centered model of voluntary work behavior: Some parallels between counterproductive work behavior (CWB) and organizational citizenship behavior (OCB). *Human Resources Management Review*, 12, 269–92.

Staw, B.M. and Barsade, S.G. (1993). Affect and managerial performance: A test of the sadder-but-wiser vs. happier-and-smarter hypotheses. *Administrative Science Quarterly*, 38, 304–31.

Staw, B.M., Sutton, R.R. and Pelled, L.H. (1994). Employee positive emotion and favorable outcomes at the workplace. *Organization Science*, 5, 51–71.

Strutton, D. and Pelton, L.E. (1998). Effects of ingratiation on lateral relationship quality within sales team settings. *Journal of Business Research*, **43**, 1–12.

Sutton, R.I. (1991). Maintaining norms about expressed emotions: The case of bill collectors. *Administrative Science Quarterly*, **36**, 245–68.

Thoits, P.A. (1996). Managing the emotions of others. *Symbolic Interaction*, **19**, 85–109.

Thoresen, C.J., Kaplan, S.A., Barsky, A.P., Warren, C.R. and Chermont, K. (2003). The affective underpinnings of job perceptions and attitudes: A meta-analytic review and integration. *Psychological Bulletin*, **129**, 914–45.

Tiedens, L.Z. (2001). Anger and advancement versus sadness and subjugation: The effect of negative emotion expressions on social status conferral. *Journal of Personality and Social Psychology*, **80**, 86–94.

Tiedens, L.Z., Ellsworth, P.C. and Mesquita, B. (2000). Stereotypes about sentiments and status: Emotional expectations for high- and low-status group members. *Personality and Social Psychology Bulletin*, **26**, 560–75.

Tsai, W. (2001). Determinants and consequences of employee displayed positive emotions. *Journal of Management*, **27**, 497–512.

Valle, M. and Perrewé, P.L. (2000). Do politics perceptions relate to political behaviors? Test of an implicit assumption and expanded model. *Human Relations*, **53**, 359–86.

Van Maanen, J. and Kunda, G. (1989). 'Real feelings': Emotion expression and organizational culture. In L.L. Cummings and B.M. Staw (eds), *Research in organizational behavior* (Vol. 11, pp. 43–103). Greenwich, CT: JAI Press.

Vigoda, E. (2000). Internal politics in public administration systems: An empirical examination of its relationship with job congruence, organizational citizenship behavior, and in-role performance. *Public Personnel Management*, **29**, 185–211.

Vigoda, E. (2001). Reactions to organizational politics: A cross-cultural examination in Israel and Britain. *Human Relations*, **54**, 1483–518.

Vigoda, E. (2002). Stress-related aftermaths to workplace politics: The relationships among job distress, and aggressive behavior in organizations. *Journal of Organizational Behavior*, **23**, 571–91.

Vigoda, E. and Cohen, A. (2002). Influence tactics and perceptions of organizational politics: A longitudinal study. *Journal of Business Research*, **55**, 311–24.

Vigoda-Gadot, E., Vinarski-Peretz, H. and Ben-Zion, E. (2003). Politics and image in the organizational landscape: An empirical examination among public sector employees. *Journal of Managerial Psychology*, **18**, 764–87.

Vredenburgh, D.J. and Maurer, J.G. (1984). A process framework of organizational politics. *Human Relations*, **37**, 47–66.

Wayne, S.J. and Liden, R.C. (1995). Effects of impression management on performance ratings: A longitudinal study. *Academy of Management Journal*, **38**, 232–60.

Wayne, S.J., Liden, R.C., Graf, I.K. and Ferris, G.R. (1997). The role of upward influence tactics in HR decisions. *Personnel Psychology*, **50**, 978–1006.

Weiss, H.M. (2002). Deconstructing job satisfaction: Separating evaluations, beliefs and affective experiences. *Human Resource Management Review*, **12**, 173–94.

Weiss, H.M. and Cropanzano, R. (1996). Affective events theory: A theoretical discussion of the structure, causes and consequences of affective experiences at work. In B.M. Staw and L.L. Cummings (eds), *Research in organizational behavior* (Vol. 18, pp. 1–74). Greenwich, CT: JAI.

Wharton, A.S. and Erickson, R.J. (1993). Managing emotions on the job and at home: Understanding the consequences of multiple emotional roles. *Academy of Management Review*, **18**, 457–86.

Yukl, G. and Tracey, J.B. (1992). Consequences of influence tactics used with subordinates, peers, and the boss. *Journal of Applied Psychology*, **77**, 525–35.

11 The strain-related reactions to perceptions of organizational politics as a workplace stressor: Political skill as a neutralizer

Robyn L. Brouer, Gerald R. Ferris, Wayne A. Hochwarter, Mary Dana Laird and David C. Gilmore

Introduction

Organizational politics often is viewed in a negative manner by scholars and practitioners alike, and is thought to predominantly produce negative effects not only at the organizational level, but also at the individual level. Previous research has consistently found that perceptions of organizational politics demonstrate a positive relationship with various individual strain reactions, such as job tension, somatic tension and burnout (Ferris, Adams et al., 2002). Furthermore, depression is a growing concern among the general population, and as a strain reaction to workplace difficulties. We contend that depression represents a strain reaction to perceptions of politics at work. This premise is consistent with previous research demonstrating that as individuals' perceptions of organizational politics increase, their strain reactions increase as well (Cropanzano et al., 1997).

However, the positive relationship between politics perceptions and strain reactions may not operate in the same fashion for all individuals. Certain individuals possess skills that allow them to function adequately in a political environment (Ferris, Davidson and Perrewé, 2005). One such set of characteristics, collectively know as political skill, enables individuals to influence others in the work environment in ways that lead to personal success (Ferris et al., 2005; Ferris, Treadway et al., 2005). Furthermore, political skill represents a coping resource that enables individuals in political environments to navigate successfully through obstacles resulting from others' self-serving behavior. Political skill assists individuals in garnering other key coping resources, such as control and social support. Working in unison, these coping resources minimize the strain reactions that politically skilled individuals experience in political environments.

The purpose of this chapter is to investigate the role of political skill in the relationship between politics perceptions and depressive symptoms. Depression, although considered a mental disorder, manifests itself as minor depressive symptoms in over 10 million people in the USA alone (McGrath et al., 1990). Chronic life stressors, such as unfavorable job characteristics, often trigger these symptoms (e.g. Baugher and Roberts, 2004; Dormann and Zapf, 2002). Therefore, it is important to investigate the role of politics perceptions as a workplace stressor that can produce depressive symptoms as strain reactions, and political skill as a potential neutralizer of such dysfunctional consequences. To date, no research has examined these relationships in a field environment.

In order to accomplish this, we begin the chapter with a brief overview of the politics perceptions literature. We then examine politics perceptions as a workplace stressor and as a possible trigger for depressive symptoms. This is followed by a review of political skill and its role as a coping mechanism for workplace stressors. After presenting the results from three studies, implications of the research are discussed and directions for future research are suggested.

Literature review

Nature and consequences of organizational politics perceptions
Perceptions of organizational politics 'involve an individual's attribution to behaviors of self-serving intent, and are defined as an individual's subjective evaluation about the extent to which the work environment is characterized by co-workers and supervisors who demonstrate such self-serving behavior' (Ferris, Harrell-Cook and Dulebohn, 2000, p. 90). Although some studies have shown direct relationships with politics perceptions and favorable outcomes (e.g. Hochwarter, 2002), most of the empirical research has documented negative individual and organizational consequences (Ferris, Adams et al., 2002).

For example, not only did Cropanzano et al. (1997) find a negative correlation between perceptions of organizational politics and job satisfaction, job involvement and organizational commitment, but also a positive relationship between politics perceptions and psychological withdrawal, turnover intentions, antagonistic work behaviors, job tension, somatic tension, general fatigue and burnout. Furthermore, Witt (1999) reported a significant positive relationship between perceptions of organizational politics and actual turnover, thus supporting the positive politics perceptions–intent to turnover relationship that has been found in a number of other studies (e.g. Cropanzano et al., 1997; Hochwarter et al., 1999; Kacmar et al., 1999; Valle and Perrewé, 2000). Although numerous studies have examined the negative outcomes of politics perceptions, Vigoda (2003) suggested that not enough attention has been paid to the stress-related outcomes.

Politics perceptions as a workplace stressor
Although a series of empirical studies have supported its stress-inducing qualities (Ferris, Frink, Galang et al., 1996; Kacmar and Baron, 1999; Vigoda, 2003), the idea that organizational politics might be a work-related stressor is relatively new to organizational scientists. Initially, Matteson and Ivancevich (1987) identified politics as a potential stressor in the work environment. Building on this work, several theoretical and empirical studies have investigated the stress-related implications of organizational politics (e.g. Gilmore et al., 1996; Ferris, Frink, Galang et al., 1996; Jex and Beehr, 1991; Vigoda, 2003). In order to integrate stress and organizational politics, these studies have highlighted the three main features that these constructs share: (1) both are perceptual in nature, (2) both have uncertain characteristics, and (3) both can be viewed as either threats or opportunities (Ferris, Frink, Galang et al., 1996).

Just as the study of perceptions of organizational politics is concerned with individuals' subjective evaluations, stress often is viewed as an individually experienced phenomenon rather than a characteristic of the environment (McGrath, 1976; Schuler, 1980; Schuler and Jackson, 1986). Individuals respond to their perceptions of reality, not to objective reality *per se* (Lewin, 1936). Therefore it is clear that individual perceptions are integral to both stress and perceptions of organizational politics (Ferris, Frink, Galang et al., 1996), because comparable anxiety-provoking stimuli may be perceived as noxious by one individual and virtually harmless by another.

Uncertainty is a second characteristic that integrates job stress and organizational politics. According to Ferris, Fedor et al. (1989), uncertainty leads to increases in both political behavior and perceptions of organizational politics. For instance, if an organization's policy on bonuses is ambiguous, the process might be deemed political because individuals may not understand why some employees received bonuses and others did not. Researchers have highlighted the role of process and outcome uncertainty in their definitions of stress (e.g. Beehr, 1998; Schuler, 1980). For example, Schuler and Jackson (1986) argued that stress represents the level of uncertainty that individuals encounter, and that a careful examination of uncertainty should provide a greater understanding of stress.

The third and final feature that unifies stress and perceptions of organizational politics is the possibility of labeling each as either an opportunity or a threat. For example, stress has been viewed in terms of constraints (e.g. threats) and/or opportunities (McGrath, 1976). Furthermore, Schuler (1980) defined anxiety as a dynamic condition in which individuals deal with opportunities, constraints, or demands. According to Ferris, Frink, Galang et al. (1996, p. 236), 'it seems quite reasonable to conceive of politics as providing situations of potential gain, as well as situations of potential loss.'

Evidence for the politics perceptions–strain relationship has been substantiated in the literature. For example, Valle and Perrewé (2000) found a direct positive relationship between perceptions of politics and job anxiety. Cropanzano et al. (1997) also identified significant direct associations between perceptions of politics and several forms of strain, including job tension, somatic tension, general fatigue and burnout. Vigoda (2002) found job distress to be an immediate response to organizational politics perceptions in three distinct organizations. More recently, Vigoda (2003) found politics perceptions to be related to job stress in three samples and supported both a direct and indirect relationship with burnout.

Perceptions of organizational politics as a trigger for depression symptoms
Despite the fact that a series of studies have reported a positive relationship between perceptions of organizational politics and strain, there has been a lack of research on the relationship between politics perceptions and depressive symptoms. This omission is surprising given the theoretical underpinnings of politics perceptions and psychological distress. Evidence for examining this relationship comes from the multiple studies demonstrating relationships between work stress and mental health (Ganster, 1989; Karasek and Theorell, 1990; Menaghan, 1994), emotional distress (Spector, 1986) and depression (Braun and Hollander, 1988; Kawakami et al., 1990; Nadaoka et al., 1997).

Furthermore, empirical studies also have shown job characteristics to contribute to the onset of depression (e.g. Baugher and Roberts, 2004; Mackie et al., 2001; Dormann and Zapf, 2002). Given the veracity of these findings, it is reasonable to assume that perceptions of organizational politics, which have been characterized as a workplace stressor that is prevalent in virtually all work domains, would be positively associated with depressive symptoms.

In order to explore the relationship between politics perceptions and depressive symptoms, it is necessary to define both indices of psychological distress. According to Kaplan and Sadock (1981), depression is viewed as a group of disorders that are characterized by a disturbance of mood that is accompanied by related cognitive, psychomotor, psychophysiological and interpersonal difficulties. In the clinical sense, major depression refers to a disorder that includes five of the following nine symptoms: depressed mood, the inability to gain enjoyment from normally pleasurable experiences, weight gain or loss, sleep disturbances, psychomotor problems, loss of energy, excessive guilt, loss of concentration and suicidal thoughts (Kaplan and Sadock, 1981).

In order to be classified as depression, the previously listed symptoms must last for two weeks and cause clinically significant social or occupational disturbances (American Psychiatric Association, 1994). Depressive symptoms are indicators of depression, such as those listed above. These indicators uncover general affective, cognitive, motivational and physiological symptoms of depression occurring for more than two weeks (Kaplan and Sadock, 1981).

Despite these stringent guidelines for diagnosis, depression and depressive symptoms have become among the most common forms of mental disorders. In 2000, approximately 330 million people were suffering from depression worldwide (American Psychiatric Association, 2000). In the USA alone, it was estimated that 7 million women and 3.5 million men suffer from major depression, and equally large numbers experience depressive symptoms (McGrath et al., 1990). Furthermore, the American Psychiatric Association (1994) predicts that depression may lead to psychiatric hospitalizations for 6 percent of all women and 3 percent of all men.

Not only is depression prevalent; it is also costly to organizations. Depressive disorders now account for over 50 percent of healthcare costs related to mental health problems (Conti and Burton, 1994). Furthermore, depression is the leading cause of physical disability claims, and has been classified as a risk factor for cardiovascular mortality (Saz and Dewey, 2001; Wulsin et al., 1990). By the early 1990s, the economic impact of depression and depressive symptoms on organizations had grown to a staggering $24 billion, in large part due to excessive absenteeism and reductions in productive capacity (Greenburg et al., 1993).

Due to the prevalence of depression and the substantial problems that it creates, researchers have attempted to identify factors that may be useful in detecting and diagnosing it. Many studies have linked individual factors, such as gender (Nolen-Hoeksema et al., 1999), genetics (National Institute of Mental Health Genetics Workgroup, 1998) and personality traits (Barnett and Gotlib, 1988; Jorm et al., 2000), with depression. Furthermore, studies also have examined the effects of situational factors, such as social isolation (Barnett and Gotlib, 1988; Joiner and Coyne, 1999; Lara et al., 1997), stressful life events, and chronic life strains (e.g. Monroe and Simons, 1991; Nolen-Hoeksema and Morrow, 1991), on the developments of depression and depressive symptoms.

In addition to the previously mentioned factors, a number of studies have investigated the relationship between job characteristics and depressive symptoms. For example, Baugher and Roberts (2004) surveyed chemical plant employees and found that perceived exposure to fire and explosions at work increased anxiety and depression. Furthermore, the use of problem-focused coping strategies, such as joining a union, moderated the relationship between environmental risks and depression, lowering experienced depression. Dormann and Zapf (2002) also examined the effects of workplace characteristics on depression. However, like many other studies that propose that stressors and health outcomes often are mediated by one or more variables (e.g. Kahn and Byosiere, 1992;

McGrath, 1976), results found that jobs characterized by social conflict and animosities led to irritation, which, in turn, caused depressive symptoms.

The work of Mackie et al. (2001) provides further support for the relationship between job characteristics and depressive symptoms. Armed with research that suggests that jobs without control, autonomy, influence, participation, decision latitude (e.g. Baker et al., 1996; Barnett and Brennan, 1995; Bourbonnais et al., 1996; Dyer and Quine, 1998; Glass and McKnight, 1996; Narayanan et al., 1999; Spector, 1986) and supervisor support (e.g. Baker et al., 1996; Jones-Johnson and Johnson, 1992) are related to negative outcomes, Mackie and colleagues (2001) investigated the relationship between management practices and depression. Their results, which showed support for the previously mentioned research on which they built their argument, indicated that jobs characterized by high levels of employee involvement contributed to lower levels of depression among employees.

Politics perceptions, as noted earlier, reduce control and increase uncertainty (Ferris Frink, Galang et al., 1996; Gilmore et al., 1996). Further, previous research has supported the notion that these factors may influence depressive symptoms. Therefore, it is reasonable to assume that a job characterized by perceptions of organizational politics may lead an employee to experience depressive symptoms.

Based on the definition of depression, it must permeate all aspects of one's life, not just one aspect. Therefore, one must wonder whether depressive symptoms at work would permeate other areas of the individual's life or be restricted to the employee's time at work. Vigoda (2003) suggested that the stress one feels at work resulting from sources such as organizational politics is significant across boundaries. In other words, depressive symptoms might affect individuals' work *and* home life. Research on work–family conflict (WFC), or the goodness of fit between work and family life (Frone et al., 1992), may shed some light on this issue. Several studies have begun to examine work–family conflict (WFC) as a source of stress that may influence well-being (e.g. Greenhaus and Parasuraman, 1986; Voydanoff, 1987). One study by Frone et al. (1992) found that family–work conflict, or the situation where family interferes with work, is both indirectly (via job distress) and directly related to depression.

Furthermore, 'spillover' of mood, in which feelings caused by events in one domain affect the other domain, is a commonly cited phenomenon in the work–family conflict literature. For example, Williams and Alliger (1994) found distress and fatigue to spill over from work to family and from family to work. Based on this research, it is presumable that depressive symptoms caused by organizational politics, much like those caused by work–family conflict, would affect individuals inside, as well as outside, of the work environment.

Political skill and organizational politics
Although politics perceptions may cause strain reactions such as depressive symptoms in certain individuals, this reaction may not hold for everyone. Individuals who possess certain characteristics (i.e. political skill) will be better equipped to participate in work environments perceived to be political (Ferris et al., in press). In order to understand why certain individuals are able to avoid the deleterious effects of perceived political environments, it is necessary to understand the manner in which these individuals successfully influence their environments. Therefore, it is essential to investigate political skill.

Although research in the area of politics is abundant (e.g. Vigoda, 2002; Ferris et al., 2002), more recent studies have examined the skill set necessary to work successfully in political environments (e.g. Ferris et al., in press). In such environments, it is necessary to effectively employ influence tactics and strategies to minimize the harmful effects of politics (Pfeffer, 1981). Surprisingly, the examination of the 'style or execution of the influence behaviors' has been largely overlooked (Ferris, Perrewé et al., 2000, p. 30). Yet researchers have argued that the success of influence attempts is largely determined by the verbal and non-verbal style through which it is presented (Liden and Mitchell, 1989). Therefore, it is important to examine individual differences that may affect the implementation and results of the influence behavior. By successfully influencing their work environment, individuals should experience an increased sense of control and a reduced sense of uncertainty, thus reducing the onset of depressive symptoms.

Mintzberg (1983) first introduced the term political skill, defining it as an individual characteristic that engenders effectiveness in political arenas. Specifically, he suggested that political skill referred to the implementation of influence through manipulation, persuasion and negotiation. More recently, Ahearn and his colleagues provided an updated and more specific definition, suggesting that political skill represents 'the ability to effectively understand others at work, and to use such knowledge to influence others to act in ways that enhance one's personal and/or organizational goals' (Ahearn et al., 2004, p. 311; see also Ferris, Treadway et al., 2005, p. 2).

Political skill is a set of positive traits that are critical in contemporary work environments (Ferris, Treadway et al., 2005). Indeed, although political skill bears directly on the nature of interpersonal influence in organizations, it is somewhat similar to the construct of 'political efficacy' from the political science literature, which is defined as 'the feeling that political and social change is possible, and that the individual citizen can play a part in bringing about this change' (Campbell et al., 1954, p. 188).

Politically skilled individuals combine social astuteness with the ability to adapt behavior to various situations. This skill allows individuals to influence others in ways that appear to be sincere, thus inspiring both support and trust (Ferris, Treadway et al., 2005). Specifically, politically skilled individuals are able to read social situations and the interpersonal interactions occurring in these situations. Based on their assessment, these individuals are able to select the most appropriate influence tactics (Ferris, Treadway et al., 2005). Moreover, politically skilled individuals are able to develop diverse networks, which allow them to build alliances, coalitions, and social capital (Ferris, Treadway et al., 2005; Perrewé et al., 2000). They can use these networks for many benefits such as information access and increased cooperation (Baron and Markman, 2000). The way in which politically skilled individuals employ influence tactics is subtle, because influence attempts will be successful only when no ulterior motives are perceived to exist (Jones, 1990).

Political skill, although partly innate, can be developed and improved (Ferris, Perrewé et al., 2000). Specifically, individuals gain tacit knowledge by utilizing their political skill (Perrewé et al., in press). Moreover, political skill can be developed through training programs that are designed for developmental purposes (Ferris, Perrewé et al., 2000). Political skill does not have to be developed in the context of a work environment. It can be developed in any situation which requires the management of interpersonal interactions in order to achieve personal goals (Ferris et al., in press).

As with depression, there can also be a spillover effect of political skill. The tacit knowledge gained when developing political skill in either a work or non-work environment also can be applied in either a work or non-work environment. Thus experiences and development available only in a non-work environment can become a valuable source of success in the work environment and vice versa (Cohen and Vigoda, 1999). For instance, Cohen and Vigoda (2000) found support for the view that participation in non-work environments fostered usable skills that could be transferred to work environments. This supports the notion that political skill can be nurtured and developed outside of work and transferred into the work environment.

Political skill is related to emotional, practical and social intelligence (Ferris, Perrewé and Douglas, 2002). However, research has shown that it is a distinct construct, displaying both appropriate construct and discriminant validity (Ferris, Treadway et al., 2005). For example, political skill is unique in that it is designed to focus on interactions in the work environment (Ferris, Perrewé et al., 2000). Social effectiveness constructs are more general and relate to everyday contexts (Ferris, Perrewé and Douglas, 2002). As such, political skill should have modest, positive relationships with such concepts as self-monitoring and conscientiousness (Ferris, Treadway et al., 2005). Indeed, Ferris, Berkson et al. (1999) found that political skill was moderately related to self-monitoring ($r = 0.13$ and 0.21, $p < 0.01$, in two samples), and conscientiousness ($r = 0.25$, $p < 0.01$). However, these correlations are not so high as to indicate construct redundancy (Ferris, Treadway et al., 2005).

Moreover, political skill has been assessed based on discriminant validity with the goal of demonstrating that political skill is not correlated with cognitive ability. Several studies have supported the hypothesis that political skill is not a sub-dimension of cognitive ability. Specifically, these studies have typically shown a zero correlation between political skill and measures of cognitive ability (Ferris, Treadway et al., 2005).

Furthermore, political skill can be distinguished from social skill (Ferris et al., in press). At first blush, these two concepts might seem very similar. However, social skill refers to a facility with communication, and a comfort with interpersonal interactions (Ferris et al., in press). Political skill involves more than just communication efficacy; it implies that there is specific management of interactions with others, which enables individual accomplishment (e.g. Ferris et al., in press; Luthans et al., 1988; Peled, 2000). The key is that politically skilled individuals can actively manipulate their relationships with those in the workplace (Peled, 2000), whereas social skill only implies a competence with communication and efficacy in dealing with others (Peled, 2000).

In addition to demonstrating construct and discriminate validity, political skill also has been shown to predict important work criteria, such as job performance and effectiveness ratings (Ferris, Treadway et al., 2005), and team effectiveness (Ahearn et al., 2004). Additionally, researchers have begun to examine the role of political skill in alleviating strain reactions in response to work-related stressors (Perrewé et al., in press; Perrewé et al., 2004).

Political skill as antidote to dysfunctional effects of politics perceptions

Because of their ability to successfully influence others, individuals high in political skill should have a greater sense of self-confidence and personal security than those not possessing this proficiency. As stated earlier, politically skilled individuals are adept at the 'development and leveraging of social capital' (Perrewé et al., 2000, p. 117). The management of this social capital not only gives the politically skilled individual greater control in their work environment, but also an enhanced social support system. The control and social support obtained by politically skilled individuals enhance their ability to cope with work stressors, such as those promoted in political environments.

Resource theories of coping are helpful in delineating the processes by which political skill assists individuals to cope with work stressors. Resource theories, largely examined by social psychologists, are intended to explain how individuals' resources affect resistance to stress (Hobfoll, 2002; Thoits, 1994). Individuals possessing key resources 'might be more capable of selecting, altering, and implementing their other resources to meet stressful demands' (Hobfoll, 2002, p. 308). Resources, such as control (Seligman, 1975), self-efficacy (Bandura, 1997) and social support (Cohen and Wills, 1985), are argued to represent key resources. However, much of the research has focused on a single, central form (e.g. Bandura, 1997; Cohen and Wills, 1985), and key resources do not act in isolation, but work to accumulate others (Hobfoll, 2002).

In light of this view, political skill can be perceived as a key resource for coping with political environments. Political skill enables individuals to assess the environment accurately to determine the correct courses of action. Further, politically skilled individuals also are better at resource implementation. Additionally, political skill enhances the development of at least two other key resources: perceived control and social support.

Politically skilled individuals possess a fundamental understanding of their work environment, which manifests in feelings of self-confidence and control at work. Individuals high in political skill have a greater understanding of a political environment because they are adept at perceiving situations, thus reducing uncertainty (Ferris et al., 1999; Perrewé et al., 2000; Perrewé et al., 2004). Their ability to understand and manage their work environment enables politically skilled individuals to successfully influence and, therefore, control others (Ferris, Treadway et al., 2005). Ferris, Frink and colleagues (1996) found that the extent to which individuals perceived environmental control significantly weakened the positive relationship between perceptions of organizational politics and job anxiety. Furthermore, research indicates that increased control on one's job can lessen negative mental outcomes such as depressive symptoms (Mackie et al., 2001; Baker et al., 1996).

Moreover, individuals high in political skill may view a political environment as an opportunity to utilize their expertise instead of as a stressor. Conversely, individuals low in political skill, and thus low in perceived control, are likely to see a political environment as a threat, leading to various strain reactions including depressive symptoms (Ferris, Russ and Fandt, 1989). Individuals low in political skill lack the appropriate coping resources, which increases the negative impact of politics perceptions (Hobfoll et al., 2003).

Social support is another key resource that is enhanced by political skill. Social support refers to the instrumental, informational, and/or emotional assistance others can offer (Thoits, 1994). In the case of politically skilled individuals, co-workers can become a source of social support. Because politically skilled individuals are proficient at regulating interpersonal interactions, they are able to establish friendships and alliances (Perrewé et al., 2000; Perrewé et al., 2004). The benefits of having large social networks are many. These networks enable politically skilled individuals to obtain important information as well as provide other forms of social support. In terms of political science, political skill enables individuals to achieve goals through the use of proper influence (Vigoda, 2003).

In support, Perrewé and her colleagues (2004) found that political skill was used as a coping resource in the stressor–strain relationships of role conflict and psychological anxiety and role conflict and somatic complaints. Specifically, political skill was found to alleviate the negative effects of role overload and the strain reactions of job tension, job dissatisfaction and general anxiety (Perrewé et al., in press). Furthermore, Ferris, Treadway et al. (2005) found political skill was significantly and negatively related to trait anxiety. Therefore, we hypothesize:

Hypothesis 1 The relationship between perceptions of politics and depressive symptoms is moderated by political skill such that increases in politics perceptions will be associated with increases in depressive symptoms for those low in political skill. For those high in political skill, the negative relationship between perceptions of politics and depressive symptoms will be attenuated.

Method

Participants – Sample 1
Surveys were distributed to all 80 leadership development personnel of a large hospital located in the southeastern USA. A total of 62 surveys were returned directly to the researchers through the mail (78.5 percent response rate). The sample consisted of 38 females (62 percent), with an average age of approximately 47 years. Organization and position tenure were roughly 11 and five years, respectively. Archival data provided by the organization confirmed that the responding sample did not differ from the surveyed population in terms of age and gender.

Participants – Sample 2
All 108 individuals employed by a branch of a state agency received surveys at work, of which 102 were returned directly to the researchers (response rate of 94 percent). The sample consisted of 59 (58 percent) females, while the average age was approximately 36 years. Organizational and position tenure were roughly eight and three years, respectively. Archival data indicated that the 102 respondents did not differ from the population of 108 in terms of age and gender.

Participants – Sample 3
Students in two upper-level business courses were given five surveys to be completed by individuals working full-time. Course credit was received for participation. A wide range of blue-collar (i.e. machinist, heavy equipment operator) and professional (i.e. vice-president of finance, computer sales) employees were included in the sample. A total of 227 completed surveys were returned. The sample consisted of 125 females (55 percent) while the average age was 36 years. Organization and position tenure were approximately eight and five years, respectively.

Measures

Optimism Optimism was measured using an eight-item scale developed by Scheier and Carver (1985). Sample items include 'In uncertain times, I expect the best' and 'I hardly ever let things get in my way.' A five-point scale was used (1 = strongly disagree to 5 = strongly agree). Reliability estimate were adequate in each sample ($\alpha = 0.72$ – Sample 1; $\alpha = 0.73$ – Sample 2; $\alpha = 0.75$ – Sample 3).

Politics perceptions   Politics perceptions were measured using a six-item measure developed by Hochwarter et al. (2003). 'In this organization, there is a lot of self-serving behavior going on' and 'In this organization, individuals are stabbing each other in the back to look good in front of others' represent scale items. A five-point scale was used (1 = strongly disagree to 5 = strongly agree). Reliability estimates were adequate in each sample ($\alpha = 0.89$ – Sample 1; $\alpha = 0.91$ – Sample 2; $\alpha = 0.92$ – Sample 3).

Political skill   Political skill was measured using the four-item interpersonal influence subscale developed by Ferris, Treadway et al. (2005). The items were 'I find it easy to develop good rapport with most people,' 'I am able to make most people feel comfortable and at ease around me,' 'I can communicate easily and effectively with others' and 'I am good at getting people to like me.' A five-point scale was used (1 = strongly disagree to 5 = strongly agree). Reliability estimates were adequate in each sample ($\alpha = 0.86$ – Sample 1; $\alpha = 0.91$ – Sample 2; $\alpha = 0.89$ – Sample 3).

Depressive symptoms   Six items were used to measure depressive symptoms (Schroevers et al., 2001). Items included 'Over the past month, things that usually don't bother me have bothered me' and 'Over the past month, I've felt like I could not shake off the blues even with help from my family and friends.' A five-point scale was used (1 = strongly disagree to 5 = strongly agree). Reliability estimates were adequate in each sample ($\alpha = 0.89$ – Sample 1; $\alpha = 0.87$ – Sample 2; $\alpha = 0.88$ – Sample 3).

Data analysis

Moderated regression analyses (Cohen and Cohen, 1983) were conducted to evaluate the politics perceptions–political skill interactive relationship on performance. In step one, demographic variables (i.e. age, gender), length of service variables (i.e. organization and position tenure) and optimism were included. Optimism was included due to its potential overlap with political skill. In step two, politics perceptions and political skill were entered followed by the interaction term in the final step. Significance is demonstrated if the interaction term explains incremental criterion variance over and above that contributed by variables in the previous steps (i.e. control variables and main effects).

Results

Descriptive statistics and moderated regression results

Tables 11.1 and 11.2 contain descriptive statistics and regression results. In several cases, politics perceptions and political skill are correlated with depressive symptoms. However, the magnitude of these associations does not support a manifestation of common method variance.

In each study, politics perceptions × political skill interaction terms were significant, explaining between 4 percent (Sample 2) and 12 percent (Sample 1) of criterion variance. Consistent with Stone and Hollenbeck (1989), these significant effects were plotted in

Table 11.1 *Correlations among study variables*

Variable	Study 1[a]							Study 2[b]							Study 3[c]						
	1	2	3	4	5	6	7	1	2	3	4	5	6	7	1	2	3	4	5	6	7
1. Age																					
2. Gender	-0.24							-0.30							0.06						
3. Org. tenure	0.27	0.01						0.51	-0.16						0.50	0.10					
4. Pos. tenure	0.25	-0.30	0.28					0.41	-0.05	0.58					0.47	0.04	0.55				
5. Optimism	0.18	-0.23	0.17	0.04				-0.01	-0.01	-0.09	0.01				0.10	-0.01	-0.05	-0.05			
6. Politics	-0.03	0.01	-0.13	0.15	-0.27			-0.09	0.06	-0.10	-0.08	-0.06			-0.11	0.04	-0.02	-0.02	0.01		
7. Political skill	0.01	0.11	-0.01	-0.01	0.46	-0.15		-0.10	0.16	-0.01	-0.04	0.35	0.01		0.08	0.05	0.03	0.05	0.34	-0.21	
8. Depressive symptoms	-0.15	0.10	0.07	-0.13	-0.38	0.25	-0.36	-0.14	-0.08	-0.17	-0.08	-0.10	0.29	-0.10	-0.20	0.07	-0.06	-0.06	-0.18	0.39	-0.20

	Study 1		Study 2		Study 3	
	Mean	S.D.	Mean	S.D.	Mean	SD
Age	46.73	12.42	36.46	16.97	38.22	11.42
Gender	–	–	–	–	–	–
Org. tenure	11.19	8.75	8.09	7.70	7.81	7.97
Pos. tenure	4.54	4.90	3.39	3.27	5.31	6.78
Optimism	3.70	0.51	3.13	0.46	3.34	0.55
Politics	3.23	0.89	3.20	0.80	2.85	0.93
Political skill	4.03	0.50	3.82	0.62	4.00	0.63
Depressive symptoms	2.60	0.97	2.31	0.77	2.46	0.92

Notes:
[a] $N = 62$ ($r > 0.25, p < 0.05$).
[b] $N = 102$ ($r > 0.22, p < 0.05$).
[c] $N = 279$ ($r > 0.13, p < 0.05$).

Table 11.2   Regression analyses for depressive symptoms

Predictors	Study 1[a]		Study 2[b]		Study 3[c]	
	β	ΔR^2	β	ΔR^2	β	ΔR^2
Step 1:						
Age	−0.01		0.01		−0.01	
Gender	−0.18		−0.01		−0.14	
Organizational tenure	0.02*		−0.04*		−0.01**	
Position tenure	−0.04		0.03		0.01*	
Optimism	−0.98**	0.29	−0.32	0.11	−0.06	0.06
Step 2:						
Politics perceptions (A)	0.20		0.29**		0.39**	
Political skill (B)	−0.29	0.05*	−0.15	0.07*	−0.05	0.16**
Step 3:						
A × B	−0.88**	0.12**	−0.34*	0.04*	−0.30**	0.05**

Notes:
[a] $N = 62$.
[b] $N = 102$.
[c] $N = 279$.
** $p < 0.01$.
* $p < 0.05$.

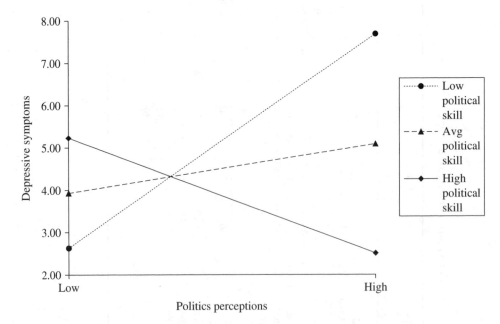

Figure 11.1   The interactive effects of politics perceptions and political skill on depressive symptoms (Sample 1)

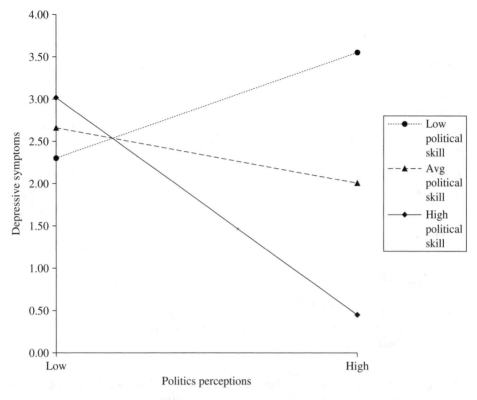

Figure 11.2   The interactive effects of politics perceptions and political skill on depressive symptoms (Sample 2)

Figures 11.1–11.3. In each case, low levels of political skill were associated with increased levels of depressive symptoms when politics increased. Interestingly, depressive symptoms declined as politics perceptions increased for highly politically skilled individuals in Samples 1 and 2.

Additional data analyses
Additional data analyses were conducted in order to investigate two remaining issues: (1) that political skill can result in positive effects by investigating job satisfaction as a criterion variable, not simply a reduction of negative effects, using depressive symptoms as the outcome; and (2) that it is political skill, and not optimism, that is the most important moderator of the politics perceptions–depressive symptoms relationship.

Positive effects of political skill   In each sample the politics perceptions × political skill interaction was significant for job satisfaction, explaining 3 percent (Sample 1) or 4 percent (Samples 2 and 3) of criterion variance (Sample 1: $\beta = 0.14$, $\Delta R^2 = 0.03$, $p > 0.10$; Sample 2: $\beta = 0.17$, $\Delta R^2 = 0.04$, $p > 0.05$; Sample 3: $\beta = 0.19$, $\Delta R^2 = 0.04$, $p > 0.01$). Individuals with low political skill reported significantly reduced levels of job satisfaction as politics perceptions increased. Conversely, job satisfaction increased as

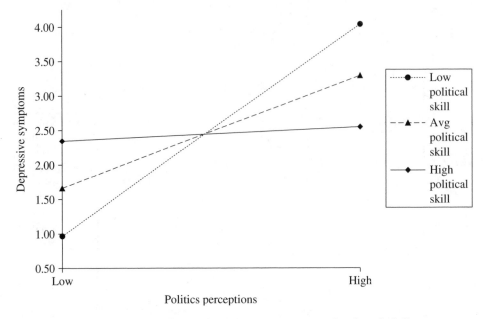

Figure 11.3   *The interactive effects of politics perceptions and political skill on depressive symptoms (Sample 3)*

politics perceptions increased for those individuals with high levels of political skill (figures depicting these relationships are available from the authors).

Political skill versus optimism as moderator   In order to assure that political skill was the most important moderator of the politics perceptions–depressive symptoms relationship, we ran the regression analysis using optimism as the moderator, while controlling for political skill. The results of these analyses demonstrated that the politics perceptions × optimism interaction term failed to reach significance in any of the three samples. Therefore, it appears that it is political skill that is the mechanism that operates to affect the politics perceptions–depressive symptoms relationship.

Discussion

As hypothesized, the relationship between perceptions of a political climate in the workplace and depressive symptoms was moderated by political skill. The negative relationship between the perception of politics and depressive symptoms, although evident for those with low political skill, had the opposite effect for those with high political skill. Based on these results, it is apparent that political skill enables people to ward off the potentially harmful effects of a work environment perceived to be political.

Those participants reporting low political skill seemed to be negatively impacted by the political environment in their workplace. Depressive symptoms were much more pronounced in environments where politics perceptions were high for individuals with low political skill. Conversely, those with high political skill reported fewer depressive symptoms in highly political environments than was the case in less political workplaces.

Political skill not only enables individuals to cope with organizational politics, but also, in some ways, actually enables them to enjoy a less troubling existence with fewer expressed depressive symptoms.

Results indicate that organizational politics may not necessarily be a negative feature of an organization, and, in fact, can be good for the politically skilled. Perhaps the level of political activity in an organization creates opportunities for politically skilled individuals to influence their environment, and the result appears to be fewer reported depressive symptoms and increased job satisfaction. For the less politically skilled, organizational politics perceptions create a threat, and this is associated with a higher rate of depressive symptoms and reduced job satisfaction.

The results of this research illustrate the difference between the potential opportunity or threat offered by a political environment. For the politically skilled, a political environment offers an opportunity that ultimately could result in positive outcomes including fewer depressive symptoms and increased job satisfaction. Conversely, the workplace perceived as highly politicized when viewed through the eyes of a low political skill person must be seen as a hostile environment.

The hostile environment creates a threat, which ultimately results in low political skill individuals expressing more depressive symptoms and job satisfaction. Those who possess the key resource of being politically skilled are likely to assess their environments more accurately, perceive that they have some control over the situation, adjust their behavior to match the politics of the situation, and utilize their social support to meet the demands of the situation. Under these circumstances, the likelihood of success is enhanced and most individuals would report feeling positive about life. Those lacking the key resource of political skill are likely to misread their environment, feel as though they have little control over the situation, may engage in inappropriate behavior, and may isolate themselves from others, increasing the onset of depressive symptoms.

A further interpretation of these finding concerns the fit of the person to the work environment. It may be that individuals high in political skill fit in work environments that are perceived to be political. The concept of fit has evolved into a multidimensional construct subsuming the notions of person–organization fit, person–job fit, person–vocation fit, person–team fit, and person–preferences fit (Wheeler et al., in press). This last sub-dimension, person–preferences fit (P–P fit), is the most applicable to high politically skilled individuals who perceive the work environment as political and vice versa (i.e. low politically skilled individuals in a work environment perceived as nonpolitical).

P–P fit represents the relationship between individual preferences and contributions of the work environment (Wheeler et al., in press). Christiansen et al.'s (1997) study concerning political compatibility found that an individual's preferences for political influence processes, when aligned with the perceived organizational processes, were positively related to numerous work attitudes, such as satisfaction with co-workers and perceptions of procedural fairness. This suggests that individuals who are effective at influencing others (i.e. highly politically skilled individuals) might prefer to work in environments that afford the opportunity to utilize their skills (i.e. an environment perceived as highly political). This fit between what individuals prefer and what the environment offers may lead to less adverse effects and possibly explain why highly politically skilled individuals reported fewer depressive symptoms and higher job satisfaction when in environments perceived as political.

P–P fit provides further explanation for why those who possess low political skill in environments of high politics perceptions would, in fact, show increased depressive symptoms and reduced job satisfaction. These individuals are experiencing misfit, or an incongruence of P–P fit (Wheeler et al., in press). The political environment does not match with the low politically skilled individuals' abilities or preferences, thus potentially leading to heightened reports of depressive symptoms.

Strengths and limitations
A major strength of this study is that our results were consistent across three samples, which included leaders from a large hospital, state agency employees, and a fairly wide ranging sample of white-collar and blue-collar individuals. These findings offer evidence of external validity due to our ability to conduct literal replications across diverse environments.

Because the data were self-reports contained in a single survey, there is a possibility of single-source bias in this research. Additionally, the measure of political skill contained only four items and the depressive symptoms measure contained only six items. These constructs of political skill and depressive symptoms may be more complex. Although the reliability estimates for each of these scales were good, additional research may be needed to capture the nuances of each construct more completely.

Directions for future research
In this research, political skill neutralized the impact of a political environment on depressive symptoms. Obviously, strains other than depressive symptoms should be included in future research. Self-report measures of depressive symptoms represent only one outcome that people could experience in a work environment. Measures of anxiety, somatic complaints, fatigue and burnout should be considered in future research on this topic. Additionally, obtaining reports from others to gauge interpersonal difficulties or other behavioral manifestations of strain would be desirable. Psychophysiological measures reflecting increased strain (e.g. increased blood pressure, heart rates, etc.), although often difficult to obtain, would provide highly objective measures of the impact of these variables on individuals.

An unanswered question that logically follows concerns the extent to which politically skilled people are more likely to be satisfied in highly political organizations. Related to perceived satisfaction, are people attracted to potential employers based on assessments of political climate in the organization? Consistent with the attraction–selection–attrition (ASA) notion of Schneider et al. (1998), are politically skilled people attracted to and more likely to remain in organizations with high levels of political behavior?

Because it has been established that political skill can minimize depressive symptoms, organizations should consider either selecting those with good political skill and/or developing the political skill of their employees. Developing the political skill of their employees should reduce symptoms of strain and depression, which ultimately will be reflected in reduced healthcare costs and improved productivity. As such, the potential return on investment of developing political skill in organizational members is significant.

Also, whereas politically skilled people should report fewer depressive symptoms and other strains, there may be some additional benefits to having a workforce that is more politically skilled. One significant aspect of political skill is the interpersonal sensitivity that enables people to adjust their behavior to the situation. A politically skilled workforce should help an organization in all endeavors that require interpersonal savvy. Research has shown that interpersonal acuity is a significant predictor of both group (Ahearn et al., 2004) and individual (Ferris et al., 2001) performance. The 'politics' of dealing with internal or external customers cannot be minimized in today's workplace.

Research should examine the assumption that politically skilled individuals are more successful in dealing with the vagaries that permeate all work settings. We contend that political skill can assist employees in dealing with the myriad uncertainties that they face in their workplace. To date, the intermediate linkage of reduced uncertainty has not been examined in political skill–work outcomes research.

References

Ahearn, K.K., Ferris, G.R., Hochwarter, W.A., Douglas, C. and Ammeter, A.P. (2004). Leader political skill and team performance. *Journal of Management*, **30**, 309–27.

American Psychiatric Association (1994). *Diagnostic and statistical manual of mental disorders* (4th edn). Washington, DC: American Psychiatric Association.

American Psychiatric Association (2000). *Diagnostic and statistical manual of mental disorders* (4th edn, text revision). Washington, DC: American Psychiatric Association.

Baker, E., Isreal, B. and Schurman, S. (1996). Role of control and support in occupational stress: An integrated model. *Social Science and Medicine*, **43**, 1145–59.

Bandura, A. (1997). *Self-efficacy: The exercise of control*. New York: W.H. Freeman.

Barnett, R.C. and Brennan, R.T. (1995). The relationship between job experiences and psychological distress: A structural equation approach. *Journal of Organizational Behavior*, **16**, 259–76.

Barnett, P.A. and Gotlib, I.H. (1988). Psychosocial functioning and depression: Distinguishing among antecedents, concomitants, and consequences. *Psychological Bulletin*, **104**, 97–126.

Baron, R.A. and Markman, G.D. (2000). Beyond social capital: How social skills can enhance entrepreneurs' success. *Academy of Management Executive*, **14**, 106–16.

Baugher, J.E. and Roberts, T. (2004). Workplace hazards, unions and coping styles. *Labor Studies Journal*, **29**, 83–106.

Beehr, T.A. (1998). Research on occupational stress: An unfinished enterprise. *Personnel Psychology*, **51**, 835–44.

Bourbonnais, R., Brisson, C., Moisan, J. and Vezina, M. (1996). Job strain and psychological distress in white-collar workers. *Scandinavian Journal of Work Environment and Health*, **22**, 139–45.

Braun, S. and Hollander, R.B. (1988). Work and depression among women in the Federal Republic of Germany. *Women and Health*, **14**, 5–24.

Campbell, A., Gurin, G. and Miller, W. E. (1954). *The voter decides*. Evanston, IL: Row, Peterson.

Christiansen, N., Villanova, P. and Mikulay, S. (1997). Political influence compatibility: Fitting the person to the climate. *Journal of Organizational Behavior*, **18**, 709–30.

Cohen, A. and Vigoda, E. (1999). Politics and the workplace. *Public Productivity and Management Review*, **22**, 389–406.

Cohen, A. and Vigoda, E. (2000). Do good citizens make good organizational citizens? *Administration and Society*, **32**, 596–624.

Cohen, J. and Cohen, P. (1983). *Applied multiple regression/correlation analysis for the behavioral sciences*. Hillsdale, NJ: Lawrence Erlbaum.

Cohen, S. and Wills, T. A. (1985). Stress, social support, and the buffering hypothesis. *Psychological Bulletin*, **98**, 310–57.

Conti, D.J. and Burton, W.N. (1994). The economic impact of depression in a workplace. *Journal of Management*, **36**, 983–8.

Cropanzano, R., Howes, J.C., Grandey, A.A. and Toth, P. (1997). The relationship of organizational politics and support to work behaviors, attitudes, and stress. *Journal of Organizational Behavior*, **18**, 159–80.

Dormann, C. and Zapf, D. (2002). Social stressors at work, irritation, and depressive symptoms: Accounting for unmeasured third variables in a multi-wave study. *Journal of Occupational and Organizational Psychology*, **75**, 33–58.

Dyer, S. and Quine, L. (1998). Predictors of job satisfaction and burnout among the direct care staff of a community learning disability service. *Journal of Applied Research in Intellectual Disabilities*, **11**, 320–32.

Ferris, G.R., Fedor, D.B., Chachere, J.G. and Pondy, L.R. (1989). Myths and politics in organizational contexts. *Group and Organizational Studies*, **14**, 83–103.

Ferris, G.R., Russ, G.S. and Fandt, P.M. (1989). Politics in organizations. In R.A. Giacalone and P. Rosenfeld (eds.), *Impression management in the organization* (pp. 143–70). Hillsdale, NJ: Lawrence Erlbaum.
Ferris, G.R., Frink, D.D., Bhawuk, D.P.S., Zhou, J. and Gilmore, D.C. (1996). Reactions of diverse groups to politics in the workplace. *Journal of Management*, **22**, 23–44.
Ferris, G.R., Frink, D.D., Galang, M.C., Zhou, J., Kacmar, K.M. and Howard, J.L. (1996). Perceptions of organizational politics: Predictors, stress-related implications, and outcomes. *Human Relations*, **49**, 233–66.
Ferris, G.R., Berkson, H.M., Kaplan, D.M., Gilmore, D.C., Buckley, M.R., Hochwarter, W.A. and Witt, L.A. (1999). Development and initial validation of the political skill inventory. Paper presented at the Academy of Management, 59th Annual National Meeting, Chicago, IL.
Ferris, G.R., Harrell-Cook, G. and Dulebohn, J.H. (2000). Organizational politics: The nature of the relationship between politics perceptions and political behavior. In S.B. Bacharach and E.J. Lawler (eds), *Research in the sociology of organizations* (pp. 89–130). Stamford, CT: JAI Press.
Ferris, G.R., Perrewé, P.L., Anthony, W.P. and Gilmore, D.C. (2000). Political skill at work. *Organizational Dynamics*, **28**, 25–37.
Ferris, G.R., Witt, L.A. and Hochwarter, W.A. (2001). The interaction of social skill and general mental ability on work outcomes. *Journal of Applied Psychology*, **86**, 1075–82.
Ferris, G.R., Adams, G., Kolodinsky, R.W., Hochwarter, W.A. and Ammeter, A.P. (2002). Perceptions of organizational politics: Theory and research directions. In F.J. Yammarino and F. Dansereau (eds), *Research in multi-level issues, Volume 1: The many faces of multi-level issues* (pp. 179–254). Oxford, UK: JAI Press/Elsevier Science.
Ferris, G.R., Perrewé, P. and Douglas, C. (2002). Social effectiveness in organizations: Construct validity and research directions. *Journal of Leadership and Organizational Studies*, **9**, 49–64.
Ferris, G.R., Davidson, S.L. and Perrewé, P.L. (2005). *Political skill at work*. Palo Alto, CA: Davies–Black Publishing.
Ferris, G.R., Treadway, D.C., Kolodinsky, R.W., Hochwarter, W.A., Kacmar, C.J., Douglas, C. and Frink, D.D. (2005). Development and validation of the political skill inventory. *Journal of Management*, **31**, 1–28.
Ferris, G.R., Brouer, R.L., Laird, M.D. and Hochwarter, W.A. (in press). The consequences of organizational politics perceptions as a workplace stressor. In P. Perrewé (ed.), *Stress and quality of working life: Current perspectives in occupational health*. São Paulo, Brazil: Editora Atlas.
Frone, M.R., Russell, M. and Cooper, M.L. (1992). Antecedents and outcomes of work–family conflict: Testing a model of the work–family interface. *Journal of Applied Psychology*, **77**, 65–78.
Ganster, D. (1989). Worker control and well-being: A review of research in the workplace. In S.I. Sauter, J.J. Hurrell and C.C. Cooper (eds.), *Job control and worker health* (pp. 3–24). New York: Wiley.
Gilmore, D.C., Ferris, G.R., Dulebohn, J.H. and Harrell-Cook, G. (1996). Organizational politics and employee attendance. *Group and Organization Management*, **21**, 481–94.
Glass, D.C. and McKnight, J.D. (1996). Perceived control, depressive symptomatology and professional burnout: A review of the evidence. *Psychology and Health*, **11**, 23–48.
Greenburg, P.E., Stiglin, L.E., Finkelstein, S.N. and Berndt, E.R. (1993). The economic burden of depression in 1990. *Journal of Clinical Psychiatry*, **54**, 405–18.
Greenhaus, J.H. and Parasuraman, S. (1986). A work–nonwork interactive perspective of stress and its consequences. *Journal of Organizational Behavior Management*, **8**, 37–60.
Hobfoll, S.E. (2002). Social and psychological resources and adaptation. *Review of General Psychology*, **6**, 307–24.
Hochwarter, W. (2002). The interactive effects of pro-political behavior and politics perceptions on job satisfaction and affective commitment. *Journal of Applied Social Psychology*, **33**, 1360–78.
Hochwarter, W., Perrewé, P.L., Ferris, G.R. and Guercio, R. (1999). Commitment as an antidote to the tension and turnover consequences of organizational politics. *Journal of Vocational Behavior*, **55**, 277–97.
Hochwarter, W., Kacmar, C., Perrewé, P. and Johnson, D. (2003). Perceived organizational support as a mediator of the relationship between politics perceptions and work outcomes. *Journal of Vocational Behavior*, **63**, 438–56.
Jex, S.M. and Beehr, T.A. (1991). Emerging theoretical and methodological issues in the study of work-related stress. In G.R. Ferris and K.M. Rowland (eds.), *Research in personnel and human resources management* (Vol. 9, pp. 311–65). Greenwich, CT: JAI Press.
Joiner, T. and Coyne, J.C. (eds) (1999). *The interactional nature of depression: Advances in interpersonal approaches*. Washington, DC: American Psychological Association.
Jones, E.E. (1990). *Interpersonal perception*. New York: W.H. Freeman.
Jones-Johnson, G. and Johnson, W.R. (1992). Subjective underemployment and psychological stress: The role of perceived social and supervisor support. *Journal of Social Psychology*, **132**, 11–21.
Jorm, A.F., Christensen, H., Henderson, A.S., Jacomb, P.A., Korten, A.E. and Rodgers, B. (2000). Predicting anxiety and depression from personality: Is there a synergistic effect of neuroticism and extraversion? *Journal of Abnormal Psychology*, **109**, 145–9.

Kacmar, K.M. and Baron, R.A. (1999). Organizational politics: The state of the field, links to related processes and an agenda for future research. In G.R. Ferris (ed.), *Research in personnel and human resources management* (Vol. 17, pp. 1–39). Stamford, CT: JAI Press.

Kacmar, K.M., Bozeman, D.P., Carlson, D.S. and Anthony, W.P. (1999). A partial test of the perceptions of organizational politics model. *Human Relations*, **52**, 383–416.

Kahn, R.L. and Byosiere, P. (1992). Stress in organizations. In M.D. Dunnette and L.M. Hough (eds), *Handbook of industrial and organizational psychology* (2nd edn, Vol. 2, pp. 571–650). Palo Alto, CA: Consulting Psychology Press.

Kaplan, H.I. and Sadock, B.J. (1981). *Modern synopsis of comprehensive textbook of psychiatry IV*. Baltimore, MD: Wilkins and Wilkins.

Karasek, R. and Theorell, T. (1990). *Healthy work: Stress, productivity and the reconstruction of working life*. New York: Basic Books.

Kawakami, N., Araki, S. and Kawashima, M. (1990). Effects of job stress on occurrence of major depression in Japanese industry: A case-control study nested in a cohort study. *Journal of Occupational Medicine*, **32**, 722–5.

Lara, M.E., Leader, J. and Klein, D.N. (1997). The association between social support and course of depression: Is it confounded with personality? *Journal of Abnormal Psychology*, **106**, 478–82.

Lewin, K. (1936). *Principles of topological psychology*. New York: McGraw-Hill.

Liden, R. and Mitchell, T.R. (1989). Ingratiation in the development of leader–member exchanges. In R.A. Giacalone and P. Rosenfeld (eds), *Impression management in the organization* (pp. 343–61). Hillsdale, NJ: Lawrence Erlbaum.

Luthans, F., Hodgetts, R.M. and Rosenkrantz, S.A. (1988). *Real managers*. Cambridge, MA: Ballinger.

Mackie, K.S., Holahan, C.K. and Gottlieb, N.H. (2001). Employee involvement, management practices, work stress, and depression in employees of a human services residential care facility. *Human Relations*, **54**, 1065–89.

Matteson, M.T. and Ivancevich, J.M. (1987). *Controlling work stress*. San Francisco, CA: Jossey-Bass.

McGrath, J.E. (1976). Stress and behavior in organizations. In M.D. Dunnette (ed.), *Handbook of industrial and organizational psychology* (pp. 390–419). Chicago, IL: Rand McNally.

McGrath, E., Keita, G.P., Strickland, N.F. and Russo, N.F. (1990). *Women and depression*. Washington, DC: American Psychological Association.

Menaghan, F.G. (1994). The daily grind: Work stressors, family patterns and intergenerational outcomes. In W.R. Avison and I.H. Gotlih (eds), *Stress and mental health: Contemporary issues and prospects for the future* (pp. 115–47). New York: Plenum.

Mintzberg, H. (1983). *Power in and around organizations*. Englewood Cliffs, NJ: Prentice-Hall.

Monroe, S.M. and Simons, A.D. (1991). Diathesis–stress theories in the context of life stress research: Implications for the depressive disorders. *Psychological Bulletin*, **110**, 406–25.

Nadaoka, T., Kashiwakura, M., Ojii, A., Morioka, Y. and Tosuka, S. (1997). Stress and psychiatric disorders in local government officials in Japan in relation to their employment level. *Acta Psychiatrica Scandinavica*, **96**, 176–83.

Narayanan, L., Menon, S. and Spector, P.F. (1999). Stress in the workplace: A comparison of gender and occupations. *Journal of Organizational Behavior*, **20**, 63–73.

National Institute of Mental Health Genetics Workgroup (1998). *Genetics and mental disorders* (NIH Publications No. 98–4268). Rockville, MD: National Institute of Mental Health.

Nolen-Hoeksema, S. and Morrow, J. (1991). A prospective study of depression and posttraumatic stress symptoms after a natural disaster: The 1989 Loma Prieta earthquake. *Journal of Personality and Social Psychology*, **61**, 115–21.

Nolen-Hoeksema, S., Larson, J. and Grayson, C. (1999). Explaining the gender differences in depressive symptoms. *Journal of Personality and Social Psychology*, **77**, 1061–72.

Peled, A. (2000). Politicking for success: The missing skill. *Leadership and Organization Development Journal*, **21**, 20–9.

Perrewé, P., Ferris, G.R., Frink, D.D. and Anthony, W.P. (2000). Political skill: An antidote for workplace stressors. *Academy of Management Executive*, **14**, 115–23.

Perrewé, P.L., Zellars, K.L., Ferris, G.R., Rossi, A.M., Kacmar, C.J. and Ralston, D.A. (2004). Neutralizing job stressors: Political skill as an antidote to the dysfunctional consequences of role conflict stressors. *Academy of Management Journal*, **47**, 141–52.

Perrewé, P., Zellars, K.L., Rossi, A.M., Ferris, G.R., Kacmar, C.J., Lui, Y., Zinko, R. and Hochwarter, W.A. (in press). Political skill: An antidote in the role overload–strain relationship. *Journal of Occupational Health Psychology*.

Pfeffer, J. (1981). *Power in organizations*. Boston, MA: Pitman.

Saz, P. and Dewey, M.E. (2001). Depression, depressive symptoms and mortality in persons aged 65 and over living in the community: A systematic review of the literature. *International Journal of Geriatric Psychiatry*, **16**, 622–30.

Scheier, M.F. and Carver, C.S. (1985). Optimism, coping and health: Assessment and implications of general-ized outcome expectancies. *Health Psychology*, **4**, 219–47.

Schneider, B., Smith, D.B., Taylor, S. and Fleenor, J. (1998). Personality and organizations: A test of the homo-geneity of personality hypothesis. *Journal of Applied Psychology*, **83**, 462–70.

Schroevers, M.J., Sanderman, R., van Sonderen, E. and Ranchor, A.V. (2001). The evaluation of the Centre for Epidemiologic Studies Depression (CES-D) scale: Depressed and positive affect in cancer patients and healthy reference subjects. *Quality of Life Research*, **9**, 1015–29.

Schuler, R. (1980). Definitions and conceptualizations of stress in organizations. *Organizational Behavior and Human Performance*, **25**, 184–215.

Schuler, R.S. and Jackson, S.E. (1986). Managing stress through PHRM practices: An uncertainty interpreta-tion. In K.M. Rowland and G.R. Ferris (eds), *Research in personnel and human resources management* (Vol. 4, pp. 183–224). Greenwich, CT: JAI Press.

Seligman, M.E.P. (1975). *Helplessness*. San Francisco, CA: Freeman.

Spector, P.E. (1986). Perceived control by employees: A meta-analysis of studies concerning autonomy and par-ticipation in decision-making. *Human Relations*, **39**, 1005–16.

Stone, E.F. and Hollenbeck, J.R. (1989). Clarifying some controversial issues surrounding statistical procedures for detecting moderator variables: Empirical evidence and related matters. *Journal of Applied Psychology*, **74**, 3–10.

Thoits, P. (1994). Stressors and problem-solving: The individual as psychological activist. *Journal of Health and Social Behavior*, **35**, 143–60.

Valle, M.P. and Perrewé, P.L. (2000). Do politics perceptions relate to political behaviors? *Human Relations*, **53**, 359–86.

Vigoda, E. (2002). Stress-related aftermaths to workplace politics: The relationship among politics, job distress and aggressive behavior in organizations. *Journal of Organizational Behavior*, **23**, 571–91.

Vigoda, E. (2003). *Developments in organizational politics: How political dynamics affect employee performance in modern work sites*. Cheltenham, UK and Northampton, MA, USA: Edward Elgar.

Voydanoff, P. (1987). *Work and family life*. Newbury Park, CA: Sage.

Wheeler, A.R., Buckley, M.R., Halbesleben, J.R.B., Brouer, R.L. and Ferris, G.R. (in press). 'The elusive crite-rion of fit' revisited: Toward an integrative theory of multidimensional fit. In J.J. Martocchio (ed.), *Research in personnel and human resources management* (Vol. 24). Oxford, UK: JAI Press/Elsevier Science.

Williams, K.J. and Alliger, G.M. (1994). Role stressors, mood spillover, and perceptions of work–family conflict in employed parents. *Academy of Management Journal*, **37**, 837–68.

Witt, L.A. (1999). I am outta here: Organizational politics vs. personality predicting turnover. Paper presented at the Academy of Management, 59th Annual Meeting, Chicago, IL.

PART IV

SYSTEMS AND PERFORMANCE: STRATEGY, CHANGE AND DECISION MAKING AS A POLITICAL PROCESS

12 A micro-political perspective of strategic management
Jane Gunn and Stephen Chen

Introduction

Strategic management processes have been shown to be worthwhile activities that contribute to organizational success (Miller and Cardinal, 1994). The dominant theories of strategic management emphasize the value of rationality and comprehensiveness in the process. While a small number of authors have considered the political angle, strategic management processes are largely considered to be effective because they enable planning, encourage rationality and enable control of political and other factors which detract from rationality of decision making and the logic of strategy implementation processes.

In contrast, intra-organizational political behaviour is predominantly considered to have a negative impact on individuals and on organizations, and is seen as something that organizations should therefore seek to minimize, or even eliminate. Perhaps as a consequence of this view and the perception that an effective strategy process will eliminate politics, only minimal attention has been paid to politics within the field of strategic management. At a more detailed level, this lack of consideration of organizational politics (OP) by strategic management scholars has meant that there has been minimal attention paid to the stream of literature that considers the potential for organizational politics to have a positive impact on organizational processes.

In this chapter, we seek to contribute towards the development of a micro-political perspective on strategic management. As Kacmar et al. (1999) note, 'the investigation of political behaviour in organizations is of extreme importance if management theory and research are to provide relevant information and sound prescriptive advice about dealing effectively with politics in organizations to business practitioners' (p. 385). To achieve our aim, we critically review the literature on strategic management and micro-organizational politics, and propose a challenge to the assumptions that continue to dominate strategic management practice. We articulate a set of assumptions based on a micro-political perspective of strategic management and identify opportunities for further research.

The treatment of strategic management and organizational politics in the literature

Strategic management

No comprehensive theory of strategy making has yet emerged (see for example Boyd and Reuning-Elliott, 1998), and it is unlikely that a single paradigm will ever exist in the field (Lowendahl and Revang, 1998). However, it is possible to define strategy and strategic management so as to take account of the major themes in the literature. We define 'strategy' as a firm's overall direction and goals, along with the consciously intended and emergent actions directed at achieving these goals, which are developed and implemented by the organization in response to its environment. In terms of strategy content, these strategic goals are likely to revolve around achieving financial success for the benefit of shareholders in private sector firms, while in public sector and other not-for-profit firms, the strategic goals are more likely to focus on the achievement of community or social outcomes.

Important aspects of this definition of strategy include the recognition that strategy involves both the objectives that the organization aims to achieve, and the sets of activities or initiatives put in place to achieve the goals. Additionally the definitions recognize that strategy goals and actions must be coordinated; that is, strategy is not random behaviour and completely autonomous actions (Farjoun, 2002), and neither is it purely actions specified in a plan prior to action. Rather, it incorporates both planned and emergent activity, guided by a documented plan, a guiding sense of purpose or a set of simple rules which guide response to the internal and external environment (Farjoun, 2002). Third, strategy does not occur in an organizational vacuum; it is fundamentally about how the firm will act in the context of its external environment, including the political, economic, industry and competitive landscape. The internal environment is also important, as suggested by proponents of the resource-based view of the firm, who suggest that the firm's internal resources or competences are the basis for competitive advantage (see for example Peteraf, 2004). These two latter elements also indicate that strategy is not static, but changes over time in response to changes in the external and internal environments. These environment changes are partly caused by the firm's strategy (Farjoun, 2002).

Therefore the term 'strategic management process' describes the ongoing steps and associated behaviours by which these courses of action are determined and implemented by organizations in their environment. There is much variation in views of what this process includes; however, the process is commonly considered in terms of the two processes of strategy formulation and strategy implementation, recognizing that these are not discrete processes, but overlap conceptually as well as in time. As the definition of strategy identified above suggests, strategic management processes must be continuous and overlapping, which enables strategy to be defined, refined, implemented and adjusted according to changes both within and external to the firm. Strategy formulation includes behaviours and activities, such as the analysis of the firm's internal and external environments, the development of a vision or purpose, the identification of guiding sets of values, development of goals and actions such as entry into new markets or measures to counter competitive threats, financial decisions concerning these actions, and the development of action plans and associated project planning. Strategy implementation involves the activities required to achieve the specified or planned actions, and to enable strategy to emerge, such as the management of initiatives to budgets and timetables, performance management of both company goals and individuals, communication of goals, vision and values, and other aspects associated with managing change in the organization. 'Strategic planning', 'strategy making' and 'strategy formulation' are often used interchangeably with 'strategic management'; however, on closer investigation they are usually found to have a more limited meaning, associated with the strategy formulation or decision-making element of strategy development, rather than including implementation. This view of strategic management is limited, as the realization of the strategy is at least as important as, if not more important than, the planning of it.

We should also consider why organizations put strategic management processes in place. Fundamentally, strategic management processes are implemented because 'organizational survival depends to a significant extent on the adjustment and renewal capacities of strategy-making processes' (Burgelman, 1991, p. 255). However, there are also other important goals of strategic management pertaining to the process itself, which facilitate the realization of the ultimate goal of organizational survival. These include the degree to which the firm's plan effectively guides and stimulates organizational members' actions and behaviour, the creation of legitimacy for the company in the eyes of stakeholders, the achievement of cooperation across organizational boundaries, and the degree to which the firm's strategies/action plans provide effective competitive strategies to influence and direct the firm's behaviour (see for example Brews and Hunt, 1999; Farjoun, 2002; Stone and Brush, 1996).

Limited consideration of organizational politics in strategic management

Despite extensive and ongoing research into strategic management over more than 30 years, there has been only limited consideration of strategic management from a political perspective. 'Power used to be viewed as a kind of fifth column in this field. Everyone knew about it but nobody studied it' (Mintzberg et al., 1998, p. 235). In the early 1980s, Narayanan and Fahey (1982) identified that valuable efforts to conceptualize strategy formulation as a political process were under way, but that a 'coherent framework in which to study strategic decision making from a political perspective' was lacking. Similarly Zahra (1987) noted that despite an increasing awareness of the ramifications of organizational politics in organizational success, 'there is a paucity of empirical studies that articulate the link between organizational politics and the strategic process. In fact, most of the contributions in this area are normative in nature or based on limited case studies' (p. 579). Nearly 20 years on, the situation remains the same. Among the ten distinct schools of strategic management thought identified by Mintzberg et al. (1998), politics does not figure prominently. The definitional schema includes prescriptive schools, design, planning and positioning schools, the 'configurational school' which attempts to integrate the other schools, and six descriptive schools that describe strategy-making processes from different perspectives. This grouping includes a 'thin, but quite different stream' (Mintzberg, 1999, p. 25) of research into strategy as a construct associated with power and politics.

Organizational politics

Like strategic management, organizational politics is a highly complex construct. 'While certain similarities may be said to exist among the definitions proposed thus far, at present there is no widely shared definition of organizational politics' (Kacmar et al., 1999, p. 384). This lack of a coherent view of organizational politics is partly attributable to the different perspectives brought to bear on the issue, including the functionalist, interpretive and radical perspectives (Bradshaw-Camball and Murray, 1991). Depending on the perspective brought to the discussion, the starting point for defining and investigating the occurrence of politics differs. For example, politics is variously seen as an objective and inherent reality of organizations, as unimportant and therefore ignored, and as reality constructed by the powerful (Bradshaw-Camball and Murray, 1991).

One important distinction in considering organizational politics is that of scope of the treatment of the construct. This chapter is concerned with 'micro-politics', which describes politics within the firm, rather than 'macro-politics', which describes the firm's engagement in influencing and other political behaviours beyond the firm, for example in relation to alliance building and political lobbying of government (Mintzberg, 1999).

The study of macro-politics considers the entire organization and its relationship with the social and political systems in the country (Vigoda, 2003). Macro-politics is also an important area of investigation within the strategic management field, not least because the ability of firms to influence their macro-political environment can be critical in the achievement of an organization's strategy.

Despite the lack of a clear theory of OP, three aspects of defining micro-organizational politics are widely agreed. First, political behaviour is associated with influencing behaviours. For example Dean and Sharfman (1993) describe political behaviour as 'intentional acts of influence'. Second, politics is usually associated with the use of power; for example Pfeffer (1992) defines politics as 'the exercise or use of power' (p. 33). A third common element in the definition of OP is that it arises in cases of conflict or potential conflict. Drory and Romm (1990), for example, suggest that conflict 'can be considered as a necessary underlying element which is present in all political situations regardless of whether the two parties to the political exchange are keenly aware of it or not' (p. 1144). Further, OP is commonly described as 'non-sanctioned' (for example Zanzi and O'Neill, 2001) or 'informal' behaviour, and this commonly has negative associations. However, as we will discuss further below, restricting the definition to only those behaviours that are negative or have negative consequences limits our understanding of OP.

Beyond this description, complexity exists due to the multifaceted nature of defining OP. Definitions commonly include two elements: how politics is enacted (the behaviours or tactics) and the result of the behaviours. Drory and Romm (1990) use the terms 'means' and 'ends' to describe these definitional elements. Less commonly, situational variables are also included in the definition. Table 12.1 shows a summary of definitions of organizational politics, broken down in this manner. Additionally, definitions vary according to whether politics is considered to be a positive or negative force.

Some authors have focused on defining politics according to the 'means'. For example, Kipnis et al. (1980), in one of the most widely used taxonomies of interpersonal influence processes, defined eight dimensions of influence as assertiveness, ingratiation, rationality, sanctions, exchange of benefits, upward appeal, blocking and coalitions. Schriesheim and Hinkin (1990) refined the Kipnis et al. tool to develop an 18-item instrument, which they tested to ensure theoretically valid content, perceptual distinctiveness, and adequate scale reliabilities (Table 12.2). Their instrument was developed specifically around influence tactics used by subordinates to influence their superiors, as one of their key criticisms of the Kipnis et al. (1980) work is that it examined tactics from three different perspectives: how I influence my boss, my co-workers and my subordinates. This approach to defining politics has been criticized as potentially too broad, in that it 'runs the risk of widening the scope of the discussion too much and may lead to a blurring of the real boundaries of political behaviour in the organization' (Vigoda, 2003, p. 11).

Zanzi et al. (1991) and Zanzi and O'Neill (2001) also developed the work of Kipnis et al. (1980) further. Zanzi and O'Neill (2001) refine the definition of OP as influence tactics by identifying that these tactics can be either sanctioned – considered positive, tolerated, expected or even encouraged in organizations – or non-sanctioned – considered unacceptable, undesirable and negative. This view of politics is in contrast with that of scholars who restrict the definition of politics to those tactics that are negative or non-sanctioned. For example, Eisenhardt and Bourgeois (1988) describe political behaviour as 'observable, but often covert actions to influence', while behaviour which is not political

Table 12.1   Definitions of organizational politics

What is done?	For what purpose?	Situation	Author
'Intentional acts of influence'	'To enhance or protect the self-interest of individuals and groups'		Allen et al. (1979)
'The intentional use of power'	'In the service of one's own interests'		Gray and Ariss (1985)
When individuals make decisions and take actions to satisfy their own needs	'Designed to benefit particular individuals and groups rather than the organizational as a whole'		Jones (1985)
'The process by which individuals and groups attempt to influence decision making'	'Essentially intended to win the support of the powers that be'		Prasad and Rubenstein (1992)
'Observable but often covert actions' (as opposed to straightforward influence tactics of open and forthright discussion with full sharing of information, open to all decision makers)	'To influence a decision'		Eisenhardt and Bourgeois (1988)
'The exercise of power'	'To promote interests'. Notes that these interests can be self-serving – 'to defeat one another' or they can be to achieve something together that couldn't have been achieved separately		Baum (1989)
(Political behaviour) 'Procedures for promoting interests'		'To allocate scarce resources'	
'Informal means of influence'	'When goal attainment is sought'	'In the face of potential conflict'	Drory and Romm (1990)
'The exercise or use of power, with power being defined as a potential force'			Pfeffer (1992)
'Intentional acts of influence'	'For one's own ends'		Dean and Sharfman (1993)
'Activities to acquire, develop and use power and other resources'	'To obtain one's preferred outcome'	'Where there is uncertainty or	Voyer (1994) developed from Pfeffer (1981)

Table 12.1   (continued)

What is done?	For what purpose?	Situation	Author
		disagreement about choices'	
'The practical domain of power in action, worked out through the use of techniques of influence and other (more or less) extreme tactics'	For own and organizational goals, as needed		Buchanan and Badham (1999b)
'Organizationally non-sanctioned behaviour'	'May be detrimental to organizational goals or to the interests of others in the organization . . . the underlying but concealed intent of political behaviour is assumed to be self serving in nature'		Harrell-Cook et al. (1999)
Behaviour that is 'highly covert, symbolic and subject to differences in perception . . . the same behaviour may be interpreted as either political or nonpolitical by different observers, depending on each observer's prior experience and frame of reference'	'Represents a threat to overall organizational efficiency and effectiveness' (p. 385)		Kacmar et al. (1999)
'The exercise of tactical influence by individuals'	'Strategically goal directed, rational, conscious and intended to promote self interest, either at the expense of or in support of others' interests'		Valle and Perrewé (2000)
'Actions that are inconsistent with acceptable norms'	'Are designed to promote self interest, and are taken without regard for and even at the expense of organizational goals'		Valle and Witt (2001)
'Behaviours that occur on an informal basis within an organization and involve intentional acts of influence'	'Designed to project or enhance individuals' professional careers'	'When conflicting courses of action are possible'	O'Connor and Morrison (2001)
'Broad, general set of social behaviours'	'Can contribute to the basic functioning of the		Zanzi and O'Neill (2001)

Table 12.1   (continued)

What is done?	For what purpose?	Situation	Author
	organization – can be either functional or dysfunctional' (from Pfeffer, 1981, p. 246)		
'The constructive reconciliation of competing causes and central to managing'			Butcher and Clarke (2002)
'The things people engage in'	'To get power when it might not come naturally'		Lewis (2002)
'Activities not required as part of one's formal role in the organization to influence or attempt to influence'	'Designed to influence outcomes'	'The distribution of advantage and disadvantage within the organization'	Sussman et al. (2002)
'Constructive management of shared meaning' (p. 751)	'Neutral and inherently necessary component of organizational functioning' (p. 751)		Ammeter et al. (2002)
'Intra-organizational influence' tactics used by organization members'	'To promote self interests or organizational goals in different ways'		Vigoda (2003)
	'Achieving the goal regardless of how it is achieved'		Parker (2003)
'A fact of life in every organization'	'Probably necessary to their effective operation'		Davis and Gardner (2004)
'Unsanctioned actions or those that deviate from formal or rational procedures'			Darr and Johns (2004)

is described as straightforward influence tactics of open and forthright discussion with full sharing of information open to all decision makers.

Others have defined organizational politics according to the 'ends'. Many equate organizational politics with negative impacts such as behaviour that is self-serving in nature and contrary to organizational interests. For example, Darr and Johns (2004) suggest that organizational politics is 'generally understood as involving behaviour that is directed toward furthering self or group interest at the expense of others' well being' (p. 171).

The impact of organizational politics on strategic management
The few studies that have examined the linkage between OP and strategic management have commonly identified that politics has a negative impact on strategic management.

Table 12.2   Influence tactics

Kipnis et al. (1980)	
Assertiveness	Keep checking up on him or her
	Simply ordered him or her to do what was asked
	Demanded that he or she do what I requested
	Bawled him or her out
	Set a time deadline for him or her to do what I asked
	Told him or her that the work must be done as ordered or he or she should propose a better way
	Became a nuisance (kept bugging him/her until he/she did what I wanted)
	Repeatedly reminded him or her about what I wanted
	Expressed my anger verbally
	Had a showdown in which I confronted him or her face to face
	Pointed out that the rules required that he or she comply
Ingratiation	Made him or her feel important ('only you have the brains, talent to do this')
	Acted very humbly to him or her while making my request
	Acted in a friendly manner prior to asking for what I wanted
	Made him or her feel good about me before making my request
	Inflated the importance of what I wanted him or her to do
	Praised him or her
	Sympathized with him/her about the added problems that my request has caused
	Waited until he or she appeared in a receptive mood before asking
	Showed my need for their help
	Asked in a polite way
	Pretended I was letting him or her decide to do what I wanted (act in a psuedo-democratic fashion)
Rationality	Wrote a detailed plan that justified my ideas
	Presented him or her with information in support of my point of view
	Explained the reasons for my request
	Used logic to convince him or her
	Wrote a memo that described what I wanted
	Offered to compromise over the issue (I gave in a little)
	Demonstrated my competence to him or her before making my request
Sanctions	Gave no salary increase or prevented the person from getting a pay raise
	Threatened his or her job security (e.g. hint of firing or getting him or her fired)
	Promised (or gave) a salary increase
	Threatened to give him or her an unsatisfactory performance evaluation
	Threatened him or her with loss of promotion
Exchange	Offered an exchange (e.g. if you do this for me, I will do something for you)
	Reminded him or her of past favours that I did for them
	Offered to make a personal sacrifice if he or she would do what I wanted (e.g. work late, work harder, do his/her share of the work etc.)
	Did personal favours for him or her
	Offered to help if he/she would do what I wanted

Table 12.2 (continued)

Upward appeal	Made a formal appeal to higher levels to back up my request
	Obtained the informal support of higher-ups
	Filed a report about the other person with higher-ups (e.g. my superior)
	Sent him or her to my superior
Blocking	Threatened to notify an outside agency if he or she did not give in to my request
	Threatened to stop working with him or her until he or she gave in
	Engaged in a work slowdown until he or she did what I wanted
	Ignored him or her and/or stopped being friendly
	Distorted or lied about reasons he or she should do what I wanted
Coalitions	Obtained the support of co-workers to back up my request
	Had him or her come to a formal conference at which I made my request
	Obtained the support of my subordinates to back up my request
Unclassified items	Kept kidding him or her until they did what I wanted
	Ignored him or her and went ahead and did what I wanted
	Provided him or her with various benefits that they wanted
	Challenged his or her ability ('I bet you can't do that')
	Pretended not to understand what needed to be done so that he or she would volunteer to do it for me
	Concealed some of my reasons for trying to influence him/her

Schriesheim and Hinkin (1990)

Ingratiation	Acted very humbly to him or her while making my request
	Acted in a friendly manner prior to asking for what I wanted
	Made him or her feel good about me before making my request
Exchange of benefits	Reminded him or her of past favours that I did for him/her
	Offered an exchange (e.g. if you do this for me I will do something for you)
	Offered to make a personal sacrifice if he or she would do what I wanted (e.g. work late, work harder, do his/her share of the work, etc.)
Rationality	Used logic to convince him or her
	Explained the reasons for my request
	Presented him or her with information in support of my point of view
Assertiveness	Had a showdown in which I confronted him or her face to face
	Expressed my anger verbally
	Used a forceful manner; I tried such things as demands, the setting of deadlines, and the expression of strong emotion
Upward appeal	Obtained the informal support of higher-ups
	Made a formal appeal to higher levels to back up my request
	Relied on the chain of command – on people higher up in the organization who have power over him or her
Coalitions	Obtained the support of co-workers to back up my request
	Obtained the support of my subordinates to back up my request
	Mobilized other people in the organization to help me in influencing him or her

Table 12.2   (continued)

Zanzi and O'Neill (2001)

Sanctioned:

Use of expertise	Using particular skills, unique knowledge or solutions to enhance one's position
Superordinate goals	Attempting to generate support by linking one's argument to the greater good of the organization
Networking	Taking advantage of one's access to a network of organizational and/or occupational incumbents, specialists or power holders (special ties with professional, social, or family groups)
Coalition building	A temporary or permanent alliance with other individuals or groups to increase the support of one's position or to achieve a particular objective
Persuasion	Seeking to win another party over to one's own point of view through selective use of rational argumentation
Image building	To promote self-interests through creating and maintaining a favourable image with the power holders

Non-sanctioned:

Intimidation and innuendoes	Using language, situations or oblique allusions
Manipulation	Seeking to win another party over to your point of view through distortion of reality or misrepresentation of intentions (including selective disclosure and 'objective' speculation about individuals or situations
Cooptation	Merging or incorporating another power group or individual for the purpose of controlling or silencing a counterpart
Control of information	Selective use of what information is distributed and who are the recipients of it
Using surrogates	Having an intermediary secure compliance in others
Organizational placement	Controlling or supporting the promotion of agreeable people into strategic positions or isolating/removing potential opponents
Blaming or attacking others	Blaming other parties for one's failure or minimizing their accomplishments

OP has been seen as distracting people from the goals of the company, distorting factual information and restricting information flow. However, there have also been some findings, notably Zahra's (1987) study, which found a positive association between politics and successful elements of strategic management. Of particular note are the articles by Narayanan and Fahey (1982), Jones (1985), Zahra (1987) and Voyer (1994), which specifically look at politics and strategic management, and the research into politics and decision making, for example Eisenhardt and Bourgeois (1988), Eisenhardt and Zbaracki (1992) and Dean and Sharfman (1993). These are reviewed briefly below.

Jones (1985) is particularly scathing in his consideration of the impact of OP on strategic management, concluding that 'when managers engage in internal politics, the effects on the development and implementation of the strategic business plan can be disastrous' (p. 33). He claims that politics is displayed in the business planning process in four ways: coalition building, information control, empire building and budget distortion. He concludes that these political behaviours lead to a factionalized organization, rather than a cohesive cooperative one, that a distorted picture and inaccurate profile of the organization's strengths and weaknesses emerges and that they create advantages for individual parts of the organization, rather than for the organization as a whole.

Voyer (1994), in a qualitative study, identified that, while politics does not have a direct negative impact on the strategic planning process, it does negatively impact the quality of management, which in turn has an indirect negative impact on the strategic planning process. Zahra (1987) conducted one of the rare empirical studies into the impact of politics on strategic planning. He found that organizational politics impacted positively on some aspects of the strategic management process, and negatively on others, with an overall negative impact on firm performance. Specifically, this research found that there was a positive association between organizational politics intensity and quality of long-range planning, effective selection of strategy, effective resource allocation among competing units and effective strategy implementation. A negative relationship was found between organizational politics intensity and consensus among key executives concerning corporate goals, comprehensiveness of long-range plans, coordination between units, quality of interdepartmental communications and effective evaluation of department goal achievement.

Eisenhardt and Bourgeois (1988), in their qualitative and quantitative study of strategic decisions in eight firms, considered political behaviours such as the degree of full disclosure of information in meetings, the formation of insurgency groups, internal and external alliances, withholding information, agenda control and private attempts to coopt or lobby key executives. They found that the greater the use of politics, the poorer the firm performance. They surmised that the reasons for this included time wasted engaging in politics, restricted information flow and distortion of people's perceptions. Dean and Sharfman (1993) found that rationally based decisions are associated with more successful strategic decisions than are politically based decisions. Zanzi and O'Neill (2001) provide one explanation why the impact of politics is negative. They summarize research findings that organizational politics creates less focus on organizational goals, restriction of the flow of information and decision-making slowness, and a reduction in the excitement about innovation. Baum (1989) also sheds light on why politics can have a negative impact on strategic management processes: 'when workers think in terms of individual achievement and when they concentrate on attacking co-workers, they become isolated and are unlikely to affiliate deeply with an organization' (p. 202). Further, they find it difficult to work alongside their co-workers, making the resolution of issues and collaborative working difficult to achieve.

Rather than offer a judgement on the positive or negative impact of organizational politics, Narayanan and Fahey (1982) simply present it as a reality of organizations which must be integrated into strategic management thinking. Their framework considers strategic decision making from a political perspective, with particular emphasis on the role of coalitions. They compare the rational model of strategy formulation with a political one, concluding that decision making depends on power/influence distribution within and across coalitions, strategic issues recognition is at least partially a result of the power of the organizational actors, that rationally based decision-making tools such as strategic planning and portfolio analysis are also used for symbolic purposes by political actors, and that the management of context and process is just as important as strategy content. Context includes such issues as conflict management, team building and organizational development. Eisenhardt and Zbaracki (1992) undertook a review of strategic decision-making literature, concluding, 'Organizations are accurately portrayed as political systems in which strategic decision makers have partially conflicting objectives and limited cognitive capability.' They propose that strategic decision making is both boundedly rational because people do engage in some rational processes, and political since decision makers engage in politics, and power is important.

While few studies have identified the positive impacts of politics in the strategy process, two examples of research in the information technology field demonstrate the potential positive impact of OP. Wainwright and Waring (2004) looked at the impact of politics in information services (IS) project implementation. They found that there is a high rate of failure of IS integration projects and they suggest that this is in part due to a failure to integrate organizational behaviour theory into IS, due to a strong focus on technical and rational approaches. When approached from a broader perspective, they conclude that IS projects will be better implemented using an organizational analysis, which takes account of political issues. Peled (2000) more specifically analyses the impact of the presence of organizational politics in the implementation of IT projects. He concludes that the effective display of politics is not only positive; it is critical in the success of these projects, and the lack of political skill prevents success. He defines political skills as 'the manager's ability to manipulate his/her interpersonal relationships with employees, colleagues, clients and supervisors to ensure the ultimate success of the project' (p. 26). Similarly the positive impact of politics has been investigated in leadership theory. Ammeter et al. (2002), in their research into politics and leaders, found that politics can have a positive impact in enabling leaders 'to minimize the amount of ambiguity that occurs in organizations and to give meaning to organizational phenomena where uncertainty exists' (p. 754).

Revising assumptions in strategic management theory

Building on the literature described above, we propose a challenge to prevailing assumptions, which have seen organizational politics often ignored in strategic management. Additionally, we challenge the view that politics is an inherently negative force in organizations and therefore in strategic management. Three key assumptions have informed the majority of strategic management literature. First is the assumption that organizations are rational and, therefore, strategic management processes are also rational. We propose instead that organizations and strategic management are political. Second is the assumption that politics is negative and needs to be eliminated from the strategic management process. We suggest that politics can also be positive, and that positive politics can be used to advantage in the strategic management process. Third is the assumption that effective strategic management should be used to overcome politics and restore rationality. We propose instead that strategic management account for politics and seek to incorporate positive aspects of it within the management processes.

First consider the assumption that organizations and strategic management are inherently political. There is increasing acceptance in the organizational literature that politics is an inherent part of organizations. Davis and Gardner (2004) note that 'political behaviour is a fact of life in every organization and probably necessary to their effective operation' (p. 441). Narayanan and Fahey (1982) also adopt this view, stating that the rational model of organizations and associated unitary perspective is not relevant to the reality of organizations. Instead, organizations can be viewed as 'loose structures of interests and demands, competing for organizational attention and resources, and resulting in conflicts which are never completely resolved' (p. 27).

This differs markedly from rationalist assumptions, which underlie much of strategic management literature and practice. Lewis (2002) suggests that the dominant unitarist assumptions of management theorists mean that they 'largely ignore the role of power in organizational life and prefer to think of authority, leadership and control as strategies of the managerial prerogative of guiding the organization towards achieving common goals' (p. 29). Similarly, Butcher and Clarke (2002) note that the accepted rational view of the organization requires that employees 'appreciate the rational logic of working collaboratively in order to share effort and knowledge in the wider interests of the enterprise' (p. 39).

Organizationally, this rational approach has called for the use of a formal strategic planning system (Hart, 1992). Dean and Sharfman (1993) note that 'most of the strategic management literature is explicitly or implicitly based on the assumption of rationality' (p. 1070). This approach remains dominant in teaching and practice (Boyd and Reuning-Elliott, 1998; Mintzberg et al., 1998), and can be characterized by words such as analysis, synthesis, formal, structured and timetabled. Farjoun (2002) describes it as 'mechanistic' and it is exemplified by the design school approach (Mintzberg, 1990). The term 'synoptic', meaning comprehensive, formal and sophisticated, has also been used (see for example Hendrick, 2003). Perhaps a reflection of the extreme to which these rational views of organizations underlie the strategic management literature is the paper by Lyles and Lenz (1982), which identifies the human 'problems' which emerge in planning. The term 'problem' implies that the dominant planning process designs do not account for the fact that people would be using them, and therefore people's behaviour became recognized as a problem to be solved, rather than an inherent part of the planning process itself.

Parallels with the treatment of politics in strategic management can be drawn in other areas of organizational theory. In their consideration of the implementation of business process re-engineering (BPR), Knights and McCabe (1998) make a similar point that politics has been largely ignored, that BPR is seen by its proponents as a 'technical process untrammeled by human aspects of the organization' rather than operating 'within a context of organizational politics and indeed representative of these politics' (Taylor, 1995 in Knights and McCabe, 1998, p. 774). Vigoda's (2000) explanation of why public sector organizations were long neglected in the study of organizational politics demonstrates the strength of the assumption that the implementation of formal processes will overcome politics. He points out that it was assumed that formal structures and bureaucracy prevented politics from emerging. Similarly, Ammeter et al. (2002) note that traditional theories of leadership have ignored politics and have 'labored under implicit assumptions of rationality' (p. 753).

If the assumption that organizations behave rationally is accepted, it becomes clear why strategic management has not embraced a political perspective: it simply isn't necessary. However, as Pfeffer (1992) comments, 'it is not clear that by ignoring the social realities of power and influence we can make them go away' (p. 30). Masking political behaviour with rational processes does not reduce its effect: 'all organizations strive for the appearance of rationality and the use of proper procedures, including using information and analysis to justify decisions, even if this information and analysis is mustered after the fact to ratify a decision that has been made for other reasons (Pfeffer, 1992, p. 71). Similarly, Narayanan and Fahey (1982) point out that strategic planning doesn't actually overcome politics, despite appearances; rather it creates the 'appearance of rationality, rather than rationality per se, defined in organizational terms' (p. 28).

Further, strategic management is, by its very nature, associated with change and with bringing new and different ideas and initiatives into the organization. This is almost certain to threaten entrenched personal or organizational interests. The introduction of new ideas will generate opposition from those who are affected by change. Dean and Sharfman (1993) point out that 'decisions are arenas where individuals compete to satisfy their interest. Preferences are based on subunit and individual goals, rather than organizational goals; thus conflicts of interest and political behaviour are seen as inevitable' (p. 1071). Opposition to the introduction of new ideas is likely to be associated with conflict. Since it is widely recognized that OP occurs in the face of conflict or potential conflict (Bradshaw-Camball and Murray, 1991; Darr and Johns, 2004; Drory and Romm, 1990), it is clear that politics will arise in the strategic management process.

Our second revised assumption is that, while politics can have a negative impact on the strategic management process, it can also have a positive impact. A second, and perhaps more important, reason that politics has been ignored in strategic management may be the assumption that organizations are political, but that they *shouldn't be* – that is, that politics is aberrant and negative behaviour that needs to be minimized or eliminated. Typically, political behaviours are defined in the negative, for example, informal, non-sanctioned, manipulative, covert actions which are inconsistent with acceptable norms. Other authors have focused on the purpose of the behaviour, suggesting that OP is behaviour that is inherently negative because the purpose or intent behind it is negative; that is, its intention is self-serving. Additionally, it is assumed to have an adverse organizational impact. For example, political behaviour is believed to be displayed for the purpose of promoting self-interest 'without regard for and even at the expense of organizational goals' (Valle and Witt, 2001, p. 380), and 'for one's own ends' (Dean and Sharfman, 1993, p. 1072).

This negative view of the impact of politics on organizations extends to consideration of the impact of politics on strategy. As summarized above, the few studies which empirically considered the impact of politics on strategic management have found the impact to be largely negative. For example, Voyer (1994) found that politics had an indirectly negative impact on strategic management by adversely affecting the quality of management, Eisenhardt and Bourgeois (1988) found an association between high levels of politics in strategic decision making and poor firm performance, and Dean and Sharfman (1993) found that rationally based decisions are associated with more successful strategic decisions than are politically based decisions.

While the majority of scholars have defined politics as inherently negative, a smaller proportion of definitions find that political behaviour can be positive. As noted above,

Zahra (1987) found that some elements of the strategic planning process were positively impacted by the presence of OP, including quality of long-range planning, effective selection of strategy, effective resource allocation among competing units and effective strategy implementation. While Zahra did not differentiate between positive and negative political tactics, Zanzi and O'Neill (2001) suggest that the political tactic used can be either positive (sanctioned) or negative (non-sanctioned), regardless of the purpose for which the tactic is used. They suggest that positive or sanctioned political tactics include 'use of expertise', 'super-ordinate goals', 'networking', 'coalition building', 'persuasion' and 'image building'. Non-sanctioned or negative political tactics are: 'intimidation and innuendoes', 'manipulation', 'co-optation', 'control of information', 'using surrogates', 'organizational placements', and 'blaming or attacking others'.

Likewise, Pfeffer (1992), in arguing that politics is an inherent part of organizations, finds that politics can be negative or positive and it is the intent behind the behaviour that is the determining factor. He suggests that influence and power should not be viewed negatively as they can be used for evil purposes *and* to accomplish great things. In commenting on the commonly negative view of organizational politics, he suggests that 'the end may not always justify the means, but neither should it be used automatically to discredit the means' (p. 35). Buchanan and Badham (1999a) also find that the techniques of influence can be used for own and organizational goals, as needed. Vigoda (2003) argues for a balanced perspective on organizational politics. He suggests that research into OP 'should carefully examine the conditions under which organizational politics is harmful for the organization and/or its surroundings and on the other hand, the conditions under which it becomes a functional component that has a positive influence on organizations and their employees' (p. 25).

Baum (1989) similarly defines politics in a way that allows it to be considered as both negative and positive, based on a combination of behaviours and intent. He finds that positive, or collaborative organizational politics has the potential to add significant value to the organization and the individual. He identifies four types of politics: subordinacy, in which people look for others who are strong on whom they can depend; isolation, in which people try to become self-sufficient by accumulating as many resources as possible; interpersonal conflict, which is the conventional organizational politics of win–lose competition for resources; and career opportunities. This type of politics is interested in preserving personal goals and winning rather than being collaborative, and prevents people from being able to identify with the organization. The fourth type of politics is what he terms 'collaboration', which begins with the assumption that co-workers, including managers, will continue to support one another despite conflicts over real differences and they can, therefore, assert their interests vigorously but securely. It is this fourth type of politics that he suggests is necessary for the effective functioning of organizations.

Existing research on politics and strategic management has not differentiated between positive and negative political tactics. However, we propose that positive political behaviours will positively impact the strategic management process (A), while negative politics will negatively impact success (B) as shown in Figure 12.1. For instance, the use of positive political tactics such as persuasion, reference to superordinate goals, development of coalitions and networking (Zanzi and O'Neill, 2001) will enhance the effectiveness of the strategic management process by, among other things, encouraging debate, improving collaborative behaviour and improving implementation (Baum, 1989; Zahra, 1987). This is

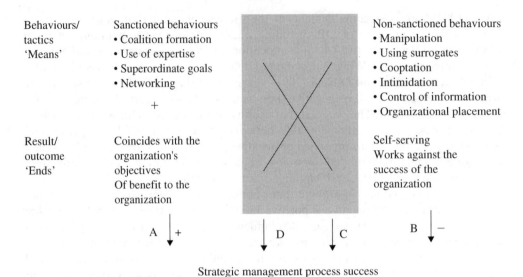

Figure 12.1   Separating political means and ends

because such positive political tactics are consistent with the goals of strategic management, which include the generation of commitment of organizational members, creation of cooperation across organizational boundaries, full consideration of alternatives, and involvement of stakeholders. On the other hand, as is well documented, negative political tactics such as manipulation, control of information and cooptation to pursue self-interest at the expense of others' and the organization's goals will detract from the success of the strategic management process, creating a factionalized organization, distorting information and reducing focus on organizational goals (Eisenhardt and Bourgeois, 1988; Jones, 1985; Zahra, 1987).

A key point that arises from the literature on organizational politics is that to define politics as positive or negative, it is necessary to distinguish political 'means' and 'ends' (Drory and Romm, 1990). Second, both means and ends can be either 'positive' or 'negative', depending on the definition (Figure 12.1). Some authors, such Zanzi and O'Neill (2001), suggest that the political tactic used can, of itself, be either positive (sanctioned) or negative (non-sanctioned), regardless of the purpose for which the tactic is used. Others, such as Pfeffer (1992) and Buchanan and Badham (1999a), suggest it is the purpose of the behaviour or 'ends' which defines it as negative or positive.

Considering the elements of 'means' and 'ends' separately suggests that the relationships between sanctioned behaviour and negative outcome and non-sanctioned behaviour and positive outcome (relationships C and D respectively in Figure 12.1) require further exploration. While a distinction has been made by Zanzi and O'Neill (2001) and others in relation to both the purpose and the behaviour themselves, there remain outstanding questions concerning the distinction between negative and positive political behaviour. This is highlighted by Zanzi and O'Neill's (2001) conclusion that, despite defining positive and negative political behaviour according to the 'means', some political behaviours can be used for both positive and negative outcomes. This suggests that the intent behind the behaviour is also important in indicating whether political tactics are positive or negative. For example, how should one view the use of non-sanctioned political behaviour such as control of information, which has the impact of assisting in the implementation of an organizationally beneficial outcome? Or the use of a positive or sanctioned political behaviour, such as networking, used for a negative outcome, such as the undermining of an agreed course of action?

This brings us to the third revised assumption, which is that effective management of politics is necessary for effective strategic management and that this will involve the proactive use of positive political tactics and the minimization of negative politics. This is in sharp contrast to the assumption that strategic management processes should be designed to overcome politics. Many strategy practitioners have been frustrated that a carefully designed and project-managed strategic planning process, based on the latest management text or MBA school case studies, has been stymied by management 'games', or they are annoyed that managers commit to a strategy in the boardroom about which they later appear to suffer short-term amnesia. However, perhaps the strategy practitioner is not as frustrated as the managers who perceive that the analytical processes they are being 'forced through' are wasting their precious time, or that the head office staff simply don't understand what it is like 'in the real world'.

A micro-political perspective of strategic management

The gaps between strategic management theory and practice will continue while we design strategic management processes based on outdated assumptions of rationality and the inherent negativity of political behaviour, which suggests that enforcing rational processes would help to control politics, restore rationality and result in successful strategic management. These approaches remain dominant in theory and practice (Boyd and Reuning-Elliott, 1998; Mintzberg et al., 1998). One of the reasons that this remains the case may be the existence of sophisticated and highly developed tools which help to create the appearance of rationality. It is difficult to discard these tools, which have the appearances of using logic to produce the 'right' answers and the 'best' plan, despite the fact that they, and the plans they produce, may be rendered useless by politics. As Dean and Sharfman (1993) point out, 'the many complex, prescriptive frameworks for strategic management are pointless unless we believe that top managers carefully and systematically make choices intended to promote organizational success' (p. 1070).

A strategic management process that has been designed from a political perspective recognizes instead that individuals will pursue their own interests. As Stone and Brush (1996) suggest, 'individuals can have goals for the organization but these do not exist independently of participant interests'. In this environment, consensus among organizational participants is not a given; it must be nurtured and developed (Narayanan and Fahey, 1982). Therefore, a strategic management process is needed that recognizes that OP is an ongoing activity requiring continual facilitation of strategy development and implementation, not just a dedicated effort in the three to six months before the development of the company's annual budget.

Moreover, a political approach to strategic management recognizes that strategy is not something decided upon by senior managers and the rest of the organization simply implements it willingly (see for example Burgelman, 1996; Noda and Bower, 1996). As Pfeffer (1992) points out, there are three problems with this hierarchical perspective on implementation of strategic decisions: it is inconsistent with current democratized work-places and participative management practices; it fails to recognize that people must achieve cooperation with those outside a direct chain of command; and individuals at the top of the hierarchy cannot possibly know everything and may make poor decisions. Further, consideration of the broader purpose of strategy identified by recent authors operating from an organic rather than mechanistic perspective (for example Farjoun, 2002; Liedtka, 1998) helps to change the focus of strategic management processes from being purely on the production of a plan to recognizing that the process itself requires management.

Therefore, effective strategic management requires active management of the process and the politics which that involves, rather than an attempt to remove politics. While there may have been some hope for strategy practitioners to ensure that politics did not domi-nate in a 'plan then do' model, there is very little hope of it in an ongoing, iterative process. That is, if the underlying assumption is that strategic management processes are rational, formal decision-making processes, followed by hierarchically controlled implementation of the decision, the use of rational control mechanisms such as performance indicators and performance contracts can be seen to be useful in countering political tactics and achieving strategic goals. In a model where strategy decisions are made in an ongoing and continuous way, and where emergent strategy is encouraged, control mechanisms imple-mented in the traditional way can be expected not only to be ineffective in controlling behaviour; they may actually work against the sorts of behaviour needed for effective strategy to emerge. Narayanan and Fahey (1982) support this view in their argument that the politics of strategic management must be managed in the same way that the rational or analytical aspects are managed. Similarly, Pfeffer (1992) suggests that people in organ-izations must be prepared to use power to accomplish tasks.

Using the political tactics identified by Zanzi and O'Neill (2002) a number of other sug-gestions for the explicit use of political tactics in strategic management are made. First, the political tactic of using coalitions will assist in bringing conflict into the open (Eisenhardt and Zbaracki, 1992), thus enhancing the effective consideration of alterna-tives and helping to ensure that decisions are well considered. Liedtka (2000) notes that strategy is contestable and reflective of the values of those making the choice and, there-fore, strategic conversations will involve the sharing of conflicting points of view. Thus a key strategic management activity is the deliberate encouragement of existing and new coalitions to generate debate and bring issues out into the open for challenge and debate. The ability of people to express their interests 'vigorously but securely' (Baum, 1987, p. 200) is critical to this process.

Another example is the use of political tactics such as persuasion and networking to improve the success of implementation of strategic initiatives. Zahra (1987) found a posi-tive relationship between effective strategy implementation and political intensity. This may be because managers who use tactics of persuasion can help to bring about a higher degree of understanding of initiatives and elicit any opposition to the issues throughout the development of a strategic initiative concept, the decision to implement it, and the realization of its benefits. Furthermore, the use of networks and personal relationships can overcome resistance to ideas in a way that rational argumentation is unlikely to achieve. Strategic management processes should therefore encourage the use of political skills by emphasizing the importance of presenting the case for change to co-workers and managers, and using networks to generate support and impetus for the implementation of ideas. A manager who is not 'equipped, or not willing, to deal with political issues and power plays is thus likely to be outmanoeuvred – and will probably fail' (Buchanan and Badham, 1999a, p. 5). Useful parallels can be drawn with how organizational change practitioners are being urged to deals with politics. Lewis (2002) argues that there is a need for balanced thinking. 'Managers need to retain some control over their organizations' futures. However, political motives will also sometimes drive change and political tactics will always be used in some measures in the implementation of change' (p. 33).

Successful implementation of strategic initiatives depends, in part, on people identifying with and being prepared to work with co-workers to achieve organizational goals. The use of the tactic of superordinate goals whereby activities are justified on the basis of the greater good and purpose of the organization may be useful. As Baum (1989) suggests, for workers to identify with their co-workers and the organization, they 'must participate in politics that enables them to discover and serve collective interest', p. 205. Strategic management activities must establish the environment in which people have the opportunity to debate, understand and contribute to the ongoing development of the organization's purpose and identity. The use of positive political tactics can help people to express opinions and resolve issues honestly on the understanding that they will continue to support one another despite conflicts over real differences (Baum, 1989). For example, strategy practitioners might work to diagnose patterns of dependence and interdependence in the organization, including which individuals are influential (Pfeffer in Buchanan and Badham, 1999a), identify the key players and their main interests, use informal networks to gather intelligence and to send unobtrusive messages, and develop relations with those they know will support them (Jackall, 1988 in Buchanan and Badham, 1999a).

Conclusion

This chapter contributes towards the development of a micro-political perspective on strategic management. A critical review of the existing literature highlights the assumptions that have traditionally informed strategic management theory and practice and suggests that these assumptions must be rejected in favour of assumptions that account for the political nature of organizations. Taking a micro-political perspective helps to identify that strategic management is inherently political, that politics can also be positive, and that positive politics can be used to advantage in the strategic management process; further, effective management of politics is necessary for effective strategic management. Development of the ideas and concepts contained in this chapter will be important in enabling scholars and practitioners to effectively manage politics in organizations. Strategic management processes are important to organizational success, and we should therefore conceive of these processes in a way that allows us to manage the politics that is an inevitable part of them.

Clearly there is an opportunity to further investigate the relationship between organizational politics and the strategic management process. More research is needed into whether political behaviour occurs in the strategic management process in the positive and negative manner surmised above, and whether or not these behaviours have a subsequent positive and negative impact on the strategic management process. Among others, Zahra's (1987) empirical study, Eisenhardt and Bourgeois's (1988) case studies and Narayanan and Fahey's (1982) theoretical model provide significant insight into these issues; however, it is clear that more work is required to understand what occurs and whether and how the success of the strategic management process is affected. Additionally, the assumptions outlined suggest a new way of perceiving strategic management and suggestions are made as to what this might mean for the effective management of strategy processes. Further work is required to identify how strategic management processes can be managed to take full advantage of positive and minimize negative political behaviours.

References

Allen, R.W., Madison, D.L., Porter, L.W., Renwick, P.A. and Mayes, B.T. (1979). Organizational politics: Tactics and characteristics of its actors. *California Management Review*, **22** (1), 77–83.

Ammeter, A.P., Douglas, C., Gardner, W.L., Hochwarter, W.A. and Ferris, G.R. (2002). Toward a political theory of leadership. *The Leadership Quarterly*, **13**, 751–96.

Baum, H.S. (1989). Organizational politics against organizational culture: A psychoanalytic perspective. *Human Resource Management*, **28** (2), 191–206.

Boyd, B.K. and Reuning-Elliott, E. (1998). A measurement model of strategic planning. *Strategic Management Journal*, **19** (2), 181–92.

Bradshaw-Camball, P. and Murray, V.V. (1991). Illusions and other games: A trifocal view of organizational politics. *Organization Science*, **2** (4), 379–98.

Brews, P.J. and Hunt, M.R. (1999). Learning to plan and planning to learn: Resolving the planning school/learning school debate. *Strategic Management Journal*, **20** (10), 889–913.

Buchanan, D. and Badham, R. (1999a). *Power, Politics and Organizational Change*. London: Sage Publications.

Buchanan, D. and Badham, R. (1999b). Politics and organizational change: The lived experience. *Human Relations*, **52** (5), 609–29.

Burgelman, R.A. (1991). Intraorganizational ecology of strategy making and organizational adaptation: Theory and field research. *Organization Science*, **2** (3), 239–62.

Burgelman, R.A. (1996). A process model of strategic business exits: Implications for an evolutionary perspective on strategy. *Strategic Management Journal*, **17** (special issue), 193–214.

Butcher, D. and Clarke, M. (2002). Organizational politics: The cornerstone for organizational democracy. *Organizational Dynamics*, **31** (1), 35–46.

Darr, W. and Johns, G. (2004). Political decision-making climates: Theoretical processes and multi-level antecedents. *Human Relations*, **57** (2), 169–200.

Davis, W.D. and Gardner, W.L. (2004). Perceptions of politics and organisational cynicism: An attributional and leader–member exchange perspective. *The Leadership Quarterly*, **15**, 439–65.

Dean, J.W. and Sharfman, M.P. (1993). The relationship between procedural rationality and political behavior in strategic decision making. *Decision Sciences*, **24** (6), 1069–83.

Drory, A. and Romm, T. (1990). The definition of organizational politics: A review. *Human Relations*, **43** (11), 1133–55.

Eisenhardt, K.M. and Bourgeois, L.J. (1988). Politics of strategic decision making in high-velocity environments: Toward a midrange theory. *The Academy of Management Journal*, **31** (4), 737–70.

Eisenhardt, K.M. and Zbaracki, M.J. (1992). Strategic decision making. *Strategic Management Journal*, **13** Special Issue: Fundamental Themes in Strategy Process Research (Winter), 17–37.

Farjoun, M. (2002). Towards an organic perspective on strategy. *Strategic Management Journal*, **23** (7), 561–94.

Gray, B. and Ariss, S.S. (1985). Politics and strategic change: Across organizational life cycles. *Academy of Management Review*, **10** (4), 707–23.

Harrell-Cook, G., Ferris, G.R. and Dulebohn, J.H. (1999). Political behaviors as moderators of the perceptions of organizational politics–work outcomes relationships. *Journal of Organizational Behavior*, **20** (7), 1093–105.

Hart, S.L. (1992). An integrative framework for strategy-making processes. *The Academy of Management Review*, **17** (2), 327–51.

Hendrick, R. (2003). Strategic planning environment, process, and performance in public agencies: A comparative study of departments in Milwaukee. *Journal of Public Administration Research and Theory*, **13** (4), 491–519.

Jones, R.E. (1985). Internal politics and the strategic business plan. *Journal of Small Business Management*, **23** (1), 31–7.

Kacmar, K.M., Bozeman, D.P., Carlson, D.S. and Anthony, W.P. (1999). An examination of the perceptions of organizational politics model: Replication and extension. *Human Relations*, **52** (3), 383–415.

Kipnis, D., Schmidt, S.M. and Wilkinson, I. (1980). Intraorganizational influence tactics: Explorations in getting one's way. *Journal of Applied Psychology*, **65** (4), 440–52.

Knights, D. and McCabe, D. (1998). When 'Life is but a dream': obliterating politics through business process reengineering? *Human Relations*, **51** (6).

Lewis, D. (2002). The place of organisational politics in strategic change. *Strategic Change*, **11** (1), 25–34.

Liedtka, J.M. (1998). Linking strategic thinking with strategic planning. *Strategy and Leadership*, **26** (4), 30–36.

Liedtka, J.M. (2000). In defense of strategy as design. *California Management Review*, **42** (3), 8–31.

Lowendahl, B. and Revang, O. (1998). Challenges to existing strategy theory in a postindustrial society. *Strategic Management Journal*, **19** (8), 755–73.

Lyles, M.A. and Lenz, R.T. (1982). Managing the planning process: A field study of the human side of planning. *Strategic Management Journal*, **3** (2), 105–18.

Miller, C.C. and Cardinal, L.B. (1994). Strategic planning and firm performance: A synthesis of more than two decades of research. *Academy of Management Journal*, **37** (6), 1649–65.

Mintzberg, H. (1990). The design school: Reconsidering the basic premises of strategic management. *Strategic Management Journal*, **11** (3), 171–95.

Mintzberg, H. (1999). Reflecting on the strategy process. *Sloan Management Review*, **40** (3), 21–30.

Mintzberg, H., Ahlstrand, B. and Lampel, J. (1998). *Strategy Safari*. Harlow: Pearson Education.

Narayanan, V.K. and Fahey, L. (1982). The micro-politics of strategy formulation. *Academy of Management Review*, **7** (1), 25–34.

Noda, T. and Bower, J.L. (1996). Strategy making as iterated processes of resource allocation. *Strategic Management Journal*, **17** (special issue), 159–92.

O'Connor, W.E. and Morrison, T.G. (2001). A comparison of situational and dispositional predictors of perceptions of organizational politics. *The Journal of Psychology*, **135** (3), 301–12.

Parker, M. (2003). Introduction: Ethics, politics and organizing. *Organization*, **10** (2), 187–203.

Peled, A. (2000). Politicking for success: The missing skill. *The Leadership and Organization Development Journal*, **21** (1), 20–29.

Peteraf, M. (2004). Research complementarities: A resource-based view of the resource allocation process model (and vice versa). Unpublished manuscript, Oxford.

Pfeffer, J. (1981). *Power in Organizations*, Boston: Pitman.

Pfeffer, J. (1992). Understanding power in organizations. *California Management Review*, **34** (2), 29–50.

Prasad, L. and Rubenstein, A.H. (1992). Conceptualising organisational politics as a multidimensional phenomenon: Empirical evidence from a study of technological innovation. *IEEE Transactions on Engineering Management*, **39** (1), 4–12.

Schriesheim, C.A. and Hinkin, T.R. (1990). Influence tactics used by subordinates: A theoretical and empirical analysis and refinement of the Kipnis, Schmidt, and Wilkinson subscales. *Journal of Applied Psychology*, **75** (3), 246–57.

Stone, M.M. and Brush, C.G. (1996). Planning in ambiguous contexts: The dilemma of meeting needs for commitment and demands for legitimacy. *Strategic Management Journal*, **17** (8), 633–52.

Sussman, L., Adams, A.J., Kuzmits, F.E. and Raho, L.E. (2002). Organizational politics: Tactics, channels, and hierarchical roles. *Journal of Business Ethics*, **40** (4), 313–29.

Valle, M. and Perrewé, P.L. (2000). Do politics perceptions relate to political behaviors? Tests of an implicit assumption and expanded model. *Human Relations*, **53** (3), 359–86.

Valle, M. and Witt, L.A. (2001). The moderating effect of teamwork perceptions on the organizational politics–job satisfaction relationship. *The Journal of Social Psychology*, **141** (3), 379–88.

Vigoda, E. (2000). Internal politics in public administration systems: An empirical examination of its relationship with job congruence, organizational citizenship behavior and in-role performance. *Public Personnel Management*, **29** (2), 185–210.

Vigoda, E. (2003). *Developments in Organizational Politics: How political dynamics affect employee performance in modern worksites*. Cheltenham, UK and Northampton, MA, USA: Edward Elgar.

Voyer, J. (1994). Coercive organizational politics and organizational outcomes: An interpretive study. *Organization Science*, **5** (1), 72–85.

Wainright, D. and Waring, T. (2004). Three domains for implementing integrated information systems: Redressing the balance between technology, strategic and organisational analysis. *International Journal of Information Management*, **24**, 329–46.

Zahra, S.A. (1987). Organizational politics and the strategic process. *Journal of Business Ethics*, **6** (7), 579–87.

Zanzi, A. and O'Neill, R.M. (2001). Sanctioned versus non-sanctioned political tactics. *Journal of Managerial Issues*, **13** (2), 245–62.

Zanzi, A., Arthur, M.B. and Shamir, B. (1991). The relationship between career concerns and political tactics in organizations. *Journal of Organizational Behavior*, **12**, 219–33.

13 Organizational politics: Affective reactions, cognitive assessments and their influence on organizational commitment and cynicism toward change

Simon Albrecht

Introduction

Organizational politics as a topic has generated significant popular and academic interest. Indeed there is a rapidly growing literature focused on defining the nature of organizational politics and determining the impact it can have on organizational climate and organizational outcomes (Andrews et al., 2003; Vigoda, 2000; Witt et al., 2002).

Most researchers define organizational politics as a negatively valenced construct which negatively impacts on the achievement of organizational goals (Ferris et al., 1989). Mayes and Allen (1977), for example, defined organizational politics as 'the management of influence to obtain ends not sanctioned by the organization, or to obtain sanctioned ends through non-sanctioned means' (p. 675). In a similar vein, Cropanzano et al. (1997) defined organizational politics as 'strategically designed behaviours that maximize self-interest' (p. 160).

The negative impact that organizational politics can have on organizational outcomes has been demonstrated by a number of researchers. Vigoda (2000), for example, found that organizational politics was positively associated with 'negligent' behaviour ($\beta = 0.25$, $p < 0.001$). Similarly, Cropanzano et al. (1997) found a significant positive association between organizational politics and antagonistic work behaviours ($r = 0.23$). Cropanzano et al. also found negative attitudinal consequences associated with organizational politics. They reported significant associations between organizational politics and intention to turnover ($r = 0.29$), job satisfaction ($r = -0.60$) and organizational commitment ($r = -0.63$). Randall et al. (1999) also found a strong negative association between organizational politics and affective commitment ($r = -0.70$).

Attitude theorists (Eagly and Chaiken, 1993; Fishbein and Ajzen, 1975; Forgas, 1994; Rosenberg and Hovland, 1960) have argued that both cognition and affect play an important role in shaping attitudes and determining behavioural intention. A considerable amount of empirical research supports the utility of differentiating between cognitive and affective dimensions of psychological experience. McAllister (1995), for example, identified distinct cognitive and affective dimensions of organizational trust. Organ and Konovsky (1989) identified different cognitive and affective determinants of organizational citizenship behaviour. However, some researchers have argued that the cognitive and affective dimensions of attitudes are not always defined and operationalized in ways that are conceptually clear. Brief and Robinson (1989), Brief and Weiss (2002) and Weiss and Cropanzano (1996), for example, argued that while job satisfaction is generally construed to be an affective state, more often than not, and mistakenly, only its cognitive aspects are measured. Weiss and Cropanzano highlighted the need for researchers to ensure that measures of constructs accurately reflect their intended affective or hedonic tone.

Despite the empirical support and the clear conceptual basis for distinguishing between cognitive and affective dimensions of psychological constructs, measures of these dimensions are often highly correlated. Within the organizational trust literature, for example, McAllister (1995), Clark and Payne (1997) and Cummings and Bromiley (1996) all reported very high correlations between cognitive and affective dimensions of trust. Given such findings, it is incumbent on researchers who distinguish between cognitive and affective dimensions of constructs to provide clear empirical evidence in support of the independence of those dimensions.

Cognitive perceptions of organizational politics
The Perceived Organizational Politics Scale (POPS), developed by Kacmar and Ferris (1991), is arguably the most widely used and accepted measure of organizational politics. The original POPS assessed three negatively valenced dimensions of political activity and behaviour: 'general political behaviour', 'pay and promotion policies' and 'go along to get ahead behaviour'. These dimensions, in part, overlap with negatively valenced 'non-sanctioned' political tactics such as 'intimidation', 'blaming or attacking others', 'manipulation' and 'control of information' identified by Zanzi and O'Neill (2001). Although empirical evidence has been presented in support of the three-dimensional model (Kacmar and Carlson, 1997), most researchers use a unidimensional set of items drawn from the 'general political behaviour' and 'go along to get ahead' subscales to measure organizational politics (e.g. Cropanzano et al., 1997; Hochwarter et al., 1999; Randall et al., 1999; Vigoda, 2000; Witt et al. 2002).

To complete the POPS, respondents rate the extent to which they agree or disagree with items such as 'there is always one group that gets their way in this organization', 'you can usually get what you want around here if you know the right person to ask' and 'in this organization favouritism, not merit, gets people ahead'. Moorman (1993) argued that such traditional 'agree–disagree' Likert scales prompt cognitive, rather than affective, responses. Responses to the POPS can therefore be said to represent employees' cognitively weighted evaluative judgements about the political climate of their organization. Responses to the POPS therefore reflect more closely what employees think about organizational politics as opposed to what they feel about it.

Affective reactions to organizational politics
A number of researchers have called for more research aimed at determining how affective experiences influence attitudes, behaviour and outcomes in organizational settings (e.g. Alimo-Metcalfe and Alban-Metcalfe, 2002; Brief and Weiss, 2002; Fox and Spector, 1999; George, 2000). Despite a resurgence of interest in the role of affective experience in the world of work (Brief and Weiss, 2002; Payne and Cooper, 2001; Mossholder et al., 2000; Wright and Doherty, 1998) very little research has been directed towards identifying how the affective experience of organizational politics might influence organizational outcomes.

In order to progress our understanding of affective experiences at work, a number of methodological issues need to be addressed. First, the questions used to assess affective experience need to be phrased quite differently to those used to assess cognitive evaluations. Moorman (1993) discussed how different measures of job satisfaction tap differentially into cognitive or affective experience depending on the types of questions asked. Affective experience might best be assessed by determining the extent to which people experience particular feelings, moods and emotions (Eagly and Chaiken, 1993). Therefore, as is done when measuring well-being (Warr, 1990), positive mood (Eisenberger et al., 2001), and positive and negative affectivity (Watson et al., 1988), more 'internally focused' questions tapping the extent to which employees *feel* 'enthusiastic', 'motivated', 'fearful' or 'nervous' might provide the most appropriate means of measuring the affective dimensions of organizational politics.

Secondly, George (2000) noted that it is important to be clear about the type of affect being researched, and to distinguish between emotions and mood. Emotions refer to intensely felt and brief affective experiences which are triggered by specific persons or events. In contrast, mood refers to longer-term, less transient and less specifically targeted affective states (Weiss and Cropanzano, 1996). Moods, because of their longer-term duration, will probably have a stronger and more reliable influence on organizational attitudes and outcomes than more transient emotional responses. Consistent with this line of reasoning Watson et al. (1988) developed alternative priming instructions for measures of positive and negative emotions, moods and dispositions. Respondents are asked to focus on how they feel 'right now' (emotions), how they have 'been feeling over the past few weeks' (mood) or 'how they feel in general' (disposition). Similar direction would need to be given when asking respondents to assess the affective experience they associate with political activity in their organization.

A third issue centres on establishing the causal relations between cognitive and affective dimensions of various work-related constructs. The social-psychological and information-processing literature currently provides no unequivocal indication as to whether affect influences cognition or whether cognition influences affect. Although there is clear evidence that affect can influence cognitive evaluations (Forgas and Bower, 1988), and that affect can occur independently of deliberate and high level cognitive functioning (Fiske and Taylor, 1984; Lazarus, 1982), there is also considerable evidence showing that affect arises out of cognitive appraisals (Frijda, 1988; Morrison and Robinson, 1997; Clore et al., 1994; Schwarz, 1990). Morrison and Robinson, for example, showed that the affective experience associated with psychological contract violation is a consequence of cognitive interpretational processes. Similarly, Eisenberger et al. (2001) showed that cognitively based perceptions of organizational support directly influence employee experiences of positive mood.

A final research issue centres on identifying and operationalizing the positive dimensions of organizational politics. Just as models of affective disposition (Watson et al., 1988) and affective well-being at work (Warr, 1990) incorporate both positive and negative dimensions, any examination of employees' affective responses to organizational politics should canvass both positive and negative reactions. Indeed, given that theorists and researchers (e.g. Ferris et al., 1994; Ferris and Kacmar, 1992; Morgan, 1997; Pfeffer, 1992; Williams and Dutton, 2000) have argued that political behaviour is a normal and necessary part of organizational life, political 'tactics' (Kipnis, 1990; Mayes and Allen, 1977; Pfeffer, 1981; Zanzi et al., 1991) such as 'coalition building', 'mentoring', 'persuasion' and 'networking' need not be seen in a negative light. Indeed the exercise of such tactics may be regarded as an acceptable, desirable and positive part of organizational functioning (Zanzi and O'Neill, 2001). Positive affective states might well be felt by people engaging in or experiencing such 'sanctioned' and positive forms of organizational political activity.

In summary, given that organizational politics has been found to be associated with important organizational outcomes, and given that further research needs to be conducted into the role of affect in organizational contexts (George, 2000), the present research focused on establishing the relative importance of cognitively versus affectively weighted dimensions of organizational politics as predictors of key organizational outcome variables. The two outcome variables of particular interest were affective commitment and attitudes toward change. Both of these outcomes are critical characteristics of 'new paradigm' organizations (Bryman, 1996) and are reported to be associated with sustained competitive advantage (Dessler, 1999; Pfeffer and Veiga, 1999).

Research model
The research model (see Figure 13.1) shows the cognitive and affective dimensions of political experience and organizational support influencing affective commitment and cynicism toward change. Given the general paucity of research on the affective dimensions of political experience and the exploratory nature of the study, no unique paths linking to the outcome variables were proposed. Similarly, while being mindful that the affective dimensions may mediate the associations between cognitively framed assessments and the outcome variables, given the exploratory nature of the study, no mediating paths were initially hypothesized. The rationale for each of these associations is outlined below.

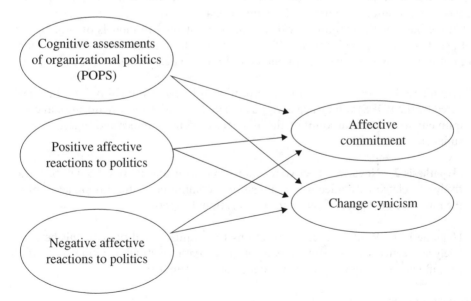

Figure 13.1   Affective and cognitive-based dimensions of organizational politics and their proposed influence on affective commitment and cynicism towards organizational change

Organizational politics and affective commitment
Theoretical frameworks modelling antecedents, correlates and consequences of organizational politics (Ferris et al., 1989; Vigoda, 2000) consistently show organizational commitment as a direct consequence of organizational politics. Consistent with social exchange theory (Blau, 1964), Vigoda argued that when an employee feels adversely affected by organizational politics, 'he/she will be inclined to react initially by reducing . . . attachment to the organization' (p. 330). Given that attachment is a defining feature of affective organizational commitment (Mowday et al., 1979; Allen and Meyer, 1990; Meyer et al., 1993), significant associations between all three dimensions of organizational politics and affective commitment might well be expected.

It needs to be noted, however, that despite strong theory linking organizational politics and organizational commitment, the empirical evidence in support of this link is mixed. For example, although Vigoda (2000) reported a significant association between politics and commitment, Randall et al. (1999) reported that when politics and support were simultaneously entered into regression equations, 'at least one of them always dropped to nonsignificance' (p. 156). Cropanzano et al. (1997) reported similar results. Recent research by Hochwarter et al. (2003) suggests that organizational support fully mediates the relationship between organizational politics and affective commitment. Moreover, given the strength of association between organizational politics and organizational support ($r = -0.83$; Rhoades and Eisenberger, 2002) and the limited amount of research that has included both variables, further research is needed to identify the relative salience of each variable and to identify the direct and indirect pathways by which these variables influence affective commitment. More generally, Cropanzano et al. (1997) argued that organizational support should routinely be included in studies looking at associations between organizational politics and organizational outcomes.

On the basis of the empirical evidence and consistent with models of organizational politics (Ferris et al., 1989; Vigoda, 2000), both the affective and cognitive dimensions of organizational politics were here predicted to be associated with affective commitment.

Hypothesis 1 Cognitively framed perceptions of organizational politics (as measured by the POPS) will be negatively associated with affective organizational commitment after taking account of the influence of demographics and organizational support.

Hypothesis 2 Negative affective reactions to organizational politics will be negatively associated with affective organizational commitment after taking account of the influence of demographics and organizational support.

Hypothesis 3 Positive affective reactions to organizational politics will be positively associated with affective organizational commitment after taking account of the influence of demographics and organizational support.

Attitudes to change
Given that organizational change is a necessary and constant feature of contemporary organizational experience (Weick and Quinn, 1999), it is important to understand which organizational factors influence positive and negative attitudes toward change.

Involvement in change and trust in senior management have been shown to positively influence attitudes toward change (Albrecht, 2003). Organizational politics has been shown to adversely influence attitudes toward change and impede the implementation of change (Beer et al., 1990; Beer and Eisenstat, 1996; Maurer, 1996; Rousseau and Tijoriwala, 1999; Rummelt, 1995). Rousseau and Tijoriwala, for example, found that if employees view politics in a negative light, they will be less inclined to trust managerial communication about change and more likely to have negative attitudes towards it.

Within the literature focused on understanding employee attitudes toward organizational change (Armenakis et al., 1993; Judge et al., 1999; Rousseau and Tijoriwala, 1999; Wanberg and Banas, 2000), a number of researchers have focused more specifically on employee cynicism toward change (Abraham, 2000; Andersson and Bateman, 1997; Dean et al., 1998; Reichers et al., 1997). Wanous et al., (2000), in part, defined cynicism about organizational change as 'a pessimistic viewpoint about change efforts being successful' (p. 133). Extrapolating from the more general organizational change research, it was expected that this 'pessimistic' viewpoint would probably be associated with cognitive and affective dimensions of organizational politics. More formally, it was hypothesized that the affectively and cognitively framed dimensions of organizational politics would influence cynicism to change in the following ways:

Hypothesis 4 Cognitively framed assessments of organizational politics (as measured by the POPS) will be positively associated with cynicism toward change after taking account of the influence of demographics and organizational support.

Hypothesis 5 Negative affective reactions to organizational politics will be positively associated with cynicism toward change after taking account of the influence of demographics and organizational support.

Hypothesis 6 Positive affective reactions to organizational politics will be negatively associated with cynicism toward change after taking account of the influence of demographics and organizational support.

Method

Procedure
Questionnaire data were collected from full-time employees working in a diverse range of occupational settings. Questionnaires were administered by students who, as part of their course of studies, were trained in survey administration techniques and exposed to the practical and ethical imperatives of administering survey questionnaires (Kraut, 1996). Each student was tasked with personally administering ten questionnaires to full-time employees who had been working at their place of employment for more than one year. Each questionnaire was accompanied by a cover letter, a participant information sheet and a return envelope addressed to the researcher. Participants were assured that their responses would remain confidential and that under no circumstances would their employing organization receive information about individual responses.

Of the 440 questionnaires distributed, 364 usable responses were received. This represents a response rate of 83 per cent. The final sample consisted of 187 females (51 per cent) and 177 males (49 per cent). The average age of the respondents was 32 years (S.D. = 10.77) and ranged from 19 to 60 years. All respondents were full-time employees who, on average, had been working within their organization for 5.6 years (S.D. = 6.98, range = 1–38 years). Two hundred and twenty-eight respondents (63 per cent) were employed in the private sector, 118 (32 per cent) in the public sector, 14 (4 per cent) in the not-for-profit sector, and 4 (1 per cent) did not indicate the sector within which they work. Finally, 125 (35 per cent) respondents classified their job as professional, 115 (31 per cent) as clerical, sales and service, 47 (13 per cent) as manager/administrator, 35 (9 per cent) as associate professional, 28 (8 per cent) as trades and related, 11 (3 per cent) as labourer and related, and 3 (1 per cent) as production and transport.

Measures
Cognitively framed organizational politics was assessed with a set of items drawn from Kacmar and Ferris's (1991) Perceived Organizational Politics Scale (POPS). The eight-item scale consisted of items drawn from the 'general political behaviour' and the 'go along to get ahead' subscales. Alpha coefficients for similar adaptations of the POPS have ranged from 0.79 (Cropanzano et al., 1997) to 0.93 (Nye and Witt, 1993). Items included 'you can usually get what you want around here if you know the right person to ask' and 'I have seen policy changes here that only serve the purposes of a few individuals, not the work unit or organization as a whole'. The full set of items is presented in the Appendix. Response alternatives were anchored on a five-point Likert scale where 1 corresponded to 'strongly disagree' and 5 corresponded to 'strongly agree'.

Negative affective reactions to organizational politics were assessed with a self-devised scale consisting of six items drawn from previously published measures of work-related affect (Warr, 1990; Watson et al., 1988). The six items represented the highest-loading items resulting from preliminary factor analysis of a larger 23-item set. Respondents were asked to rate, for example, the extent to which the politics in their organization had made them feel 'nervous', 'uncomfortable', 'fearful' and 'upset'. The full set of items is presented in the Appendix. Response alternatives were anchored on a seven-point scale where 1 corresponded to 'not at all' and 7 corresponded to 'to a very great extent'.

Positive affective reactions to organizational politics were similarly assessed with a self-devised scale consisting of six items drawn from previously published measures of work-related affect (Warr, 1990; Watson et al., 1988). The six items represented the highest-loading items resulting from preliminary factor analysis of a larger 13-item set. Respondents were asked to rate the extent to which the politics in their organization made them feel 'enthusiastic', 'motivated', 'optimistic' and 'energized'. The full set of items is presented in the Appendix. Response alternatives were anchored on a seven-point scale where 1 corresponded to 'not at all' and 7 corresponded to 'to a very great extent'.

Affective commitment was measured using a six-item scale adapted from Meyer et al. (1993). Extensive validity and reliability data support the psychometric properties of the scale (Meyer et al., 2002). Consistent with arguments proposed by Magazine et al. (1996), all items were positively phrased. Response alternatives ranged from 'strongly disagree' (1) to 'strongly agree' (7). Items included 'I feel emotionally attached to this organization', 'This organization has a great deal of personal meaning for me' and 'I feel a strong sense of belonging to this organization'. The full set of items is presented in the Appendix.

Alpha reliabilities ranging from 0.85 to 0.87 have been reported for similar scales (e.g. Meyer et al., 1993).

Cynicism towards change was measured with a four-item scale developed by Wanous et al. (2000). Items included 'suggestions on how to solve problems won't produce much real change', 'plans for future improvements won't amount to much' and 'attempts to make things better around here won't produce much real change'. The full set of items is presented in the Appendix. Employees were asked to rate the extent to which they agreed with each statement on a five-point scale ranging from 'strongly disagree' (1) to 'strongly agree' (5). Higher scores therefore suggest higher levels of cynicism. Wanous et al. reported an acceptable full-scale (eight-item) alpha reliability coefficient for their cynicism about organizational change (CAOC) scale ($\alpha = 0.86$). They did not report the reliability for the four-item 'pessimism' subscale, as used in the current study. Albrecht (2003) reported an alpha of 0.92 for the four-item subscale.

Perceived organizational support was measured with a shortened version of Eisenberger et al.'s (1986) well-validated measure of organizational support (SPOS). The eight positively worded items included: 'the organization where I work values my contribution to its well-being', 'the organization where I work really cares about my well-being' and 'the organization where I work is willing to help if I need a special favour'. The full set of items is presented in the Appendix. Responses were made on a seven-point scale ranging from 'strongly disagree' (1) to 'strongly agree' (7). Armeli et al. (1998), Eisenberger et al. (1986), Hutchison and Garstka (1996), and Wayne et al. (1997), using similar scales, have reported alpha reliability coefficients ranging from 0.75 to 0.96.

Analyses
As a first step in the analyses, exploratory and confirmatory factor analyses were conducted to ascertain whether respondents could reliably distinguish between the three dimensions or components of organizational politics. Descriptive statistics were then generated for all variables of interest. Next, a correlation matrix was generated in order to make an initial assessment of the strength and direction of the relationships between the politics measures and the outcome variables. Multiple regression analyses were then conducted to determine the extent to which the demographics, organizational support, and the affective and cognitive dimensions of organizational politics explained unique variance in each of the outcome variables. The predictor variables were entered in blocks. First, demographic variables (age, tenure, education, employment level) were entered into the regression equation. Then, given the substantial amount of research showing that both organizational support (SPOS) and organizational politics (POPS) predict affective commitment, these two variables were entered into the next block. Finally, the newly developed measures of affective reactions were entered to determine whether they explained additional variance in the outcomes beyond that explained by the variables entered previously.

Results

Factor analyses and scale validation
When presenting new measures it is important to provide evidence in support of their construct, convergent and discriminant validity (Hinkin, 1995). Therefore exploratory factor analysis was conducted on the eight POPS items, the six items assessing negative affective

reactions, and the six items assessing positive affective reactions to politics. The resulting pattern matrix, after maximum likelihood extraction and oblimin rotation, is reproduced as Table 13.1. In support of the convergent and discriminant validity of all three measures, the items clearly split into three unique factors (each with eigenvalues greater than 1) and all items loaded strongly on their designated factor. The factor loadings ranged from 0.54 to 0.86. The cognitive assessment of politics (as assessed by the POPS) explained approximately 30 per cent of the variance in the final solution. The positive affective factor explained approximately 21 per cent of the variance in the final solution while the negative affective factor accounted for approximately 10 per cent of the variance in the final solution.

As an additional test, confirmatory factor analysis (CFA), using AMOS (5) (Arbuckle, 2003) and the raw data as the input, was used to assess the construct, convergent and discriminant validity of the three-dimensional measurement model. Table 13.2 shows how competing measurement models compared against a number of recommended 'fit indices' (Marsh et al., 1996): the comparative fit index (CFI), the normed fit index (NFI), the

Table 13.1   Pattern matrix showing loadings of items from POPS, negative affective reactions to politics (NARP) and positive affective reactions to politics (PARP) (n =364)

	Factor		
	1	2	3
POPS 4	0.843		
POPS 6	0.776		
POPS 7	0.746		
POPS 3	0.738		
POPS 5	0.682		
POPS 1	0.676		
POPS 2	0.667		
POPS 8	0.540		
Motivated		0.858	
Excited		0.835	
Optimistic		0.823	
Inspired		0.817	
Enthusiastic		0.813	
Energized		0.787	
Fearful			−0.855
Uncomfortable			−0.806
Threatened			−0.802
Nervous			−0.802
Upset			−0.685
Agitated			−0.651
Eigenvalue	6.0	4.2	1.9
% of Variance	29.8	20.8	9.6

Note: Extraction method: maximum likelihood; rotation method: oblimin with Kaiser normalization; rotation converged in six iterations.

Table 13.2 Fit indices of alternative measurement models (n = 364)

Model	χ2	DF	NFI	GFI	CFI	RMSEA	RMSEA (90% CI)
Null model	4520.40	190					
One-factor	2706.66	170	0.40	0.44	0.41	0.208	(0.201–0.215)
Two-factor	1998.59	169	0.56	0.53	0.58	0.177	(0.170–0.184)
Three-factor	387.87	167	0.91	0.90	0.95	0.063	(0.055–0.071)

Note: NFI = normed fit index, GFI = goodness-of-fit index, CFI = comparative fit index, RMSEA = root-mean-square error of approximation, 90% CI = RMSEA 90% confidence interval.

goodness-of-fit index (GFI) and the root-mean-square error of approximation (RMSEA). NFI and GFI values greater than 0.90, CFI values of 0.95 and above, and RMSEA values less than 0.08 indicate relatively good fit between a hypothesized model and observed data (Browne and Cudeck, 1993).

Table 13.2 shows that the three-dimensional measurement model provided acceptable fit to the data. It also shows that neither the null model nor an alternative one-factor model, where all 20 items were forced to load on a single factor, provided acceptable fit. Similarly, an alternative two-factor model, where all 12 affective items were forced to load on one dimension and all eight POPS items on the other, did not provide acceptable fit.

Furthermore, and in support of the convergent validity of the three-dimensional measurement model, the output showed that all items loaded strongly on their designated factor with standardized parameter estimates ranging from 0.56 to 0.86. Finally, the discriminant validity between each pair of constructs was assessed by comparing chi-square values when the covariance between the two constructs was fixed at 1 to when the covariance between the two constructs were freely estimated (Anderson and Gerbing, 1988). A significant difference in chi-square (with 1 degree of freedom) assures discriminant validity (Bagozzi and Phillips, 1982). Consistent with the moderate and low correlations evidenced in Table 13.2, the three chi-square different tests confirmed the independence of the constructs.

Descriptive statistics
Means, standard deviations and alpha reliabilities for the primary study variables are shown in Table 13.3. The mean score for negative affective reactions to politics (mean = 2.6) corresponded to a scale rating between 'very little' and 'a little'. The mean score for positive affective reactions to politics (mean = 3.4) corresponded to a scale rating between 'a little' and 'to some extent'. The mean score for cognitively framed assessment of politics (POPS; mean = 2.9) was close to the scale mid-point and corresponded to a scale rating of 'neither agree nor disagree'. Moderate levels of affective commitment (mean = 4.4), cynicism toward organizational change (mean = 2.6) and organizational support (mean = 5.1) were indicated.

The alpha reliabilities for each of the scales ranged from 0.88 to 0.93 and clearly suggest acceptable levels of internal consistency. Importantly, the alpha coefficients of the newly developed measures of positive and negative affective reactions to politics ($\alpha = 0.91$, $\alpha = 0.93$, respectively) and the cognitively framed politics scale ($\alpha = 0.90$) clearly exceeded a widely accepted criterion value ($\alpha = 0.80$; Nunnally, 1978).

Table 13.3   Scale ranges, means, standard deviations and alpha reliabilities for affective and cognitive dimensions of organizational politics and outcomes variables $(n=364)$

Measure	Scale range	Mean	Standard deviation	Alpha
Negative affective reactions to politics	1–7	2.6	1.22	0.91
Positive affective reactions to politics	1–7	3.4	1.42	0.93
Cognitive assessments of politics (POPS)	1–5	2.9	0.93	0.90
Organizational support (SPOS)	1–7	5.1	1.04	0.90
Affective commitment	1–7	4.4	1.38	0.88
Cynicism to change	1–7	2.6	0.84	0.80

Note: Number of valid observations varies from $n=361$ to $n=364$ according to listwise deletion of cases.

Correlations

Correlations between the main study variables are shown in Table 13.4. As hypothesized, cognitively framed perceptions of organizational politics (as measured by the POPS) and organizational support (as measured by the SPOS) were both significantly associated with each of the outcome variables. Perceptions of organizational politics was negatively correlated with affective commitment ($r=-0.20$, $p<0.01$) and positively correlated with cynicism toward organizational change ($r=0.44$, $p<0.01$). Organizational support was positively correlated with affective commitment ($r=0.53$, $p<0.001$) and negatively correlated with cynicism toward change ($r=-0.38$, $p<0.01$). These correlations are generally consistent with those previously reported in the literature (Meyer et al., 2002; Vigoda, 2000).

Table 13.4 shows that the correlation between the two newly developed measures of affective reactions to organizational politics was non-significant ($r=0.005, p>0.05$). This result is consistent with the substantial amount of research showing that employee experiences of positive and negative affect are not related (e.g. Bradburn, 1969; Watson et al., 1988; Russell, 1980; Warr, 1990).

Table 13.4 also shows that each of the new measures of affective reactions to politics was significantly related to cognitively framed perceptions of organizational politics (as measured by the POPS). However, the negative affective reactions were more strongly related to POPS ($r=0.46, p<0.001$) than were the positive affective reactions ($r=-0.14$, $p<0.05$).

Table 13.4 also shows that both the positive and negative affective reactions to organizational politics were significantly correlated with the outcome variables. Positive affective reactions were more strongly related to affective commitment ($r=0.41$, $p<0.001$) than to cynicism toward change ($r=-0.11, p<0.05$). Negative affective reactions were more strongly related to cynicism toward change ($r=0.41$, $p<0.001$) than to affective commitment ($r=-0.12, p<0.05$).

Regression analyses

Hierarchical multiple regression analyses were then conducted to ascertain the unique influence of the politics variables on each of the two outcome variables. As mentioned in

Table 13.4   *Correlations between affective and cognitive dimensions of organizational politics, organizational support and outcomes variable (n=364)*

	1 NARP	2 PARP	3 POPS	4 SPOS	5 AC	6 Cyn
1 Negative affective reactions to politics (NARP)	–					
2 Positive affective reactions to politics (PARP)	0.01	–				
3 Cognitive assessments of politics (POPS)	0.46**	−0.14**	–			
4 Organizational support (SPOS)	−0.31**	0.33**	−0.41**	–		
5 Affective commitment (AC)	−0.12*	0.41**	−0.20**	0.53**	–	
6 Change cynicism (Cyn)	0.34**	−0.11*	0.44**	−0.38**	−0.14**	–

Note: *significant at $p<0.05$; ** significant at $p<0.01$ (2-tailed); ns = not significant.

the methods section, the analyses took account of the influence of demographic variables and of perceived organizational support. The results of these analyses are shown in Table 13.5. The table shows the standardized beta weights at each successive step of the regression, with statistically significant predictors indicated by an asterisk, and non-significant beta weights indicated by 'ns'.

Table 13.5 shows that tenure was the only demographic variable significantly associated with affective commitment at the final stage of the hierarchical regression procedure. None of the demographic variables predicted cynicism towards change.

Consistent with Hypothesis 4, cognitively framed perceptions of organizational politics, as measured by the POPS, was significantly associated with cynicism toward change ($\beta = 0.31$, $p<0.001$). In contrast, and contrary to expectations, the cognitively framed perceptions of organizational politics, as measured by the POPS, was not significantly associated with affective commitment ($\beta = 0.01$, ns). Consistent with previous research Table 13.5 also shows that organizational support, as measured by SPOS, was significantly associated with both affective commitment ($\beta = 0.45$, $p<0.001$) and cynicism towards change ($\beta = −0.23$, $p<0.001$).

In partial support of Hypotheses 2, 3, 5 and 6, the newly developed measures of affective reactions to organizational politics each explained additional variance in the outcome variables beyond that explained by the demographic variables, organizational support and cognitively framed perceptions of organizational politics. However, the negative and the positive affective reactions predicted different outcomes. Negative affective reactions to organizational politics predicted additional variance in cynicism towards change ($\beta = 0.14$, $p<0.01$; $\Delta r^2 = 0.02$) but not affective commitment. Positive affective reactions to organizational politics predicted additional variance in affective commitment ($\beta = 0.27$, $p<0.001$; $\Delta r^2 = 0.07$) but not cynicism towards change.

Supplementary analysis – mediation effects
Eisenberger et al. (2001) reported that positive mood mediates the relationship between perceived organizational support and affective commitment. Extrapolating from this finding, it was decided to test whether negative affective reactions to organizational politics mediate the relationship between cognitive perceptions of organizational politics

Table 13.5   Output of regression analyses showing the influence (standardized beta weights) of affective reactions to, and cognitively framed assessments of organizational politics on outcome variables (n = 364)

Variables	Affective commitment	Change cynicism
Step 1 Demographic variables		
Age	ns	ns
Gender	ns	ns
Education level	ns	ns
Tenure	0.17**	ns
R^2 (Adj R^2)	0.08*** (0.07)	0.02 ns (0.00)
Step 2 POPS and SPOS		
Age	ns	ns
Gender	ns	ns
Education level	ns	ns
Tenure	0.22***	ns
Cognitive assessments of politics (POPS)	0.02 ns	0.37***
Organizational support (SPOS)	0.52***	−0.24***
R^2 (Adj R^2)	0.33*** (0.32)	0.27*** (0.26)
ΔR^2	0.25***	0.26**
Step 3 Affective reactions to politics		
Age	ns	ns
Gender	ns	ns
Education level	ns	ns
Tenure	0.20***	ns
Cognitive assessments of politics (POPS)	0.01 ns	0.31***
Organizational support (SPOS)	0.45***	−0.23***
Negative affective reactions to politics	0.03ns	0.14**
Positive affective reactions to politics	0.27***	−0.02ns
R^2 (Adj R^2)	0.40*** (0.39)	0.29*** (0.27)
ΔR^2	0.07***	0.02*

Note: ** significant at $p < 0.01$; *** significant at $p < 0.001$; ns = not significant.

(POPS) and cynicism toward organizational change. Mediating effects involving affective commitment were not assessed given that neither cognitive perceptions of organizational politics nor negative affective reactions to organizational politics influenced affective commitment at the final step of the regression analysis.

A number of steps recommended by Baron and Kenny (1986) were used to determine whether negative affective reactions to politics partially or fully mediated the relationship between perceived organizational politics (POPS) and cynicism towards change. At step 1, it was first established that the independent variable (POPS), in the absence of the mediator variable (negative affective reactions to politics), predicted the dependent variable, cynicism toward change ($\beta = 0.44$, $p < 0.001$). At step 2, it was shown that the independent variable (POPS) predicted the mediator variable ($\beta = 0.44$,

$p < 0.001$). At step 3 it was shown that mediator predicted the dependent variable ($\beta = 0.33$, $p < 0.001$). At step 4, when the dependent variable was simultaneously regressed on the independent variable and the mediator variable, the influence of the independent variable on the dependent variable was diminished. This result suggests partial mediation. Calculation of the Sobel test (Sobel, 1982) and the Goodman (I) version of the Sobel test, confirmed that the indirect effect of the independent variable (POPS) on the dependent variable (cynicism towards change) via the mediator was significantly different from zero ($z = 2.99$, $p < 0.01$; $z = 2.98$, $p < 0.01$, respectively). These results provide clear evidence that negative affective reactions to politics partially mediate the relationship between cognitive perceptions of organizational politics and cynicism toward organizational change.

Discussion
On the basis of data derived from full-time employees in a diverse array of organizations, the relative influence of affective reactions and cognitive perceptions of organizational politics on affective commitment and cynicism towards change was assessed.

The results show that respondents were able to clearly distinguish between a measure used to assess cognitive perceptions of organizational politics (POPS) and the newly developed measures of affective reactions to organizational politics. The positively and negatively framed affective reactions to organizational politics were found to reliably factor into two distinct dimensions, with each occupying roughly equal amounts of the affective space. Consistent with previous research on affect in organizational contexts (e.g. Bradburn, 1969; Watson et al., 1988; Russell, 1980; Warr, 1990), the correlation between the positive and the negative dimensions was close to zero. This suggests that the constructs, rather than defining opposite poles of a single continuum, are independent. In effect, employees who report positive affective reactions to politics will be neither more nor less likely than others to report negative affective reactions.

Positive affective reactions to organizational politics were characterized by feelings of enthusiasm, motivation, optimism and energy. These upbeat and positive feelings were shown to influence affective commitment but not cynicism towards change. It appears therefore that employees who feel 'inspired' and 'motivated' by political behaviour in their organization are more likely to feel connected to their organization than those who do not. The finding that positive affect influences positively valenced outcomes is consistent with previous research. Staw and Barsade (1993), Staw et al. (1994) and Wright and Staw (1999) showed that positive affective states will more likely be associated with positive outcomes (e.g. performance, creativity, efficacy judgements) than will negative affective states. Similarly, Thoresen et al. (2003) argued that job satisfaction, organizational commitment and personal accomplishment, being positively valenced attitudes, would be more strongly correlated with positive affective reactions than with negative affective reactions. Given that this line of argument was supported in the present research, additional research might usefully be directed toward establishing whether positive affective reactions to organizational politics are associated with additional positive outcomes such as organizational citizenship behaviour and job satisfaction.

On the issue of positive reactions to politics, further research might also usefully be directed towards developing a positively valenced equivalent to the POPS. Such a measure, focused for example on 'coalition building', 'mentoring', 'persuasion' and 'networking' (Kipnis, 1990; Mayes and Allen, 1977; Pfeffer, 1981; Zanzi et al., 1991), would probably be strongly associated with positive affective states which, in turn, would be more strongly associated with positive organizational outcomes (e.g. performance, creativity, commitment).

Negative affective reactions to organizational politics were characterized by feelings of fearfulness, discomfort, nervousness and threat. Such reactions have obvious implications for the psychological well-being of affected employees and for organizational climate and morale. Stress researchers and organizational climate researchers have clearly identified that adverse individual and organizational outcomes are associated with negative affective experiences at work (Hochwarter et al., 2003; Parker et al., 2003; Viswesvaran et al., 1999). Irrespective of the negative organizational consequences that might accrue from employees experiencing prolonged negative affective reactions to their work environment, organizational decision makers might also consider their moral responsibility to ensure that employees are not unduly subjected to such distress-related feelings for any protracted period of time.

Negative affective reactions to organizational politics were shown to influence attitudes to change. Consistent with arguments proposed by Thoresen et al. (2003), negative affective reactions were more strongly associated with the negatively valenced construct of cynicism towards change than were positive affective reactions. Supplementary analysis identified that negative affective reactions to politics partially mediated the relationship between POPS and cynicism towards organizational change. This finding suggests that it is the fear, nervousness, threat and upset associated with perceived political behaviour which, in part, explains why employees will be cynical towards change. Additional research might usefully be focused on determining the extent to which negative affective reactions to politics influence additional negatively valenced constructs such as intention to turnover, negligent behaviour (Vigoda, 2000), emotional exhaustion and depersonalization (Thoresen et al., 2003).

The correlations between both measures of affective reactions to organizational politics and the cognitive perceptions of organizational politics (as measured by the POPS) were significant. However, and in contrast to previous researchers who found very high correlations between affective and cognitive dimensions of constructs (Clark and Payne, 1997; Cummings and Bromiley, 1995), in this case, the correlations were either moderate or low. It therefore appears that the constructs were operationalized in a way which enabled respondents to clearly discriminate between them. In addition, and again consistent with arguments proposed by Thoreson et al. (2003), the correlation between the negatively valenced POPS scale and the negative affective reactions to organizational politics scale was higher than the correlation between the POPS and the positive affective reactions to organizational politics scale.

In broad terms, the results therefore have implications for how researchers should operationalize measures of affect in organizational contexts. The form of the new scales, drawn from the wider affect literature (Warr, 1990; Watson et al., 1988), asking respondents to report the extent to which they feel a range of single-word affective indicators, appears to have conceptual and psychometric merit. Although explaining modest amounts of variance in the outcome variables (beyond that explained by demographic factors, organizational support and cognitive perceptions of organizational politics), the format of the scales resulted in reliable measures with explanatory utility. Overall, the unambiguous factor solution and the high alpha reliability coefficients for each of the new affective scales provided strong evidence in support of their measurement properties. Researchers and practitioners can therefore, with some degree of confidence, begin to use these measures to assess the affective domain of organizational politics across a wider range of organizational settings and in relation to a broader set of outcome variables.

Contrary to expectations, the data did not support the prediction that cognitive perceptions of organizational politics (as measured by POPS) would predict affective commitment. When simultaneously assessing the effects of organizational support and organizational politics on affective commitment, only organizational support was significant. As previously noted, Randall et al. (1999) and Cropanzano et al. (1997) reported similar results. By way of explanation, Randall et al. argued that organizational politics and organizational support each have a somewhat different focus and a slightly different frame of reference. They argued that political perceptions are more likely to be made with reference to co-workers and superiors, while perceptions of organizational support are more likely to be made with reference to the organization as a whole. Given that affective commitment is also referenced to the organization as a whole (Meyer et al., 2002), organizational support rather than organizational politics will probably be the more salient predictor. Alternatively, and consistent with the arguments proposed by Thoresen et al. (2003), it may simply be the case that positively valenced constructs (e.g. organizational support) explain more variance in positively valenced outcomes (e.g. affective commitment) than do negatively valenced constructs (e.g. organizational politics). It may also be the case that the relationship between organizational politics and affective commitment is fully mediated by organizational support (Hochwarter et al., 2003; Rhoades and Eisenberger, 2002). Mediation would account for why the relatively strong bi-variate association between organizational politics and affective commitment disappears in the presence of organization support. Overall, further research is warranted to help progress our understanding of how organizational politics and organizational support, after consideration of common variance, differentially predict and influence a wider range of outcome variables.

In summary, the results support the argument that increasing importance should be placed on researching the affective dimensions of organizational experience (George, 2000; Alimo-Metcalfe and Alban-Metcalfe, 2001). Not only did the results support the viability of the measures of the affectively framed dimensions of organizational politics; they showed that the positive and negative affective experiences have differential effects on the important organizational outcomes. Given the clear evidence that organizational benefits accrue from high levels of commitment (Rousseau, 1998; Dessler, 1999), significant opportunities to improve organizational efficiency and effectiveness may be realized by actively monitoring and managing affective reactions to organizational politics. Monitoring and managing more cognitively based perceptions and negatively valenced reactions may not yield the same effects.

At a practical level, the monitoring and managing of organizational politics can be achieved through a range of organizational development initiatives. Climate surveys, for example, which include the variables used in this study, could routinely be administered to diagnose and monitor employee perceptions of and reactions to organizational politics. The measures presented here, being relatively short, reliable and focused, are well suited to this purpose. Climate surveys should help identify areas within an organization where organizational politics is having a positive or negative effect. Survey feedback processes (Golombiewski and Hilles, 1979) could then be used to involve employees in developing strategies aimed at identifying and promoting more conducive and adaptive political behaviour.

The monitoring and managing of organizational politics could also be achieved through a range of training and development initiatives. For example, 360-degree feedback could be used to provide selected managers with feedback on the extent to which they are perceived by their colleagues to be engaging in positive or negative political behaviour. Such feedback processes might help managers gain an appreciation of how their behaviour is interpreted and the impact that it has on the thoughts, feelings and behaviour of others. Similarly, emotional intelligence coaching (e.g. Mayer and Salovey, 1997) might usefully be used to assist senior leaders and managers to better recognize, understand and manage their thoughts, feelings and behaviour.

The research described here represents a first attempt to identify reliable measures of the affective dimensions of organizational politics. These measures may be of use to researchers and practitioners interested in understanding and managing the dynamics of organizational politics. Future research using longitudinal data and structural equations modelling will serve to provide stronger evidence in support of the relationships presented here. Such methods will allow researchers to more rigorously test alternative and expanded models. Future research might for instance focus on how variables such as psychological contract breach (Robinson and Morrison, 1995; Rousseau, 1990), trust (Podsakoff et al., 1990), procedural justice (Cropanzano and Greenberg, 1997; Folger and Konovsky, 1989; Moorman, 1991) and distributive justice (McFarlin and Sweeney, 1992) interact with the various dimensions of organizational politics to predict a range of outcome variables. The influence of dispositional factors, such as positive affectivity, dispositional trust, openness to experience and risk aversion, might also be considered (see Judge and Bono, 2000; Judge et al., 1999). Future research should also look to link the effects of both cognitive and affectively framed organizational politics with more objectively defined criteria.

References

Abraham, R. (2000). Organizational cynicism: Bases and consequences. *Genetic, Social, and General Psychology Monographs*, **126** (3), 269–92.
Albrecht, S.L. (2003). Cynicism toward change in the public sector. In M.A. Rahim, R.T. Golembiewski, and K.D. Mackenzie (eds), *Current Topics in Management* (Vol. 8). Stamford, CT: JAI Press.
Alimo-Metcalfe, B. and Alban-Metcalfe, R.J. (2002). Leadership. In P. Warr (ed.), *Psychology at Work*. London: Penguin.
Allen, N.J. and Meyer, J.P. (1990). The measurement and antecedents of affective, continuance and normative commitment. *Journal of Occupational Psychology*, **63**, 1–18.
Anderson, J.C. and Gerbing, D.W. (1988). Structural equation modeling in practice: A review and recommended two-step approach. *Psychological Bulletin*, **49**, 411–23.
Andersson, L.M. and Bateman, T.S. (1997). Cynicism in the workplace: Some causes and effects. *Journal of Organizational Behavior*, **18**, 449–69.
Andrews, M.C., Witt, L.A. and Kacmar, K.M. (2003). The interactive effects of organizational politics and exchange ideology on manager ratings of retention. *Journal of Vocational Behavior*, **94**, 357–69.
Arbuckle, J.L. (2003). *Amos 5.0: Update to the Amos User's Guide*. Chicago, IL: Smallwaters.
Armeli, S., Eisenberger, R., Fasolo, P. and Lynch, P. (1998). Perceived organizational support and police performance: The moderating influence of socioemotional needs. *Journal of Applied Psychology*, **83** (2), 288–97.

Armenakis, A.A., Harris, S.G. and Mossholder, K.W. (1993). Creating readiness for organizational change. *Human Relations*, **46**, 681–703.

Bagozzi, R.P. and Phillips, L.W. (1982). Representing and testing organizational theories: A holistic construal. *Administrative Science Quarterly*, **27**, 459–89.

Baron, R.M. and Kenny, D.A. (1986). The moderator–mediator variable distinction in social psychological research: Conceptual, strategic, and statistical considerations. *Journal of Personality and Social Psychology*, **51**, 1173–82.

Beer, M. and Eisenstat, R.A. (1996). Developing an organization capable of implementing strategy and learning, *Human Relations*, **49**, 597–617.

Beer, M., Eisenstat, R.A. and Spector, B. (1990). Why change programs don't produce change. *Harvard Business Review*, **68** (6), 158–66.

Blau, P.M. (1964). *Exchange and Power in Social Life*. New York: John Wiley.

Bradburn, N.M. (1969). *The Structure of Psychological Well-being*. Chicago, IL: Aldine.

Brief, A.P. and Robinson, B.S. (1989). Job attitude organization: An exploratory study. *Journal of Applied Social Psychology*, **19**, 717–27.

Brief, A.P. and Weiss, H.M. (2002). Organizational behavior: Affect in the workplace. *Annual Review of Psychology*, **53**, 279–307.

Browne, M.W. and Cudeck, R. (1993). Alternative ways of assessing model fit. In K.A. Bollen and J.S. Long (eds), *Testing structural equation models* (pp. 136–62). Newbury Park, CA: Sage.

Bryman, A. (1996). Leadership in Organizations. In S.R. Clegg, C. Handy and W.R. Nord (eds), *Handbook of Organizational Studies* (pp. 276–92). London: Sage.

Clark, M.C. and Payne, R.L. (1997). The nature and structure of workers' trust in management. *Journal of Organizational Behavior*, **18**, 205–24.

Cropanzano, R. and Greenberg, J. (1997). Progress in organizational justice: Tunnelling through the maze. *International Review of Industrial and Organizational Psychology*, **12**, 317–72.

Cropanzano, R., Howes, J.C., Grandey, A.A. and Toth, P. (1997). The relationship of organizational politics and support to work behaviors, attitudes, and stress. *Journal of Organizational Behavior*, **18**, 159–80.

Cummings, L.L. and Bromiley, P. (1996). The Organizational Trust Inventory (OTI): Development and validation. In R.M. Kramer and T.R. Tyler (eds), *Trust in Organizations: Frontiers of theory and research*. Thousand Oaks, CA: Sage.

Dean, J.W., Brandes, P. and Dhwardkar, R. (1998). Organizational cynicism. *Academy of Management Review*, **23**, 341–52.

Dessler, G. (1999). How to earn your employees' commitment. *Academy of Management Executive*, **13** (2), 58–67.

Eagly, A.H. and Chaiken, S. (1993). *The Psychology of Attitudes*. Fort Worth, TX: Harcourt Brace Janovich College Publishers.

Eisenberger, R., Huntington, R., Hutchison, S. and Sowa, D. (1986). Perceived organizational support. *Journal of Applied Psychology*, **71**, 500–507.

Eisenberger, R., Armeli, S., Rexwinkel, B., Lynch, P.D. and Rhoades, L. (2001). Reciprocation of perceived organizational support. *Journal of Applied Psychology*, **86** (1), 42–51.

Ferris, G.R. and Kacmar, K.M. (1992). Perceptions of organizational politics. *Journal of Management*, **18** (1), 93–116.

Ferris, G.R., Russ, G.S. and Fandt, P.M. (1989). Politics in organizations. In R.A. Giacalone and P. Rosenfeld (eds), *Impression Management in Organizations* (pp. 143–70). Newbury Park, CA: Sage.

Ferris, G.R., Fedor, D.B. and King, T.R. (1994). A political conceptualization of managerial behavior. *Human Resource Management Review*, **4**, 1–34.

Ferris, G.R., Frink, D.D., Galang, M.C., Zhou, J., Kacmar, K.M. and Howard, J.L. (1996). Perceptions of organizational politics: Prediction, stress-related implications, and outcomes. *Human Relations*, **49** (2), 233–66.

Fishbein, M. and Ajzen, I. (1975). *Belief, Attitude, Intention, and Behavior: An introduction to theory and research*. Reading, MA: Addison-Wesley.

Fiske, S.T. and Taylor, S.E. (1984). *Social Cognition*. New York: Random House.

Folger, R. and Konovsky, M. (1989). Effects of procedural and distributive justice on reactions to pay raise decisions. *Academy of Management Journal*, **32**, 115–30.

Forgas, J.P. (1994). The role of emotion in social judgements: An introductory review and an Affect Infusion Model (AIM). *European Journal of Social Psychology*, **24**, 1–24.

Forgas, J.P. and Bower, G.H. (1988). Affect in social judgements. *Australian Journal of Psychology*, **40**, 125–45.

Fox, S. and Spector, P.E. (1999). A model of work frustration–aggression. *Journal of Organizational Behaviour*, **20**, 915–31.

Frijda, N.H. (1988). The laws of emotion. *American Psychologist*, **43**, 349–58.

George, J.M. (2000). Emotions and leadership: The role of emotional intelligence. *Human Relations*, **58**, 1027–55.

Golembiewski, R.T. and Hilles, R.J. (1979). *Toward the Responsive Organization: The theory and practice of survey feedback*. Salt Lake City, UT: Brighton.

Hinkin, T.R. (1995). A review of scale development practices in the study of organizations. *Journal of Management*, **21**, 967–88.

Hochwarter, W.A., Perrewé, P.L., Ferris, G.R. and Guercio, R. (1999). Commitment as an antidote to the tension and turnover consequences of organizational politics. *Journal of Vocational Behavior*, **55**, 277–97.

Hochwarter, W.A., Kacmar, C., Perrewé, P.L. and Johnson, D. (2003). Perceived organizational support as a mediator of the relationship between politics and work outcomes. *Journal of Vocational Behavior*, **63**, 438–56.

Hutchison, S. and Garstka, M.L. (1996). Sources of perceived organizational support: Goal setting and feedback. *Journal of Applied Social Psychology*, **26** (15), 1351–66.

Judge, T.A. and Bono, J.E. (2000). Five-factor model of personality and transformational leadership. *Journal of Applied Psychology*, **84** (5), 751–65.

Judge, T.A., Thoresen, C.J., Pucik, V. and Welbourne, W. (1999). Managerial coping with organizational change: A dispositional perspective. *Journal of Applied Psychology*, **84**, 107–22.

Kacmar, K.M. and Carlson, D.S. (1997). Further validation of the perceptions of politics scale (POPS): A multiple sample investigation. *Journal of Management*, **23**, 627–58.

Kacmar, K. M. and Ferris, G.R. (1991). Perceptions of organizational politics scale (POPS): Development and construct validity. *Educational and Psychological Measurement*, **51**, 193–205.

Kipnis, D. (1990). *Technology and power*. New York: Springer-Verlag.

Kraut, A.I. (ed.) (1996). *Organizational Surveys: Tools for assessment and change*. San Francisco, CA: Jossey-Bass.

Lazarus, R.S. (1982). Thoughts on the relations between emotions and cognition. *American Psychologist*, **37**, 1019–24.

Magazine, S.L., Williams, L.J. and Williams, M.L. (1996). A confirmatory factor analysis of reverse coding effects in Meyer and Allen's affective and continuance commitment scales. *Educational and Psychological Measurement*, **56**, 241–50.

Marsh, H.W., Balla, J.R. and Hau, K.-T. (1996). An evaluation of incremental fit indices: A clarification of mathematical and empirical properties. In G.A. Marcoulides and R.E. Schumacker (eds), *Advanced Structural Equation Modeling* (pp. 315–52). Mahwah, NJ: Lawrence Erlbaum.

McAllister, D.J. (1995). Affect- and cognition-based trust as foundations for interpersonal cooperation in organizations. *Academy of Management Journal*, **38**, 24–59.

McFarlin, D.B. and Sweeney, P.D. (1992). Distributive and procedural justice as predictors of satisfaction with personal and organizational outcomes. *Academy of Management Journal*, **35**, 626–37.

Maurer, R. (1996). Using resistance to build support for change. *The Journal for Quality and Participation*, **19** (3), 56–66.

Mayer, J.D. and Salovey, P. (1997). What is emotional intelligence? In P. Salovey and D. Sluyter (eds), *Emotional Development and Emotional Intelligence* (pp. 3–31). New York: Basic Books.

Mayes, B.T. and Allen, R.W. (1977). Toward a definition of organizational politics. *Academy of Management Review*, **2**, 672–8.

Meyer, J.P., Allen, N.J. and Smith, C.A. (1993). Commitment to organizations and occupations: Extension and test of a three-component conceptualization. *Journal of Applied Psychology*, **78**, 538–51.

Meyer, J.P., Stanley, D.J., Herscovitch, L. and Topolnytsky, L. (2002). Affective, continuance, and normative commitment to the organization: A meta-analysis of antecedents, correlates and consequences. *Journal of Vocational Behavior*, **61** (1), 20–52.

Moorman, R.H. (1991). Relationship between organizational justice and organizational citizenship behavior: Do fairness perceptions influence employee citizenship? *Journal of Applied Psychology*, **76** (6), 845–55.

Moorman, R.H. (1993). The influence of cognitive and affective based job satisfaction measures on the relationship between satisfaction and organizational citizenship behavior. *Human Relations*, **46** (6), 759–76.

Morgan, G. (1997). *Images of Organization*. Thousand Oaks, CA: Sage.

Morrison, E.W. and Robinson, S.L. (1997). When employees feel betrayed: A model of how psychological contract violation develops. *Academy of Management Review*, **22**, 226–56.

Mossholder, K.W., Settoon, R.P., Armenakis, A.A. and Harris, S.G. (2000). Emotion during organizational transformations: An interactive model of survivor reactions. *Group and Organization Management*, **25**, 220–43.

Mowday, R.T., Steers, R.M. and Porter, L.W. (1979). The measurement of organizational commitment. *Journal of Vocational Behavior*, **14**, 244–7.

Nunnally, J. (1978). *Psychometric Theory*. New York: McGraw-Hill.

Nye, L.G. and Witt, L.A. (1993). Dimensionality and construct validity of the Perceptions of Politics Scale (POPS). *Educational and Psychological Measurement*, **53**, 821–9.

Organ, D.W. and Konovsky, R. (1989). Cognitive versus affective determinants of organizational citizenship behavior. *Journal of Applied Psychology*, **74**, 157–64.

Parker, C.P., Baltes, B.B., Young, S.A., Huff, J.W., Altmann, R.A., Lacost, H.A. and Roberts, J. E. (2003). Relationship between psychological climate perceptions and work outcomes: A meta-analytic review. *Journal of Organizational Behavior*, **24**, 389–416.

Payne, R.L. and Cooper, C.L. (eds). (2001). *Emotions at Work: Theory, research and applications in management.* Chichester: Wiley.

Pfeffer, J. (1981). *Power in Organizations.* Boston, MA: Pitman.

Pfeffer, J. (1982). *Managing with power: Politics and influence in organizations.* Boston, MA: Harvard Business School Press.

Pfeffer, J. (1992). *Managing with power: Politics and influence in organizations.* Boston, MA: Harvard Business School Press.

Pfeffer, J. and Veiga, J.F. (1999). Putting people first for organizational success. *The Academy of Management Executive*, **13** (2), 37–48

Podsakoff, P.M., MacKenzie, S.B., Moorman, R.H. and Fetter, R. (1990). Transformational leader behaviors and their effects on followers' trust in leader, satisfaction, and organizational citizenship behaviors. *Leadership Quarterly*, **1**, 177–92.

Randall, M.L., Cropanzano, R., Bormann, C.A. and Birjulin, A. (1999). Organizational politics and organizational support as predictors of work attitudes, job performance, and organizational citizenship behavior. *Journal of Organizational Behavior*, **20**, 159–74.

Reichers, A.E., Wanous, J.P. and Austin, J.T. (1997). Understanding and managing cynicism about organizational change. *Academy of Management Executive*, **11**, 48–59.

Rhoades, L. and Eisenberger, R. (2002). Perceived organizational support: A review of the literature. *Journal of Applied Psychology*, **87** (4), 698–714.

Robinson, S.L. and Morrison, E.W. (1995). Psychological contracts and OCB: The effect of unfulfilled obligations on civic virtue behaviour. *Journal of Organizational Behavior*, **16**, 289–98.

Rosenberg, M.J. and Hovland, C.I. (1960). Cognitive, affective, and behavioral components of attitude. In M.J. Rosenberg, C.I. Hovland, W.J. McGuire, R.P. Abelson and J.W. Brehm (eds). *Attitude Organization and Change: An analysis of consistency among attitude components* (pp. 1–14). New Haven, CT: Yale University Press.

Rousseau, D.M. (1990). Assessing organizational culture: The case for multiple methods. In B. Schneider (ed.), *Organizational Climate and Culture* (pp. 153–94). San Francisco, CA: Jossey-Bass.

Rousseau, D.M. (1998). Why workers still identify with organizations. *Journal of Organizational Behaviour*, **19**, 217–33.

Rousseau, D.M. and Tijoriwala, S.A. (1999). What's a good reason to change? Motivated reasoning and social accounts in promoting organizational change. *Journal of Applied Psychology*, **84**, 514–28.

Rummelt, R.P. (1995). Inertia and transformation. In C.A. Montgomery (ed.), *Resource-based and Evolutionary Theories of the Firm* (pp. 101–32). Boston, MA: Kluwer Academic Publishers.

Russell, J.A. (1980). A circumplex model of affect. *Journal of Personality and Social Psychology*, **39**, 1161–78.

Schwarz, N. (1990). Feelings as information: Informational and motivational functions of affective states. In E.T. Higgins and R.M. Sorrentino (eds), *Handbook of Motivation and Cognition* (Vol. 2, pp. 527–61). New York: Guilford Press.

Sobel, M.E. (1982). Asymptotic intervals for indirect effects in structural equations models. In S. Leinhart (ed.), *Sociological Methodology 1982* (pp. 290–312). San Francisco, CA: Jossey-Bass.

Staw, B.M. and Barsade, S.G. (1993). Affect and managerial performance: a test of the sadder-but-wiser vs. happier-and-smarter hypotheses. *Administrative Science Quarterly*, **38**, 304–31.

Staw, B.M., Sutton, R.I. and Pelled, L.H. (1994). Employee positive emotion and favorable outcomes at the workplace. *Organizational Science*, **5**, 51–71.

Thoresen, C.J., Kaplan, S.A., Barsky, A.P., Warren, C.R. and de Chermont, K. (2003). The affective underpinnings of job perceptions and attitudes: A meta-analytic review and integration. *Psychological Bulletin*, **129** (6), 914–45.

Vigoda, E. (2000). Organization politics, job attitudes, and work outcomes: Exploration and implications for the public sector. *Journal of Vocational Behavior*, **57**, 326–47.

Viswesvaran, C., Sanchex, J.I. and Fisher, J. (1999). The role of social support in the process of work stress: A meta-analysis. *Journal of Vocational Behavior*, **54**, 314–34.

Wanberg, C.R. and Banas, J.T. (2000). Predictors and outcomes of openness to changes in a reorganising workplace. *Journal of Applied Psychology*, **85** (1), 132–42.

Wanous, J.P., Reichers, A.E. and Austin, J.T. (2000). Cynicism about organizational change: Measurement, antecedents, and correlates. *Group and Organization Management*, **25**, 132–53.

Warr, P. (1990). The measurement of well-being and other aspects of mental health. *Journal of Occupational Psychology*, **63**, 193–210.

Watson, D., Clarke, L.A. and Tellegen, A. (1988). Development and validation of brief measures of positive and negative affect: The PANAS scales. *Journal of Personality and Social Psychology*, **54**, 1063–70.

Wayne, S.J., Shore, L.M. and Liden, R.C. (1997). Perceived organizational support and leader–member exchange: A social exchange perspective. *Academy of Management Journal*, **40**, 82–111.

Weick, K.E. and Quinn, R.E. (1999). Organization change and development. *Annual Review of Psychology*, **50**, 361–86.

Weiss, H.M. and Cropanzano, R. (1996). Affective events theory: A theoretical discussion of the structure, causes, and consequences of affective experiences at work. *Research in Organizational Behavior*, **18**, 1–74.

Williams, M. and Dutton, J.E. (2000). Corrosive political climates: The heavy toll of negative political behavior in organizations. In R.E. Quinn, R.M. O'Neill and L. St Clair (eds), *The Pressing Problems of Modern Organizations: Redefining the agenda for research and practice* (pp. 3–30). San Francisco, CA: New Lexington Press.

Witt, L.A., Kacmar, K.M., Carlson, D.S. and Zivnuska, S. (2002). Interactive effects of personality and organizational politics on contextual performance. *Journal of Organizational Behavior*, **23**, 911–26.

Wright, T.A. and Staw, B.M. (1999). Affect and favorable work outcomes: Two longitudinal tests of the happy-productive worker thesis. *Journal of Organizational Behavior*, **20**, 1–23.

Zanzi, A., Arthur, M.B. and Shamir, B. (1991). The relationship between career concerns and political tactics in organizations. *Journal of Organizational Behavior*, **12**, 219–33.

Zanzi, A. and O'Neill, R.M. (2001). Sanctioned versus non-sanctioned political tactics. *Journal of Managerial Issues*, **13**, 245–63.

Appendix

Organizational politics (POPS)
1. There is one group that always gets their way in this organization.
2. There is an influential group in this department that no one ever crosses.
3. I have seen policy changes here that only serve the purposes of a few individuals, not the work unit or organization as a whole.
4. In this organization favouritism, not merit, gets people ahead.
5. People here generally do not speak up for fear of retaliation.
6. People build themselves up by tearing others down.
7. There are 'cliques' or 'in-groups' which hinder effectiveness here.
8. You can usually get what you want around here if you know the right person to ask.

Organizational politics – positive (+) and negative affective (−) reactions
How do you *feel* about the politics in your organization? To what extent does the politics in your organization make you feel:

1. enthusiastic (+)
2. motivated (+)
3. optimistic (+)
4. upset (−)
5. inspired (+)
6. nervous (−)
7. uncomfortable (−)
8. excited (+)
9. agitated (−)
10. threatened (−)
11. fearful (−)
12. energized (+)

Perceived organizational support
The organization where I work

1. . . . values my contribution to its well-being.
2. . . . is willing to help me when I need a special favour.
3. . . . really cares about my well-being.
4. . . . takes pride in my accomplishments at work.
5. . . . strongly considers my goals and values.
6. . . . helps when I have a problem.
7. . . . cares about my general satisfaction at work.
8. . . . would not ignore any complaint from me.

Organizational commitment
1. I would be very happy to spend the rest of my career at this organization.
2. I really feel as if this organization's problems are my own.
3. I feel a strong sense of 'belonging' to this organization.

4.   I feel 'emotionally attached' to this organization.
5.   This organization has a great deal of personal meaning for me.
6.   I enjoy discussing my organization with people outside of it.

Cynicism towards change
1.   Most of the programmes that are supposed to solve problems around here will not do much good.
2.   Attempts to make things better around here will not produce good results.
3.   Suggestions on how to solve problems will not produce much real change.
4.   Plans for future improvement will not amount to much.

14 The relationship between perceptions of politics, social support, withdrawal and performance
Jonathon R.B. Halbesleben and Anthony R. Wheeler

Introduction

The interest in organizational politics as a research construct and practitioner phenomenon has grown considerably over the last decade. To this point, several major reviews of organizational politics have been published summarizing the state of organizational politics concerning individual political behaviors (Johns, 1999), perceptions of politics (POP; Kacmar and Baron, 1999), and theory guiding future organizational politics research (Ferris et al., 2002). These major summaries of organizational politics research have outlined several robust lines of future research that will ultimately lead to multi-level, multi-variable models of how organizational politics influences the behaviors of employees, the processes of human resource management (HRM), and the performance of employees and organizations. However, one clear theme that emerges from major summaries of the organizational politics literature is the need to conduct theoretically grounded empirical research that includes more complex models of how organizational politics, in terms of employee behaviors and employee perceptions, influences important organizational outcomes such as performance.

The goal of the present chapter is to utilize the conservation of resources (COR; Hobfoll, 1989) model to explain the complex relationship between employee POP, social support, withdrawal behavior and employee performance. We accomplish this goal by first providing a brief review of the relevant literature related to these variables, and we develop the hypotheses tested in this research based on the COR model of burnout. We then conduct two empirical studies on two diverse samples that provide constructively replicated findings in support of our hypotheses, and we finally discuss the applications of our findings to organizations, specifically relating to HRM systems and employee performance. Thus we add to the existing organization politics literature by utilizing the COR model of burnout to explain how political behaviors and POP influence both withdrawal and performance behaviors.

Review of political behavior and perceptions of politics

As previously mentioned, most organizational politics research exclusively focuses on either political behaviors or perceptions of politics. While we will not provide an exhaustive review of these areas of organizational politics research, as Johns (1999) and Kacmar and Baron (1999) have comprehensive reviews of each, we discuss pertinent findings of each area of research that are of note to the hypothesized conceptual model of the present study.

In terms of political behavior, referred to as self-serving behavior in the literature, self-serving behavior includes 'self-enhancing perceptions, [taking] undue credit for successes, [avoiding] due responsibility for failure, or [making] self-flattering presentations' (Johns, 1999, p. 2).[1] Volition or intent, whether it be conscious or unconscious, underlies self-serving behavior in that an individual chooses (at some level of consciousness) to distort reality through false perceptions, attributions, or self-presentations (Johns, 1999). The motives of self-serving behavior include a threat to an individual's identity (Ashforth and Mael, 1996) and an individual's desire to accumulate resources (Greenberg and Scott, 1996). Moreover, these motives are heightened in an uncertain environment so that uncertainty will moderate the relationship between identity threat and self-serving behaviors (Johns, 1999). That is, when individuals feel threatened with the loss of resources central to their identity, self-serving behavior increases as environmental uncertainty increases. A main consequence of self-serving behavior is the *actor–observer* bias (Watson, 1982), whereby the actor's attributes of behavior differ from the observer's attribution of behavior. This process inevitably leads to conflict between individuals, which can result in myriad negative individual and organizational outcomes (cf. Johns, 1999).

In terms of POP, Ferris et al. (1989) proposed a theoretically grounded model that explains the antecedents, moderators and outcomes of POP. Their model, which has received extensive empirical support (cf. Ferris et al., 2002; Kacmar and Baron, 1999), proposes that individuals within organizations form subjective POP that lead to attributions about others' political behaviors, which then influence the perceivers' subsequent behaviors (Ferris et al., 1989). Their model also proposes that POP influence employee job satisfaction, job involvement and withdrawal behaviors (Ferris et al., 1989). Subsequent empirical examinations of the POP model have included several moderators of the relationship between POP and organizational outcomes (cf. Ferris et al., 2002; Kacmar and Baron, 1999); however, the relationship between POP and employee performance, both in-role and extra-role, is equivocal (Randall et al., 1999; Vigoda, 2000). In terms of the POP–performance relationship, empirical evidence suggests that environmental or contextual variables influence this relationship (Witt, 1998).

In the present research, we combine the two organizational politics paradigms by including a political behavior, perceptions of managerial social support (Randall et al., 1990), as a moderator of the relationship between POP and withdrawal behaviors, specifically employee burnout. While some research has examined political behavior as a moderator between POP and work outcomes (e.g. Harrell-Cook et al., 1999; Valle and Perrewé, 2000) and found mixed results for these relationships, we examine the influence of political behavior as a moderator of a more complex relationship between POP and work outcomes. This more complex model of the relationship between POP and work outcomes, specifically employee performance, includes employee disengagement as a mediator between the two variables.

Conceptual model
We provide the conceptual model that guides this research in Figure 14.1. We hypothesize that POP lead to withdrawal behaviors, conceptualized as a key symptom of employee burnout. This POP–withdrawal behaviors relationship is moderated by social support, such that employees who perceive higher levels of social support will feel less burned out by their POP than will employees who perceive lower levels of social support. Furthermore, we hypothesize that employee withdrawal behaviors, again conceptualized as employee burnout, mediate the POP–employee performance relationship such that employees who feel burned out as a response to their POP will show a decrease in their performance.

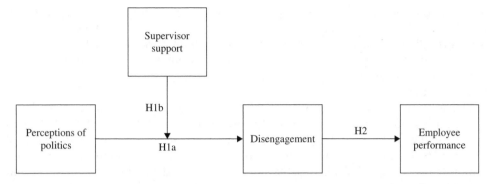

Figure 14.1   Proposed relationships between perceptions of politics, supervisor support, disengagement and performance

POP–performance
As noted by both Ferris et al. (2002) and Kacmar and Baron (1999), most research examining the relationship between POP and employee performance has yielded equivocal findings. Recently, two empirical studies found significant moderated relationships between POP and performance. Treadway et al. (2005) established a relationship between POP and performance, with age as a moderator of the relationship. Moreover, they replicated this finding in three independent studies. Zivnuska et al. (2004) found that impression management moderated the relationship between POP and performance in that employees engaging in impression management reduced the negative relationship between POP and performance. These studies are notable, along with Witt et al.'s (2002) study of Big Five personality traits moderating the POP–performance relationship, in that these researchers demonstrated significant negative relationships between POP and performance. The inclusion of moderators clarifies the relationship between POP and performance, further underscoring the complexity of the relationship (Harris and Kacmar, 2005).

Conservation of resources model
While there have been a number of comprehensive models presented to understand POP (e.g. Ferris et al., 2002), we propose an alternative theory to understand the relationship between POP, disengagement and performance by looking to research in stress and burnout. Hobfoll (1988, 1989, 1998, 2001; Hobfoll and Freedy, 1993) proposed that the key to understanding stress and strain and their effects is to understand the processes underlying resources, which he defined as those aspects of life that we value. The COR model proposes that stress is the result of a threat to resources (e.g. the perception that one might lose one's job), the actual loss of a resource (e.g. the actual loss of the job), or the insufficient gain of additional resources following significant investment of other resources (e.g. the inability to obtain employment following the resources invested obtaining a college degree). In a work context, the stress caused by one of the three paths will lead employees to burn out over time, particularly because the rate at which work demands use up employee resources is typically greater than the rate at which those resources are replenished (Freedy and Hobfoll, 1994). Over the long term, this may lead

to disengagement from work, a key manifestation of strain (Hobfoll and Freedy, 1993). In other words, as employees are faced with demands (perceptions of politics), those demands will lead them to withdraw psychologically from work. One might think of this as a form of coping, as psychologically withdrawing from work allows the employee to regain resources (at least psychological resources) that would have otherwise been invested in the workplace.

The notion of conserving resources helps to explain the link between POP and disengagement. As POP serve as a demand on the worker, they increase the likelihood of stress and, subsequently, burnout (Hobfoll, 1998). POP act as a demand by forcing the employee to expend psychological resources concerned with the political environment in the organization (cf. Vigoda, 2002), whether they choose to avoid the political environment and experience anxiety concerning it or try to use the political situation to serve as an advantage in their own work (Harris and Kacmar, 2005). Over time, the continued demand on the employee's resources will lead the employee to experience burnout, and thus to disengage from work.

Organizational politics scholars conceptualize and operationalize employee withdrawal behaviors in many ways (Vigoda, 2003), including intent to turnover (Valle and Perrewé, 2000; Vigoda, 2001), absenteeism (Ferris et al., 1993), and psychological withdrawal from stress (Gilmore et al., 1996; Vigoda, 2002). Most of these relationships between POP and withdrawal behaviors have been empirically established; however, researchers have yet to link these conceptualizations of withdrawal to the relationship between organizational politics and performance. One possible explanation of this finding, and the findings of other POP–withdrawal research, is that researchers operationalized withdrawal behaviors in the form of organizational withdrawal, not as psychological withdrawal. In other words, by studying withdrawal behaviors such as turnover and absenteeism, researchers may be studying rather distal forms of withdrawal that may not reflect a person's actual response to POP and social support. For that reason, we focus on disengagement. Disengagement is a psychological and behavioral experience of 'breaking away' from work and those people associated with it. It has been commonly studied as a symptom of burnout (Maslach, 1982) and has been found to be associated with subsequent withdrawal behaviors such as turnover and absenteeism (Drake and Yadama, 1996; Geurts et al., 1998; Koeske and Koeske, 1993). As such, disengagement antecedes other withdrawal behaviors and, therefore, may serve as a more direct withdrawal variable for understanding the effects of POP on workers. With that in mind, we hypothesize that POP will be associated with higher levels of disengagement among workers.

Hypothesis 1a   Perceptions of politics are associated with higher levels of the disengagement component of burnout.

As noted by Harris and Kacmar (2005), researchers have examined a variety of moderators to the POP–strain relationship. The COR model suggests that employee resources might offer a potential moderator, as resources serve as a buffer between demands and strain (Hobfoll, 2001). Social support has been a key resource in understanding the stressor–strain relationship, particularly in the context of burnout research (Baruch-Feldman et al., 2002; Carlson and Perrewé, 1999; Schaufeli and Greenglass, 2001). The COR model suggests that as a resource, social support (in this study, we will focus on perceived emotional and instrumental support from one's supervisor) should reduce the relationship between a demand (POP) and strain (disengagement). A such, we hypothesize that for those individuals who perceive higher levels of supervisor social support, the relationship between POP and disengagement will be reduced, as they will have resources that keep them from disengaging.

Hypothesis 1b The relationship between POP and disengagement is moderated by perceived supervisor social support, whereby participants with higher levels of reported social support will experience less burnout as a result of POP.

As we have noted, empirical studies of the relationship between POP and performance have led to unclear results. We have suggested that this is because researchers have not fully considered variables that might influence this relationship. We return to the COR model to understand how disengagement moderate the POP–performance relationship. Hobfoll (2001), based on the work of Baltes and Baltes (1990; Baltes, 1997) has argued that as resources are depleted, we become more careful about how we invest resources in the future. Halbesleben and Bowler (2005) have argued that this leads workers to be more careful about how they invest motivational resources, leading to reductions in job perfor-mance. This suggests that employees who are disengaging from their work will be more careful about how they invest resources such as motivation; as such, supervisors may observe lower job performance among these workers. Therefore, we predict that disen-gagement mediates the POP–performance relationship, where POP leads to disengage-ment, leading the disengaged employee to have lower job performance.

Hypothesis 2 The relationship between POP and employee performance is medi-ated by disengagement, such that POP leads to higher disengagement and the higher disengagement is associated with lower job performance.

Plan of present research
As we plan to test a complex model that includes both moderating and mediating effects, the use of constructive replication should help us to increase the reliability and validity of our results and how we interpret them (Lykken, 1968; Tsang and Kwan, 1999). In Study 1, we test our hypothesized model using a small sample of employees from a single organi-zation. To increase the reliability and validity of the findings in Study 1, we constructively replicated these findings using a large, diverse sample of employees from several organi-zations in Study 2.

Method

Study 1

Participants and procedure Study 1 was conducted with the cooperation of the profes-sional staff at a federal fire department (i.e. firefighters and management). This sample was primarily male ($n = 81$, 98 percent), with an average age of 38.4 years (S.D. = 4.5). Included in the sample were firefighters ($n = 64$, 77 percent), dispatch personnel ($n = 6$, 7 percent), fire inspectors ($n = 3$, 4 percent), and managers/administrative staff ($n = 10$,

12 percent). The fire department was located on a US military base; however, all of the employees of the department were non-military.

Surveys were distributed to the fire department staff in-group sessions and were returned directly to the first author. Of the 91 employees of the fire department, two declined to participate, allowing for a potential sample of 89 respondents. Eighty-five surveys were returned, for an initial response rate of 95 percent.

One year later, we returned to administer a follow-up survey. Again, the surveys were distributed in-group sessions and returned directly to the first author. In the second wave of surveys, 83 surveys were returned, for a final response rate of 93 percent. The measures utilized for this study were part of a larger packet of research measures.

Measures   Perceptions of politics were measured using Kacmar and Carlson's (1997) Perceptions of Politics Scale (POPS). It is a 14-item measure that utilized a five-point Likert-type scale (strongly agree to strongly disagree). A sample item was 'When it comes to pay raises and promotion decisions, policies are irrelevant.'

The *social support* measure of Caplan et al. (1975) was utilized to measure perceived instrumental and emotional support from each participant's supervisor. It has been one of the most widely used social support measures in the study of stress and burnout (cf. Fenlason and Beehr, 1994; Ganster et al., 1986; Ray and Miller, 1994). For the purposes of this study, we collapsed the measures of instrumental and emotional support to create one overall measure of supervisor support.

To measure *disengagement*, we utilized the disengagement subscale of the Maslach Burnout Inventory–General Survey (MBI–GS; Schaufeli et al., 1996). The disengagement subscale includes 5 questions that were scored on a five-point, Likert-type scale; a sample question is 'I just want to do my job and not be bothered.'

To assess *job performance*, the employees were asked to self-report the ratings they received from their supervisor on their most recent performance appraisal. They were asked to provide ratings on each of the nine performance dimensions that comprised their performance appraisal. Because of the very high internal consistency of the nine perform-ance ratings, a mean aggregate score of the dimensions was used as a supervisor job per-formance rating score. The fire department employees were also asked to provide self-ratings for each of the nine performance dimensions. These ratings were also aggre-gated to form a mean self-job performance rating score.

Study 2

Participants and procedure   The participants were discerned from a larger-scale data col-lection that included 606 working adults. Responses from 85 participants were not ana-lyzed because of incomplete data (e.g. missing supervisor data, incomplete surveys), leaving a final usable sample of 521 participants.

The sample included 240 males and 369 females with a mean age of 37.98 years (S.D. = 11.11). The participants had been working for their current organization for a mean of 11.67 years (S.D. = 8.52). A significant majority (76 percent) of the participants indicated that they were Caucasian. A wide variety of industries were represented, including edu-cation (*n* = 102), health care (*n* = 76), government/military (*n* = 72), banking or financial services (*n* = 69), manufacturing (*n* = 52), telecommunications (*n* = 45), and retail (*n* = 29).

The data were collected with the assistance of approximately 230 introductory management students at two universities (one in Oklahoma and one in California) as part of a research experience assignment. The students collected measures from three to five working adults. To ensure that the surveys were indeed completed by the working adults, we randomly selected 50 percent of the surveys and directly contacted the participant to verify their participation. Of those contacted, all of the participants verified that they had completed the survey. This method of survey collection has been effectively used by field researchers in organizational settings (cf. Ferris et al., 2005; Kolodinsky et al., 2004) and is particularly well suited to situations where it can be matched with field data from one organization as it offers an opportunity to generalize beyond the single setting offered by one organization.

Measures To maintain consistency, the measures used for *perceptions of politics, social support* and *burnout* utilized in Study 1 were also used in Study 2. Perceptions of politics were measured using Kacmar and Carlson's (1997) Perceptions of Politics Scale (POPS). The social support measure of Caplan et al. (1975) was utilized to measure perceived instrumental and emotional support from each participant's supervisor. Disengagement was measured using the disengagement subscale of the Maslach Burnout Inventory–General Scale (MBI–GS; Schaufeli et al., 1996). Its five items are intended to be general enough to apply to a wide range of occupations; as such, it was well suited for the present sample.

We assessed *performance* by utilizing the in-role performance subscale of the performance measure developed by Williams and Anderson (1991). This scale was used because it is general enough to fit with a variety of jobs, providing us with a measure that could be used with such a general sample. The subscale is a seven-item, five-point Likert-scaled measure that assessed in-role (task) performance behaviors (sample item included 'adequately completes assigned duties'). This scale was completed by the participant's supervisor. To collect this scale, the participant gave the performance measure to the supervisor, who completed it and returned it directly to the researchers.

Based on a review of the literature, we identified five additional variables that may covary with perceptions of politics, social support and/or burnout, and thus were treated as *control variables* in the analysis. These variables included age, organization tenure, education level, race and negative affectivity. The demographic variables were measured with single-item scales. Negative affectivity was measured using the negative affectivity subscale of Watson et al.'s (1988) positive and negative affect schedule (PANAS).

Results

Study 1
The descriptive statistics from Study 1 and Study 2 are displayed in Table 14.1. To analyze the data, we utilized hierarchical regression as recommended by Baron and Kenny (1986). Specifically, we began the analysis by adding the control variables and main effects into the model (Steps 1 and 2), then added the interaction between perceptions of politics and perceived supervisor social support that was predicted in Hypothesis 1b (Step 3). Finally, we entered all previous variables, including disengagement, as predictors of supervisor-rated performance (Step 4).

After accounting for the control variables, we found that perceptions of politics were not

Table 14.1 Scale means, standard deviations, internal reliability estimates and interscale correlations

	Study 1		Study 2		1	2	3	4	5	6	7	8	9
	Mean	S.D.	Mean	S.D.									
1. Gender	—	—	0.60	0.49	—	0.11*	-0.12**	-0.05	-0.05	-0.07	0.09*	-0.04	0.09*
2. Age	39.25	6.68	37.98	11.11	—	—	0.05	-0.16**	-0.23***	-0.01	-0.14**	0.15**	0.24***
3. Education	—	—	3.41	0.92	—	—	—	-0.02	-0.09*	-0.02	-0.05	0.09*	0.08*
4. Race	—	—	1.64	1.29	—	—	—	—	0.15**	0.07	0.07	0.00	-0.18***
5. Neg. affect.	3.18	0.67	1.92	0.70	—	-0.03	—	—	0.93/0.87	0.14**	0.39***	-0.26***	0.20***
6. POPS	4.04	0.78	2.84	0.79	—	-0.10	—	—	-0.12	0.92/0.90	0.25***	-0.12**	-0.09*
7. Disengagement	3.02	1.24	2.56	0.91	—	0.05	—	—	-0.02	-0.08	0.93/0.86	-0.48***	-0.27***
8. Support	3.09	1.41	3.59	0.91	—	-0.03	—	—	0.00	0.02	-0.82***	0.94/0.81	0.23***
9. Performance	7.38	0.94	4.02	0.75	—	-0.08	—	—	0.05	0.07	-0.51***	-0.51***	0.96/0.85

Note: Study 1 (Firefighters) data are below the diagonal; Study 2 (working adults) data are above the diagonal. Internal consistency estimates (Cronbach's alpha) are along the diagonal, with Study 1 alpha before the slash (/) and Study 2 alpha after the slash. Gender was coded 0 = male, 1 = female. Education level was divided into four categories: 1 = high school diploma, 2 = two-year degree, 3 = bachelor's degree, and 4 = graduate degree. Race was coded 1 = white/Caucasian, 2 = black/African-American, 3 = Hispanic/Latino, 4 = Asian/Pacific Islander, 5 = Native American, 6 = Other. * indicates $p < 0.05$, ** indicates $p < 0.01$, *** indicates $p < 0.001$.

Table 14.2   Study 1 regression results

	Step 1		Step 2		Step 3		Step 4	
	β	SE	β	SE	β	SE	β	SE
Age	0.00	0.02	0.00	0.01	0.00	0.01	−0.01	0.01
Negative affectivity	−0.05	0.21	−0.04	0.12	−0.01	0.12	0.08	0.13
Perceptions of politics	−0.12	0.18	−0.10	0.10	0.69*	0.32	−0.46	0.37
Social support			−0.72***	0.06	0.13	0.33	0.58	0.38
Social support * POPS					−0.21*	0.08	−0.11	0.09
Disengagement							−0.26*	0.13
R^2	0.01		0.67		0.70		0.31	
ΔR^2			0.66***		0.03*		n/a	

Note: * indicates $p<0.05$; ** indicates $p<0.01$; *** indicates $p<0.001$.

associated with disengagement ($\beta = -0.12, p = 0.49$; see Table 14.2), contrary to Hypothesis 1a. Upon entering supervisor social support into the regression equation, we found that support was inversely associated with disengagement ($\beta = -0.72, p<0.001$) and perceptions of politics were not a significant predictor of disengagement ($\beta = -0.10, p = 0.36$); the addition of support resulted in an increase in the variance in disengagement accounted for by 0.66 ($p<0.01$). Next, we entered the interaction between perceptions of politics and support into the regression equation, finding that it was a significant inverse predictor of disengagement ($\beta = -0.21, p = 0.01, \Delta R^2 = 0.03, p<0.05$). The negative direction of the interaction supported the contention that those who perceive higher social support have less of a relationship between perceptions of politics and disengagement; this relationship is depicted graphically in Figure 14.2. This finding lent support to Hypothesis 1b. Finally, when we conducted the regression that included the previous steps predicting supervisor-rated performance and added disengagement, we found that disengagement was a significant inverse predictor of performance ($\beta = -0.26, p = 0.04$), supporting Hypothesis 2.

Study 2
In Study 2, we used a similar analysis strategy as had been utilized in Study 1. After accounting for the control variables, we found that perceptions of politics were positively associated with emotional disengagement ($\beta = 0.22, p<0.001$; see Table 14.3), supporting Hypothesis 1a. Upon entering supervisor social support into the regression equation, we found that support was inversely associated with disengagement ($\beta = -0.37, p<0.001$) and perceptions of politics remained a significant predictor of disengagement ($\beta = 0.17$, $p<0.001$); moreover, the addition of support resulted in an increase in the variance in disengagement accounted for by 0.13 ($p<0.01$). Next, we entered the interaction between perceptions of politics and support into the regression equation, finding that it was a significant inverse predictor of disengagement ($\beta = -0.14, p<0.001, \Delta R^2 = 0.02$, $p <0.05$). The negative direction of the interaction supported the contention that those who perceive higher social support have less of a relationship between perceptions of politics and disengagement; this relationship is depicted graphically in Figure 14.3. This finding supported Hypothesis 1b. Finally, when we conducted the regression that

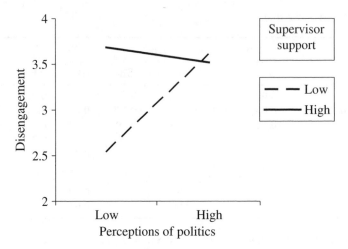

Figure 14.2   The interactive effect of perceptions of politics and supervisor support on disengagement in Study 1

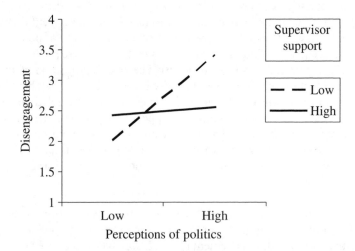

Figure 14.3   The interactive effect of perceptions of politics and supervisor support on disengagement in Study 2

included the previous steps predicting supervisor-rated performance and added disengagement, we found that disengagement was a significant inverse predictor of performance ($\beta = -0.08$, $p < 0.001$), supporting Hypothesis 2.

General discussion
The findings in the present studies support the notion that conservation of resources may be a driving factor in the relationship between POP, withdrawal and performance. The relative consistency across the two studies provided a constructive replication (Tsang and

Table 14.3   Study 2 regression results

	Step 1		Step 2		Step 3		Step 4	
	β	SE	β	SE	β	SE	β	SE
Gender	0.16*	0.07	0.14*	0.07	0.13	0.07	0.14*	0.06
Age	0.00	0.00	0.00	0.00	0.00	0.00	0.01	0.00
Education	0.01	0.04	0.05	0.04	0.06	0.04	0.02	0.03
Race	0.00	0.03	0.01	0.03	0.01	0.03	−0.08*	0.02
Negative affectivity	0.48***	0.05	0.40***	0.05	0.38***	0.05	−0.06	0.05
Perceptions of politics	0.22***	0.05	0.17***	0.04	0.69***	0.16	−0.33*	0.16
Social support			−0.37***	0.04	0.04	0.12	−0.17	0.12
Social support * POPS					−0.14**	0.04	0.09*	0.04
Disengagement							−0.08*	0.04
R^2	0.20		0.33		0.35		0.14	
ΔR^2			0.13**		0.02*		n/a	

Note: Gender was coded 0 = male, 1 = female. Education level was divided into four categories: 1 = high school diploma, 2 = two-year degree, 3 = bachelor's degree, and 4 = graduate degree. Race was coded 1 = white/Caucasian, 2 = black/African-American, 3 = Hispanic/Latino, 4 = Asian/Pacific Islander, 5 = Native American, 6 = Other. * indicates $p < 0.05$; ** indicates $p < 0.01$; *** indicates $p < 0.001$.

Kwan, 1999) and offered further credence to our predictions concerning the relationships between the variables of interest.

Overall, the findings supported our contention that the relationship between perceptions of politics and burnout was moderated by social support. Moreover, the pattern of interaction suggested that those higher in perceived supervisor social support had a less strong relationship between perceptions of politics and burnout than those who perceived lower social support. Finally, the results supported the prediction that disengagement would be associated with lower job performance.

Interestingly, perceptions of politics were not associated with disengagement in Study 1, as had been expected in Hypothesis 1a. While this was unexpected, it may give further credence to the argument that the perceptions of politics–strain relationship is complex and that other variables, such as social support, must be considered to fully understand the relationship between these two variables.

The present research adds to the existing literature in several ways. First, it provides a framework for understanding the processes underlying outcomes of perceptions of politics. While we will not suggest that the COR framework replace previously proposed models of perceptions of politics, it does add to the previous theoretical work by providing an explanatory process that underlies the relationship between POP and their outcomes. Our model suggests that understanding the interplay between demands (POP) and resources (support) will allow managers to better understand the potentially negative outcomes of POP. It allows managers an opportunity to avoid the negative outcomes of POP by supplementing employee resources through support. Moreover, as Drory and Romm (1990) noted, politics, through its links with power, represents a resource within organizations. This suggests that resource-based theories of politics and perceptions of politics may be useful in understanding underlying political processes in organizations.

This work also extends previous work in POP by using a more primary form of withdrawal behavior, disengagement. Disengagement is likely to occur before other withdrawal behaviors such as turnover and, as such, may be a more valuable variable to study as it allows us to better understand the initial withdrawal process. Moreover, it helps to bypass a number of the methodological concerns with studying turnover (e.g. using intention as a proxy and access to individuals who have turned over). It is also consistent with the application of the COR model, as that model was developed as a theory to understand stress and strain variables.

Finally, this is one of the first studies to integrate social support as a buffer between POP and its outcomes. It suggests that the negative effects of POP might be ameliorated when supervisors can provide support to their employees. This is consistent with the COR model, as it suggests that support serves as a resource; when supervisors provide support they are reducing the likelihood of the negative outcomes associated with demands. It also underscores the role that supervisors play in both creating and reducing the political environment.

Practical applications

The findings of the present study, in concert with the notions of resources and demands, suggest a variety of practical approaches that organizations can use to either reduce the demands associated with POP or provide resources to deal with the political environment. The importance of social support in reducing the level of employee burnout implicates the role of HRM in organizations; moreover, clearly communicated and properly run HRM systems should reduce the level of demand in the organizational environment that often leads to political behaviors. Organizations have several HRM processes at hand to mitigate the influence of organizational politics. The earliest moment in which organizations can reduce the role of POP in the POP–disengagement–performance relationship is during organizational recruitment. Organizations send signals and provide information to potential employees through recruitment materials about what they should expect from the job and the organization upon entry into it (Dineen et al., 2002; Rynes, 1991). These signals and pieces of information build employee expectations so that the applicants begin to form a psychological contract with the organization, even before they enter it (Schalk and Rousseau, 2002). Upon entry to the organization, any discrepancy between the signals and information transmitted during recruitment and the actual environment of the organization will lead to the violation of the psychological contract and cause several negative individual and organizational outcomes (Breaugh and Starke, 2000). The information provided by such HRM practices may serve as a further resource to address the potential demands associated with POP. Thus it seems appropriate for organizations to consider POP during recruitment and modify recruitment materials to help set employee expectations, pre-hire, about not only organizational politics but also the level of social support given to employees.

One method of tailoring recruitment materials to address employee pre-hire expectations is through 'realistic job previews' (RJPs). RJPs provide applicants with both positive and negative job and organization information (Hom et al., 1998; Wanous, 1992), and the use of pre-hire RJPs has been found to increase job satisfaction and organizational commitment and reduce intent to turnover (Breaugh and Starke, 2000; Phillips, 1998). While some of the findings associated with RJPs are equivocal (Phillips, 1998), and some researchers posit that RJPs might cause highly attractive applicants to self-select out of the recruitment and selection phases of employment (Bretz and Judge, 1998), the presentation of more realistic information, in lieu of providing only positive information, should help to modify employee expectations (Wanous and Reichers, 2000). We do not recommend that every organization include RJP-type information relating solely to POP; however, we do suggest that organizations begin the consistent communication of social support availability to employees as this will improve the resources available to them.

Once employees enter the organization, there are few opportunities to set realistic expectations about the job and organization so that pre-employment expectations are not violated. The organizational socialization process, whether formal or informal, generally lasts between 12 and 18 months (Bauer et al., 1998; Cable and Parsons, 2001). During this period of socialization, employee work-related expectations, values, goals and norms become enduring. If organizations are interested in mitigating the influence of POP on employee burnout and performance through providing social support, it seems appropriate to address these issues during organizational socialization. Again, we do not recommend that organizations devote hours of formal socialization to the topic of organizational politics; however, we do encourage organizations to address the issues of politics and social support during this critical period of employee development. Otherwise, organizations might miss the last opportunity to develop and stabilize employee expectations about POP and social support.

Buckley et al. (1998) developed an organizational socialization program called 'expectation lowering procedures' (ELPs) specifically designed to lower employee expectations context-free. That is, the ELP primes employees to think about their expectations in general, not just at work, so that these employees will be amenable to changing their expectations without necessarily violating their established psychological contracts. Buckley et al. (1998) and Buckley et al. (2002) found that ELPs provide similar positive individual and organizational outcomes as RJPs. This suggests that organizations weary of discussing organizational politics during recruitment or formal socialization can foster realistic employee expectations through a simple ELP.

After employee socialization, the issue of employee performance evaluation becomes an important driver of organizational politics. As organizations normally link performance evaluation to compensatory outcomes (e.g. promotions, raises, etc.), it is not difficult to imagine how organizational politics can increase during the performance evaluation process (Wayne et al., 1997). Hochwarter et al. (2000) maintained that organizations increase POP and political behavior among employees when they are placed in an ambiguous or uncertain environment. This suggests that for those HRM functions that might elicit natural organizational politics tendencies, organizations should implement rigorously adhered-to HRM functions. In terms of performance evaluation, this requires organizations to implement and communicate objective performance evaluation processes.

One possible method of reducing political behavior and POP and of increasing perceived supervisor support during performance evaluation is through frame of reference (FOR) training (Bernardin and Buckley, 1981). FOR training establishes a common conceptualization of employee performance across performance raters in an organization, and FOR training has been found to reduce performance rating errors (Fletcher and Perry, 2002); moreover, the process of training raters and communicating performance standards has been found to increase employee perceptions of fairness (Bernardin et al.,

2001). While components of the FOR training protocol, namely the development of true performance scores, has proved elusive in field replications (Hauenstein, 1998), Chirico et al. (2004) recently demonstrated the costly and time-consuming process of developing true scores can be effectively eliminated from the FOR training protocol without sacrificing rater accuracy. As HRM processes tend to influence employee perceptions and attitudes (Bretz and Judge, 1994), formalized HRM process, such as FOR training in the performance evaluation process, should increase employee perceptions of social support and mitigate the influence of POP on performance.

Organizations might also utilize teams as a mechanism to reduce political behavior and POP, thereby mitigating the influence of organizational politics on work outcomes, such as performance. Johns (1999) suggests that reducing the actor–observer bias can be achieved through increasing group identity among team members. Kramer (1993) indeed found that identification with a group or a team reduced self-serving behavior. Witt et al. (2001) similarly found that individual–team goal congruence reduced POP among team members. Witt et al.'s (2001) findings are consistent with two theoretical perspectives on motivation. Social identity theory (Tajfel and Turner, 1986) would predict that belonging to a group should reduce individual self-serving behavior, as individuals possess a strong motive to attain group membership. In terms of individual–team goal congruence, Karau and Williams (1993), in a meta-analytic summary of social loafing findings, proposed an expectancy-based model of reducing undesirable individual behaviors within a group. They argued that individual accountability of behavior directed toward group achievement of goals is the primary mechanism to reduce undesirable behaviors.

Finally, in terms of reducing uncertainty and increasing social support resources to reduce the influence of POP on work outcomes, organizations might consider the use of mentors. While research indicates that mentoring can lead to negative individual outcomes for the people involved in the mentoring relationship (Scandura, 1998), a carefully developed mentoring program can be used to create structured and supportive work environments (Mullen, 1998). This type of direct social support given to employees, so long as the mentors do use protégés as a political tool, should help to reduce POP in the organization as well as serve as a buffer against its potentially negative effects.

Limitations
While these findings were generally supportive of the proposed model, we recognized that there were some key limitations in the manner in which Study 1 was conducted. First, the performance data were collected from the participants. While they had just received the performance appraisal (and many referred directly to their copy of their most recent appraisal to ensure accuracy), the possibility exists for inaccuracies in reporting performance data. We hoped to temper this by asking them to report their self-ratings of performance, with the idea that such a procedure would reduce the need for impression management by inflating ratings. Nonetheless, we recognize that we cannot rule out inaccurate reporting of performance data. We attempted to address this concern by collecting performance data directly from supervisors in Study 2.

Along those lines, given the data are entirely self-reported, the possibility of common method bias exists. To test for the effect of common method bias, we conducted Harmon's one-factor test to determine whether the measured (non-demographic) scales were influenced significantly by a common measurement factor (cf. Korsgaard and

Roberson, 1995; Mossholder et al., 1998). Using confirmatory factor analysis, we tested a model that loaded all of the measured variables (including control variables) on to one factor, finding that it provided relatively poor fit to the data (Study 1: $\chi^2 = 113.41$, df = 6, TLI = 0.39, CFI = 0.61, RMSEA = 0.22; Study 2: $\chi^2 = 78.11$, df = 6, TLI = 0.57, CFI = 0.77, RMSEA = 0.19). While this test cannot rule out the possibility of common method bias (Podsakoff et al., 2003), when considered along with the pattern of results consistent with the hypotheses the test suggests the effect of common method bias is limited.

Conclusion

The objective of this chapter was to explore the relationship between perception of politics, social support, disengagement and performance. In doing so, we proposed a framework for understanding the links between these variables in the form of conservation of resources. While future research is needed to fully understand the reach of COR theory in explaining the outcomes of POP and the nature of its integration with other models of POP, this research offers an initial investigation to serve as a springboard for future COR-based studies of POP.

Note

1. While we are focusing on a conceptualization of political behaviors that centers on self-serving behavior, we recognize that political motives can also involve group-level or organizational-level outcomes.

References

Ashforth, B.E., and Mael, F. (1996). Social identity and the organization. *Academy of Management Review*, **14**, 20–29.

Baltes, M.M. and Baltes, P.B. (1990). Psychological perspectives on successful aging: The model of selective optimization with compensation. In P.B. Baltes and M.M. Baltes (eds). *Successful aging: Perspectives from the behavioral sciences* (pp. 1–34). New York: Cambridge University Press.

Baltes, P.B. (1997). On the incomplete architecture of human ontogeny: Selection, optimization, and compensation as foundation of development theory. *American Psychologist*, **52**, 366–80.

Baron, R.M. and Kenny, D.A. (1986). The moderator–mediator distinction in social psychological research: Conceptual, strategic, and statistical considerations. *Journal of Personality and Social Psychology*, **51**, 1173–82.

Baruch-Feldman, C., Brondolo, E., Ben-Dayan, D. and Schwartz, J. (2002). Sources of social support and burnout, job satisfaction, and productivity. *Journal of Occupational Health Psychology*, **7**, 84–93.

Bauer, T.N., Morrison, E.W. and Callister, R.R. (1998). Organizational socialization: A review and directions for future research. *Research in Personnel and Human Resource Management*, **6**, 149–214.

Bernardin, H.J. and Buckley, M.R. (1981). Strategies in rater training. *Academy of Management Review*, **6**, 205–12.

Bernardin, H.J., Buckley, M.R., Tyler, C.L. and Wiese, D.S. (2001). A reconsideration of strategies for rater training. In G.R. Ferris (ed.), *Research in personnel and human resources management* (Vol. 20, pp. 221–74). Stamford, CT: JAI Press.

Breaugh, J.A. and Starke, M. (2000). Research on recruitment: So many studies, so many remaining questions. *Journal of Management*, **26**, 405–34.

Bretz, R.D. Jr and Judge, T.A. (1994). The role of human resource systems in job applicant decision processes. *Journal of Management*, **20**, 531–51.

Bretz, R.D. Jr and Judge, T.A. (1998). Realistic job previews: A test of the adverse self-selection hypothesis. *Journal of Applied Psychology*, **83**, 330–37.

Buckley, M.R., Fedor, D.B., Veres, J.G., Wiese, D.S. and Carraher, S.M. (1998). Investigating newcomer expectations and job-related outcomes. *Journal of Applied Psychology*, **83**, 452–61.

Buckley, M.R., Mobbs, T.A., Mendoza, J.L., Novicevic, M., Carraher, S.M. and Beu, D.S. (2002). Implementing realistic job previews and expectation-lowering procedures: A field experiment. *Journal of Vocational Behavior*, **61**, 263–78.

Cable, D.M. and Parsons, C.K. (2001). Socialization tactics and person–organization fit. *Personnel Psychology*, **54**, 1–23.

Caplan, R.D., Cobb, S., French, J.R., Harrison, R.U. and Pinneau, S.R. (1975). *Job demands and work health.* US Department of Health, Education, and Welfare Publication No. 75–160. Washington, DC: Institute for Social Research.

Carlson, D.S. and Perrewé, P.L. (1999). The role of social support in the stressor–strain relationship: An examination of work–family conflict. *Journal of Management*, **25**, 513–40.

Chirico, K.E., Buckley, M.R., Wheeler, A.R., Facteau, J.D., Bernardin, J.H. and Beu, D.S. (2004). A note on the need for true scores in frame-of-reference (FOR) training research. *Journal of Managerial Issues*, **16**, 382–95.

Dineen, B.R., Ash, S.R. and Noe, R.A. (2002). A web of applicant attraction: Person–organization fit in the context of web-based recruitment. *Journal of Applied Psychology*, **87**, 723–34.

Drake, B. and Yadama, G.N. (1996). A structural equation model of burnout and job exit among child protective services workers. *Social Work Research*, **20**, 179–87.

Drory, A. and Romm, T. (1990). The definition of organizational politics: A review. *Human Relations*, **43**, 1133–54.

Fenlason, K. and Beehr, T. (1994). Social support and occupational stress: Effect of talking to others. *Journal of Organizational Behavior*, **15**, 157–75.

Ferris, G.R., Russ, G.S. and Fandt, P.M. (1989). Politics in organizations. In R.A. Giacalone and P. Rosenfeld (eds), *Impression management in the organization* (pp. 143–70). Hillsdale, NJ: Lawrence Erlbaum.

Ferris, G.R., Brand, J.F., Brand, S., Rowland, K.M., Gilmore, D.C., King, T.R., Kacmar, K.M. and Burton, C.A. (1993). Politics and control in organizations. In E.J. Lawler, B. Markovsky, J. O'Brien and K. Heimer (eds), *Advances in group processes* (Vol. 10, pp. 83–11). Greenwich, CT: JAI Press.

Ferris, G.R., Adams, G., Kolodinsky, R.W., Hochwarter, W.A. and Ammeter, A.P. (2002). Perceptions of organizational politics: Theory and research directions. In F. Dansereau and F.J. Yammarino (eds), *Research in multi-level issues* (Vol. 1, pp. 179–254). Oxford, UK: Elsevier Science/JAI Press.

Ferris, G.R., Treadway, D.C., Kolodinsky, R.W., Hochwarter, W.A., Kacmar, C.J., Douglas, C. and Frink, D.D. (2005). Development and validation of the political skill inventory. *Journal of Management*, **31**, 126–52.

Fletcher, C. and Perry, E.L. (2002). Performance appraisal and feedback: A consideration of national culture and a review of contemporary research and future trends. In N. Anderson, D.S. Ones, H.K. Sinangil and C. Viswesvaran (eds), *Handbook of industrial, work and organizational psychology* (Vol. 1, pp. 127–44). Thousand Oaks, CA: Sage Publications.

Freedy, J.R. and Hobfoll, S.E. (1994). Stress inoculation for reduction of burnout: A conservation of resources approach. *Anxiety, Stress and Coping*, **6**, 311–25.

Ganster, D.C., Fusilier, M.P. and Mayes, B.T. (1986). Role of social support in the experience of stress at work. *Journal of Applied Psychology*, **71**, 102–10.

Geurts, S., Schaufeli, W. and De Jonge, J. (1998). Burnout and intention to leave among mental health-care professionals: A social psychological approach. *Journal of Social and Clinical Psychology*, **17**, 341–62.

Gilmore, D.C., Ferris, G.R., Dulebohn, J.H. and Harrell-Cook, G. (1996). Organizational politics and employee attendance. *Group and Organization Management*, **21**, 481–94.

Greenberg, J. and Scott, K.S. (1996). Why do workers bite the hand that feeds them? Employee theft as a social exchange process. In R.I. Sutton and B.M. Staw (eds), *Research in organizational behavior* (Vol. 18, pp. 111–56). Stamford, CT: JAI Press.

Halbesleben, J.R.B. and Bowler, W.M. (2005). Organizational citizenship behaviors and burnout. In D.L. Turnipseed (ed.), *A handbook on organizational citizenship behavior: A review of 'good soldier' activity in organizations* (pp. 399–414). Hauppauge, NY: Nova Science Publishers.

Harrell-Cook, G., Ferris, G.R. and Dulebohn, J.H. (1999). Political behaviors as moderators of the perceptions of organizational politics–work outcomes relationships. *Journal of Organizational Behavior*, **20**, 1093–106.

Harris, K. and Kacmar, K.M. (2005). Organizational politics. In J. Barling, E.K. Kelloway and M.R. Frone (eds), *Handbook of work stress* (pp. 353–74). Thousand Oaks, CA: Sage.

Hauenstein, N.M. (1998). Training raters to increase accuracy of appraisals and the usefulness of feedback. In J.W. Smither (ed.), *Performance appraisal: State of the art in practice* (pp. 404–41). San Francisco, CA: Jossey-Bass.

Hobfoll, S.E. (1988). *The ecology of stress.* New York: Hemisphere.

Hobfoll, S.E. (1989). Conservation of resources: A new attempt at conceptualizing stress. *American Psychologist*, **44**, 513–24.

Hobfoll, S.E. (1998). *Stress, culture, and community.* New York: Plenum.

Hobfoll, S.E. (2001). The influence of culture, community, and the nested self in the stress process: Advancing conservation of resources theory. *Applied Psychology: An International Review*, **50**, 337–70.

Hobfoll, S.E. and Freedy, J. (1993). Conservation of resources: A general stress theory applied to burnout. In W.B. Schaufeli, C. Maslach and T. Marek (eds), *Professional burnout: Recent developments in theory and research*. Washington, DC: Taylor & Francis.

Hochwarter, W.A., Witt, L.A. and Kacmar, K.M. (2000). Perceptions of organizational politics as a moderator of the relationship between conscientiousness and job performance. *Journal of Applied Psychology*, **85**, 472–8.

Hom, P.W., Griffeth, R.W., Palich, L.E. and Bracker, J.S. (1998). An exploratory investigation into theoretical mechanisms underlying realistic job previews. *Personnel Psychology*, **51**, 421–51.

Johns, G. (1999). A multi-level theory of self-serving behavior in and by organizations. In R.I. Sutton and B.M. Staw (eds), *Research in organizational behavior* (Vol. 21, pp. 1–38). Stamford, CT: JAI Press.

Kacmar, K.M. and Baron, R.A. (1999). Organizational politics: The state of the field, links to related processes, and an agenda for future research. In G. Ferris (ed.), *Research in personnel and human resources management* (Vol. 17, pp. 1–39). Stamford, CT: JAI Press.

Kacmar, K.M. and Carlson, D.S. (1997). Further validation of the Perception of Politics Scale (POPS): A multi-sample approach. *Journal of Management*, **23**, 637–58.

Karau, S.J. and Williams, K.D. (1993). Social loafing: A meta-analytic and theoretical investigation. *Journal of Personality and Social Psychology*, **65**, 681–706.

Koeske, G. and Koeske, R. (1993). A preliminary test of the stress–strain-outcome model for reconceptualizing the burnout phenomenon. *Social Service Research*, **17**, 107–35.

Kolodinsky, R.W., Hochwarter, W.A. and Ferris, G.R. (2004). Nonlinearity in the relationship between political skill and work outcomes: Convergent evidence from three studies. *Journal of Vocational Behavior*, **65**, 294–308.

Korsgaard, M.A. and Roberson, L. (1995). Procedural justice in performance evaluation: The role of instrumental and noninstrumental voice in performance appraisal decisions. *Journal of Management*, **21**, 657–69.

Kramer, R.M. (1993). Cooperation and organizational identification. In J.K. Murnighan (ed.), *Social Psychology in Organizations* (pp. 244–69). Englewood Cliffs, NJ: Prentice-Hall.

Lykken, D.T. (1968). Statistical significance in psychological research. *Psychological Bulletin*, **70**, 151–9.

Maslach, C. (1982). *Burnout: The cost of caring*. Englewood Cliffs, NJ: Prentice-Hall.

Mossholder, K.W., Bennett, N., Kemery, E.R. and Wesolowski, M.A. (1998). Relationships between bases of power and work reactions: The mediational role of procedural justice. *Journal of Management*, **24**, 533–52.

Mullen, E.J. (1998). Vocational and psychosocial mentoring functions: Identifying mentors who serve both. *Human Resource Development Quarterly*, **9**, 319–31.

Phillips, J.M. (1998). Effectiveness of realistic job previews on multiple organizational outcomes: A meta-analysis. *Academy of Management Journal*, **41**, 673–90.

Podsakoff, P.M., MacKenzie, S.B., Lee, J.Y. and Podsakoff, N.P. (2003). Common method biases in behavioral research: A critical review of the literature and recommended remedies. *Journal of Applied Psychology*, **88**, 879–903.

Randall, M.L., Cropanzano, R., Borman, C.A. and Birjulin, A. (1999). Organizational politics and organizational support as predictors of work attitudes, job performance, and organizational citizenship behaviors. *Journal of Occupational Behavior*, **20**, 159–74.

Ray, E.B. and Miller, K.I. (1994). Social support, home/work stress, and burnout: Who can help? *Journal of Applied Behavioral Science*, **30**, 357–73.

Rynes, S.L. (1991). Recruitment, job choice, and post-hire consequences: A call for new research directions. In M.D. Dunnette and L.M. Hough (eds), *Handbook of industrial and organizational psychology*, 2nd edn (pp. 399–444). Palo Alto, CA: Consulting Psychologists Press, Inc.

Scandura, T.A. (1998). Dysfunctional mentoring relationships and outcomes. *Journal of Management*, **24**, 449–67.

Schalk, R. and Rousseau, D.M. (2002). Psychological contracts in employment. In N. Anderson, D.S. Ones, H.K. Sinangil and C. Viswesvaran (eds), *Handbook of industrial, work and organizational psychology* (Vol. 2, pp. 133–42). Thousand Oaks, CA: Sage Publications.

Schaufeli, W.B. and Greenglass, E.R. (2001). Introduction to special issue on burnout and health. *Psychology and Health*, **16**, 501–10.

Schaufeli, W.B., Leiter, M.P., Maslach, C. and Jackson, S.E. (1996). The Maslach Burnout Inventory – General Survey. In C. Maslach, S.E. Jackson and M.P. Leiter (eds), *'Maslach Burnout Inventory*. Palo Alto, CA: Consulting Psychologists Press.

Tajfel, H. and Turner, J.C. (1986). The social identity theory of intergroup behavior. In S. Worchel and W.E. Austin (eds), *Psychology of intergroup relations* (pp. 7–24). Chicago: Nelson-Hall Publishers.

Treadway, D.C., Ferris, G.R., Hochwarter, W., Perrewé, P.L., Witt, L.A. and Goodman, J.M. (2005). The role of age in the perceptions of politics–job performance relationship: A three-study constructive replication. *Journal of Applied Psychology*, **90**, 872–81.

Tsang, E.W. K. and Kwan, K. (1999). Replication and theory development in organizational science: A critical realist perspective. *Academy of Management Review*, **24**, 759–80.

Valle, M. and Perrewé, P.L. (2000). Do politics perceptions relate to political behaviors? Tests of an implicit assumption and expanded model. *Human Relations*, **53**, 359–86.

Vigoda, E. (2000). Internal politics in public administration system: An empirical examination of its relationship with job congruence, organizational citizenship behavior, and in-role performance. *Public Personnel Management*, **29**, 185–210.

Vigoda, E. (2001). Reactions to organizational politics: A cross-cultural examination of Israel and Britain. *Human Relations*, **54**, 1483–518.

Vigoda, E. (2002). Stress-related aftermaths to workplace politics: The relationship among politics, job distress, and aggressive behavior in organizations. *Journal of Organizational Behavior*, **23**, 571–91.

Vigoda, E. (2003). *Developments in organizational politics*. Cheltenham, UK and Northampton, MA, USA: Edward Elgar.

Wanous, J.P. (1992). *Organizational entry*. Reading, MA: Addison-Wesley.

Wanous, J.P. and Reichers, A.E. (2000). New employee orientation programs. *Human Resource Management Review*, **10**, 435–51.

Watson, D. (1982). The actor and the observer: How are their perceptions of causality divergent? *Psychological Bulletin*, **92**, 682–700.

Watson, D., Clark, L.A. and Tellegren, A. (1988). Development and validation of brief measures of positive and negative affect: The PANAS scales. *Journal of Personality and Social Psychology*, **54**, 1063–70.

Wayne, S.J., Liden, R.C., Graf, I.K. and Ferris, G.R. (1997). The role of upward influence tactics in HR decisions. *Personnel Psychology*, **50**, 978–1006.

Williams, L.J. and Anderson, S.E. (1991). Job satisfaction and organizational commitment as predictors of organizational citizenship and in-role behaviors. *Journal of Management*, **17**, 601–17.

Witt, L.A. (1998). Enhancing organizational goal congruence: A solution to organizational politics. *Journal of Applied Psychology*, **83**, 666–74.

Witt, L.A., Hilton, T.F. and Hochwarter, W.A. (2001). Addressing politics in matrix teams. *Group and Organization Management*, **26**, 230–47.

Witt, L.A., Kacmar, K.M., Carlos, D.S. and Zivnuska, S. (2002). Interactive effects of personality and organizational politics on contextual performance. *Journal of Organizational Behavior*, **23**, 911–26.

Zivnuska, S., Kacmar, K.M., Witt, L.A., Carlson, D.S. and Bratton, V.K. (2004). Interactive effects of impression management and organizational politics on job performance. *Journal of Organizational Behavior*, **25**, 627–40.

15 Competing perspectives on the role of understanding in the politics perceptions–job performance relationship: A test of the 'antidote' versus 'distraction' hypotheses

Wayne A. Hochwarter, Robert W. Kolodinsky,
Lawrence A. Witt, Angela T. Hall, Gerald R. Ferris
and Michele K. Kacmar

Introduction

Politics is simply a fact of organizational life (Vigoda-Gadot et al., 2003). Whether the behavior is taking credit for the accomplishments of others or influencing important decision makers to fund a project deemed worthy of support, politics is largely inescapable. Because of its pervasive influence, considerable research has examined the role of politics on a host of work outcomes over the past 20 years (Ferris et al., 1989; Vigoda, 2003).

According to Ferris and colleagues (Ferris et al., 2002), research in organizational politics has followed two, largely independent, streams. One stream has focused on political behavior, and includes influence tactics and strategies used mostly for self-serving intentions. The other, politics perceptions, is a subjective *evaluation* (Gandz and Murray, 1980) made by workers about 'actions by individuals that are directed toward the goal of furthering their own self-interests without regard for the well-being of others within the organization' (Kacmar and Baron, 1999, p. 4). The second stream, politics perceptions, is the focus of the current research.

Both theory and research (cf. reviews by Ferris et al., 2002; Kacmar and Baron, 1999) have noted that organizational politics, and particularly politics perceptions, largely have negative consequences. Even so, Ferris et al. (1989) suggested that worker *understanding* of organizational decisions and events – that is, 'the extent to which one comprehends why and how things happen the way they do' (p. 162) in organizational settings helps to reduce the impact of such adverse outcomes. Indeed, empirical studies examining the interaction between politics perceptions and understanding, and its effect on worker outcomes, have validated the positive efficacy of the understanding moderator (e.g. Ferris, Frink, Galang et al., 1996; Ferris et al., 1994; Vigoda, 2003).

To date, politics perceptions research, using the understanding moderator, has focused exclusively on employee *reactions*. For example, understanding has been found to reduce the negative effects of politics perceptions on job anxiety (e.g. Ferris, Frink, Galang et al., 1996; Ferris et al., 1994; Vigoda-Gadot, 2002), satisfaction with one's supervisor (Ferris, Frink, Galang et al., 1996), and job satisfaction (Ferris, Frink, Bhawuk et al., 1996; Kacmar et al., 1999; Vigoda et al., 2003). Unfortunately, the understanding moderator has not been evaluated in politics studies for *behavioral* outcomes, such as job performance.

Whereas politics has typically been inversely correlated with job performance (e.g. Hochwarter et al., 2000; Kacmar et al., 1999; Randall et al., 1999; Vigoda, 2000; Witt, 1998), research to date has failed to examine whether understanding moderates this relationship. To address this limitation, the current study examines the impact that worker understanding has on the typically negative relationship between politics perceptions and job performance.

The investigation of the effect of politics perceptions on job performance as moderated by understanding raises interesting questions concerning the process dynamics of this association. For example, plausible arguments can be made for alternative results that either complement previous 'antidote' findings for employee reaction variables, or differ from them substantially. Specifically, we argue that there are two competing perspectives concerning the form of the politics perceptions–understanding interaction on job performance. One perspective might be referred to as the amelioration or 'antidote' hypothesis. This is the perspective initially suggested by stress researchers (e.g. Sutton and Kahn, 1986), implied in the Ferris et al. (1989) model, and more explicitly articulated in subsequent research (Ferris et al., 1994; Ferris, Frink, Galang et al., 1996). This argument suggests that increased understanding diminishes the negative effects of politics perceptions on job performance by easing worker perceptions of ambiguity and uncertainty (Ferris et al., 1989).

An alternative viewpoint can be referred to as the 'distraction' hypothesis, a perspective that has received considerable attention in advertising (e.g. Festinger and Maccoby, 1964) and in social facilitation research (e.g. Zajonc, 1965; Baron et al., 1978). In the current context, the distraction argument suggests that increases in understanding in highly political situations may serve as a distracting function that diverts attention from one's work, where one focuses too much attention on politics and less on job tasks. Doing so likely exacerbates the negative effects that politics perceptions have on job performance.

With data from three separate samples, the present research examines whether increased understanding distracts workers away from job tasks, thus hindering job performance, or supplies them with clarity and additional organizational data that facilitates task focus. Instead of formulating a single hypothesis in this study, we attempt to establish two reasonable and logically compelling perspectives regarding the form of the politics perceptions–understanding interaction on job performance, and allow these two perspectives to compete against each other in a 'strong inference' framework (Platt, 1964).

Furthermore, we seek to establish the results in Study 1, and then confirm the form and magnitude of that interaction in subsequent studies, using different measures for focal constructs, in a partial constructive replication approach (Lykken, 1968). Compared to a strict 'literal replication,' which employs identical operationalizations of constructs across studies, this more conservative approach provides more confidence in the validity of convergent findings for the politics perceptions–understanding interaction.

Organizational politics
The study of organizational politics began at least four decades ago (e.g. Burns, 1961), but serious scientific inquiry began to rapidly increase in the late 1970s and early 1980s (e.g. Allen et al., 1979; Gandz and Murray, 1980; Porter, 1976; Schein, 1977). A politics perceptions theoretical model by Ferris and colleagues (Ferris et al., 1989), and validated measurement tools (Ferris and Kacmar, 1992; Hochwarter et al., 2003; Kacmar and

Carlson, 1997; Kacmar and Ferris, 1991), helped foster the rapid growth of empirical work that has occurred during the last 15 years.

Ferris et al. (1989) suggested that most workers view high levels of organizational politics as either an opportunity or a threat, and offered several possible responses. One response is to 'not play the political game' (p. 161) and withdraw from the organization entirely. Another response is to ignore politics and immerse oneself in work, 'which could prove to be a functional distraction from the political behavior surrounding them' (ibid.). A third response is to explore opportunities to take part in the political behavior. These differential worker responses are, in part, a function of 'the extent to which they understand the nature of politics as they are played out in the particular organization' (p. 162).

In the current context, with job performance as the behavioral outcome of focus, increased worker understanding is seen as either aiding job performance by reducing the negative effect that politics appears to have on job performance (e.g. Hochwarter et al., 2000; Kacmar et al., 1999; Randall et al., 1999; Witt, 1998), or hindering it. Thus, when politics perceptions are high, understanding may operate either as an antidote or as a distraction in the politics perceptions–job performance relationship.

The 'antidote' hypothesis
In their model of organizational politics perceptions, Ferris et al. (1989) argued that individuals are less affected by their perceptions of politics when they have an understanding of organizational events and workplace decisions that affect them. Normally, this understanding takes the form of knowledge or awareness of why decisions or events at work take place. High levels of understanding in political work environments are seen as helpful in reducing uncertainty and ambiguity, giving the worker a greater sense of control (Sutton and Kahn, 1986). Alternatively, workers saddled with low levels of understanding in such settings may be blissfully ignorant, simply unaware of the political activities taking place around them, or 'lost in the dark' and feeling threatened by the volatility surrounding them.

According to Ferris et al. (1989), reducing uncertainty and ambiguity through greater comprehension of organizational functioning should help ameliorate the typically negative reactions that occur in highly political work environments. Therefore, particularly for those perceiving politics as a threat, increased understanding may serve to help temper any negative reactions they may have when confronted with the 'realities' of organizational politics, and hence will lessen the adverse effects that politics perceptions have on employee reactions.

At least for employee reaction outcomes, the 'antidote' hypothesis has been generally supported in the politics perceptions literature. For example, Ferris et al. (1994) found support for the moderating effect of understanding (i.e. operationalized as tenure) on the politics perceptions–job anxiety relationship, which led to the conclusion that understanding 'serves as an antidote of sorts for the dysfunctional consequences of politics perceptions as a stressor' (p. 1215). In addition, Kacmar et al. (1999) found that understanding lessened the negative effect of politics perceptions on job satisfaction. Further, Ferris, Frink, Galang et al. (1996) reported that understanding helped reduce the adverse effects of politics perceptions on job anxiety and satisfaction with supervision.

The politics perceptions–understanding interaction was the focus of one behavioral outcome study. Gilmore et al. (1996) examined the moderating potential of understanding, operationalized as tenure working for one's immediate supervisor, on the relationship between politics perceptions and worker attendance. After controlling for the quality of the supervisor–subordinate relationship, increases in politics perceptions were associated with lower attendance for those with limited understanding (i.e. low tenure), as hypothesized. Also as proposed, no politics perceptions–attendance relationship was found under conditions of high understanding (i.e. higher tenure).

The findings above support the notion that understanding serves to lessen the negative effects of politics perceptions on many outcome variables. However, the 'antidote' hypothesis was developed for, and tested on, primarily employee reaction outcomes. A similarly positive result could occur for job performance, because increased cognitive understanding may help to reduce the negative effect politics perceptions have on job performance. As workers become more aware of organizational processes, the rationale behind decisions, and the reasons why certain events take place, they feel less vulnerable.

Moreover, because they understand 'the system,' they may be able to use such insider knowledge in 'working the system' to their advantage in promoting more favorable images and impressions of performance to their supervisors who rate them. Hence, under conditions of high understanding, the 'antidote' hypothesis suggests that increases in politics perceptions will be associated with increases in job performance. Under conditions of low understanding, where contextual knowledge is largely absent, job performance should be inhibited by politics such that increases in politics perceptions should be associated with decreases in job performance.

The 'distraction' hypothesis

Distractions refer to 'psychological reactions triggered by external stimuli or secondary activities that interrupt focused concentration on a primary task' (Jett and George, 2003, p. 500). In the current context, expectancy and equity theory perspectives offered by Kacmar et al. (1999) may be helpful in making a case for the 'distraction' hypothesis. According to expectancy theory, work motivation depends on the performance–reward link. However, the distribution of rewards in a political climate is based on factors typically not linked to contribution (Kacmar and Ferris, 1991). It might be the case that individuals who believe that organizational decisions are made politically (i.e. those with high understanding) recognize that no matter how hard they work, the expected payoff may not materialize. In this regard, making an investment in the workplace through a commitment to maximizing individual performance may be viewed as a risky investment (Randall et al., 1999).

In addition, understanding that decisions are made politically may compel individuals to reduce their job performance (or work less hard) in an effort to reduce or eliminate feelings of inequity (Moorman, 1991). However, for those individuals with a low understanding of how decisions are made, there may be no recognition of the break in the performance–reward link. Consequently, their job performance is likely to be affected to a much lesser extent.

Furthermore, the case for the 'distraction' hypothesis also stems from arguments based in the social information-processing literature on attentional focus and salience. According to Fiske and Taylor (1984), for one to process social information in organizational settings, encoding and attention must occur. Encoding is the interpretative process of transforming external stimuli into internal representations. During this process of interpretation, 'some details are lost, others altered, and still others are fabricated' (p. 184), resulting in inference distortions that are stored in memory.

Attention is related to encoding and involves a focus on either what is currently being interpreted from external stimuli or on information retrieved from memory. Attention has two components – direction and intensity. Because workers are often bombarded with stimuli that are not related to their jobs, a certain amount of directional focus, along with intensity of effort, typically is required for workers to effectively complete tasks. A stimulus that is prominent relative to its context is considered salient, and individuals tend to focus on these cues, and reduce attention on stimuli that are less relevant (Fiske and Taylor, 1984).

When stimuli associated with organizational politics are perceived to possess a potentially detrimental effect on one's promotability, for example, it likely will be seen as salient and require that attention be mobilized in that direction. Unfortunately, efforts to attend to (i.e. understand) stimuli perceived as political may serve to distract workers from job tasks, potentially resulting in reduced job performance. In fact, Ferris et al. (1989) suggested that organizational politics can 'represent a potential source of distraction for those not wishing to play the political game' (p. 162). Further, it may be that the negative effects of distraction may be occurring even for those who desire to 'play politics,' because it diverts their attention away from job-related tasks and toward activities deemed necessary to minimize the harmful effects of others' self-serving behavior.

Hence the distraction hypothesis suggests that, under conditions of high understanding, increases in politics perceptions will be associated with decreases in job performance due to interruption from central job tasks. Under conditions of low understanding, increases in politics perceptions will be associated with increases in job performance because these individuals largely are unaware of, and thus not distracted by, politics. Consequently, performance on the job is made more salient and thus improves. The prediction for this condition is consistent with Ferris et al.'s (1989) reaction to politics perceptions that indicated that some people ignore the politics going on around them, increase their involvement in their jobs, and thus are not distracted. Though this does not definitively establish an increase in job performance in itself, there is sufficient empirical evidence to support the positive linear relationship between job involvement and job performance (Diefendorff et al., 2002).

Finally, the distraction hypothesis is consistent with related research in the cognitive sciences (Christie and Geis, 1970; McIlwain, 2003). For example, research suggests that the goal of the influencer is to create confusion, power imbalances, and generally cause the target(s) to react to cues that are manipulated to promote self-serving objectives (O'Hair et al., 1981). In this regard, politicians cognitively monitor the amount and intent of information presented to targets (Leary and Kowalski, 1990). As such, increases in externally manipulated understanding by politicians have a useful purpose. Targets may acknowledge a high level of understanding, but in fact the information perceived is determined by the overarching goals of the politician. Consequently, higher levels of perceived understanding may have adverse effects on performance in environments where politicking is extensive because the information presented for evaluation is purposely intended to draw the target away from the foremost task of contributing to the organization.

Tenure as operationalization of understanding
Although previous research has demonstrated the utility of using tenure as a proxy for understanding (Ferris et al., 1994; Gilmore et al., 1996), we thought it necessary to further elaborate upon the association between these conceptualizations of workplace

comprehension discussed in previous literature (Fisher, 1986). The organizational adaptation literature, for example, explicates a strong theoretical association between understanding and tenure. Katz (1980) indicated, 'employees are constantly seeking to interpret, understand, and organize the world of their experiences' (p. 82).

Logically, the more time that an individual spends in a particular work setting, the more likely that the cognitive gaps in understanding will be minimized. In support, Ashford and Taylor (1990) noted the salient link between effective adaptation and increased tenure, such that those who are unable to acclimatize themselves to the inner working of the organization are more prone to withdraw (either through self-selection or organizational decisions). Furthermore, recent research has demonstrated the significant relationship between personal learning (and understanding) in the organization and organization tenure (e.g. Chao et al., 1994; Lankau and Scandura, 2002), further reinforcing the use of tenure as a proxy for, or operationalization of, understanding.

Finally, career stage research offers evidence that tenure represents one of the many forms of workplace understanding (Hall, 1976; Katz, 1980). This research suggests that increases in tenure are not only associated with general increases in understanding (e.g. what's going on around here), but that those with more years of service in a particular organization focus their sensemaking activities in a different direction than more junior associates as well (Gordon and Johnson, 1982; Orlikowski and Yates, 2002; Wagner et al., 1987). For example, at low levels of tenure, individuals focus almost exclusively on developing the skills needed to demonstrate job mastery. As tenure increases, individuals expand their scanning activities to include contextual factors. In this line of thought, increases in tenure are concurrently associated with increases in workplace understanding because one's knowledge base is enhanced when more opportunities for 'filling in the gaps' are available.

Plan of the present research

Three studies were conducted to establish the moderating effect of understanding on the politics perceptions–job performance relationship. A number of scholars (i.e. Lykken, 1968; Popper, 1959; Tsang and Kwan, 1999) have advocated the use of replications as a means of demonstrating consistency of findings that is not possible when results from a single-study design are presented. As noted by Popper (1959, p. 45): 'We do not even take our own observations quite seriously, or accept them as scientific observation, until we have repeated and tested them.' Although replications are unable to definitively verify or falsify theories, they can build evidence to either question or support particular conceptualizations (Tsang and Kwan, 1999).

Method

Participants and procedures

Study 1   Students in two upper-level business courses were given five surveys to be completed by individuals working full-time. Course credit was received for participation. Respondents were not identified and a total of 337 completed surveys were returned. The sample consisted of 54 percent females ($N = 182$), 46 percent males ($N = 155$), while the average age was 37 years (M = 36.92, S.D. = 11.30). A wide range of blue-collar (i.e. machinist, heavy equipment operator) and professional (i.e. vice-president of finance, computer sales) employees were included in the sample.

Study 2   All 108 individuals employed by a branch of a state agency received surveys at work, of which 102 were returned directly to the researchers (response rate of 94 percent). The sample consisted of 43 (42 percent) males and 59 (58 percent) females, while the average age was approximately 36 years (S.D. = 16.97). Archival data indicated that the 102 respondents did not differ from the population of 108 in terms of age and gender.

Study 3   Surveys were distributed to all 220 members of a financial services firm located in the southeastern USA. A total of 103 usable questionnaires were returned directly to the researchers (47 percent response rate). The sample consisted of 55 women (52 percent) and 49 men (48 percent), while the average age of respondents was approximately 44 years (M = 44.25, S.D. = 8.31). Archival data indicated that the sample mirrored the population in terms of age and gender representation.

Measures

Understanding   Respondents were asked to report their length of service with their current organization as an operationalization of tenure in all three studies.

Perceptions of politics   A six-item scale developed by Hochwarter et al. (2003) was used to measure politics perceptions in all three studies. Representative items include 'In this organization, there is a lot of self-serving behavior going on' and 'In this organization, people do what's best for them, not what's best for the organization' ($\alpha = 0.92$, $\alpha = 0.91$, $\alpha = 0.93$ for Studies 1–3 respectively). A five-point response format was used (1 = strongly disagree to 5 = strongly agree).

Job performance   Performance was measured using four items from Van Dyne et al.'s (1994) organizational obedience scale in Studies 1 and 2 ($\alpha = 0.78$, $\alpha = 0.81$ for Studies 1 and 2 respectively). Items included 'I rarely waste time while I am at work' and 'Regardless of the circumstances, I am effective at work.' A five-point response format was used (1 = strongly disagree to 5 = strongly agree). In Study 3, supervisor-rated performance was assessed with a four-item scale drawn from the firm's yearly evaluation form ($\alpha = 0.72$). Supervisors responded to work attributes (e.g. 'Adaptable and flexible,' 'Demonstrates mature judgment,' 'Demonstrates creativity/innovation' and 'Effectively influences and negotiates') using a three-point response format (i.e. 1 = needs improvement, 2 = accomplished, 3 = exemplary).

Control variables   Age and gender were controlled to assess their potentially spurious effects on performance in all three studies (Greenhaus and Parasuraman, 1993; Waldman and Avolio, 1986).

Data analysis
Hierarchical moderated multiple regression analysis (Cohen and Cohen, 1983) was used to test the competing perspectives on the form of the politics perceptions–understanding

interaction on job performance. Age and gender were entered in the first step, followed by the main effect terms (e.g. understanding and politics perceptions) in steps 2 and 3. The cross-product term was included in the final step.

Results

Correlation and regression analyses

Descriptive statistics and regression analyses for the three studies are shown in Tables 15.1 and 15.2. As exhibited, the politics perceptions–understanding cross-product terms (Study

Table 15.1   Correlations among study variables

Variable	Study 1[a]				Study 2[b]				Study 3[c]			
	1	2	3	4	1	2	3	4	1	2	3	4
1. Age												
2. Gender	0.10				**−0.30**				0.08			
3. Understanding	**0.50**	**0.11**			−0.09	0.06			**0.25**	0.01		
4. Politics	−0.10	0.07	−0.04		**0.51**	−0.16	−0.10		−0.08	0.01	0.02	
5. Performance	**0.20**	**0.16**	**0.11**	**−0.18**	−0.06	0.16	0.06	0.06	**−0.18**	**−0.11**	**−0.11**	−0.04

	Mean	S.D.	Mean	S.D.	Mean	S.D.
Age	36.98	11.30	36.46	16.97	44.25	8.31
Gender	0.56	0.52	0.59	0.51	0.54	0.51
Understanding	7.48	8.17	8.09	7.70	6.54	3.86
Politics	2.93	0.94	3.20	0.80	4.29	1.21
Performance	3.62	0.70	3.54	0.68	2.11	0.33

Notes:
[a] $N = 337$; [b] $N = 102$; [c] $N = 103$.
Correlations in bold are significant ($p < 0.05$).

Table 15.2   Regression analyses

Predictors	Study 1[a]		Study 2[b]		Study 3[c]	
	β	ΔR^2	β	ΔR^2	β	ΔR^2
Step 1:						
Age	0.01**		−0.01		−0.01	
Gender	0.20**	0.06	0.20	0.02	−0.06	0.04
Step 2:						
Politics perceptions (A)	−0.13**	0.03**	−0.09	0.01	−0.01	0.01
Step 3:						
Understanding (B)	0.01	0.00	0.01	0.01	−0.01	0.00
Step 4:						
A × B	−0.01*	0.03*	−0.04*	0.03*	−0.03**	0.14**

Note:
[a] $N = 337$; [b] $N = 102$; [c] $N = 103$.
** $p < 0.01$; * $p < 0.05$; [†] $p < 0.10$.

1: $\beta = -0.01, p < 0.05$; Study 2: $\beta = -0.04, p < 0.05$; Study 3: $\beta = -0.03, p < 0.01$) explained incremental criterion variance (Study 1: $\Delta R^2 = 0.03, p < 0.05$; Study 2: $\Delta R^2 = 0.03, p < 0.05$; Study 3: $\Delta R^2 = 0.14, p < 0.01$).

To graphically depict the interaction, we employed a procedure advocated by Stone and Hollenbeck (1989), plotting slopes at three levels of understanding: at the mean, at one standard deviation above the mean, and at one standard deviation below the mean. As shown in Figures 15.1–15.3, perceptions of organizational politics were related to job performance when understanding was either high or low. The form of the interaction provides support for the distraction hypothesis because job performance increased with increases in politics perceptions for those low in understanding. Further, job performance decreased with increases in politics perceptions for those high in understanding.

Discussion

Convergent results from three separate studies demonstrated that a distraction effect may be a viable hypothesis when considering underlying dynamics of the relationship between perceptions of organizational politics, understanding and job performance. Specifically, under conditions of high understanding, increases in politics perceptions were associated with decreases in job performance in all five studies. Workers with high understanding may continue to work hard, but the time taken and effort made to better understand organizational events and decisions, in particularly uncertain or ambiguous environments (i.e. where high politics is perceived), may hinder their ability to focus directly on tasks, resulting in lower job performance.

These findings, when considered in their entirety, are consistent with those reported in other research domains. For example, Wagner et al. (1987) noted that individuals low in tenure are more apt to insulate themselves from their immediate environment by focusing on skill acquisition (e.g. working on the computer) rather than participating in the social milieu. If this view were adopted, politics would likely have a minimal effect on these individuals due to an emphasis on external data gathering. As skills become acceptably honed, the potentially noxious consequences of adverse contextual factors become prominent. With regard to the current series of studies, highly tenured individuals likely see others' politicking as an effort to pilfer their deserved share of rewards and resources. To head off these advances, individuals likely become more involved in the political domain, thus dedicating fewer resources toward performance mastery.

Strengths and limitations of the research

The study has several strengths. The most notable strength is the fact that convergent results were found in three diverse samples, thus providing constructive replication evidence (Lykken, 1968). In each instance, the form and magnitude of the interaction effects were comparable. The analogous findings are particularly compelling when considering that samples had both narrow and broad occupational ranges, helping to provide initial evidence of generalizability, pending additional research.

An additional strength was the manner with which job performance data were obtained. In Study 3, we were able to gather performance measures from a source other than the job incumbent. Hence concerns regarding common method variance, a problem that often surfaces when same-source data are utilized, are somewhat abated. In the remaining studies, respondents were responsible for providing performance scores that were supplied

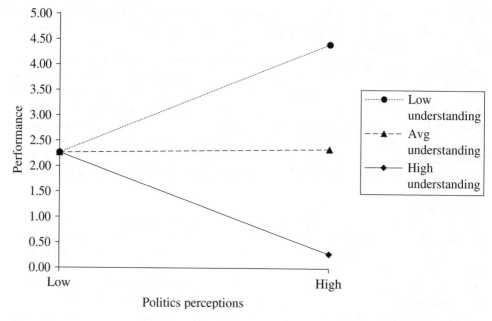

Figure 15.1   The interactive effects of politics perceptions and understanding on performance (Study 1)

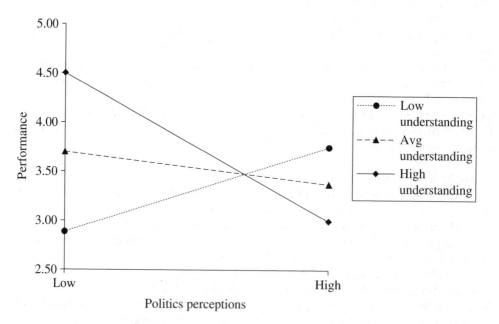

Figure 15.2   The interactive effects of politics perceptions and understanding on performance (Study 2)

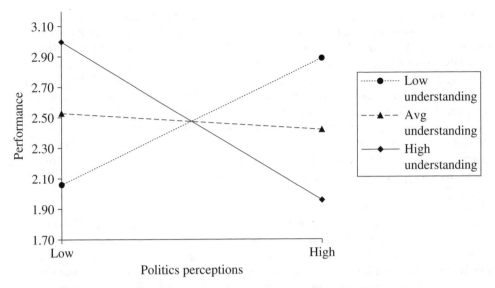

Figure 15.3 *The interactive effects of politics perceptions and understanding on performance (Study 3)*

by an external source during their most recent appraisal or self-report perceptions of contribution. Although this may represent a non-traditional way of collecting performance scores, there are reasons to feel confident about their accuracy and adequacy.

First, we compared respondents' self-report scores to those of the entire sampled population and found no discernible statistical differences. Moreover, it may be useful to view employee performance scores in Studies 1 and 2 from a 'perception is reality' perspective. Even if the performance scores provided by incumbents deviated from supervisor-rated performance, the results are clear: respondents *reported* lower performance scores in conditions reflecting higher politics and understanding. Finally, correlations noted in Table 15.1 are not high enough to offer evidence of common method variance.

This research is not without limitations. One limitation is that although past research has supported the use of organization tenure as a proxy for, or operationalization of, understanding, definitive conclusions regarding this research cannot be made until understanding is measured directly and results are confirmed. Another potential limitation might have to do with the nature of the distraction causing performance detriments, since distraction was not measured directly in the current study. It remains merely speculative, although intuitively compelling, that distracting elements in the organizational environment are, in fact, accounting for the effects found in this case. Future politics perceptions–understanding research should consider specific ways of directly measuring forms of work distraction in organizations.

Implications for practice
In addition to theoretical advances, the findings reported here offer prescriptions for management, one of which is briefly discussed. The environment facing most employees is increasingly becoming uncertain due to rapid workforce modifications (e.g. layoffs

and restructurings). Consequences include concurrent increases in politicking and employee-designed information searches. In the current study, we examined *perceived* or implicit understanding, which may not accurately reflect the level of understanding preferred by decision makers. When individuals seek understanding in response to deficiencies promulgated by the organization, biases and misinterpretations are likely to surface, leading to consequences best described as adversarial. In response, management may find it especially useful to commit more resources to the dissemination of information that promotes individual and organizational objectives (i.e. lower stress, higher productivity). For example, organizations may increase the use of weekly meetings, newsletters, or town hall meetings with executives to ensure that making sense of the external environment is not subjected entirely to individual interpretation.

Directions for future research
Future research should explore constructs not subjected to scrutiny in previous politics perceptions research. For example, a construct that has yet to be investigated with respect to its influence on the politics perceptions–work outcomes relationship is mentoring. Implications for including mentoring in studies that assess the relationship among understanding, politics and work outcomes are abundant, especially if we assume that a primary role of a mentor is to help the protégé develop a richer understanding of the immediate work environment.

Lankau and Scandura (2002) found that the presence of a mentoring relationship was associated with personal learning, and that this form of understanding was related to a host of work outcomes (i.e. job satisfaction, intent to leave and actual turnover). In addition, they found that mentoring increased personal learning, which, in turn, affected experienced role ambiguity. As noted earlier, workplace ambiguity represents a salient environmental condition that directly contributes to politics perceptions' association with adverse outcomes (Ferris et al., 1989). Perhaps by leading to increased understanding, mentoring can help serve to ameliorate many of politics perceptions' harmful effects by minimizing ambiguity.

Further, researchers may find utility is more fully exploring the various conceptualizations of understanding in organizations. For example, research in virtually all organizational domains would be benefited if studies were able to elucidate (1) the dispositional factors that predict understanding, (2) the role that reciprocity relationships have on understanding, and (3) whether fit relationships increase understanding. Initial work in this area, focusing on politics perceptions, has been conducted by Vigoda-Gadot (Vigoda, 2003; Vigoda and Cohen, 2002). However, there appears to be room for much further deliberation in this area.

With regard to the complexity of the understanding–politics perceptions relationship, examining linear effects exclusively may fail to generate the best representation of these constructs. For example, it may be that examining nonlinear forms offers a viable alternative. Arguments used in distraction–conflict theory (e.g. Baron et al., 1978) may help to explain additional variance and complexity. As any stressor may serve as a distraction (Cohen, 1978), and given that politics perceptions has exhibited a strong link with increased stress (Ferris, Frink, Galang et al., 1996), one's initial understanding that the work environment is political will likely arouse attention and cause stress and distraction. However, depending on the degree of distraction intensity (e.g. Baron, 1986) and other factors (e.g. one's subjective evaluation of the situation; one's political skill), the negative effects of increased distraction on performance may be exacerbated for some, but reduced for others.

In summary, future politics perceptions research may best be served by including moderators such as understanding in the variable mix. Furthermore, the continued exploration of the effects of the politics perceptions–understanding interaction appears to be worthwhile. The results of the present research provide politics researchers with an alternative view of politics outcomes, indicating that the interaction between politics perceptions and understanding may produce different dynamics for behavioral outcomes than for employee reaction outcomes. Hence, although increased understanding of highly political environments may cause many workers to feel better (i.e. reduce job dissatisfaction and job tension), additional attention on stimuli not necessarily related to their jobs may distract them from the work at hand, resulting in reduced job performance.

References

Allen, R.W., Madison, D.L., Porter, L.W., Renwick, P.A. and Mayes, B.T. (1979). Organizational politics: Tactics and characteristics of its actors. *California Management Review*, **22**, 77–83.

Ashford, S. and Taylor, M. (1990). Adaptations to work transitions: An integrative approach. In G. Ferris and K. Rowland (eds), *Research in personnel and human resources management* (pp. 1–39). Greenwich, CT: JAI Press.

Baron, R. (1986). Distraction – conflict theory: Progress and problems. *Advances in Experimental and Social Psychology*, **19**, 1–40.

Baron, R.S., Moore, D. and Sanders, G.S. (1978). Distraction as a source of drive in social facilitation research. *Journal of Personality and Social Psychology*, **36**, 816–24.

Burns, T. (1961). Micropolitics: Mechanisms of institutional change. *Administrative Science Quarterly*, **6**, 257–81.

Chao, G.T., O'Leary-Kelly, A.M., Wolf, S., Klein, H.J. and Gardner, P.D. (1994). Organizational socialization: Its content and consequences. *Journal of Applied Psychology*, **79**, 730–43.

Christie, R. and Geis, F. (1970). *Studies in Machiavellianism*. Academic Press: New York.

Cohen, J. and Cohen, P. (1983). *Applied multiple regression/correlation analysis for the behavior sciences*. Hillsdale, NJ: Lawrence Erlbaum.

Cohen, S. (1978). Environmental load and the allocation of attention. In A. Baum, J. Singer and S. Valins (eds), *Advances in environmental psychology: Volume 1. The urban environment* (pp. 1–29). Hillsdale, NJ: Lawrence Erlbaum.

Diefendorff, M., Brown, D., Kamin, A. and Lord, R. (2002). Examining the roles of job involvement and work centrality in predicting organizational citizenship behavior and job performance. *Journal of Organizational Behavior*, **23**, 93–108.

Ferris, G.R. and Kacmar, K.M. (1992). Perceptions of organizational politics. *Journal of Management*, **18**, 93–116.

Ferris, G.R., Russ, G.S. and Fandt, P.M. (1989). Politics in organizations. In R.A. Giacalone and P. Rosenfeld (eds), *Impression management in the organization* (pp. 143–70). Hillsdale, NJ: Lawrence Erlbaum.

Ferris, G.R., Frink, D.D., Gilmore, D.C. and Kacmar, K.M. (1994). Understanding as an antidote for the dysfunctional consequences of organizational politics as a stressor. *Journal of Applied Social Psychology*, **24**, 1204–20.

Ferris, G.R., Frink, D.D., Bhawuk, D.P., Zhou, J. and Gilmore, D.C. (1996). Reactions of diverse groups to politics in the workplace. *Journal of Management*, **22**, 23–44.

Ferris, G.R., Frink, D.D., Galang, M.C., Zhou, J., Kacmar, K.M. and Howard, J.L. (1996). Perceptions of organizational politics: Prediction, stress-related implications, and outcomes. *Human Relations*, **49**, 233–66.

Ferris, G.R., Adams, G., Kolodinsky, R.W., Hochwarter, W.A. and Ammeter, A.P. (2002). Perceptions of organizational politics: Theory and research directions. In F.J. Yammarino and F. Dansereau (eds), *Research in multi-level issues, Volume 1: The many faces of multi-level issues* (pp. 179–254). Oxford, UK: JAI Press/Elsevier Science.

Festinger, L. and Maccoby, N. (1964). On resistance to persuasive communication. *Journal of Abnormal and Social Psychology*, **68**, 359–66.

Fisher, C. (1986). Organizational socialization: An integrative review. In K. Rowland and G. Ferris (eds), *Research in personnel and human resources management* (pp. 101–45). Greenwich, CT: JAI Press.

Fiske, S.T. and Taylor, S.E. (1984). *Social cognition*. New York: Random House.

Gandz, J. and Murray, V. (1980). The experience of workplace politics. *Academy of Management Journal*, **23**, 237–51.

Gilmore, D.C., Ferris, G.R., Dulebohn, J.H. and Harrell-Cook, G. (1996). Organizational politics and employee attendance. *Group and Organization Management*, **21**, 481–94.

Gordon, M. and Johnson, W. (1982). Seniority: A review of its legal and scientific standing. *Personnel Psychology*, **35**, 255–80.

Greenhaus, J. and Parasuraman, S. (1993). Job performance attributions and career advancement prospects: An examination of gender and race effects. *Organizational Behavior and Human Decision Processes*, **55**, 273–98.

Hall, D. (1976). *Career in organizations*. Santa Monica, CA: Goodyear.

Hochwarter, W.A., Witt, L.A. and Kacmar, K.M. (2000). The moderating effects of perceptions of organizational politics on the conscientiousness–sales performance relationship. *Journal of Applied Psychology*, **85**, 472–8.

Hochwarter, W., Kacmar, C., Perrewé, P. and Johnson, D. (2003). Perceived organizational support as a mediator of the relationship between politics perceptions and work outcomes. *Journal of Vocational Behavior*, **63**, 438–65.

Jett, Q.R. and George, J.M. (2003). Work interrupted: A closer look at the role of interruptions in organizational life. *Academy of Management Review*, **28**, 494–507.

Kacmar, K.M. and Baron, R.A. (1999). Organizational politics: The state of the field, links to related processes, and an agenda for future research. In G.R. Ferris (ed.), *Research in personnel and human resources management* (Vol. 17, pp. 1–39). Stamford, CT: JAI Press.

Kacmar, K.M. and Carlson, D. (1997). Further validation of the Perceptions of Politics Scale (POPS): A multiple sample investigation. *Journal of Management*, **23**, 627–58.

Kacmar, K.M. and Ferris, G.R. (1991). Perceptions of Organizational Politics Scale (POPS): Development and construct validation. *Educational and Psychological Measurement*, **51**, 193–205.

Kacmar, K.M., Bozeman, D.P., Carlson, D.S. and Anthony, W.P. (1999). An examination of the perceptions of organizational politics model: Replication and extension. *Human Relations*, **52**, 383–416.

Katz, R. (1980). Time and work: Toward an integrative perspective. In B. Staw and L. Cummings (eds), *Research in organizational behavior* (pp. 81–127). Greenwich, CT: JAI Press.

Lankau, M. and Scandura, T. (2002). An investigation of personal learning in mentoring relationships: Content, antecedents, and consequences. *Academy of Management Journal*, **45**, 779–90.

Leary, M.R. and Kowalski, R.M. (1990). Impression management: A literature review and two-component model. *Psychological Bulletin*, **107**, 34–47.

Lykken, D.T. (1968). Statistical significance in psychological research. *Psychological Bulletin*, **70**, 151–9.

McIlwain, D. (2003). Bypassing empathy: A Machiavellian theory of mind and sneaky power. In B. Repacholi and V. Slaughter (eds), *Individual differences in theory of mind* (pp. 39–66). New York: Psychology Press.

Moorman, R.H. (1991). Relationship between organizational justice and organizational citizenship behaviors: Do fairness perceptions influence employee citizenship? *Journal of Applied Psychology*, **76**, 845–55.

O'Hair, H.D., Cody, M.J. and McLaughlin, M.L. (1981). Prepared lies, spontaneous lies, Machiavellianism, and nonverbal communication. *Human Communication Research*, **7**, 325–39.

Orlikowski, W. and Yates, J. (2002). It's about time: Temporal structuring in organizations. *Organizational Science*, **13**, 684–701.

Platt, J.R. (1964). Strong inference. *Science*, **146**, 347–53.

Popper, K. (1959). *The logic of scientific discovery*. London: Hutchison.

Porter, L.W. (1976). Organizations as political animals. Presidential address, Division of Industrial–Organizational Psychology, 84th Annual Convention of the American Psychological Association, Washington, DC, September.

Randall, M.L., Cropanzano, R., Bormann, C.A. and Birjulin, A. (1999). Organizational politics and organizational support as predictors of work attitudes, job performance, and organizational citizenship behavior. *Journal of Organizational Behavior*, **20**, 159–74.

Schein, V.E. (1977). Individual power and political behaviors in organizations: An inadequately explored reality. *Academy of Management Review*, **2**, 64–72.

Stone, E.F. and Hollenbeck, J.R. (1989). Clarifying some controversial issues surrounding statistical procedures for detecting moderator variables: Empirical evidence and related evidence. *Journal of Applied Psychology*, **74**, 3–10.

Sutton, R.I. and Kahn, R.L. (1986). Understanding, prediction, and control as antidotes to organizational stress. In J. Lorsch (ed.), *Handbook of organizational behavior* (pp. 272–85). Englewood Cliffs, NJ: Prentice-Hall.

Tetrick, L.E. and LaRocco, J.M. (1987). Understanding, prediction, and control as moderators of the relationship between perceived stress, satisfaction, and psychological well-being. *Journal of Applied Psychology*, **72**, 538–53.

Tsang, E. and Kwan, K. (1999). Replication and theory development in the organizational sciences: A critical realistic perspective. *Academy of Management Review*, **24**, 759–80.

Van Dyne, L., Graham, J. and Dienesch, R. (1994). Organizational citizenship behavior: Construct redefinition, measurement, and validation. *Academy of Management Journal*, **37**, 765–802.

Vigoda, E. (2000). Internal politics in public administration systems: An empirical examination of its relationship with job congruence, organizational citizenship behavior, and in-role performance. *Public Personnel Management*, **29**, 185–210.

Vigoda, E. (2003). *Developments in organizational politics: How political dynamics affect employee performance in modern work sites*. Cheltenham, UK and Northampton, MA, USA: Edward Elgar.

Vigoda, E. and Cohen, A. (2002). Influence tactics and perceptions of organizational politics: A longitudinal study. *Journal of Business Research*, **55**, 311–24.

Vigoda-Gadot, E. (2002). Stress-related aftermaths to workplace politics: An empirical assessment of the relationship among organizational politics, job stress, burnout, and aggressive behavior. *Journal of Organizational Behavior*, **23**, 571–91.

Vigoda-Gadot, E., Vinarski-Peretz, H. and Ben-Zion, E. (2003). Politics and image in the organizational landscape: An empirical examination among public sector employees. *Journal of Managerial Psychology*, **18**, 764–87.

Wagner, J., Ferris, G., Fandt, P. and Wayne, S. (1987). The organizational tenure–job involvement relationship: A job–career experience explanation. *Journal of Occupational Behavior*, **8**, 63–70.

Waldman, D. and Avolio, B. (1986). A meta-analysis of age differences in job performance. *Journal of Applied Psychology*, **71**, 33–8.

Witt, L.A. (1998). Enhancing organizational goal congruence: A solution to organizational politics. *Journal of Applied Psychology*, **83**, 666–74.

Zajonc, R.B. (1965). Social facilitation. *Science*, **149**, 269–74.

16 The symbiosis of organizational politics and organizational democracy

David Butcher and Martin Clarke

Introduction

It is widely recognized that organization leaders have to cope with being more responsive both to the external interests of shareholders, supply chain relationships and strategic alliances, and to the internal concerns of employees for greater 'voice' and consultation (Child and Rodrigues 2003, Gratton and Ghoshal 2003, Friedman and Miles 2002). Understandably, from this multiple stakeholder perspective, the role of business leadership is often linked to the notion of governance (Kakabadse and Kakabadse 2001). Yet progress towards corresponding levels of organizational democracy and participation has been limited (Heller 1998), and the idea that organizations can be viewed as democratically governable political systems has usually been confined to 'interesting experiments', as with such notable successes as the Spanish Mondragon Cooperative, or simply dismissed as inimical to rational management and unitary organizational purpose. Despite advocacy of so-called 'bottom–up' approaches to change (Hamel 2000, Lipmann-Blumen and Leavitt 2001), business leaders, it appears, have yet to see a meaningful alternative to rational bureaucracy as a way of providing organizational direction, coherence and efficiency (Child and McGrath 2002).

But experiments aside, there is even less dispute that organizations are inherently pluralistic in terms of their goals, that this diversity of view must be given voice, and thus that managers should and certainly do exercise power in pursuit of conflicting objectives (Pfeffer 1992, Child and Rodrigues 2003, Etzioni 1998, Cludts 1999). This raises two fundamental questions: how is that power to be used, and to achieve whose objectives? The principles of democracy, of course, stipulate clear answers to both in terms of a supporting political system (Held 1987). But if the use of politics is itself illegitimate, or even inadmissible, then what is the basis for an appropriate organizational democratic process? Does the acceptability of organizational democracy depend on the legitimization of organizational politics?

Along with many other scholars (Pfeffer 1992, Greco 1996, Ferris et al. 2002, Ammeter et al. 2002, Vigoda 2003, Davis and Gardner 2004), we argue that organizational politics is not only an important and necessary managerial discipline, but that models of political behaviour are central to the development of real organizational democracy.

Since the call from House and Aditya (1997) for the development of a political theory of leadership, much has been done to reframe political activity as a neutral and inherently necessary component of organizational functioning (Ammeter et al. 2002). In this vein, in the editorial of a recent special edition of *The Leadership Quarterly* (2004: 15), Ammeter et al. promote a definitional basis for politics as being concerned with the influence and management of meaning, rather than as an implicitly negative and self-serving activity.

Building on this position, much recent research provides important insights into the relationship between political skill and perceptions of leadership effectiveness (Ferris et al. 2000, Treadway et al. 2004, Douglas and Ammeter, 2004, Hall et al. 2004): however, an additional perspective provided by Novicevic and Harvey (2004) lies in the notion of organizational politics as a 'democratic asset', distributed across all employees. In this conceptualization, political capital represents the varying capacity of employees to influence the way they are governed and it is this idea that represents the point of departure for this chapter.

To this end we first consider the evolution of organizational democracy, and the way in which notions of managerial rationality appear to have curtailed its wider adoption. Building on recent contributions to the discourses on both organizational and institutional politics, we then highlight the inherent compatibility of organizational politics with democracy. Drawing on recent exploratory research, we provide an example of how the adoption of constructive political behaviour derived from a political institutional leadership setting offers a potential model for the leadership of more democratic organizational forms. Advice is provided on how to work with a constructive political 'mindset', and we consider how the progress towards redistributing organizational influence may be accelerated through individual action.

The evolution and impact of organizational democracy

The move to redistribute workplace influence has a long history. It can be traced from European feudalism, through the industrial revolution, the many attempts to introduce participation schemes and co-operative enterprises over the past hundred years, to the more recent emphasis on de-layering and empowerment. Today democratization is centre stage (Gratton 2003, Cloke and Goldsmith 2002).

Whilst there are divergent views about the nature and form of democratized organizations, there is some agreement that they are likely to share the following principles: (1) devolved power and responsibility for many more organizational decisions, leading to smaller, self-organizing communities (Child and Rodrigues 2003, Daboub 2002, Courpasson and Dany 2003); (2) acceptance of diverse internal and external interests based on power as a function of successful relationships rather than just structure (Butcher and Clarke 2001, Cludts 1999, Coopey and Burgoyne 2000); (3) high levels of psychological ownership of organizational activities that depend on individual contribution, knowledge and leadership (Handy 1997, Gratton and Ghoshal 2003, Rajagopalan et al. 2003).

However, instances where these principles are to be found in practice do not arise simply as a result of the well-intentioned application of democratic values. Rather they are a response to very real business imperatives. Technological advancement, innovation, globalization and an increasing concern for business ethics are forcing management to reconsider its approach to this issue (see Box 16.1).

All of these trends reflect the increasing importance of many voices in the management of contemporary organizations (Etzioni 1998, Denis et al. 2001). They act incrementally on society at national and global levels, edging organizations closer to accepting the need to reconcile different aims as the basis for managing. Yet there remains a question as to the real impact these changes are having. Newspapers and management journals regularly report on surveys highlighting worrying levels of employee dissatisfaction and stress, often fuelled by issues such as poor communication, race and gender discrimination,

---

BOX 16.1   THE DRIVERS OF ORGANIZATIONAL
DEMOCRACY

- The need for continual innovation and improvement has led to the recognition that individual knowledge is a valuable organizational asset that necessitates acceptance of the power of the possessor.
- The recognition that customer satisfaction is critical to organizational success has facilitated the idea of employee empowerment and de-layering. For example in AT&T Universal Card Services front-line staff are trusted to handle 95 per cent of requests on the first call, even credit extensions.
- The benefits of managing knowledge and reducing hierarchy are realized through attracting, retaining and developing key talent. In the words of Charles Handy, employees are increasingly treated as 'members of voluntary clubs' rather than as organizational assets or human resources.
- As organizations align ever more closely with the needs of specific customer groups, individual business units become more specialized. The resulting fragmentation of organizational structures transfers power away from the corporate centre in the service of particular customer needs.
- The interdependence of organizations with their suppliers and customers has led to increasing acceptance that external stakeholders influence decision making and, ultimately, competitive advantage. Democratization, therefore, is also being driven by the need for organizational boundaries to be permeable and, at times, altogether removed.
- The need to secure greater levels of employee commitment has led organizations to democratize their approach to rewards and ownership. Stock ownership plans are now commonplace, and in some organizations, such as the UK-based John Lewis Partnership, include all employees as owners.
- At an institutional level, the democratization process has also been influenced on a global scale by growing legislation in the areas of employee protection, participation and communication. For example in Europe, an EU directive will, in due course, force organizations with more than 50 employees to consult staff about decisions that may lead to substantial changes in work organization.

---

organizational injustices and corporate scandals (Dean et al. 1998, Andersson 1996). Even in areas where progress has supposedly been made there is considerable evidence that change has been patchy at best. The benefits of autonomous work teams, for example, have been known since Pehr Gyllenhammer's experiments at Volvo over 40 years ago, yet this organizing principle has never been widely adopted. Or consider the move towards empowerment. As Chris Argyris points out, 'like the emperor's new clothes, we praise it loudly in public and ask ourselves privately why we can't see it. There has been no transformation in the workforce, and there has been no sweeping metamorphosis' (1998: 99).

Furthermore, this gap between public praise and reality devalues the efforts of management to democratize organizations and, worse, creates cynicism. A recent survey by Gallup (Buckingham 2001) revealed that 80 per cent of employees in the UK are not engaged at work; that is, they are not psychologically bonded to their organization even though they may be productive. It is not hard to find reasons for this in the everyday experience of managers. For example, enlightened management's efforts to treat employees as corporate citizens by enhancing their employability falls into disrepute when training and development budgets are slashed in the face of poor trading performance. Much the same tension arises when 'independent' business units are subject to top–down budgeting processes. Examples are legion because they are routine. Evidently something beyond good intentions and the changing business environment is required to effect a fundamental redistribution of organizational power.

The rational mindset and democracy
There are of course well-rehearsed explanations for this continuing disconnection: management simply does not want to relinquish power; most employees do not want power, because with it comes responsibility. No doubt the arguments around these positions will continue, but let us consider an altogether more powerful reason for the discontinuity between the desire for democratization and organizational practices – the rational mindset (Butcher and Atkinson 2001) or rational myth (Czarniawski 2003).

Mindsets are the particular ways that individuals come to think about everyday experience, saturating attention to the exclusion of all else. They are driven by values that are created and reinforced at an institutional level, and define what is appropriate and inappropriate in specific contexts (Giddens 1984, Hales 1999). In the context of 'rational organization', the mindset is governed by values about rationality, creating a deeply held belief system that governs what is assumed about organizations as they are worked in each and every day. Thus despite their self-evident diversity of goals and need for dispersed power, organizations implicitly remain places of unity where employees work with consistent strategies towards clear corporate goals (Brunson 2002). Top management continue to provide direction through vision and value statements that reflect prescriptions about desired behaviours. Key to these behaviours is still the need for employees to appreciate the logic of working collaboratively in order to share effort and knowledge in the wider interests of the enterprise (Butcher and Atkinson 2001, Cludts 1999).

Yet these principles of rational organization are not in themselves in opposition to those of democracy. Indeed, the argument in support of organizational democracy is persuasive particularly because of its emphasis on combining the best of both value systems. But, in practice, the rational mindset implicitly undermines the democratization process.

Consider the first principle of the democratized organization we highlighted earlier – the idea that power must be hierarchically devolved. This of course does not obviate the need for hierarchy. Rather, it ensures that decisions are made by those best placed to take them. In rational terms it promotes efficiency and effectiveness. Yet there are countless examples of management embarking on empowerment strategies only to wrest decision-making control again in times of economic downturn. Significantly, one longitudinal research programme led by Frank Heller designed to assess the devolution of power at work concludes 'that organizational influence sharing appears to have made only limited progress during the last 50 years' (1998: 1425).

The second principle of democratized organizations, the reconciliation of diverse interests, is also accommodated within the rational model in theory, but not necessarily in practice. Stakeholders, particularly employees, can be satisfied through a range of motivational devices and management tools that 'balance' potentially clashing demands. The 'business scorecard' concept does just that. Likewise, the separate and often conflicting interests of business units, projects, product lines and even brands can be managed as an in-house market democracy. Businesses like 3M, Apple Computer Inc. and MCI have done it successfully for years. Yet the intention to meet this diversity of interests is easily submerged in the pursuit of corporate goals. Not surprisingly, research has consistently shown that employees tend to surface-act espoused corporate goals (Ackers and Preston 1997, Dopson and Neumann 1994, Hope and Hendry 1995) rather than wholeheartedly embrace them, raising the question of whether congruity of interests is the means to a corporate goal or an end in itself.

This priority of corporate vision and values also serves to undermine the establishment of the 'psychological ownership' principle. Even small organizations can be sufficiently complex and fragmented such that corporate goals and values become disconnected from the *raison d'être* of constituent business units, or become too generic to provide meaningful ownership. Yet there is firm research evidence (Denis et al. 2001, Van Den Ende 2003, O'Reilly and Tushman 2004) that employees often attach greater psychological ownership to local issues having a direct impact on them than they do to distant corporate business agendas. This simple understanding underpins the massively devolved structures of successful companies like engineering giant ABB, and WPP, the global marketing services company. Consider, for example, the energy often invested by front-line workers in recommending improvements within their sphere of activities. Consider also how easily this commitment can be extinguished by management inaction born of desire for corporate neatness. Again, the concept of local identification does not itself contradict the principle of organizational unity. But in practice, psychological ownership of organizational activities that depends on individual contribution, leadership and knowledge is limited by the rational mindset.

Organizational democracy and organizational politics

If rational thinking undermines the practice rather than the principles of organizational democracy, it can only be because the mindset has failed to evolve beyond a conception of organizations that did not need to legitimize diversity of goals and agendas. In society at large the means of achieving such democratic reconciliation is not at issue. We call it the political system (March and Olsen 1995, Held 1987). But rather than recognize the possibility of systematizing the administration of diverse agendas, the rational mindset has the closed-loop effect of associating 'organizational politics' with misuse of power, secrecy and backroom deals (Vigoda 2003, Ferris et al. 2002, Buchanan and Badham 1999). That this may sometimes be the case further obscures the conception of politics as a constructive organizational mechanism for resolving partisan agendas.

Certainly, the use of power to promote partisan interests is open to abuse. In the context of governing through the political system, this process is judged principled so long as a cause is just (Starrat 2001). But if a just cause is at times an elusive concept in government, it is doubly so in organizations. There, one person's just cause may be another's slashed budget, leading, as in government, to the question of who decides what is in the best interests of whom. If motives are perceived as self-serving, the resulting behaviour will surely be deemed as negative political behaviour (Ammeter et al. 2002, Davis and Gardner 2004). Within democratic systems, political activity is institutionalized as a legitimate mechanism for reconciling just causes (Elgie 1995, March and Olsen 1995). As political theorists have shown, these mechanisms are both formal and informal – as with 'behind the scenes' lobbying (DeGregorio 1997, Preston and t'Hart 1999). Those with formal power (elected members of an administration) have the great responsibility of both representing the interests of the (theoretical) majority and preserving the integrity of a system that represents the interests of all. The organizational parallel lies in the role of top management – often now argued to be one of stewardship and grand social design (Kets de Vries 1998), achieved through the mediation of many strong interests internal and external to their organization.

Organizations, of course, do not have the same constitutions as governments, nor can they fully emulate the principles of democracies (Armbruster and Gebert 2002). For one thing, most organizations do not elect their managers (Peters and Williams 2002, Etzioni 1998), and for another, managerial agendas are not usually associated with great social causes. Furthermore, unlike organizations, government itself does not have corporate goals. Rather, it is the institution through which the corporate goals of consecutive administrations are realized. Nevertheless, the principles of democracy, representing as they now widely do the ideal of constructive politics, arguably contain the model for organizational democracy. They do this in three key respects.

First, constructive politics, in this general sense, represents the *logical process* by which diverse interests and stakeholders may be reconciled in organizations. Given that it is in the nature of organizations for powerful interest groups to form, more than ever in today's decentralized corporations, how else can this reconciliation be achieved? Not through hierarchical control – the evidence for that is overwhelmingly clear. Indeed, within the model of constructive politics, significant interest groups check the power invested in formal hierarchy (Ammeter et al. 2002, Kan and Parry 2004). Thus, far from being an irrational organizational response, therefore, the political system, as with institutional government, is the only judicious way of managing inevitable differences. Also, like its institutional counterpart, constructive political behaviour in organizations can only be considered legitimate if individuals are able to demonstrate civic virtue, to forgo, or at least balance, personal interests with the interests of other communities (Starrat 2001, Ruscio 2004, Davis and Gardner 2004). This is similar to Buchanan's (1999) notion of a 'logic of political action' in which politically skilled individuals justify their behaviour by reference to the maintenance of their reputations, being able to account for their actions and being able to identify positive organizational outcomes.

Second, in recognizing the multi-goal nature of organizations, the political model implicitly *values diversity*. Generic corporate goals (survival, growth or profit) become an umbrella under which (competing) top management visions and disparate local interests can be balanced. The democratic management of these differences, that is, balancing the need for coherence and diversity, is thus a primary component of organizational working (Denis et al. 2001, Malnight 2001, Ashmos et al. 2002), as it is for political institutions (see for example Leach and Wilson 2000), and many examples are to be found. Some are well-documented experiments in democracy such as St Luke's, the UK advertising agency, a collective in which all employees become shareholders. No job descriptions exist, and employees work in 'citizen cells' of no more than 35 people which have complete control over their budgets and income streams, and can question their own direction and that of the parent organization, at any time. Care has therefore been given to creating processes for dealing with the inevitable differences that arise. These include monthly operational meetings, shareholder days and company days where all employees discuss the future direction of the business, in formal meetings and informally, in the bar. There are many other unsung, yet nonetheless successful examples. Such organizations have one notice-able feature in common – diversity is considered both desirable and essential.

Finally, leadership, defined here as a collective phenomenon distributed at all levels of an organization (Barker 1997, Denis et al. 2001), is central to the maintenance and pro-motion of both organizational and political institutional democracy. Whilst at face value the concept of leadership appears antithetical to democracy, it is also implicit in its enact-ment (Ruscio 2004). True, it is the fear of leaders using personal power in a coercive manner that forms the rationale for the institutional checks and balances of government, yet formalized processes of representative accountability are simply not enough to secure democratic governance (Stuckey 1999, Patten 2001). If trust and power are central to good organizational governance (Grandori 2001), when set against the backdrop of a rational mindset that often undermines the ethical application of such principles, it is a leader's personal stewardship of them, and how this is perceived by others (Hall et al. 2004), that is critical to their enactment, not just the establishment of institutionalized structures. As Ruscio confirms from a liberal political institutional standpoint, 'it is impossible to imagine a strong healthy democracy without leaders' (2004: ix). Whilst to be effective, organizational democracy must reflect processes for participation, good citi-zenship behaviour and other tenets of political institutions, democratic governance is justified in terms of people exercising influence over their collective destiny and leader-ship is implicit in this endeavour (Ruscio 2004).

Political leadership
This analysis suggests that constructive politics results when individuals willing to take leadership action work in ways that make sense of, rather than close off, the conflicting tensions of civic virtue and self-interest, and of cohesion and diversity. Our own exploratory research into this area suggests that this may well be the case.

That research is reported more fully elsewhere (Clarke 2004), but in summary consisted of interviews with 31 managers from five organizations of varying plurality in very different industries. We asked them about their understanding of the organizations in which they worked and how they went about influencing and leading within that envir-onment. Responses varied from those reflecting a rational mindset to those demonstrat-ing behaviours consistent with a political model of leadership (see Table 16.1). In the absence of any formally agreed model of working, the latter group of managers largely 'made it up for themselves'. That is, in seeking to work with the tensions of plurality, they arrived at their own conclusions largely irrespective of organizational circumstance. In consequence, they tended to see themselves as independent of the goals of the organiza-tion, while also working within them.

Table 16.1   Leadership behaviours research

From (rational leadership)	To (political leadership)
• Preference for formal meetings and processes	• Extensive use of informal processes, e.g. covert activity, corridor meetings
• Focus on senior management approval/buy-in	• Focus on working with personal agendas
• Relationship building focused at senior levels	• Relationship building and networking at all levels
• Debating and challenging amongst small coterie	• Encouraging debate and challenge at all levels
• Carefully prescribed delegation and empowerment	• Providing others with space and autonomy to experiment, stimulating bottom–up change
• Tendency to influence through operational control	• Influencing by focusing on broad direction
• Working on formally agreed priorities/issues	• Working outside of agreed responsibilities, often on unofficial initiatives
• Challenging through established processes	• Challenging the status quo, irreverent and subversive
• Exclusive and involving few	• Inclusive and involving many
• Representing legitimate organization interests, e.g. own department, customers	• Representing the interests of quasi legitimate constituencies, often external to own responsibilities, e.g. other functions, unofficial issues

This cluster of managers were delineated from the rest of the sample by a combination of three factors. First, they each viewed diversity of interest as a critical organizing principle to be encouraged in order to enhance organizational effectiveness. Second, this orientation encouraged a mindset in which individuals felt able to make a personal difference, to pursue their own goals legitimately. However, this perspective was balanced by an orientation in which personal success was inextricably interwoven with the success of others' agendas, suggesting that these managers attached real value to the achievement of others' goals. This approach brought them into conflict with their colleagues. Third, therefore, in order to ameliorate accusations of self-interest, individuals attached importance to building legitimacy of action through transparency of motive.

The resulting behaviour was far from self-serving, and demonstrated how constructive political activity enabled a more democratic reconciliation of diverse internal agendas. For example, one manager deliberately created a silo around her business, in contravention of the prevailing culture, in order to develop a more customer-focused approach with shared values of debate, challenge and autonomy. This was extremely successful and the manager, after publicizing the advantages of her approach, secured agreement to extend the model to the rest of the organization.

In this study, legitimacy of plurality and reciprocity of success were significant in enabling managers to work with the conflicting tensions of civic virtue and self-interest, and cohesion and diversity. By accepting their inherent contradiction as a form of 'organized dissonance' (Ashcraft 2001: 1304) they were able to move beyond the notion that more of one necessitates less of the other.

Accelerating the process of democratization
In the light of the above discussion, the problem of how to accelerate the process of organizational democratization is perhaps better cast as one of how to hasten the legitimization of organizational politics. However, it is a daunting prospect given that the values underlying the rational mindset run as deep as those of democracy. After all, the language of rationality applies alike to military organizations, churches, universities and Wal-Mart. So how might constructive politics gain a rightful place as an organizing principle?

Executive development seems an obvious answer until we remind ourselves that this activity does not exist independently of the rational mindset. Consider corporate university programmes. These have become a prevalent means of ensuring that managers live the organizational values that align behaviours to the mission and strategy (Case and Selvester 2002). The values of rationality that lie behind such interventions remain deeply embedded (Clarke 1999), even though much of this effort appears to have little long-term impact on the persistence of alternative agendas. Part of the problem lies in what is meant by executive development. Many activities so described are not in practice developmental, in that they do not enable managers to consider their own values and beliefs, and how these influence behaviour (Burrell 1989). Yet it is those personal values that managers must consider before alternative models of organizing can be explored.

In contrast, business schools should provide the independent intellectual critique required to address alternative organizational models. In practice, however, they too are caught in the same rational mindset trap as their client world (Reed and Anthony 1992, Willmott 1994, Holman 2000). Indeed, the academic communities of North America and Europe have played a substantial role in articulating and encouraging the use of the rational mindset. In any case, business schools are also businesses and, like most businesses, not given to alienating their clients with unpalatable messages (Pfeffer and Fong 2002, Friga et al. 2003). Furthermore, development is not often on the curriculum because the intellectual heritage of many business school faculty members leads them to emphasize the cerebral rather than the emotional domain of learning. Case studies, models and research findings tend to be the established currency, not in-depth personal development (Mintzberg 1992, Pfeffer and Fong 2002).

Whilst there are pockets of academics who critique the institutionalized values and processes of executive development (see for example Reynolds 2000 and Pfeffer and Fong 2002), it seems unlikely that there will be any rapid alteration of existing priorities. This is only likely to come with a societal-level shift that influences education as a whole, a process of transformation almost certainly measurable in decades rather than years. However, this does not mean that the individual in a given organization has to wait for sea changes in society. The ability of individuals to promote alternatives is, after all, the cornerstone of democracy, and in the context of a single organization, it is this notion that probably provides the most realistic way of accelerating the process of democratization.

As our research demonstrates, in any one business it may be the determination of individuals and groups to promote their alternative organizational agendas, to act on principled causes, which serves to dislodge the rational mindset. In other words, within the context of any one organization, constructive political action may legitimize itself. Consider how progress towards democratization has been made in particular enterprises, the impression made by champions of organizational innovation such as Percy Barnevik, the ex-CEO of ABB, Andy Grove of Intel, or Richard Branson of Virgin. They and others like them impact, not just on their own organizations, but on popular consciousness as well. Whilst their businesses, like all businesses, enjoy mixed fortunes over the long term, this does not eclipse their greater contribution – they create organizations that become models for other organizations. Moreover, in terms of the power of individual action they are but the tip of the iceberg, for in many corporate businesses it is possible to find champions of constructive politics who have won widespread respect and admiration for their opposition to ill-conceived corporate policies. Those organizations, or pockets of good practice within them, provide glimpses of how truly democratized large-scale organizations might be managed.

Similarly, many smaller organizations experiment with radical approaches to managing. For example, at Acer, the personal computer company, Stan Shih, co-founder of the group, has built a federation of self-managing firms held together by mutual interest rather than legal ownership. Some companies are R&D centres, others marketing organizations. The group's management and home country investors jointly own each one, with (usually) only a small minority ownership stake held by Acer. At Oticon, an international hearing aid manufacturer, they have gone one step further still in ushering democratization into the process of management (see Box 16.2).

BOX 16.2   OTICON

This highly successful company is defined by a number of features. First, there is an underlying assumption that all employees are responsible adults who come to work to do their best. They are also considered to be unique individuals with diverse interests and ways of working. This means that work is established on an internal market: whilst project managers pursue the people they would like on their projects, individuals are free to work on any project that will accept them or to propose their own initiative. In effect, employees design their own jobs, but everyone must find projects in which they can take roles outside of their own core expertise in order to encourage a broad perspective. Employees are developed by 'mentors', whose responsibility is to support their 'pupils'' professional development, review performance and co-ordinate salary adjustments. The allocation of time and attention to different tasks is not controlled by central authority but arises out of a negotiation process. The resolution of conflicts is left to mutual agreement between employees, project leaders and mentors. Strategic priorities are discussed with all employees by a development group which also co-ordinates the overall process, evaluates project initiatives, and allocates financial resources. William Demant, the holding company for Oticon, was named European Company of the Year 2003.

These are organizations where action by leaders at the top makes it possible for the values of democracy to flourish. But not that many organizations are led by enlightened entrepreneurs or radical corporate visionaries, so what are the possibilities for individual or group action working from less favourable organizational starting points?

Clearly the transition for individuals to constructive political management is daunting because it requires both unlearning the official model of management and developing demanding new capabilities. (Box 16.3 offers an outline development agenda.) For this

---

BOX 16.3   CONSTRUCTIVE POLITICS: AN OVERVIEW OF KEY CAPABILITIES

Conceptual understanding

- Power and politics – evaluating the complexity of the influence process and the role of motives
- Relationships – evaluating the different barriers to organizational relationships
- Political mechanisms – recognizing the value of lobbying, stealth and apparent adherence to formal procedure
- Pockets of good practice – appreciating the value of establishing worthwhile causes to stimulate organizational change

Self understanding

- Civic virtue – balancing personal and organizational motivations
- Managerial irreverence – a healthy scepticism about the limits to what is possible through formal organization
- Personal success – inextricably interwoven with the success of others

Awareness

- Stakeholder knowledge – knowing the agendas and motivations of key players
- Organizational knowledge – knowing who makes key decisions and how they are made
- Knowledge of the business environment – knowing the issues critical for the organization

Interpersonal skills

- Persuasive presentation – developing collaborative outcomes through personal enthusiasm, suggestion, logical connections and the disclosure of motives
- Productive challenge – causing others to analyse their assumptions
- Reading others – a continual observation and evaluation of the motives and actions of others

---

reason, processes of self-development must reflect the need for individuals to take a more irreverent and critical perspective of their organization in order to accept the limitations of the rational mindset.

If senior executives cannot embrace a political perspective in their business, individuals must think and act as politicians for themselves. As we have tried to show in this chapter, to do so they must see political action as constructive, and understand that personal gain must be in the service of others, not just self-seeking. Worthy causes are the key.

Many managers appear to have the beginnings of such a cause. They hold high ambitions for their team, or their business unit. They wish their professional values to guide their actions and those of others. They can feel deeply about mistaken strategic decisions, or the neglect of huge opportunities in their markets. Or again, what of the frustrations they sometimes feel because obvious organizational improvements never happen? Each such fledgling agenda on its own may appear insignificant. But in the context of any one organization they provide a point of departure in legitimizing politics, and individual action is axiomatic in this process.

Conclusion

We have argued in this chapter that organizational politics, far from being antithetical to individual choice and autonomy, should be considered as symbiotic with the move toward greater organizational democracy. In an environment where organizations are increasingly called upon to respond to a multitude of internal and external stakeholder interests, our case is built upon three principles. First, that constructive politics represents an entirely logical process by which these diverse interests and stakeholders may be reconciled. Wherever there is conflict, political processes are at work. The effective reconciliation of these causes depends on the ability of individuals to balance personal interests with those of other stakeholders, to demonstrate civic virtue. Second, that in recognizing the multi-goal nature of organizations, the political model implicitly values the diversity these competing agendas provide, and views their reconciliation as a constructive process. This requires that managers are able to work with the need for both coherence and diversity by promoting debate and justifying outcomes to those involved. Third, that management is essentially all about the reconciliation of competing causes and therefore managers are, *de facto*, politicians by the nature of their role. Indeed, as in a political institutional setting, individual leadership action provides a central platform from which to promote the stewardship of more democratic organization forms. Our exploratory research suggests that individual cognitions reflecting transparency of motive and reciprocity of success are significant in enabling managers to work constructively with politics for the benefit of themselves and their organizations.

Nevertheless, such is the capacity of the rational mindset to undermine the notion of constructive politics that progress toward more democratic organization forms, despite encouraging environmental trends, has been limited. Current management development practices are also influenced by rational thinking such that little impact is likely to be made through these mechanisms. In practical terms, therefore, we argue that rather than by grand design, progress towards organizational democracy may best be made by exploiting the loopholes and contradictions of the rational mindset from within, since the benefit of constructive political behaviour appears to be best appreciated when experienced in practice. Our research case studies highlight this opportunity. The challenge for senior management is to harness the diversity inherent in their businesses so as to better realize the value of competing political agendas. As a starting point senior executives could contemplate some of the following:

1. Coaching those who work for them to question assumptions about corporate unity. Doing the same with colleagues at executive level, but calling it 'scenario painting' or 'brainstorming'.
2. Recruiting and nurturing organizational 'misfits' so that they blossom into leaders of pockets of good practice. Protecting the pockets once they begin to take shape, and until they can stand on their own success.
3. Suggesting to their HRM specialists that political skills should be included in their competency framework, and that they should question the value of team development for the organization.
4. Leading a special project to evaluate the benefits of radical approaches to employee ownership and rewards.
5. Tasking business school academics and consultants working with their business to show how their models challenge managers, not merely support their assumptions.

But in terms of creating a wholesale shift in organizational democratization it is a gradual process. That said, it is important to remember that the rational model of organizing has guided managerial values for at least two centuries, if not much longer, yet in the last 20 years there has been a significant unfreezing of organizing principles. Contemporary organizational forms and management models allow greater scope for individual agendas to be voiced. On a more optimistic note, then, true organizational democratization, built on principles of constructive politics, may be closer than its painstakingly slow emergence suggests.

References

Ackers, P. and Preston, D. (1997). Born again? The ethics and efficacy of the conversion experience in contemporary management development. *Journal of Management Studies*, **34**, 677–701.
Ammeter, A., Douglas, C., Gardner, W., Hochwater, W. and Ferris, G. (2002). Toward a political theory of leadership, *The Leadership Quarterly*, **13**, 751–96.
Ammeter, A., Douglas, C. and Gardner, W. (2004). Introduction to: *The Leadership Quarterly* special issue on political perspectives in leadership, *The Leadership Quarterly*, **15**, 433–5.
Andersson, L. (1996). Employee cynicism: An examination using a contract violation framework. *Human Relations*, **49**, 1395–417.
Argyris, C. (1998). Empowerment: The emperor's new clothes, *Harvard Business Review*, May–June, 98–105.
Armbruster, T. and Gebert, D. (2002). Uncharted territories of organizational research: The case of Karl Poppers's open society and its enemies. *Organization Studies*, **23**, 169–88.
Ashcraft, K. (2001). Organized dissonance: Feminist bureaucracy as hybrid form. *Academy of Management Journal*, **44**, 1301–22.
Ashmos, D., Duchon, D., McDaniel, R. and Huonker, J. (2002). What a mess! Participation as a simple managerial rule to 'complexify' organizations. *Journal of Management Studies*, **39**, 189–206.
Barker, R. (1997). How can we train leaders if we do not know what leadership is? *Human Relations*, **50**, 343–63.
Brunson, N. (2002). *The organization of hypocrisy: Talk, decisions and actions in organizations*. Chichester, UK: John Wiley and Sons.
Buchanan, D. (1999). The logic of political action: An experiment with the epistemology of the particular, *British Journal of Management*, **10**, S73–S88.
Buchanan, D. and Badham, R. (1999). *Change, power and politics, winning the turf game*. London: Sage.
Buckingham, M. (2001). What a waste. *People Management*, October, London: Personnel Publications.

Burrell, G. (1989). The absent centre: The neglect of philosophy in Anglo-American management theory. *Human Systems Management*, **8**, 307–12.

Butcher, D. and Atkinson, S. (2001). Stealth, secrecy and subversion: The language of change. *Journal of Organizational Change Management*, **14**, 554–69.

Butcher, D. and Clarke, M. (2001). *Smart Management, Using Politics in Organizations*, Basingstoke, UK: Palgrave Macmillan.

Case, P. and Selvester, K. (2002) Watch your back: Reflections on trust and mistrust in management. *Management Learning*, **33**, 231–47.

Child, J. and McGrath, R. (2002). Organizations unfettered: organizational form in an information-intensive economy. *Academy of Management Journal*, **44**, 1135–48.

Child, J. and Rodrigues, S. (2003). Corporate governance and new organizational forms: Issues of double and multiple agency. *Journal of Management and Governance*, **7**, 337–60.

Clarke, M. (1999), Management development as a game of meaningless outcomes. *Human Resources Management Journal*, **9**, 38–49.

Clarke, M. (2004). A study of the role of representative leadership in pluralistic settings: Preliminary findings. Paper presented at the European Academy of Management (EURAM) Conference, 'Governance in Managerial Life', Edinburgh, May.

Cloke, K. and Goldsmith, J. (2002). *The end of management and the rise of organizational democracy*. San Francisco, CA: Jossey Bass.

Cludts, S. (1999). Organization theory and the ethics of participation. *Journal of Business Ethics*, **21**, 157–71.

Coopey, J. and Burgoyne, J. (2000). Politics and organizational learning. *Journal of Management Studies*, **37**, 869–85.

Courpasson, D. and Dany, F. (2003). Indifference or obedience? Business firms as democratic hybrids. *Organization Studies*, **24**, 1231–60.

Czarniawska, B. (2003), Forbidden knowledge: Organization theory in times of transition. *Management Learning*, **35**, 353–65.

Daboub, A. (2002). Strategic alliances, network organizations, and ethical responsibility. *SAM, Advanced Management Journal*, **67**, 40–48.

Davis, W. and Gardner, W. (2004). Perceptions of politics and organization cynicism: An attributional and leader–member exchange perspective. *The Leadership Quarterly*, **15**, 439–65.

Dean J., Brandes, P. and Dharwadkar, R. (1998). Organizational cynicism, *Academy of Management Review*, **23**, 341–52.

DeGregorio, C. (1997). *Networks of champions*. Ann Arbor, MI: University of Michigan Press.

Denis, J., Lamothe, L. and Langley, A. (2001). The dynamics of collective leadership and strategic change in pluralistic organizations. *Academy of Management Journal*, **44**, 809–37.

Dopson, S. and Neumann, J. (1994). Uncertainty, contrariness and the double bind: Middle managers' reactions to their changing contracts. Templeton Working Paper MRP/94/7.

Douglas, C. and Ammeter, A. (2004). An examination of leader political skill and its effect on ratings of leader effectiveness. *The Leadership Quarterly*, **15**, 537–50.

Elgie, R. (1995). *Political leadership in liberal democracies*. London: Macmillan.

Etzioni, A. (1998). A communitarian note of stakeholder theory. *Business Ethics Quarterly*, **8**, 679–91.

Ferris, G., Perrewé, P. and C. Douglas (2002). Political skill at work. *Organization Dynamics*, **28**, 25–37.

Ferris, G., Perrewé, P., Anthony, W. and Gilmore, D. (2004). Political skill at work. *Organization Dynamics*, **28**, 25–37.

Friedman, A. and Miles S. (2002). Developing stakeholder theory. *Journal of Management Studies*, **30**, 1–21.

Friga, P., Bettis, R. and Sullivan, R. (2003). Changes in management education and new business school strategies for the 21st century. *Academy of Management, Learning and Education*, **2**, 233–49.

Giddens, A. (1984). *The constitution of society*. Berkeley, CA: University of California Press.

Grandori, A. (2001). Methodological options for an integrated perspective on organization. *Human Relations*, **54**, 37–47.

Gratton, L. (2003). *The democratic exercise: Liberating your business with individual freedom and shared purpose (universal history)*. London: Financial Times/Prentice-Hall.

Gratton, L. and Ghoshal, S. (2003). Managing personal human capital: New ethos for the 'volunteer' employee. *European Management Journal*, **21**, 1–10.

Greco, J. (1996). Stories for executive development: an isotonic solution, *Journal of Organizational Change Management*, **9**, 43–65.

Hales, C. (1999). Why do managers do what they do? Reconciling evidence and theory in accounts of managerial work. *British Journal of Management*, **10**, 335–50.

Hall, A., Blass, R., Ferris, G. and Massengale, R. (2004). Leader reputation and accountability in organizations: Implications for dysfunctional leader behavior. *The Leadership Quarterly*, **15**, 515–36.

Hamel, G. (2000). Waking up IBM: How a gang of unlikely rebels transformed big blue. *Harvard Business Review*, July/August, 137–44.

Handy, C. (1997). Unimagined futures. In F. Hesslebein, M. Goldsmith and R. Beckhard (eds), *The organization of the future* (pp. 377–83). San Francisco, CA: Jossey Bass.

Heller, F. (1998). Influence at work: A 25 year program of research. *Human Relations*, **51**, 1425–56.

Held, D. (1987). *Models of democracy*, Cambridge, UK: Polity Press.

Holman, D. (2000). Contemporary models of management education in the UK, *Management Learning*, **31**, 197–217.

Hope, V. and Hendry J. (1995). Corporate culture change – is it relevant for the organizations of the 1990s? *Human Resource Management Journal*, **5**, 61–73.

House, R. and Aditya, R. (1997). The social scientific study of leadership: Quo vadis? *Journal of Management*, **23**, 409–73.

Kakabadse, A. and Kakabadse, N. (2001). *The geopolitics of governance*. Basingstoke, UK: Palgrave Macmillan.

Kan, M. and Parry, K. (2004). Identifying paradox: A grounded theory of leadership in overcoming resistance to change. *The Leadership Quarterly*, **15**, 467–91.

Kets de Vries, M. (1998). Charisma in action: The transformational abilities of Virgin's Richard Branson and ABB's Percy Barnevik. *Organization Dynamics*, **26**, 6–22.

Leach, S. and Wilson, D. (2000). *Local political leadership*, Bristol, UK: Policy Press.

Lipman-Blumen, J. and Leavitt, H. (2001). *Hot groups – feeding them, seeding them and using them to ignite your organization*, Oxford, UK: Oxford University Press.

March, J. and Olsen J. (1995). *Democratic governance*, New York: Free Press.

Malnight, T. (2001). Emerging structural patterns within multinational corporations: Toward process-based structures. *Academy of Management Journal*, **44**, 1187–210.

Mintzberg, H. (1992). Debate, *Harvard Business Review*, Nov.–Dec., 128–40.

Novicevic, M. and Harvey, M. (2004). The political role of corporate human resource management in strategic global leadership development, *The Leadership Quarterly*, **15**, 569–88.

O'Reilly, C. and Tushman, M. (2004). The ambidextrous organization. *Harvard Business Review*, April, 74–81.

Patten, S. (2001). Democratizing the Institutions of Policy Making: Democratic Consultation and Participatory Administration. *Journal of Canadian Studies*, **35**, 221–39.

Peters, R. and Williams, C. (2002). Does organizational leadership theory apply to legislative leaders? *Organization Dynamics*, **30**, 257–68.

Pfeffer, J. (1992). *Management with Power*, Boston, MA: Harvard School Press.

Pfeffer, J. and Fong, C. (2002). The end of business schools? Less success than meets the eye. *Academy of Management Learning and Education*, **1**, 78–95.

Preston, T. and t'Hart, P. (1999). Understanding and evaluating bureaucratic politics: The nexus between political leaders and advisory systems. *Political Psychology*, **20**, 49–98.

Rajagopalan, B., Peterson, R. and Watson, S. (2003). The rise of free agency: Is it inevitable? *Organization Dynamics*, **32**, 93–105.

Reed, M. and Anthony, P. (1992). Professionalizing management and managing professionalization: British management in the 1980's. *Journal of Management Studies*, **29**, 591–613.

Reynolds, M. (2000). Bright lights and pastoral idyll: Ideas of community underlying management education methodologies. *Management Learning*, **31**, 67–81.

Ruscio, K. (2004). *The Leadership Dilemma in Modern Democracy*. New Horizons in Leadership Studies, Cheltenham, UK and Northampton, MA, USA: Edward Elgar.

Starrat, R. (2001). Democratic leadership theory in late modernity: An oxymoron or ironic possibility? *Leadership in Education*, **4**, 333–52.

Stuckey, M. (1999). Power, policy and accountability. In S. Schull (ed.), *Presidential policy making: An end of century assessment* (pp. 263–74). New York: Sharpe.

Treadway, D., Hochwater, W., Ferris, G., Kacmar, C., Douglas, C., Ammeter, A. and Buckley, M. (2004). Leader political skill and employees' reactions. *The Leadership Quarterly*, **15**, 493–513.

Van den Ende, J. (2003). Organizing innovative projects to interact with market dynamics: A coevolutionary approach. *European Management Journal*, **21**, 273–85.

Vigoda, E. (2003). *Developments in Organizational Politics: how political dynamics affect employee performance in modern work sites*. Cheltenham, UK and Northampton, MA, USA: Edward Elgar.

Willmott, H. (1994). Management education, provocations to a debate. *Management Learning*, **25**,105–36.

PART V

THE PROFESSIONALS' PERSPECTIVE: HUMAN RESOURCE MANAGEMENT AND CONSULTING IN A POLITICAL ENVIRONMENT

17 Speaking truth to power: Three perspectives on consultation
Robert T. Golembiewski

Introduction

The literature on consultation for, and reporting to, hierarchical superiors does not dwell on power phenomena, even though strong evidence supports the view that traditional views imply significant costs. No one can confidently explain this neglect. In part, the emphasis on legitimacy is dominant, perhaps especially because this view is so attractive to formal elites in all collective systems. Perhaps relatedly, 'power' or 'politics' in organizations is seen as beneath attention, if not 'dirty' and somehow underhanded. Here, however, 'power' is seen as a necessity in all collective life, whether its manifestation can be good, bad, or somewhere in-between.

This chapter has two objectives. It seeks to help remedy this shortfall which, typically, conceptually defines power arenas as out of bounds in most organization theory and practice, as well as in consultation. And it sketches two related applied ways of moving beyond the traditional neglect.

Three features dominate, whether 'power' is viewed as derived from legitimate or formal authority or from skills, personality, or other bases. The primary focus is on public organizations but has general applicability to all sectors and NGO contexts as well.

Moreover, brief attention will be given to two useful changes in perspective that derive from the admission of power phenomena: a distinction between two patterns of power or influence in organizations, and then a few 'clinical' examples of how non-verbal designs can help in isolating and dealing with power phenomena. Both variants draw attention to contextual differences relevant in dealing with how things get done in organizations.

Finally, the present focus sees power phenomena from the point of view of stakeholders, in two senses: the experience gained through the lens of that technology-cum-values for personal and organizational change usually labeled OD or organization development; and also from the perspective of the profession commonly called OD consultant or intervenor (Golembiewski 2002, 2003).

Introductory conceptual boundaries

The public sector literature in management has not encouraged attention to influence or power phenomena as contrasted with narrowly legitimate authority, and in this it shares substantial territory with business (e.g. Harrison 1972; De Luca 1983). To illustrate in the public sector, the bureaucratic model is role- and rule-bound, and provides for neutralized management that is without compassion or anger and which follows the vertical 'chain of command' (e.g. Golembiewski 1995b). Relatedly, the basic politics versus administration distinction puts the former 'on tap' and the latter 'on top,' despite the volume of knowledge and discretion that could be used (and is used!) by staff to influence operations as well as policy (e.g. Golembiewski 1967; 1995b). In sum, organizational authority is said to flow in one vertical line – from top to bottom, as from the president through political appointees at executive levels. Beyond that, the 'neutral civil servants' carry on.

Throughout this chapter, 'power' or 'influence' refers to the ability to make things happen in organizations, whether the source is legitimate authority and/or 'informal authority' that derives from personal and group sources beyond the formal structure or beyond statements of roles and responsibilities (French and Raven 1959). In the most popular formulation, several sources of power often get distinguished in addition to legitimate authority or influence (French and Raven 1959). These can include the power of knowledge or education, the power of informal status, and so on.

Perhaps to oversimplify, four types can be identified to include all organization members (see Figure 17.1).

The focus here is on Types 1, 2 and 3, and the 'influence' phenomena associated with them. Note that the types can have different sources, and be either supportive of organization purposes or subversive of them. Classical analysis focuses on formal authority, with the two plus signs in Type 1 indicating major attention to matters of structure, roles and jurisdictions. Adding the present focus on 'informal organization' is indicated by the two plus signs in that column, and adds huge scope and coverage to the traditional emphases via enlarged focus on 'power' or 'influence' to relate to the rich textures of dynamics resulting from history, personalities, the exigencies of time and space, and the quicksilver of behavioral dynamics, among other features. Absent this added scope, classical observers were left with unsatisfactory speculations about 'deviant cases' or residual categories, especially in connection with what should have been Types 2 and 3. Witness the once-common view of slums as the chaotic consequences of anomic responses by a dysfunctional rabble. In contrast, as those such as Whyte (1952) established, slums were nuanced and rich products of an often-neglected 'informal' or 'underground' society. The common finesse missed many opportunities for theoretical and practical enrichment of knowledge about social organization. The combinatory emphases in this volume and this chapter seek to avoid such losses.

As a final note in this brief introduction, note a basic parallelism. The present volume and this chapter commonly seek to relate to the same arena – 'organization politics,' or Types 1–3 above. Given a similar pattern, the scope of the volume is obviously greater, while this chapter is content with drawing attention to consulting activities only, and even there with very selective coverage.

	Formal authority	Informal authority
1	+	−
2	+	+
3	−	+
4	−	−

Figure 17.1   Sources of influence for four types of organization members

Three exemplars of consulting approaches
Numerous ways exist to take influence into explicit theoretical and practical account in consulting, with many of them applicable in business as well as in public sector contexts. Here, three exemplars get attention: the first is narrowly descriptive; the second has a clinical flavor associated with a direct intervention in an evolving situation; and the third provides substantial detail about the reach-and-grasp of a focus on stakeholders.

Describing patterns of influence settings
To begin with a general orientation, organization contexts often will differ with respect to the prevailing mix of patterns of kinds of power, the traditional claims about homogeneity notwithstanding. Two tables establish the point, economically if selectively. Much greater elaboration is possible, but space limitations require that the temptation to risk bloviating will be resisted.

Figure 17.2(a) comes as no surprise to most commentators on organizations. That figure provides, in stark outline, the classical view that degree of influence does and should increase directly, as one goes up the level of the hierarchy. In short, no challenge to the bureaucratic model inheres in Figure 17.2(a), although some might wish to increase the slope of the line expressing the basic relationship. But the general form encountered in practice will encourage two views: that is the way that things should be, as well as the way they are.

In contrast, Figure 17.2(b) comes as a surprise to consultants in both business and government. There, middle levels exert the most influence and the 'control graph' is inverted, in contrast to Figure 17.2(a).

Data for such distinct patterns of influence estimates typically derive from surveys of organization members (e.g. Tannenbaum 1968; Tannenbaum and Cooke 1979; and Tannenbaum et al. 1974), and these cannot be detailed here, because of space limitations. But one point seems obvious – neither diagnosis nor interventions can neglect the

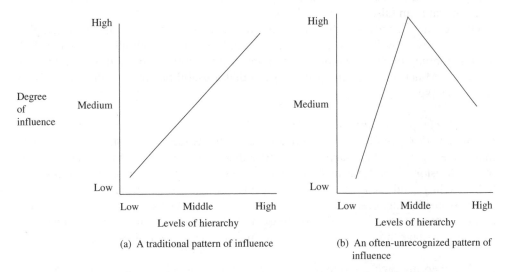

(a) A traditional pattern of influence   (b) An often-unrecognized pattern of influence

Figure 17.2   Two patterns of influence in organizations, by hierarchical level

prototypic distinction between Figure 17.2(a) and 17.2(b). A consultant does so only at multiple peril – to self as well as to clients, or perhaps even innocent bystanders.

Despite its general neglect, Figure 17.2(b) may be especially relevant in the public sector. Thus Edwards (1994; 1997) found that this pattern dominated in a state department – Extension Services in Georgia – and ostensibly due to the flows of funds coming from local as well as federal sources. One larger flow predominantly went from state sources to the service providers at county or mid-organization levels, while top state agency levels relied on a second and lesser flow from the US federal level of government. In short, practical budgeting details reflecting multiple historic and political realities changed that shape of the control graph.

The inverted control graph in Figure 17.2(b) also has been observed in several inter-national settings (e.g. Tannenbaum et al. 1974), but no convenient rationale seems available. Arguably, in addition, this pattern also may be found in the numerous US federal agencies led by political appointees of the president who have short tenures in office – let us say two years or thereabouts – which allows the accumulation of discretion at mid-organization levels of expertise and hence influence. No doubt this reflects con-gressional desires for influence or power beyond the legitimate 'checks and balances' pre-scribed in the US Constitution but absent in parliamentary forms of governance. Such an effect is consistent with virtually all observers of US dynamics at the federal level.

Whatever the relative incidence of the two patterns in Figure 17.2, and perhaps of others as well, consultants obviously are advised to be clear about which pattern exists. In addition, specific organizations may contain mixtures of such patterns. Why this care? At the very least, to illustrate, ill-targeted consultant requests for authoritative judgments may be directed at the less authoritative locus. This may inspire inter-level conflict, or at least will raise questions about the consultant's competencies. For similar reasons and for equally obvious reasons, consultants are well advised to be clear about the pattern of influence which they are serving, for fear of running afoul of it. Without fear of redun-dancy, consultants seeking guidance or making recommendations obviously should dis-tinguish real from false influence holders.

The view here is narrowly illustrative, but the general point can hardly be overempha-sized. Tomorrow's well-stocked consultant certainly will have a well-filled tool kit, includ-ing a taxonomy of organization types to which intervention can be fitted. Provisional work (e.g. Miller and Friesen 1984) suggests that a useful taxonomy will contain 12 or more archetypes.

Intervening in specific patterns of influence

Envision working as a consultant with a team of 20 members or so, which seems 'stuck': that is, ideas get raised, but action plans are either shot down or seem to come unraveled so that decisions do not stay made, even if apparently made. Generally, such groups seem to be 'circling,' and even showing signs of being in a 'downward spiral.'

A reasonable diagnosis of such a situation emphasizes the isolation of unresolved and perhaps unrecognized influence dynamics, and clinical judgments must be made, as it were. A two-stage 'non-verbal' design seems reasonable, in such a case:

I.   Members are each asked to occupy a vertical position relative to all the members – in effect, to provide a human graphic of the degree of power each person exercised over some definite period. Discussion to validate these relative levels of influence often follow.

II. Members are directed by the consultant to occupy a second, and perhaps very different, level in the vertical space of the meeting room, with discussion again following. Here, the focus is on how much influence or power each member intended to desire – an intent as distinguished from accomplishment in the first design stage.

Such 'non-verbal' designs may help people recognize and deal openly with topics that are generally taboo, and influence is often one of the topics least amenable to easy public analysis. What are the illustrative effects?

Stage I normally does not require much validation. Members tend to see degrees of their successful influence exertions in shared terms. In one case, all members might lie on the floor, with their group really being stuck. This group was 'going nowhere' because none of its members was providing energy, let alone direction. In the typical case, members distribute themselves in space – reclining on the floor, sitting on a chair, standing on a chair, climbing upon a table, and so on.

Stage II tends to be *sui generic*, and may be deeply revealing. In one case, almost all individuals had located themselves in space in ways that, agreeably to all, indicated their relative desires to exert influence. One individual was not satisfied – he first stood on a table, then went on tip-toe, but neither level satisfied. Suddenly, he grasped a colleague, forced him to his knees, and then used the surprised colleague as a foundation from which to express his desire for exerting influence by leaping upward to a western-style chandelier. Hanging there, well above his colleagues, he was finally satisfied with the representation of his intent, about which talk had not earlier been possible.

His colleagues needed no prodding. 'That's you, OK. Willing to climb on us to achieve your needs, and often without recognizing it.' They added a sharp thrust: 'Variably, also, you fail and, it seems to us, with little insight about why.'

This briefly characterizes a breakthrough event for all. In sum, an approach for getting their group beyond stuckness became available to members, and this knowledge implied a vehicle for motivating action.

Such a dramatic revelation provides much grist for the mill of a group seeking to avoid stuckness due to covert, repressed data that hence could neither trigger nor suggest effective analysis.

Stakeholder analysis and influence
Let us shift focus here to materials that have been published elsewhere in substantial detail (Golembiewski 2003; 267–71). To begin, stakeholders are those who have an interest in influencing a consultation, or should have such an interest. Obviously, the underlying concept of authority is a broad one.

Distinctions about stakeholders
Here, the approach is harshly selective, making only these three distinctions relevant to stakeholding:

● Basic differences in types of stakeholders
● Differential power of types of stakeholders

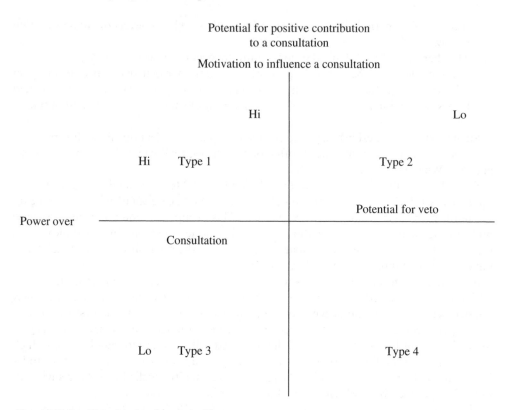

Figure 17.3   Four kinds of stakeholders

- Differentiated strategies for dealing with different types of stakeholders with variable power.

Although simple, these distinctions should not be bad-mouthed. All three often are important for consultants to keep in mind. Often, indeed, the distinctions are essential.

Four types of stakeholders
Here, we focus on a generic and simple 2 × 2 table to distinguish stakeholders. This approach parallels the approach of Savage et al. (1991), who also differentiate four kinds of stakeholders by high versus low status on two dimensions. Briefly, the analysis here begins with a brief introduction to the four cells of Figure 17.3.

Type 1: Two-way powerhouse   Such stakeholders get most of what they want, if not all. They can help a consultation, or stop it dead. Consultants can attempt to encourage the choice of obvious attractiveness to them, but consultants cannot avoid the potency of such stakeholders.

Type 2: Naysayers   These stakeholders can inhibit a consultation, but if they behave in normal fashion they can add little or nothing to positive choice making or implementation.

Naysayers come in various styles. Typically, they have position power exerted in a narrow arena, but little or no motivation or perhaps capability to develop a broader impact. In business, the heirs of the original owner–entrepreneur of a firm can have position power via stock ownership, and may be interested only in seeing that dividends remain high. Otherwise, they may be preoccupied with preserving the status quo. More broadly, naysayers may be single-interest persons or groups protecting what exists or pursuing their narrow ideal; or they may be collections of personal counterdependents who have become stereotyped into playing Dr No.

Naysayers need to be accounted for in a consultation, although proactive expectations usually will be inappropriate. Such naysayers have enough influence to make the results of their role play stick in a high-enough percentage of cases that they cannot simply be neglected. In any case, they are profoundly resistant to or uninterested in change except in a narrow arena.

Type 3: Supporting powerhouses Examples of this third type can be a consultant's dream, because they are often profoundly impactful on any forward-looking consultation, but they also are rare. They have what it takes – formal status as well as skills, resources, attributes, or whatever – to help move a consultation along. And they are supportive of the consultation, by definition, for whatever reasons and for an indeterminate period.

Perhaps curiously, the local Communist officials in Polish plants in the late 1970s often fit this profile when the consultation involved improving the quality of working life of employees. Obviously, those elites saw an unfavorable future facing them, absent finding new ways for new days. Hence their support for consultations that often would threaten old elites. Recent events proved that the elites were correct.

Type 4: Fringe players Fringe players neither have veto power, nor are they powerfully proactive players. For example, mid-managers often are fringe players, as are many employee constituencies in non-union settings or with weak union representation. Many single-interest groups also are fringe players in the present sense: they pursue their narrow interest, perhaps with a passion, but they cannot initiate, veto, or contribute significantly to most consultations. Hence their fringe-player status, despite their occasional potency (e.g. Golembiewski 1995a).

Stakeholder orientations by issue arenas
Many times, further, it is insufficient and even dangerous to make general judgments about specific stakeholders. Above all, consultants are well advised to remember the 'fallacy of misplaced concreteness.' Stakeholders are never solid and homogeneous through and through, although it may be convenient in the short run to speak of them as if they were. Stakeholders are better seen as central tendencies evolving in protean ways rather than as 'things,' as more potential quicksilver than unalterable granite. So, the present observations apply as cautious generalizations, as more or less.

In addition, different issue arenas also may see specific stakeholders shift between the four types. Indeed, the OD consultation essentially rests on such a dynamic (e.g. Golembiewski 2003).

We illustrate here this important point, if only briefly. Type 1s in issue arena A, for example, may be Type 4s in another arena. With a little consultant help, such stakeholders might get together in arena A in order to build a coalition relevant in other arenas. Even fringe players have information, for example, that may be critical in a consultation, if appropriately made public. Typically, also, fringe players might be targeted to improve their status on humanitarian grounds, if only because the implementation of change programs typically relies on having willing stakeholders with sufficient status to be taken seriously.

Detailing stakeholder status by issue arenas has much to recommend it, then. Such information can add to a consultant's effectiveness, and it will certainly increase available options.

A whimsical example comes to mind. A team of researchers was studying power and influence on decision making among fraternity members. The researchers observed a neglected but reasonable regularity in the behavior of a critical set of stakeholders – fraternity officers. The regularity depended on the decision-making task at hand. On some issues perhaps best labeled 'marginal' to fraternity life – for example choices between various political candidates or policies – the officers tended to behave in power-sharing or even *laissez-faire* ways. They aggressively sought to encourage leadership by individual members with special interests or expertise, and deferred to them.

However, on issues more central to fraternity life – rating the relative pulchritude of *Playboy* covergirls, for example – the officers/stakeholders were energized into determined action. They tried hard to influence choices. The officers were not above exercising the muscle that came with their office to get the correct choices made, with 'correct' referring to their perspectives about what choices a 'good fraternity' should make, even given that the choices were in a real sense 'academic.' In short, the officers remained the 'same,' but acted very differently in the two issue arenas. The assessment of female pulchritude was seen as central to the fraternity mission, while the assessments of political candidates and policies were much less so, if not irrelevant. In the latter case, they tended to defer to others – perhaps because of lack of knowledge, lack of interest, or as a way of saving themselves for the 'big issues' while perhaps gaining a few points from their less well-situated fraternity brothers who enjoyed the deference, even if temporary.

So it can be with other stakeholders in different issue arenas. Consultant failure to be flexibly aware of such contextual variations can be costly, or even deadly.

Strategies for dealing with types of stakeholders
Assume that a consultant has a good sense of the stakeholder types in the issue arena(s) relevant to a particular consultation. What strategies might a consultant adopt? This discussion is illustrative only.

Type 1: Two-way powerhouse Here the consultant obviously needs to be wary. Remember: 800-pound gorillas usually get what they want, even if things or people in between them and what they want get trampled in the process.

So it is tough to have a Type 1 stakeholder who comes to oppose a consultant's orientation or recommendations. A research team (Savage et al. 1991, 65) advises that one should 'collaborate' with such stakeholders. Some would even advise clients to learn what Type 1s want, and then see that they get all or most of it!

But both suggestions oversimplify. Not infrequently, a consultant may have to try to moderate the stance of a Type 1 stakeholder, or even to seek a change of direction that preserves the influence of the stakeholder in the process. The probabilities of success here usually are low, but the need may nonetheless exist. Witness a consultant facing a Type 1 stakeholder adamantly stonewalling on an issue that threatens the public health or safety. The consultant cannot simply 'collaborate' here. That option may be closed to the consultant – ethically, or perhaps even legally.

Moreover, a consultant 'in solid' with a Type 1 stakeholder is not necessarily in the clear. Other stakeholders may suspect a consultant who is 'too close' to a Type 1, and the need here may be for a suitable 'distance' or 'independence' for the consultant intent on remaining a credible third party. But the trick is accomplishing these while preserving the status of the stakeholder, except in extraordinary cases, as when illegal or unethical collaboration is required to maintain the support of a two-way powerhouse. For OD consultants, much progress has been made on defining what their professional status requires in terms of ethical as well as caring and competent service (e.g. Gellerman et al. 1990).

Type 2: Naysayers Such stakeholders may pose special kinds of problems, if only because a consultant may find it difficult to deal with them without uncomfortable pandering or without counterproductive defensiveness.

One mature approach involves gaining perspective on the naysayer. For example, the mode may be a reasonable response by a stakeholder who was an underdog for a long time, or even a punching bag for some stakeholders who were bullies. The issue here may simply be to see that the stakeholder gets the credit deserved for hanging in there, if that credit is necessarily delayed.

Of course, such a consulting perspective does not necessarily provide the 'frame breaking' to get the support of a naysaying stakeholder. I recall one union leadership that would have opposed management's announcement that the day after Sunday was Monday, so poisonous were the relationships between them. And vice versa. Since there were longstanding reasons for the union attitude, the effects remained strong and stable. Hence getting a start on the simplest initiatives usually was very tough even after management, in pursuit of its self-interest, sought to bury the hatchet while temporarily remaining cautious or even suspicious about the union leaders.

My up-front consulting strategy was to get *some* initial agreement on *something* – even if minor – to slowly begin to build trust beyond bitter-end adversarial postures of two powerhouse naysayers. It was at best one step forward, and seven-eighths of a step back. I vividly recall one very long afternoon spent on seeing whether management and union officials could get together on an initiative that was attractive to one stakeholder and had a very small cost to the other (Golembiewski and Varney 2000).

Manipulative consultants may try to provide Type 2 stakeholders with something (or even someone) they can pummel, but which (or who) is not central to the issues of the consultation. This approach seeks to distract attention of Type 2 stakeholders, to allow expression of their veto power on a 'pesky tar baby', which is beside the essential point. At times, indeed, the OD consultant ends up playing this sad role. But scapegoating is not an ethically attractive option; and, moreover, it can have a very distinctive backlash in practice.

Type 3: Supporting powerhouse Ah, the consultant's dream. Such stakeholders can help, and hugely. Cherish them, cultivate them, and (above all) make as sure as you can that they stay involved or at least plugged into the communication network relevant to the consultation and your activities.

Why? One reason is obvious, beyond the simple courtesy and acknowledgement of relationships – perhaps past, present, and maybe in the future. Directly, today's supporting powerhouse may become tomorrow's naysayer, a two-way powerhouse, or even a fringe player (see Type 4 below). The wise consultant takes heed in preserving or even enhancing such a supporter, as by heads-up warnings of coming events of which a player might be unaware.

Type 4: Fringe players   The temptation here may be to let sleeping dogs lie, as it were. As is, they can't help, but they can't hurt either. One research team advises that such stakeholders be 'monitored' (Savage et al. 1991, 67)

This low-energy orientation may be seriously misguided, however, for both normative and practical reasons. For example, an OD consultant might find it useful or even necessary to help empower Type 4 stakeholders, as happens in many cases of team building; and broadly OD interventions often involve mobilizing latent power in stakeholders who once were fringe players. They may well return to that status after a short time; or they might remain empowered for an indefinite period.

References

Carnevale, David G. (2002). *Organizational development in the public sector*. Cambridge, MA: Westview Press.
Dalton, Melville (1950). *Men who manage*. New York: Wiley.
De Luca, J.R. (1983). *Politics of H.R. planning*. Mimeo. Philadelphia, PA.
Dyer, William (1988). *Team building*. Reading, MA: Addison-Wesley.
Edwards, J. David. (1997). Measuring influence distribution in a public agency: A test of the control graph technique. *Public Administration Quarterly*, **20** (4), 81–113.
French, John R.P. and B. Raven (1959). The bases of social power. In Darwin Cartwright (ed.), *Studies in social power*. Ann Arbor, MI: Institute for Social Research, University of Michigan.
Gellerman, William, Frankel, M:S. and Ladenson, R.F. (1990). *Values and ethics in organization and human systems development*: San Francisco, CA: Jossey-Bass.
Golembiewski, Robert T. (1967). *Organizing men and power: Problems of behavior and line-staff models*. Chicago, IL: Rand McNally.
Golembiewski, Robert T. (1995a). *Managing diversity in organizations*. Tuscaloosa, AL: University of Alabama Press.
Golembiewski, Robert T. (1995b). *Practical public management*. New York: Marcel Dekker.
Golembiewski, Robert T. (2002). *Handbook of organizational consultation*. New York: Marcel Dekker.
Golembiewski, Robert T. (2003). *Ironies in organizational development*. New York: Marcel Dekker.
Golembiewski, Robert T. and Glenn H. Varney (eds) (2000). *Cases in organization development*. New York: Marcel Dekker.
Harrison, Roger (1972). Understanding your organization's character. *Harvard Business Review*, **50**: 121–3.
Miller, Danny and P.H. Friesen (1984). *Organizations: A quantum view*. Englewood Cliffs, NJ: Prentice-Hall.
Savage, G.T., T.W. Nix, C.J. Whitehead and J.D. Blair (1991). Strategies for assessing and managing organizational stakeholders. *Academy of Management Executive*, **5** (2), 61–75.
Tannenbaum, Arnold S. (1968). *Control in organizations*. New York: McGraw-Hill.
Tannenbaum, Arnold S. and Robert A. Cooke (1979). Organizational control: A review of studies employing the control graph method. In Cornelis J. Lammers and David J. Hickson (eds), *Organizations alike and unlike: International and interinstitutional studies in the sociology of organizations* (pp. 183–210). London: Routledge & Kegan Paul.
Tannenbaum, Arnold S., Bogdan Kavcic, Menachem Rosier, Mino Vianello and Georg Wieser (1974). *Hierarchy in organizations: An international comparison*. San Francisco, CA: Jossey-Bass.
Whyte, W.F. (1952). *Street corner society: The social structure of an Italian slum*. Chicago, IL: University of Chicago Press.

18 Twelve foundations for the power position of consultants

Astrid I. Boogers-van Griethuijsen, Ben J.M. Emans, Janka I. Stoker and Arndt M. Sorge

Introduction

Power within an organization is an indispensable entity for any individual with interests linked to occurrences in that organization. Consultants involved in change projects form one category of those individuals. Kubr (2002, p. 10) defines their job as 'an independent professional advisory service assisting managers and organizations in achieving organizational purposes and objectives by solving management and business problems, identifying and seizing new opportunities, enhancing learning and implementing changes'. As long as the last element (implementing changes) forms a substantive part of their role, 'getting things done' becomes pivotal for the successful completion of their projects. A solid power position, defined as the chance to influence the behavior of other people, is then a requisite for them to do their job well. The aim of this chapter is to get insight into the foundations of that position. The question to be answered reads: what are the roots of consultant power, that is, what are the qualities consultant power is based on?

Consultancy and organizational politics

The assumption behind the question mentioned above is that consultants are supposed to be engaged in the game of organizational politics. Organizational politics is like a coin with two sides (cf. Vigoda and Cohen, 2002), one of them representing the influence tactics displayed by actors in the organization and the other representing the perception and the evaluation of those behaviors by the organization members who are the targets of it. The latter equals attributed power. To the degree that intended targets attribute a fair amount of power to an actor, the influence attempts displayed by him/her will be appreciated, invoking true commitment rather than sheer compliance or – even worse – flat resistance. Politics, then, constitutes a positive force in the organization, encompassing room for influence attempts (side one of the coin) as well as positive reactions to those attempts (side two). Having, developing and maintaining a reliable power position therefore may be called a prerequisite for successful initiative taking in organizations. This applies to consultants no less than it does to other people in and around organizations.

This assumption may seem to be at odds with the way the consultancy job most often is viewed. An overview by Harrison (1991) shows that until the 1970s most authors in the field tended to assume that successful consultants must remain aloof from organizational politics. This view, which essentially reflects a negation of power and politics, is embraced by those who see consultants primarily as social engineers (the so-called rational–analytical view), as well as those who see them as therapists–facilitators (the humanistic view). Both conceptualizations imply that there is neither room nor need for political elements in the role of consultants, because the steps taken by them are supposed to be unrelated to their own interests. Political non-involvement is said to promote objectivity and consequently to facilitate the access to people and groups with divergent interests and outlooks. This view still pervades the world of consultancy. Change professionals have continued to be cautious and conservative in grappling with the political realities involved in the implementation of planned organizational change (Kumar and Thibodeaux, 1990). According to Harrison's overview, however, competing views emerge after the 1970s.

One of the new views is still only slightly different from the power negation position. Acknowledging that politics is part and parcel of organizational processes, the authors advocating this view argue that consultants should diagnose political processes (but without taking part in them) in order to fit their actions and recommendations to the organization's political realities. Other views are more radical, asserting that successful consultants must play the role of political operator (next to the roles of social engineer and therapist/facilitator) by actively gaining power and subsequently using it to further their consulting goals. Authors representative of this view are Beer (1976), Cobb (1987), Cobb and Margulies (1981), Kakabadse (1984), Margulies and Raia (1984) and Mastenbroek (1986). Still more radical notions are expressed, finally, by authors who argue that political activism by consultants is unavoidable (Pettigrew, 1975) or even desirable (Alinsky, 1971; Borum, 1980; Chesler et al., 1978, Elden, 1986; Greiner and Schein, 1988).

The position adopted in this chapter fits in with the political operator role of consultants. Power of consultants is considered as a quality that is instrumental to perform their job, not because that job would imply any form of political activism for or against certain interest groups, but due to the plain fact that organizational change is inextricably linked with organizational politics. While in the consultancy literature the skills and contributions of the 'social engineer' and the 'therapist–facilitator' have been explored at length, the role of change agent as political operator is less well defined and understood (Buchanan and Badham, 1999). Exploring the types of power available for consultants may be helpful for filling up this gap. Rather than being at odds with fundamental consultant attitudes, such an endeavor will help to mark out those attitudes in a meaningful way.

Power bases for managers

The concept of power in organizations has been articulated rather well in relation to the position of formal managers. Categorizations of so-called power bases of managers have been elaborated (French and Raven, 1959; Mulder et al., 1986; Pettigrew, 1975, Emans and Van Tuuren, 1998). Something similar is not available regarding the position of consultants. Due to the sheer fact that consultants are devoid of formal and related forms of power, we cannot simply assume that categorizations developed for formal leaders are unrestrictedly applicable to them. These categorizations may, however, serve as a suitable starting point for a discussion of consultants' power bases.

Power bases of managers can be distinguished by dividing the power dynamics underlying them. According to Emans (1995), three different types of power dynamics, and thus three different categories of power bases, can be distinguished.

The first category is labeled 'attributes'. It contains power bases that are effective because the actors are characterized by some specific attribute, irrespective of how targets are approached by them. This type of base is related to what an actor is. The second category is labeled 'dependencies'. The effectiveness of power bases in this category depends on whether an actor has valuable resources at his disposal while, at the same time, targets are dependent upon that actor for obtaining those resources. It thus roots in the fact that the resources that the power holder can credibly control are positively valued by targets (Clegg, 2002). In short, this type of base is related to what an actor has. The third category, labeled 'abilities', has to do with the action repertory of actors in that it enables them to influence and persuade targets. This type of base is related to what actors can do.

Table 18.1 is an overview of models of power bases of managers as they are found in social psychological and other literature, grouped in accordance with the above categorization. The first column presents an integrated summary of these models, resulting in a synoptic model of eight items: expert power, referent power, formal power, network/information power, means of exchange, reward power, coercive power and rational persuasion.

Method

With the synoptic model of eight managerial power bases as a starting point, the remaining sections of this chapter aim at redressing that model in such a way that it can serve as a tool for describing consultants' power positions in change projects. In a first step, the model is adapted to the situation of consultants on strictly theoretical grounds. The result is an extended model consisting of 12 consultant power bases. This theoretical step is explained in the next section. In a second step, based on the results of a series of interviews, each of these power bases is elaborated in detail in the section after that.

The interviews, held with 28 management consultants involved in change processes, took approximately two hours per respondent. We used a structured interview schedule, consisting of two parts. In the first part, respondents were asked to describe the change project they were involved in. We needed to get insight into the context of the change project, in order to understand the answers of the second (main) part of the interview, which was entirely devoted to the power position of the consultant.

The main purpose of the second part of the interview was to validate and articulate the 12 power bases. We introduced them only very briefly. We just named the constructs, classified according to the attributes, dependencies and ability categories, without providing any definition or explication, leaving room for articulations in the answers of the interviewees. We asked the respondents whether these power bases were foundations for their own power position in this change project. We also asked them to illustrate their answers with examples. In order to further validate our model, we concluded the interview by asking whether the respondents were of the opinion that the model of power bases was complete. If not, we asked them what kind of power bases should be added.

The sample of interviewed consultants consists of 5 women and 23 men. Their average age is 38 years, with a minimum of 28 years and a maximum of 52 years. Seventeen consultants are categorized as 'younger' (age between 25 and 40 years) and 11 consultants are categorized as 'older' (age between 40 and 60 years). On average, the consultants in our sample have had almost 11 years of experience as consultant. Eight consultants are categorized as 'having little experience' (years of experience as a consultant between 0 and 7 years), 13 consultants are categorized as 'having moderate experience' (years of experience as a consultant between 7 and 15 years) and 7 consultants are categorized as 'having extensive experience' as consultant (more than 15 years of experience as a consultant).

Table 18.1 Power bases relevant for managers

Summary	French and Raven (1959)	Pettigrew (1975)	Harrison (1991)	Mulder et al. (1986)	Benfari et al. (1986)
Attributes					
• Expert power • Referent power	• Expert • Referent	• Assessed stature	• Personal and professional assessed stature	• Expert power • Referent power	• Expert • Referent • Affiliation
• Formal power	• Legitimate	• Political access and sensitivity • Group support	• Access to powerful members of the organization • Support of internal and external power groups	• Formal power	• Authority • Group power
Dependencies					
• Network/ information power		• Control over information	• Control over information	• Upward influence • Outward influence	• Information
• Means of exchange		• Expertise	• Expertise • Ability to develop mutually beneficial exchanges with powerful members	• Expertise	
• Reward power • Coercive power	• Reward • Coercive			• Sanction power • Sanction power	• Reward
Abilities					
• Rational persuasion				• Reciprocal open consultation	

Note: The first column summarizes the elements found in the models displayed in the other columns; empty cells reflect non-correspondence between those models.

Three respondents have a one-person business, 10 respondents work for small consultancy firms (between 2 and 10 consultants), 8 respondents work for medium consultancy firms (between 10 and 100 consultants) and 7 respondents work for large consultancy firms (more than 100 consultants).

From power bases for managers to power bases for consultants: theoretical step

In order to apply the synoptic model to the world of consultancy, some adjustments need to be made. As will be argued below, these adaptations relate to three elements in the model: formal power, reference power and the total abilities category.

Concerning 'formal power', consultants have none in their client organization because they have no formal position in the organization's hierarchical structure (Pettigrew, 1975; Benfari et al., 1986; Mulder et al., 1986). This does not imply, however, that power is by definition non-existent in their situation. In an indirect way, they may take advantage of the existing formal power in the client organization. They can use the formal, legitimate power of – for instance – members of the management team in order to get commitment with respect to the change project. In order to do so, they need good relationships with these members of the management team. More generally speaking, we may define indirect formal power, that is, strong relationships with those high in formal power, as a power base on its own (comparable bases are found in Pettigrew, 1975 and Harrison, 1991), which is particularly applicable to the position of consultants. As a replacement for simple formal power, this power base can be included as an additional element in a model suitable for consultants.

The power base called 'referent power' originates from the identification of power targets (in our case members of the client organization) with the power holder (in our case the consultant) (French and Raven, 1959). Identification represents a feeling of oneness that the client organization's members have in respect of the consultant, or a desire for such an identity. One may wonder whether this type of power, in the case of consultants, is fully linked to the person who actually exercises the power. Actually, consultants are more or less strangers in the client organization. At least, they may be at the start of their project. Does this then mean that referent power is non-existent? We propose that, in case they are considered to represent either their office or their profession, something like referent power is possible, even when consultants are strangers. Next to the one linked to the consultant's person, this kind of representativeness may give rise to two additional types of referent power. One is the power derived from the association with a (well-known, highly valued) consultancy firm. The other power base is derived from the association with the consultancy profession and the status connected to it. The latter is visible in all kinds of status symbols that refer to the profession, such as cars and clothes. Thus reputation of the consultancy firm and professional status symbols come into view as two additional power bases relevant to consultants as power holders.

The 'abilities' category of the synoptic model in Table 18.1 contains just one power base. It is the rational persuasiveness of power holders. In the consultancy literature, however, at least two other abilities, communicative skills and analytical skills respectively, are claimed to form part of the consultants' repertory when he/she is involved in influence attempts *vis-à-vis* the organization (e.g. Buchanan and Boddy, 1992).

Effective communication in a change project is of vital interest. In a survey on consultants in the ICT field, Buchanan and Boddy (1992) found that communication is one of the five competence clusters relevant to change managers. According to them, communication skills are used to transmit effectively, to the people involved, the need for changes in project goals as well as in individual tasks and responsibilities. These skills clearly encompass more than the use of rational persuasiveness. For that reason, being a good communicator can be considered as a power base on its own for consultants (if not for other actors as well).

In addition to communication skills, analytical skills are a necessary part of the consultant's métier. Buchanan and Boddy (1992) call this the helicopter perspective: standing back from the immediate project and taking a broader view of priorities. Being able to take that perspective, the consultant provides the members of the client organization with a wider, broader and longer-term view of their situation. By doing so he/she brings about changes in their mindsets, and accordingly paves the way for further influence attempts. According to Buchanan and Boddy (1992), this is important when one has to do with strategic technological or organizational changes. In this way, analytical skills emerge as an additional ability increasing the power of consultants.

By adding the four additional power bases described above, we come to a model of 12 power bases for consultants. They are listed in the first two columns of Table 18.2.

From power bases for managers to power bases for consultants: results of the interview study

As described above, we tested the model of the 12 power bases for consultants in an interview study. The outcomes of these interviews serve for further articulation and validation of the 12 bases. The results, which are summarized in the third column of Table 18.2, are presented in the 12 following sections.

Power base 1 (attributes): Expert power

According to the interviewed consultants, members in the client organization value two kinds of expertise. They first value knowledge about and/or experience in the same type of industry and, second, they value expertise that is focused on knowledge about and/or experience with the content of the change project. Obviously, these kinds of expertise are not mutually exclusive.

Respondents distinguish 'demonstrated' and 'perceived' amount of expertise as a source for expert power. In general, the younger consultants in this interview study have to prove their expertness, for example by showing their business card together with their university degree, by showing their expertise during interventions in the change project or by talking about earlier projects and their background. The older consultants more often told us that members in their client organization assume a certain amount of expertise without having to see any evidence. One respondent told us to be content with his grey hair, because to members of the client organization it is a symbol of experience. On the other hand, the older consultants told us more than once that in their opinion members of the client organization attribute too much expertise to them, and are, as a consequence, passive and docile. French and Raven (1959) argue that the strength of expert power varies with the extent of the knowledge the power holder (in our case the consultant) possesses. Based on the results of the interview study, we extend this statement, stressing that the demonstrated as well as the perceived expertise is relevant to the strength of expert power.

The interviewed consultants gave different examples of situations in which they recognized their power position to be based on expert power. Some consultants told us that

Table 18.2   The 12 bases of the consultant's power

Main categories	Potential power bases for external consultants	Qualifications
Attributes 'to be'	1. Expert power	Power based on perceived or demonstrated knowledge and experience related to the client's industry as well as the content of the change project
	2. Personal power	Members of the client organization and the consultant 'clicking' with each other
	3. Power based on the reputation of the consultancy firm	Recognition of name, useful in the beginning of the change project
	4. Power based on professional status symbols	Useful in the beginning of the project, because of the raised expectations
	5. Indirect formal power	Reflection of formal, hierarchical power of members in the client organization to the consultant
Dependencies 'to have'	6. Network power	Network contacts of the consultant valued by members of the client organization
	7. Means of exchange	Knowledge made available in exchange for support for the change project
	8. Reward power	Positive feedback
	9. Coercive power	Negative feedback
Abilities 'to be able'	10. Power based on persuasive skills	Showing advantages of proposals, making use of examples, and so on
	11. Power based on communicative skills	Adapting language, understanding client's jargon, and so on
	12. Power based on analytical skills	Not only the analysis itself, but also translation into practice

members of the client organization asked them questions about topics which were not related to the change project. These consultants experienced those questions as evidence for attributed expertise. Several consultants noticed that their proposals most often did not meet with much resistance. According to the consultants, members of the client organization did not bring up these proposals for discussion, because they expected a certain degree of expertness in advance and therefore considered the proposals of the consultants as unconditionally good. Other examples of remarks reflecting the client members' belief in the expertise of the consultant are: 'You have to become project manager, because you know our organization and industry and you have knowledge about this kind of project' and 'The manager asked me: "Tell me what will work and what not. You know our organization, our people, and you know critical success factors."'

Summarizing, expert power of a consultant can be defined as the power based on perceived or demonstrated knowledge and experience related to the client's industry as well as the content of the change project.

Power base 2 (attributes): Personal power
The respondents of the interview study recognize power derived from personality as an important power base. The consultant and the members of the client organization have to 'click' personally with each other. In general, personal characteristics that add to the consultant's personal power are, according to the respondents, being an open person, being calm, especially in difficult situations, being accessible, willing to cooperate with members in the client organization, and showing interest in and commitment to the client organization.

Although almost every respondent values the importance of personality as a source of power, not every respondent is positive about the impact of this power base. Three consultants stated that they always visit client organizations with a colleague because of the risk of a mismatch between the personality of the consultant and the members of the organization. This is especially important at the start of the project. In one of the three cases, the colleague of the respondent did not match with members in the client organization and therefore a third colleague took his place.

Both younger and older consultants as well as more experienced and less experienced consultants agree with the notion that trust is an important indication of power based on personality. Other indications are that the client organization explicitly asks for a specific consultant or expresses the wish to continue the cooperation.

Power base 3 (attributes): Power derived from the status of the consultancy firm
Consultants working for firms with general name recognition agreed that this name recognition leads to power. The so-called Big Five and other well-known, leading consultancy firms are associated with quality, reliability and the possibility of involvement of more specialized colleagues if necessary. The names function as a brand name. Expectations associated with these brand names result in respect and status, and therefore power for the consultant. It has been claimed that members of the client organization feel that they are taken seriously if a consultant from a respectable firm is hired.

Almost every consultant working for a one-person business or working for small consultancy firms (between 2 and 10 consultants) argued that the name of their firm does not affect their power position. It is the person himself/herself who will affect his/her power position. Consultants working for medium consultancy firms (between 10 and 100 consultants) did not answer unequivocally. Some of these consultants told us that the name of their consultancy firm did not give them any power. The names of their firms are not known by members of the client organization. The other consultants agreed with the notion that at least at some levels in the organization, especially the top level, or in some branches name recognition is a foundation of their power position. However, although their firm was lacking general name recognition, in these and comparable situations members did impute power to the consultant based on associations with and expectations of the consulting firm.

Respondents possessing power based on the status of their firm stressed that this power base is only relevant at the beginning of the change project or when establishing new contacts. After that, other bases will replace power based on the status of the firm. If the progress of the change process does not meet the expectations raised by the name of the consultancy firm, the strength of the power bases will also decrease. So, management consultants can only use this power base during the time when they lay the foundation of their power position.

Power base 4 (attributes): Professional status symbols
Status symbols reflecting a certain image were recognized as important by a considerable part of the interviewed respondents. Included symbols are clothes, motorcars, ICT means (such as GSMs and laptop computers) and the costs connected with the change project. Professional status symbols can be used to either increase or reduce the distance between the consultant and members in the client organization. According to the respondents, both increasing and reducing distance can create a power position.

Most older consultants argued that in order to reduce the distance it is important to adapt to requirements and habits of members of the client organization. One of the respondents said: 'You should respect your customers, which means that you have to think about your clothes. It is important to adapt to the client organization rather than to create a distance.' Half of the younger consultants also argued that it is better to reduce distance. The others used status symbols, especially their clothes, to increase the distance. One respondent told us that he used his clothes to compensate for his age.

These two different methods of working can be found in the discussion of Rosenfeld et al. (1995) on the question of whether or not to act like chameleons. According to the respondents, there are no general rules for how to use status symbols. However, they agree with the non-existence of a linear relationship between distance and amount of power.

Power base 5 (attributes): Indirect formal power
Although the respondents of the interview study lacked formal power in the client organization, they all used its existing formal power structure to develop their own power position. We define this power base as indirect formal power, which contains the formal, hierarchical power of members in the client organization that is transferred to the consultant and, as such, forms a part of the power position of the consultant in the client organization.

However, a difference exists between older and younger consultants. According to their examples, a considerable part of the younger consultants makes explicit use of the formal power of management team members. For example, they ask managers to attend a number of meetings to emphasize the importance of the change project. This attendance is then announced to the other members of the meeting to stimulate them to attend and prepare it. One consultant told us: 'I explicitly focus on wishes of the management team in order to legitimate their request of my cooperation.' Older consultants used the formal power of the client organization's members more implicitly. The consultants recognized the importance of their social position which was created by the management and partly due to their introduction as well as pointing to their contacts; however, they did not use this power explicitly in a way the younger consultants said they did. Here is an example from an older consultant: 'I show my relationship with the members of the management team by for example having lunch together and walking into the office without an appointment, especially because this is no common use for members of the client organization.'

Power base 6 (dependencies): Network power

The interviewed consultants defined network contacts as valuable possibilities to get to know relevant people inside and outside the organization. The distinction between inside and outside contacts is made by the respondents. As an example of inside contacts, some recognized the interest that the client organization's members had in their contacts with top management. They would ask consultants to be positive about them or to ask the top management about its opinion of them regarding relevant issues.

More experienced respondents considered outside contacts a power source. According to the respondents, members in the client organization are sometimes impressed by the outside contacts of the consultants, even without the necessity to meet these contacts themselves. Consultants with more experience were able to compare the client organization with other organizations in the same industry. Furthermore, in some cases, they were actually able to benchmark, which is valuable for the client organization.

Consultants working for larger firms considered the network inside their consulting firm as relevant. Their colleagues, who could be experts in a certain area, would for example conduct a workshop to provide extra information about a special topic of the change project.

Power base 7 (dependencies): Means of exchange

We asked consultants whether they provided members in the client organization with means to exchange in order to get them to participate and support their change project. Some consultants recognized this exchange relationship. They used knowledge and information as means of exchange. One consultant said: 'The fact that we give knowledge and models to the teams attributes to our power position. It helps to create support, because if you hand them a model (try to fill in this model, use this model as a way of thinking), they use it to continue their part in the change project.' Some other respondents argued that they did not characterize their relationships with members of the client organization as exchange relationships and therefore did not recognize this power base as a foundation of their power position.

With respect to the exchange relationship, a distinction should be made between knowledge as an attribute and knowledge as a source. Emans (1995) distinguishes expert power from expertise. In his terms, in a relationship characterized by expertise, targets depend upon an actor with regard to assistance in problem solving. According to this definition, knowledge is a means of exchange, which the consultant can possess and make available to members of the organization. This is different from expert power as an attribute, in which targets rely upon the way in which they perceive the expertise of an actor. In a clearly unequal relationship, targets (members of the client organization) attribute a lesser amount of relevant abilities and/or knowledge to themselves than to the power holder (the consultant). Due to the perceived knowledge gap, they tend to agree with whatever the consultant says.

Summarizing, knowledge and information are recognized as means of exchange that consultants can use for the benefit of support for the change project and can therefore be considered as the foundation of their power position in the client organization.

Power base 8 (dependencies): Reward power

According to the definition of Mulder et al. (1986), rewards consist of material as well as psychological components. The interviewed consultants recognized the possibilities to psychologically reward members of a client organization. Psychological rewarding mainly implies recognition: recognition of the proven effort of members regarding the change project, recognition of the individual qualities of members and trust in their capabilities, and recognition and understanding of the complex work situation of members. However, in our interview study, the respondents did not recognize possibilities of material rewards.

Respondents argue that the amount of reward power differs in all levels of the organization and also during the project. In general, members at the lower levels depend to a larger degree on recognition and compliments than members at the top levels. Especially if complimenting is not a common practice in the client organization, compliments can motivate the members. However, if members get used to compliments, the effect will decrease.

In summary, reward power can be defined as the possibility to provide psychological rewards to members in the client organization by recognizing and respecting their efforts and capabilities which, in exchange, stimulates them to behave in the direction desired by the consultant.

Power base 9 (dependencies): Coercive power
The importance of immaterial coercive power is recognized by the interviewed consultants. They distinguished content-related negative feedback and process-related negative feedback. The former involves the ability of consultants to point out weak characteristics of both the organization and the individual members. To show their ability to hold a mirror up to members of the client organization, some management consultants, in most cases more experienced ones, consciously ask some critical questions during a first (orienting) meeting. In order to create a solid starting point for change, they use the negative content-related feedback to show the problems of the client organization to establish a sense of urgency.

The process-related negative feedback is defined as feedback that stimulates members of the client organization to participate in the change project and, more important, to have them hold on to their commitment to it. An example of this type of feedback is talking to members about their conduct (e.g. using a GSM during a meeting, not delivering documents in time). According to the respondents, members try to avoid such feedback by complying with the requests of the consultant. This is in line with, for example, the definition of French and Raven (1959), who argue that coercive power stems from the expectation of the targets (members in the client organization) that they will be punished by the power holder (the consultant) if they fail to conform to influence attempts (requests of the consultant).

Summarizing, coercive power of management consultants consists of two parts: power derived from the recognition of content-related negative feedback, and power derived from the willingness of members of the client organization to prevent process-related negative feedback.

Power base 10 (abilities): Power based on persuasive skills
Concerning persuasive skills, an obvious distinction should be made between the effective use of these skills, which leads to successful influence attempts (persuasive skills as influence tactics), and the recognition of the consultant's persuasive skills by members in the client organization, which leads to the attribution of power to them (persuasive skills as a power base). We refer to the latter.

Most of the respondents in the interview study agreed with the notion that persuasive skills are important as a power base. Persuasive skills include showing members the advantages of the proposed changes, using content-related arguments to promote the changes, making use of examples of other change projects to promote the changes, and making sure that members in the client organization conclude by themselves what is best for their organization. These skills operate as a power base. Members of the client organization recognize and value them, and therefore they attribute power to the consultant.

Power base 11 (abilities): Power based on communicative skills
According to the respondents of the interview study, effective communication skills is about adapting your own language to the language of the client organization, which includes understanding the technical jargon of the industry, avoiding the use of management jargon, assessing the level of the audience appropriately, using clear written as well as oral communication, and being able to really listen to the people one is speaking with. Respondents of the interview study argued that these skills are a very important foundation in establishing their power position in change projects.

Power base 12 (abilities): Power based on analytical skills
Respondents of the interview study agreed that analytical skills are very important for consultants. Sometimes, members of client organizations only see problems instead of solutions. Others do not see the real problem, which makes it difficult to change in the right way. According to the interviewed consultants, being able to diagnose situations quickly is a skill that many members in the client organization value.

An important remark several respondents made is that analytical skills relate not only to the analysis itself, but also to the translation of this analysis to the practice of the client organization. Members in the client organization value these analytical skills and consequently attribute power to the consultant.

Conclusions
The results presented above, with all of the interviewees readily describing their work conditions in terms of power bases, underscore the meaningfulness of the concept of consultant power for understanding the consulting job. More specifically, the three categories of power bases (attributes, dependencies and abilities) appeared to play a role in the consultant profession no less than they tend to do in the world of managers. Simultaneously, the specific contents of each of the three categories appeared to be different in the case of consultants (compared to managers) as power holders. Among other things, this had to do with their position in the organization as an outsider devoid of formal authority. That position evidently affects the nature of their power bases, but not the significance of them.

This aspect of consulting tends to be largely overlooked in textbooks such as Kubr (2002), Fombrun and Nevins (2004) and Wickham (2004), which, as far as they deal with power-related issues, focus on the ability category of power bases only. This may be because power and consultancy are often seen as two incompatible entities, as consultancy is assumed to always allow clients their own 'free, informed choice', as Argyris (1973) phrased it. If embraced unrestrictedly, though, this assumption tends to deny the reality of organizational politics. In its positive form, organizational politics may be an extra force that enables clients to be free and informed rather than restricting their freedom and involvement. Indeed, power is a necessary condition for high-quality consulting, while influencing members of the client organization, and thus being politically active, is one of the core responsibilities of consultants.

The concept of consultant power seems to constitute a paradox. More precisely: a political active consultant – in a sense – plays a paradoxical role. On the one hand, political activities enable him/her to get things done and thus to promote intended developments. In short: the more power, the more consulting. On the other hand, those activities induce the involved members of the organization to perceive the consulting project as a political game, whereas that perception, in turn, tends to reduce the willingness of these members to whole-heartedly join the project. In short: the more power, the more opposition to consulting (see Vigoda, 2003, ch. 2 and *passim* for an overview of the negative impacts of the perception of organizational politics on organizational attitudes). In sum, the power game seems to be both a requirement and an impediment for the consulting job. The findings in our interviews help to unravel this paradox.

Each of the 12 power bases in our model is associated with a repertory of influence attempts in such a way that they confer a connotation of normality to those attempts. As exemplified by the illustrations given by the interviewed consultants, the power bases tend to add to the acceptability of influence attempts and thus actually to reduce the perception of organizational politics. Viewed this way, the power bases of consultants play a role similar to the role played by procedural and interactional justice (Folger and Greenberg, 1985; Folger and Cropanzano, 1998, ch. 2). These are two phenomena that are highly relevant for understanding organizational politics as they tend to justify the outcomes of decisions in organizations in the eyes of involved organization members, irrespective of the actual contents of those decisions. This is accomplished through a strict obedience to formally institutionalized and agreed-upon decision-making rules (procedural justice) and/or through the use of decent and friendly ways of approaching the people concerned (interactional justice). For consultants who make influence attempts *vis-à-vis* people in organizations, this means that they may enhance the responsiveness to those attempts by carefully following the rules of procedural and interactional justice. Based on the outcomes of our interviews study we can now conclude that similar effects can be produced by building and maintaining power bases alongside actually making power attempts. Along with high levels of enacted procedural and interactional justice, strong power bases can attenuate the causal relation between political behavior displayed by consultants on the one hand, and resistance evoked by the perception of organizational politics on the other. Far from being a paradox in itself, consultant power reduces the paradox inherent in political activities displayed by consultants. It paves the way for fruitfully playing political games in consulting projects.

As yet, this conclusion, however pertinent it may be, is evidently a somewhat crude one. It would merit further investigation into to what extent specific power bases are invoked and combined, when consultants practice specific influence styles and tactics such as rational persuasion, inspirational appeals, personal appeals, exchange, assertiveness, sanctions and pressure (Yukl and Falbe, 1990; Yukl, 2004; Emans et al., 2003). Conceivably, this depends on the nature of consultancy jobs, the specification of consultancy objectives, and the politics involved not only on the part of commissioning management but also on the part of different sections of the client organization, sections whose compliance is important for the success of the consultancy operation. Progressing further along the contingency theory of organizational politics sketched out by Vigoda (2003) may hold out the prospect of eventually explaining the exercise of power by consultants as subject to project and client organization contingencies, and geared to apply specific combinations of influence tactics by invoking related power bases. Last but not least, the refined deployment of organizational power and politics by consultants may shed light on tactics implemented by line managers, in a situation where access to hierarchical power is not sufficient or productive. In this respect, the resourceful manager may learn from the diligent consultant's experience. The study of consultants' politics thus may enlarge our understanding of organizational politics in general.

References

Argyris, C. (1973). *Intervention theory and method*. Reading, MA: Addison-Wesley.
Alinsky, S. (1971). *Rules for radicals*. New York: Random House/Vintage.
Beer, M. (1976). On gaining influence and power for OD. *Journal of Applied Behavioral Science*, **12**, 45–51.
Benfari, R.C., Wilkinson, H.E. and Orth, C.D. (1986). The effective use of power. *Business Horizons*, **7**(3), 12–16.
Borum, F. (1980). A power-strategy alternative to organization development. *Organization Studies*, **1**, 123–46.
Buchanan, D. and Badham, R. (1999). Politics and organizational change: The lived experience. *Human Relations*, **52**(5), 609–29.
Buchanan, D. and Boddy, D. (1992). *The expertise of the change agent: public performance and backstage activity*. New York: Prentice-Hall.
Chesler, M., Crawfoot, J. and Brayant, B. (1978). Power training: an alternative path to conflict management. *California Management Review*, **21**, 84–91.
Clegg, S. (2002). Power. *International Encyclopedia of Business and Management*, 2nd edn, vol. 6: 5369–80. London: Thomson Learning.
Cobb, A. (1987). The politics of consultation. *Consultation: An International Journal*, **6**, 71–89.
Cobb, A. and Margulies, N. (1981). Organization development: A political perspective. *Academy of Management Review*, **6**, 49–59.
Elden, M. (1986). Socio-technical systems ideas as public policy in Norway: Empowering participation through worker-managed change. *Journal of Applied Behavioral Science*, **22**, 239–55.
Emans, B.J.M. (1995). Macht en machtgebruik van leidinggevenden. In R. van der Vlist, H. Steensma, A. Kampermann and J. Gerrichhauzen (eds), *Handboek leiderschap in arbeidsorganisaties*. Utrecht: Lemma.
Emans, B.J.M. and Van Tuuren, M.J.J. (1998). Restructuring welfare organizations: The power and powerless of local authorities. *European Journal of Work and Organizational Psychology*, **7**(2), 145–61.
Emans, B.J.M., Munduate, L., Klaver E. and Van de Vliert, E. (2003). Constructive consequences of leaders' forcing influence styles. *Applied Psychology*, **52**, 36–54.
Folger, R. and Cropanzano, R. (1998). *Organizational justice and human resource management*. Thousand Oaks, CA: Sage Publications.
Folger, R. and Greenberg, J. (1985). Procedural justice: An interpretive analysis of personnel systems. *Personnel and Human Resources Management*, **3**, 141–83.
Fombrun, C.J. and Nevins, M.D. (2004). *The advice business: Essential tools and models for management consulting*. Upper Saddle River, NJ: Pearson/Prentice-Hall.
French, J.R.P. and Raven, B. (1959). The bases of social power. In D. Cartwright (ed.), *Studies of social power* (pp. 150–67). Ann Arbor, MI: University of Michigan Press.
Greiner, L. and Schein, V. (1988). *Power and organizational development: Mobilizing power to implement change*. Reading, MA: Addison-Wesley.
Harrison, M.I. (1991). The politics of consulting for organizational change. *Knowledge and Policy: The International Journal of Knowledge Transfer*, **4**(3), 92–107.
Kakabadse, A. (1984). Politics of a process consultant. In A. Kakabadse and C. Parker (eds), *Power, politics and organizations: A behavioral science review* (pp. 169–83). Chichester, UK: Wiley.
Kubr, M. (2002). *Management consulting: A guide to the profession*, 4th edn. Geneva: International Labour Office.
Kumar, K. and Thibodeaux, M.S. (1990). Organizational politics and planned organization change. *Group and Organization Studies*, **15**(4), 357–66.
Margulies, N. and Raia, A. (1984). The politics of organization development. *Training and Development Journal*, **38**(8), 20–23.

Mastenbroek, W. (1986). The politics of consultancy. *Journal of Management Consulting*, **3**, 20–26.

Mulder, M., Koppelaar, L., De jong, R.D. and Verhage, J. (1986). Power, situation, and leaders' effectiveness: An organizational field study. *Journal of Applied Psychology*, **71**(4), 566–70.

Pettigrew, A.M. (1975). Towards a political theory of organizational intervention. *Human Relations*, **28**(2), 191–208.

Rosenfeld, P., Giacalone, R.A. and Riordan, C.A. (1995). *Impression management in organizations: theory, measurement, practice*. London and New York: Routledge.

Vigoda, E. (2003). *Developments in organizational politics: How political dynamics affect employee performance in modern work sites*. Cheltenham, UK and Northampton, MA: Edward Elgar.

Vigoda, E. and Cohen, A. (2002). Influence tactics and perceptions of organizational politics: A longitudinal study. *Journal of Business Research*, **55**, 311–24.

Wickham, P.A. (2004). *Management consulting: delivering an effective project*. Harlow: Prentice-Hall.

Yukl, G. (2004). Interactions in organizational change: Using influence tactics to initiate change. In J.J. Boonstra (ed.), *Dynamics of Organizational Change and Learning* (pp. 301–15). Chichester, UK: John Wiley.

Yukl, G. and Falbe, C.M. (1990). Influence tactics in upward, downward and lateral influence attempts. *Journal of Applied Psychology*, **75**, 525–35.

19 Organizational politics: Building positive political strategies in turbulent times

Ronnie Kurchner-Hawkins and Rima Miller

Introduction

Organizational politics is alive and well, and turbulent times can create cutthroat political action. Despite the extent of political action that takes place, organizational politics remains something that most managers do not want to talk about openly. Like many of the stereotypes about politics, it remains in the 'dark, smoke-filled room' of organizational behavior. In his book, *The empowered manager: Positive political skills at work*, Peter Block (1991) refers to organizational politics – 'like sex was in the 1950's – we knew it was going on, but nobody would really tell us about it' (p. 5). Huotari and Iivonen (2004) note that most employees are aware of organizational politics and influence and even use it when needed. This chapter is an attempt to open up the discussion of politics in organizations and shed light on this topic so practitioners will be more adept at coping and responding to political behavior and researchers can focus efforts at providing insight into the range of political strategies that will support organizational and individual success.

In reviewing different definitions of organizational politics, politics and self-serving behavior are often described synonymously (Kuzmits et al., 2002; Narayanan and Fahey, 1982; Egan, 1994; Drory, 1993). Malan and Bredemeyer (2002) state that politics is 'sullied by manipulative, power-grubbing behavior of a few individuals.' Reardon (2000) describes politics as – 'the messy stuff of getting things done.' Mayes and Allen (1977) present a complex definition about the management of means and ends, that is, using influence to achieve acceptable goals not approved by the organization or to achieve unacceptable goals that are approved by the organization through acceptable means. Parker et al. (1995) and Ferris et al. (1989) discuss organizational politics as a social influence process aimed at achieving both short- and long-term individual interests through a strategic and planned approach.

In a summary of three organizational models, rational, process and political, Drory (1993) describes the political model as one in which decision making and actions are determined through the process of conflict, power struggles and consensus building. Individual and group self-serving interests constitute the building blocks of the political process (p. 1).

The acquisition or use of power is another approach to defining organizational politics (Pfeffer, 1994; Dubrin, 2001; LaBarre, 1999). Egan (1994) refers to power as 'the essence of politics' and the core of political action, while Vigoda (2003) and Pfeffer (1994) refer to political behavior simply as the use of influence tactics and interpersonal influence. Although there is a wide range of definitions, for many organizational members, politics remains a dirty word, something to be avoided, for example, 'I don't play politics', says an upright employee. Not possible! This all too familiar response by employees may limit their contribution to the organization and their own effectiveness. According to Egan

(1994, p. 195), 'Decrying the fact that the system is political is like complaining that the water is wet . . . all systems have some kind of politics' (p. 195). Politics is an organizational reality and, as Pericles noted long ago, 'Just because you do not take an interest in politics does not mean that politics does not take an interest in you.' As Kuzmits et al. (2002) suggest, 'Politics are firmly embedded in any social structure and impossible to control or remove' (p. 79). Vigoda (2003, p. 10) concludes that organizational politics is 'an acceptable, common, and socially functional phenomenon' (p. 10).

Some of the more emotive and negative-sounding language used to describe organizational politics – self-serving, manipulative, intimidating and the like – may be due to the current turbulence and uncertainties in many organizational environments. In fact, there are several sources thought to contribute to negative political action. They include such factors as unpredictable and uncertain environments, survival, unclear goals and standards of performance, poorly defined decision processes, internal competition for resources and power (Egan, 1994; Toupin, 2001; Jinkner, 2004). Bureaucracy and traditional hierarchical organizational structures are also seen as sources of political behavior (Mitchell, 2003; Block, 1987; Pfeffer, 1994). Despite hierarchical structures, organizational politics is not necessarily the domain of top executives or leaders but involves organizational members interested in influencing decision processes from both formal and/or informal power positions (Mintzberg, 1983; Pettigrew, 1973). In fact, political behavior takes place at all different levels of an organization (Mayes and Allen, 1977).

Politics is pervasive in organizations. However, most of the attention for theory and practice has been on understanding the impact and antecedents of negative political behaviors in organizations. The model presented in this chapter is an initial step aimed at understanding the essential components for creating positive political action in an organizational environment. It is intended to describe how individuals can impact outcomes for themselves and their organization through positive strategic political behavior.

Moving from the negative to the positive

Despite the negative tone and feel to the discussion of organizational politics, there is a small but growing belief that a more positive approach to political behavior is possible and worthwhile.

> The best of politics is, however, about working to achieve consensus, to effectively align people through integration of interests, and persuasion and influence rather than authority or dominance. It is about decision making by representatives, with bottom-up delegation from the many to a trusted few. It is about caring passionately enough about an outcome to work at overcoming objections and resistance – not by any means at all, but with personal integrity and insight into the hopes, values, and concerns, that all play a role in making or obstructing progress. (Malan and Bredemeyer, 2002, p. 2)

Egan (1994) refers to positive politics as 'the politics of institutional enhancement' where 'players lobby for the agendas that they believe will advance the fortunes of the company' (p. 205). Block (1987) describes positive politics as 'enlightened self-interest' that begins with articulating a compelling, lofty and strategic vision.

The construct of organizational citizenship behavior (OCB) seems to emphasize the positive side of political action and opens the field to exploring positive aspects of political behavior. Using a term such as 'organizational citizenship behavior' reflects the biased connotation that politics is inherently negative and a different term is needed to describe positive behaviors. Tepper et al. (2004) describe OCB as discretionary actions that promote organizational effectiveness. Their following discussion indicates the overlap of the concept with politics and reflects the possibility of both negative and positive outcomes.

> However, more recent contributions to the OCB literature suggest that the consequences of OCB may not always be favorable (Bolino, 1999). Several authors have asserted that, on the surface, OCBs share much in common with actions that might be regarded as antithetical to OCB, such as impression management (Schnake, 1991), politics (Ferris, Judge, Rowland, and Fitzgibbons, 1994), and ingratiation (Eastman, 1994). For example, Ferris, Bhawuk, Fedor, and Judge (1995) argued that the key distinction between organizational politics and OCB has to do with perceivers' attributions of intentionality; observers regard behavior as prosocial when they can attribute sincerity to the actor's intent, and they attach the label 'politics' to the same behavior when they attribute self-interest and manipulation to the actor's intent. (Ibid., p. 456)

OCB may be political behavior by another name.

> What are the consequences of self-serving OCB? Contributors to this literature disagree as to whether the consequences of self serving OCB differ from the consequences of well-intentioned OCB. For example, Podsakoff, MacKenzie, and Hui (1993) asserted that acts of citizenship, regardless of their motive, contribute to organizational effectiveness: 'Does it really matter why an employee comes to work extra early or stays extra late? As long as the employee is really working, it should enhance the effectiveness of the organization' (p. 33). Schnake (1991) took a different tack, arguing that, in the long term, OCB motivated by self-interest produces dysfunctional outcomes. Bolino's (1999) position lies somewhere in the middle because he believed that self-serving OCB does not necessarily detract from organizational effectiveness, though its contribution to effective organization functioning is not as strong as well-intentioned OCB. (Ibid.)

To develop positive political strategies, a more neutral and less emotive definition and way of thinking about politics is needed that takes into account the range of behaviors that are political. It is naïve to believe that positive behavior cannot be political. For example, in his discussion of the political process, Pettigrew (1973) lays out a neutral position in which politics is about setting goals, and generating support for achieving them and managing the distribution of resources. Vigoda (2003) argues the utility of a more neutral perspective on politics.

> Politics is not necessarily a negative term implying illegitimate behavior. When discussing the use of force and influence in the national arena the term 'politics' allows researchers to objectively express a social phenomenon (behavioral or bureaucratic) describing the force and influence relations in the state. Similarly there is no need for the term 'organizational politics' to be loaded with negative meanings. It should serve organizational and management theory researchers as an analytical tool and natural term which contributes to the analysis and examination of organizational force and influence relations and their influence on organizational products. (pp. 11–12).

The utility of this neutral perspective is appealing to practitioners who experience the range of behaviors in daily organizational life and need tools to respond and act effectively.

Politics, leadership and organizational effectiveness

Organizational politics is an important leadership issue considering the potential impact of political behavior on organizational climate and productivity. Windsor (2003) notes a fundamental shift in the conceptualization of leadership. Leadership is a political art rather than a strategic science. 'Leadership involves a complex interaction of several dimensions; human management skill, strategic insight and business acumen, business ethics, and political skills (intra and extra-organizational)' (p. 14). Burke and Litwin (1989) in their seminal work on organizational performance demonstrated a clear relationship between leadership and management practice, climate and performance. The link between political behavior and its impact on job attitudes and performance is an important one (Drory, 1993). Vigoda (2003) notes that many theoretical arguments that politics damages productivity and performance both at the individual and organizational level are not clearly supported by the research.

The lack of a clear link between political behavior and organizational effectiveness may in fact be due to how the concept is defined and operationalized and in particular a bias towards the negative connotations of the term. Vigoda (2003) found that organizational politics had a strong impact on negligent behavior and job performance. Job attitudes mediated the relationship between organizational politics and work outcomes. Interestingly, O'Connor and Morrison (2001) found that organizational climate appear to be related to perceptions of organizational politics. Also, the lower a person's job autonomy in the organization, the greater the likelihood that he or she perceives the organization as political. The negative interpretation of behavior as political may derive from a lack of control of one's situation. The idea that political behavior influences people's feelings about their work and productivity makes sense and supports the need for developing a positive approach to organizational politics.

Pfeffer (1994) reinforces the importance of the study of power and politics and the need to learn to use both effectively. Perhaps it is useful to think of positive political behavior as a skill set that organizational leaders need to recognize, understand and develop in order to positively influence their organizations and use power in an ethical way to achieve results.

A working definition

This chapter has been developed on several assumptions about politics. Organizational politics is a neutral concept that can be either positive or negative in how it occurs. The negative connotations come from historical practice, not definition. It is an organizational reality that members have choices about the way they engage in political action. Politics can be strategic and focused on achievement. It is possible to practice politics in a positive way.

Organizational politics is an exercise of power and influence that primarily occurs outside of formal organizational processes and procedures. The behavior is based upon influence tactics designed to further self and/or organizational interests and is aimed at reconciling potential competing interests. Those interests may be the individual's ones versus the organizational ones, or they may be the individual interests versus the interests of others and/or groups. It is the manner in which the competing interests are managed that this chapter explores.

Political mindset shift continuum

Negative or hostile political action does occur, especially during times of uncertainty, ambiguity, and/or volatility where access to clear information is often lacking. However, if it is agreed that politics is an organizational reality (Pfeffer, 1994; Mitchell, 2003; Kuzmits et al., 2002; Block, 1987; Egan, 1994), the choice for organizational actors is not *if* they participate, but *how* they participate. Politics does not need to be a game of back-stabbing or intimidation. Instead, it can be about 'contribution, diplomacy, collaboration, cooperation and conducting a personal public relations campaign' (Toupin, 2001, p. 3).

Positive political action is possible but does require a shift in thinking and behaving. It is a shift that requires moving from the worst of the negative political stereotyping, for example manipulation, intimidation, power grabbing, controlling, to a more optimistic approach that has at its core a belief in a positive vision for the future (Miller and Kurchner-Hawkins, 2004).

On the left side of the political mindset shift continuum (Figure 19.1) are those political behaviors that are most often associated with organizational politics today. They represent the 'dark side' of political action: egocentrism, power grabs, intimidation and

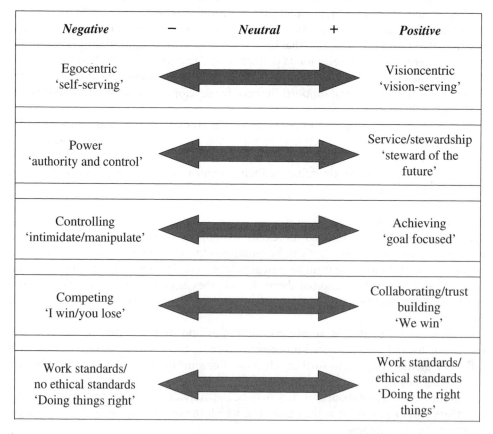

Figure 19.1   Political mindset shift continuum

manipulation, competition, and lack of ethical standards. On the right side of the continuum are the positive behaviors: serving a positive vision of the future, achievement-oriented, collaboration and trust building, and working to ethical standards.

Egocentric versus visioncentric

In *Working the shadow side*, Egan (1994) describes two different types of politics: the politics of self-interest and 'institution-enhancing' politics. These two types of politics reflect the first relationship in the political mindset shift continuum. In the first case, being political results in serving one's own job, career, team and so on at the expense of others (Block, 1987) or the well-known 'me first' that some consider embedded in human nature (Miletich, 1988). 'Institution-enhancing' politics is in the service of a vision that expresses values, purpose, contribution and optimism and promotes positive dialogue and debate (Egan, 1994; Block, 1987). A vision is only an idea for the future, but the 'right vision' is an idea so energizing that it in effect jump-starts the future by calling forth the skills, talents and resources to make it happen (Nanus, 1992). According to Block (1987), in articulating a vision we declare our independence as well as our dream of 'how we would like the organization to be' (p. 107). Block notes that a 'great vision' will have three qualities:

- It comes from the heart
- It's personal
- It's compelling.

Building support for the vision and for projects and activities aligned to that vision is one of the first steps for building positive political strategies. It appears that there are positive outcomes that arise from creating this congruence between the employees and the vision and goal presented by the organization. Witt (1998) noted that efforts to build congruence between employees and supervisors on organizational goal priorities impacted the perception of political behaviors.

Power versus stewardship

Block (1993) believes the 'antidote' to self-serving behavior is to commit to a cause, 'to something outside of ourselves' (p. 10). This is the clue to the second set of relationships in the mindset continuum. Is power used for the purpose of asserting control and authority or is power used to commit to a cause? Block (1993) introduced the concept of 'stewardship' to the political arena. He discusses stewardship as an exercise of accountability that 'centers on service rather than control' and is a 'means to impact the degree of ownership and responsibility each person feels' for the success of our organizations, our society and our lives (p.19). Mitchell (2003) suggests that by moving from the exercise of power for the sake of maintaining authority and control to stewardship, we make a choice to work in partnership with colleagues rather than through the traditional hierarchy and its pyramid-shaped structure.

Controlling versus achieving

Controlling traditionally means maintaining a clear line of authority and, some believe, dominance and dependence (Block, 1993; Pfeffer, 1994). If this is true, then the political activity is geared to maintaining the status quo. On the 'dark side,' control is maintained through intimidation and manipulation (Malan and Bredemeyer, 2002; Greenleaf, 1998). Moving away from maintaining control through manipulation and intimidation leads us to focusing on achieving the vision. Instead of attempting to maintain control, we direct energy to achieving the vision and the values embedded within it.

What does tight control achieve? According to Cooke (1994) tightly controlled and rule-bound organizations produced people following rules to avoid reprisals versus more self-expressive achieving cultures where 'people invent, teach, and learn from one another, to achieve as much as they are capable of achieving' (Klein and Napier, 2003, p. 45).

Competing versus collaborating

Political activity that values competition is taking the position that winning is all that matters. And sometimes winning is not enough unless there is a clear loser (Miller and Kurchner-Hawkins, 2004). Especially in times of scarce resources, teams, units and departments find themselves competing neck and neck for those resources and 'for visibility, for time, and for executive support' (Klein and Napier, 2003, p. 16). Political activity that values winning and losing over achieving makes it difficult to stay focused on the vision and values. At the opposite end of the continuum is collaboration, which moves away from 'I win, you lose' to 'we both win', stressing collaboration and trust. The culture becomes one of true working together to achieve goals with values of collaboration as the glue (Klein and Napier, 2003). Trust becomes a form of social capital that influences cooperation, collaboration and behavior that 'enhance collective well being and further the attainment of collective goals' (Kramer, 1999, p. 11).

There is a sense of reciprocity to trust (Messick et al., 1983) – we share common interests. My interests are your interests. Where trust is high, cooperation can increase and be less affected by the competitive 'I win, you lose' messages (Parks et al., 1996).

Work standards and ethical standards

Any technique of exercising power may be unethical if done with negative intentions and in the extreme (Mitchell, 2003). According to Art Brief, a business professor and director of the Burkenroad Institute for the Study of Ethics and Leadership in Management, 'Good people do bad things . . . Good people do horrendous things in the workplace because they don't see the situation as an ethical dilemma. They see it as a business problem to be solved' (Teuke, 2004, p. 58). For this very reason, defining business ethics is difficult and must consider the interaction between the needs of people to find meaning at work, the social responsibility of business and the interest of business stakeholders (Pava, 1999).

Demonstrating this difficulty, there are real business cases emerging where decisions were made that were consistent with prevailing practices. But the practices were not ethical or right. It is not enough to have accepted work practices and standards. To practice positive politics, one's work standards need to pass an ethics test. The Center for Business Ethics at Bentley College has developed six questions to measure the ethics of a decision or tactic.

1.   Is it right?
2.   Is it fair?

3. Who gets hurt?
4. Would you be comfortable if the details of the decision were made public?
5. What would you advise your child, brother or sister, or best friend to do?
6. What does your common sense tell you? (Mitchell, 2003)

Beyond the political mindset shift

This political mindset shift continuum represents the shift that organizational members need to make in order to move away from the 'dark side' of organizational politics and into the positive political arena. Both ends of the continuum represent a context for problem solving and decision making and could be motivating factors for personal behavior. Moving from the 'dark side' represents moving away from self-serving behavior and the politics of self-interest where the exercise of power is for the purpose of maintaining authority and control. It is a move away from manipulation and intimidation. And it is a move away from the politics of winners and losers. By making the mindset shift, you increase the likelihood of positive political actions because your political behavior is directed towards a positive vision of the future where there is accountability, dialogue, collaboration and trust. Political action is bound by the context in which it occurs. The mindset shift presents the context for determining the degree to which the behavior within an organization is positive or negative.

Having the right mindset for positive political behavior is not enough. There are skills required to be a positive political player. Goleman (1998) suggested that conscientiousness without social skill could lead to problems. In other words, when highly conscientious people lack social skills, working with them may be particularly difficult. Conscientious individuals without social skill can be seen as unreasonably demanding, inflexible and micromanaging. Thus highly conscientious, yet socially unskilled, workers likely pursue matters well beyond the point desired by others. They might be seen as not just fighting the wrong battles but rather as fighting almost every battle, perhaps in their minds 'for the good of the company' or 'to do what is right' (Witt and Ferris, 2003, p. 811). Wanting to be a positive political player is not the same as being one. The mindset shift is necessary but not sufficient to become a positive political force in an organization.

Developing a positive political strategy

The model presented in this chapter is an initial step aimed at understanding the essential components for creating political action in an organizational environment. It is intended to describe how individuals can impact outcomes for themselves and their organization through strategic political behavior. The model incorporates factors that reflect both macro- and micro-organizational levels of analysis and action. Vigoda (2003) summarized three key components needed to capture the essence of political behavior:

1. It must incorporate both the macro-organizational level and the micro-organizational level.
2. It must relate to behavior other than those that focus on asset distribution in organizations (economic perspective).
3. It must distinguish between political and non-political behaviors.

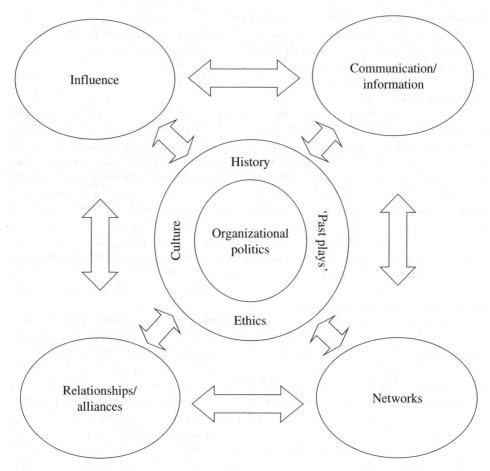

Figure 19.2   Model of organizational politics

When developing a political strategy, we propose that there are eight factors that affect political outcomes (see Figure 19.2). These factors are:

1. Influence
2. Communication/information
3. Relationships/alliances
4. Networks
5. History
6. Organizational culture
7. 'Past plays'
8. Ethics.

The first four factors are behavioral factors or 'levers' that can be directly affected by individual behaviors and are the means through which political behavior occurs. We use the term lever to denote actions one might take to activate and deactivate the behaviors associated with these factors. When creating a strategy, one or any combination of the factors may be used to achieve the desired results. The eight factors are now described in more detail:

- *Influence*: degree to which one can change others' behaviors, beliefs, or actions. The focus of this factor ('lever') is on tactics that will increase control over outcomes.
- *Communication/information*: the communication process and tools that allow information to move through the system. The focus of this factor ('lever') is on clarity, accuracy, quality, quantity, access to information, and movement of information in order to affect outcomes.
- *Relationships/alliances*: building relationships and alliances through the management of trust and agreement to combine capabilities to gain control.
- *Networks*: the systems of connections among people, teams, units, functions and so on in organizations. The focus is on identifying, understanding and tapping these crucial connections.

The last four factors are mediating factors that affect strategizing and outcomes. They are contextual, and are essential determinants of the effectiveness of the political behavior. These need to be considered and understood since they can affect outcomes and may color and help to determine the most appropriate strategy. These four mediating factors are now described in more detail:

- *History*: the recreation of past events into a coherent framework.
- *Organizational culture*: 'how things are done,' 'what is valued or not valued,' 'what is recognized or rewarded and conversely punished,' and 'what is revered or demonized' in an organization.
- *'Past plays'*: an individual's experience of interaction with other people or groups.
- *Ethics*: the value system that guides behavior in the organization.

The model presented thus far is of political behavior and can represent both positive and negative political action. Positive politics occurs when behaviors are congruent with the positive side of the political mindset shift. The behaviors must be in the service of the vision, help to steward the future, are goal focused, build collaboration and trust, and are considered ethically congruent – 'the right thing.' The model provides a starting point for effecting change in how politics occurs in organizations. This approach assumes that we continue to enact the organization in which we exist and with each behavior we create new contexts for behavior (Weick, 1995). Over time the four mediating factors will change as a result of how the four behavioral factors (influence, communication/information, relationships/alliances and networks) occur in the organization. Simply said, if we behave in a way that is effective and positive politically and others start to do the same, over time we may change the culture, history, ethics and 'past plays' that provide the context for political behavior. The following sections describe the four behavioral factors and four mediating factors.

Influence   The first behavioral factor (lever) to be considered in creating a positive political strategy is influence. 'Influence' has been defined as the degree to which one can change others' behaviors, beliefs, decisions or actions. It is often related to one's use of power and persuasion (e.g. French and Raven, 1959; Lee and Bohlen, 1997). Vigoda (2003) concludes after an extensive review of definitions of organizational politics that influence tactics are a major component of political behavior. Influence strategies or tactics are the processes individuals use to get others to do their bidding and act or comply with their desired response, for example, accept advice, agree with decisions. There is a range of skills and knowledge that comprise effective influence behavior. Included in these skills is the ability to effectively understand, read and control social situations. Witt and Ferris (2003) note that

> socially skilled individuals are more likely than those low in social skill to effectively use those social perceptions to identify the appropriate timing for an influence attempt, improvise when they perceive that their planned impression management strategy is likely to fail, and know when to remain silent or speak up. Thus, social skill effectively captures the cognitive element of reading and understanding social situations and also captures the behavioral or action component of being able to act on that insight to influence others. (p. 811)

In a seminal work that categorized and described these influence strategies, Kipnis et al. (1980) introduced the Profiles of Organizational Influence Strategies (POIS) scales. These scales describe types of influence strategies and associated behaviors. Falbe and Yukl (1992) further refined this concept. Frequently identified tactics include: assertiveness, blocking, coalitions, consultation, exchange, ingratiation, rational persuasion, sanctions and upward appeals (Judge and Bretz Jr., 1994; Schilit and Locke, 1982, Schriesheim and Hinkin, 1990; Voyer, 1994; Yukl and Falbe, 1990; Kipnis et al., 1980; Mintzberg, 1983). These influence tactics maybe grouped into: 'hard tactics', in which authority, coercion and force were prominent, 'soft tactics', in which more subtle forms of persuasion and appeal were employed, 'rational tactics', such as logical arguments, presentation of information and benefits, and 'bargaining' (Falbe and Yukl, 1992; Kipnis and Schmidt, 1988). Chery and Wilkinson (2002) also identify tactics that cannot be categorized in the three groups. They describe the tactics as 'non-strategies' that may still accomplish desired results. The deliberate use of no influence strategy becomes a strategy of influence. For example, 'Chinese torture' uses friendliness and rational persuasion over repeated influence episodes to try to persuade the target to change his or her mind about a decision. Four characterizations of non-strategies include:

- *The non-use of strategy*: strives to be seen as a neutral third party in order to preserve relations with two parties involved in a dispute.
- *The non-use of strategy*: in an ongoing *influence* relationship between two hostile parties, in which giving in to the other side's demand creates a temporary ceasefire until the next skirmish begins.
- *The non-use of strategy*: in an ongoing *influence* relationship between two cooperative parties (close allies), with one party accepting the other party's *influence* attempt without exerting any counter-*influence* tactics out of friendship and goodwill.
- *Exclusion from decision-making*: 'when this first started, we didn't get much of a say. It was all the purchasing people who had the say [who went to all the meetings], not the people on the ground who are using the products' (Chery and Wilkinson, 2002, p. 11)

Empirical studies of preferences for different types of political tactics have shown that rational and informational persuasion tactics are generally preferred over soft, and that soft are preferred over hard tactics (Kipnis and Schmidt, 1988; Mowday, 1978; Schilit and Locke, 1982). Yukl and Falbe (1990) have also found that the relative frequency of use of various influence tactics is consistent regardless of directionality (upward, lateral and downward). Tactic preferences and effectiveness are not the same. The research on preferences does not indicate the effectiveness of the strategy. Influence tactics need to be considered in the context of the organizational environment, characteristics of the individuals and the desired outcomes. It is not simply a matter of whether political behavior works or does not work. The effectiveness of political behavior depends on the type of strategy employed. While the differential effectiveness of influence behaviors has been found in other areas of human resource management (Ferris and Judge, 1991), it is important to think also about this distinction in terms of career and organizational effectiveness (Judge and Bretz Jr, 1994).

For influence strategies to be positive, they must be congruent with the political mindset shift. They must be in the service of the vision, help to steward the future, be goal focused, build collaboration and trust, and considered ethically congruent – 'the right thing.'

Communication/information   The second behavioral factor ('lever') is 'communication/ information'. This factor is focused on the communication process and how information moves through the system. It is the means by which coordination and meaning are created in organizations (Weick, 1995). Communication is a process in which senders make choices about the content and channel through which the message is conveyed. These choices may reflect sensitivity to the receivers' response and interpretation of messages sent. It is an iterative process of sender and receiver switching roles. Organizational reality is defined through these communication and information processes (Morgan, 1986). In the real world, problems are messy and are not clearly laid out as givens. They must be constructed from the gathering of information about these problematic situations, which may be puzzling, troubling and uncertain. In order to convert a problematic situation into a problem, a practitioner must do certain kind of work. He/she must make sense of an uncertain situation that initially makes no sense. Information and communication are the means for creating these understandings and the subsequent actions. Meanings are created in an evolutionary and iterative process between people. Information and communication are the means for gaining control of situations. Information/communication can be used to 'enlighten the receiver' and help them understand and advance the vision of the organization or be used for self-serving purposes (Weick, 1995; Morgan, 1986). Communication and information are the linchpins in the political process. Control of information and communication are of great importance to the political process in organizations. Creating messages that are clear and accurate and monitoring the quality, quantity, access to and movement of information requires vigilance and skill.

Channel selection can be a key component in the creation of communication that is effective and has the desired impact. Kuzmits et al. (2002) explored how e-mail becomes an enabler of organizational politics. They found that face-to-face channels were used most often to convey political messages while e-mail was the next most often used channel. They describe how e-mail can be used for self-serving purposes. Sussman et al. (2002) found that the creation and transmission of self-serving messages was dependent on the target for the message (e.g. boss, subordinate, or peer) and the channel used (face to face, telephone, e-mail).

Competence in managing communication and information is essential for positive political behavior. The simple intention to be clear, accurate and 'audience oriented' is not enough. Even though open communication may constrain the impact of negative political behavior (Mitchell, 2003), the perception of such behavior can occur as a result of misinformation or miscommunication. Open communication could in some cases create unintended negative consequences for the sender. How we communicate and the timing of the communication may be as important as what we are communicating.

Relationships/alliances   The third behavior factor ('lever') is 'relationships/alliances'. Relationships and alliances are based on a direct connection between individuals. They create value by combining capabilities of separate individuals to gain control through an implied open-ended informal agreement. An alliance or relationship is a way to manage incompleteness. Individuals do not have access to all information, knowledge, resources and so on. Through others one can grow, obtain clarity and understanding, learn, and respond to situations. Relationships/alliances are important in helping us to see our blind spots. Being fluid, they provide us with more control in responding to events. Gargiulo (1993) found that leaders build cooptive ties with people in a position to affect their performance in the firm directly. Gresov and Stephens (1993) in a study of inter-unit influence attempts reinforced the notion that influence activity is not simple and occurs with a complex multi-faceted environment. They found that even if other units engage in influence attempts, units that have loosely coupled relationships or relationships that are unproblematic or predictable were less likely to resort to influence behavior, even if they are the targets of such behavior.

Relationships/alliances are achieved through trust and agreement. It is a two-way process and continues to be subject to negotiation. Trust hinges on the expectation that the other will look out for your interests as if they were their own. Blomqvist and Stahle (2000) define trust as an 'actor's expectation of the other party's competence, goodwill and behavior' (p. 3). The added component of competence, for example technical capabilities and know-how, suggests that expectations are based more on the ability and capability to deliver than simply looking out for one's own interest. Trust has also been described as 'a safety net of the work community which helps people to tolerate uncertainty, but also produces commitment and accountability' (Huotari and Iivonen, 2004, p. 10). Robinson (1996) describes this delicate balancing act as built on the person's expectations, assumptions, or beliefs about the likelihood of another person's actions being beneficial, not detrimental. In a sense, when we create these relationships we 'trust' that the other will hold up their end of the implicit 'deal' and look out for our interests. Das and Teng (2001) note that trust and control are linked with risk in strategic alliances and that risk management in alliances is a complex endeavor.

> Trust can be understood as a means that allows informational gaps to be bridged, but – uno actu – it often produces considerable risk, since, unavoidably, it can be betrayed and turn out to be misplaced. While the willingness and capacity to take such risks may vary between individual social actors, it seems that 'blind trust' is anything but a favourable option. In other words, even

if trust is the dominant element, it usually occurs as one element in a complicated process of co-ordinating and controlling organizational relations. (Bachman et al., 2001, p. 1)

Because trust is based on others' expectations, an understanding of these expectations is essential to building a trusting relationship (Huotari and Iivonen, 2004). Consequently, relationships and alliances built on trust and agreement that are competently activated in the service of the vision of the organization may be politically positive. Empathy and network centrality have been linked with task and interpersonal citizenship behavior (Settoon and Mossholder, 2002). Gomes-Casseres (2003) provides insight into the positive use of alliances between organizations to support business strategy that is relevant to individuals. He proposes four principles to follow:

- Use business strategy to drive alliance decisions.
- Design alliances to fit the strategy and grow relationships; that is, 'don't do deals.'
- Use portfolios of alliances, not stand-alones.
- Organize internally to cooperate externally.

This advice is well taken in the creation of relationships and alliances for supporting positive political action. Using relationships/alliances should be in the service of the organizational vision, be viewed from a long-term perspective, and include a number of alliances in a range of places.

Networks The last behavioral factor ('lever') focuses on the network of relationships that can be mobilized. An individual's network value can be quantified in terms of the 'social capital' it can provide. This reflects the advantages that accrue from one's location in the social structure (Burt, 2000). Huotari and Iivonen (2004) refer to 'social capital' as 'the sum of the actual and potential resources embedded within, and available through, and derived from the network of relationships possessed by an individual or social unit. Social capital thus comprises both the network and the assets that may be mobilized through that network' (p. 30). Basically this would imply that the better connected one is, the more social capital one has. Hedin (2001), when describing the 'logic of interpersonal trust' for decision making in organizations, provides insight into the operationalizaton of the social capital metaphor. In her view, agency following this logic is conditioned by

- preexisting, trust-carrying social network ties ('Whom do I trust?');
- deliberation and social influence through these social network ties to others who are trusted ('What do they say?');
- mobilization of resources through social network ties ('Can they help me with that?'); and
- the social network basis of collective action ('cooperate with trusted others'). (p. 83)

Burt (2000) further refines the thinking on social capital as a function of location in the structure of the network when he identifies 'brokerage across structural holes' as a key to higher social capital. Using this, he sees individuals who bridge different areas within the network as having higher social capital, being potentially more efficient in obtaining information and being more effective organizationally. Burt (2000) built on Granovetter's

(1973) theory of the 'strength of weak ties' which proposed that the people with whom a person has weak ties are less likely to be connected to one another; that is, the person is embedded in a structural hole. These weak ties were less likely to be redundant and more likely to be unique, thereby making them 'information rich.'

Location and embeddedness in networks are clearly important in determining one's capacity to foster positive political action. Settoon and Mossholder (2002) tested a model of interpersonal citizenship behavior (ICB) and found links between network centrality and interpersonal and task-related ICB. Gargiulo (1993) describes how networks may be activated in response to political behavior.

> The structural approach, in turn, grounds causal force in the relations of interdependence among the players, whatever the sources of this interdependence. The analytical focus is not on resources and goals but on interdependence and constraint. Second, the literature on coalition maneuvers has often revolved around the weak-against-strong theme. This approach typically assumes that the motive behind the members of the coalition is to join forces against a powerful third party. Two-step maneuvers do not need such an assumption. Although A's cooptive tie with C is aimed at neutralizing the power of a strong party (i.e., B), the theory makes no assumption about C's 'goals' or 'weakness.' It would therefore be inaccurate to say that A and C have formed a coalition against B, at least in the usual sense given to this term. Thus, although coalitions may take the form of two-step maneuvers, not all two-step maneuvers can be properly discussed as coalitions. (pp. 4–5)

A few examples of using networks to influence others' behavior include: the case of the subordinate whose old friendship with his boss's supervisor prevents the boss from effectively controlling his behavior (Thurman, 1979), the local leader who builds political contacts in higher circles to deal with a troublesome local official (Tarrow, 1977), and the manager who seeks a mentor–protégé relation with senior players to bypass the authority of his or her immediate supervisor (Kram, 1985; Burt, 1992). The irritation that such maneuvers breed in the bypassed actor attest to their potential effectiveness (Gargiulo, 1993). Reichheld (2003) notes that superior leaders create networks of mutually beneficial trust-inspiring partnerships. These networks can be important for both the individual's and the organization's success. The network of relationships that can be mobilized and the social capital inherent in these relationships can be a positive force when used for the 'right' reasons. There are also risks in mobilizing weak ties in one's network that should be considered in building positive political strategies.

Mediating factors

There are four additional factors that mediate the effects of the strategies created using the behavioral factor ('levers') of influence, communication/information, relationships/alliances and networks. These are not factors that can be directly acted on but rather mediate the effectiveness of the behavioral factors levers. They may in fact be affected over time by the actions linked to the first four levers.

History 'History' is the re-creation of past events into a coherent framework. It is the facts as viewed from a particular perspective, the accumulation of experience, information and communication. It may include how things were done or occurred in the past, for example past interactions, responses, problems, successes, conflicts, structures or similar situations. It is comparable to the concept of organizational memory. Each organization has its own way of doing things. Being aware of this history when creating a strategy may help navigate the 'potholes' or 'bumps' in the road. Forray and Woodilla (2002) demonstrate how invoking the future or the past is used as a means of sustaining a dominant reality. They suggest that such temporal spans, created interactively in talk, are a way in which human resource managers use consistency to construct the image of a fair organization. Reputation and word of mouth were found to be important determinants of trust in one's manager (Cherry, 2000). Understanding and in some cases respecting the past will support building a positive strategy. Understanding history may include learning about what happened before you came along, where the problem areas are, who the survivors of reorganizations, downsizing, mergers and feuds between organizational units are, and how the structure has shifted.

Organizational culture   Organizational culture, simply put, is 'how things are done around here,' 'what we value or do not value,' 'what is recognized or rewarded and conversely punished,' and 'what we revered or demonized.' Weick (1995) describes it as 'shared experience'. Schein (1992) says that culture of any type manifests itself at three levels, from the deepest level of tacit assumptions to espoused values, that is what people say they wish to be, and then up to day-to-day behavior, that is what people are actually doing. To get at the essence of culture, Schein says we have to surface the tacit assumptions, and look at the alignment or lack of alignment among these levels within a particular culture as well as across cultures. Garsten (2003) argues that culture must be viewed as more than unevenly distributed and constantly negotiated 'networks of perspectives' – rather that culture is a context for organizing. Hofstede (1983) notes that 'culture is the collective programming of the mind that distinguishes the members of one group or category of people from another' (p. 139). In organizations, this may occur by group or category of people, by occupation, type of business, or a corporation. Hofstede (1983) uses socialization, the way in which a person is conditioned by environments, to distinguish types of culture and to associate this with their sources of socialization. Culture affects how one understands and perceives events. It is not surprising that what is considered negative or political in one culture is viewed differently and interpreted differently in another. Vigoda's (2001) comparative study of Israeli and British reactions to organizational politics found culture as a moderating variable. Culture at various levels of analysis, for example group, unit, organization, country, may mediate political behavior.

Past plays   'Past plays' as distinguished from history are an individual's experience or interaction with other people or groups. Past plays are experienced first hand or as part of a group. For example, they may include how the individual/team/division worked towards achieving goals or aligned itself to the vision of the organization and its interactions with others. Past plays may also be how the individual/team/division operated during stress, turbulence, or calm, and the reaction of others inside or outside the organizations. Past plays are how others' actions are experienced directly by an individual in their organizational capacity. The individual's prior interactions bring with them an assessment of the other that influences future interactions.

Whenever a person wants to judge the quality of a possible interaction partner, she can do so by applying the mechanism of extrapolation. Past common experience and observation of behavior in past situations form the basis for assumptions about the probable behaviour of possible interaction partners in future situations. Actors who disappoint their interaction partners at a certain time t_0 are likely to do the same in future interactions and can be treated accordingly. (Gossling, 2004, p. 680)

Past plays affect interaction. For example, 'Communication about an observation of unreliable behaviour can ruin the reputation of an actor. Other members of the social surrounding can decide whether and how to interact based upon indirect reciprocity' (Gossling, 2004, p. 680). Gargiulo (1993) found that leaders tend to avoid troublesome players. Cherry (2000) found that the trust that an employee has in his/her manager is developed through word-of-mouth or reputational information and frequent interaction with the manager.

Gresov and Stephens (1993) found that influence attempts by organizational units occur in an interactive context and are less a matter of internal pressures of unit members or a sense of politically disadvantaged position. Tepper et al. (2004) note that subordinates are more satisfied with their jobs and more committed to their organizations when their coworkers perform organizational citizenship behaviors (OCBs) with greater frequency. An interesting finding was that abusive supervision correlated negatively with coworkers' OCBs. This suggests that subordinates feel that their coworkers perform fewer OCBs when their supervisors are more abusive (p. 459). We are basically saying that our past direct experience shapes our future behavior. We assume there is learning that takes place about interacting with the target individual that directs future behavior and interaction.

Ethics　Ethics is the value system that guides behavior. It is a matter of personal integrity and responsibility. It is the crux of positive political action. We cannot be positive if what we do is ethically suspect. Begley (2004) states, 'authentic leadership is knowledge-based, values informed and skillfully executed' (p. 5). Embracing the concept of empowerment and participative management does not remove the responsibility for ethical behavior. Ethical behavior may be obscured by the complexity of the issues an individual is dealing with. Addressing complexity may involve being able to understand second- and third-order effects of decision making and actions. Ethics becomes one of the screens we use to judge our behavior. Ethics is often interpreted in culturally exclusive ways, and can be a troublesome category of values to employ as a guide for action in our increasingly global environments (Begley, 2004). Seldman and Betof (2004) describe how leaders at Becton, Dickinson and Company set the ethical tone for employees through following rules of conduct. These rules are linked to what is described as savvy political behavior that serves the company, shareholders and customers. Being a good global corporate citizen or a philanthropist is not enough to absolve unethical behavior. The recent organizational governance scandals at Enron, AES and WorldCom only serve to highlight the dilemma of 'doing things right' versus 'doing the right thing' (Windsor, 2003). In addition to the questions presented above on ethics and the mindset shift, the positive and negative implications of political behavior can be determined by asking:

- Is the action I am considering legal?
- Is the action I am considering fair and balanced?

- Is it morally right?
- Is the action I am considering consistent with my values?
- Would I feel OK if the action I'm considering were made public? (Miller and Kurchner-Hawkins, 2004)

Ethical behavior in organizations has implications for individual general ethical behavior. The meanings-based view of how ethical behavior occurs in organizations stresses that organizations are not just locations for creating goods and services; they are locations where life's meaning is interpreted. In essence, people create businesses and are created by them (Pava, 1999). Ethics is a key mediator and determinant of positive political action.

Strategy development

> In strategy, it is important to see distant things as if they were close, and see a distanced view of close things. (Miyamoto Musashi, 1584–1645)

Strategy is a plan of action for achieving a goal that links 'ends', 'ways' and 'means.' Strategy allows us to navigate volatility, uncertainty, complexity and ambiguity. For effective strategy development, we need to relinquish the idea that politics is a rational process – that we can control it – since too many factors influence outcomes, and small, seemingly inconsequential events can have a major impact. 'Rationality is always political . . . The idea of rationality is as much a resource to be used in organizational politics as a descriptive term describing the aims of organizations' (Morgan, 1986, p. 195). Creating strategy must therefore keep 'consequential decision making' in mind. Strategy involves balancing what we know with what we are clear we do not know and creating predictions about the future and how we want to affect it. The role of a strategic leader in a volatile, uncertain, complex and ambiguous environment is to be a sense-maker of phenomena, to connect the dots of random events and activities, and to bring coherence to apparent disarray.

When developing a strategy, it may be helpful to consider the following:

1. Identify the political behavior. Naming it makes it easier to understand and manage.
2. Articulate your purpose, what you are trying to achieve. Remember to be vision-centric.
3. Consider history, culture, past plays, ethics. What is driving the behavior?
4. It's time to name names! Who's involved?
5. Every action has a reaction. Anticipate! What's at stake?
6. Take responsibility for your participation. How am I contributing? What effect will my behavior have on others and the organization now and in the future?
7. Consider if any action you are taking is consistent with your values and the organization's values. Is what I am considering ethical? What are the implications for my actions beyond how they immediately affect me?
8. Push and pull those behavioral levers. What combination of levers will be most effective? What are my options? Consider your strategies around influence, communication/information, relationships/alliances and networks.

		History	Culture	Past plays	Ethics
Behavioral factors	Influence				
	Communication/ information				
	Relationships/ alliances				
	Networks				
	Mediating factors				

Figure 19.3   Determining political action: Using behavioral factors and mediating factors to determine strategic issues and actions

The grid presented in Figure 19.3 provides a tool for strategy development. The behavioral factors are presented on one axis (influence, communication/information, relationships/alliances and networks) and the mediating factors (history, culture, past plays and ethics) on the other. The grid can be used to understand and identify the issues, pitfalls or blind spots of a strategy. The box at the intersection of a behavioral factor with each mediating factor can be used to identify issues, behaviors or actions to be considered. For example, different types of influence behaviors could be viewed in the context of history, that is, what worked in the past and what didn't work in the past. As such, reviewing the situation using the grid may indicate that issues cannot be addressed with influence behaviors alone and may require additional behavior factors to be activated. Responding politically in this instance may require leveraging influence, communication/information and relationships/alliances in order to be effective. The grid can be used to think through how to support positive political action.

Although the development of strategy can be articulated as a step-by-step process in most cases, the complexity of the situation and the time constraints create an environment where improvisation may more aptly describe how the astute political participant operates. Improvisation is viewed as a deliberate creation of novel activity that takes into account the complexity of the situation (Miner et al., 2001). Miner et al. (2001) make a distinction between improvisation and rapid sequencing of distinct steps that might still be considered strategic or a compression of the strategy since it is done deliberately and methodically. Hatch (1998) observed that skilled improvisers often recombine existing routines (parts of memory) to create novel action, much as a musician reassembles previously performed bundles of notes into a novel melody (Miner et al., 2001). Memory, history and past performances will likely shape the skillful and fruitful improvisation of novel performances. This implies that skillful improvisation requires competence in routines. There are skills to master to become an effective political operative. This reinforces the notion that there are skills and routines that can be developed to be effective politically.

Discussion

Organizational politics is clearly a force in organizational life. It is the power and influence activities that often occur outside the boundaries of formal organizational processes and procedures. Researchers and members of organizations have made assumptions that the only type of political behavior that exists in organizations is self-serving and focused on individual goals. There are clearly negative attributions associated with politics in organizations. This limited view of politics has diminished the potential for understanding the richness, subtlety and range of how political behavior occurs in organizations and how it contributes to the accomplishment of organizational outcomes.

Implications for research and practice

There are four major implications of the model and approach we proposed.

Political behavior can be positive   Political behavior should be conceived as a continuum of behaviors that range from negative to positive. Political behavior is multidimensional and contextual. Attributions of negative or positive must take this into account. Some researchers, rather than look at political behavior as occurring on a continuum from positive to negative, simply label positive political behavior as something else. They seem to have assumed that political behavior by definition is negative and therefore describe behaviors that could be construed as political but aimed at advancing the organization's goals as something else, for example organizational citizenship behavior, or emotional intelligence. Unfortunately this approach may confuse the issue and reinforce the stereotype of political behavior as negative.

Viewing political behavior as only negative and studying only the impact of this aspect of the behavior diminishes the potential for understanding how political behavior occurs in organizations. It also implies that to be political is not to be concerned about the vision and goals of the organization. Practitioners may restrict the range of behaviors they use to accomplish goals for fear of being 'political.' We need to explore what makes someone a positive political actor in organizations and how this affects outcomes within the organization. We need to understand how to foster positive political behavior in organizations. More research is needed on both the antecedents and outcomes of positive political behavior for individuals and organizations. Studies show that the higher the level within the organization, the lower the perception of politics. This may be related to the fact that those who do it and do it well or positively don't perceive it as politics.

Political behavior can be learned and taught   There are skills that can be taught and practiced. It isn't enough to want to 'play politics' positively – one needs to have the skills and awareness of what constitutes positive political behavior. Wanting to, believing you can and doing are different. For positive politics to occur, individuals must both know what constitutes positive political behavior and be able to make it happen. We propose that the skills sets and routines to be honed focus on influence, communication/information, relationship/alliances and network-related behaviors. Contextual information that can guide behavior choices would focus on history, culture, past plays and ethics. Training and development opportunities for individuals in organizations could focus on these issues and behaviors. Research could assess the outcomes of the positive political strategies individuals employ.

The potential full range of strategies becomes more transparent using the model of political behavior that we propose. It takes into account the multidimensional aspects of the determinants of positive political behavior. It helps in identifying blind spots in strategy and makes them easier to detect using tools like the grid presented in Figure 19.3. For example, tools for network mapping might help to understand which individuals could influence outcomes and which links in the network might be activated to help elicit support. Indirect influence can be achieved through the network. The network also could be used to gather information in order to find out about obstacles to a particular strategy. Communication/information skills may enable the individual to think about which channel is most appropriate for providing certain types of information in order to have the desired impact, for example face to face versus e-mail versus teleconference. Although we would like to believe that one could sit down and map out a strategy to be 'politically positive' and follow it step by step, it is more appropriate to conceive of the positive political player as someone who has honed the skills outlined above so that as they confront daily life in an organization they improvise and respond effectively and positive politically. They have created effective routines that they can rely on when confronted with a variety of political situations. The decisions about how to behave take into account history, past plays, culture and ethics. Researchers and practitioners could focus on determining what these routines are and how to facilitate their effective creation and use by individuals in organizations.

Positive political behavior has the potential not only to effect change in individuals but in the organization as a whole   Over time and with significant players involved in positive political behavior, organizations can change for the better. In effect, the behaviors of these players can change the culture, history and ethics of an organization. For practitioners who are interested in making organizations better places to work, helping individuals in the organization to build and use positive political behavior is challenging. The creation of strategies is complex and not clear. A long-term view may be needed to effect these changes. Researchers could focus on the long-term effects of positive political strategies on organizational effectiveness. It might be helpful to understand what happens to culture, history and ethics over time when positive political strategies are used.

Conclusion

We have defined organizational politics as a neutral term. Unfortunately current definitions have been imbued with negative connotations. Because some politicians may be devious or underhand, all politics is assumed to be by nature negative, and we should not engage in it. This view diminishes the opportunity to view politics as a force for good, as a way to influence organizations positively and bring about productive change. We believe that understanding how to participate effectively in organizational politics can further the aims of an organization and its members. The mindset shift is offered as a way to visualize this. Political behavior does not occur in a void; it is contextual. It occurs within a social system that by definition includes interaction among participants, networks of relationships, beliefs and values, and history and memory. When forming a positive political strategy, all of these factors need to be taken into consideration.

References

Bachman, R., Knights, D. and Sydow, J. (2001). Organizational studies: Trust and control in organizational relations. *Organizational Studies*. Special Issue March **2**(22).

Begley, P.T. (2004). Understanding valuation processes: Exploring the linkage between motivation and action. *International Studies in Educational Administration (ISEA)*, **32**(2), 4–17.

Block, P. (1991). *The empowered manager: Positive political skills at work*. San Francisco: Jossey-Bass.

Block, P. (1993). *Stewardship*. San Francisco, CA: Berrett-Koehler.

Blomqvist, K. and Stahle, P. (2000). Building organizational trust. Paper presented at the 16th Annual IMP Conference, 7–9 September, Bath, UK.

Burke, W.W. and Litwin, G. (1989). A causal model of organizational performance. *The 1989 Annual: Developing Human Resources*, Vol. 18, pp. 277–88.

Burt, R. (1992). *Structural holes: The social structure of competition*. Cambridge, MA: Harvard University Press.

Burt, R. (2000). The network structure of social capital. In R.I. Sutton and B.M. Staw (eds), *Research in organizational behavior* (Vol. 22). Greenwich, CT: JAI Press.

Cherry, B.W. (2000). The antecedents of trust in a manager: The subordinate tells the story of time. *Dissertation Abstracts International*, **61**(3-A), 1065.

Chery, M. and Wilkinson, I.F. (2002). E-procurement and intra firm influence. Paper presented at the meeting of the EMAC/ANZMAC Colloquium, Kuala Lumpur, 16–17 December.

Cooke, R.A. (1994). *Organizational culture inventory manual*. Plymouth, MI: Human Synergistics.

Das, T.K. and Teng, B. (2001). Trust, control and risk in strategic alliances: An integrated framework. *Organizational Studies* **22**(2), Special Issue: Trust and control in organizational relations, 251–83.

Drory, A. (1993). Perceived political climate and job attitudes. *Organizational Studies*. Thousand Oaks, CA: Sage.

Dubrin, A. (2001). *Leadership* (3rd edn). New York: Houghton Mifflin.

Egan, G. (1994). *Working the shadow side: A guide to positive behind-the-scenes management*. San Francisco, CA: Jossey-Bass.

Falbe, C.M. and Yukl, G. (1992). Consequences for managers of using single influence tactics and combinations of tactics. *Academy of Management Journal*, **35**, 638–52.

Ferris, G.R. and Judge, T.A. (1991). Personnel/human resources management: A political influence perspective. *Journal of Management*, **17**, 447–88.

Ferris, G.R., Russ, G.S. and Fandt, P.M. (1989). Politics in organizations. In R.A. Giacalone and P. Rosenfeld (eds), *Impression management in the organization*. Hillside, NJ: Lawrence Erlbaum.

Forray, J.M. and Woodilla, J. (2002). *Organizational Studies*, **23**(6), 899–916.

French, J.R.P. and Raven, B. (1959). A formal theory of social power. In D. Cartwright (ed.), *Studies in social power* (pp. 150–67). Ann Arbor, MI: Institute for Social Research.

Gargiulo, M. (1993). Two-step leverage: Managing constraint in organizational politics. *Administrative Science Quarterly*, **38**, 1–19.

Garsten, C. (2003). The cosmopolitan organization – an essay on corporate accountability. *Global Networks*, **3**(3), 355–70.

Goleman, D. (1998). *Working with emotional intelligence*. New York: Bantam Books.

Gomes-Casseres, B. (2003). Alliance strategy: Fundamentals for success. Paper presented at the meeting of NETSEA, Burlington,VT.

Gossling, T. (2004). Proximity, trust and morality in networks. *European Planning Studies*, **12**(5), 675–89.

Granovetter, M. (1973). The strength of weak ties. *American Journal of Sociology*, **78**, 1360–80.

Greenleaf, R.K. (1998). In L.C. Spears (ed.), *The power of servant leadership*. San Francisco, CA: Berrett-Koehler.

Gresov, C. and Stephens, C. (1993). The context of interunit influence attempts. *Administrative Science Quarterly*, **38**, 252–76.

Hatch, M.J. (1998). Jazz as a metaphor for organizing in the 21st century. *Organization Science*, **9**(5), 556–7.

Hedin, A. (2001). *The politics of social networks: Interpersonal trust and institutional change in post-communist East Germany* (118). Sweden: Lund University.

Hofstede, G. (1983). The cultural relativity of organisational practices and theories. *Journal of International Business Studies*, **14**(2), 75–89.

Huotari, M. and Iivonen, M. (2004). Managing knowledge-based organizations through trust. In M. Huotari and M. Iivonen (eds), *Trust in knowledge management and systems in organizations*, IDEA Group Inc., Hersey, PA, pp. 1–29.

Jinkner, J. (2004). *Managing organizational politics*. Retrieved from www.unf.edu/~jinj0001/whyplaycompany politics.html

Judge, T. and Bretz Jr, R. (1994). Political influence behavior and career success. *Journal of Management*, **20**(1), Spring, 43–65.

Kipnis, D. and Schmidt, S.M. (1988). Upward-influence styles: Relationship with performance evaluations, salary, and stress. *Administrative Science Quarterly*, **33**, 528–42.

Kipnis, D., Schmidt, S.M. and Wilkinson, I. (1980). Intraorganizational influence tactics: Explorations in getting one's way. *Journal of Applied Psychology*, **65**(4), 440–52.

Klein, M. and Napier, R. (2003). *The courage to act*. Palo Alto, CA: Davies-Black.

Kram, K. (1985). *Mentoring at work: Developmental relationships in organizational life*. Glenview, IL: Scott Foresman.

Kramer, R.M. (1999). Trust and distrust in organizations: Emerging perspectives, enduring questions. *Annual Review of Psychology*, **50**(1), 569–97.

Kuzmits, F., Sussman, L., Adams, A. and Raho, L. (2002). Using information and e-mail for political gain. *The Information Management Journal*, **36**(5), (September/October), 76–80.

LaBarre, P. (1999). The new face of office politics. In *Fast Company* (28). Retrieved from www.fastcompany.com/magazine/28/newface.html

Lee, D. and Bohlen, G.A. (1997). Influence strategies of project managers in the information-technology industry. *Engineering Management Journal*, **9**(2), 7–14.

Malan, R. and Bredemeyer, D. (2002). *Organization Politics: Architect Competency Elaboration*. Retrieved from www.bredemeyer.com/pdf_files/PoliticsCompetency.PDF

Mayes, B.T. and Allen, R.W. (1977). Toward a definition of organizational politics. *Academy of Management Review*, **2**, 672–8.

Messick, D.M., Wilke, K., Brewer, M.B., Kramer, R.M., Zemke, P.E. and Lui, L. (1983). Individual adaptations and structural change as solutions to social dilemmas. *Journal Perspectives of Social Psychology*, **44**, 294–309.

Miletich, L.N. (1988). A business bestiary. *Administrative Management* (April), 11–13.

Miller, R. and Kurchner-Hawkins, R. (2004). Organizational politics: Positive strategies for turbulent times. Paper presented at the annual conference of the American Society for Training and Development, San Diego, CA.

Miner, A.S., Bassoff, P. and Moorman, C. (2001). Organizational improvisation and learning: A field study. *Administrative Science Quarterly*, **46**(2), 304–37.

Mintzberg, H. (1983). *Power in and around organizations*. Englewood Cliffs, NJ: Prentice-Hall.

Mitchell, R. (2003). Fundamental concepts about power. Retrieved 3 November from http://www.csun.edu/~hfmgt001/power1.doc

Morgan, G. (1986). *Images of organization*. Beverly Hills, CA: Sage.

Mowday, R. (1978). The exercise of upward influence in organizations. *Administrative Science Quarterly*, **23**, 137–56.

Nanus, B. (1992). *Visionary leadership*. San Francisco: Jossey-Bass.

Narrayanan, V.K. and Fahey, L. (1982). The micro-politics of strategy formulation. *Academy of Management Review*, **7**(1), 25–34.

O'Connor, W. and Morrison, T. (2001). A comparison of situational and dispositional predictors of perceptions of organizational politics. *Journal of Psychology*, **135**(3), 301–12.

Parker, C.P., Diboye, R.L. and Jackson, S.L. (1995). Perceptions of organizational politics: An investigation of antecedents and consequences. *Journal of Management*, **21**, 891–912.

Parks, C.D., Hanager, R.F. and Scamahorn, S.D. (1996). Trust and reactions to messages of intent in social dilemmas. *Journal of Conflict Resolution*, **40**, 134–51.

Pava, M.L. (1999). *The search for meaning in organizations: Seven practical questions for ethical managers*. Westport, CT: Quorum Books.

Pettigrew, A.M. (1973). *The politics of organizational decision-making*. London: Tavistock.

Pfeffer, J. (1994). *Managing with power: Politics and influence in organizations*. Boston: Harvard Business School Press.

Reardon, K.K. (2000). *The secret handshake*. New York: Doubleday.

Reichheld, F.F. (2003). The only number you need to grow. *Harvard Business Review*, December, 1–11.

Robinson, S.L. (1996). Trust and breach of the psychological contract. *Administrative Science Quarterly*, **41**, 574–99.

Schein, E. (1992). *Organizational culture and leadership* (2nd edn). San Francisco, CA: Jossey-Bass.

Schilit, W.K. and Locke, E.A. (1982). A study of upward influence in organizations. *Administrative Science Quarterly*, **27**, 304–16.

Schriesheim, C.A. and Hinkin, T.R. (1990). Influence tactics used by subordinates: A theoretical and empirical analysis and refinement of the Kipnis, Schmidt, and Wilkinson subscales. *Journal of Applied Psychology*, **55**, 246–57.

Seldman, M. and Betof, E. (2004). An illuminated path. *Training and Development*, **58**(12), 34–8.

Settoon, R.P. and Mossholder, K.W. (2002). Relationship quality and relationship context as antecedents of person- and task-focused interpersonal citizenship behavior. *Journal of Applied Psychology*, **87**, 255–67.

Sussman, L., Adams, A., Kuzmits, F. and Raho, L. (2002). Organizational politics: Tactics, channels, and hierarchical roles. *Journal of Business Ethics*, **40**(4), 313–29.

Tarrow, S. (1977). *Between center and periphery: Grassroots politicians in Italy and France*. New Havenv, CT: Yale University Press.

Tepper, B.J., Duffy, M.K., Hoobler, J. and Ensley, M.D. (2004). Moderators of the relationships between coworkers' organizational citizenship behavior and fellow employees' attitudes. *Journal of Applied Psychology*, **89**(3), 455–65.

Teuke, M.R. (2004). Teach the right thing. *Continental* (September), 57–59.

Thurman, B. (1979). In the office: Networks and coalitions. *Social Networks*, **2**, 47–63.

Toupin, E.B. (2001). *Corporate Survival: How to manage yourself in the political playing field*. Retrieved from http://www.sensiblesoftware.com/articles/a/Corporate-Survival-to-manage-yourself-in-the-political-playing-field.html.

Vigoda, E. (2001). Reactions to organizational politics: A cross-cultural examination in Israel and Britain. *Human Relations*, **54**(11), 1483–518.

Vigoda, E. (2003). *Developments in organizational politics: How political dynamics affect employee performance in modern work sites*. Cheltenham, UK: Edward Elgar.

Voyer, J.J. (1994). Coercive organizational politics and organizational outcomes: An interpretive study. *Organizational Science*, **5**, 72–85.

Weick, K. (1995). *Sensemaking in organizations*. Thousand Oaks, CA: Sage.

Windsor, D. (2003). Organizational Politics in Strategy Process. Paper presented at the AiSM-INSEAD Conference, Fontainbleau, 24–26 August.

Witt, L.A. (1998). Enhancing organizational goal congruence: A solution to organizational politics. *Journal of Applied Psychology*, **83**, 666–74.

Witt, L.A. and Ferris, G.R. (2003). Social skill as moderator of the conscientiousness–performance relationship: Convergent results across four studies. *Journal of Applied Psychology*, **88**(5), 809–20.

Yukl, G. and Falbe, C.M. (1990). Influence tactics and objectives in upward, downward, and lateral influence attempts. *Journal of Applied Psychology*, **75**(2), 132–40.

Index